AF478385

MAD SQUARE

Edited by Jacqueline Strecker

THE MAD SQUARE

MODERNITY IN GERMAN ART 1910–37

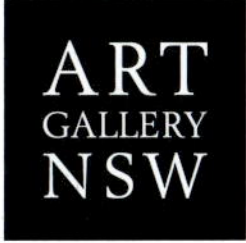

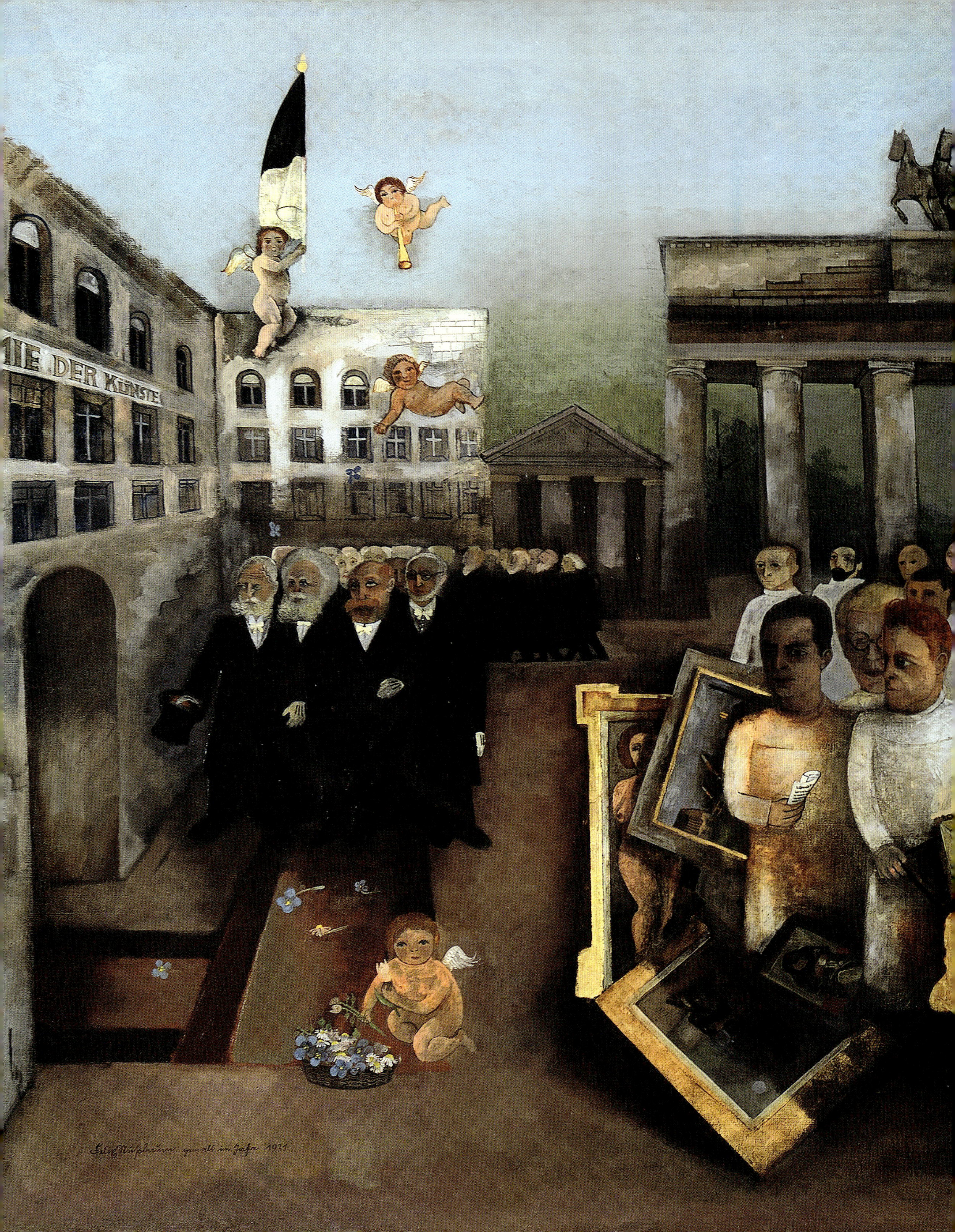
IE DER KÜNSTE

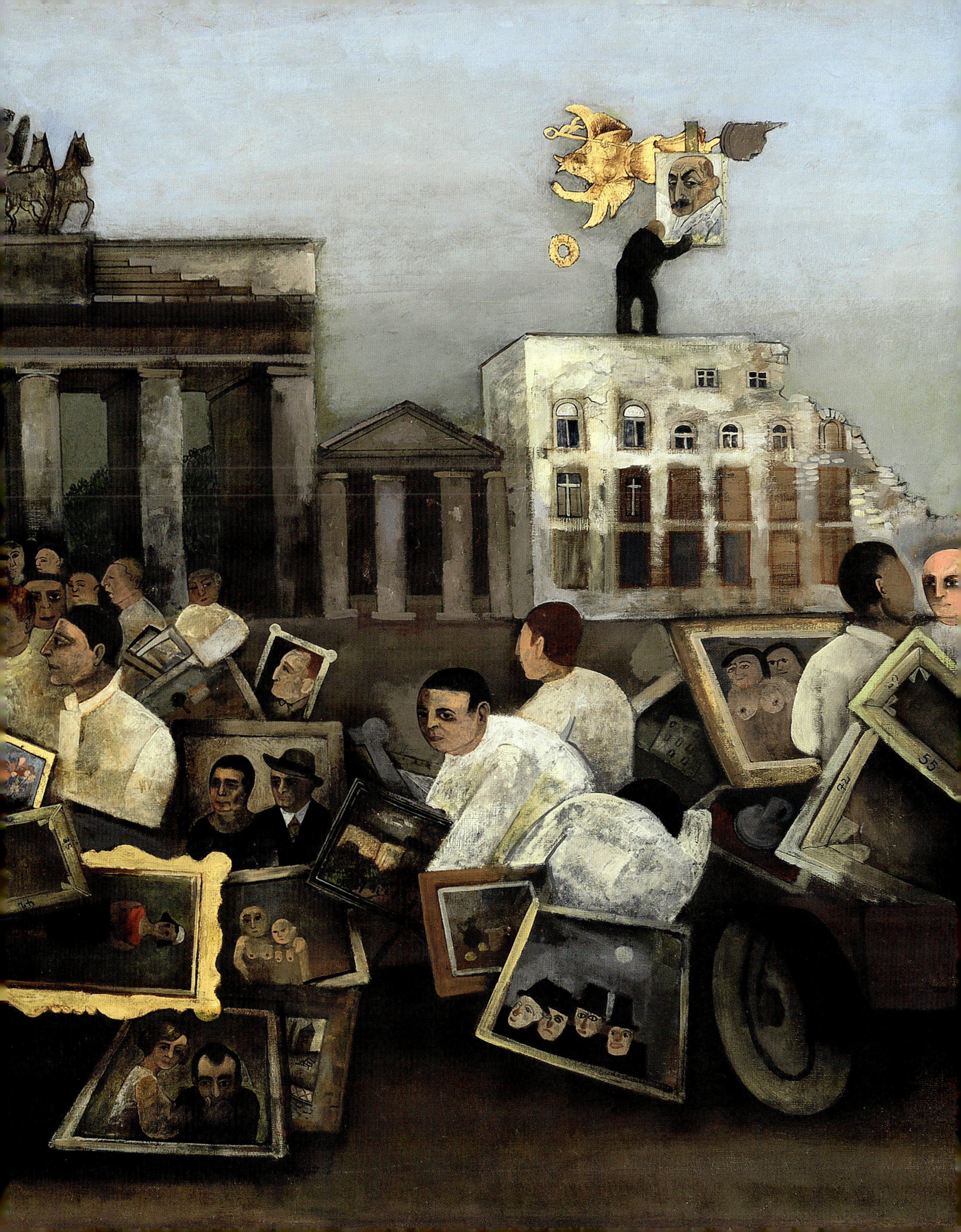

previous pages:

Felix Nussbaum
The mad square 1931 (detail)

pp 10–11:

Ludwig Meidner
Apocalyptic landscape 1913 (detail)

PAINTED DURING A PERIOD OF INTENSE POLITICAL AND INTELLECTUAL POLARISATION, HE MAD SQUARE BY FELIX NUSSBAUM CAN BE SEEN AS A SATIRISATION OF THE COLLAPSE OF SOCIETY DURING THE YEARS OF THE WEIMAR REPUBLIC AND AS A FOREWARNING OF THE CATACLYSM THAT WAS TO ENSUE.

CONTENTS

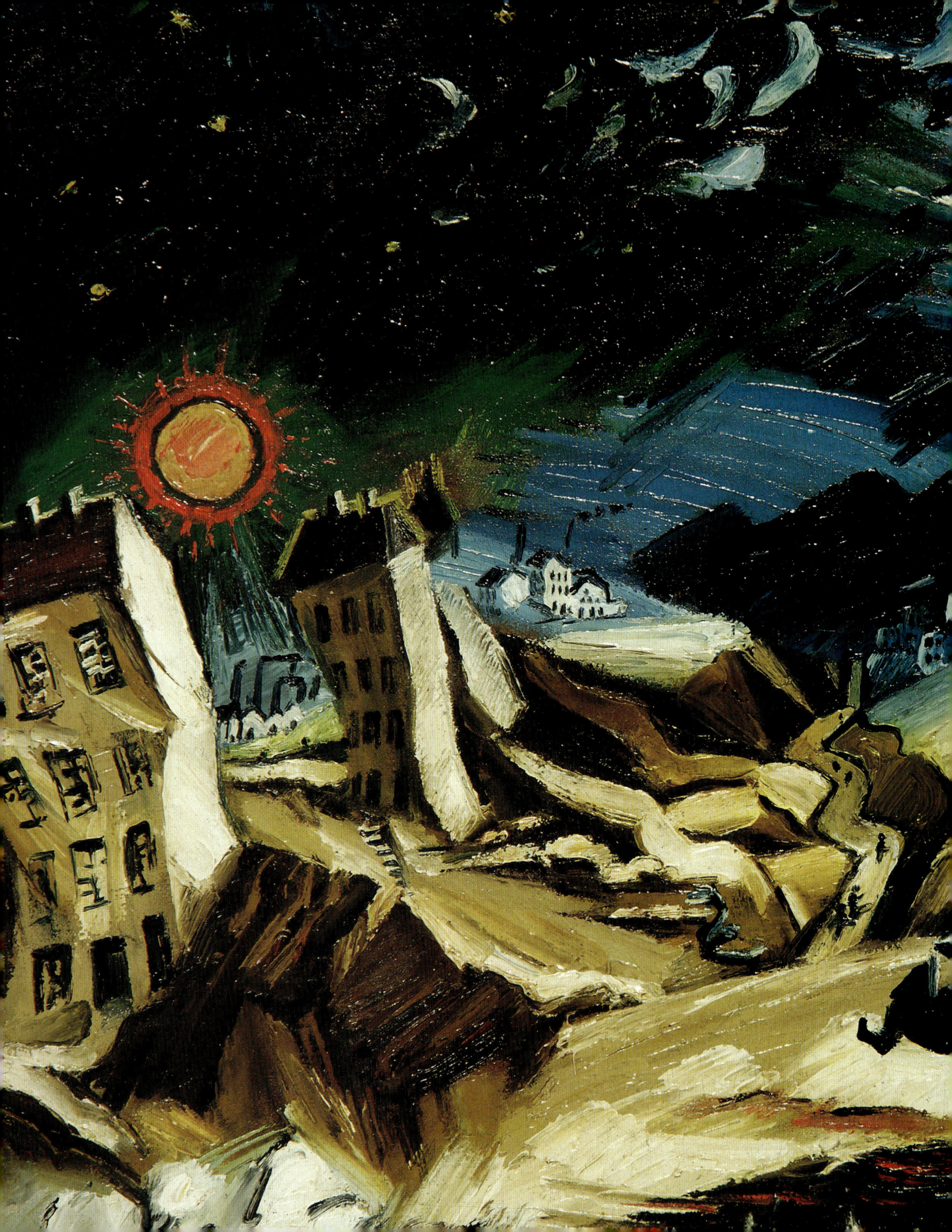

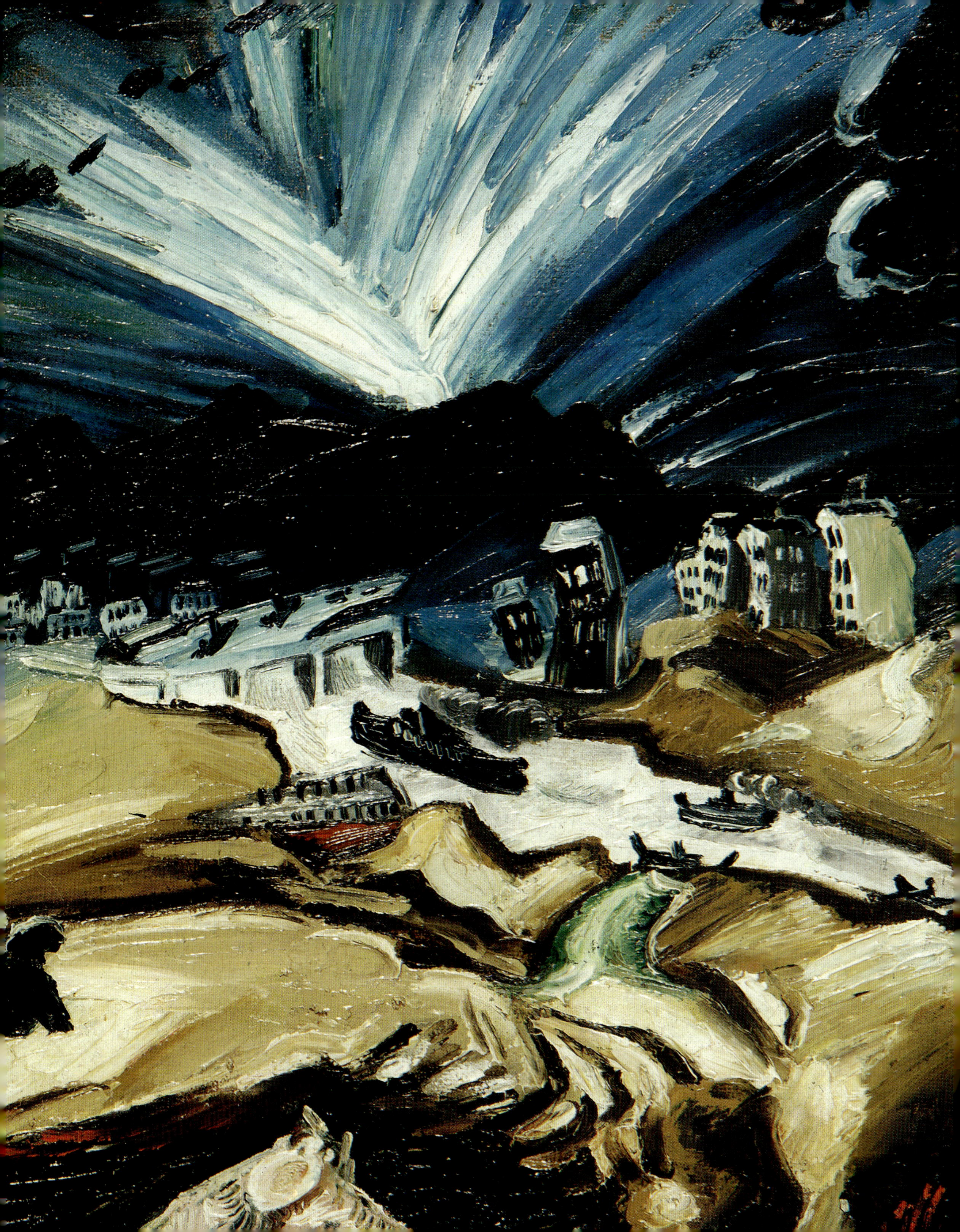

FROM THE PRESIDENT'S COUNCIL

The President's Council of the Art Gallery of New South Wales is delighted to sponsor *The mad square: modernity in German art 1910–37*. This impressive exhibition of modern German art reveals the intense creativity and innovation that characterised the diverse range of art movements that flourished before and during the years of the Weimar period.

The President's Council, whose members are Australian business leaders, provides important counsel and financial support to the Gallery. Since its inception in 1995, the Council has established a strong partnership between the corporate community and the Gallery, and has grown to become the major sponsor of the Gallery's extensive and stimulating exhibition program.

The President's Council is pleased support another important exhibition of international art in Australia.

Steven Lowy AM President

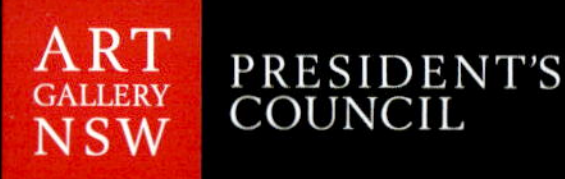

President's Council Members

Michael Fraser, AGL Energy Limited
Nigel Williams, ANZ Banking Group
John Symond AM, Aussie Home Loans
Bruce Fink, Bickham Court Group
John C Conde AO, BUPA Australia Group
Giam Swiegers, Deloitte
Greg Everett, Delta Electricity
Chum Darvall, Deutsche Bank AG
Damian Hackett, Deutscher and Hackett
Rob McLeod, Ernst & Young
Geoff Parmenter, Events New South Wales
Peter Fray, Fairfax Media Limited
Kim Williams, FOXTEL
Kathryn Everett, Freehills
Emmanuel Pohl, Hyperion Asset Management
David Clarke, Investec Bank (Australia) Limited
Stephen O'Connor, JCDecaux Australia
Rob Priestley, J P Morgan
Chris Jordan AO, KPMG
John Clayton, Marsh
Virginia Mansell, Stephenson Mansell
Paul O'Sullivan, Optus
Kerr Neilson, Platinum Asset Management
Mark Johnson, PricewaterhouseCoopers
Alan Joyce, Qantas Airways
Alfred Moufarrige OAM, Servcorp
Ryan Stokes, Seven Group Holdings
Luca Belgiorno-Nettis AM, Transfield Holdings
Philip Coleman, UBS AG Australia
Jeff Mitchell, Westpac Banking Corporation

DIRECTOR'S FOREWORD

The mad square: modernity in German art 1910–37 presents the key avant-garde movements that emerged in Germany during the early 20th century. It begins in Berlin in 1911, exactly 100 years ago, when four young, ambitious artists – Max Pechstein, Ernst Ludwig Kirchner, Karl Schmidt-Rottluff and Erich Heckel – moved to the metropolis to seek out new subject matter and audiences for their radically modern paintings, sculptures and prints. From this moment on and for the next two decades, Germany became an important centre for international avant-garde artists as they engaged with modernity and motifs derived from modern city life. Berlin was a potent stimulant for these artists, providing a thriving, vibrant, cosmopolitan culture and generating a kind of nervous, creative energy that sustained artists during the prewar years until the early 1930s. While Berlin remained the undisputed cultural capital of Germany between the wars – a powerful image that has endured until the present day – this exhibition explores the many different forms of avant-garde art that emerged in cities throughout Germany, emphasising the inter-disciplinary and diverse nature of German modernism. Finishing in 1937 with the *Degenerate art* exhibition in Munich, *The mad square* explores the National Socialists' brutal campaign against modernism.

This exciting and tumultuous period in modern European art has, until now, only been partly seen in Australia through exhibitions of single avant-garde movements, artists or collections. Since 1989, when we mounted *German Expressionism: the colours of desire* (1989–90), there has been a growing interest in and enthusiasm for early 20th-century German art. Subsequent Gallery exhibitions – which include *Prints in Germany 1880–1940* (1989–90), *Prints and drawings of the Weimar Republic* (1996), *Otto Dix: Der Krieg* (2008) and *August Sander* (2008) – have highlighted the great creativity and innovation of this period. It is timely that we present this exhibition and publication covering the broad visual culture of Weimar Germany in Sydney and Melbourne.

The mad square brings together modern German works from Australian and international public and private collections for the first time. Rather surprisingly, more than half of the 220 works included in the exhibition are held in Australian collections. We have supplemented these with major paintings, sculptures, works on paper, photographs and decorative arts from collections around the world. We are extremely grateful to our lenders for their generosity in loaning works that have enabled us to exhibit the most representative and highest quality examples of the art of this period.

The mad square has been curated by guest curator Jacqueline Strecker. I wish to thank Jacqueline for her work over four years in developing and delivering this project. I would like to acknowledge the support of members of the international curatorium: Jill Lloyd, Sean Rainbird, Carla Schulz-Hoffmann, Matthias Eberle and Gerard Vaughan; and the scholarly contribution of the writers Eric Hobsbawm, Jill Lloyd, Brigid Doherty, Karen Koehler, Petra Kayser, Maggie Finch, Matthias Eberle and Uwe Fleckner. I acknowledge and appreciate the work and commitment of the Gallery staff across all areas, who worked on this project. Finally, to the President's Council we express our gratitude for their continued and generous support of our major exhibitions.

Edmund Capon Director, Art Gallery of New South Wales

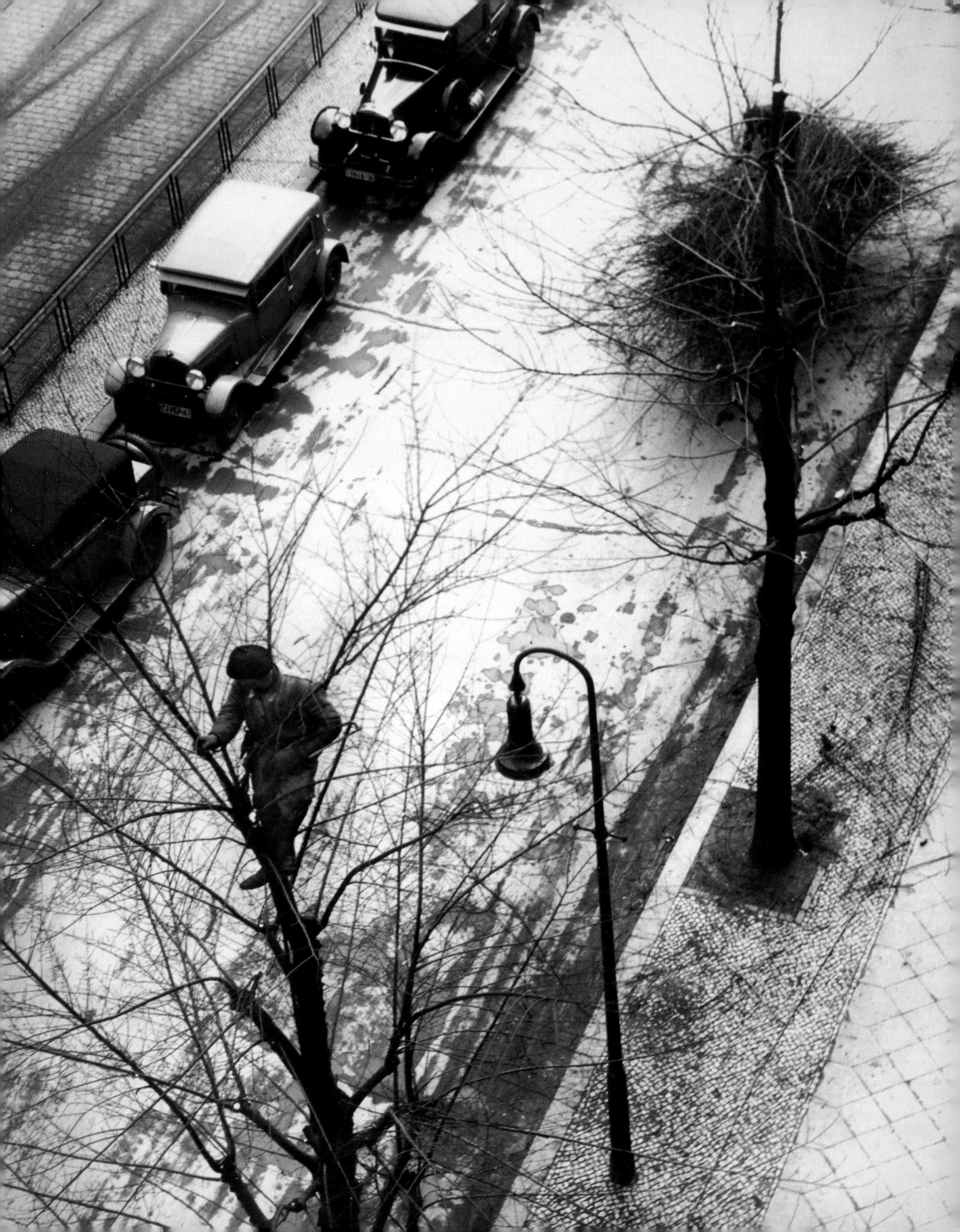

DIARY: MEMORIES OF WEIMAR

Eric Hobsbawm

I spent the most formative time of my life, the years 1931–33, as a *Gymnasiast* and would-be communist militant, in the dying Weimar Republic. I was asked to recall that time in an online German interview under the title '*Ich bin ein Reiseführer in die Geschichte*' ('I am a travel guide to history'). Some weeks later, at the annual dinner of the survivors of the school I went to when I came to Britain, the no longer extant St Marylebone Grammar School, I tried to explain the reactions of a 15-year-old suddenly translated to Britain in 1933. 'Imagine yourselves,' I told my fellow Old Philologians, 'as a newspaper correspondent based in Manhattan and transferred by your editor to Omaha, Nebraska. That's how I felt when I came to England after almost two years in the unbelievably exciting, sophisticated, intellectually and politically explosive Berlin of the Weimar Republic. The place was a terrible letdown.'

It is hard to remember, though Hitler made it the staple of his rhetoric in the ironic plethora of voting that took place in its last year, that the republic lasted only 14 years, and of these just six, sandwiched between a murderous birth-period and the terminal catastrophe of the Great Slump, had a semblance of normality. The massive international interest in it is largely posthumous, the consequence of its overthrow by Hitler. It was primarily this that raised the question of Hitler's rise to power and whether it could have been avoided, questions that are still debated among historians. It was clear to those of us who lived through 1932 that the Weimar Republic was on its deathbed. The only political party specifically committed to it was reduced to 1.2 per cent of the vote and the papers we read at home debated what room there was in politics for its supporters.

It was also Hitler who produced the community of refugees who came to play a disproportionately prominent part in their countries of refuge and to whom Weimar's memory owes so much. Certainly they were far more prominent, except in the world of ballet, than the much larger post-1917 Russian emigration. They may have made little impact on the old entrenched professions – medicine, law – but their impact on more open fields, and eventually on science and public life, was quite remarkable. In Australia and Britain émigrés transformed art history and visual culture, as well as the media through the innovations of Continental publishers, journalists, photographers and designers.

The basic achievements of the Weimar Republic and the reasons non-Germans take an interest in it are not political but intellectual and cultural. The word today suggests the Bauhaus, George Grosz, Max Beckmann, Walter Benjamin, the great photographer August Sander and a number of remarkable movies, as well as Thomas Mann, Bertolt Brecht, Kurt Weill, Martin Heidegger, the less familiar theorist Siegfried Kracauer and the artist Hannah Höch. One could as easily add, say, Carl Schmitt on the (rare) intellectual right, Ernst Bloch on the far left and the great Max Weber in the middle.

In 1933 only Thomas Mann and a few films had made much of a stir beyond the narrowest of niche-publics outside Central Europe, and possibly a small homosexual

László Moholy-Nagy
Spring, Berlin 1928
gelatin silver photograph
Collection of George Eastman House,
International Museum of Photography and Film

subculture which discovered the attractions of Berlin in the final Weimar years. Mann was an established master even before 1914. He won the Nobel Prize in 1929, though not for his Weimar masterwork, *The magic mountain*, so much as the more ancient *Buddenbrooks*. But who had heard of Franz Marc, whose blue horses adorned the corridor of my *Gymnasium* until the new regime removed them, together with our republican headmaster?

At that time Paris was the unquestioned capital of the visual arts, Vienna still the native home of both heavy and light music. German was not widely spoken in the West outside the transatlantic diaspora or read outside classical scholarship. Even today only German speakers recognise Brecht not just as a dramatist but as one of the great 20th-century lyric poets. About the only branch of Weimar literature that broke out of the Central European enclosure was the anti-war fiction of the late 1920s, headed by Remarque's *All quiet on the western front*. Naturally, it was filmed by Universal, the only Hollywood studio headed by a native German.

What, looking back, was so characteristic about the culture of a short-lived German republic that nobody had really wanted and most Germans accepted as *faute de mieux* at best? Every German had lived through three cataclysmic experiences: the Great War; the genuine, if abortive German revolution which overthrew the defeated Kaiser's regime; and the Great Inflation of 1923, a brief, man-made catastrophe that suddenly made money valueless. The political right, traditionalist, anti-Semitic, authoritarian and deeply entrenched in the institutions carried over from the Kaiser's Reich (I still remember the title of Theodor Plivier's 1932 book, *The Kaiser went, the generals remained*) refused the republic totally. It regarded Weimar as illegitimate, the Versailles Treaty as an undeserved national shame, and aimed at getting rid of both of them as soon as possible.

But almost all Germans, including the communists, were passionately against Versailles and the foreign occupiers. I can still recall as a child seeing from the train the French flag flying on Rhineland fortresses, with a curious sense that this was somehow unnatural. Being both English and Jewish (I was *der Engländer* at school) I was not tempted into the German nationalism of my school friends, let alone into Nazism, but I could well understand the appeal of both to German boys. The authoritarian right was always the main danger both politically and, through their persistent and popular hostility to *Kulturbolschewismus*, culturally.

The major centrist thinkers – Mann, Max Weber, Walther Rathenau, none of them instinctive democrats, but urged on by fear of the gun-happy right – managed to justify a democratic republic as the necessary successor to an unrestorable Reich. So, of course, did the main parties of the system: the majority Social Democrats, who had not actually wanted the Kaiser to go, and the Catholic Centre, transformed by the revolution from a confessional pressure group into a government party. Beyond these the political left, shaped largely by revulsion against the Great War, shock at the failed revolution of 1918, and hatred of the old ruling class that survived it so well, was no less rejectionist than the right. Joined by half of the anti-war independent breakaway from the Social Democratic Party, the Communist Party acquired a mass base of intransigent working-class opposition. Large enough to block the fashioning of a lasting non-right Weimar regime, this left did not wish to contribute anything to its practical politics except disgust.

For understandable reasons creative artists, radicalised by the horrors of war and the hope and fury left behind by lost revolution, were attracted to it; indeed, there are Weimar figures whose lasting achievement rests primarily on the force of their distaste for the republic. Even genuine high talents like Grosz and Weill ceased to be very interesting when, after 1933, they arrived in the United States and felt at ease. This was even more the case with lesser talents among the Expressionist writers and artists moved by pain and outrage to find temporarily memorable ways to express humourless emotion at the top of their voices. It was partly against these that Weimar found the nearest thing to its own voice after the Great Inflation, hard-nosed, unsentimental, passionate but cabaret-cool, in the *Neue Sachlichkeit* (New Objectivity). For me, Weimar still speaks now, as it did in 1932, with the voice of *Mahagonny* and *The threepenny opera*, of Alfred Döblin's *Berlin Alexanderplatz*, of the underrated Erich Kästner, or of the pawky political chansons of Erich Weinert.

But Weimar was more than a German phenomenon and its role as a crucible for what after 1917 was the major generator of intellectual and artistic innovation: post-revolutionary Central and Eastern Europe has been underestimated. The prestige of Paris, 'capital of the 19th century', obscured the fact that it no longer had major innovations to offer between the wars except for Surrealism, itself largely derived from the multinational Dada of the Zurich Central European refugees.

With its 7000 plus periodicals, 38 000 books (in 1927) and the most formidable movie industry outside Hollywood, Germany was a vast market. With the fall of the Habsburg Empire it naturally absorbed the large surplus talent of what remained of Austria. Where would Weimar films be without Vienna, without Fritz Lang, Georg Wilhelm Pabst, Billy Wilder, Otto Preminger or, for that matter, Peter Lorre? Its stable of stars – Conradt Veidt, Emil Jannings, Marlene Dietrich, Elisabeth Bergner – were trained under the Viennese Max Reinhardt, the chief influence on the German-language theatre business. In Berlin my family, themselves migrants from Vienna, went on living a social life largely centred on other Austrian expatriate relatives and friends.

For different but equally obvious reasons Germany was Russia's major window to the West. Berlin was both the main centre of the anti-Soviet emigration and the first stop on the western excursions of the new Soviet intellectuals and artistic revolutionaries, some of whom published a multilingual review there. Nor indeed should we forget that, in vain expectation of the German revolution, the official language of the Comintern was not Russian but German.

Inevitably, this cultural mix fertilised Weimar and eventually western culture. The Bauhaus was throughout its existence a collective of Germans, Austro-Hungarians, Russians, Swiss and Dutch. It is characteristic that what amounted to a 'Constructivist international', as John Willett described it, was set up by a collection of Hungarians, Dutch, Belgians, Romanians, Soviet Russians and Germans at a meeting in Weimar with prospective headquarters in Berlin. This was the culture that German émigrés imported into their countries of refuge.

The central international role of Weimar Germany in 20th-century science is equally easy to overlook. Albert Einstein and Max Planck gave glory to Berlin, while Göttingen under Max Born was, with Cambridge, the catalyst of the revolution of quantum mechanics, the 'boy physics', whose communal idiom, like the language of international communism, was German. Heisenberg, Pauli, Fermi, Oppenheimer, Teller all worked or studied there. The most dramatic evidence for the centrality of Weimar Germany are the 15 science Nobel Prizes won by Germans in its 14 years, a number it took the subsequent 50 years to equal.

This was the last time Germany was at the centre of modernity and western thought. It might have held out better if the Weimar Republic had been followed not by Hitler's wrecking crew but by a more traditional reactionary government. Yet in retrospect this option was as unreal as was the prospect of stopping Hitler's rise by a comprehensive anti-fascist union. The fact is that no-one, right, left or centre, got the true measure of Hitler's National Socialism, a movement of a kind that had not been seen before and whose aims were rationally unimaginable. Not even his intended victims fully recognised the danger. After the summer election of 1932 which left the Nazis as much the largest party, but short of a majority, the (Jewish) editor of the *Tagebuch*, a left-liberal weekly we took at home, published an article whose headline struck me even then as suicidal. I still see it before me: '*Lasst ihn heran!*' ('Why not let him in!'). A few months later, with very different intentions, the reactionaries around the aged President Hindenburg manoeuvred Hitler into office thinking that he could be controlled.

All attempts to make the Weimar Republic look more firmly established and stable, even before the world economic cataclysm broke its back, are historical whistling in the dark. It moved briefly through the debris of a dead but unburied past towards a sudden but expected end and an unknown future. For our parents it promised only an unrecoverable past, while we dreamed of great tomorrows; my 'Aryan' schoolmates in the form of a national rebirth, communists like myself, as the universal revolution initiated in October 1917.

Even its few years of 'normality' rested on the temporary quiescence of a volcano that could have erupted at any time. The great man of the theatre, Max Reinhardt, knew this. 'What I love,' he said, 'is the taste of transience on the tongue – every year might be the last.' It gave Weimar culture a unique tang. It sharpened a bitter creativity, a contempt for the present, an intelligence unrestricted by convention, until the sudden and irrevocable death. Moments when one knows history has changed are rare, but this was one of them. That is why I can still see myself walking home from school with my sister on the cold afternoon of 30 January 1933, reflecting on what the news of Hitler's appointment as chancellor meant. A few days later someone brought the duplicating machine of the SSB, my communist school's organisation, to store under my bed. They thought it would be safer in the flat of a foreigner. But from now on nowhere was safe. Still, it was a strange and wonderful time in which to discover oneself and the world in a Berlin that looked like the potential capital of the 20th century, until the barbarians took over. When I go there today, I still feel it has never recovered from 1933.

This essay is a modified version of Eric Hobsbawm's review of Eric Weitz's book *Weimar Germany: promise and tragedy*, originally published in the *London Review of Books* (24 January 2008) as 'Diary: memories of Weimar', and has been reproduced here with the kind permission of the author and the *London Review of Books*.

Margaret Michaelis
Untitled [Column with posters] c1932
gelatin silver photograph
National Gallery of Australia, Canberra

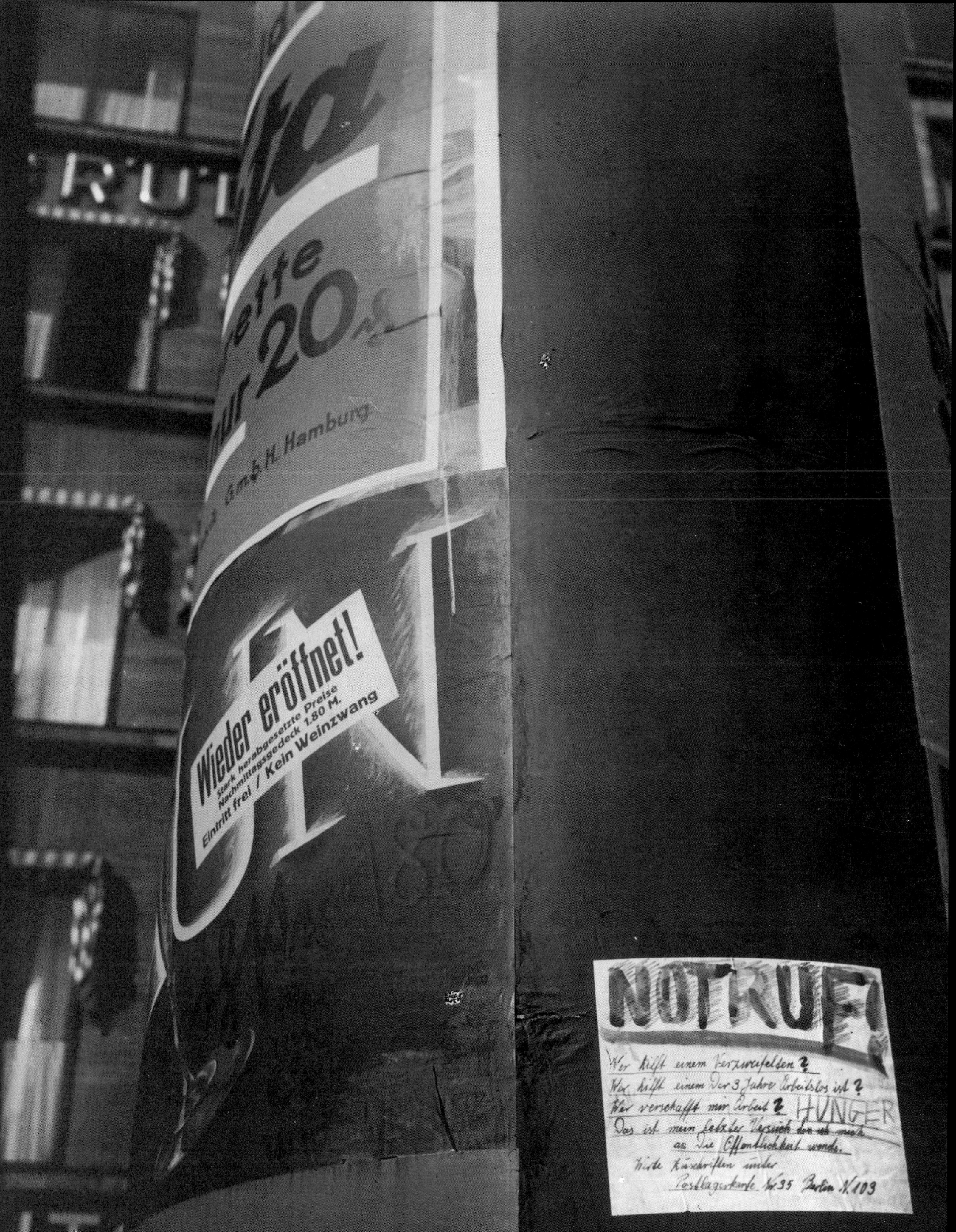

RU
ette
nur 20
G.m.b.H. Hamburg
Wieder eröffnet!
Stark herabgesetzte Preise
Nachmittagsgedeck 1.80 M.
Eintritt frei / Kein Weinzwang
NOTRUF!
Wer hilft einem Verzweifelten?
Wer hilft einem der 3 Jahre Arbeitslos ist?
Wer verschafft mir Arbeit?
HUNGER
Das ist mein letzter Versuch
an die Öffentlichkeit wende.
Bitte Zuschriften unter
Postlagerkarte Nr. 35 Berlin N. 103

INTRODUCTION

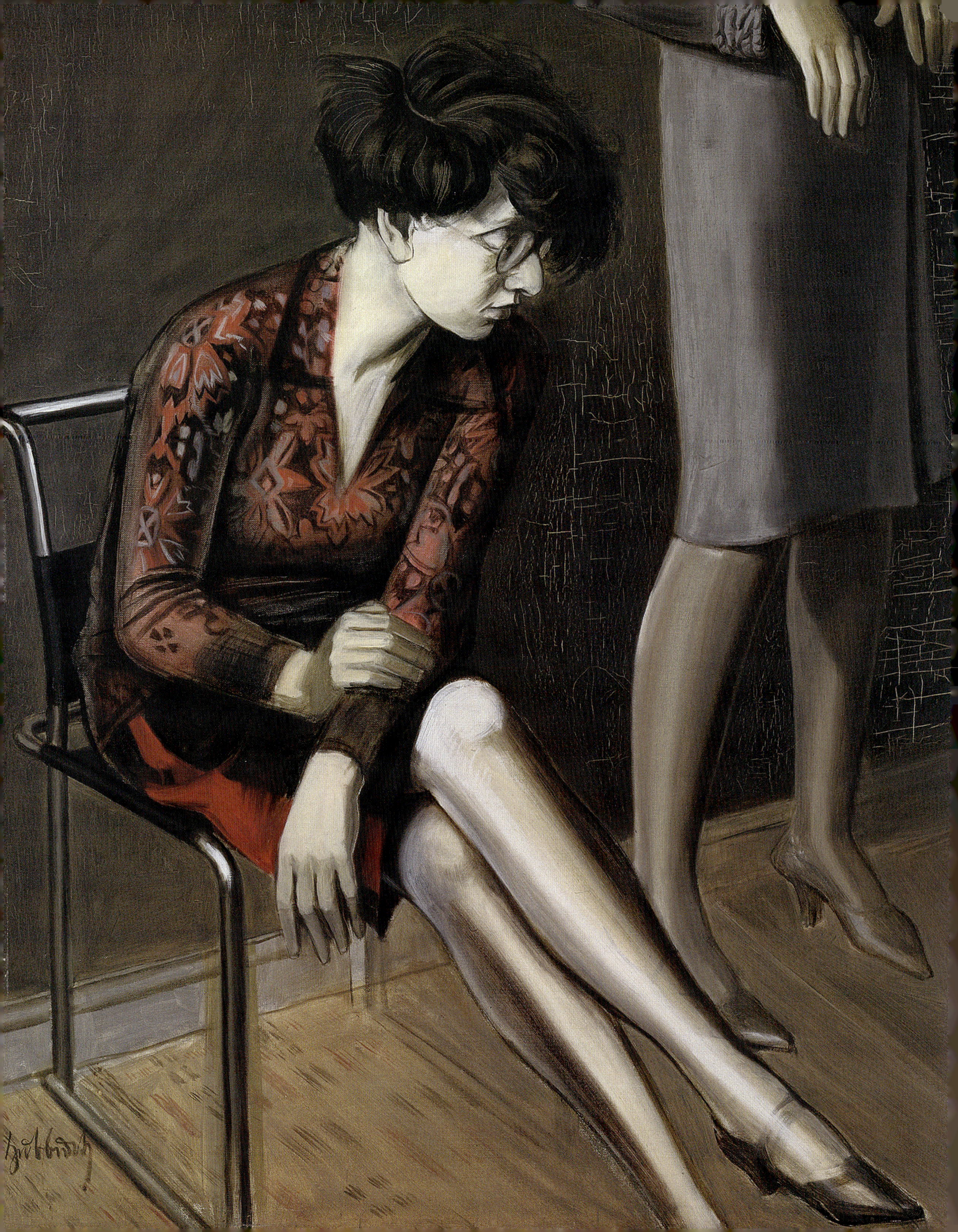

THE MAD SQUARE: MODERNITY IN GERMAN ART 1910–37

Jacqueline Strecker

The mad square: modernity in German art 1910–37 explores the development of the modernist art movements that emerged in Germany between 1910 and 1937. In bringing together such a diverse and extensive range of art, created during one of the most important and turbulent periods in modern European history, we offer new insights into our understanding of key German avant-garde movements. It explores the continuities and differences found in a range of artforms from this era, rather than presenting the art of the 1920s as unique. The impact of the First World War and the events of the 1930s are included to present a fuller, more integrated picture of modernism in Germany than in previous surveys.

One of the aims of *The mad square* is to challenge the seductive and enduring myth of 'the golden twenties' by revealing the ambivalence towards modernity expressed by many artists in Germany. While there is a strong emphasis on the art created during the tumultuous 14-year period of the Weimar Republic (1918–33), *The mad square* explores the radically different artistic responses to modern life that emerged in Germany over a 27-year period. During these years, the German population experienced a horrific world war, a violent revolution followed by an era of political and economic turmoil caused by the abdication of the Kaiser and establishment of a new democratic republic, and the gradual rise of fascism that led to Adolf Hitler's assumption of power and the subsequent devastating implementation of National Socialist policies across all areas of German society.[1] *The mad square* challenges the historical construct of Weimar as a period of artistic and cultural decadence that was doomed to fail from the outset. It presents a broad interpretation of the development of modern art in Germany that relies more on an interdisciplinary approach than on a grand, historical narrative.

The mad square also takes visitors on an emotional journey through an extraordinary moment in German art. Drawing its inspiration and title from Felix Nussbaum's painting *The mad square* of 1931 (pp 264–5), it alludes to the double meaning inherent in Nussbaum's ironic depiction of contemporary Berlin and the newest artforms as being both fabulous and crazy. Nussbaum portrays Berlin's famous city square, Pariser Platz – immediately recognisable because of the Brandenburg Gate – as a crazy place in which indignant young artists demonstrate against the exclusion of their work from the official art establishment. Painted during a period of intense political and intellectual polarisation, Nussbaum's *The mad square* can be seen as a satirisation of the collapse of society during the years of the Weimar Republic and as a forewarning of the cataclysm that was to ensue. In the context of this publication and exhibition, the 'mad square' is both a place – the city represented in so many of the works – and a modernist construct that saw artists moving away from figurative art towards increasingly abstract forms. Together with a sense of place, the 'mad square' can also be metaphorically interpreted as a state of mind, or even a prevailing sense of Zeitgeist that presides over the selected works.

Karl Hubbuch
Twice Hilde II c1929 (detail)

Traditional definitions of modernism and modernity are useful in this context[2]; however, *The mad square* challenges the representation of modernism as a series of unified developments that were primarily concerned with formal experimentation. The traditional modernist model has largely excluded artistic developments in Germany, with the exception of the Expressionist paintings and woodblock prints of the Brücke and the Blaue Reiter. In many ways, the development of modern art in Germany goes against the grain of modernism and has had a far more complex and fragmented development than in other European countries. In contrast to France and England, for example, Germany in the last decade of the 19th and first decades of the 20th centuries had no fixed cultural capital. Until the end of the First World War, the emergence of avant-garde movements in Germany was characterised by decentralisation and regionalism.

While Germany's first generation of modern artists had experimented with new approaches in landscape painting in the 1890s, it was not until the first decade of the 20th century that the well-known artists' group the Brücke emerged in Dresden, unified by a shared, albeit utopian, belief that art could facilitate the coming of a new era. Ernst Ludwig Kirchner, the leading exponent of the Brücke, moved to Berlin in 1911 searching for new audiences and a market for Expressionist art, followed by fellow Brücke artists Karl Schmidt-Rottluff and Erich Heckel. In Munich at the same time, Wassily Kandinsky and Franz Marc declared in the *Blaue Reiter Almanac* that art would pave the way towards a new era, 'a great spiritual epoch'.[3] The Blaue Reiter's move away from traditional forms and colours towards increasingly abstract compositions that were inspired by the Bavarian countryside and 'primitive' art formed a complete contrast to the urban motifs depicted by Kirchner. The scenes of prewar Berlin painted by Kirchner between 1911 and the outbreak of war offered an alienating urban alternative to the liberated sexuality of the bathers in idyllic natural landscape settings previously portrayed by the Brücke artists (fig 1 p 35). Other artists, such as George Grosz and Heinrich Maria Davringhausen, found a realm of new artistic possibilities in the thriving urban metropolis, particularly in the range of expressive subjects offered by Berlin's night-life (fig 2 p 35).

During the 1920s, the avant-garde developed as a conglomeration of complex, inter-related, fluctuating movements and groups that formed in a number of different locations, including Berlin, Dresden, Weimar, Dessau, Munich, Frankfurt, Hanover and Cologne. The avant-garde movements included in this exhibition – Expressionism, Dada, Bauhaus, Constructivism and New Objectivity – were all linked by radical artistic experimentation and innovation, intellectualism, cosmopolitanism and elite audiences. The artists' engagement with city motifs and urban themes was a direct response to their encounter with modern city life as they began to fully experience the often traumatic effects of modernity. As a result of modernisation and industrialisation, there had been significant growth in the urban population – people moved to the city in search of employment. Over the course of 35 years, Berlin's population had grown rapidly from less than 1 million to more than 2 million people in 1910.[4] By 1920, there were more than 4 million people living in Berlin, resulting in the creation of a modern metropolis.[5] The tensions and uncertainties involved in the transformation from the old world to the new were intensified in Germany, where the devastating and cataclysmic effects of the

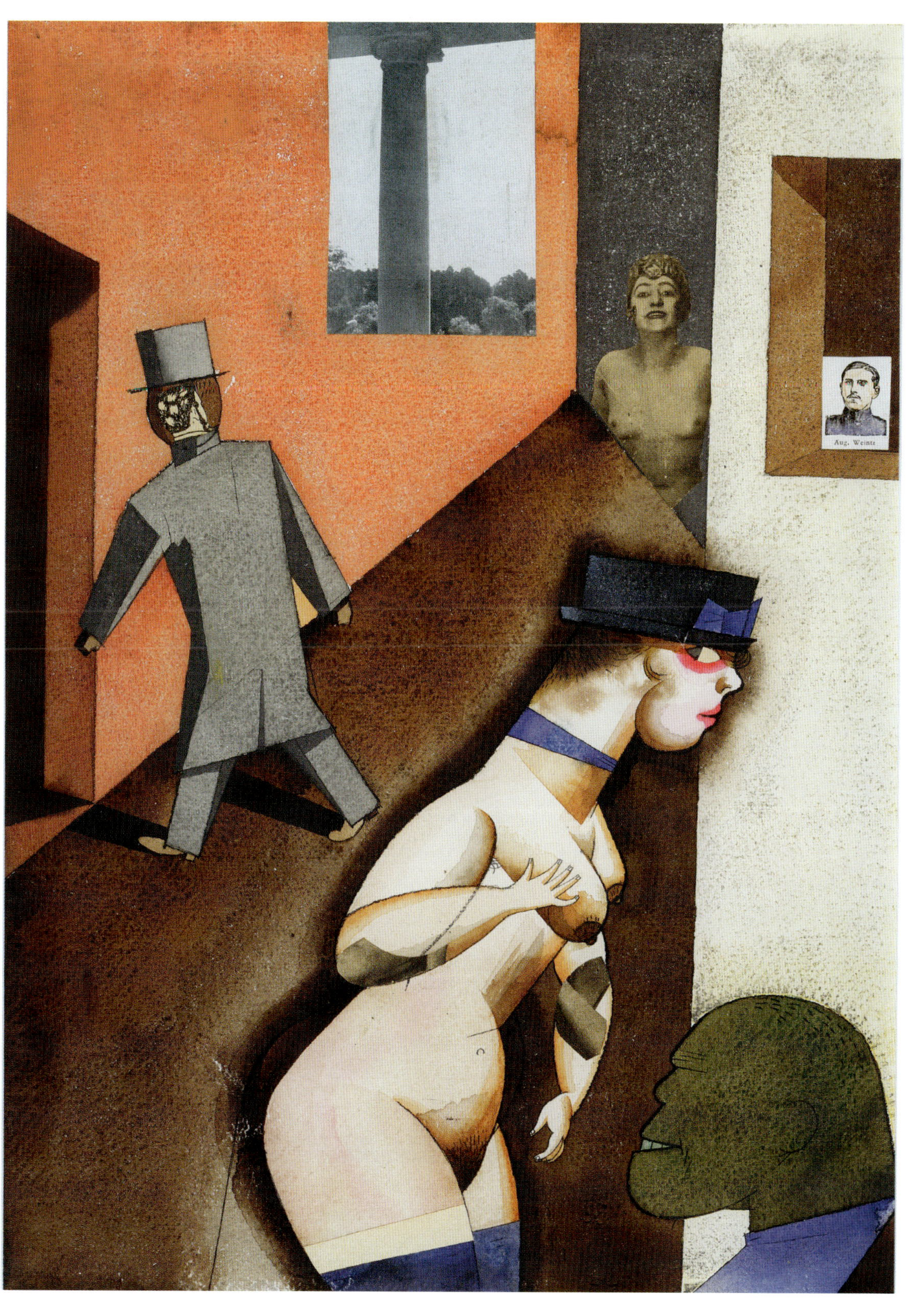

George Grosz
Tatlinesque diagram 1920
watercolour, collage, ink on paper
Museo Thyssen-Bornemisza, Madrid

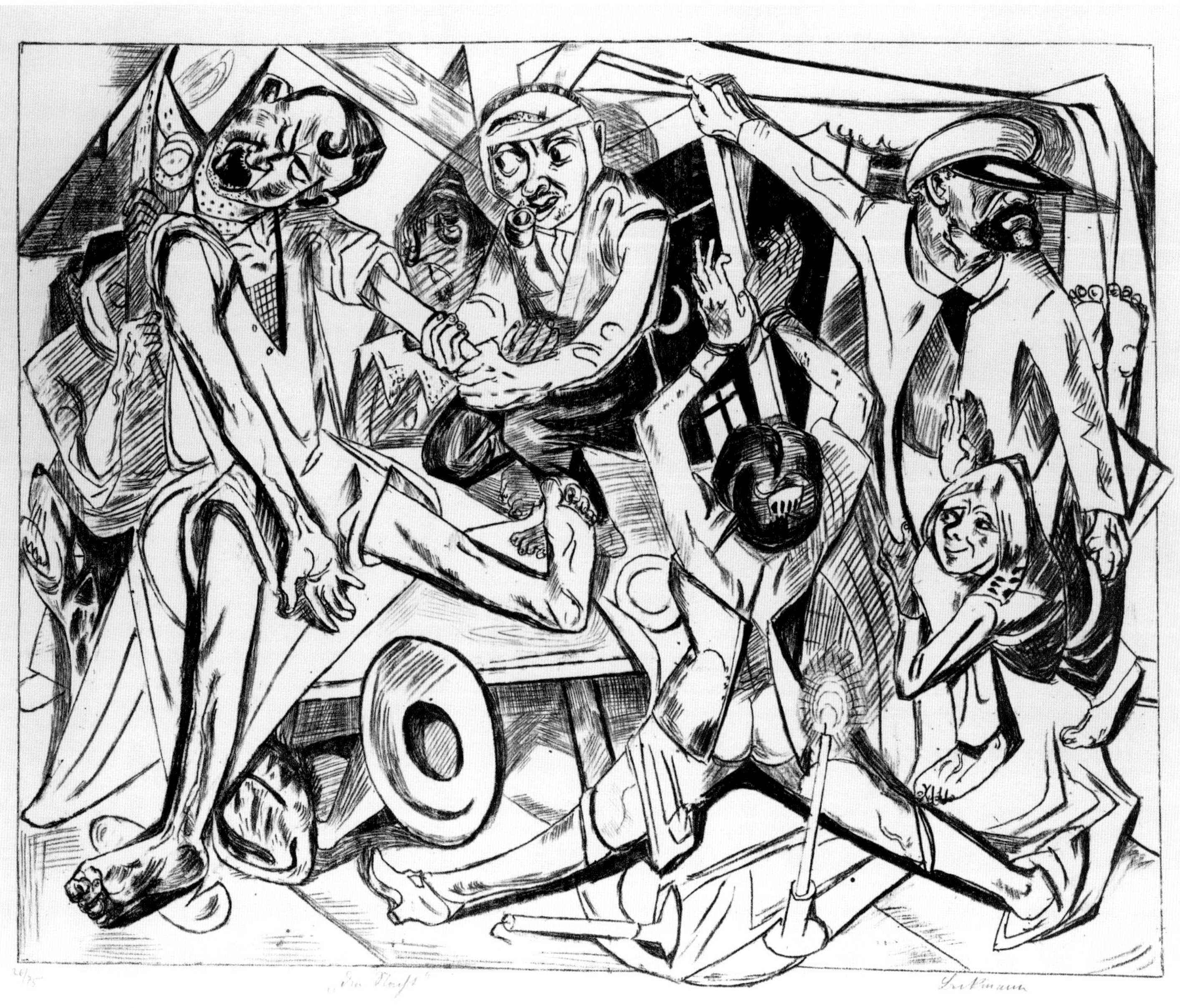

Max Beckmann
The night 1919
from the portfolio **Hell** 1919
lithograph
Kupferstichkabinett, Staatliche Museen zu Berlin

war were experienced together with sweeping changes that affected every aspect of life. The breakdown of traditional structures gave artists the freedom to reject the stifling principles of academic art and critique bourgeois society.

Most artists embraced the changes and were excited by the artistic possibilities offered by the birth of modernity and the dawn of a modern, technological age, but they were also fearful of modernity with its pressures, inherent contradictions and uncertainties. The sheer forcefulness and directness of many of the works included stem from the tension that is created by representing a view of modernity that was hopeful, dynamic and vibrant on the one hand, but dysfunctional and vulnerable on the other. The great creative spirit of the time is characterised by risk-taking, experimentation and a sense of rebelliousness as artists grappled with finding new ways to portray the modern world in painting, sculpture, photography, printmaking, drawing, film, the decorative arts, and new media such as photomontage. Germany's leading generation of interwar artists is included here – Max Beckmann, Otto Dix, George Grosz, Christian Schad, Kurt Schwitters and August Sander – as are artists from other countries who contributed to German modernism, such as László Moholy-Nagy, El Lissitzky and Marcel Breuer. Lesser-known but equally remarkable artists, such as Karl Hubbuch, Rudolf Schlichter and Hannah Höch, are also represented through major works. An overriding principle in the selection of works has been the artistic emphasis on pushing formal, intellectual and sometimes moral boundaries, so that an overall quality of edginess prevails.

The mad square: modernity in German art 1910–37 is the first exhibition held in Australia to explore the interdisciplinary nature of German modernism. This is surprising, given that more than half of the works are from public and private collections in Australia, supplemented with key works from international collections. The rationale behind the selection of works has been to bring together key artists and ideas from each of the major avant-garde groups, which will be explored in greater detail in the following thematic essays. It has not been our task to comprehensively survey each avant-garde movement or individual artist, as entire exhibitions have been recently devoted to many of these.[6] Rather, the curatorial approach is based on reconstructing a picture of the era that reflects the heterogeneity and intense creativity of German modernism, as well as the connections between art and broader social and historical issues. For this reason, and due to the fact that many artists challenged existing divisions between high art and mass culture, many different forms of art are included, ranging from small ephemeral Dada publications and large street posters, to highly complex paintings that transcend the time in which they were produced. The tendency to work across genres and media provides an opportunity to consider the cross-cultural nature of artistic expression as the visual arts converged with other artforms, including theatre, music, performance art, film, architecture and design.

The 1930s are examined as an essential part of modernism's dramatic history, rather than the usual tendency to avoid this problematic era or treat it as a separate chapter. The conservative resistance to the newest forms of art had been an undercurrent of modernism since its inception in Germany, and it is important to understand that artists often found themselves working in an environment that was hostile to modern art.

It is beyond the scope of this project to present the full range of art produced in the 1930s, and we have not included the idealised sculptures of perfect Teutonic types or traditional landscape paintings that were typically favoured under the Nazi regime and which were created as an antithesis to modernism. Rather, the focus is on the rise of fascism and the exploration of its disastrous consequences for modern art in Germany. Documentary photographs and works from the *Degenerate art* exhibition that opened in Munich in 1937 are also featured to mark the abrupt end to the artistic freedom and experimentation that had characterised the development of modern art in Germany during the previous two-and-a-half decades.

Like all great works of art, the images disturb, seduce and convince. Their themes and motifs still resonate strongly with us today and remind us of a time when artists engaged passionately with contemporary society, culture and politics. This publication and exhibition provide a context in which we can enhance our understanding of the extraordinary contribution made by these artists to modernism and to celebrate the great creativity and sense of innovation that defined the art of that era and continues to profoundly influence contemporary culture today.

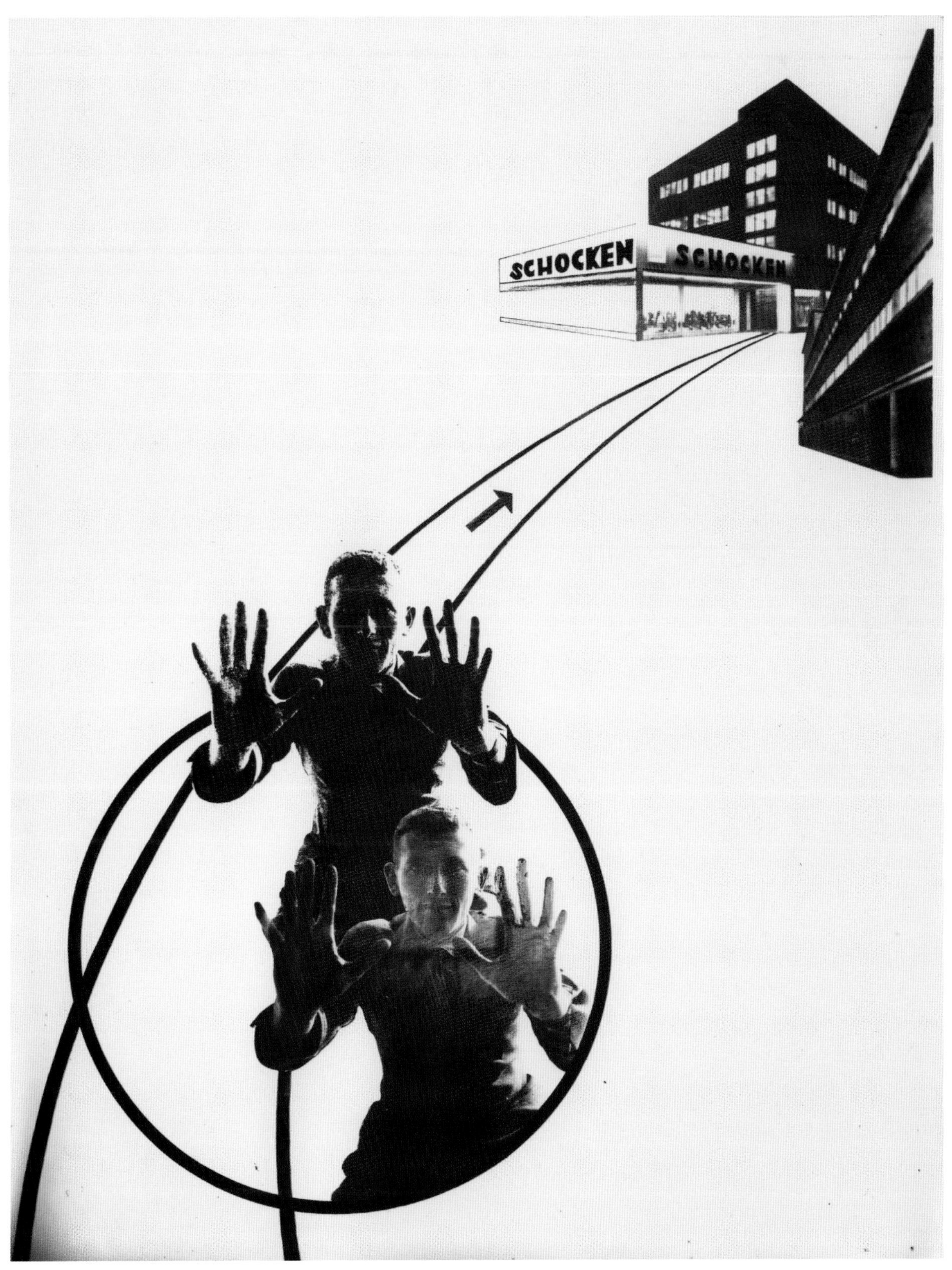

László Moholy-Nagy
[The law of the series] 1925
gelatin silver photograph
J Paul Getty Museum, Los Angeles

EXPRESSIONISM

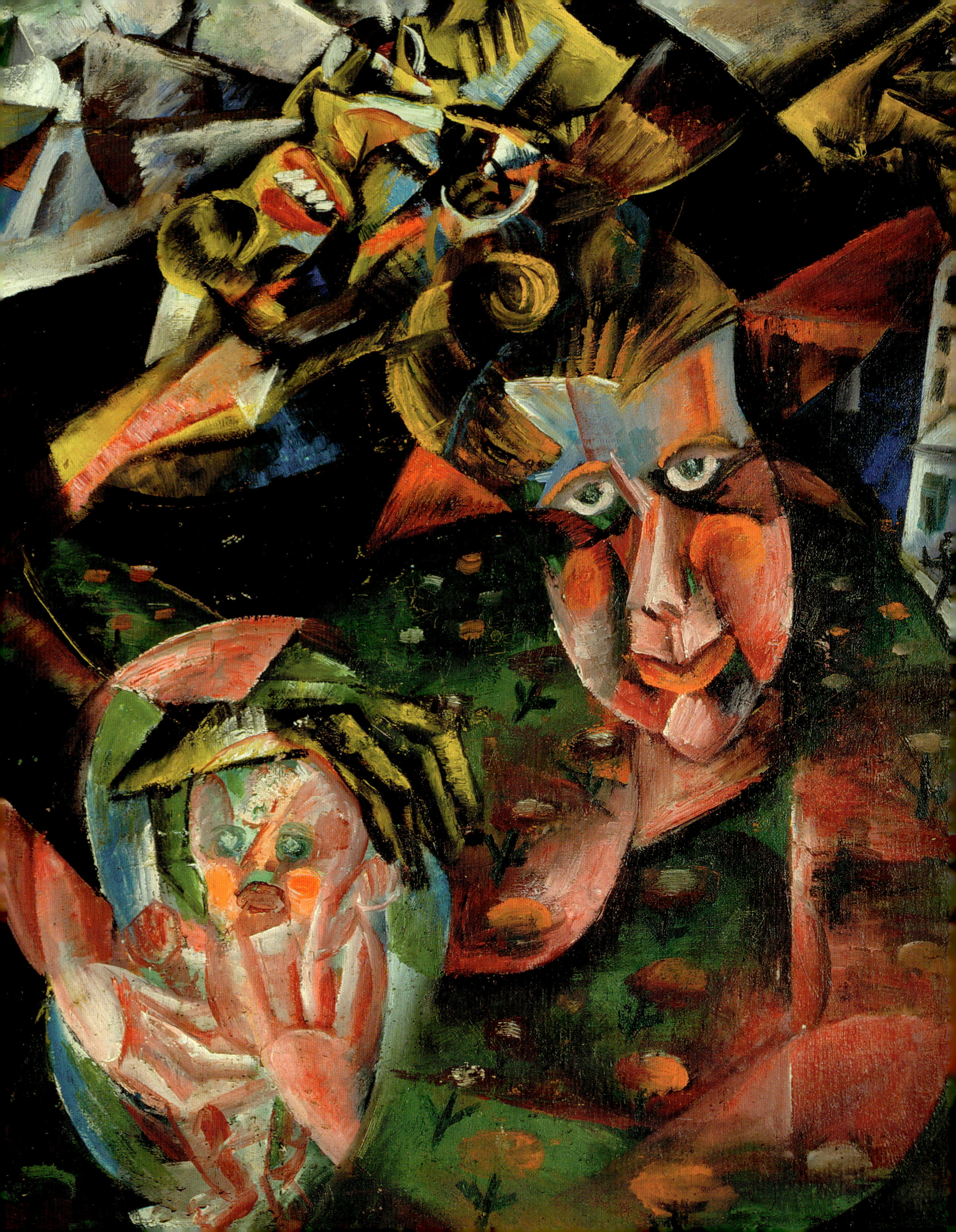

GERMAN EXPRESSIONISM: APOCALYPSE, WAR AND REVOLUTION

Jill Lloyd

Expressionism is a term that is often used to cover a bewildering variety of subjects and styles. It includes both the lively figuration practiced by the Brücke artists in the early years of the century and colourful abstract paintings by Wassily Kandinsky and other members of the Blaue Reiter. Moreover, the term is applied to two generations of artists: both the classic Expressionists of the Brücke and Blaue Reiter groups, which were founded between 1905 and 1911 and were swept up by the idealism and optimism of the new century, and those born ten years later – like George Grosz and Otto Dix – who came to maturity on the brutal battlefields of the First World War. These disparate experiences gave rise to contradictions and tensions in Expressionist art that are a source of its nervy vitality. But it remains to be seen whether Expressionism as a style and a world view was able to withstand the violent shocks of war and revolution. The searing images that Dix, Grosz and Max Beckmann made in response to these traumatic events pushed the expressive potential of 20th-century art to powerful new extremes. Can these artists who transformed an existing style still be termed Expressionists, or did they create something radically new?

Like many avant-garde artists in the early years of the 20th century – including the Cubists and Futurists – the Expressionists viewed the city as a potent symbol of modernity that would help sweep away the cobwebs of the past. Originally the Brücke artists concentrated on colourful depictions of city entertainment, such as the circus, cabaret and vaudeville, as well as lively records of street life in Dresden, where the group was based. Typically for Expressionist art, which thrives on contrast and opposition, their early exhibitions juxtaposed dynamic images of urban life with depictions of nude bathers frolicking in the lakes and forests outside the city limits. The Brücke artists infused both areas of experience with vibrant colour and energy, an approach that was inspired by their readings of Friedrich Nietzsche's vitalist philosophy. Their nudist outings with friends and models to the Moritzburg lakes near Dresden flew in the face of bourgeois convention; like other German youth movements at the beginning of the new century, the young artists escaped the burgeoning city to embrace nature as a rejuvenating force. However, there is no anti-urban sentiment in early Brücke depictions of the city – on the contrary, the cabaret and circus were celebrated as risky, alternative entertainments on the fringes of society that equally undermined the status quo.

All this changed when the Brücke artists moved to Berlin in 1911 and were confronted by the reality of life in the big city. In comparison to the elegant Baroque city of Dresden, Berlin was a fast-developing modern metropolis, undergoing an explosion of modernisation and industrialisation that eventually transformed it into the third-largest city in the world. Ernst Ludwig Kirchner's sequence of Berlin street scenes, including *Five women on the street* 1913 (fig 1 p 35), which show prostitutes stalking the city streets, chronicle the artist's response to the alienation and fragmentation associated with big-city life. Based on the iconography of contemporary fashion plates, Kirchner's mannequin-like

Otto Dix
The Felixmüller family 1919 (detail)

women are objects for sale, just like the goods they are gazing at in brightly lit shop windows. With their lurid, masked faces and extravagant feathered costumes, they inhabit a threatening urban jungle where the individual is overpowered by the anonymous city crowd. The city, in Kirchner's view, is electrified by sexual tension, and the women in his Berlin paintings – such as *Woman in a hat* 1911 (p 43) – exude both elegance and magnetic sexuality.

This crucial shift in city Expressionism and Kirchner's evocation of the powerful sexual drives that energise the city streets paved the way for Dix, Grosz and Beckmann, who all used city imagery to convey their vision of humanity's basest instincts. The destructive forces that simmer beneath the surface in Kirchner's paintings are graphically evident in a number of works by second-generation Expressionists, which take up the themes of murder, suicide and sexual crimes. Using the fragmented, prismatic devices of Futurism and Cubism, as well as the stylistic exaggerations of Expressionism, Grosz presents the city as a teeming battle for survival in *Metropolis* 1916–17 (opposite), where a medley of urban experiences collides in a headlong rush. In *Suicide* 1916 (p 51), Grosz depicts a street corner bathed in lurid red light, where a prostitute and her misshapen client overlook a scene of sordid destruction: in the foreground a man has committed suicide; another has hung himself from a nearby lamppost, while scavenging dogs prowl by. *Murder in Ackerstrasse* 1916–17 (p 37) presents a gory, sexual murder in a tight, linear style that foreshadows Grosz's depictions of the city in the 1920s, while a similar theme features in a contemporary painting by Heinrich Maria Davringhausen, *The sex murderer* 1917 (p 49), which is a variation on Edouard Manet's famous modernist painting of a prostitute, *Olympia* 1863 (Musée d'Orsay, Paris). The prostitute's client – who in Manet's rendering sent a colourful bouquet of flowers to Olympia – now lurks beneath the bed, his sinister eyes fixed on a revolver the girl apparently keeps to defend herself on her bedside table. Through the prisms of the window a lurid city view bears silent witness to the crime that is about to be enacted.

The city was the site for another violent theme in Expressionist art: apocalypse and war. Ludwig Meidner's apocalyptic paintings, for example, show the city as a wasteland torn apart by explosions and peopled by terrified figures fleeing collapsing, burning buildings. Works such as *Apocalyptic landscape* 1913 (p 45) are often interpreted as anticipating the war to come, but it was the cleansing potential of war rather than its horror that preoccupied Expressionist artists at the time. Indeed, Expressionist poets like Georg Heym, Georg Trakl and Johannes R Becher, together with artists like Meidner and Kandinsky, all took up the theme of the apocalypse in anticipation of a cataclysmic battle that would purge the modern age of its materialism and make way for a new spiritual era.

In the months leading up to the war, this idealistic message was combined with patriotic fervour and widely disseminated to German youths through propaganda encouraging them to volunteer.[1] Many members of the Expressionist avant-garde were swept up in this excitement and shared the view that Germany was not an aggressor but rather an avenging angel – envisaged by Ernst Barlach in *The avenger* 1914 (p 46) – that would crush materialism and lay the foundations for a new and better world. In 1915, the leading Berlin publisher Paul Cassirer put all his energies into a new weekly periodical titled *Kriegszeit* (*Wartime*), which contained patriotic texts and illustrations by artists including Beckmann and Barlach. Fired by their ideals, a number of Expressionist artists volunteered for active service when war was declared in 1914, although some, like Beckmann and Erich Heckel, sought to avoid direct combat by volunteering for the medical corps. Dix was just 22 years old and a student at the Academy of Art in Dresden when he enlisted. Heading off to war with the Bible and Nietzsche's *Gay science* in his hand, Dix viewed the conflict as a Nietzschean affirmation of human existence at its most violent and dramatic extreme. Even Beckmann, who was more concerned from the outset with the human cost of war, saw it as an opportunity for personal development. Writing to his wife Minna Tube in March 1915, he confirmed: 'It's good for me that there's war now. Everything I did previously was no more than an apprenticeship. I am still learning and growing.'[2]

Nobody had prepared the young men who marched off in 1914 with roses in their hands for the shock of modern mechanical warfare, which totally transformed the practice of war and caused devastation on a scale that had not previously been seen: 'the vision that was transmitted to us by history, the advice of our parents and previous writings about war are all totally false,' wrote one young student volunteer after a short period at the front.[3] Within two months of joining the fray, Blaue Reiter artist August Macke was killed and his friend Franz Marc fell in March 1916 at Verdun. The Brücke

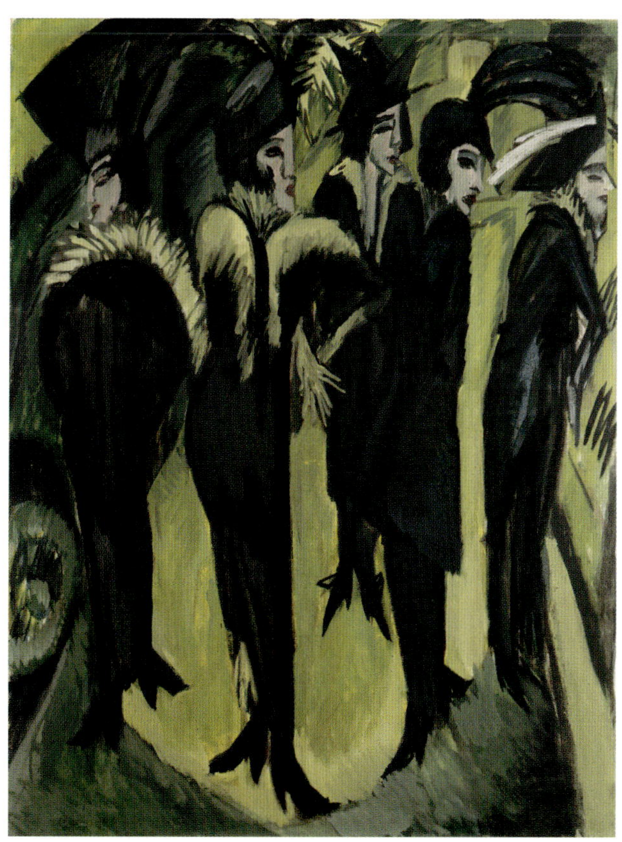

fig 1
Ernst Ludwig Kirchner
Five women on the street 1913
oil on canvas, 120 x 90 cm
Museum Ludwig, Cologne

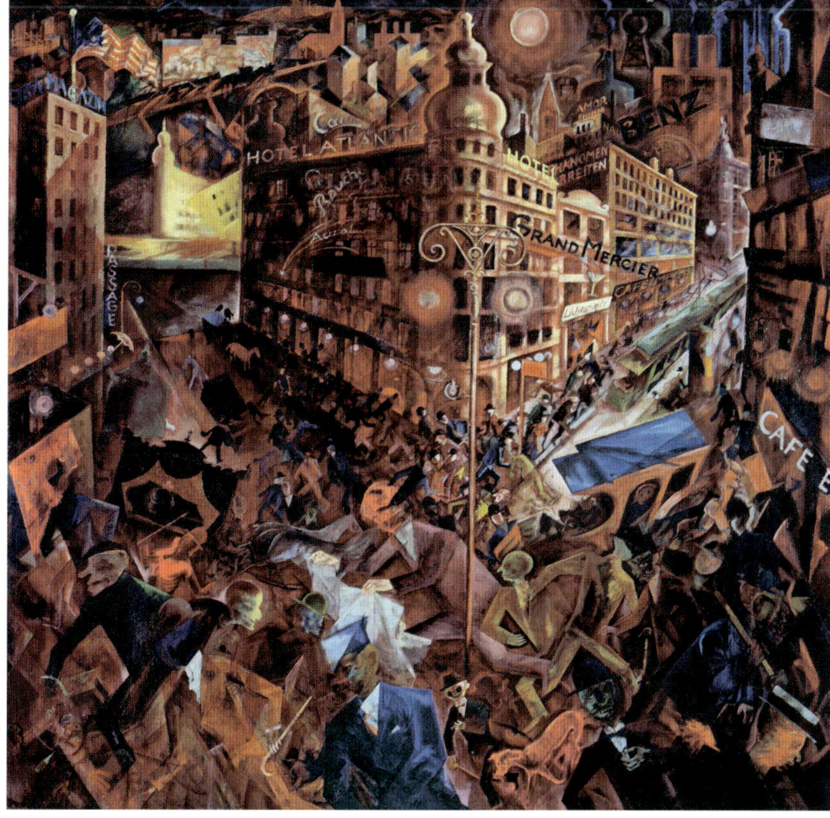

fig 2
George Grosz
Metropolis 1916–17
oil on canvas, 100 x 102 cm
Museo Thyssen-Bornemisza, Madrid

artists Kirchner and Max Pechstein, along with Beckmann and Grosz, all suffered mental breakdowns and were discharged from the army. Grosz was so disgusted by the hollow patriotism of the Germans that he Americanised his first name and began to record his bitter indictments of the German bourgeois society that had sped headlong into war in works like *Metropolis* and *Suicide*, which he executed in 1916–17.

A sign of the turning tide was Cassirer's decision to suspend his magazine *Kriegszeit* in 1916 and replace it with a series of pacifist broadsheets called *Der Bildermann* (*The picture man*). Barlach, whose *The avenger* (p 46) had represented the ideals of a generation of young Germans eager for war, now echoed Cassirer's antiwar stance, providing an illustration titled *Give us peace*, for *Der Bildermann*'s December 1916 issue.[4] The tragedies of war were experienced on the home front as well as the battlefield. Käthe Kollwitz (who lost her own son Peter in Flanders in October 1914) most memorably commemorated the heart-rending loss of husbands and sons in her graphic portfolio *War* 1924. The roughly hewn black-and-white woodcuts in this series, and the bold, simplified figures, show how the visual vocabulary of Expressionism gave eloquent voice to universal human suffering, as in *The parents* (p 64). Kollwitz stayed close to original Expressionist ideals, not only in her preference for bold, reductive forms, but also in the noble sentiments behind her work, which contain nothing of the cynicism and disillusionment we associate with artists of the second generation, such as Dix and Grosz.

Otto Dix was exceptional among artists for remaining in service throughout the course of the war. He trained as a machine-gunner, and returned again and again to active service, driven by a compulsion to experience its primal horrors: 'War is something so animal-like: hunger, lice, slime, these crazy sounds,' he later wrote, 'War was something horrible, but nonetheless something powerful ... Under no circumstances could I miss it! It is necessary to see people in this unfettered condition in order to know something about them.'[5] Although there was little opportunity to paint on the front, Dix made numerous sketches of fighting soldiers and the war-scarred landscape in a style that mixed Expressionist with Futurist and Cubist elements, while occasionally veering towards graphic realism.

The spontaneity of Expressionist style was well suited to recording fleeting impressions on the frontline, but when Dix returned to the subject in his graphic cycle *War* 1924, he recalled its horrors with studied and exaggerated realism. Although Dix maintained that he was 'no pacifist', his etchings in this cycle are a searing indictment of a war that produced victims rather than heroes. The barely human figures sporting gas masks in *Storm troopers advancing under a gas attack* 1924 (p 56) seem driven by a blind instinct to kill, while *Transplantation [Skin graft]* 1924 (p 57) dwells on the terrible disfigurations suffered by the survivors of war. Dix's delineation of horrific details – the flapping skin, crude scars and blasted features of this sad remnant of humanity – bears no relation to the style or the sentiments of prewar Expressionism. Dix still subscribed to Nietzschean vitalism, which is now expressed in disturbing images of dead bodies covered with worms and flowers sprouting beside corpses to evoke the never-ending cycle of death and new life. But this vitalism is so dramatically different from the early Expressionists' joyful affirmation of life that the artists seem to be speaking, literally, from different worlds.

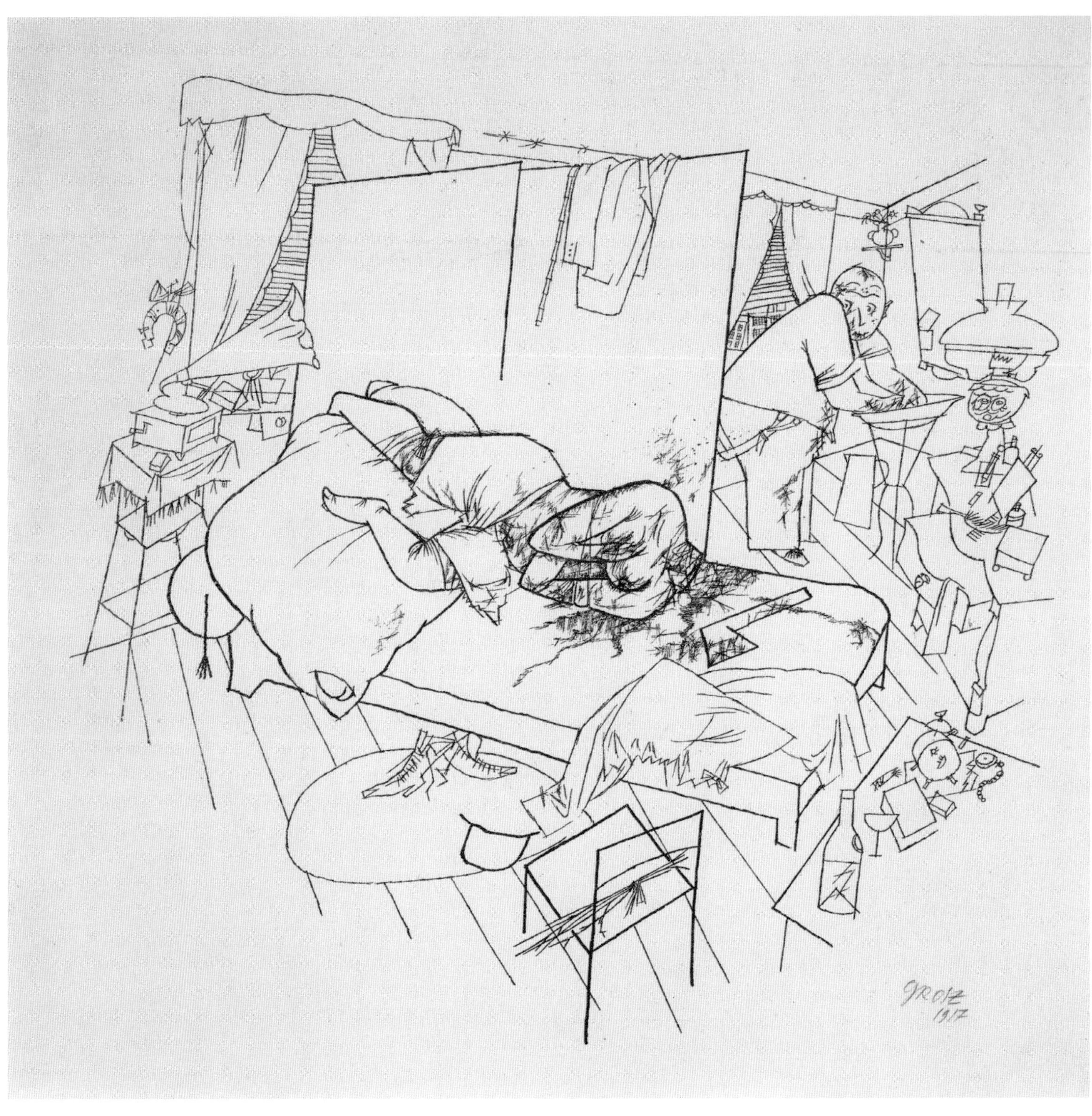

George Grosz
Murder in Ackerstrasse 1916–17
lithograph
Art Gallery of New South Wales, Sydney

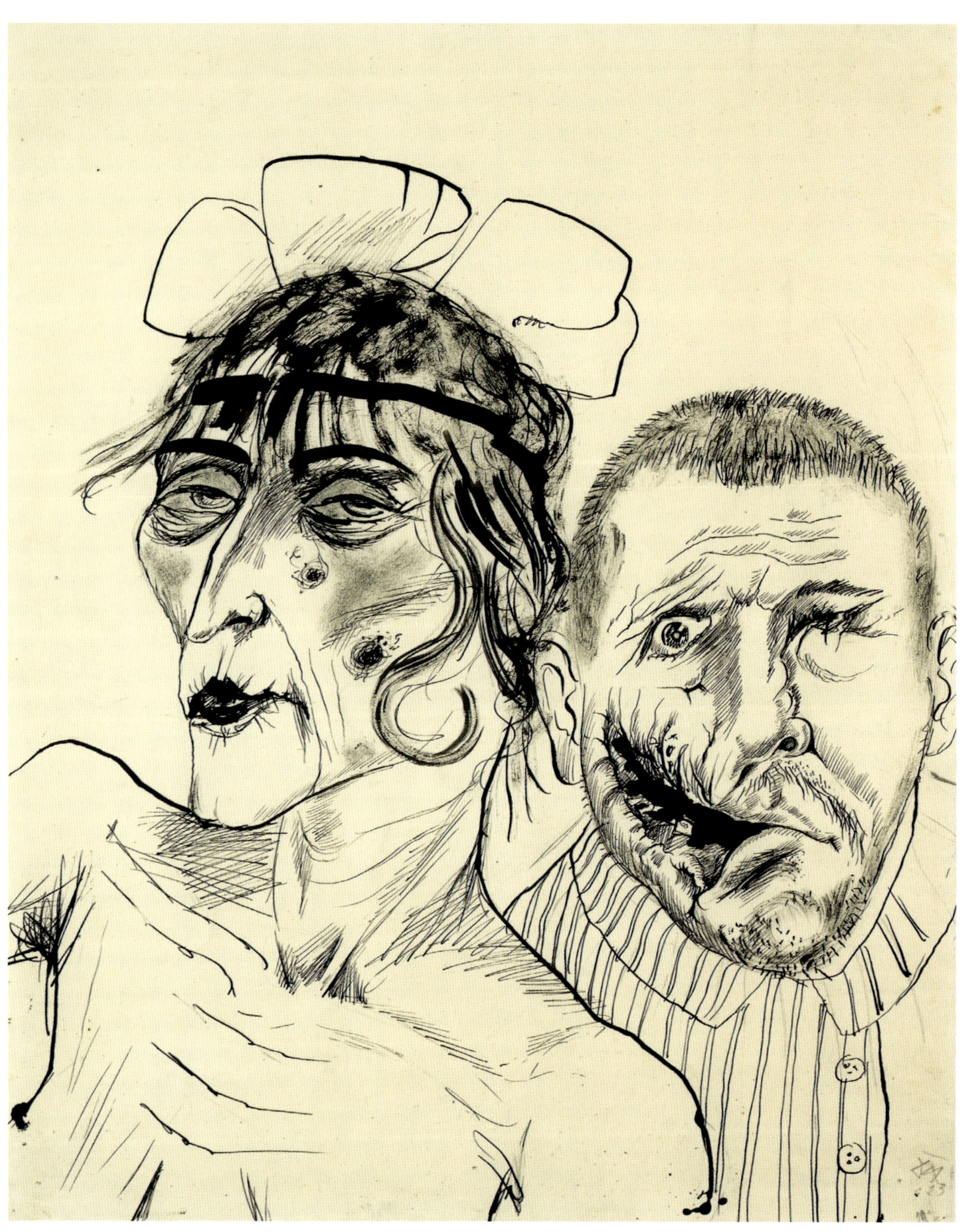

Otto Dix
Prostitute and war wounded 1923
pen, ink
LWL-Landesmuseum für Kunst und Kulturgeschichte
Westfälisches Landesmuseum, Münster

The Germany that emerged from the ashes of war in 1918 did indeed bear little relation to its prewar counterpart. When the German front collapsed in August 1918, a wave of revolutionary mutinies and strikes forced the Kaiser to abdicate and flee the country on 9 November 1918, which was the cue for the Social Democrats to proclaim a republic. This revolution, which has come to be known as the November Revolution, gave one last burst of utopian hope to Expressionist artists, who had become increasingly disillusioned during the war. Believing that Expressionism could provide the new Weimar Republic with a revolutionary art, a group led by the Brücke artist Max Pechstein entreated all the 'revolutionaries in spirit (Expressionists, Cubists, Futurists)' to unite in an association of 'radical creative artists'.[6] The following month two organisations, the *Novembergruppe* (November Group) and the *Arbeitsrat für Kunst* (Working Council for Art) were formed, in which Expressionist artists like Pechstein and Meidner played leading roles. Indeed, Pechstein issued a statement on behalf of the *Novembergruppe*, titled '*Was wir wollen*' ('What We Want'), affirming art's newly politicised role:

> We hope that a socialist republic not only will make the situation in the art world healthy, but will create a unified art epoch for our generation ... Therefore we will be able to breathe new life into the dead ideals of our age ... Let the socialist republic give us their confidence ... Then, out of the dry earth flowers will blossom to its greater glory.[7]

At first the republic was governed by an uneasy alliance of moderate and radical socialists who stopped short of the social revolution advocated by the German Communist Party (KPD), which was formed at the end of 1918. Most Expressionists leaned to the left politically and many sided with the ruling Social Democratic Party against the communists. Rudi Feld's poster *The danger of bolshevism* c1920 (p 71) goes so far as to picture Russian communism – which the Germans feared would invade their borders – as a personification of death, holding a bloody dagger between its teeth. Pechstein's political posters use the rhetorical devices of Expressionism to affirm his support for the new republican regime; although he called for a revolutionary art, he nevertheless argued for political moderation and opposed riots and strikes. Pechstein's dynamic image of a revolutionary mob streaming past a lynched man hanging from a lamppost in *To the lantern!* c1919 (p 67) is sometimes misread as advocating violent class struggle, whereas it was in fact part of a series opposing it.

Political events in 1919 soon put an end to the Expressionists' idealistic hope that a moderate revolution would win the day. When the communists staged an unsuccessful uprising in Berlin in January 1919, their leaders Karl Liebknecht and Rosa Luxemburg were brutally murdered while in the custody of military units called in by the Social Democrats to quell the riots. Even artists who supported the socialist republic, such as Kollwitz, regarded these murders as an atrocity. In her *Memorial for Karl Liebknecht* 1919–20 (p 65) she drew on traditional imagery associated with the Lamentation of Christ to commemorate the communist leader's death. By the spring of 1919, the chaotic political situation had gone from bad to worse: in March a general strike organised by radical socialists and communists was brutally crushed by the government, resulting in the loss of more than a thousand lives. The following month, a Bavarian Soviet Republic was proclaimed in Munich, which was violently crushed in May. To make matters worse, Germany was hit by an economic crisis and dramatic hyperinflation that lasted from mid 1922 to November 1923.

In the face of these events, many first-generation Expressionists retreated into their private worlds or, in the case of Kollwitz, concentrated on the humanitarian issues arising from the extreme politics of the day. It was left to the second-generation Expressionists – Dix, Grosz and Beckmann – to produce work that tackled the tough issue of political disillusionment in postwar Germany. Grosz, who was an early member of the KPD, was still motivated by political ideals; in the 1920s he evolved a graphic style influenced by graffiti to criticise the bourgeois society he detested. In his portfolio *The robbers* 1922, for example, Grosz produced numerous images of a bipolar society where the toiling proletariat and war wounded are viscously suppressed by power-hungry capitalists (p 53). However, Grosz was always more effective at criticism than praise: his capitalists are more convincing than his dispirited workers, and the communists themselves disapproved of his portrayal of the proletariat as downtrodden rather than triumphantly revolutionary.

Together with Grosz, Beckmann and Dix developed a detached, cynical, hard-edged graphic style in the immediate postwar years, which paved the way for the realist movement known as *Neue Sachlichkeit* (New Objectivity). As we have seen in Dix's etchings in the portfolio *War*, he moved away from the Expressionist élan of his early wartime images in favour of an exaggerated realism, which is also evident in his postwar drawings, such as *Prostitute and war wounded* 1923 (p 38). In contrast, Beckmann actually opposed Expressionism before the First World War. It was his experience of war and the mental breakdown he suffered in 1915 that opened his eyes to the potential of avant-garde style: the angular figures, prismatic compositions and brightened palette that feature in his immediate postwar paintings, such as *The dream* 1921 (p 61), are usually identified as aspects of Expressionist style. However, Beckmann also developed his printmaking skills during the war years; through the medium of print he developed a visual and thematic language in the postwar years that was finely attuned to the violence, depravity and political instability of the world around him. Beckmann's lithographic portfolio *Hell* 1919 provides a vividly observant picture of a Germany torn apart by war, revolution, violence and hunger. The artist is an eyewitness to the events he chronicles in his prints, confronting a horribly disfigured war veteran under a lamppost in *The way home* 1919 (opposite) or succumbing, alongside the rest of his family, to the nightmare vision of rape, murder and kidnapping he depicts in *The night* 1919 (p 26).

Like other so-called second-generation Expressionists, Beckmann absorbed the aesthetic lessons of the older generation but ultimately developed a style and range of subjects that were far more hard-edged and cynical than theirs. What little remained of Expressionist idealism after the war died out when the Weimar Republic failed to realise its goals – after this, Expressionism became a fashionable and often commercialised style that was bled of its original significance. Dix, Grosz and Beckmann, on the contrary, developed highly original ways of addressing the social and political chaos that followed, in the wake of war and revolution. Their creation of new graphic styles to convey this grim subject matter broke radical new ground in the visual arts.

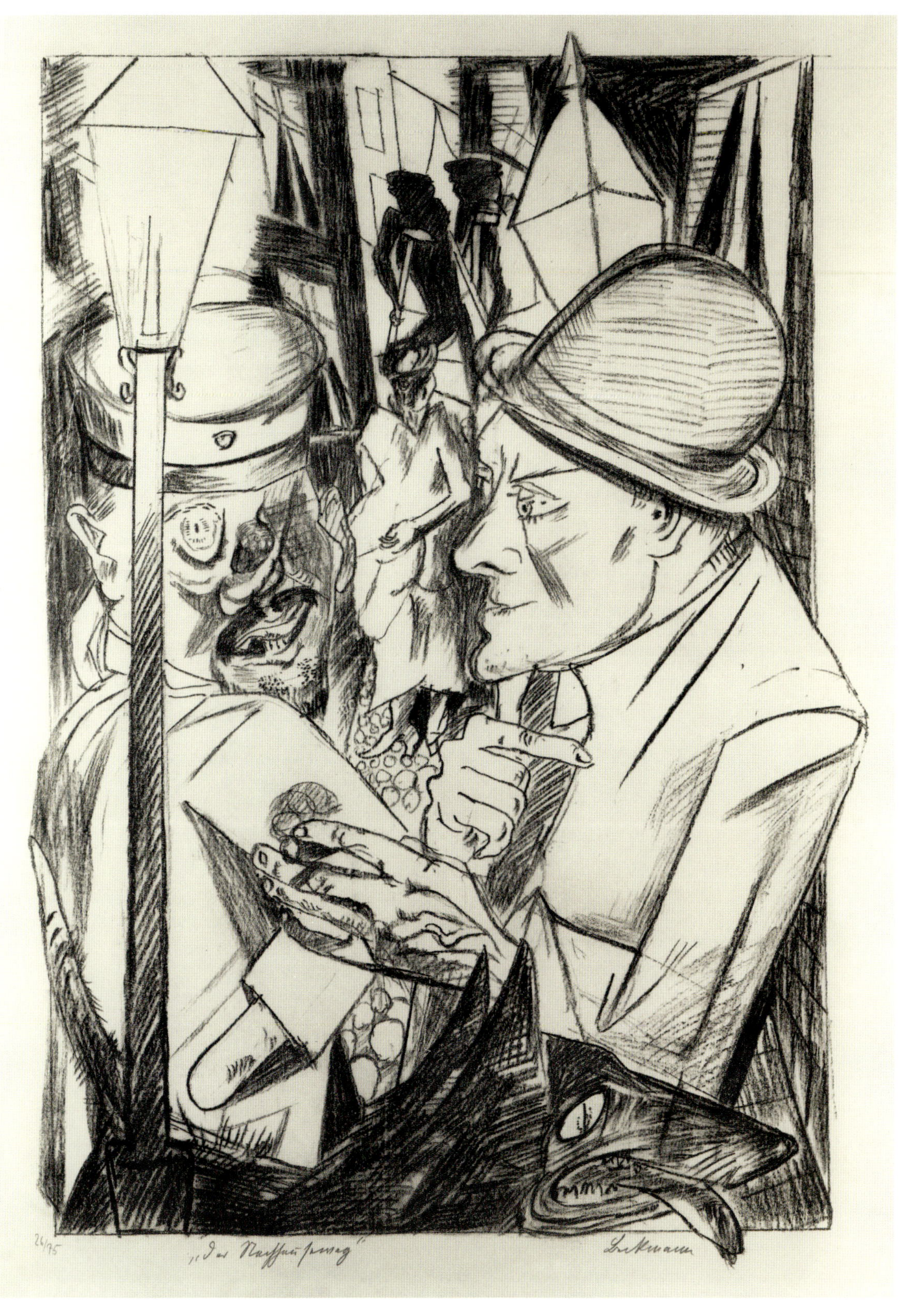

Max Beckmann
The way home 1919
from the portfolio **Hell** 1919
lithograph
Kupferstichkabinett, Staatliche Museen zu Berlin

ERNST LUDWIG KIRCHNER

Woman in a hat

In October 1911, Ernst Ludwig Kirchner moved from the provincial art centre of Dresden to Berlin, which was rapidly emerging as Germany's cultural capital and thriving metropolis. As one of the founding members of the Expressionist artists' group the Brücke, Kirchner had developed a new style of art that emphasised forms and colours derived from the imagination, rather than naturalistic modes of representation that had evolved from 19th-century academic traditions. Between 1911 and the outbreak of the First World War, Kirchner focused intensively on the representation of the female form, either in urban contexts where he portrayed women as circus performers, dancers and prostitutes, or in natural landscape settings inspired by summer visits to the Baltic island of Fehmarn. The paintings, prints and wood sculptures he produced during these years are widely accepted as the high point of his work and as critically important examples of German Expressionism.

Woman in a hat 1911 exemplifies Kirchner's early interest in portraying a distinctly modern, urban type – a motif he would develop over the coming years in the remarkable series of works now known as the Berlin street scenes. The simplified and angular rendition of the female form, and frontal placement of the figure in direct confrontation with the viewer marked a new direction in Kirchner's work; it departed significantly from his brightly coloured, Fauvist-inspired works created in Dresden. Unlike the decorative settings previously seen in his studio paintings, the background in this work appears sparse and generalised, and the perspective is distorted so that the background comes forward rather than receding.[1] The dark, boldly outlined depiction of the figure contrasts strongly with the coarsely painted, warmer tones of the background, although a highly expressive, painterly quality can be seen throughout the composition. A sense of unease is created by the lack of spatial depth and the woman's unusual pose, as she literally pushes against the edges of the canvas with her elbows.

Kirchner frequently gave his figures mask-like features, inspired by African sculpture. Yet here the woman is shown putting on the mask as a device to conceal her identity, hinting at the alienation and anonymity of city life, which would soon emerge as a major theme in Kirchner's work. With her large, midnight blue hat and matching transparent, body-hugging dress, this woman becomes the quintessential city inhabitant, dressed in the latest fashion which reveals, rather than hides, her sexually available body. As a symbol of modernity, she embodies the inherent anxieties that existed between embracing new, emancipated roles for women and the breakdown of traditional female stereotypes.

Kirchner painted *The pledge – Hutten greets Sickingen* on the reverse side of this canvas between 1923 and 1924, after he had moved to the Swiss Alps to recover from a nervous breakdown. Here he portrays a meeting between the 16th-century humanist Ulrich Hutten and the nationalist Franz von Sickingen, who fought against corruption and foreign dominance.[2] The vibrant colour and decorative style of this work reveals Kirchner's desire to return to earlier artistic influences, as illustrated in many of his paintings from the mid 1920s.

This intriguing double-sided painting was donated to the Art Gallery of Western Australia in 1979 by Baron Thyssen-Bornemisza – a passionate collector of modern art with a special interest in early 20th-century German art – as a gift to celebrate the opening of the new building. Kirchner's highly important contribution to German Expressionist painting is further represented in Australia by *Three bathers* 1913, in the collection of the Art Gallery of New South Wales. JS

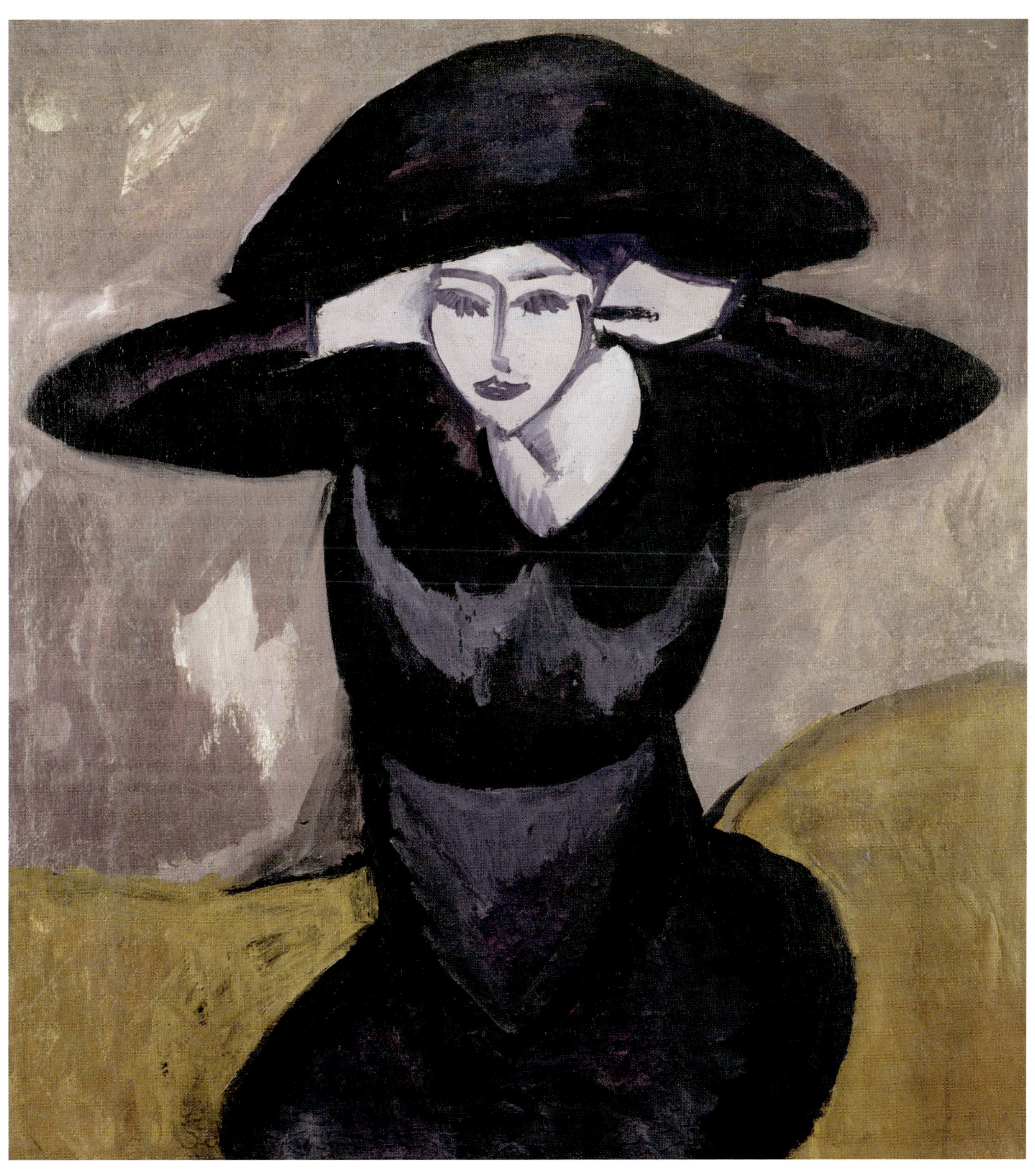

Ernst Ludwig Kirchner
Woman in a hat 1911
oil on canvas
State Art Collection, Art Gallery of Western Australia, Perth

LUDWIG MEIDNER

Apocalyptic landscape

> I trembled, all that high summer through, in front of canvases that seethed with all the fuming anguish of earth, in every patch of colour, in every scrap of cloud, and in every cascading stream ... My brain bled dreadful visions. I could see nothing but a thousand skeletons jigging in a row. Many graves and burned cities writhed across the plains ...[1]

Written from his studio in Berlin, in this statement Ludwig Meidner was referring to the series of expressionistic visions he painted between 1912 and 1916, of a world on the brink of an apocalypse. Pulsating with a sense of nervous energy and crazed intensity, these 'apocalyptic landscapes', as the series has come to be known, are uncanny in their depiction of war, destruction and revolution. Meidner's obsession with portraying catastrophe arose from a deep inner need to release the terrible anxiety he experienced prior to the outbreak of war. He depicts a world torn apart by cosmic forces creating turmoil, uncertainty and alienation in sharp contrast to the utopian future imagined by many Expressionists. Meidner remained an independent eccentric, renowned for the emotive force of his visionary landscapes which capture, more than any other Expressionist images, the social, political and human disaster that would soon unfold.

In one of the most powerful works from the series, painted in 1913 on the eve of the First World War, Meidner turned away from the bright sunlight depicted in many prewar Expressionist landscapes and represented a culture of shredded nerves and nocturnal terror. Far from yearning for Arcadia, the figures in *Apocalyptic landscape* 1913 – including the artist himself, who appears in the lower left-hand side of the composition – appear isolated and distressed, helplessly trying to escape from the ruined city that both tremors and explodes with extraordinary force. The drama of the scene is emphasised through the agitated brushwork and use of rich, dark colours in the night sky, contrasted against the bleached and barren landscape in the foreground. Though he shared an interest in the highly charged subject matter and emotional intensity of the Expressionists with whom he worked and socialised, Meidner also drew upon numerous art historical influences, ranging from the gestural mark-making of Vincent van Gogh and expressive distortion of El Greco, to the religious intensity found in German Renaissance paintings by Matthias Grünewald and Lucas Cranach.[2]

The convulsive, tormented style of Meidner's work from 1912 to 1920, for which he is best known, changed dramatically after the war. Unlike many of his contemporaries, Meidner opposed the war and did not enlist when war was declared. He was drafted in 1916, however, and spent most of his time as a translator in a prisoner-of-war camp for French soldiers. He also wrote pacifist texts and developed Catholic as well as Jewish religious subjects in his art. In 1935 he was condemned as a 'degenerate' artist and fled to England with his family in 1938. Meidner returned to Germany in the 1950s and remained there until his death in 1966, receiving wide public recognition as a prominent modern artist. JS

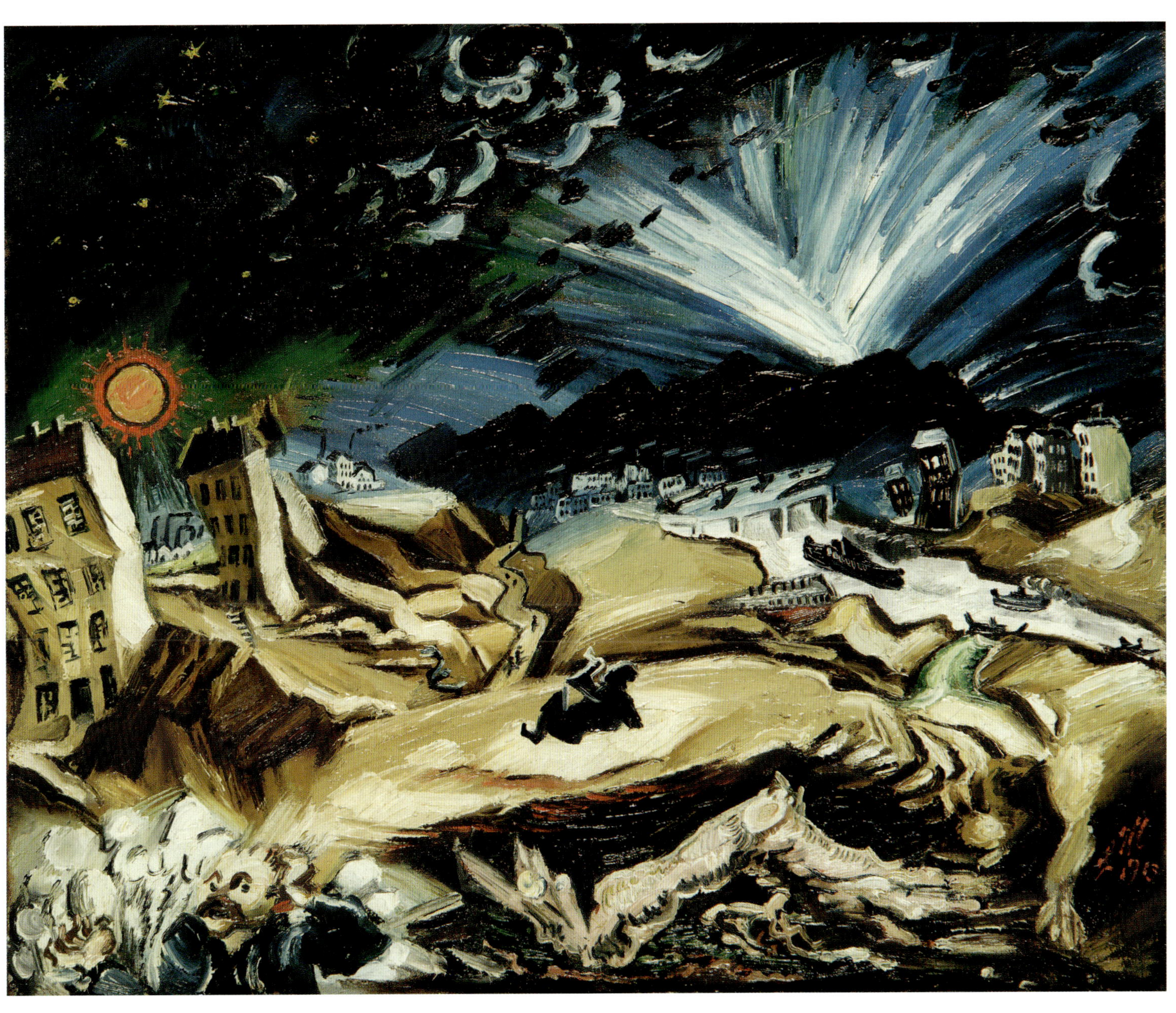

Ludwig Meidner
Apocalyptic landscape 1913
oil on canvas
Private collection, courtesy Richard Nagy, London

ERNST BARLACH

The avenger

Sculptor, writer and graphic artist Ernst Barlach trained at the School of Applied Arts in Hamburg and continued his studies in Dresden, Paris and Berlin. He travelled to Russia in 1906 and was profoundly influenced by the emotional expressiveness of eastern European culture. Throughout his working life, Barlach remained preoccupied with expressing the mental states of his figures, which often took the form of Russian peasants or beggars. These starkly simplified, almost rustic figures came to represent universal themes of human existence, suffering and sacrifice.[1]

Created in December 1914, during the early months of the First World War, *The avenger* conveys the sense of idealism and optimism with which many artists greeted what they believed would be the medium of cultural renewal and an apocalyptic cataclysm. Like many of his contemporaries, Barlach responded enthusiastically to the outbreak of war and volunteered to serve in the infantry between 1915 and 1916.[2] In this dynamic representation of the human form, Barlach depicts a heavily draped figure wielding a scythe and charging dramatically towards what many believed would be a rapid victory. The sharp angularity of the figure recalls the Cubists' emphasis on strong, linear form, while the dramatic sense of movement used by the Italian Futurists and the use of bold outlines found in Expressionist art are also evident in this striking bronze sculpture.

Barlach's initial enthusiasm for war as a dynamic, modern force soon gave way to the grim realisation of mechanised warfare's destructive potential to tear apart humanity and civilisation. After the war, Barlach produced a number of monumental public memorials that were intended as powerful antiwar statements in Lübeck, Güstrow, Kiel and other cities in Germany. He remained a highly individual and respected artist who existed outside of the institutionalised art world, although his work is considered to be generally Expressionist in character. At the height of his success in the early 1930s, Barlach was described as 'alien' and 'eastern' by the National Socialists, and his work was discredited as 'degenerate' art.[3] He was forbidden to exhibit in Germany and many of his public sculptures and memorials were destroyed shortly before his death in 1938. JS

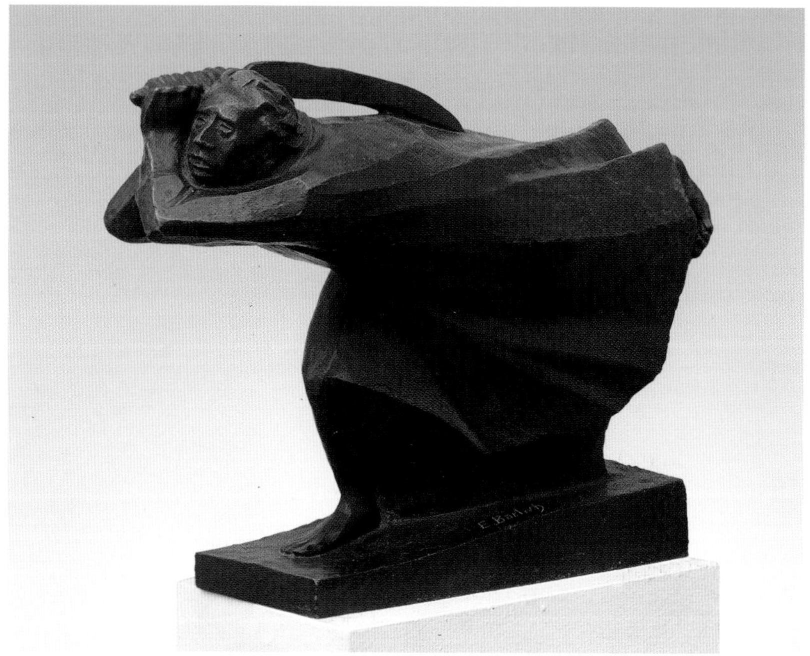

Ernst Barlach
The avenger 1914
bronze
Museum Ludwig, Cologne

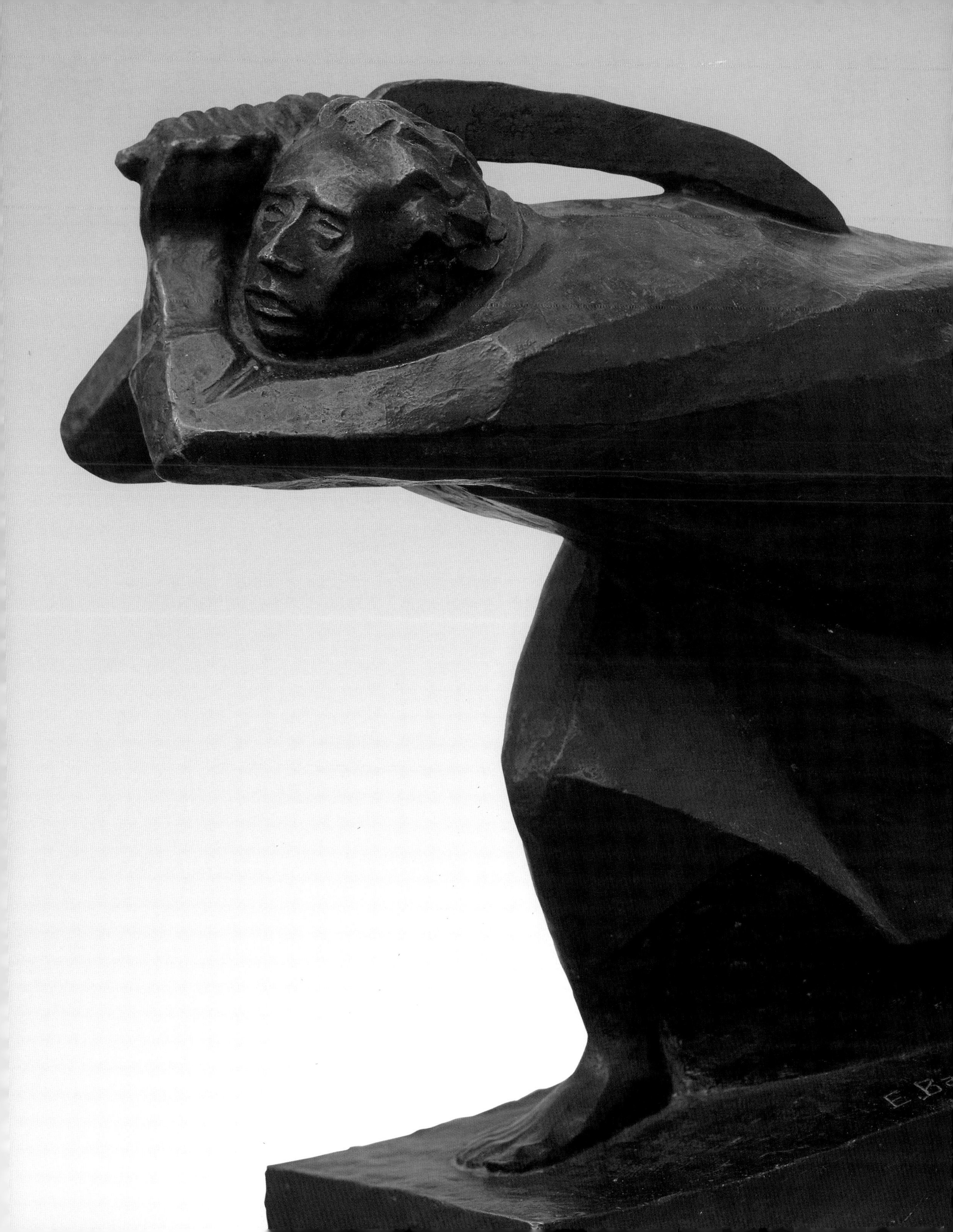

HEINRICH MARIA DAVRINGHAUSEN

The sex murderer

An essentially self-taught artist, Heinrich Maria Davringhausen moved from Aachen to Berlin during the war. There he came into contact with a range of avant-garde influences, including Expressionism, Cubism and Dada. Though he was accepted by radical, left-wing artists and writers, such as George Grosz, John Heartfield and Wieland Herzfelde, he did not become intensively engaged as a political artist.

The sex murderer 1917 was one of a series of oils painted by Davringhausen at the end of the war that portrayed the disturbing, yet frequently depicted subject of *Lustmord*, or sexual murder. The obsession of artists, writers and filmmakers of the time to represent *Lustmord* demonstrated that anxieties brought about by the war and living in the metropolis often centred around violent sexual representations of the female body (see pp 37, 49, 194).[1] Despite the shocking and powerful nature of its subject matter, *The sex murderer* has often been described in terms of its formal 'restraint' and 'lyrical sentimentality'.[2]

In this distinctly modernist representation of the female nude, Davringhausen draws upon a number of art historical precedents, most notably Edouard Manet's *Olympia* 1863 (Musée d'Orsay, Paris). Specific reference is made to Manet's well-known painting through the relaxed, yet sexually assertive posture of the reclining woman and the cat arching its back at the woman's feet. Davringhausen's female nude was also modeled on Titian's *Venus of Urbino* 1538 (Uffizi, Florence) and Francisco de Goya's *Naked Maja* 1797–1805 (Museo del Prado, Madrid).[3] Yet this image of a young prostitute who will soon be the victim of a violent sex crime portrays the cold and prosaic reality of a truly contemporary subject. The expressionistic depiction of crowded, high apartment buildings, and the stormy night sky through the window enhances the drama of the composition. The dark, midnight tones of the dimly lit and tightly composed interior are sharply contrasted against the soft hues and almost floating quality of the woman on the bed. With her expressionless, heavily made-up face and strange hat, she appears as an object – or a mannequin in a shop window. All of these pictorial elements combine to create a somewhat bizarre and jarring image that was intended as an affront to bourgeois morality during a time of extreme trauma and conflict.

At the end of the war Davringhausen moved to Munich, where he held his first one-man exhibition. Like many of his contemporaries in Munich, he was strongly influenced by the work of the Italian *Pittura metafisica* artists Carlo Carrà and Giorgio de Chirico. Around 1920, he adopted the sharper, hard-edge style of painting that came to be known as *Neue Sachlichkeit* (New Objectivity); this new style of painting is also clearly evident in Carlo Mense's 1922 portrait of Davringhausen (p 238). Davringhausen left Germany permanently in 1933 and continued to work as an artist in France, under the name Henri Davring. JS

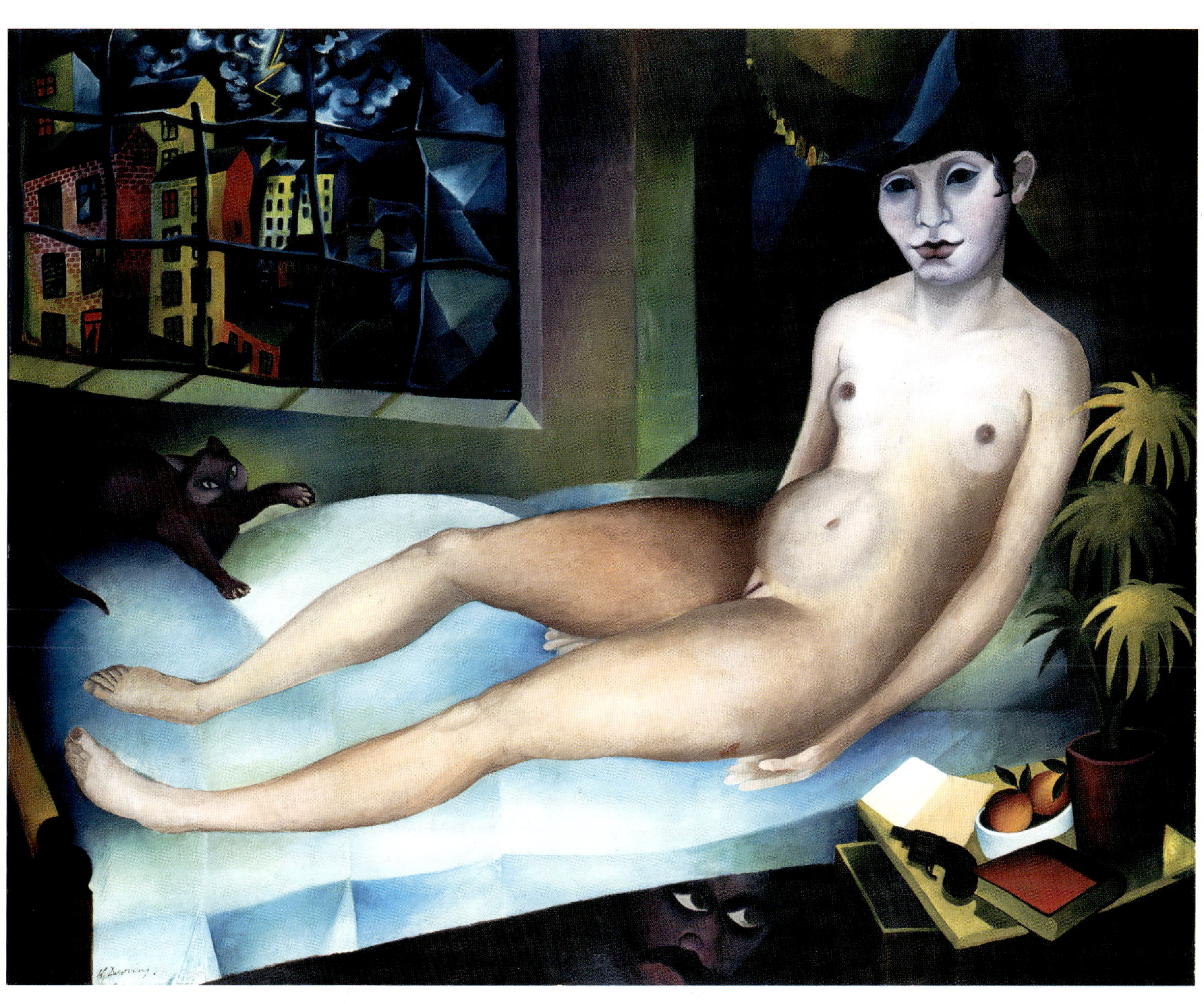

Heinrich Maria Davringhausen
The sex murderer 1917
oil on canvas
Bayerische Staatsgemäldesammlungen, Munich
Pinakothek der Moderne

GEORGE GROSZ

Suicide

In 1914, George Grosz enlisted for military service but was released as unfit for service a year later. After returning to Berlin, he began working on a major series of paintings depicting life in the metropolis during the war and exposing the dark side of modernity. Shocked and disgusted by the destructive effects of war that he saw as tearing society apart and leaving individuals physically maimed and emotionally shattered, Grosz was one of the most significant artists of the period to chronicle the excitement and energy of life in the city, but also to document its vices and excesses.

Suicide, prostitution and madness are all represented in one of Grosz's first and most powerful and engaging interpretations of modern city life, *Suicide* 1916. Now relegated to the distant past, the structures of the old world – represented here by the church – have been replaced by symbols of modernity, such as the streets, cafés and roaming dogs, as well as the grotesquely ugly prostitute and her aged client. Drawing upon the Expressionists' use of bright colour to convey emotion and desire, Grosz uses menacing red tones throughout the composition to highlight not only the scene of death but also the perverse moral corruption of life in Berlin. The tilted perspective, emphasis on sharp angles and geometric fragmentation of form further increases the disturbing nature of the subject matter.

Forced back into the army in 1917, Grosz suffered a nervous breakdown and was released permanently from military service. His art moved away from Expressionistic and Cubistic tendencies towards a sharper, more aggressive type of realism. This shift in Grosz's work took place at the same time that he became a member of the German Communist Party and joined leftist artists groups, such as the *Novembergruppe* (November Group) and Berlin Dada. Among his close friends were Ludwig Meidner, Wieland Herzfelde and John Heartfield; many of the socially and politically critical drawings and print portfolios Grosz produced during the war and in the early 1920s were printed by Herzfelde's Marxist publishing house, the Malik Verlag.

Represented in the exhibition are a number of caricatures that Grosz produced for overt political purposes, such as the *First George Grosz portfolio* 1917 (pp 86–8, 286). His intention in these hard-edged drawings of street life in Berlin was to reveal the way in which the exploiting classes under the capitalist system destroyed and betrayed the working classes. In other portfolios, such as *The robbers* of 1922, Grosz depicted what he perceived as the repulsive traits of the ruling classes – decadence, perversity and hypocrisy – contrasted against the suffering and degradation of the proletarian workers (p 53).[1] The title of *The robbers* portfolio was adopted from the drama by Friedrich Schiller, Germany's great writer of the Enlightenment. Grosz gave each work a title based on direct quotes from the 18th-century text to highlight the lawless and corrupt state of postwar, capitalist society in Germany. These print portfolios were produced in either inexpensive, mass-produced editions that could be circulated to the workers or as more expensive, fine art prints that appealed, rather ironically, to middle-class investors during the moment of peak hyper-inflation. Grosz's biting satires of German society were intended to shock viewers to the core, and the artist was forced to stand trial three times in the 1920s, facing charges of obscenity, blasphemy and offending the German military. JS

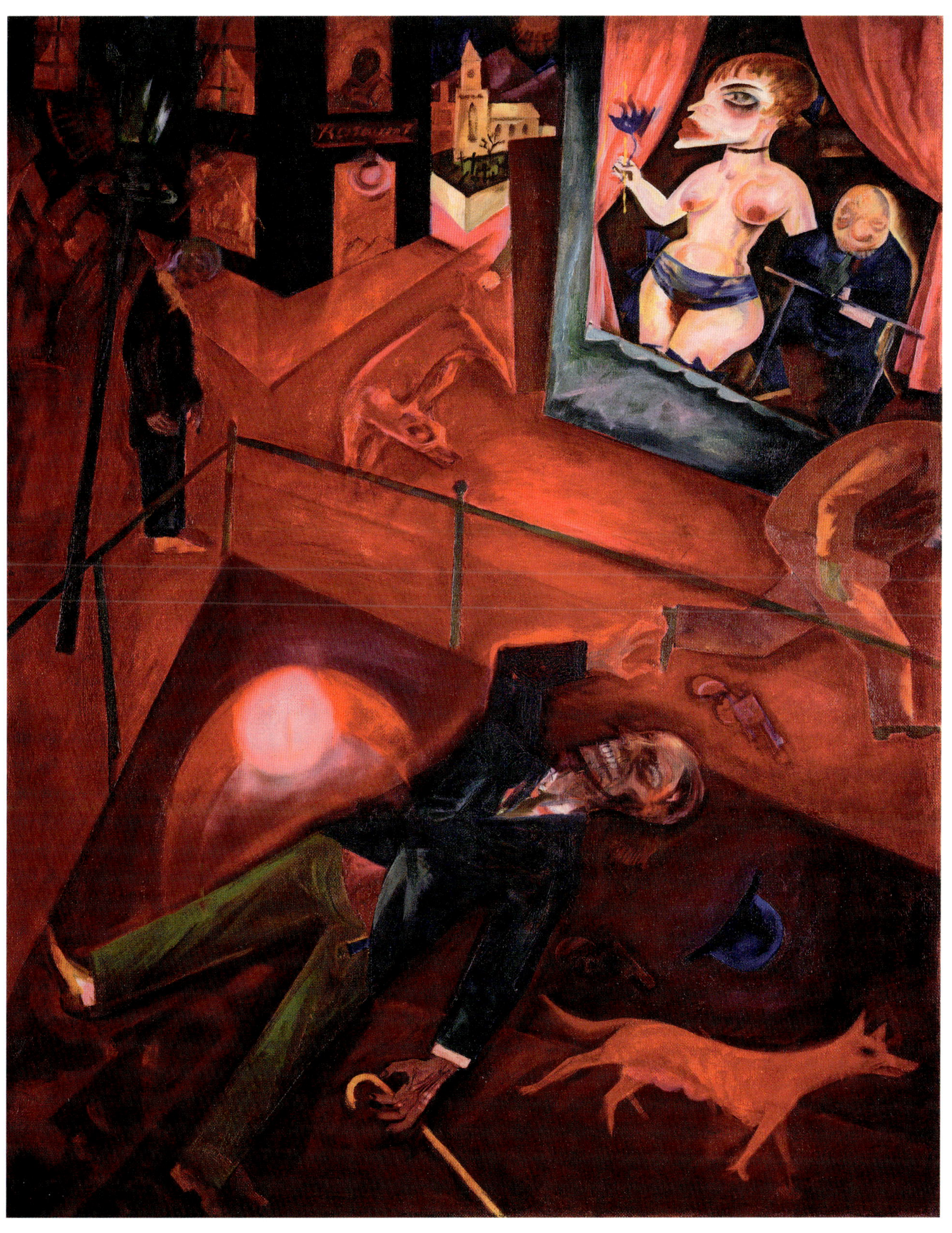

George Grosz
Suicide 1916
oil on canvas
Tate London

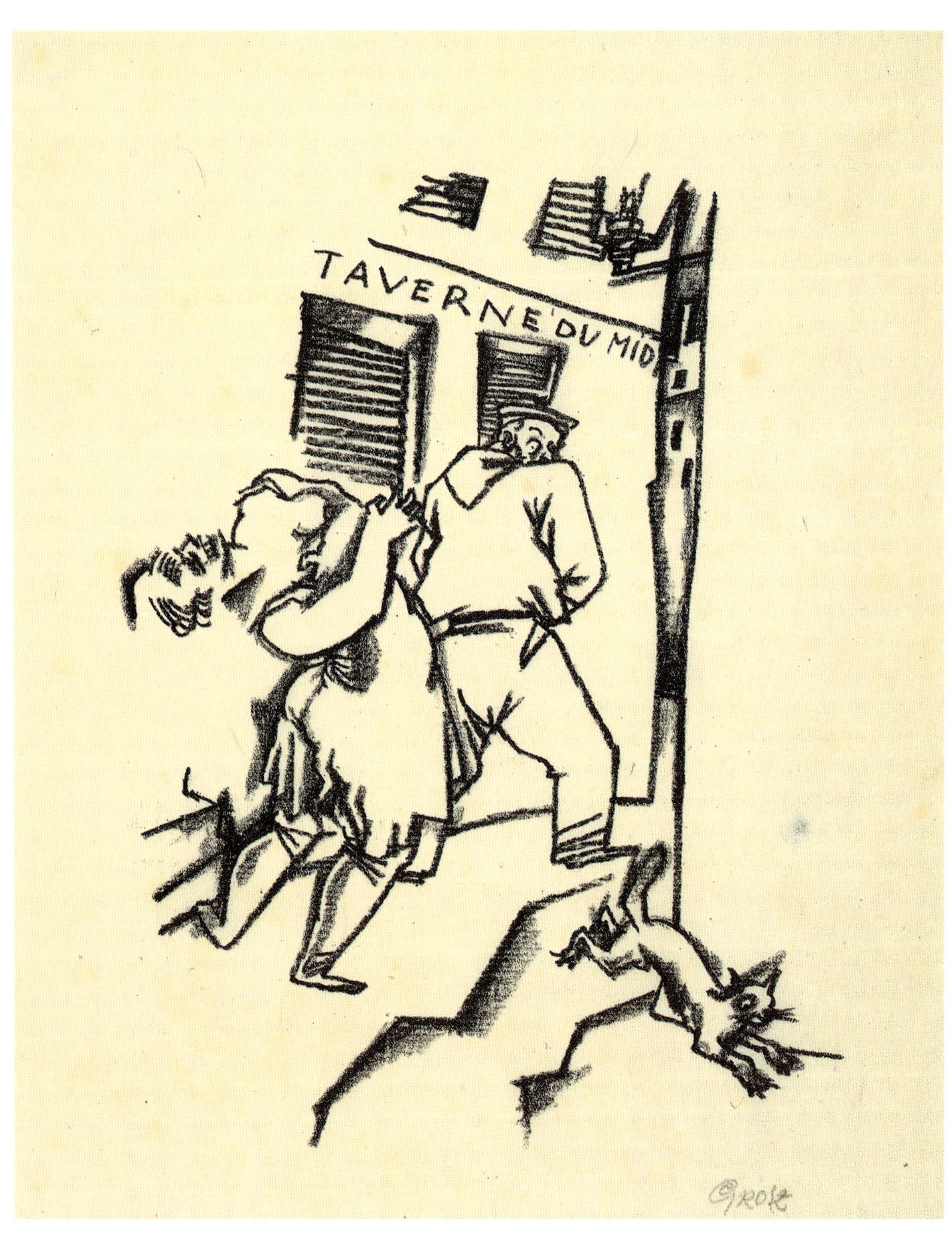

George Grosz
Taverne du Midi 1915

lithograph
National Gallery of Victoria, Melbourne

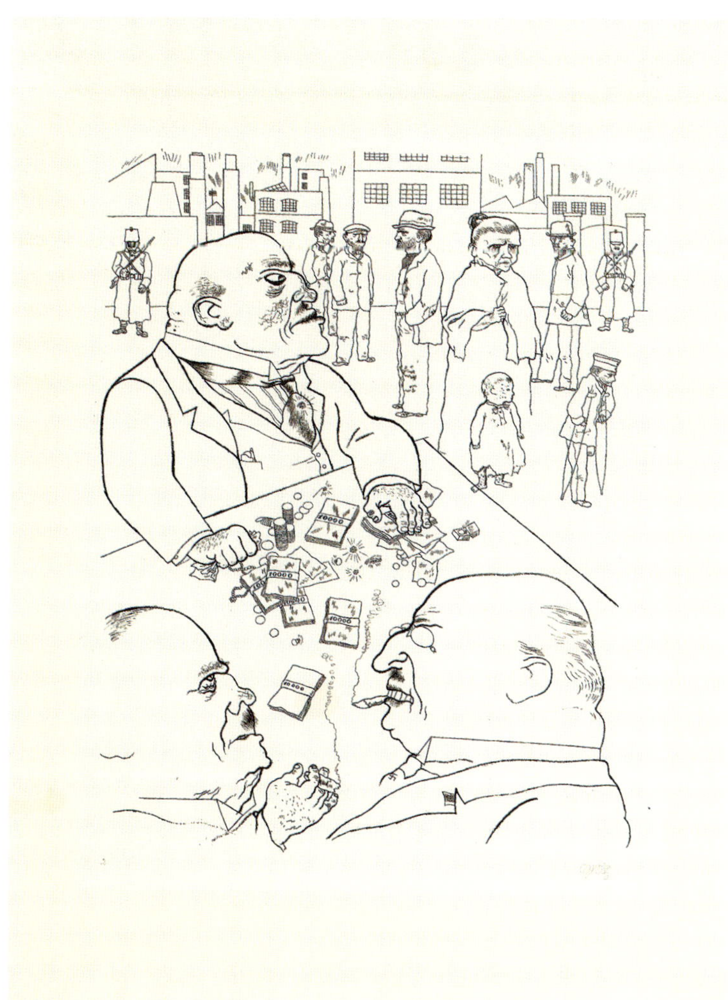

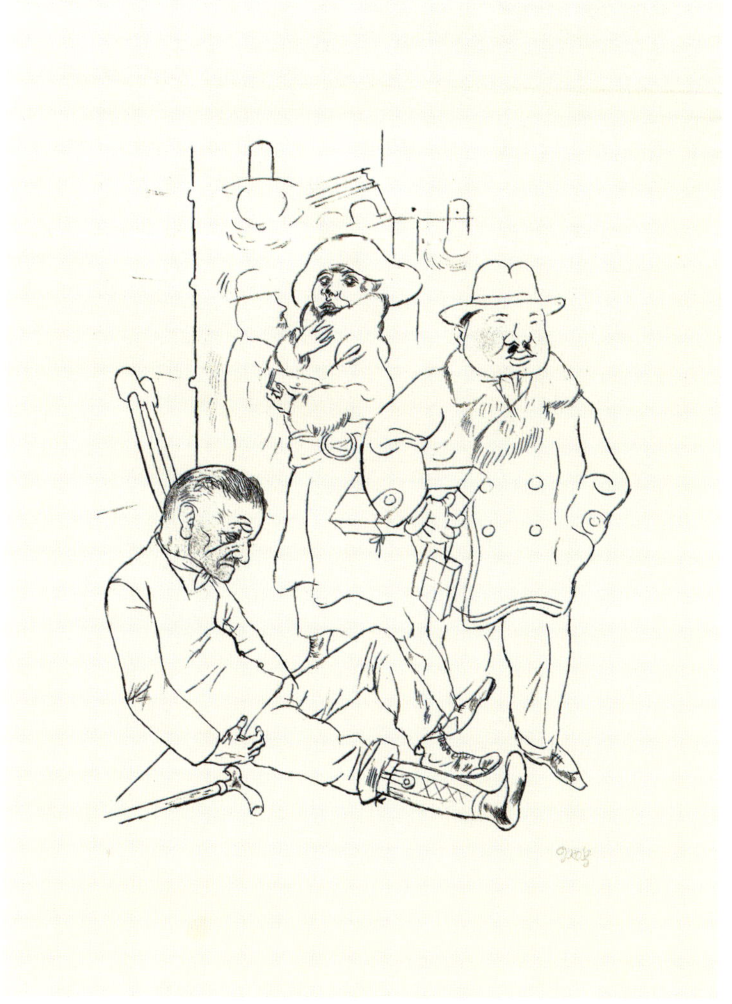

George Grosz
'Under my rule, it shall come to pass, that potatoes and small beer shall be considered a holiday treat; and woe to him who meets my eye with the audacious front of health. Haggard want, and crouching fear, are my insignia; and in this livery will I clothe ye.' 1920–21
from the portfolio The robbers 1922
photolithograph
National Gallery of Australia, Canberra

George Grosz
'I've done my bit ... the plunder is your affair!' 1922
from the portfolio The robbers 1922
photolithograph
National Gallery of Australia, Canberra

OTTO DIX

The Felixmüller family

Otto Dix fought as a machine-gunner during the First World War and witnessed some of the most horrific atrocities caused by trench warfare during his lengthy engagement on the frontline. He returned to Dresden following his discharge from the military in February 1919 and recommenced his art studies at the Dresden Academy. Over the next three years, Dix produced a large number of incredibly powerful and confronting paintings, prints and drawings that represented the horrors of trench warfare and the disastrous impact of war upon society. His views of prostitutes and war veterans, inspired by his friend Hugo Erfurth's photographs of maimed veterans, showed his intense fascination with morbid reality (pp 38, 57).[1] However, Dix also portrays these motifs as symbols of the dehumanised and demoralised state of postwar society.

The Felixmüller family 1919 is a similarly powerful interpretation of the disastrous effects of war, where the nocturnal nightmare is centred upon the depiction of the family. Since returning to Dresden, Dix had been closely associated with the painter and printmaker Conrad Felixmüller, who founded the radical artist's association the Dresden Secession Group in 1919. Felixmüller belonged to the younger generation of Expressionist artists who experienced commercial success during the war but then turned to revolutionary politics and joined the Communist Party after the November Revolution in 1918. He commissioned the impoverished Dix to paint this portrait, which related stylistically and in terms of subject matter to a portrait painted in 1918 by Felixmüller himself. In that work he depicted himself as an adoring father, with his wife Londa protectively holding their infant son Luca, and surrounded the family with trees and houses.[2]

In stark contrast to Felixmüller's tender and compassionate portrayal of his family, Dix presents the viewer with a wild, apocalyptic vision where the family unit is torn apart by the forces of violence and destruction. Felixmüller appears in the double role of revolutionary and father, yet he is thrust apart from his family as he merges into the chaotic arrangement of houses and crosses in the background. The violent colours and Cubo-Futurist treatment of this half of the composition were directly influenced by Felixmüller's own style of Expressionism, and differs from the angular and distorted, yet less sharply aggressive, treatment of the mother and baby. The woman emerges from a landscape of hills and flowers in the foreground, emphasising her 'natural' role as mother. Most of her body appears transparent and ambiguous but it is possible to decipher her face, breasts and outstretched hands that protectively cover what appears to be a kind of womb. Painted in a raw, reddish hue, the unborn foetus is perhaps the most disturbing aspect of the composition, as it is featured at the centre of this chaotic and irrational nightmare.[3] Like so many works created by Dix during the immediate postwar period, this extraordinary painting is evidence of the artist's intense need to exorcise his inner demons through the creative process. JS

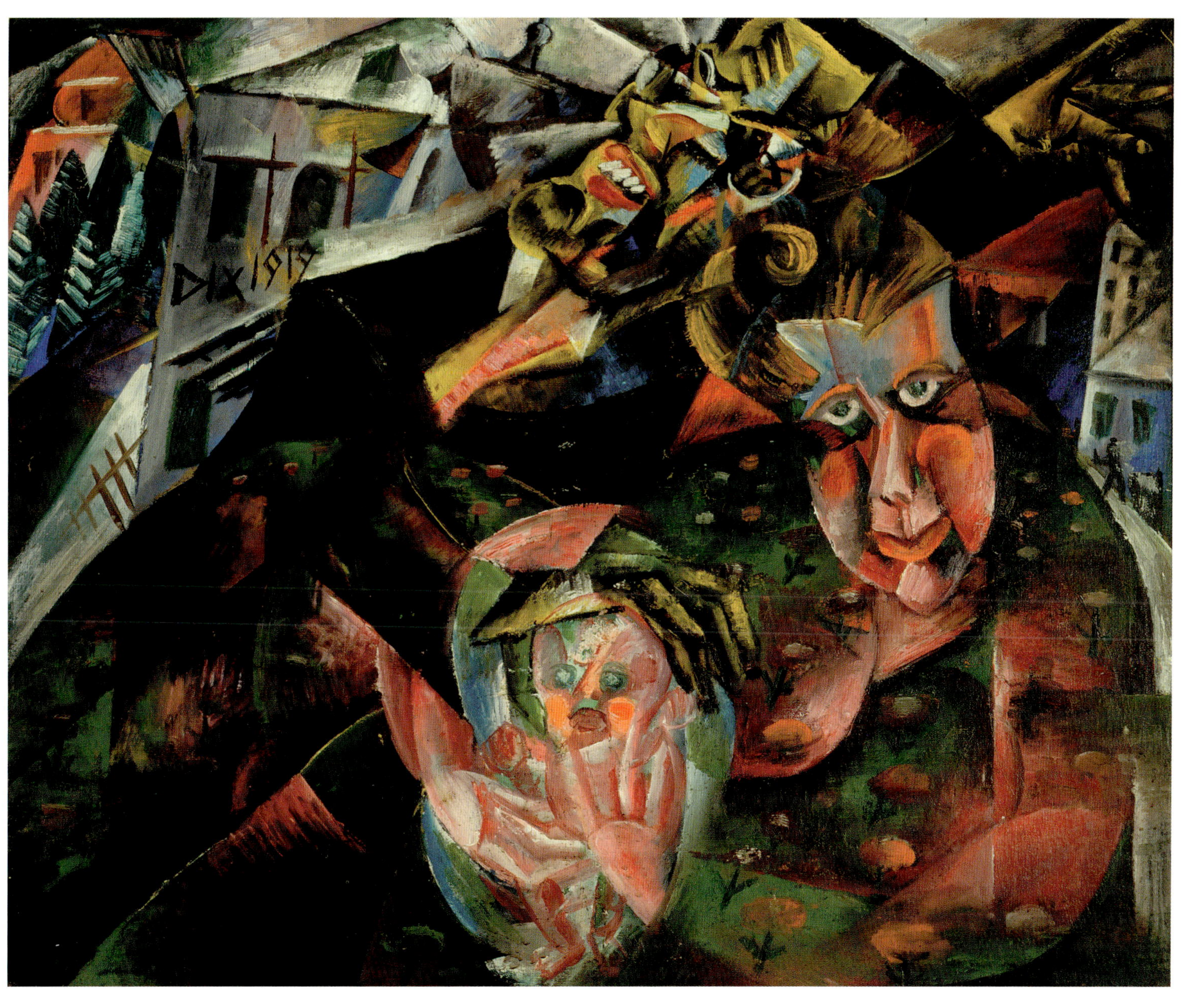

Otto Dix
The Felixmüller family 1919
oil on canvas
Saint Louis Art Museum

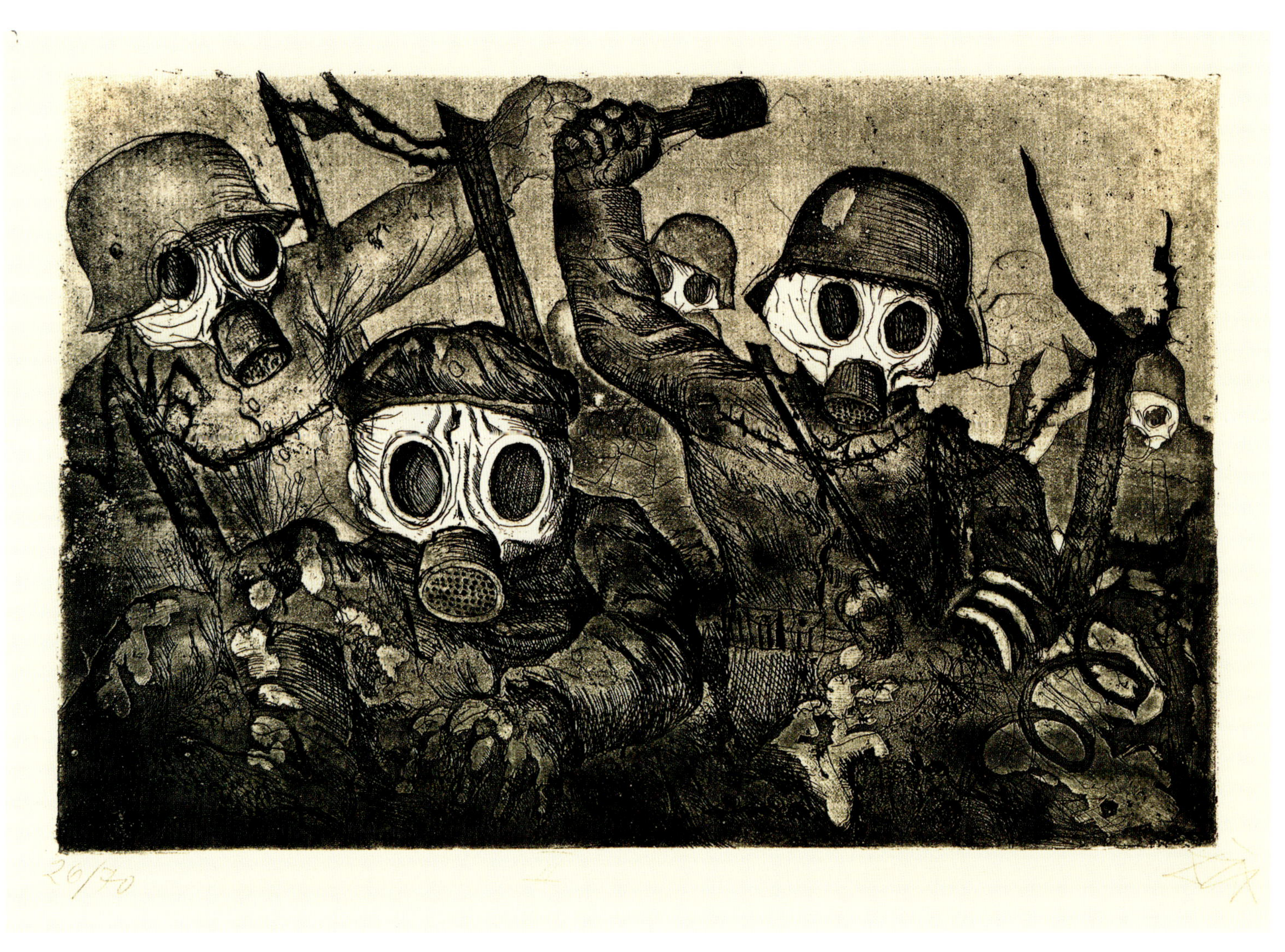

Otto Dix
Storm troopers advancing under a gas attack
from the portfolio **War** 1924

etching, aquatint, drypoint
Australian War Memorial, Canberra

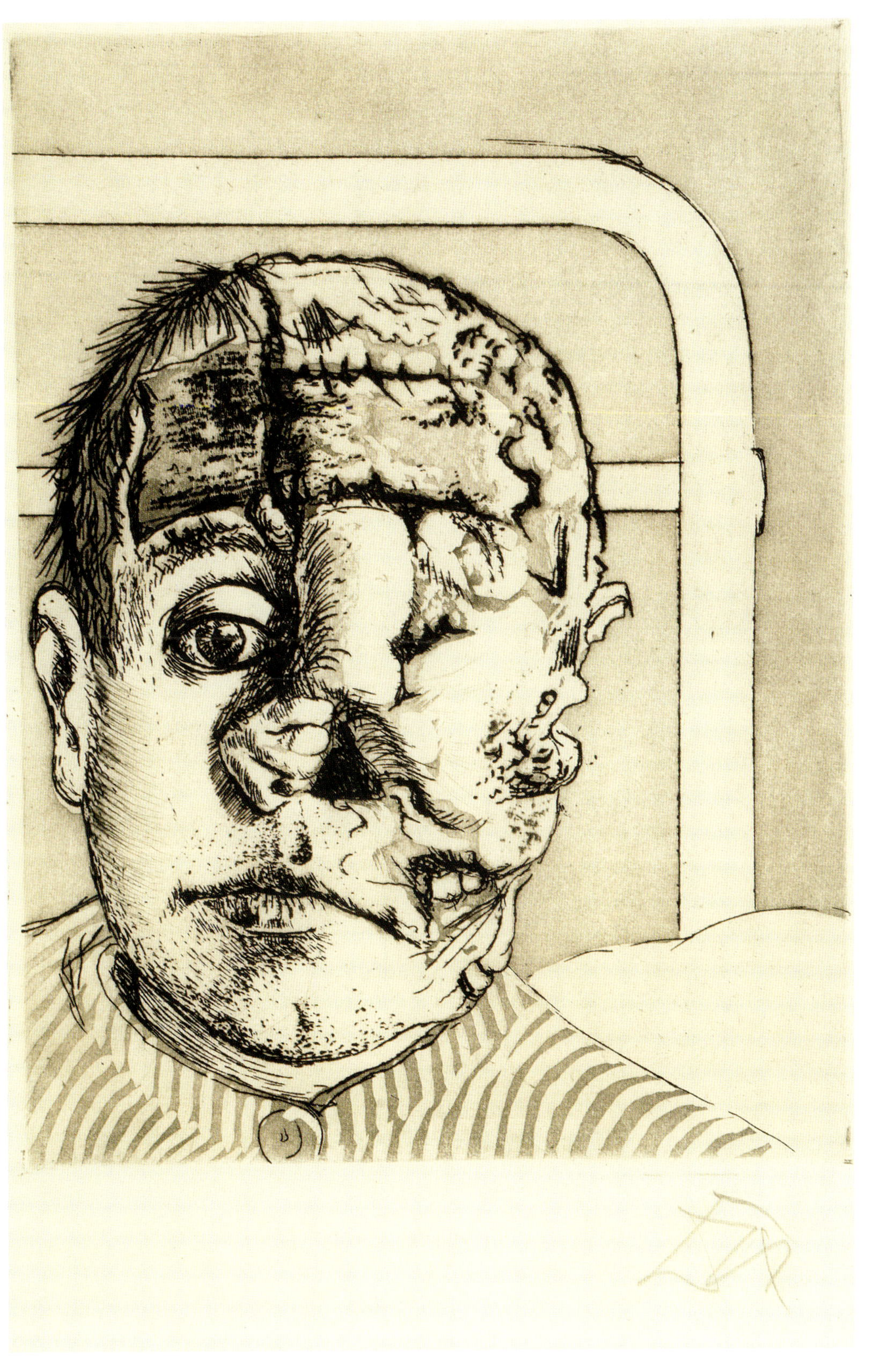

Otto Dix
Transplantation [Skin graft]
from the portfolio War 1924
etching, aquatint, drypoint
Australian War Memorial, Canberra

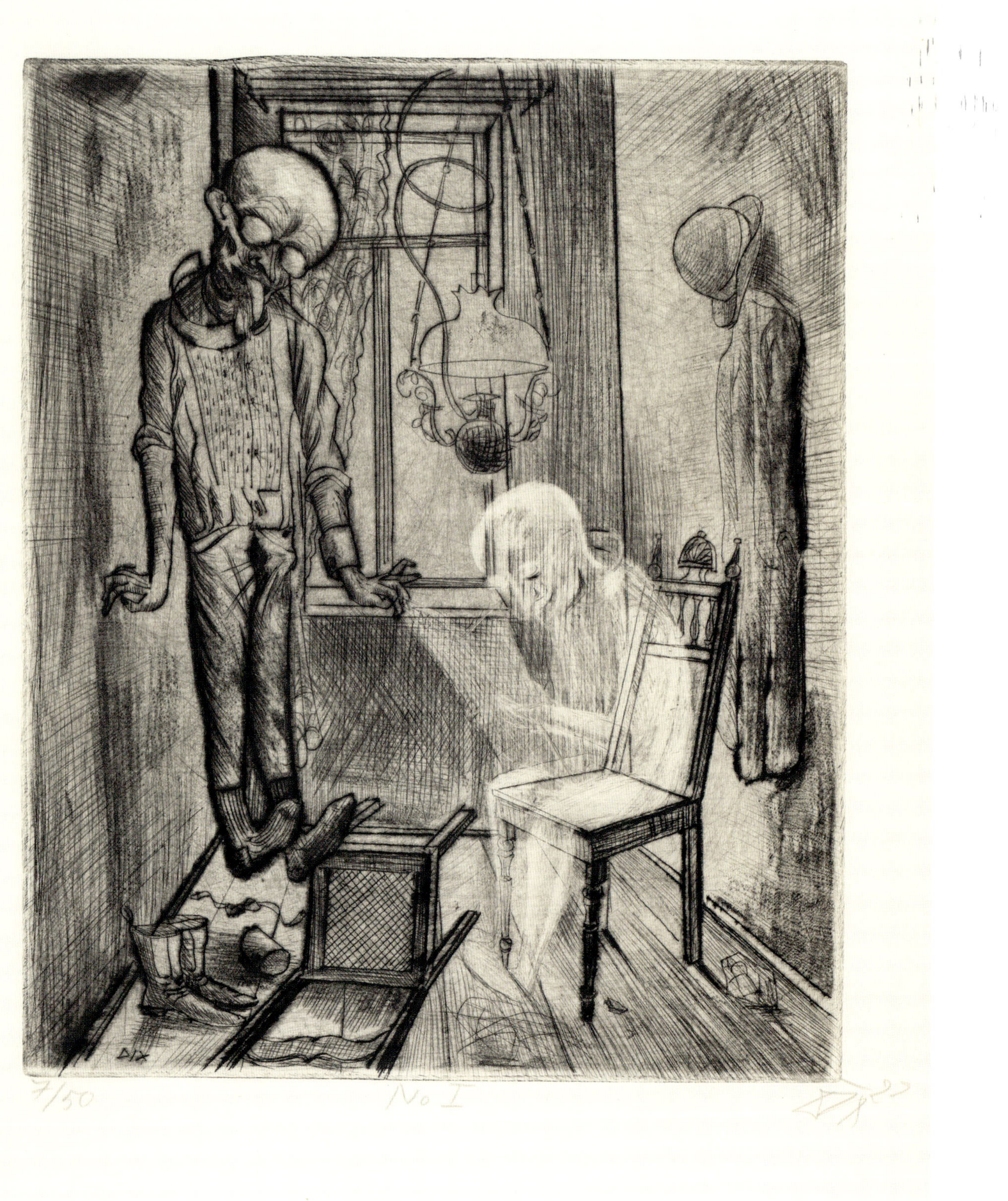

Otto Dix
The suicide 1922
from the portfolio **Death and resurrection** 1922
drypoint
Art Gallery of New South Wales, Sydney

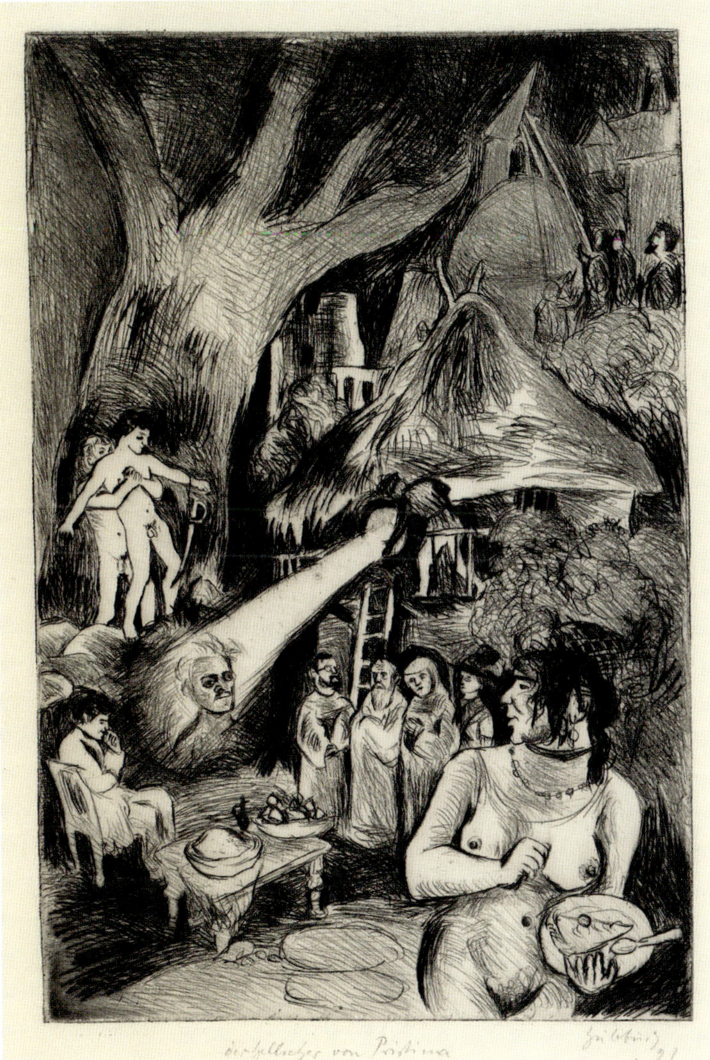

Karl Hubbuch
The clairvoyant of Pristina 1921
etching, drypoint
Art Gallery of New South Wales, Sydney

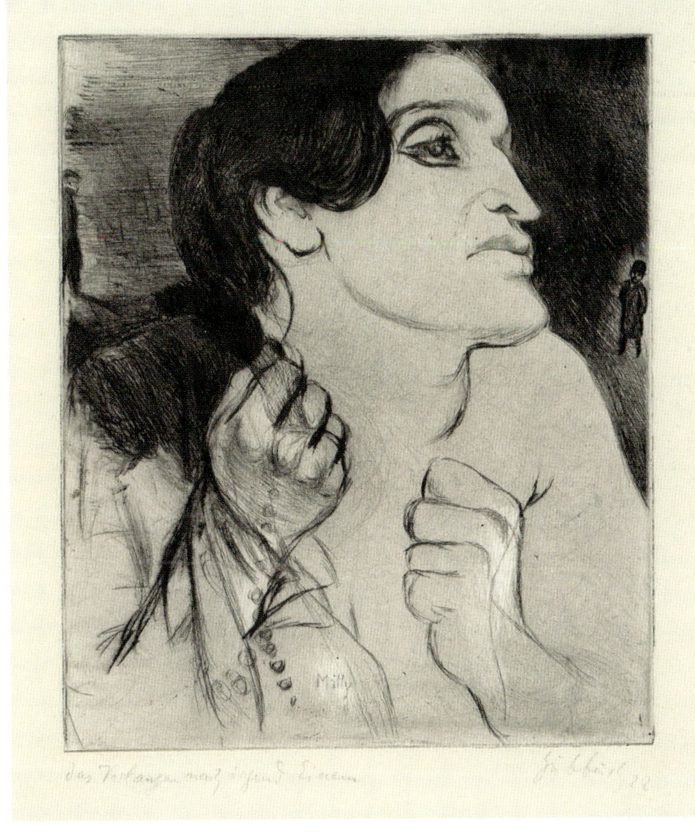

Karl Hubbuch
The longing for anyone 1922
etching, drypoint
Art Gallery of New South Wales, Sydney

MAX BECKMANN

The dream

The years immediately following the First World War were particularly formative in Max Beckmann's work. Having served as a medical orderly on the battlefields of Flanders and witnessing some of the worst atrocities, he suffered a nervous breakdown and returned to Frankfurt in 1916, where he remained until 1933. The unique and richly symbolic style of painting and printmaking he developed during this time was strongly influenced by the expressive distortion of the human figure and use of compressed, stage-like space found in German medieval painting. Beckmann was one of the few artists in Germany to work in relative isolation and kept his distance from avant-garde movements, creating penetrating self-portraits and exploring themes taken from contemporary life.

The dream 1921, one of the masterpieces of Beckmann's Frankfurt period, is a powerful representation of a society that is physically and emotionally damaged by the traumatic experiences of war. Here he depicts a group of seemingly random and unrelated characters – a drunken maid, maimed war veteran, blind organ grinder, homeless child and mutilated prisoner – who collectively represent a nightmarish vision of street life in Weimar Germany. Labelled as 'The madhouse' when it was first exhibited, this painting has been aptly described as 'a pantomime of misery, madness, and crime in which all kinds of symbols – ladder, fish, trumpet, hand organ, doll, guitar, cello, lamp, and mirror, as well as mutilated extremities – are introduced to give an allegorical meaning to the confusion'.[1] The painting's tilted perspective, confined space and complex, vertical composition glows with intense colour. It marked a radical new style of painting that coincided with the shift in Beckmann's work from religious subjects to those that engaged critically with modernity.

Two large-format lithographs in the exhibition from the *Hell* portfolio, published in 1919, are further examples of his interest in portraying the disastrous effects of war upon society. In *The way home* 1919 (p 41), Beckmann depicts himself grabbing the arm of a severely mutilated war veteran in an attempt to guide him in the right direction. The overall impression of this night scene is, however, one of misery and despair, with war cripples, prostitutes and a deranged dog intertwined tightly in the composition. This mood of social and political turbulence is also evident in *The night* 1919 (p 26), executed in 1918–19 by Beckmann (now in the Kunstsammlung Nordrhein-Westfalen, Düsseldorf), which draws directly upon a major painting of the same title. Aware of the impressive, yet disturbing nature of this work, Beckmann portrays a group of criminals forcefully interrupting a family gathering to punish the father for his political convictions. They inflict pain, fear and humiliation upon the family members as they helplessly witness the terrible scene of torture taking place before them. This poignant and technically brilliant work revealed that political extremism and violence invaded every aspect of life in post-war Germany, even the most private and domestic sphere of the home and family. JS

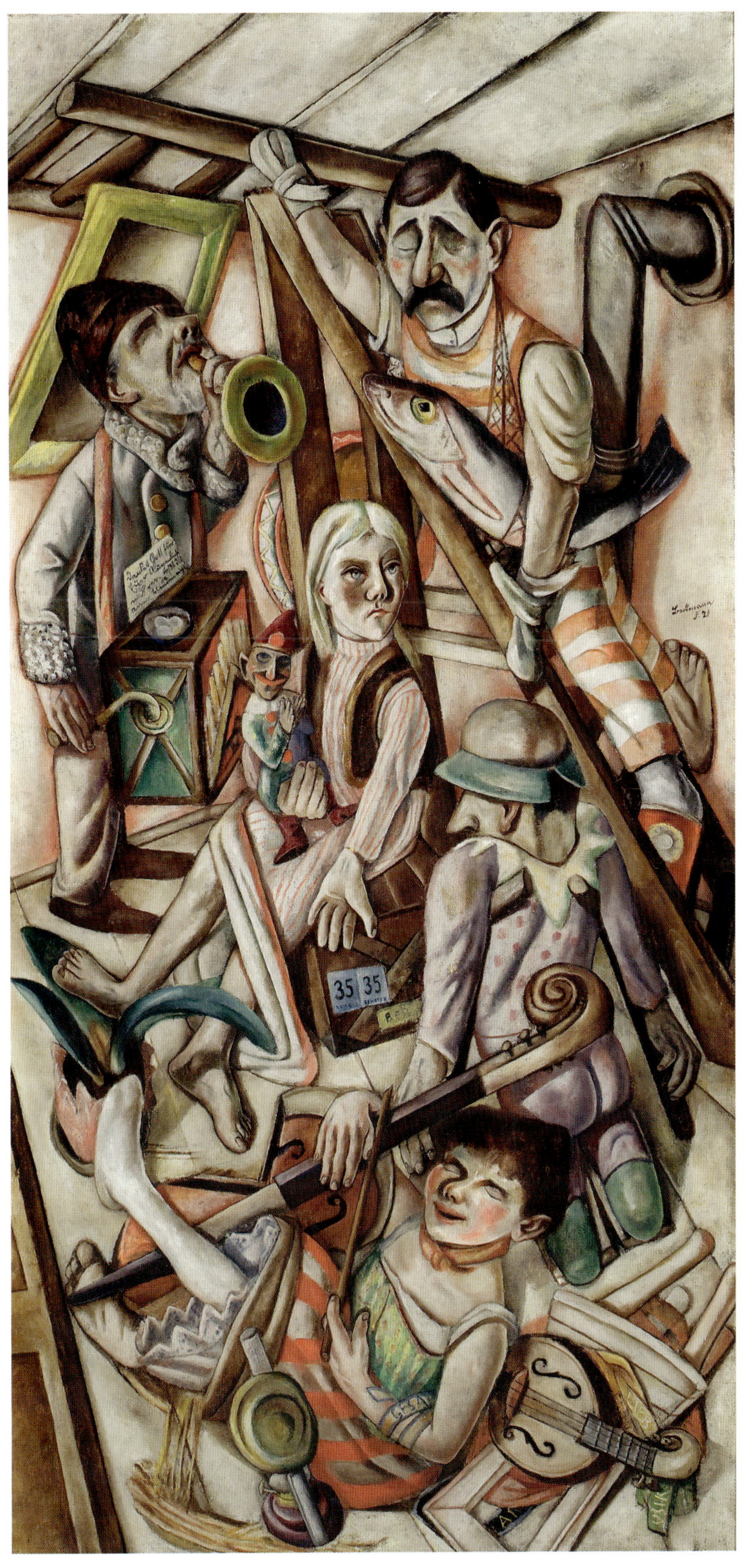

Max Beckmann
The dream 1921
oil on canvas
Saint Louis Art Museum

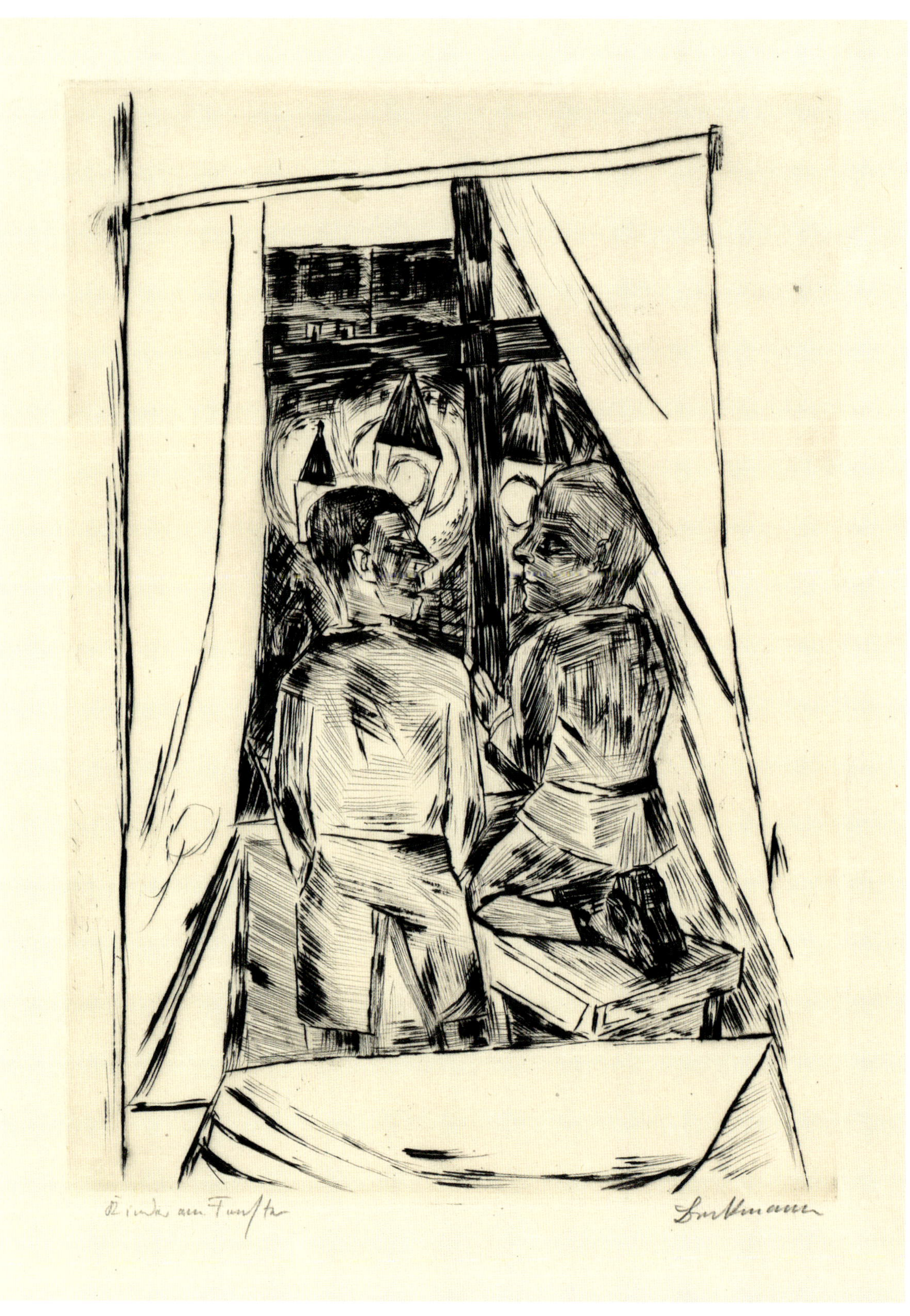

Max Beckmann
Children at the window 1922
drypoint
Art Gallery of New South Wales, Sydney

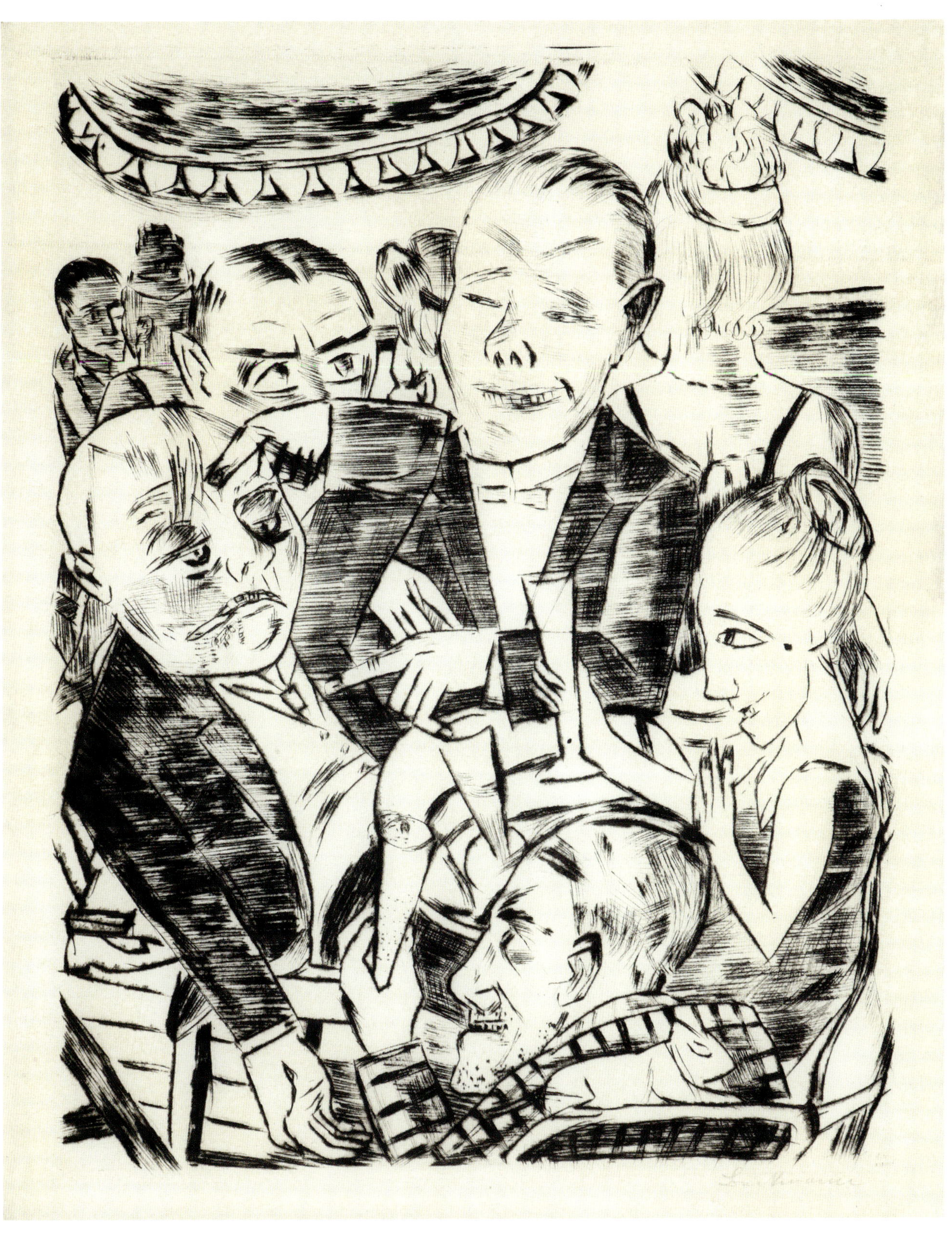

Max Beckmann
Here is intellect 1921
drypoint
Collection of James Fairfax, Sydney

KÄTHE KOLLWITZ

Memorial for Karl Liebknecht

Käthe Kollwitz belonged to the first generation of avant-garde artists in Berlin, yet she emerged as a leading artist of socially committed realism during the years immediately following the end of the First World War. Peter, the younger of her two sons, had been killed during the early stages of the war at the age of 18 and Kollwitz never fully recovered from his death. She described again and again in her diaries this deep loss, which persistently haunted her. In her art, she addressed social and political issues with a great sense of urgency and called for relief to the suffering and desperation of the working classes to whom she felt strong ties. A committed socialist and pacifist, she passionately advocated the need for a more compassionate and humane society.

There was a tremendous shift in Kollwitz's work immediately following the war, as she turned from naturalistic modes of expression in her sculptures, lithographs and etchings to the formally radical medium of the woodblock print. Adopting this technique from both Ernst Barlach and the Brücke artists, Kollwitz emphasised the stark, graphic qualities of the woodcut, as well as its effectiveness in communicating directly with the viewer. Her woodcuts from this period, such as *The parents* 1923 (below), offer an intensely personal response to the many injustices of contemporary life, which included war, poverty and hunger.

Kollwitz's *Memorial for Karl Liebknecht* 1919–20 – or, as the inscription reads, 'The Living to the Dead: Remembrance of 15 January 1919' – was one of the most

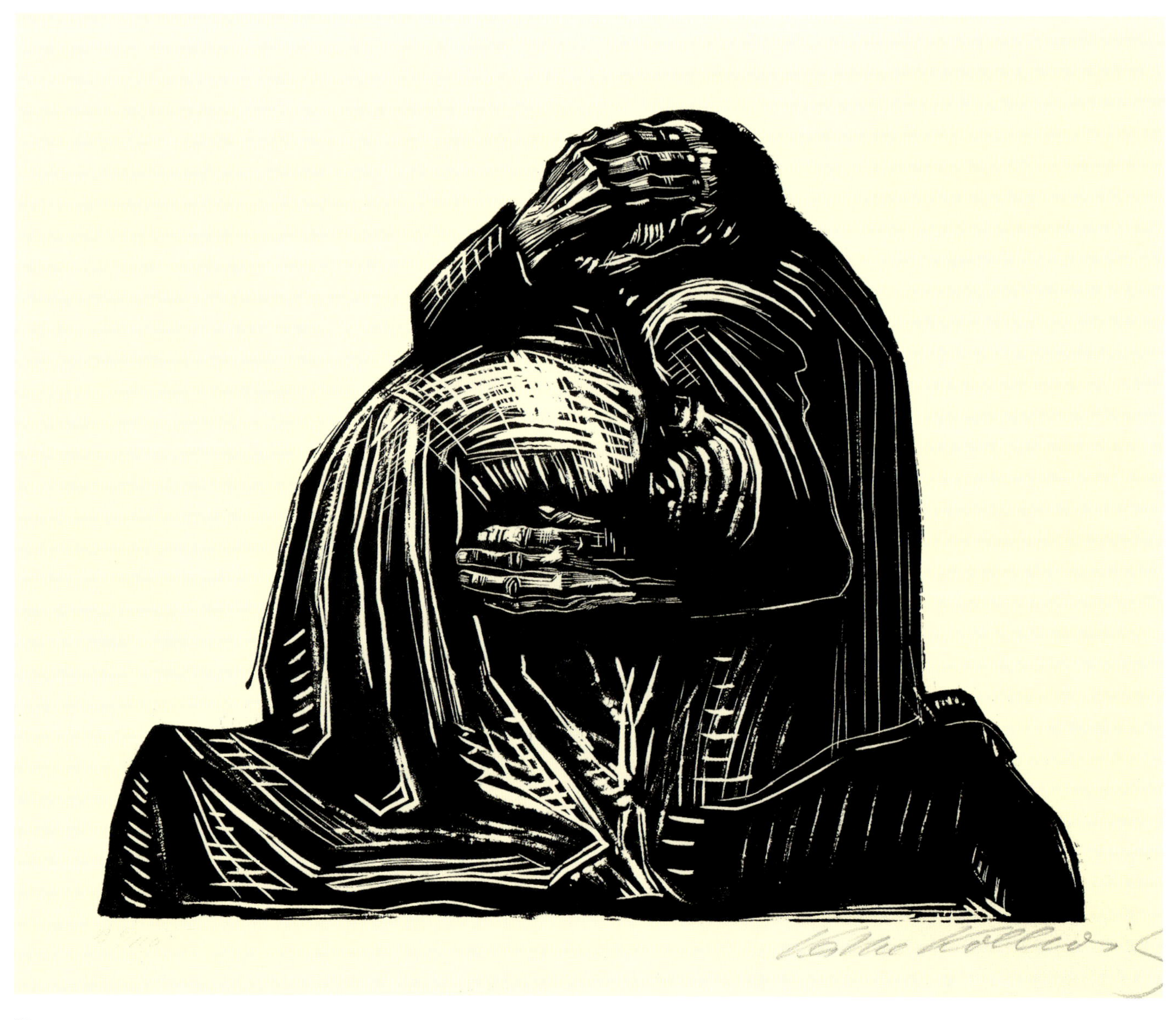

striking artistic responses to the radical and violent events that took place during the months of the November Revolution. This 'people's revolution', which took place in Germany just one year after the Russian Revolution, sought to replace the old regime with a socialist one. The socialists' short-lived seizure of power collapsed in January 1919 and was soon replaced by a parliamentary democracy. The key leaders of the revolutionary Spartacist movement – Karl Liebknecht and Rosa Luxemburg – who opposed the provisional government, were brutally murdered by police during this violent period. Public expressions of grief and mourning to mark their deaths were forbidden in Weimar Germany but Kollwitz boldly responded to the request of the Liebknecht family to make a deathbed sketch, which emphasised the communal grief of the mourners. She noted in her diary on 25 January 1919:

> Karl Liebknecht was buried today, together with 38 others who had been shot. I was allowed to make [a] drawing of him and went to the mortuary early. He was lying there in a coffin in the hall beside the other coffins, with red flowers round his bullet-holed head. His face was proud, the mouth slightly opened and twisted in pain.[1]

Kollwitz typically captures the emotional essence of her subject by focusing on the anger and resignation of the mourning workers.[2] She achieves this through the stark simplicity of the composition, which draws upon dramatic black-and-white contrasts in the depiction of the figures and facial expressions. JS

opposite:
Käthe Kollwitz
The parents 1923
from the portfolio War 1924
woodcut
Australian War Memorial, Canberra

Käthe Kollwitz
Memorial for Karl Liebknecht 1919–20
woodcut
Los Angeles County Museum of Art

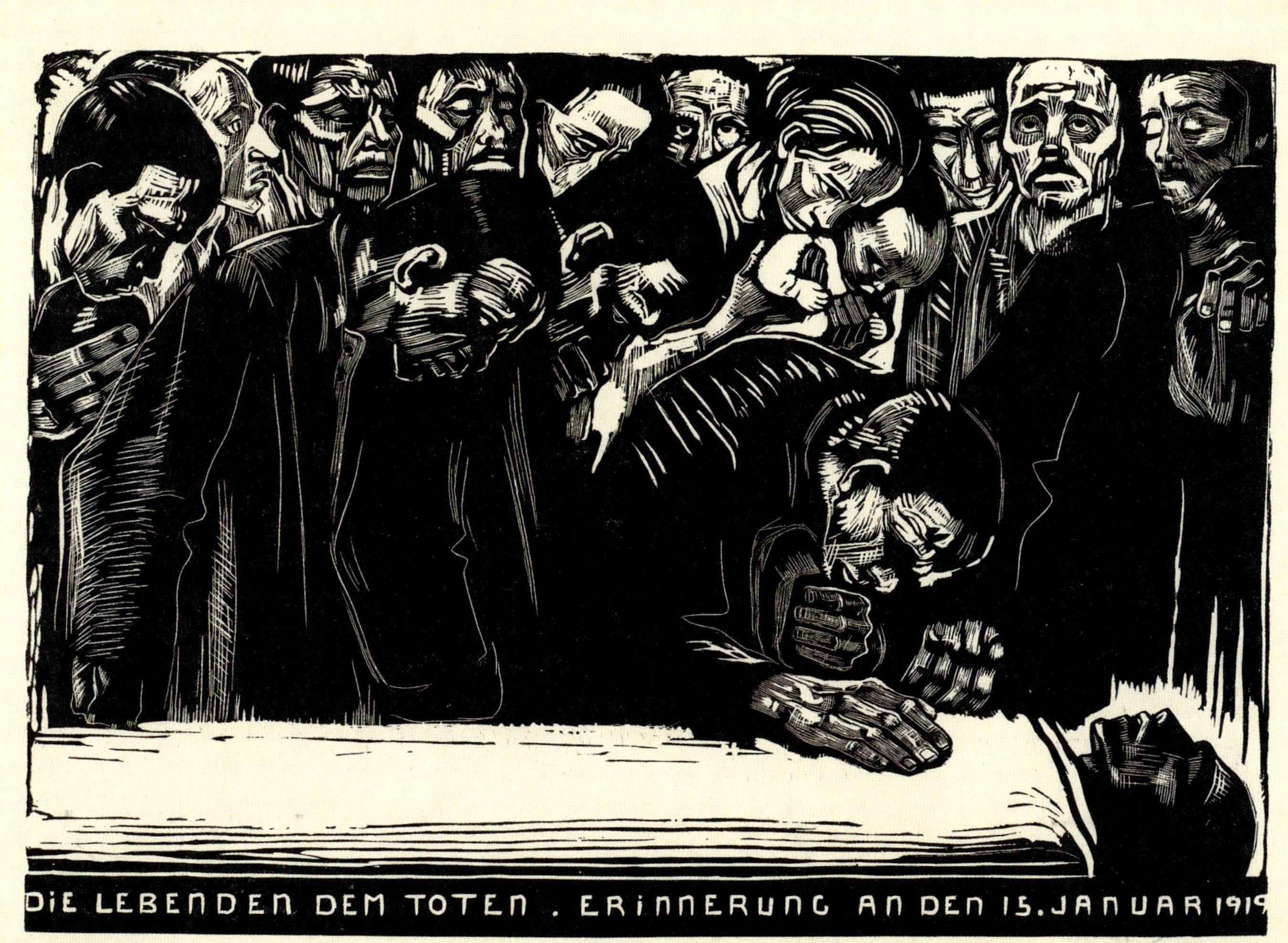

EXPRESSIONIST POSTERS

Considered both radical and revolutionary before the war, Expressionism emerged after the cessation of hostilities in November 1918 as a leading avant-garde style. It was adopted by the newly formed artists' association the *Novembergruppe* (November Group), which sought a close relationship between art and revolutionary politics. The leading members of the *Novembergruppe* – including Max Pechstein, Lyonel Feininger, César Klein, Georg Tappert and Ludwig Meidner – supported socialist politics but did not advocate radical political activity. Klein's lithograph *Whoever does not work is the gravedigger for his own children* (undated, p 69) warns against anarchy and terrorism, and urges people to keep working in order to prevent civil war. In *To the lantern!* c1919 Pechstein represents the terror and bloody street fighting that characterised the immediate postwar months in Berlin. He captures the excitement and frantic energy of this short-lived revolutionary period, but also calls for an end to the violence through his emphasis on the blood-red flags and splashes of red surrounding the hanged man, also seen in the fists and faces of the demonstrators.

Many of these artists supported the newly formed socialist coalition government and were commissioned by the National Versammlung (German National Assembly) to produce a series of posters to raise voters' support for the election in January 1919.[1] Pechstein's *The National Assembly is the cornerstone of the German Socialist Republic* 1919 (below) and Klein's *Workers citizens farmers soldiers …* 1919 (p 68) pulsate with the type of dynamic,

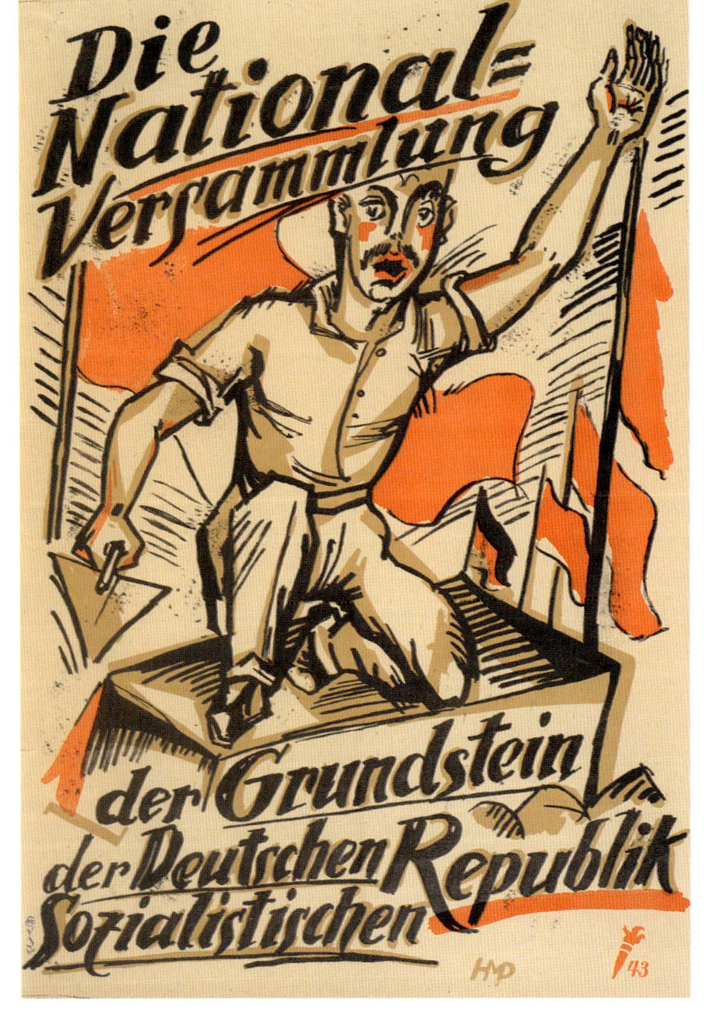

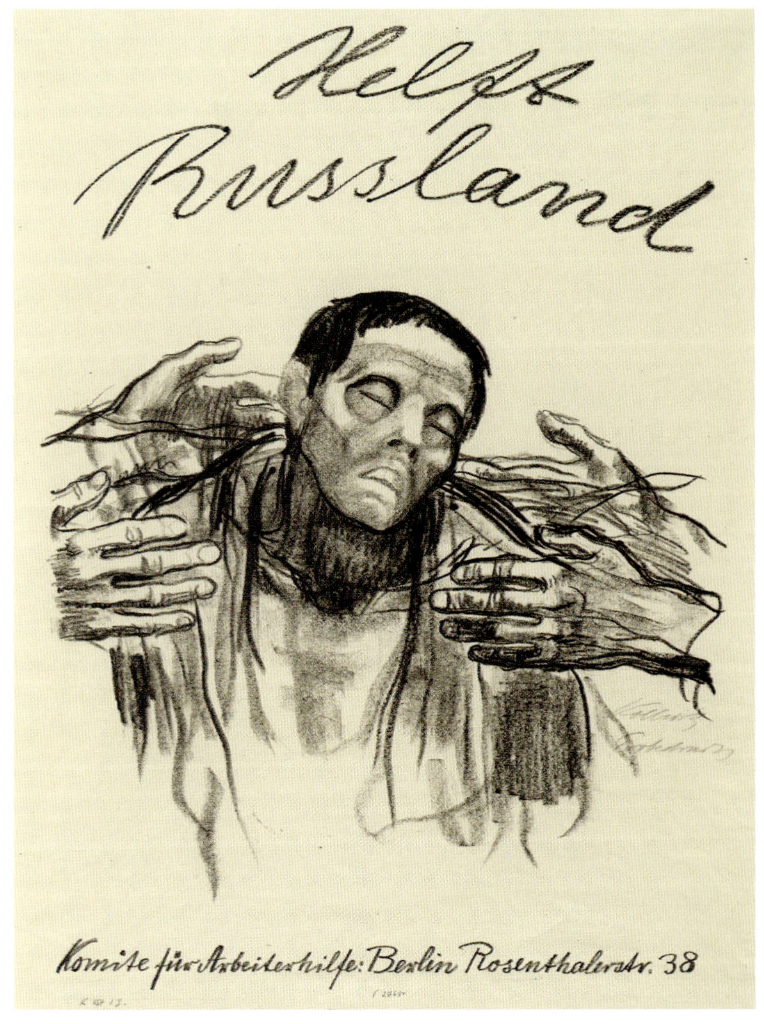

modern energy found in Expressionist works before the war. Yet the specific political message of these images is delivered with a sense of clarity and boldness that characterised avant-garde poster design in Germany. These posters demonstrate the artists' intense and passionate commitment to social reform, as well as their intention to communicate directly with the urban workers.

Johannes Safis' *Bolshevism means to drown the world in blood* 1919 (p 70) and Rudi Feld's *The danger of bolshevism* c1920 (p 71) are equally impressive posters, representing the other end of the political spectrum: the right-wing political stance of the anti-Bolshevists. These posters draw upon a recognisably Gothic – and by inference Germanic – style of imagery and text to stridently convey their political message, warning against what was perceived to be the evils of Bolshevism. While the Feld poster presents the medieval figure of a grim reaper clenching a bloody dagger in his teeth amidst a field of crosses, Safis' poster portrays a Russian wolf standing over a figure submerged in a river of blood, with a ruined city in the background.

Concentration on the stark, graphic quality of the image, combined with the integration of the text and image, were particularly strong features of poster art in Germany during and after the war. With its potential to communicate with the masses during these years of change and crisis, the poster became a very effective and highly utilised medium, representing a powerful alliance between modernism, graphic art, typography and politics. JS

left to right:

Max Pechstein
The National Assembly is the cornerstone of the German Socialist Republic 1919
colour lithograph, poster
Australian War Memorial, Canberra

Käthe Kollwitz
Help Russia 1921
lithograph, poster
National Gallery of Australia, Canberra

Max Pechstein
To the lantern! c1919
colour lithograph, poster
Los Angeles County Museum of Art

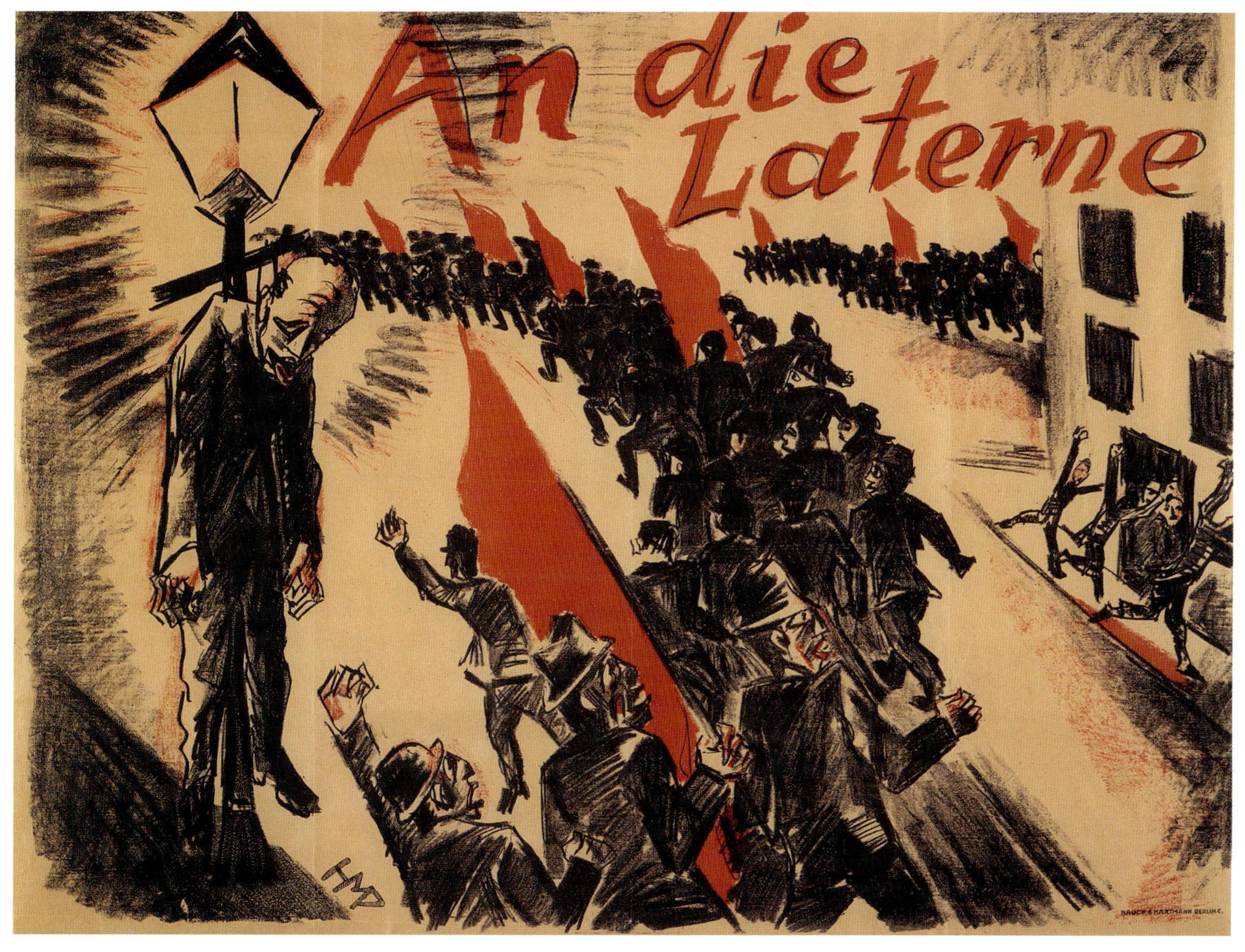

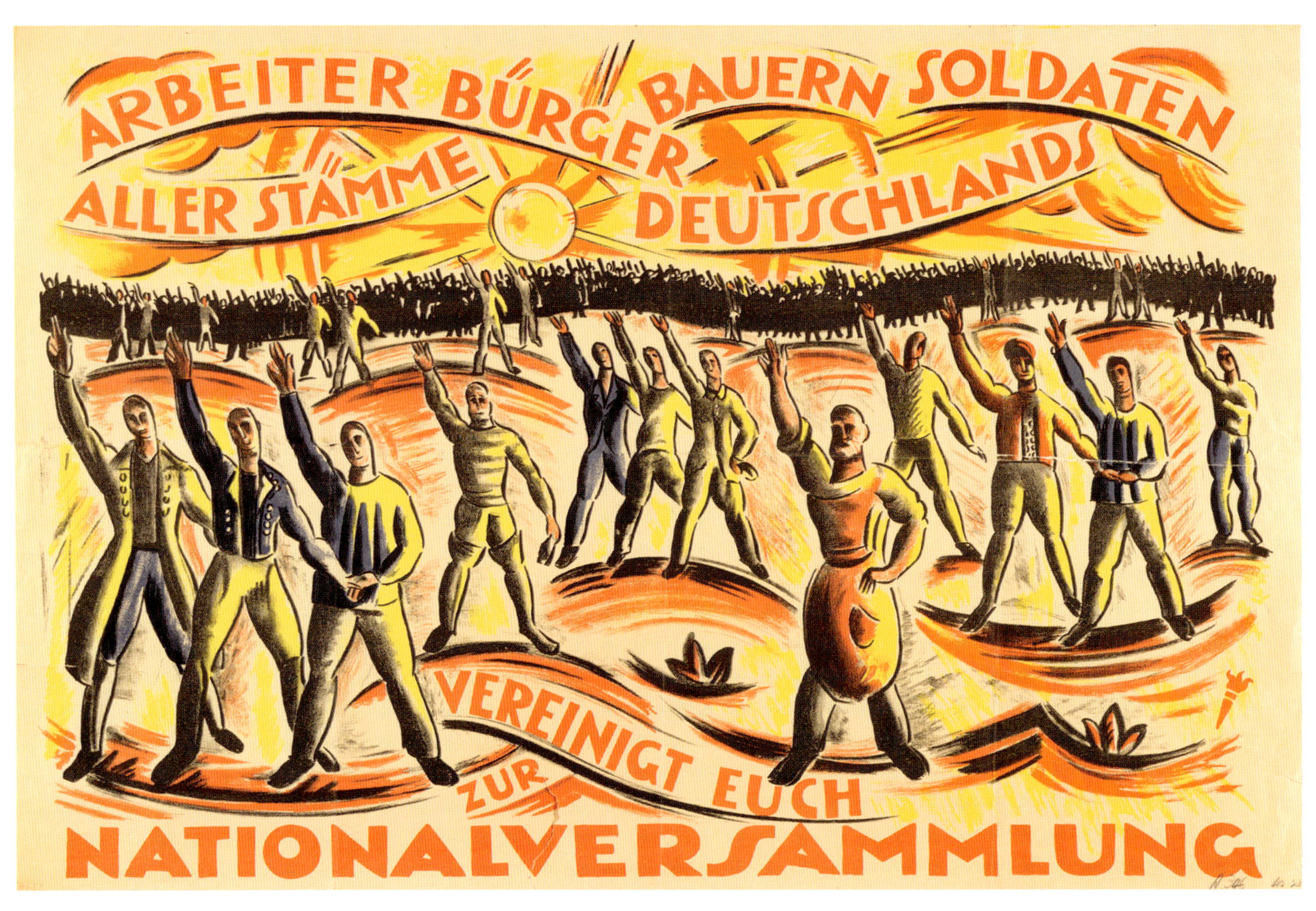

César Klein
Workers citizens farmers soldiers ... 1919
colour lithograph, poster
Australian War Memorial, Canberra

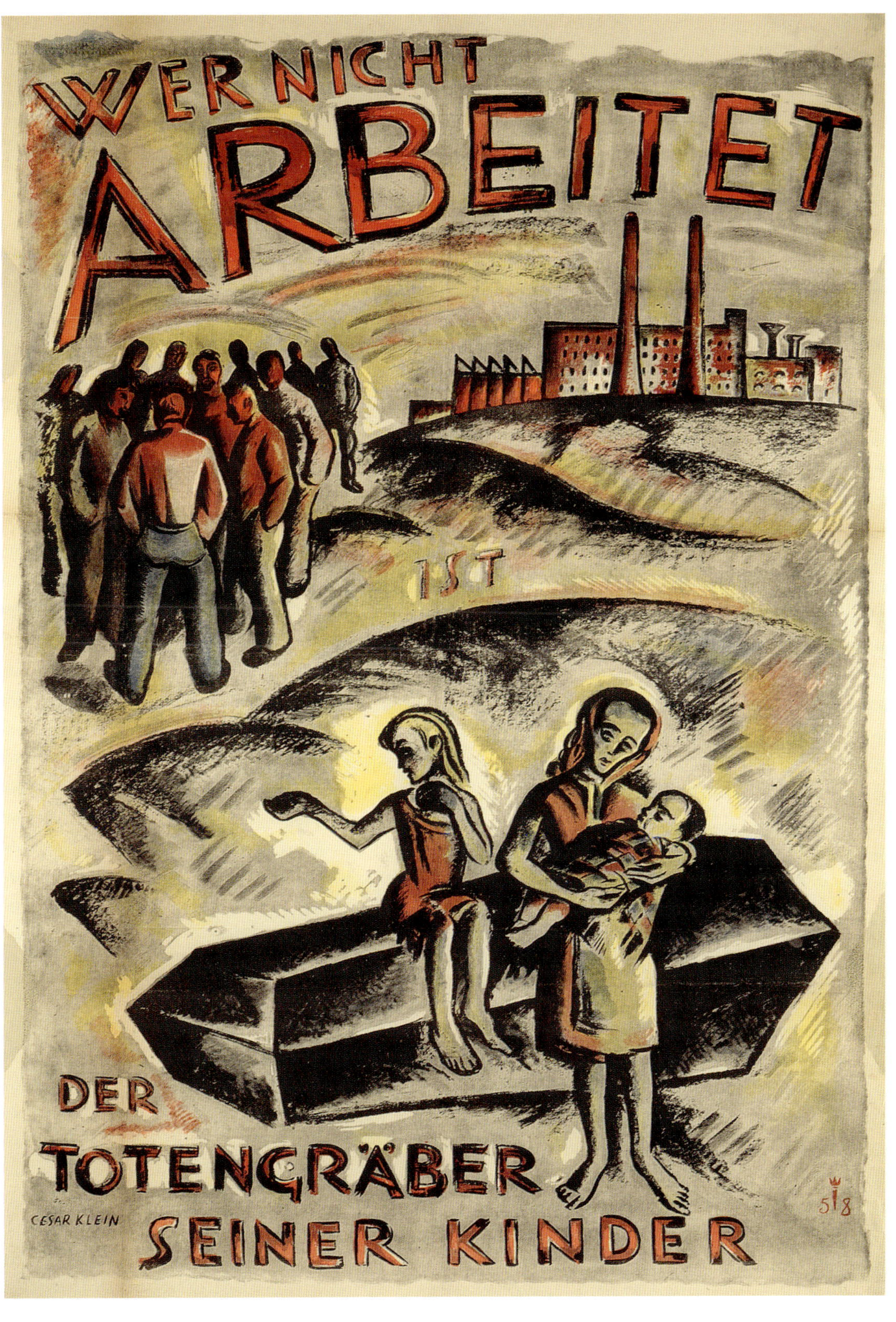

César Klein
Whoever does not work is the gravedigger for his own children nd

colour lithograph, poster
Los Angeles County Museum of Art

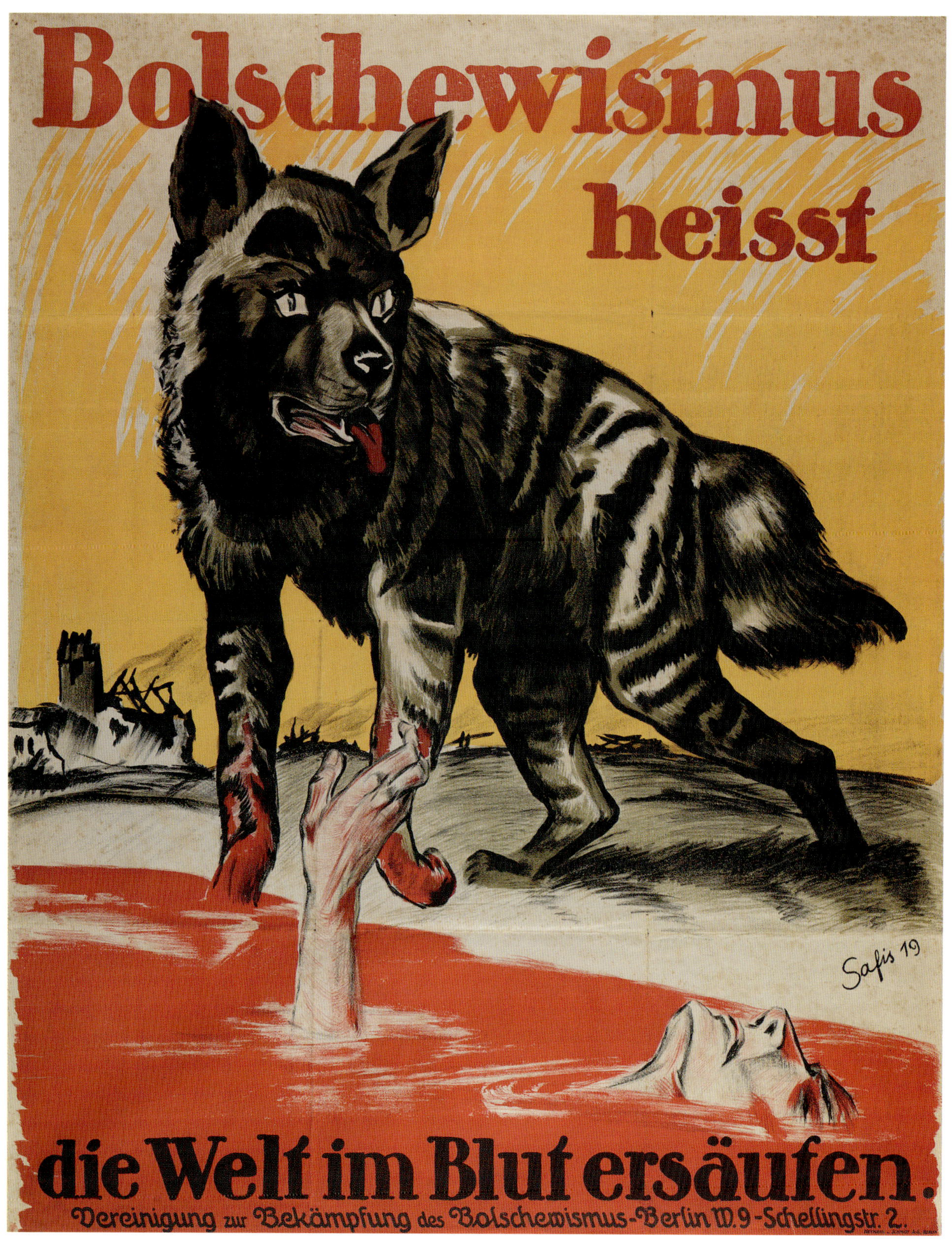

Johannes Safis
Bolshevism means to drown the world in blood
1919
colour lithograph, poster
Australian War Memorial, Canberra

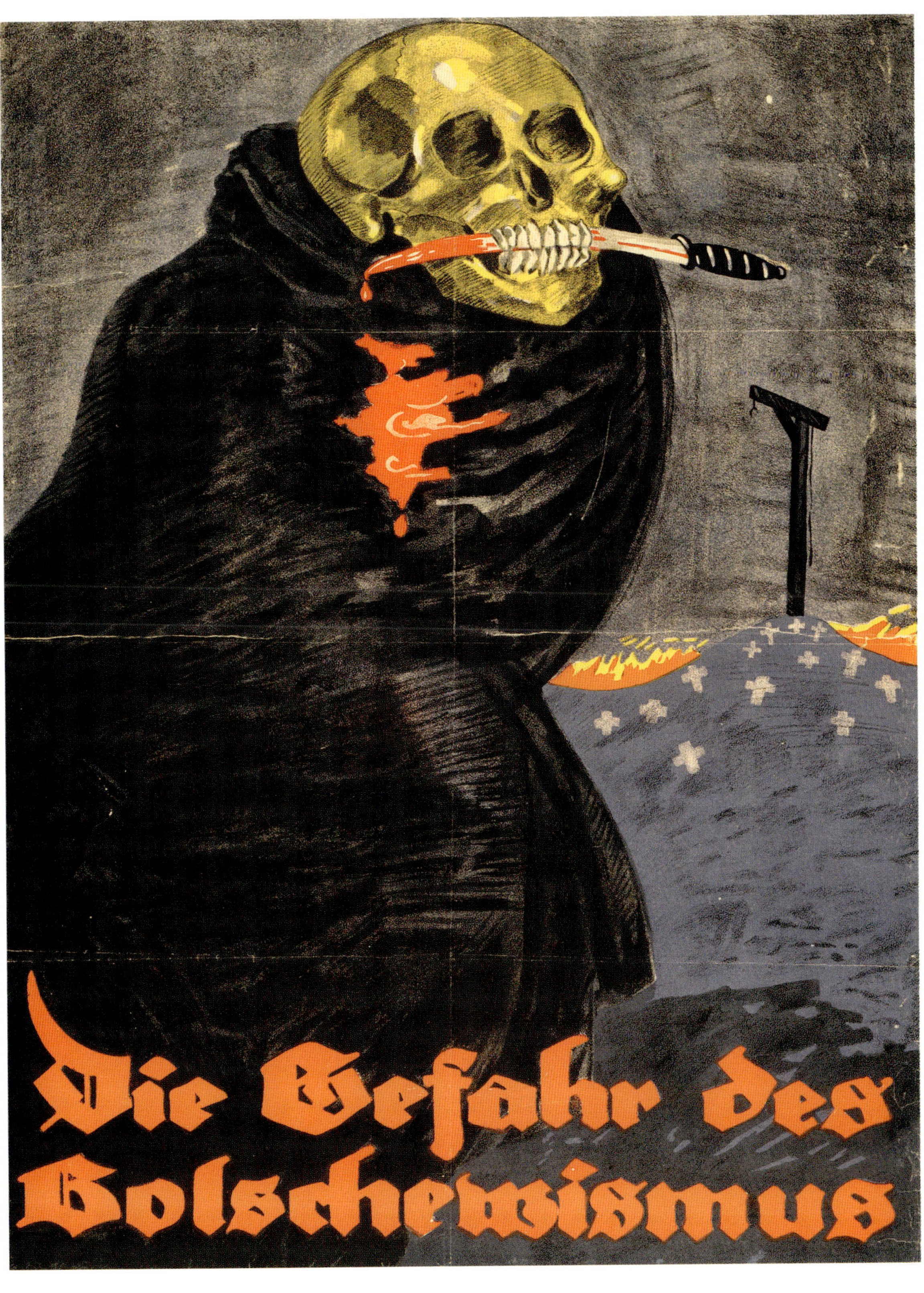

Rudi Feld
The danger of bolshevism c1920
colour lithograph, poster
Australian War Memorial, Canberra

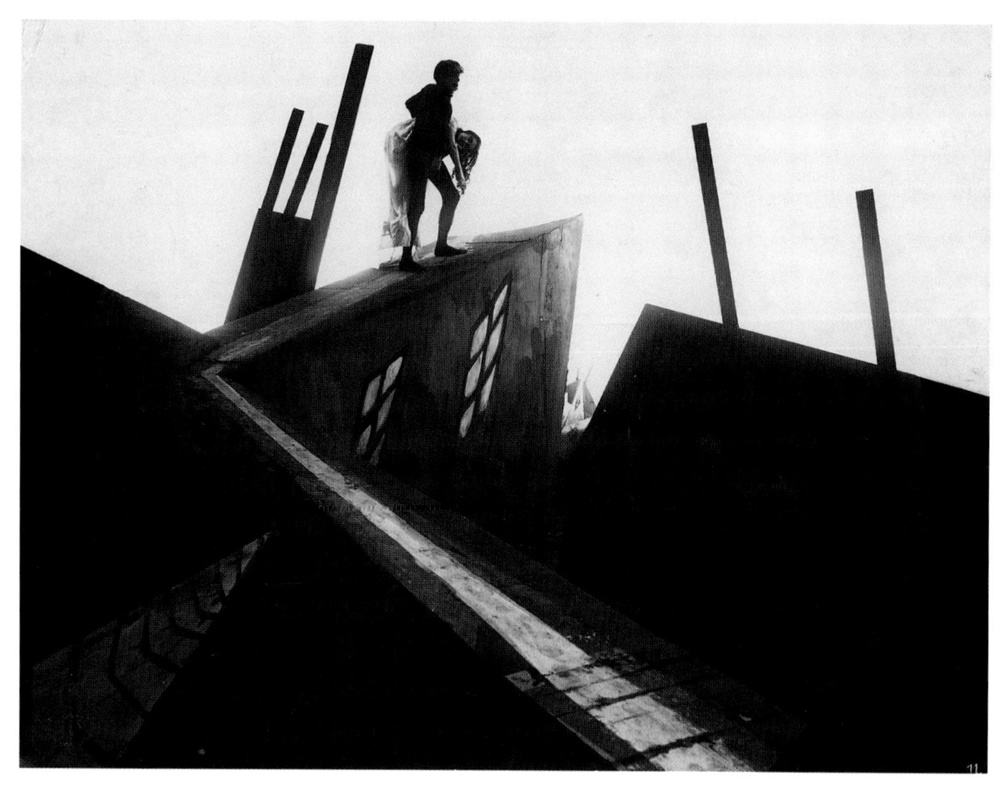

Robert Wiene
The cabinet of Dr Caligari 1919
film still

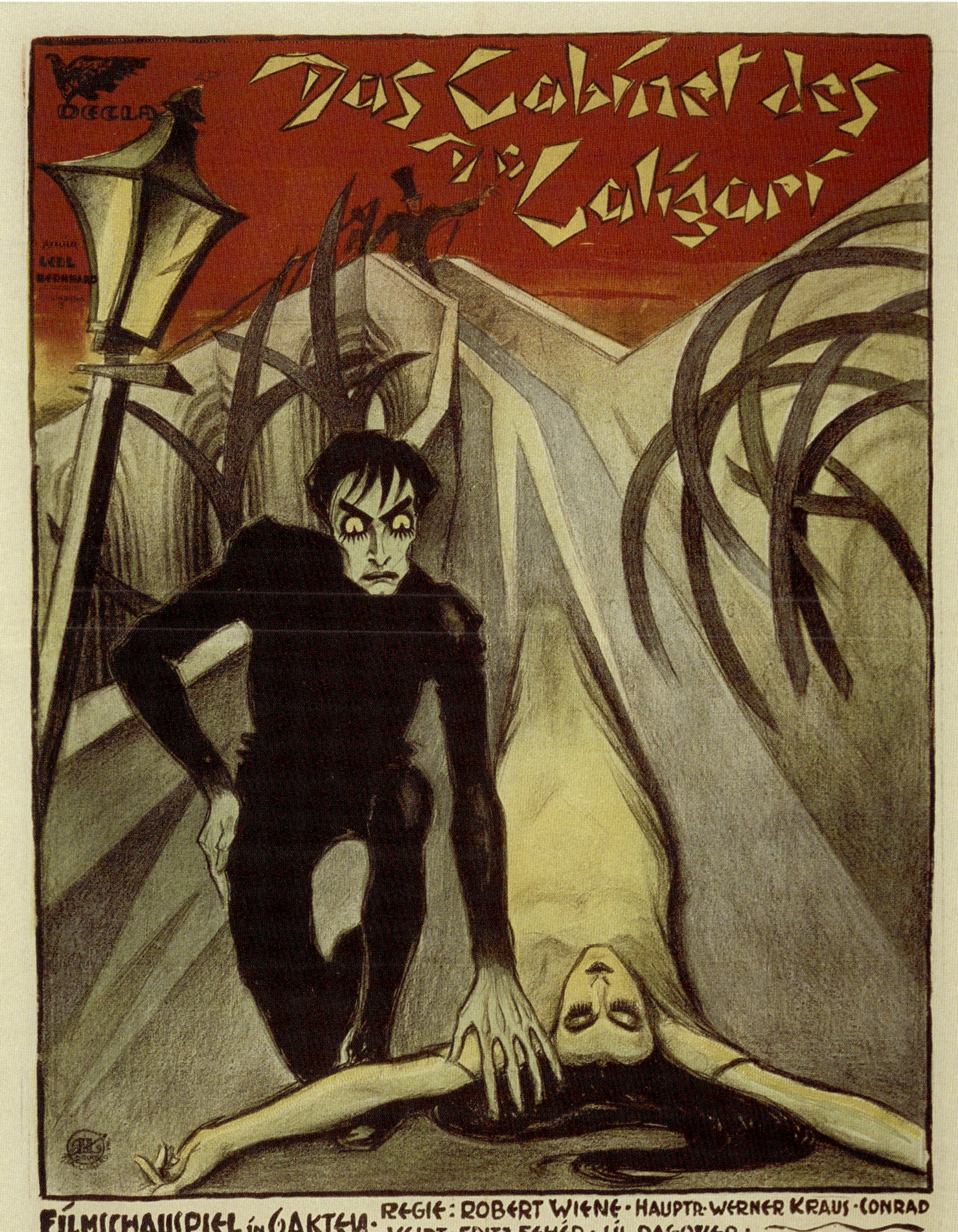

Atelier Ledl & Bernhard
The cabinet of Dr Caligari 1920
colour lithograph, poster
Austrian National Library, Vienna

DADA

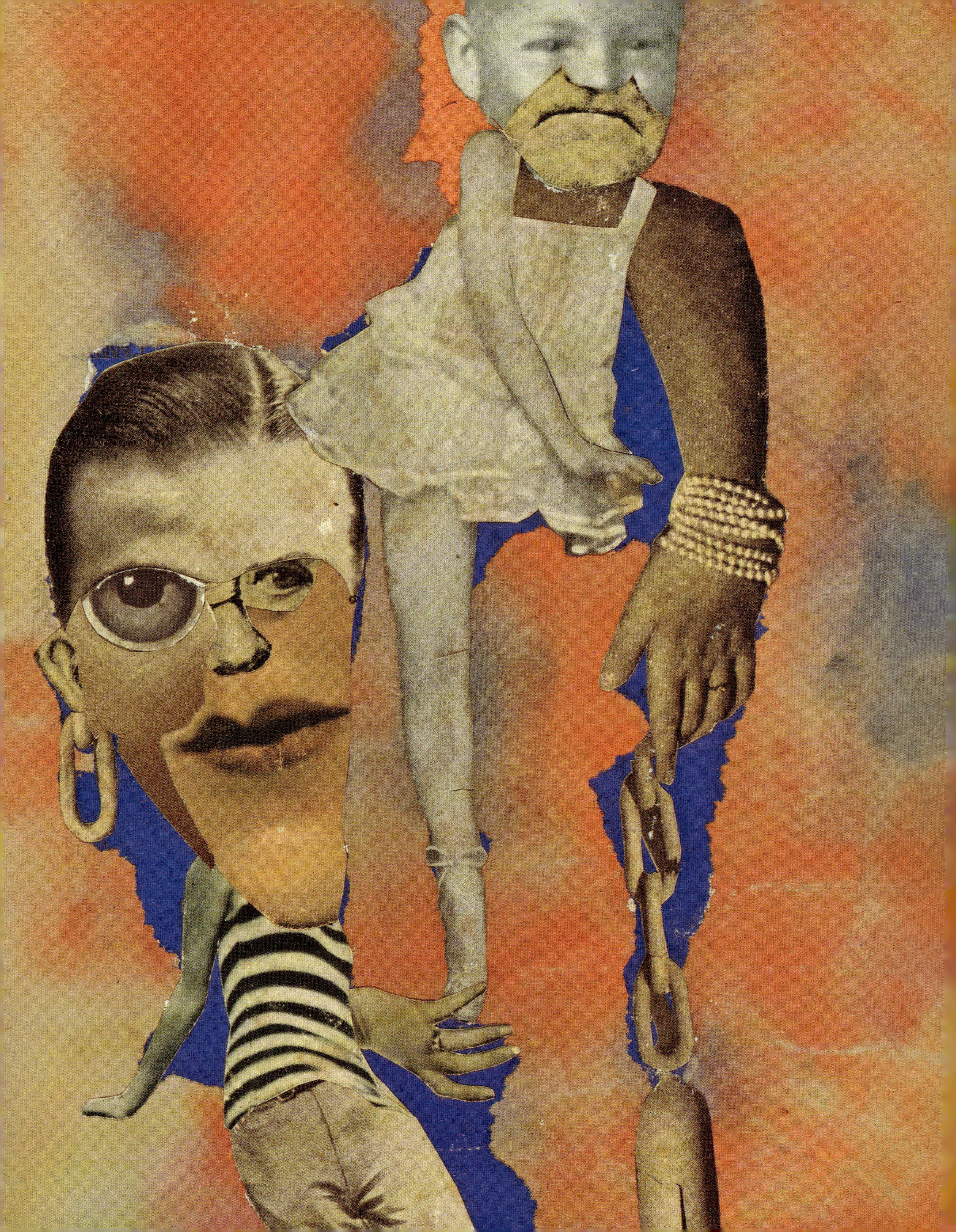

DADA IN GERMANY: 'THE DISFIGURATION OF THE CONTEMPORARY WORLD'

Brigid Doherty

Dada came on the scene in Zurich in the spring of 1916, in connection with events at the Cabaret Voltaire, where beginning in the winter of that year German poet Hugo Ball, German poet and cabaret singer Emmy Hennings, Alsatian artist Jean Arp, Romanian poet Tristan Tzara, Romanian artist Marcel Janco, Swiss artist Sophie Taeuber, and German poet and medical student Richard Huelsenbeck presented new kinds of abstract art and poetry alongside performances of idiosyncratic music-hall acts and avant-garde dance. 'The ideals of culture and of art as a program for a variety show – that is our kind of *Candide* against the times,' wrote Ball in his diary.[1] Named in honour of the French Enlightenment philosopher Voltaire, author of the satirical novel *Candide*, or *Optimism* (1759), the Cabaret Voltaire closed in June of 1916, but the impact of the Dada movement was felt throughout Europe, and perhaps most powerfully in Germany, over the next five years. The naming of the Cabaret Voltaire was a gesture that acknowledged the political and philosophical despair, as well as the artistic and ethical ambitions of Ball and his collaborators in Zurich. As a group, the Zurich Dadaists sought to invent new ways of composing both art and life in neutral Switzerland, a location in which they were at once insulated from and haunted by the perils and terrors of the First World War. Speaking of the effects of their performances and exhibitions, Ball wrote: 'The horror of our time, the paralyzing background of events, is made visible.'[2]

A journal called *Cabaret Voltaire* that was published on 4 June 1916 contained the first appearance in print of the word Dada. Part of the word's appeal was its multilingual evocativeness: 'Dada,' wrote Ball in his diary on 18 April 1916, 'is "yes, yes" in Rumanian, "rocking horse" and "hobbyhorse" in French. For Germans it is a sign of foolish naïveté, joy in procreation, and preoccupation with the baby carriage.'[3] After the Cabaret Voltaire closed, the collaborative endeavours of a number of its founders continued under the Dada name, with well-advertised public performances and the founding, in early 1917, of the Galerie Dada in Zurich. Christian Schad, who had passed through Zurich in 1915–16, participated in Dada events along with the writer Walter Serner in Geneva in 1919–20, and his art of that period, reliefs made of wood and found metal parts, as well as abstract photograms he called 'immaterial collages', declares its affinities to works in relief and in collage made by Arp, Taeuber and others in Zurich (p 94). Schad's innovative photographic works were published by Tzara, who dubbed them 'Schadographs' in the journal *Dada*, and the German artist would make his presence felt again as one of the most important painters of *Neue Sachlichkeit* (New Objectivity) in Berlin in the later 1920s.

In early 1917, Huelsenbeck returned to Berlin and quickly sought to establish the German capital as a centre of Dada activity. In the midst of the acute material deprivation and increasing social and political tension brought on by the First World War, Huelsenbeck soon began to collaborate with the artists and writers George Grosz, John Heartfield, Wieland Herzfelde and Franz Jung around the publication of *Neue Jugend*

Hannah Höch
Balance 1925 (detail)

(*New Youth*), a periodical that anticipated the posters, flyers and magazines of Berlin Dada in its experimental form and politically engaged content. In early 1918, Grosz, Heartfield, Herzfelde and Jung joined Huelsenbeck in founding Club Dada, which also counted among its members the architect and writer Johannes Baader, the artists Raoul Hausmann, Hannah Höch and Otto Schmalhausen, and the writer Walter Mehring. In Germany, Dada took on a more aggressively political character than it had shown in Zurich, with the Berlin Dadaists and their counterparts in Cologne – prominent among the latter Max Ernst – advocating radical political change in the wake of the abdication of Kaiser Wilhelm II and the November Revolution of 1918. Grosz, Heartfield, Herzfelde and Jung were all founding members of the German Communist Party, and German Dada journals and newspapers including *Der Dada*, *Jedermann sein eigner Fussball* (*Everyone His Own Football*) and *Die Pleite* (*Bankruptcy*), as well as several Dada exhibitions in Cologne and Berlin in 1919–20 that explicitly addressed contemporary political events. Indeed, those publications and exhibitions attempted to establish connections between the Dadaists' experimental artistic techniques, most prominent among them collage and photomontage, and their critiques of contemporary politics and culture.

If a renunciation of the 'dreary, lame, empty language of men in society', as well as a critique of journalism in particular and of communication in general were crucial to the development of Ball's important 'sound-poems' of the Zurich Dada period[4], the pursuit of related experiments in Berlin engaged contemporary forms of communication (newspapers, illustrated magazines, posters, advertising, photography and film) as new media for the production as well as the critique of poetry and art. In the newspaper-format catalogue for the First International Dada Fair, held in Berlin in summer 1920, Herzfelde announced as the Dadaists' 'singular program' an 'obligation to make what is happening here and now – temporally as well as spatially – the content of their pictures', and he explained that to that end they took 'the illustrated newspaper and the editorials of the press as their source'.[5]

On 15 February 1919, the Berlin Dadaists published a four-page satirical broadsheet called *Jedermann sein eigner Fussball* (opposite), which represented an effort by Grosz, Heartfield, Herzfelde and Mehring to align their work more closely with the aims of the recently founded German Communist Party. Thousands of copies of *Jedermann sein eigner Fussball* are reported to have been sold on the streets of Berlin before the broadsheet was banned that same day.[6] Designed by Heartfield, the cover includes two examples of photomontage, a medium that would emerge as central to Berlin Dada, especially in the context of the epochal 1920 Dada Fair. To the left of the title, a dashing young man doffing his hat and swinging his walking stick seems not to have noticed that his torso has been replaced by a soccer ball with the tube through which it was inflated still attached; nor does he seem to realise, more generally, that the rest of him is far too large for his head. That head is a photographic portrait of Herzfelde, who would soon spend time in jail as a consequence of the publication of *Jedermann sein eigner Fussball* and its successor, *Die Pleite* (opposite). At the centre of the page a fan displays portrait photographs of members of the administration of the recently elected Social Democratic President of the Reich, Friedrich Ebert (fourth from the left on the upper part of the fan).

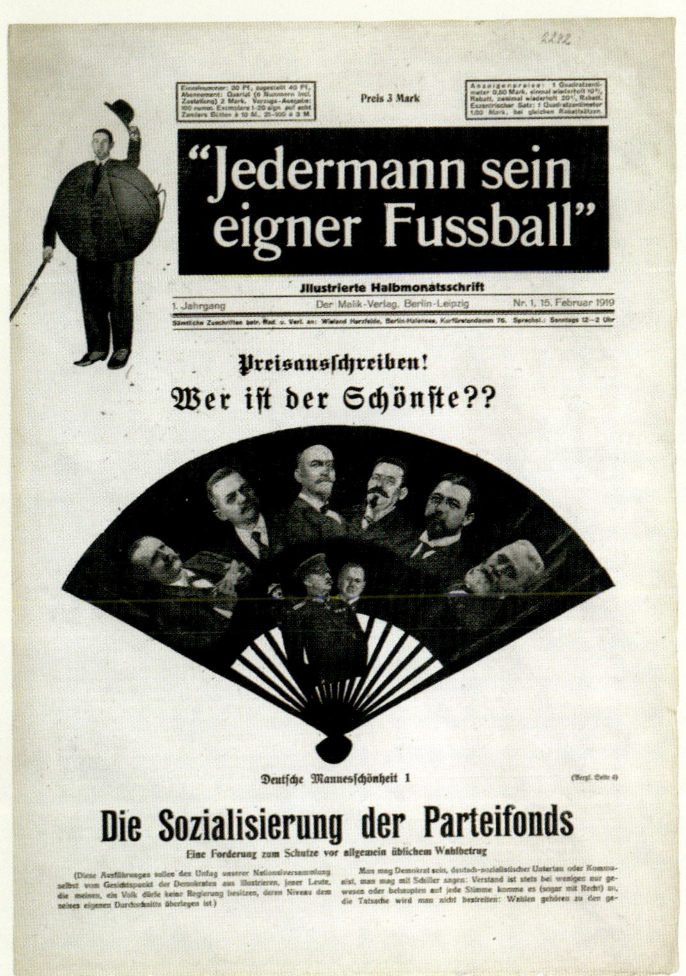

Preis 3 Mark

"Jedermann sein eigner Fussball"

Jllustrierte Halbmonatsschrift

1. Jahrgang | Der Malik-Verlag, Berlin-Leipzig | Nr. 1, 15. Februar 1919

Sämtliche Zuschriften betr. Red. u. Verl. an: Wieland Herzfelde, Berlin-Halensee, Kurfürstendamm 76. Sprechst.: Sonntags 12–2 Uhr

Preisausschreiben!

Wer ist der Schönste??

Deutsche Mannesschönheit 1

Die Sozialisierung der Parteifonds

Eine Forderung zum Schutze vor allgemein üblichem Wahlbetrug

(Diese Ausführungen sollen den Unfug unserer Nationalversammlung selbst vom Gesichtspunkt der Demokraten aus illustrieren, jener Leute, die meinen, ein Volk dürfe keine Regierung besitzen, deren Niveau dem seines eigenen Durchschnitts überlegen ist.)

Man mag Demokrat sein, deutsch-sozialistischer Untertan oder Kommunist, man mag mit Schiller sagen: Verstand ist stets bei wenigen nur gewesen oder behaupten auf jede Stimme komme es (sogar mit Recht) an, die Tatsache wird man nicht bestreiten: Wahlen gehören zu den ge-

John Heartfield
Cover of the newspaper *Everyone His Own Football*
no 1, Feb 1919

photomontages on front cover by John Heartfield and George Grosz
Akademie der Künste, Berlin, Kunstsammlung

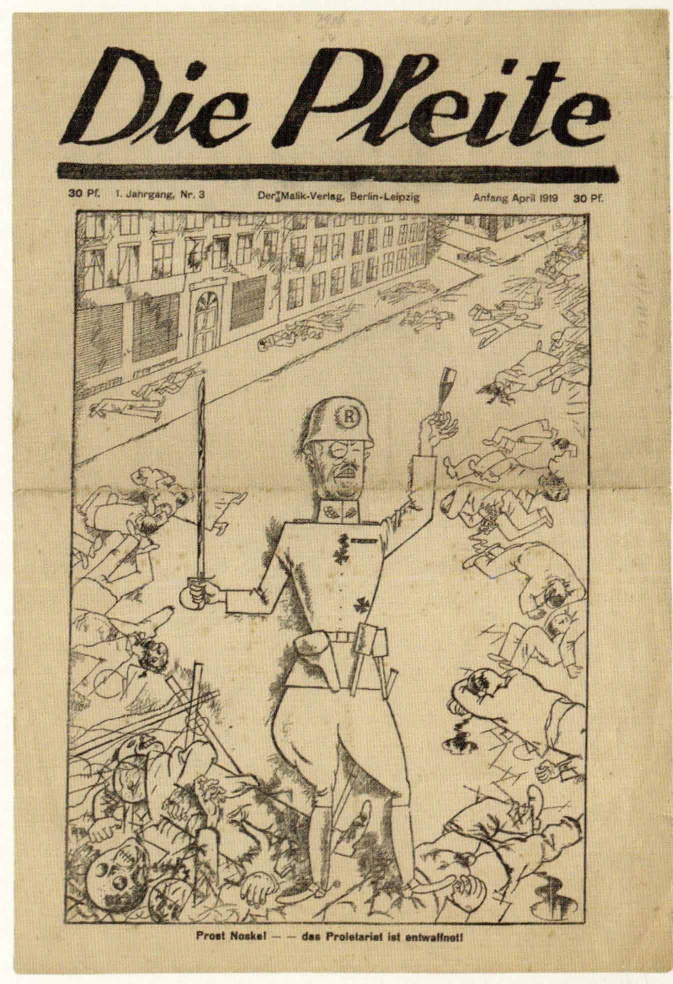

Die Pleite

30 Pf. | 1. Jahrgang, Nr. 3 | Der Malik-Verlag, Berlin-Leipzig | Anfang April 1919 | 30 Pf.

Prost Noske! — — das Proletariat ist entwaffnet!

George Grosz and Wieland Herzfelde
Cover of the journal *Bankruptcy* no 3, 1919

letterpress, gillotage
National Gallery of Australia, Canberra

Also shown is the uniformed General Ludendorff, whose military support, along with that of the counterrevolutionary *Freikorps*, had been crucial to the Social Democrats' consolidation of political power following the abdication of Kaiser Wilhelm II on 9 November 1918, and especially to their suppression of the so-called Spartacist Uprising that had been launched by the Communists in Berlin in mid January 1919. Attributed to Grosz and presented as evidence in a contest to select the most beautiful man among those represented on the fan, the photomontage was exhibited with the title *Galerie deutscher Mannesschönheit, Preisfrage 'Wer ist der schönste?'* (*Gallery of German male beauty, prize question: 'Who is the most beautiful?'*) at the Dada Fair, where it hung across the surface of Otto Dix's large montage painting, *45% Erwerbsfähig* (*45% fit for work*; see the photograph of the Dada Fair, opposite). Now lost, Dix's picture showed a parade of patriotic so-called 'war-cripples' marching along a city street.

On the cover of *Jedermann sein eigner Fussball*, the inflatable man bearing Herzfelde's head in Heartfield's photomontage appears as a mocking counterpart to the gathering of male beauties in Grosz's photomontage below, with Herzfelde's portrait affixed to a makeshift inflatable doll, and those of Ebert & Co to a hand-held accoutrement of middle-class women, both objects with a built-in readiness to change shape or collapse. When shown framed within the composition of *45% fit for work* at the Dada Fair, Grosz's *Gallery of German male beauty* found a more trenchant counterpart in the mutilated faces and reconfigured bodies of the veterans of Dix's picture. These figures were themselves based on photographs of wounded First World War soldiers and, unlike many images published in the illustrated press during and after the war, they presented evidence of the destruction of human bodies by the technologies of modern battle without showing the successful repair of that destruction by medical science and engineering. Indeed, the makeshift apparatuses Dix depicts appear markedly different from the technologically sophisticated prosthetic limbs advertised widely and often discussed in detail in newspapers and other publications of the period. A pointing hand of the sort often seen in contemporary advertising, itself a kind of minimally metaphorical emblem of the literalist pointing of Dada montage, calls attention to the presence of Grosz's photomontage as a supplement mounted on Dix's montage painting. That emblematic pointing hand asserts, in its own deictic literalism, that this assemblage of montage pictures should be recognised as a polemical presentation of montage as a technique with which the Dadaists intended to intervene in contemporary social life as it had been transformed first by the war, and then by the politics and the media culture of the early Weimar Republic.

Printed with red and black typography over a photolithographic reproduction of Heartfield and Grosz's collaborative montage, *Life and activity in universal city at 12:05 in the afternoon* (now lost), the newspaper-sized cover page of the catalogue to the First International Dada Fair (fig 3 opposite) asserts that 'the Dada movement leads to the sublation of the art trade'.[7] Organised by Grosz (who is given the military rank 'Marshal' on the cover page), Hausmann (Dadasopher) and Heartfield (Monteurdada), the Dada Fair – an 'Exhibition and Sale' of roughly 200 'Dadaist Products' that was held from 30 June to 25 August 1920 in Otto Burchard's Berlin art gallery – failed as a commercial venture.

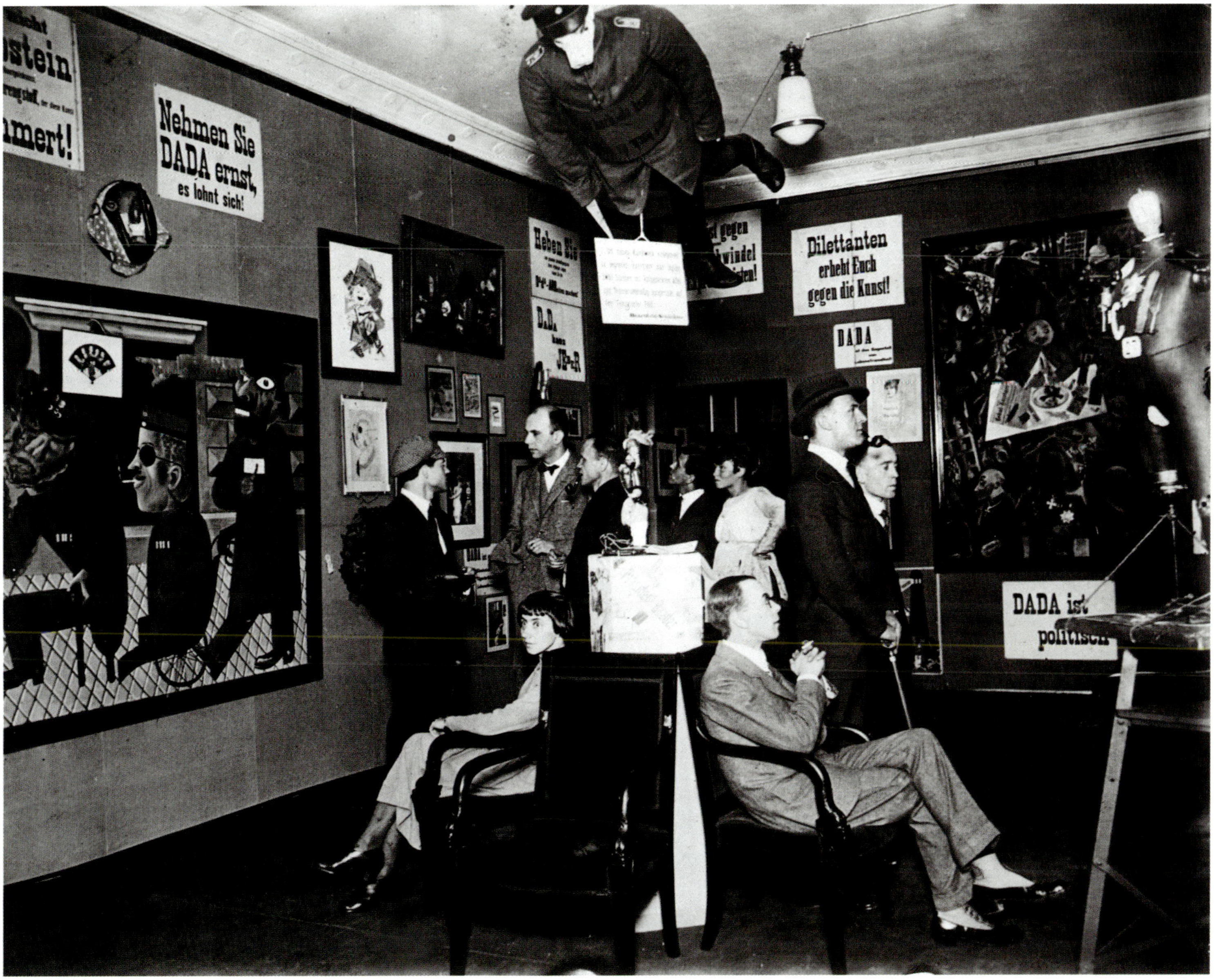

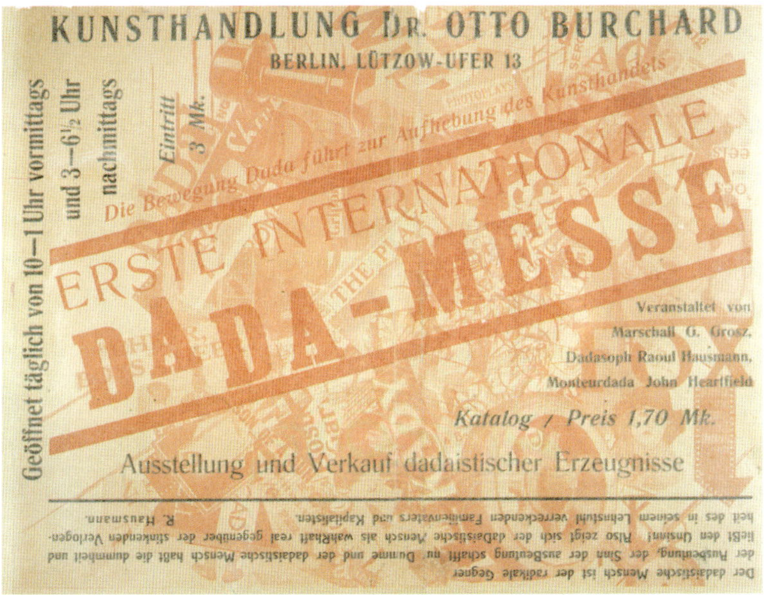

Robert Sennecke
Opening of the *First International Dada Fair* held at the Otto Burchard Gallery, Berlin, 30 June 1920

archival photograph
Bildarchiv Preussischer Kulturbesitz Berlin

left to right: Raoul Hausmann, Hannah Höch (seated), Dr Otto Burchard, Johannes Baader, Wieland Herzfelde, Margarete Herzfelde, Otto Schmalhausen, George Grosz and John Heartfield

fig 3

John Heartfield
Cover of the exhibition catalogue
First International Dada Fair 1920

photolithograph, 31.2 x 38.5 cm
Berlinische Galerie, Landesmuseum für Moderne Kunst, Photographie und Architektur

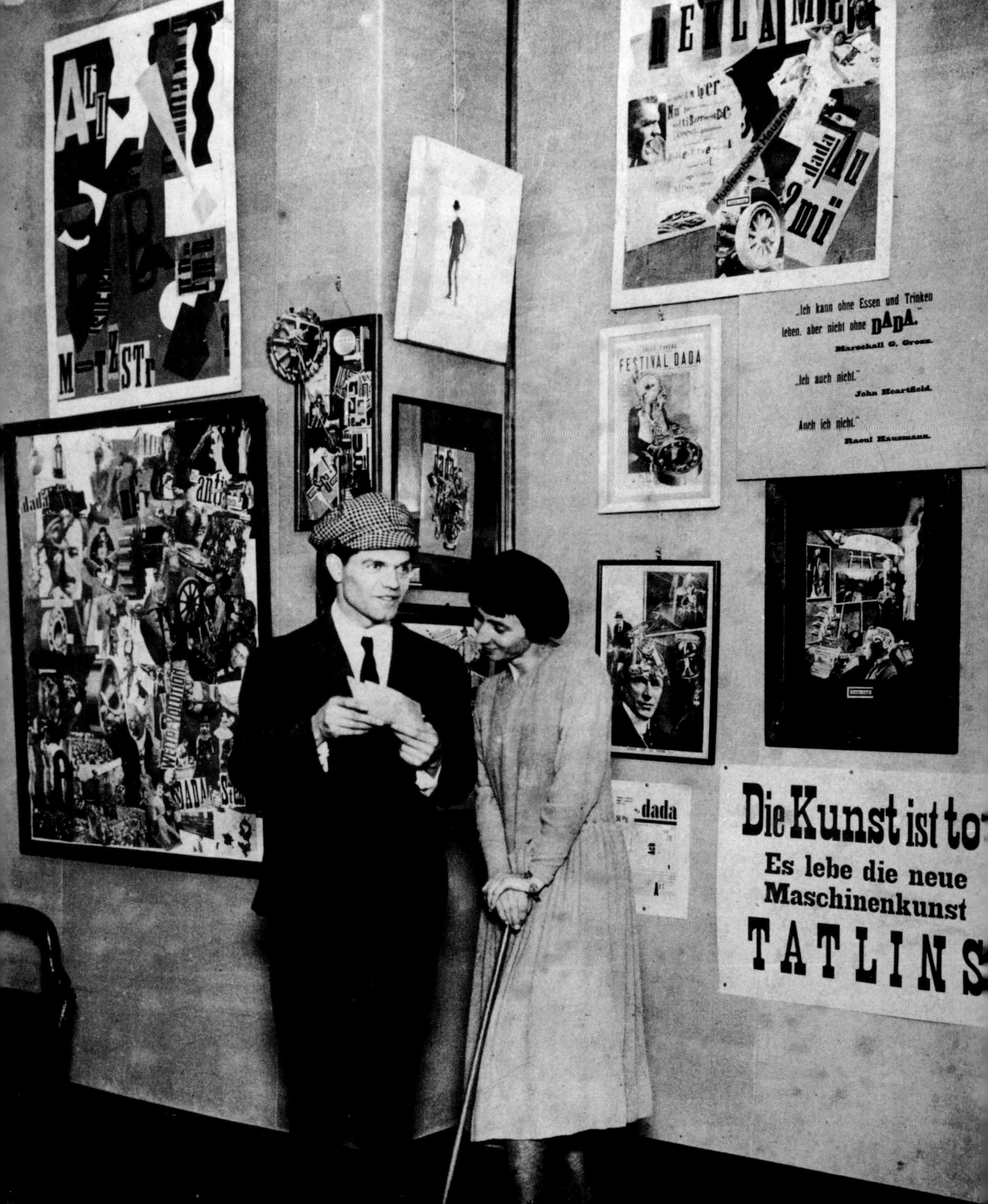
FESTIVAL DADA
„Ich kann ohne Essen und Trinken
leben, aber nicht ohne DADA."
Marschall G. Grosz.
„Ich auch nicht."
John Heartfield.
„Auch ich nicht."
Raoul Hausmann.
dada
Die Kunst ist to
Es lebe die neue
Maschinenkunst
TATLINS

Despite charging a considerable admission fee of three marks thirty (a sum even higher than the catalogue announces), while asking an additional one mark seventy for the catalogue, which was published three weeks into the run of the show, the Dadaists could not bring in enough from sales to turn a profit.[8] More successful than the Berlin Dadaists' attempts to make money on the exhibition were their efforts to generate publicity for the Dada Fair in the German and international print media. They hired a professional photographer from one of Berlin's most prominent agencies to document the show's opening, and photographs of the Dada Fair were reproduced in illustrated weeklies as far away as Amsterdam, Milan, Rome and Boston.

According to Herzfelde's published introduction to the Dada Fair, in making photomontages the Dadaists aimed neither to compete with photography nor to 'breathe a soul' into the photographic apparatus. Instead, as Herzfelde asserts, they sought to incorporate the medium's technologies and effects, above all those of the cinema's moving pictures, into the production of works that set aside an 'aspiration to art' in the service of an obligation to make 'what is happening here and now' manifest not only in their content but also in their mode of production. Herzfelde makes the case for the Dadaists' destruction of the 'cult of art' and for their invention of a new kind of artistic production that refuses to 'emancipate itself from reality' or to 'disavow the actual' – a new art, or at least a new way of making pictures, that seeks to intensify 'the pleasure of the broad masses in constructive, creative activity', for example, by taking 'the illustrated newspaper and the editorials of the press as [its] source'. Montage is the technique the Berlin Dadaists deployed in their efforts to transform the production and reception of works of art. As what Herzfelde called a 'capitulation to cinema' and a way of making objects that engage 'reality' and 'the actual' through 'means of presentation [that] are anti-illusionistic', montage connects Berlin Dada agonistically to traditions of painting and, at the same time, structures its destruction of the 'cult of art'.[9]

The Dada Fair resulted in the trial of several of its organisers on charges of having slandered the military by means of the inclusion of works such as Grosz's portfolio of lithographs *Gott mit uns* (God with us) 1920, which satirised the practices of military authorities during and after the First World War. Grosz and Herzfelde were compelled to pay 900 marks in fines as a result of their conviction at trial in April 1921. Also invoked in the charges brought against the Dadaists was a sculptural assemblage consisting of a stuffed German officer's uniform with a plaster pig's head that hung from the ceiling in the exhibition and bore the name *Prussian archangel* 1920 (2004 reconstruction of lost original in the Neue Galerie, New York). Visible in the photographs of the Dada Fair included in this exhibition (p 81), this work was made by Heartfield in collaboration with the painter Rudolf Schlichter, who (like Schad) would come to prominence in the context of *Neue Sachlichkeit*. With its caricatures of a range of contemporary social types, Schlichter's watercolour *Tingel tangel* of 1919–20 (p 209) anticipates stylistic features of *Neue Sachlichkeit*, even as the disposition of its figures in a shrilly lit café – among them two bare-breasted female performers and their tuxedo-clad band – recalls motifs of Berlin Dada photomontages and Grosz's prints and drawings of the period. The same is true for Georg Scholz's *Profiteering peasant family* 1920 (p 85), a lithograph based on

Robert Sennecke
Raoul Hausmann and Hannah Höch at the opening of the *First International Dada Fair* held at the Otto Burchard Gallery, Berlin, 30 June 1920
archival photograph
Berlinische Galerie, Landesmuseum für Moderne Kunst, Photographie und Architektur

a montage painting Scholz exhibited at the Dada Fair. Like the post-Dada paintings of Grosz, this work scrutinises and satirises its subjects in a mode that would come to be described in the 1920s as 'verist'. Scholz claimed to have based his picture of profiteering peasants on his own experience as a wounded veteran in 1919 when, seeking food for his hungry family, he asked some well-stocked farmers if they could spare something to eat, and was told in reply that the compost heap was at his disposal. Scholz's lithograph aims to answer the Berlin Dadaists' call for an art that would meet 'the requirement to further the disfiguration of the contemporary world, which already finds itself in a state of disintegration, of metamorphosis'[10], even as it departs from the tendency of Berlin Dada art to take shape by means of montage.

Grosz's *Tatlinesque diagram* 1920 (p 25) was one of a number of works shown at the Dada Fair that made reference to the Russian Constructivist artist Vladimir Tatlin, about whom the Dadaists and others in Germany had had occasion to read in a four-part series of articles on art in contemporary Soviet Russia that were published in the journal *Der Ararat* from January to June of 1920. Unrelated to Tatlin's work formally or otherwise, *Tatlinesque diagram* instead borrows elements of its construction of pictorial space from the recent so-called 'metaphysical' paintings of Italian artist Giorgio de Chirico to situate within a perspectivally constructed interior an inscrutable encounter between a male figure who resembles Grosz's self-portraits of the period and a naked woman offering him her breast. Typical stylistically of the mixed-media watercolour and montage works Grosz made in 1920 and showed at the Dada Fair that year, *Tatlinesque diagram* was reproduced as one of seven so-called 'materialisations' in Grosz's 1922 portfolio of color lithographs, *Mit Pinsel und Schere* (*With brush and scissors*).[11]

In Hannah Höch's montage *Heads of state* 1918–20 (p 91), the president of the Weimar republic, Friedrich Ebert, and his minister of defence, Gustav Noske, appear in a photographic fragment clipped from a notorious picture that had been published in Germany's most widely circulated illustrated paper, the *Berliner Illustrirte Zeitung* (*BIZ*), in August 1919. *Heads of state* features that fragment pasted on top of an iron-on needlepoint pattern created by Höch in the context of her work producing handiwork designs for the Ullstein Verlag, publishers of *BIZ*. As exemplified by *Heads of state*, Dada derided the political culture of the early Weimar republic's fledgling social democracy by exploiting the vagaries of the symbolic 'incorporation' of the Weimar republic in mass-media images of the President of the Reich and other members of the government and the military. Photographs like the one used by Höch in *Heads of state* provided the Dadaists with material for montages that would 'further the disfiguration of the contemporary world, which already finds itself in a state of disintegration, of metamorphosis,' to borrow once more the terms of Herzfelde's introduction to the Dada Fair.[12] While *Heads of state* was not shown at the Dada Fair, Höch did exhibit another photomontage, *Dada panorama* 1919 (Berlinische Galerie), in which the same picture of Ebert and Noske figures centrally. In selecting that particular photograph, Höch pointed to what the Dadaists took to be the ludicrous ambiguity of the republic's self-representation in the technological medium of the photographically illustrated press, lambasting the homely, summer-vacation pose of Weimar's elected leaders as itself a travesty of charismatic legitimacy.

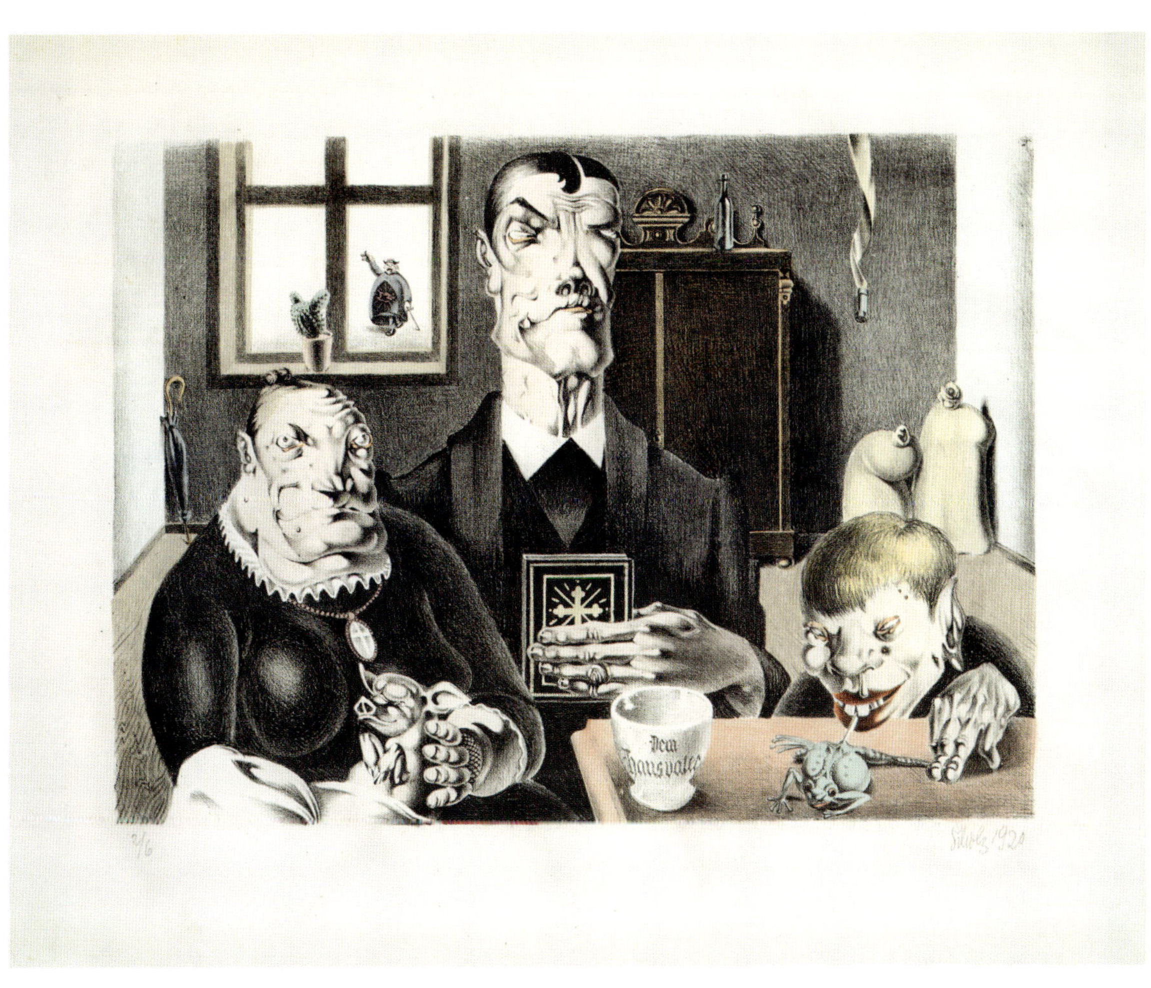

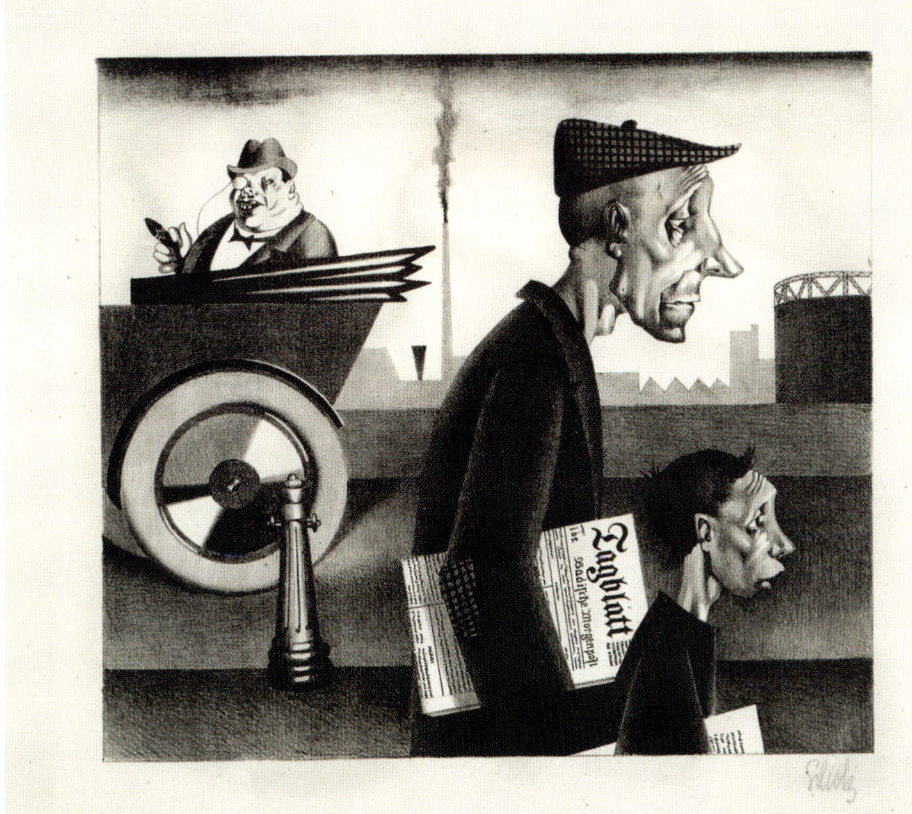

Georg Scholz
Profiteering farming family 1920
colour lithograph
Private collection

Georg Scholz
Paper boy 1921
lithograph
Private collection

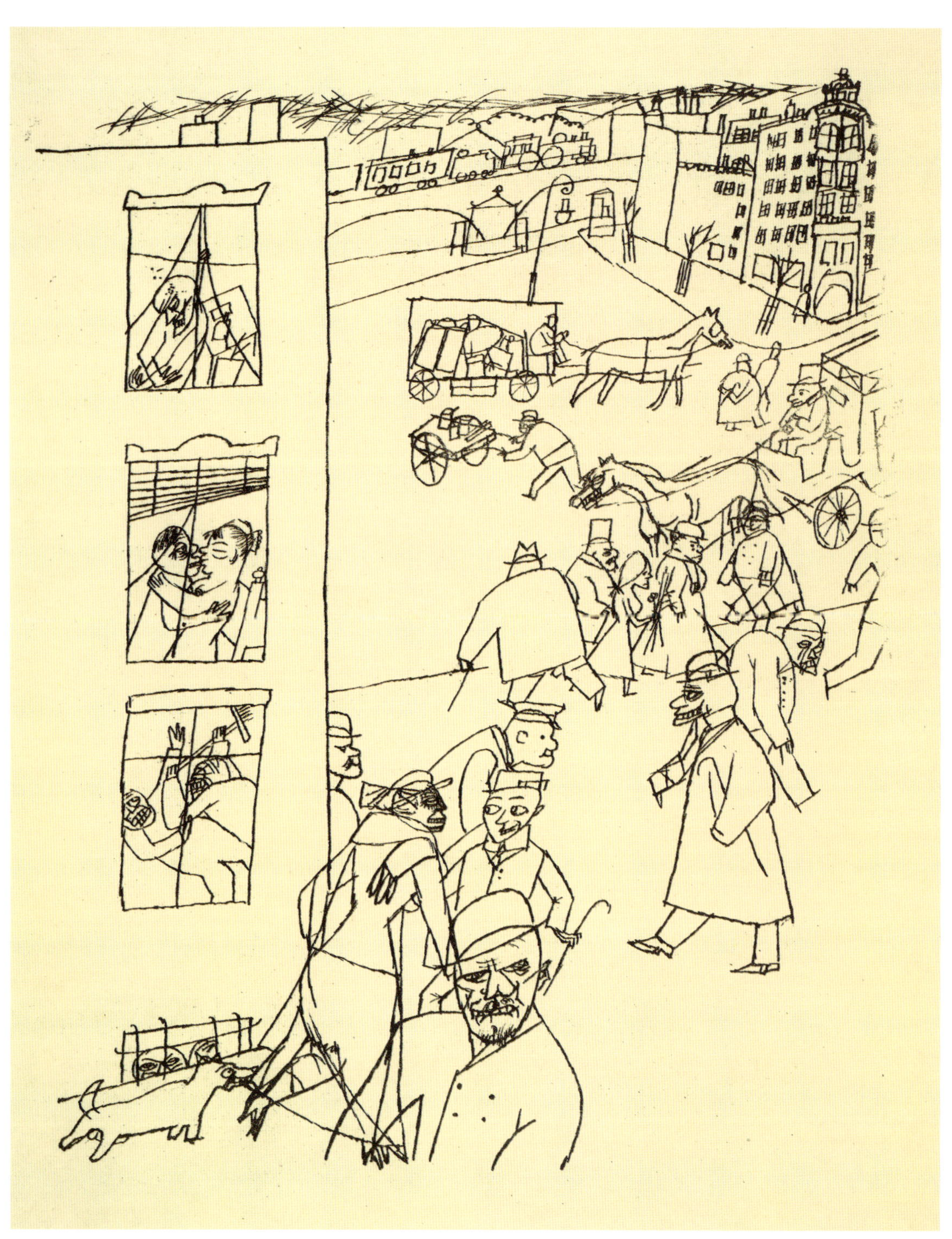

George Grosz
People in the street 1915–16
from the First George Grosz portfolio 1917
lithograph
Private collection, Melbourne

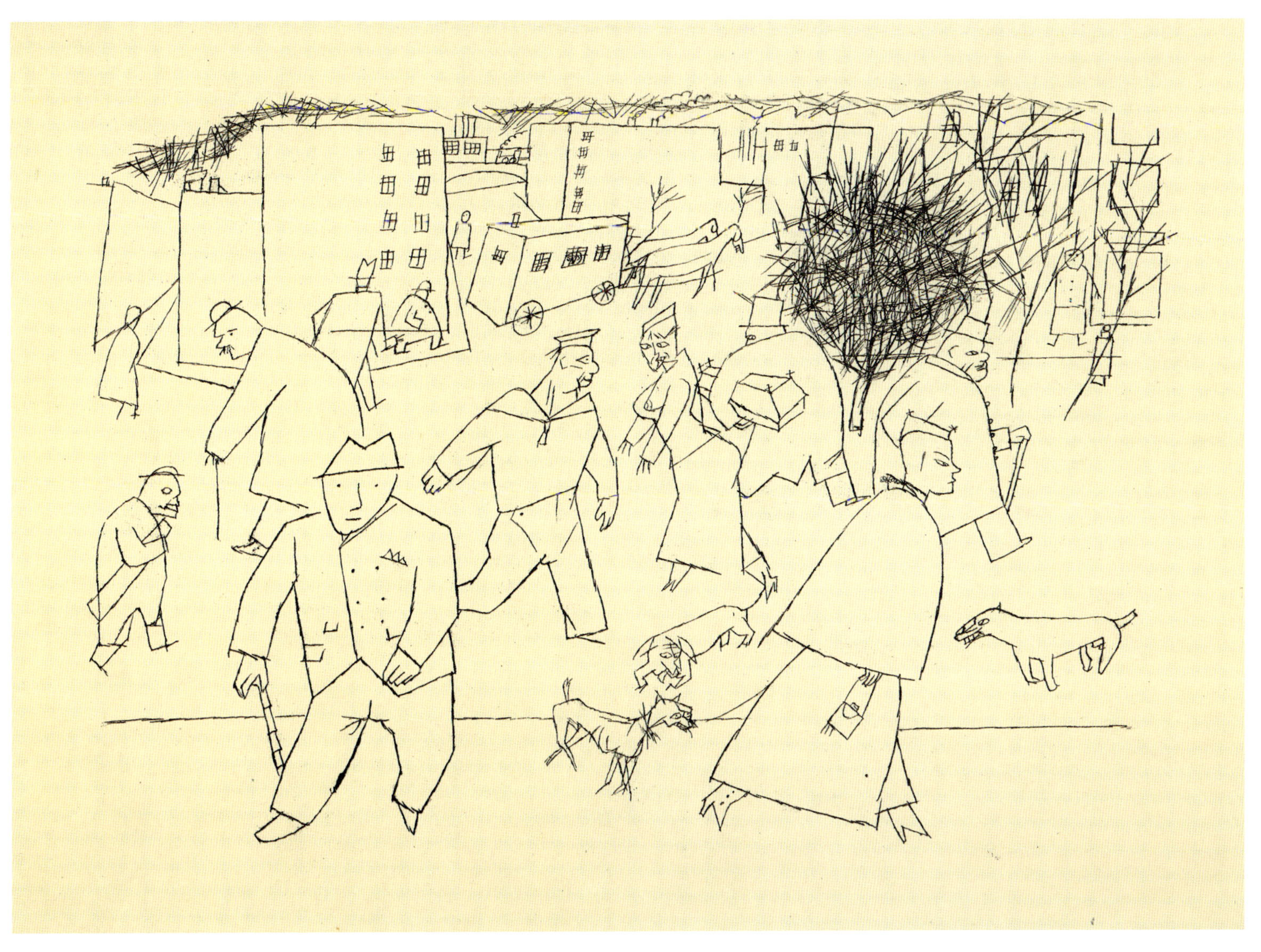

George Grosz
City street 1915–16
from the First George Grosz portfolio 1917
lithograph
Private collection, Melbourne

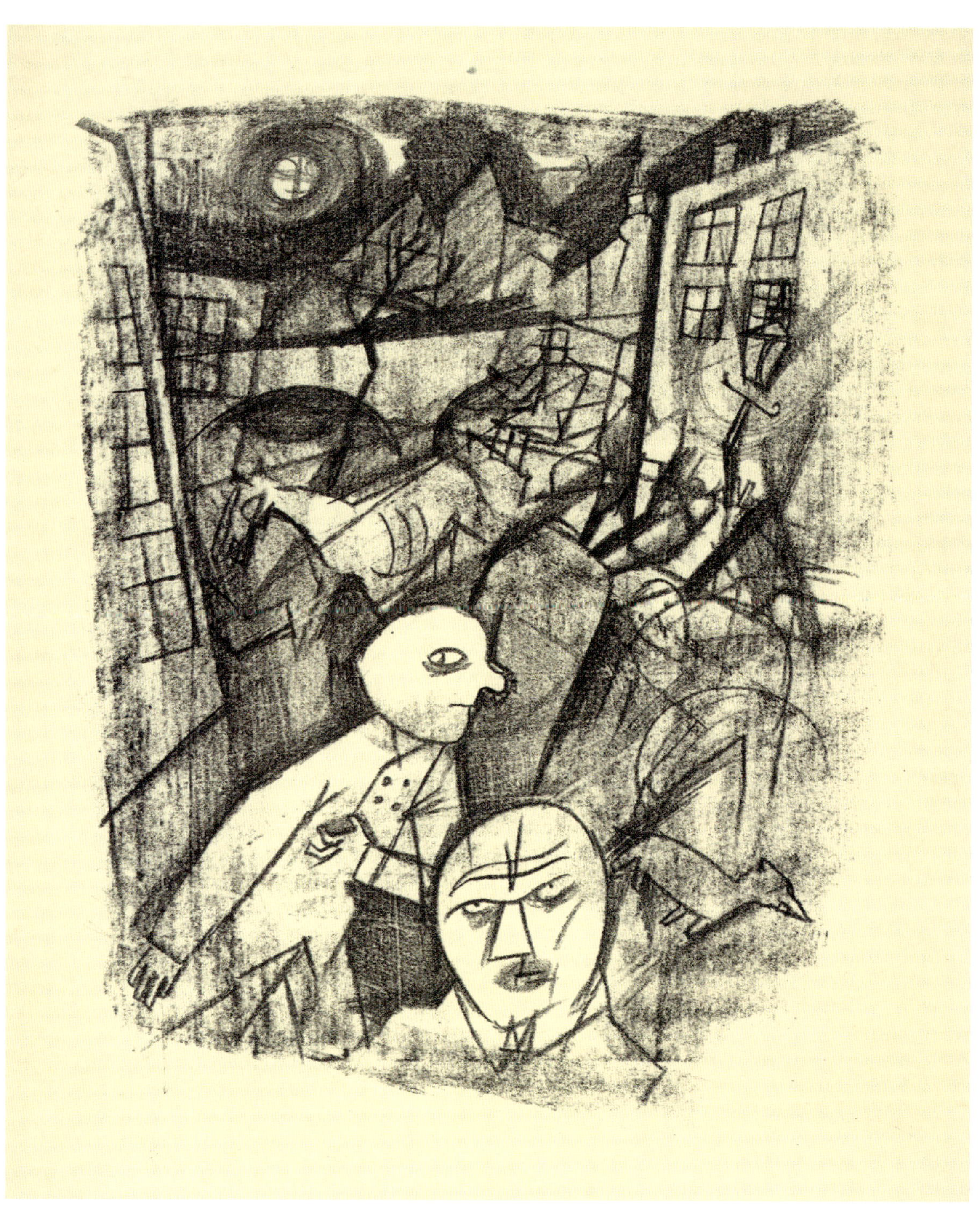

George Grosz
Moonlit night 1915–16
from the **First George Grosz portfolio** 1917
lithograph
Private collection, Melbourne

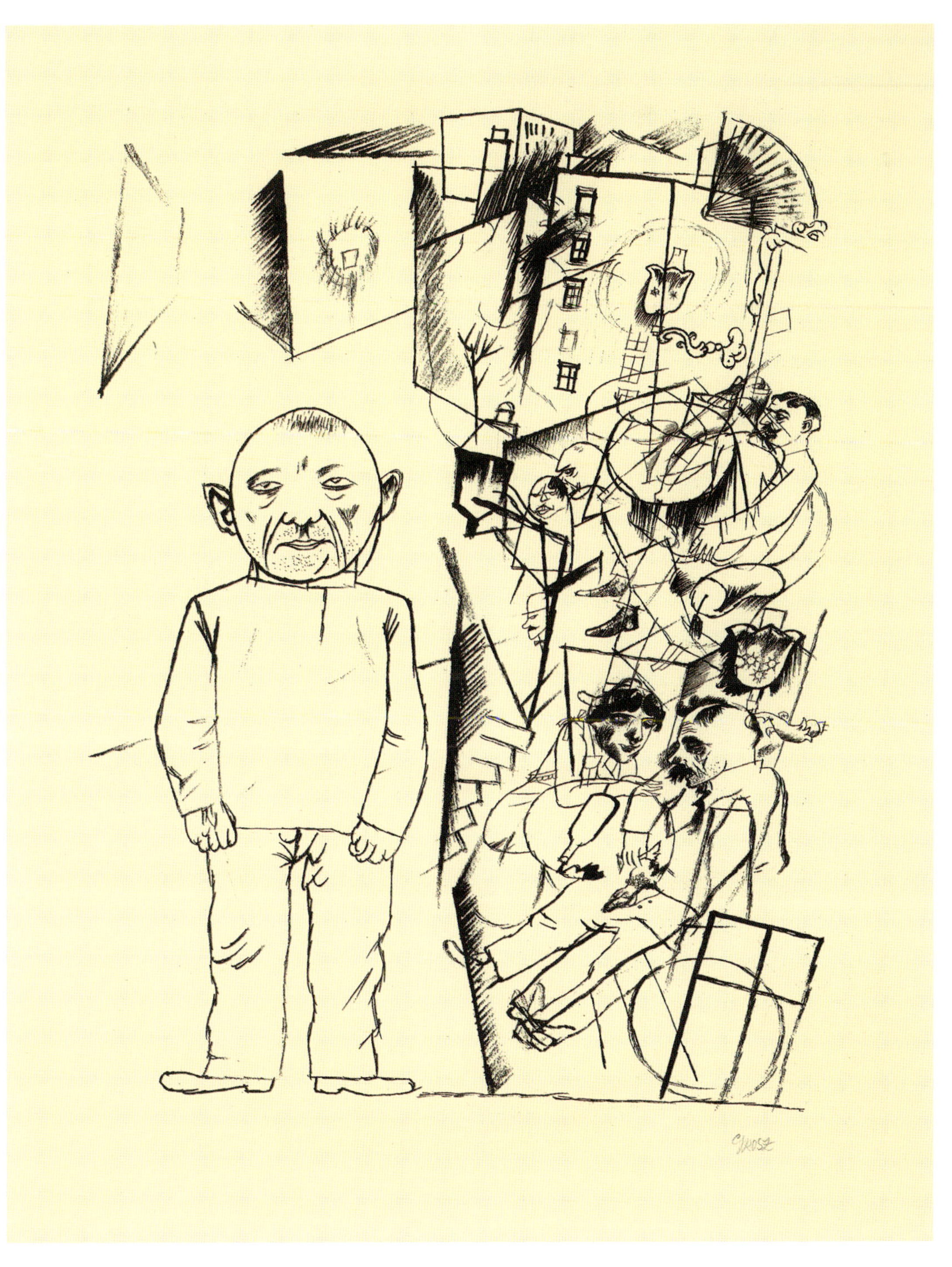

George Grosz
The convict 1919
photolithograph
National Gallery of Victoria, Melbourne

Heads of state pairs Ebert and Noske as exemplary male embodiments of the politics of the early Weimar period with an apt fantasy of femininity, a mythical creature dressed up in a costume of middle-class seaside leisure. This figure, once ready in the handicraft pattern to be stitched for domestic display, is posed in the photomontage to lounge with the tip of her tail aloft as if deriding the politicians' apparent dismemberment, which Höch's montage underscores in the layer of grey mounted below the men. The pasted paper seems to make up a lapping surf, its waves leaving room for stumpy legs (that is the anatomical logic in Ebert's case, where he still has his hips and crotch) or double, oversized penises or elephantine testicles (so suggests Noske's body, cropped just below the waist). However, the politicians fail to take up the space created by the pasted paper, as if in place of a scene of vacation bathing the montage was staging a castration fantasy in which male genitals appear at once gigantic and lacking. The seemingly tumescent photographic fragment at the lower right might suggest that fantasy's unhappy compensation: it must be the atmosphere of aquatic play (and boardwalk spectacle) associated with a mermaid (with sun hat and umbrella) that can make one see in that fragment the truncated flipper of a trained seal with its ball still attached.

Excluded from the Dada Fair and denied membership in Club Dada because of his allegedly petit-bourgeois disposition, Kurt Schwitters was derided by Huelsenbeck as a belated Romantic. Nevertheless, Schwitters undertook Dada-related activities of his own in his native Hanover and produced pictures and reliefs by means of techniques that were closely aligned with the aims set out in Herzfelde's introduction to the Dada Fair and in Dada manifestoes published in Zurich and Berlin. In 1919, Schwitters adopted the term 'Merz' – a fragment extracted from the printed word *Kommerz* ('commerce', itself in this case part of a larger phrase in the name of a bank, *Kommerz-und Privatbank*) and originally pasted into the 1919 collage *Merzbild I* (now lost) – to designate his artistic production in a wide range of media, including lyric poetry. Schwitters first exhibited his collage-based works in Berlin at Herwarth Walden's gallery *Der Sturm* (*The Storm*) in July of that year, and around that time developed close friendships with Höch and Hausmann. Following an anti-Dada Merz appearance with Hausmann in Prague, in 1921 Schwitters joined Hausmann and Höch in participating in the International Congress of Constructivists and Dadaists in Weimar in 1922. At the end of the congress, he set out with Tzara, Arp and the Dutch De Stijl artist Theo van Doesburg on a tour that ended with an evening of Dada performances and readings in Hanover, in which Hausmann and Höch also participated and which was attended by the Russian Constructivist El Lissitzsky. In early 1923, Schwitters published the first issue of the journal *Merz*, which would become an important vehicle for his experiments in typographical composition and for the publication of works of graphic art by Schwitters and others affiliated with Dada and International Constructivism.

Schwitters never abandoned the principles of collage composition that structured his Merz work beginning in 1919. Indeed, in the years after Dada, he extended the effects of those principles into the built environment of his *Merzbau* c1923–36, destroyed in a British air raid on Hanover in 1943 (it was reconstructed in the Sprengel Museum, Hanover, in 1981–83). By contrast, in September 1920 Grosz, Heartfield, Hausmann and

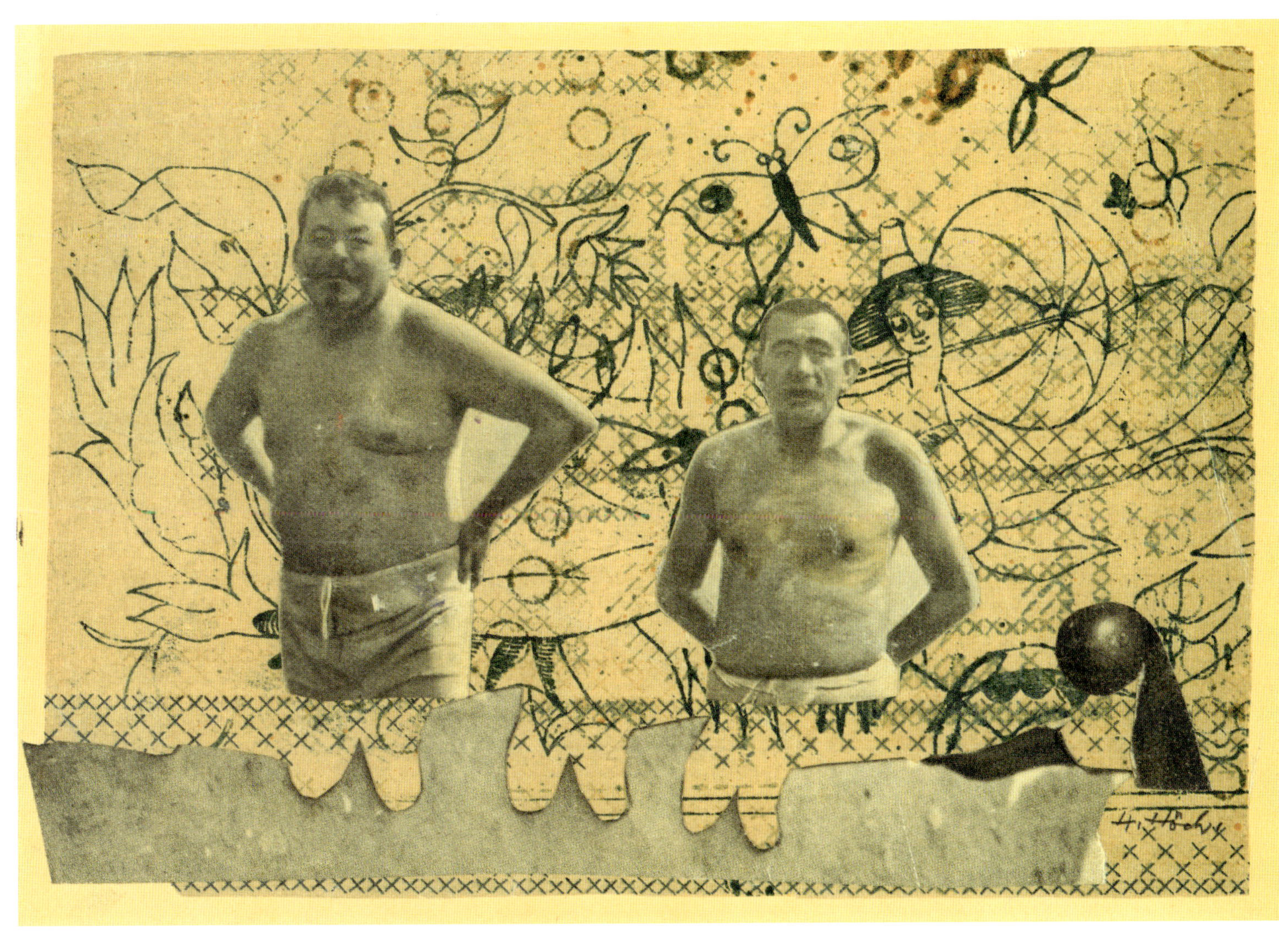

Hannah Höch
Heads of state 1918–20
collage on iron-on embroidery pattern
Institute for Foreign Cultural Relations, Stuttgart

Schlichter renounced in their manifesto 'The Rules of Painting' the principles of montage that had been presented as central to the Dada Fair just two months earlier.[13] While Grosz, Schlichter, Scholz, Dix and, intermittently, Hausmann and Höch, did return to painting and more conventional kinds of work in the graphic arts after the Dada movement dissolved, Heartfield continued to make photomontages, largely in the context of book designs for the Malik Verlag throughout the 1920s and as contributions to the *Arbeiter Illustrierte Zeitung* (*AIZ*) after 1930. Hausmann and especially Höch also made photomontages post-Dada, and Höch's prolific production in that medium in the later 1920s is featured in this exhibition with important works including *Balance* of 1925 (p 102).

According to literary critic and philosopher Walter Benjamin in his oft-cited essay 'The Work of Art in the Age of its Technological Reproducibility', in virtually 'striking' or 'jolting' the viewer by means of an evocation of tactile experience, the Dadaist artwork 'strains after effects' whose realisation demands a 'changed technical standard, that is, a new art form', specifically film. For emphasis, Benjamin announced in italics, '*Dadaism attempted to produce with the means of painting (or literature) the effects which the public today seeks in the film.*'[14] As the techniques of montage deployed by the Berlin Dadaists around 1919–20 and theorised by Herzfelde in his introduction to the Dada Fair gave way to a return to painting that would later come to be presented under the rubric of *Neue Sachlichkeit*, the Dadaists' collective efforts to produce works of art that not only presented a 'disfiguration of the contemporary world', but also demanded a non-contemplative mode of viewing, arrived at an end.

This text draws on material published previously in my entry on 'Dada' in John Merriman & Jay Winter (eds), *Encyclopedia of modern Europe: Europe since 1914 – encyclopedia of the age of war and reconstruction*, vol 2, Charles Scribner's Sons, Detroit 2006, pp 766–8; my introduction to Wieland Herzfelde, 'Introduction to the First International Dada Fair', *October*, 105, summer 2003, pp 93–9; and my contribution to the National Gallery of Art, Washington, DC, exhibition catalogue, Leah Dickerman (ed), *Dada: Zurich, Berlin, Hannover, Cologne, New York, Paris*, exh cat, National Gallery of Art, Washington, 19 Feb – 14 May 2006 and Museum of Modern Art, New York, 18 June – 11 Sept 2006, pp 84–112

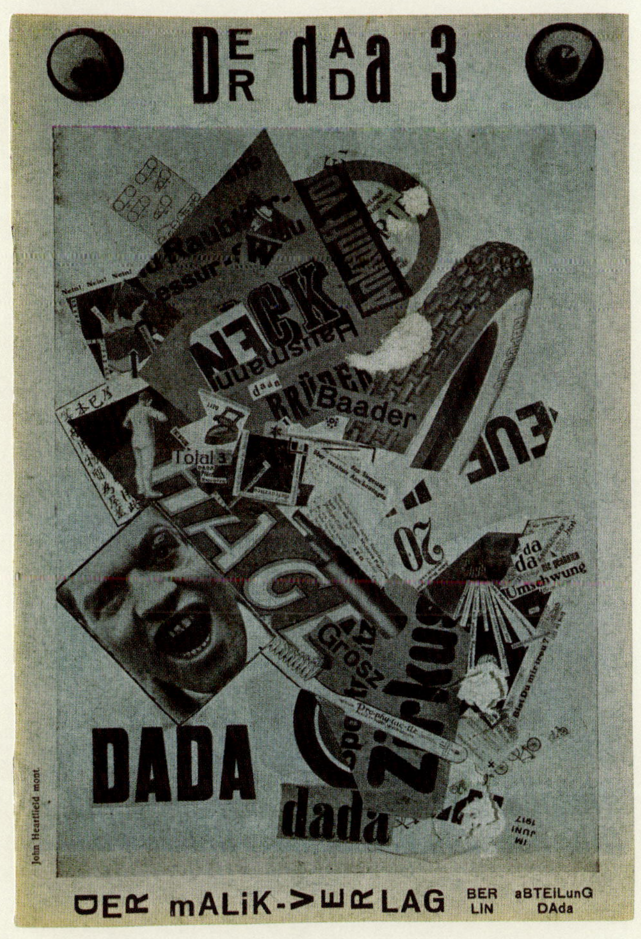

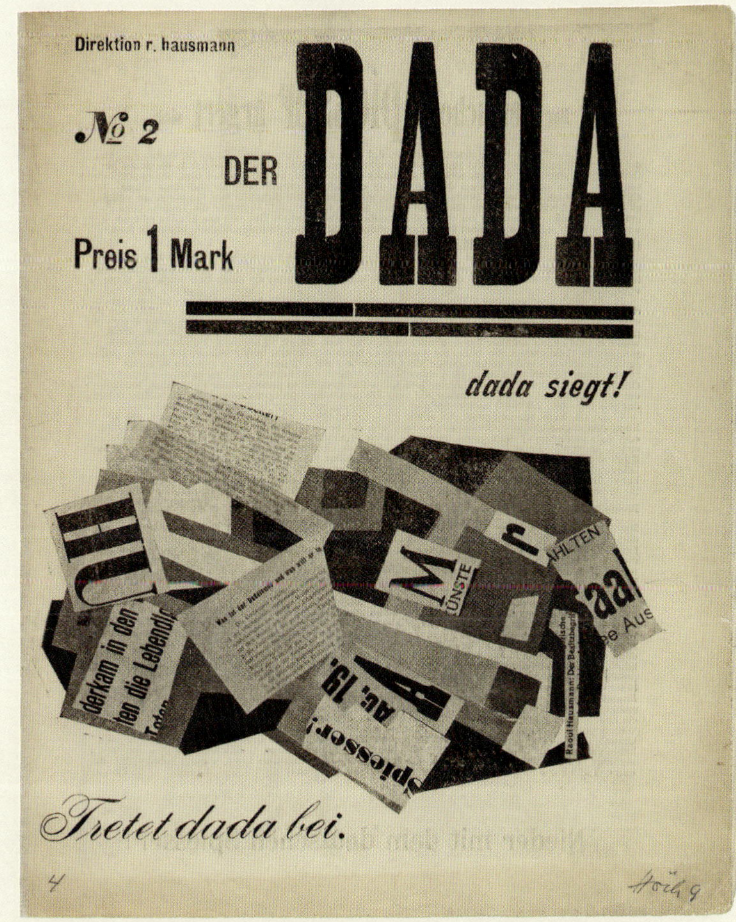

John Heartfield
Cover of the journal *Der Dada* no 3, Apr 1920
photolithograph
Akademie der Künste, Berlin, Kunstsammlung

Raoul Hausmann
Cover of the journal *Der Dada* no 2, Dec 1919
photolithograph
Berlinische Galerie, Landesmuseum für Moderne Kunst, Fotografie und Architektur

CHRISTIAN SCHAD

Portrait of a woman

Christian Schad grew up in a liberal and wealthy household in Munich, and his parents supported his early artistic aspirations. Determined not to fight in the war, he avoided military service by calling upon a doctor friend to diagnose a fictitious heart problem. He moved to neutral Zurich in August 1915 and became acquainted with members of the Dada circle, including Hans Arp, Hugo Ball and Emmy Hennings. Although he distanced himself ideologically from the Dadaists, Schad was inspired by their artistic experiments, which focused on the creation of abstract forms produced by the random placement of found objects.

In November 1916 Schad moved to Geneva, where he made an important contribution to Dada with his photograms, which were later labelled 'Schadographs' by Tristan Tzara. Created by layering scraps of paper or fabric and found objects onto light-sensitive paper, Schad's photograms, or 'immaterial collages' as he referred to them, were the first intentionally abstract creations that prefigured even Man Ray's and László Moholy-Nagy's experimentation with this form of camera-less photography.[1] Schad's remarkably intuitive sense of formalist experimentation can be seen in *Schadograph no 10* 1919, where the uneven penetration of light through the various materials creates an intensely beautiful visual effect that echoes forms found in nature. As with Dada collages by Hans Arp or Kurt Schwitters, Schad's photograms offered a challenge to traditional composition, as the end result was based upon chance and unpredictability to a certain degree. Even the jagged border around the central image, which features so prominently in this work, was intended 'to free them,' Schad said, 'from the convention of the square'.[2]

While in Geneva, Schad also created a significant series of abstract painted wood reliefs, including *Portrait of a woman* 1920. Inspired by the artistic radicalism of Dada and the wood reliefs produced by Arp in 1918, Schad created these assemblages by combining irregular pieces of wood, cut out by a carpenter, with materials associated with machine technology – heavy enamel commercial paints, mass-produced metal parts and bits of metallic paper.[3] Schad distanced himself from the romantic notion of the subjective creation of works of art – a concept the Dadaists sought to destroy – by using fragments that were industrially manufactured rather than made by the hand of the artist. Despite these avant-garde claims, this wood relief exemplifies the undeniable skill of the artist in arranging the abstract wooden shapes and metallic components into a perfectly unified composition. Schad's masterful application of colour enhances the overall effect of the composition and contributes to the partially discernable outline of a female form. These works were intended as purely abstract creations but sometimes, as with this image, a figurative aspect emerged from the random arrangement of form, which in this instance is reflected in the title: *Portrait of a woman*. JS

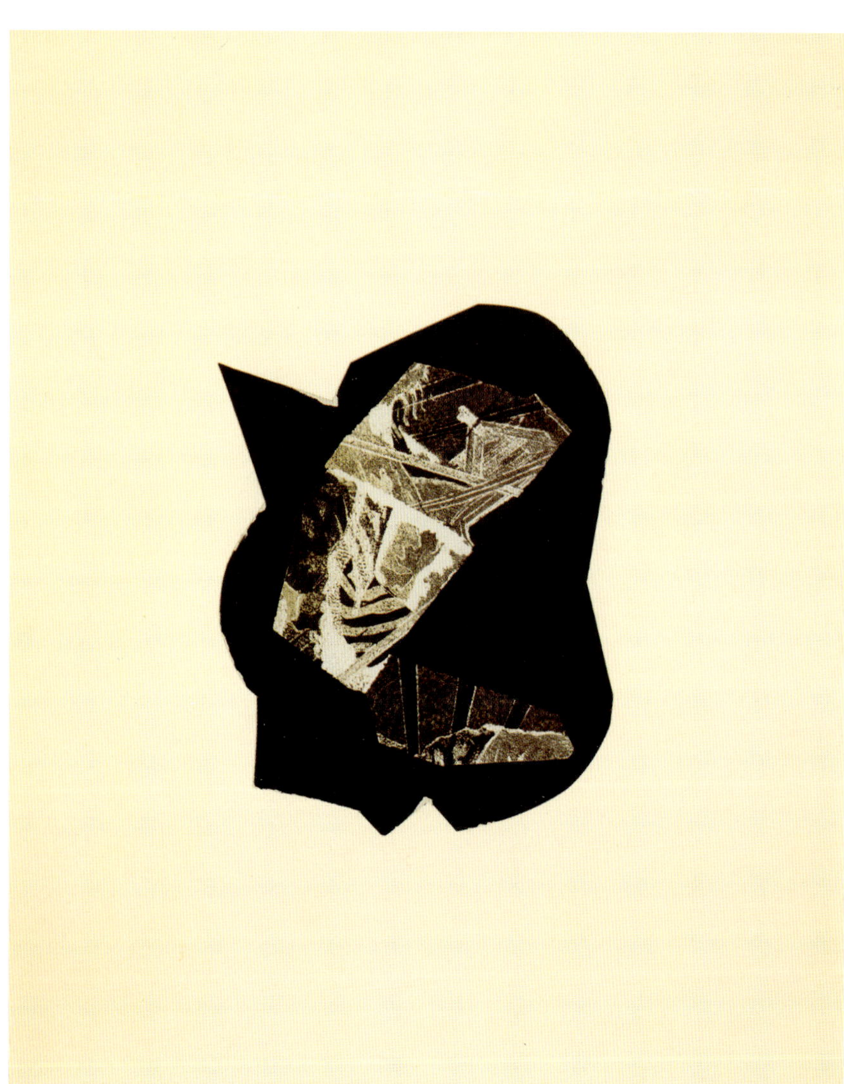

Christian Schad
Schadograph no 10 1919
photogram, gelatin silver print
Museum of Fine Arts, Houston

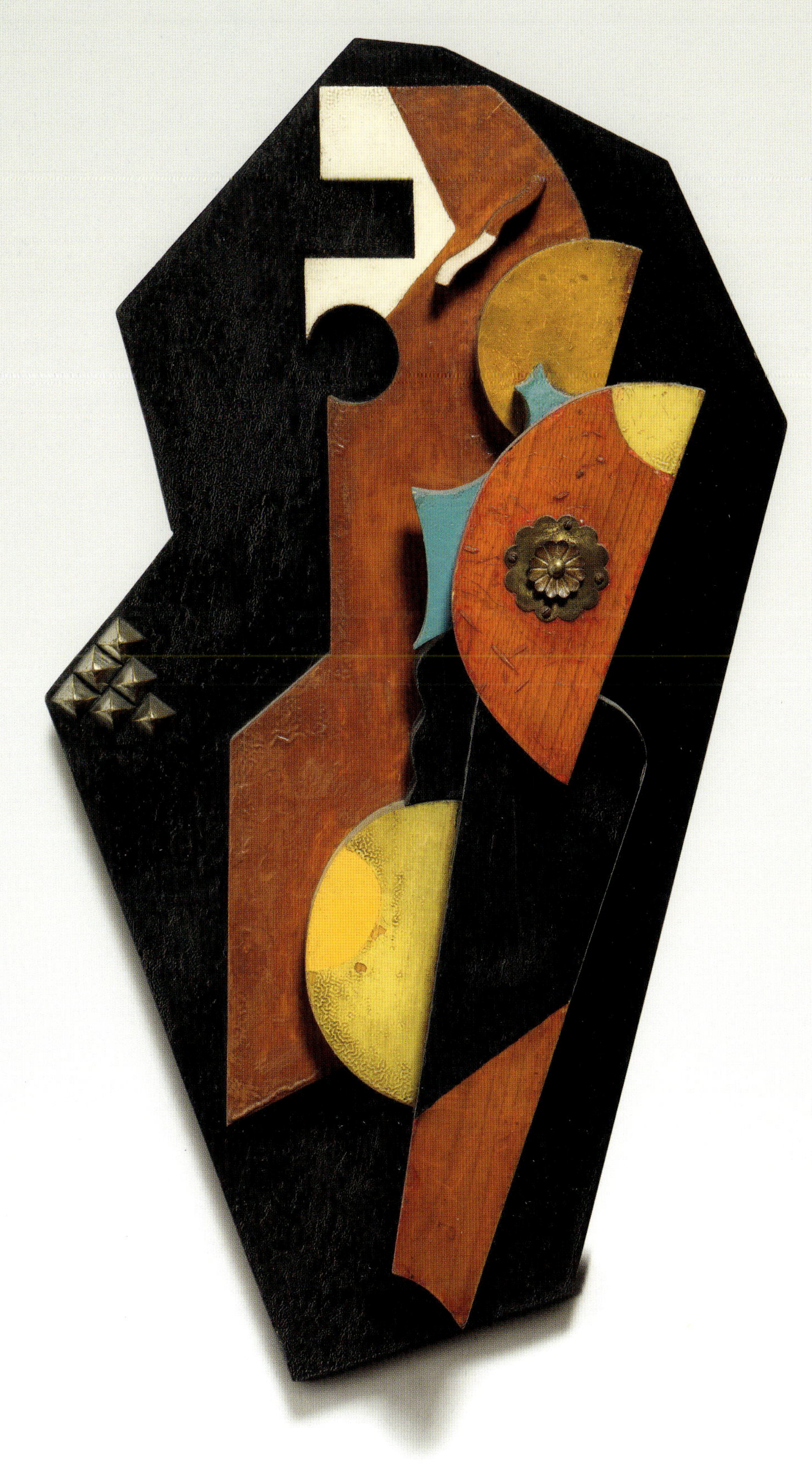

Christian Schad
Portrait of a woman 1920
painted wood, metal
Kerry Stokes Collection, Perth

MAX ERNST

Cologne Dada

Max Ernst emerged as a painter before the war but his early work was interrupted when he enlisted in the military, working as an artillery engineer at the front in France and later in Poland. After the war, he established the Dada movement in Cologne, following the same principle of the international Dada movement, which maintained that 'art is dead'. He was strongly influenced by artists such as Marcel Duchamp, Francis Picabia, Hans Arp, Giorgio de Chirico and Carlo Carrà, as well as developments that emerged from Zurich Dada. Ernst kept his distance from members of Berlin Dada, although he was certainly familiar with the work of George Grosz, John Heartfield and Wieland Herzfelde.

Ernst arrived at photographic collage between 1919 and 1920, largely through his own efforts to extend the possibilities of collage and representation beyond the limitations of Cubist formalism. In *Augustine, Thomas et Otto Flake*, an early collage from 1920 that he created collaboratively with his wife Louise Straus-Ernst, the various collage elements have been taken from engravings in old books and from photographs and advertisements in newspapers. The title of the work refers to the modern German writer Otto Flake, who wrote naively humorous fairytales. Yet the title was not intended to be read literally or as a key to understanding the meaning of the image. Rather, it adds a further dimension of humour and self-irony to the central motif, which represents a man's head on a woman's body, quizzically looking up at two carcasses hanging from the ceiling while holding onto the arm of an elegantly dressed woman who reclines upon a chair in a seductive pose. Straus-Ernst and Ernst emphasise the bourgeois nature of the domestic interior through the lace curtains and Biedermeier furniture that is echoed in the structure that frames the scene. Incongruous, witty and completely engaging, this juxtaposition of unrelated images and fragments was typical of Dada but also specific to Ernst's interest in bizarre combinations of pictorial elements that prefigured Surrealism. If any single meaning can be deciphered from this work, it is the romantic alliance between Straus-Ernst and Ernst, who were married in late 1918 but separated when Ernst moved to Paris in 1922. JS

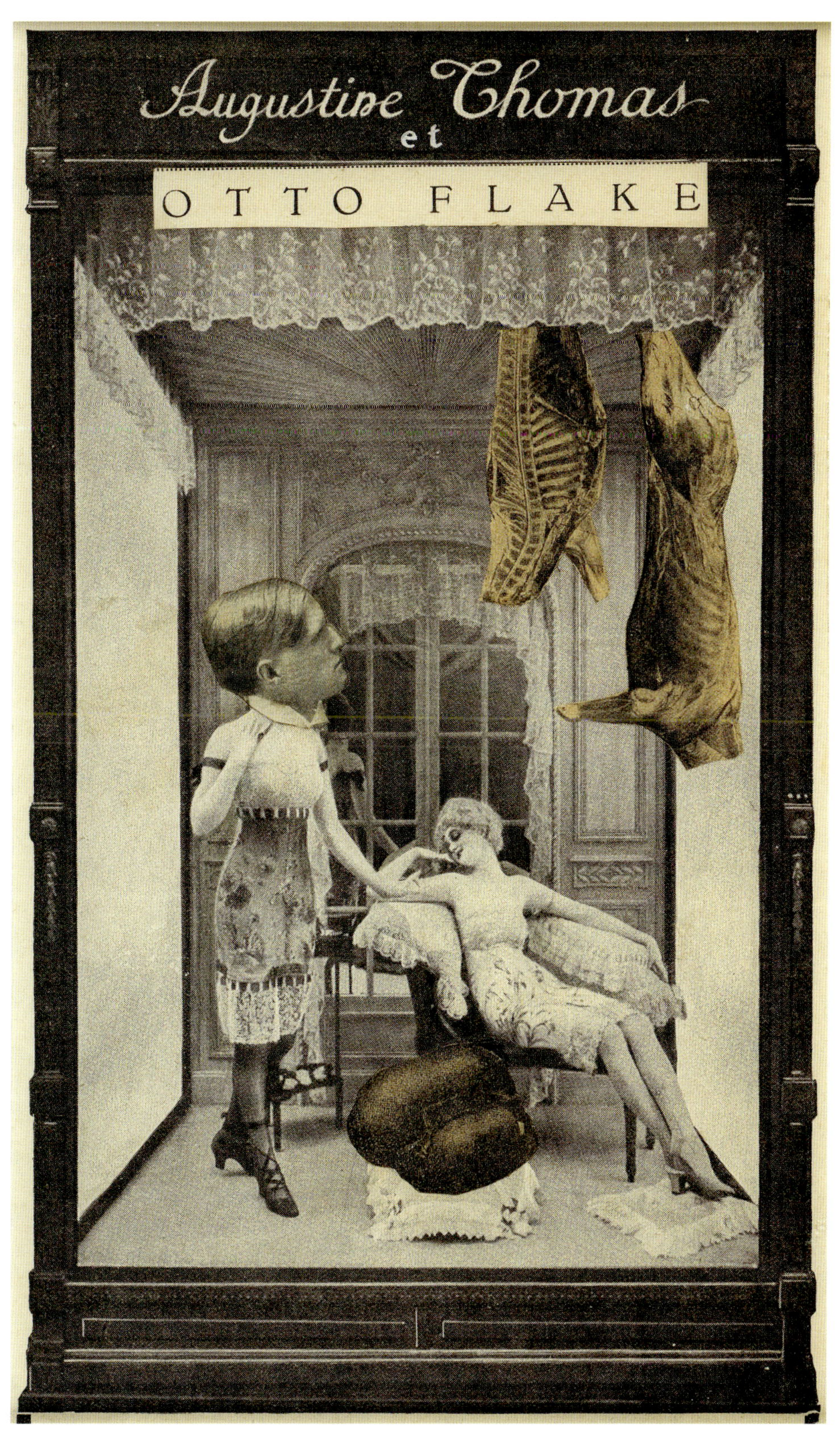

Louise Straus-Ernst with Max Ernst
Augustine, Thomas et Otto Flake 1920
collage
Sprengel Museum, Hanover

HANNAH HÖCH

Collage

Hannah Höch studied art in Berlin before and during the war, while working part-time to support herself at Berlin's major publishing house, Ullstein Verlag. From 1916 to 1926, she was a leading member of the Berlin art scene while working as a pattern designer in the handicrafts department, which produced brochures on knitting, crocheting and embroidery. Höch belonged to the new generation of professional women who emerged during the Weimar era, who were financially independent and liberated from the domestic roles that had been traditionally assigned to women. In her highly unique paintings and collages, she explored the rapidly changing roles and identities of women in the 1920s, often exposing the uneasy alliance between women and modernity in the Weimar Republic.

Two photographic portraits of Höch in the exhibition demonstrate how one of the most well-known female artists of the Weimar era deliberately styled herself in the image of the 'new woman'. Her short, bobbed hairstyle, loose modern dress, feisty expression and assertive pose in Richard Kauffmann's 1922 double-exposure (p 105) reveal Höch at the height of her creative powers, having participated in both the *Novembergruppe* (November Group) and Berlin Dada. The radical modernity of her self-image is emphasised through the radical modernity of the photographic technique, which simultaneously presents two views of the artist starkly contrasted against a natural landscape setting. An equally intimate, yet far more reflective, view of Höch can be seen in the 1931 portrait by Raoul Hausmann (p 105). Hausmann had been in a stormy relationship with Höch for many years and had supported the inclusion of her in Berlin Dada as a liberating political force. Their relationship fell apart in 1922, after Hausmann refused to have a child with her; although he was already married, he repeatedly stated that he was unable to emotionally commit to marriage and what he perceived was a bourgeois arrangement.[1] Höch fell pregnant twice to Hausmann but had both pregnancies terminated, and this unfulfilled desire to have children is evocatively portrayed in her primitivist painting entitled *Imaginary bridge* 1926 (p 104).

Höch's major contribution to modernism was the pioneering body of work she made using collage. Her compositions comprised magazine pictures that she had cut out of publications such as the highly popular *Berliner Illustrirte Zeitung* (an illustrated weekly newspaper) and *Die Dame* (the German equivalent of *Vogue*). Her collages ranged from detailed compositions that included lace and handiwork patterns or brightly coloured areas of paint, to vastly simplified designs that focus on one or two figures comprised of ill-fitting fragments.[2] Combining the traditional language of women's crafts with images taken from the mass media, Höch developed an increasingly critical attitude towards contemporary representations of gender stereotypes. In *Half-caste* 1924 (p 100), *Balance* 1925 (p 102) and *Love* 1931, for example, she has cut out and reassembled fragments of female faces and bodies, turning these women into strange and inexplicable, anthropomorphic creatures. An astonishing sense of unease and discomfort is created through these disfigurations, which not only serve to critique exalted notions of femininity generated by the mass media but also draw attention to the highly manipulated nature of media representations of women.[3] JS

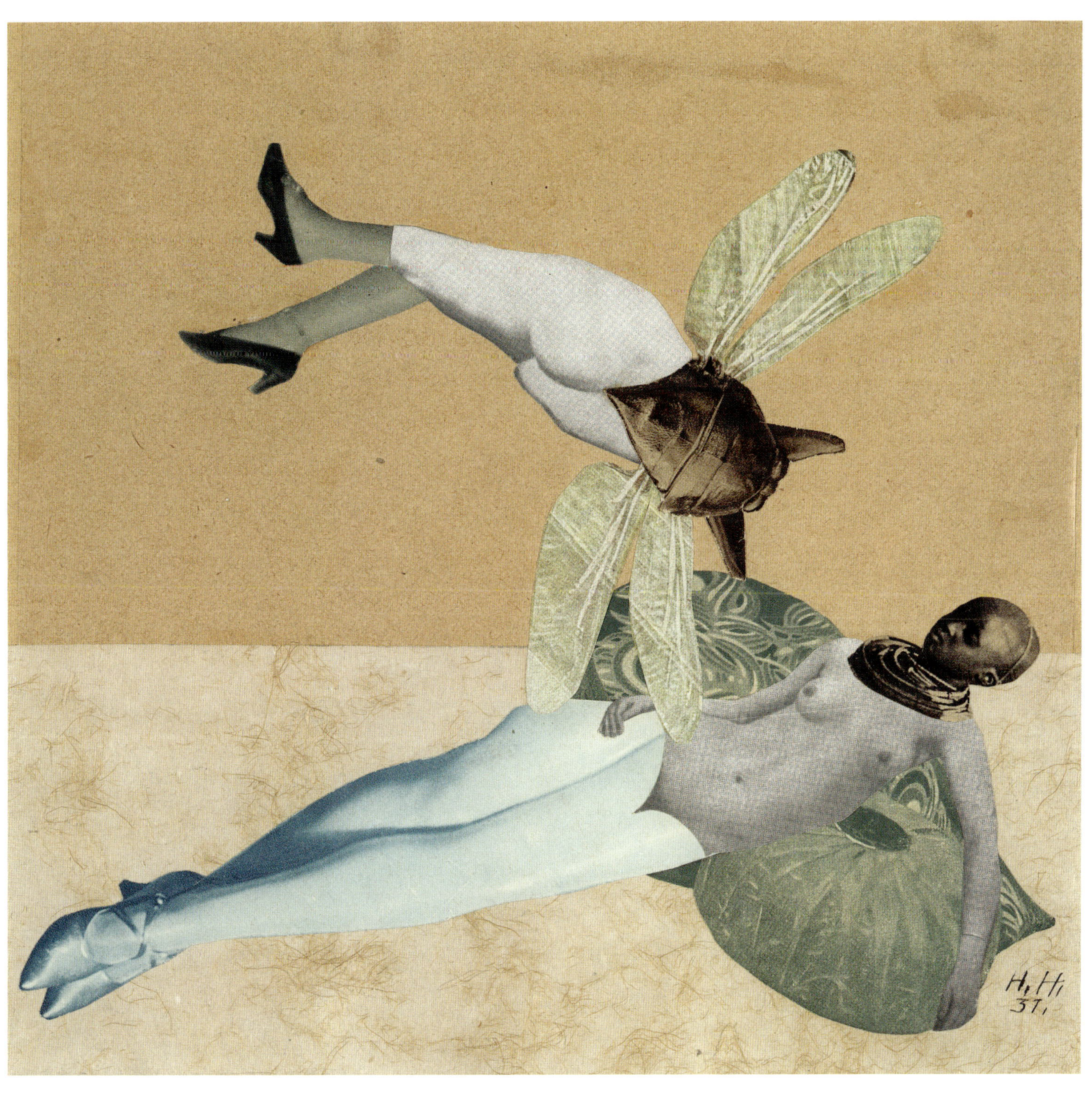

Hannah Höch
Love 1931
from the series Love
photomontage
National Gallery of Australia, Canberra

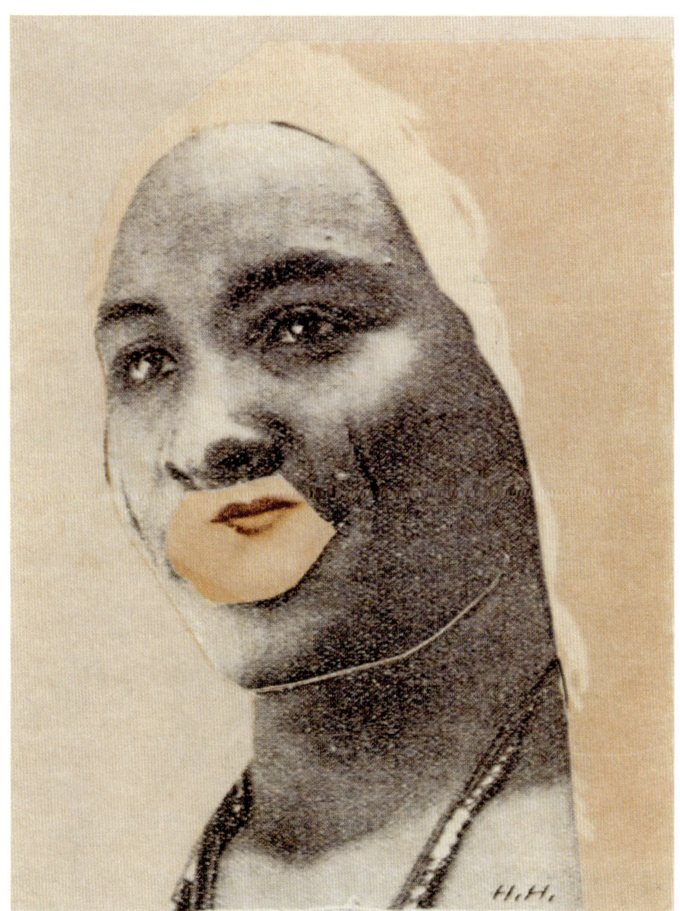

Hannah Höch
Half-caste 1924
collage
Institute for Foreign Cultural Relations, Stuttgart

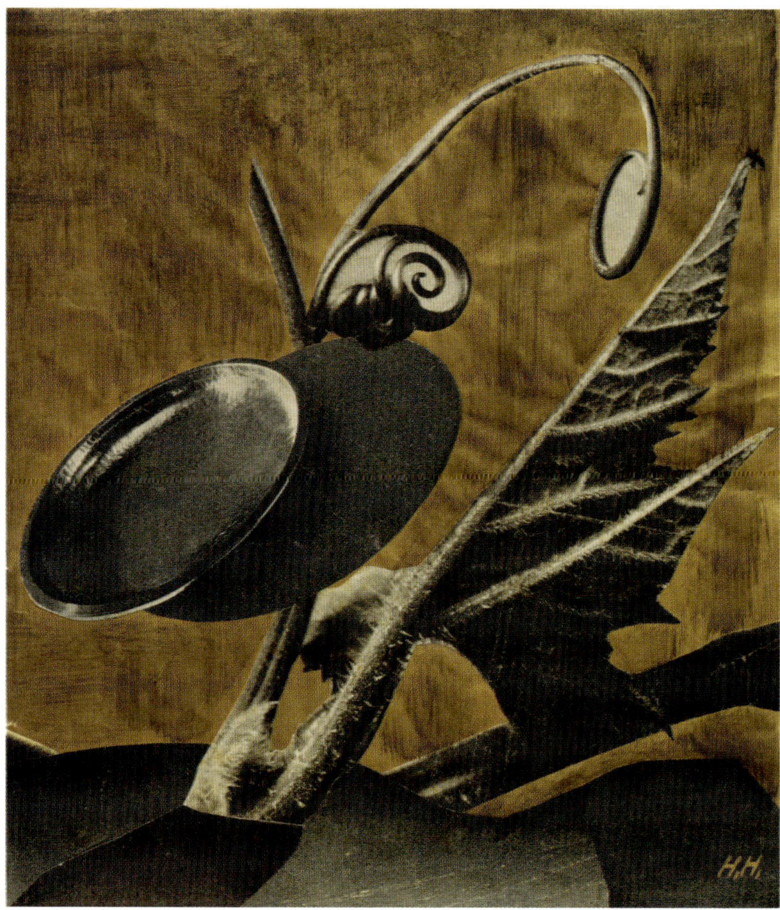

Hannah Höch
On gold paper c1920
collage
National Gallery of Australia, Canberra

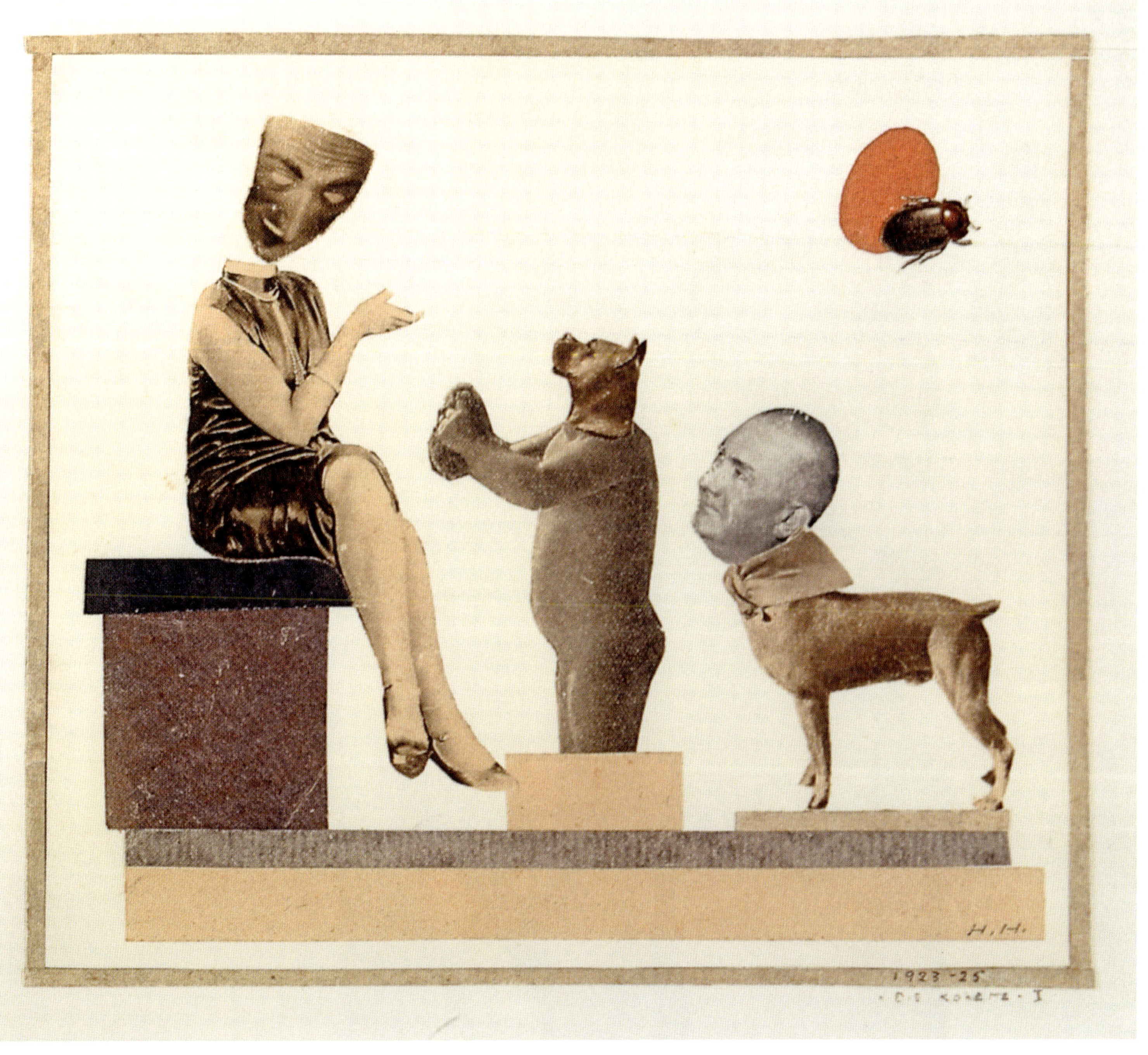

Hannah Höch
The coquette I 1923–25
collage
Institute for Foreign Cultural Relations, Stuttgart

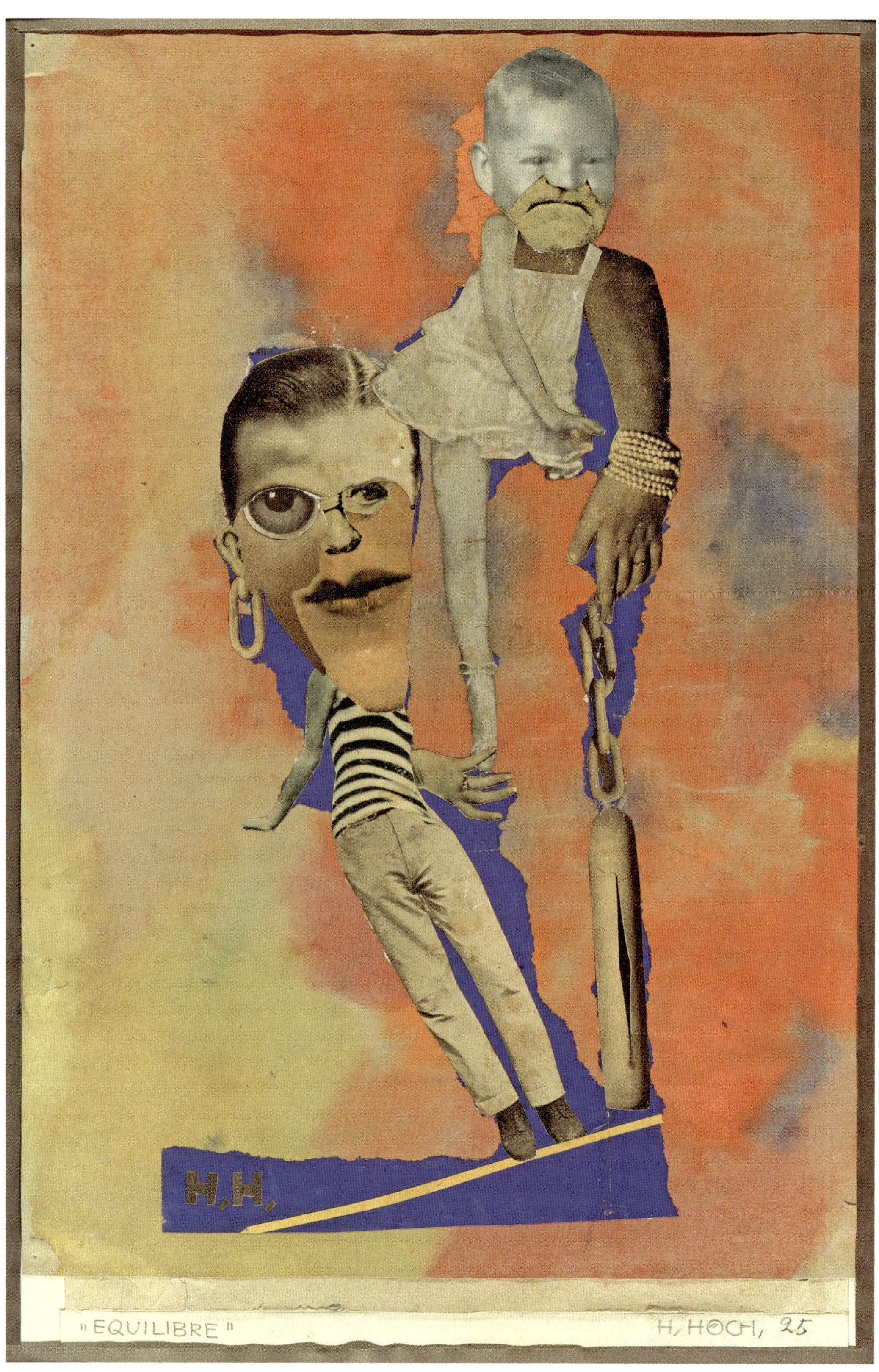

Hannah Höch
Balance 1925
collage
Institute for Foreign Cultural Relations, Stuttgart

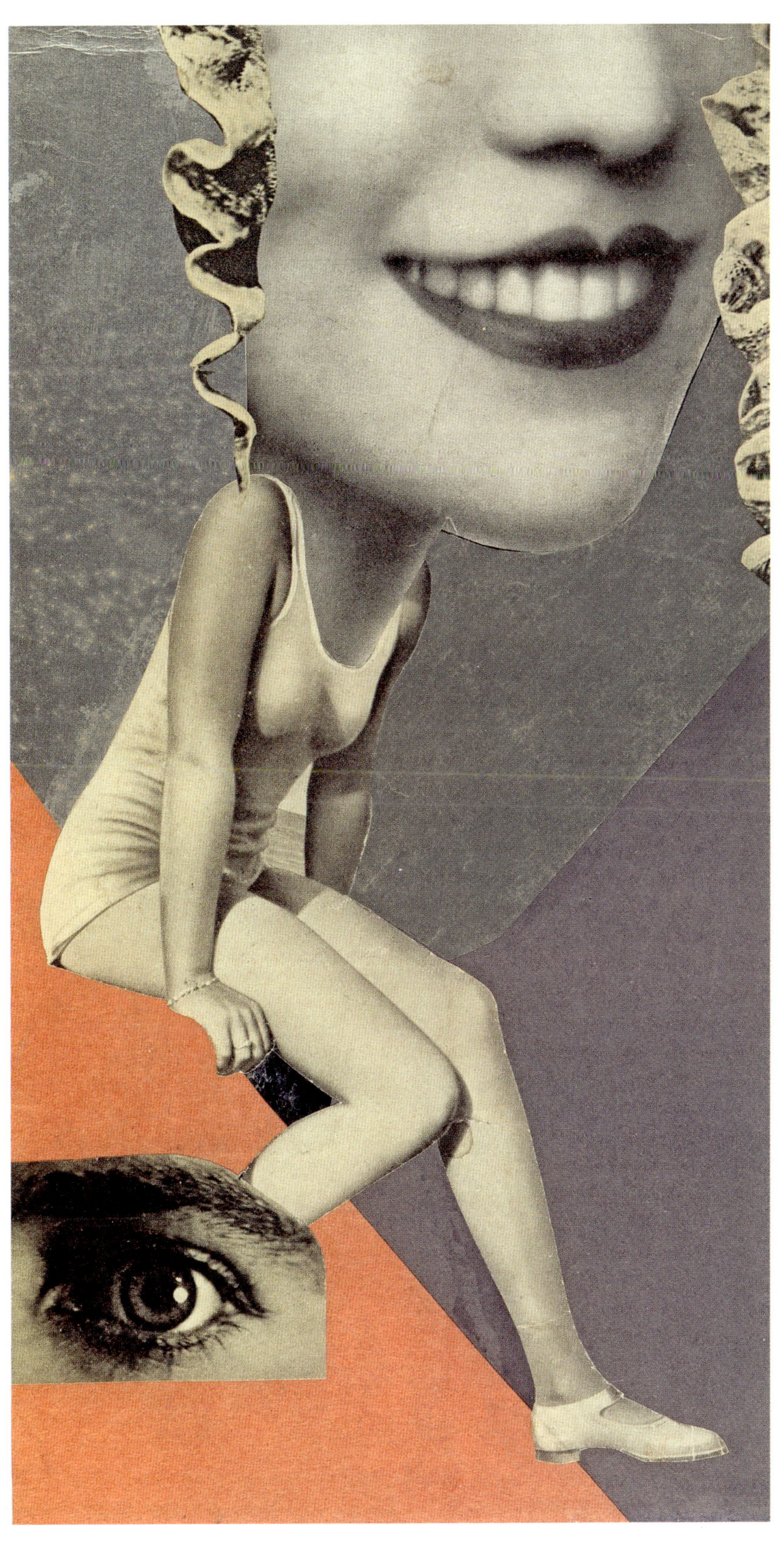

Hannah Höch
Made for a party 1936
collage
Institute for Foreign Cultural Relations, Stuttgart

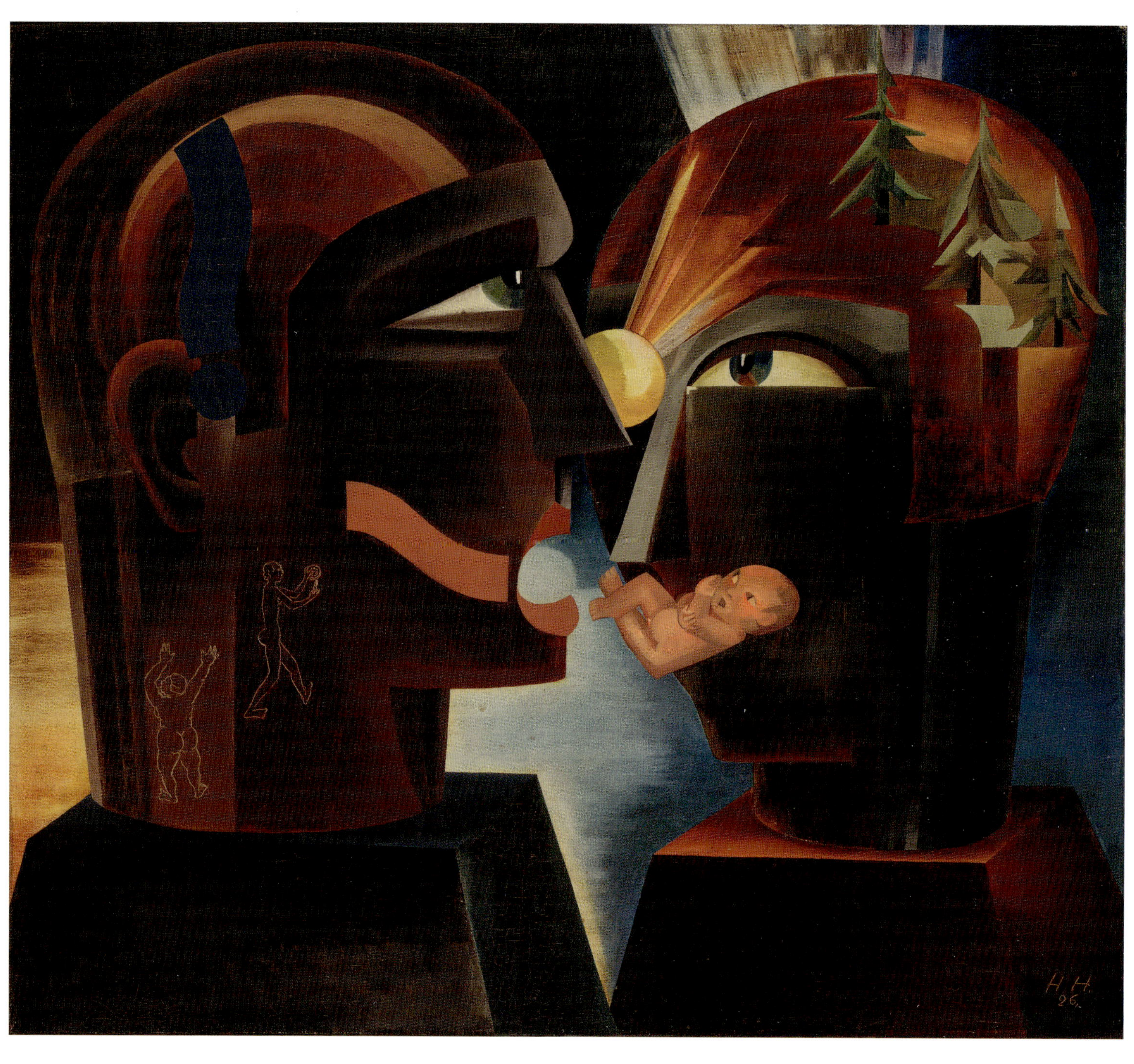

Hannah Höch
Imaginary bridge 1926
oil on canvas
National Gallery of Australia, Canberra

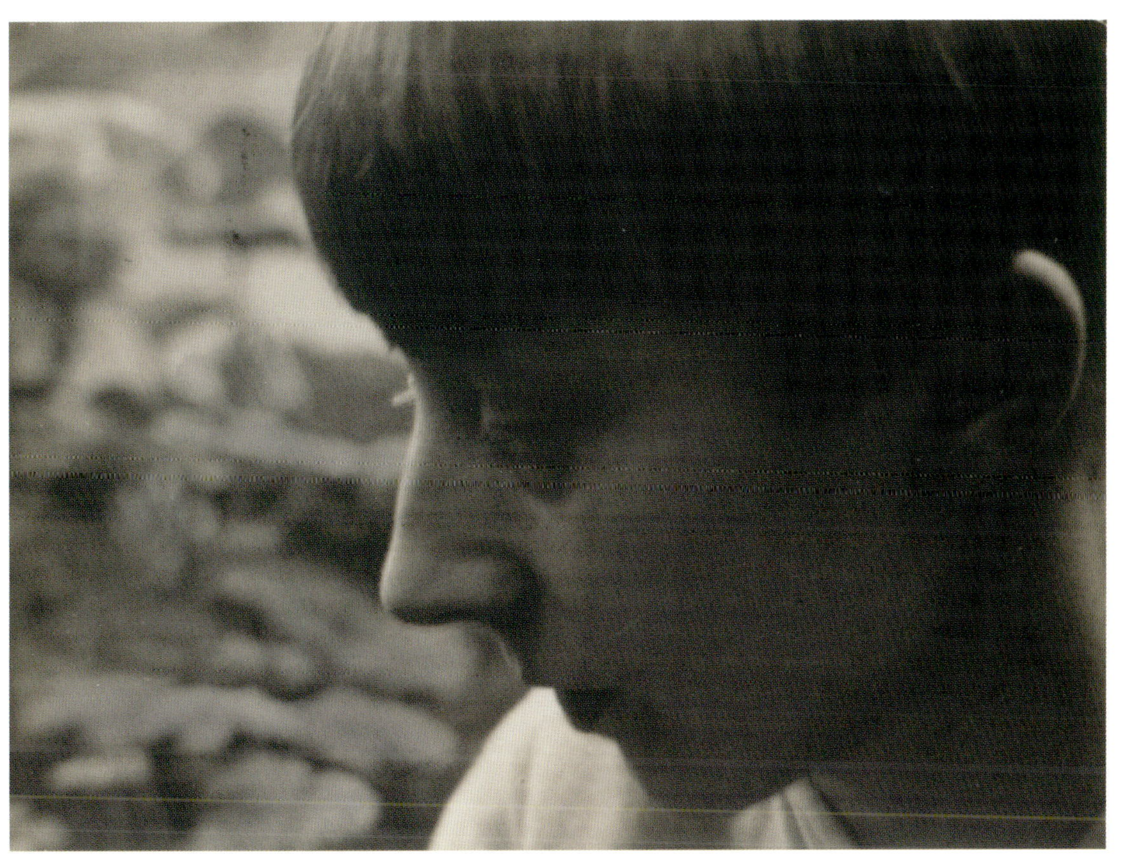

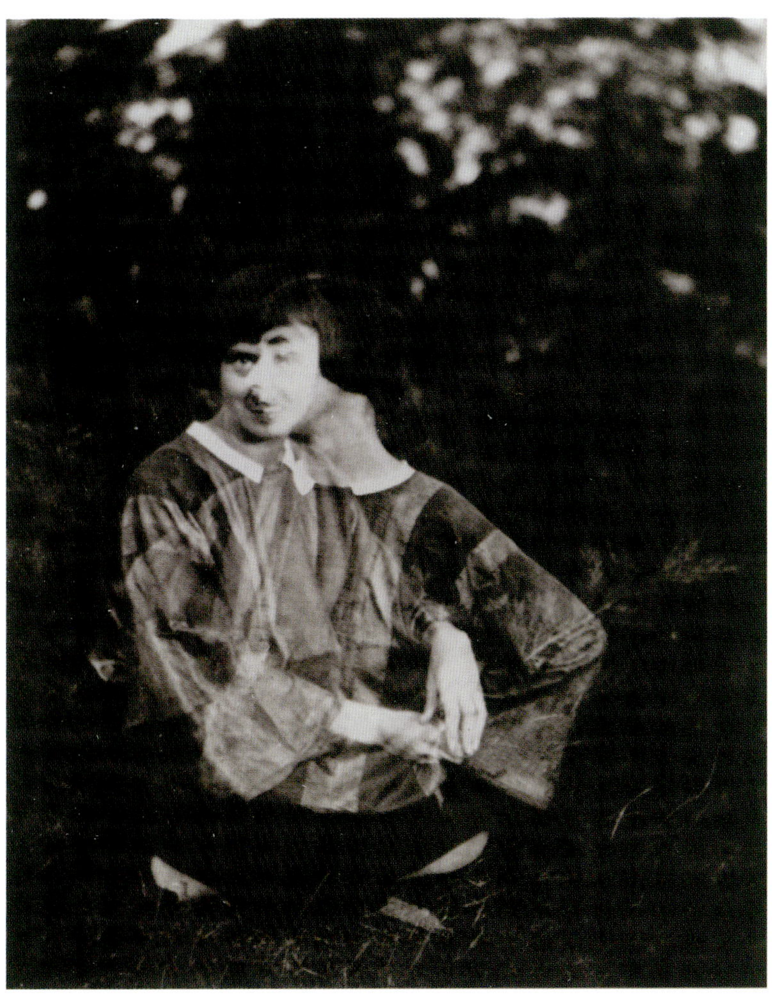

Raoul Hausmann
Untitled [Portrait of Hannah Höch] 1931
gelatin silver photograph
Berlinische Galerie, Landesmuseum für Moderne Kunst, Fotografie und Architektur

left:

Richard Kauffmann
Durchdringe Dich selbst oder: Ich umarme mich [I embrace myself] 1922
gelatin silver photograph
Berlinische Galerie, Landesmuseum für Moderne Kunst, Fotografie und Architektur

KURT SCHWITTERS

Merz

Refused official entry to the Berlin Dada group by Richard Huelsenbeck, Kurt Schwitters established a branch of Dada in his hometown of Hanover in 1918. Schwitters remained primarily concerned with aesthetic issues, unlike his fellow Dadaists in Berlin and Cologne, who criticised him for his 'bourgeois' idealisation of art and his indifference to politics. Schwitters coined the term 'Merz' from a torn newspaper advertisement containing part of the word *Kommerz-und Privatbank* (Commerce Bank) to refer to his experiments with new media, such as collage, assemblage, typography, performance, music and installation art, as well as Dada-inspired fairytales, poetry and painting.

In his small Merz collages, or *Merzzeichnungen* as he referred to them, Schwitters arranged and adjusted various ephemeral objects taken from modern city life, such as bus tickets, advertisements, pieces of fabric, bits of rubbish and pictures or pieces of text from magazines and newspapers. An important and innovative aspect of his approach to picture making was the way in which he allowed the materials to determine the overall composition and replace conventional pictorial elements, such as subject matter, perspective and technique. His Merz assemblages were revolutionary in establishing a completely new form of artistic expression but, unlike other forms of Dada, were characterised by a sense of classical order and harmony. In many of his Merz collages, he used a complicated numbering system to identify each work; in *Untitled (Hanover and Hildesheim)* 1928, however, he used a weekly train ticket to determine the title of this otherwise abstract creation composed of disparate, yet beautifully unified text and image fragments. In *Merz drawing [FOX]* 1930 (p 108), Schwitters reveals his continuing fascination for constructing collages from layers of printed and coloured paper. His addition of two hairs as an integral part of the composition draws upon Dada notions of playfulness and humour, offering a critique of the traditions of art, rather than a critique of society.

Schwitters' interest in creating new images through words was also expressed in the series of Merz publications he produced with El Lissitzky and Hans Arp from 1923 to 1932. These artists were among the few members of the international avant-garde to associate with Schwitters, although he also maintained friendships with Hannah Höch and Raoul Hausmann, and collaborated with Theo van Doesburg on Dada/Merz performance tours in the Netherlands. The *Merz* magazines were an important platform for disseminating Dada and Constructivist ideas, but they were also a highly effective marketing tool in promoting Schwitters' Merz brand to an international audience.[1] *Program for 'Merz matinées'* 1923 (p 109) reveals Lissitzky's major influence as a key innovator in the graphic arts. By 1923, he had become a major figure in the cultural life of Hanover and, like Schwitters, he pursued a vision of a new total work of art based upon avant-garde principles. This work is a brilliant example of the collaboration between the two artists, particularly in relation to typography, which was now recognised as an independent form of avant-garde art. In Lissitzky's superb photographic portrait of Schwitters, dated 1924–25 (left), the artist is portrayed midway through a Dada performance, with the word 'Merz' clearly visible in the background. This portrait rebelliously declares its intention to break with conventional forms of art and invent a completely new visual language based on photography, graphic design and performance. JS

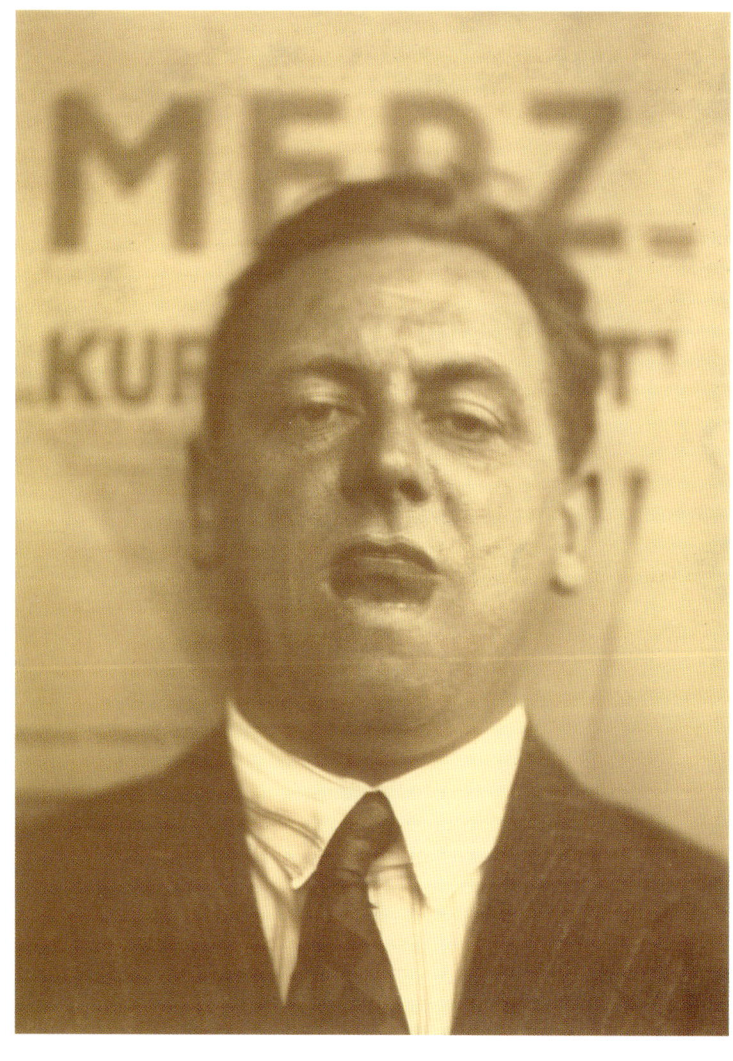

El Lissitzky
Kurt Schwitters 1924–25
gelatin silver photograph
J Paul Getty Museum, Los Angeles

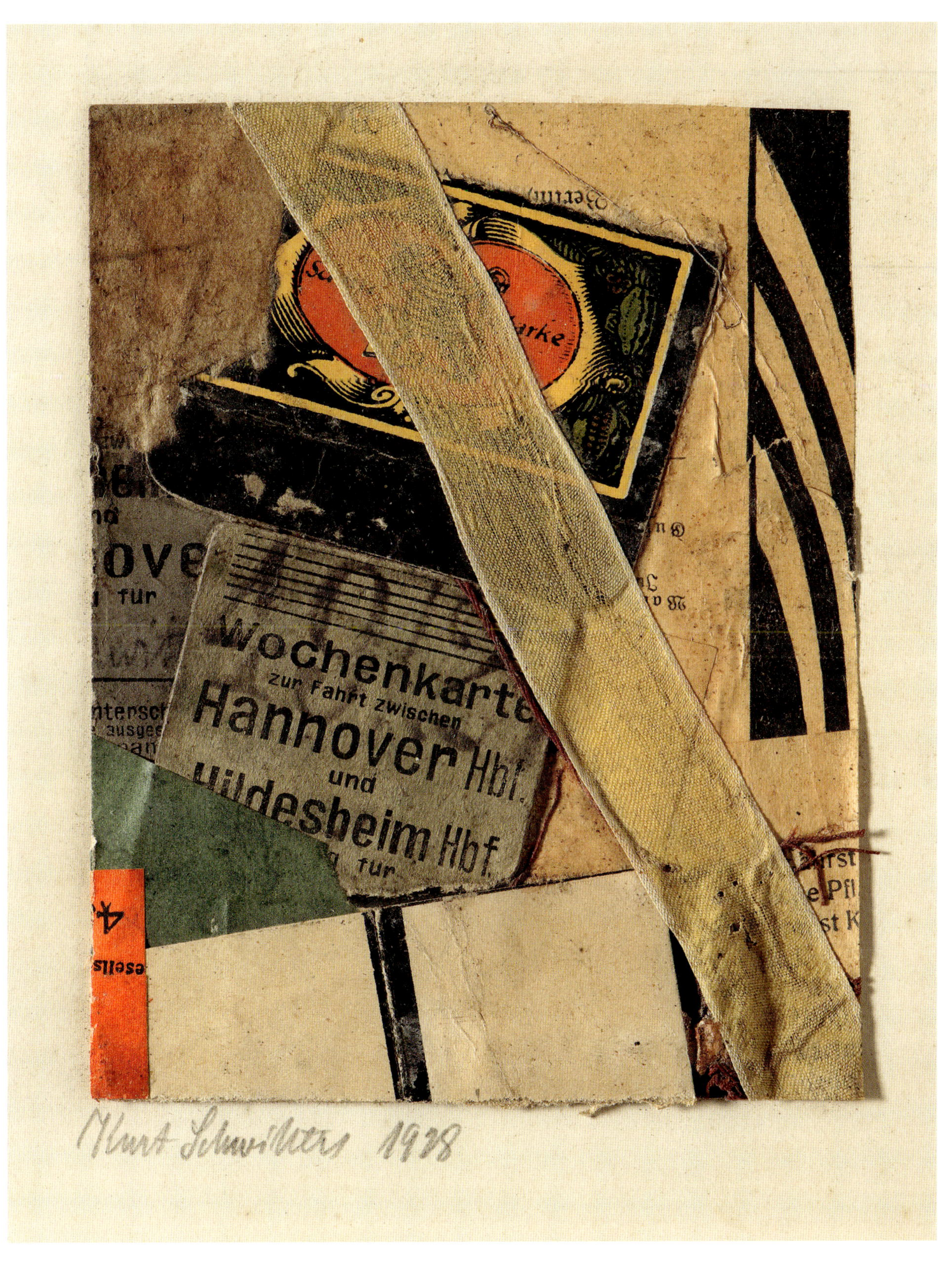

Kurt Schwitters
Untitled (Hanover and Hildesheim) 1928
collage, pasteboard, ribbon, threads, paper on paper
Kurt und Ernst Schwitters Stiftung, Hanover

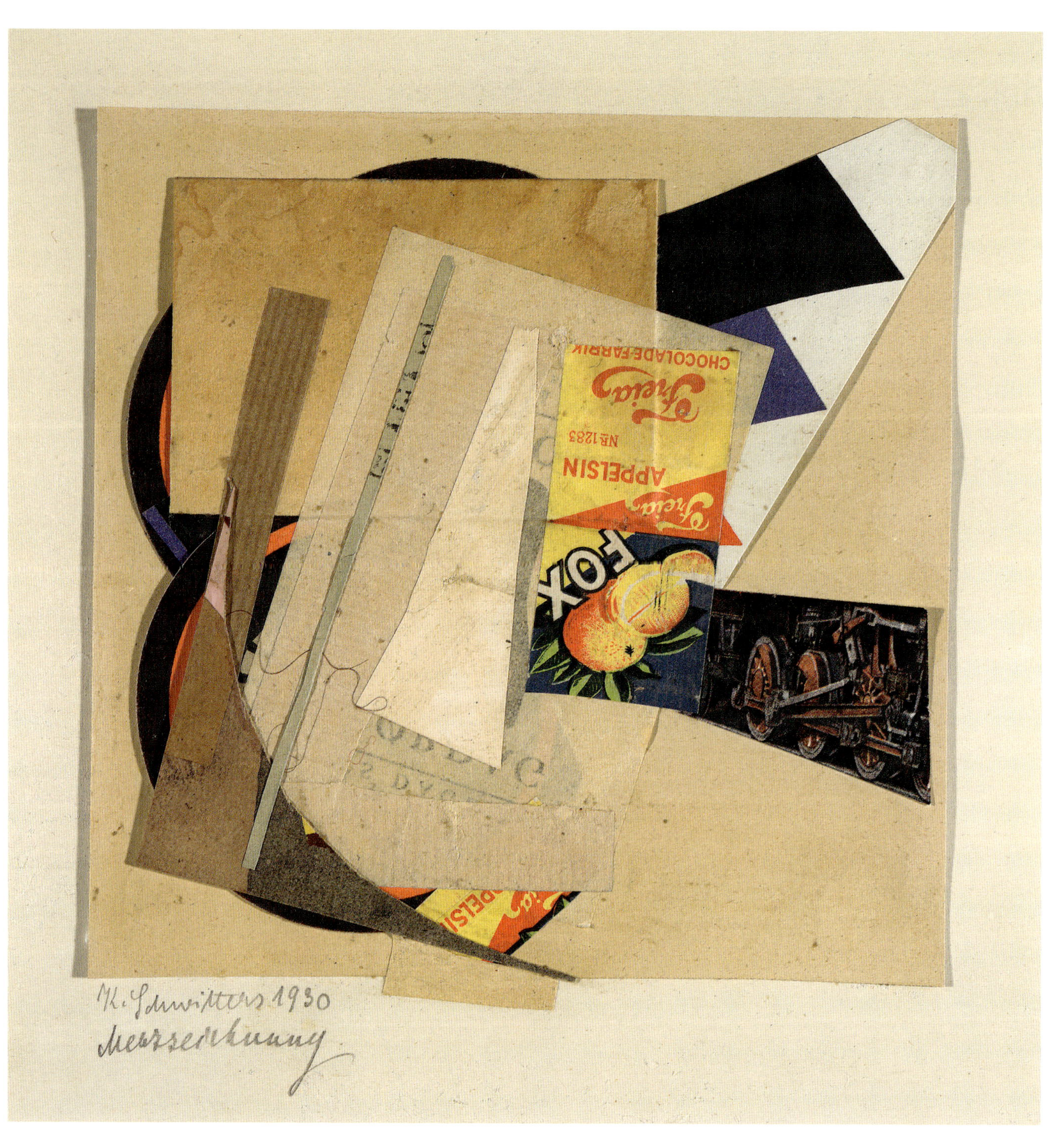

Kurt Schwitters
Merz drawing [FOX] 1930
collage
National Gallery of Australia, Canberra

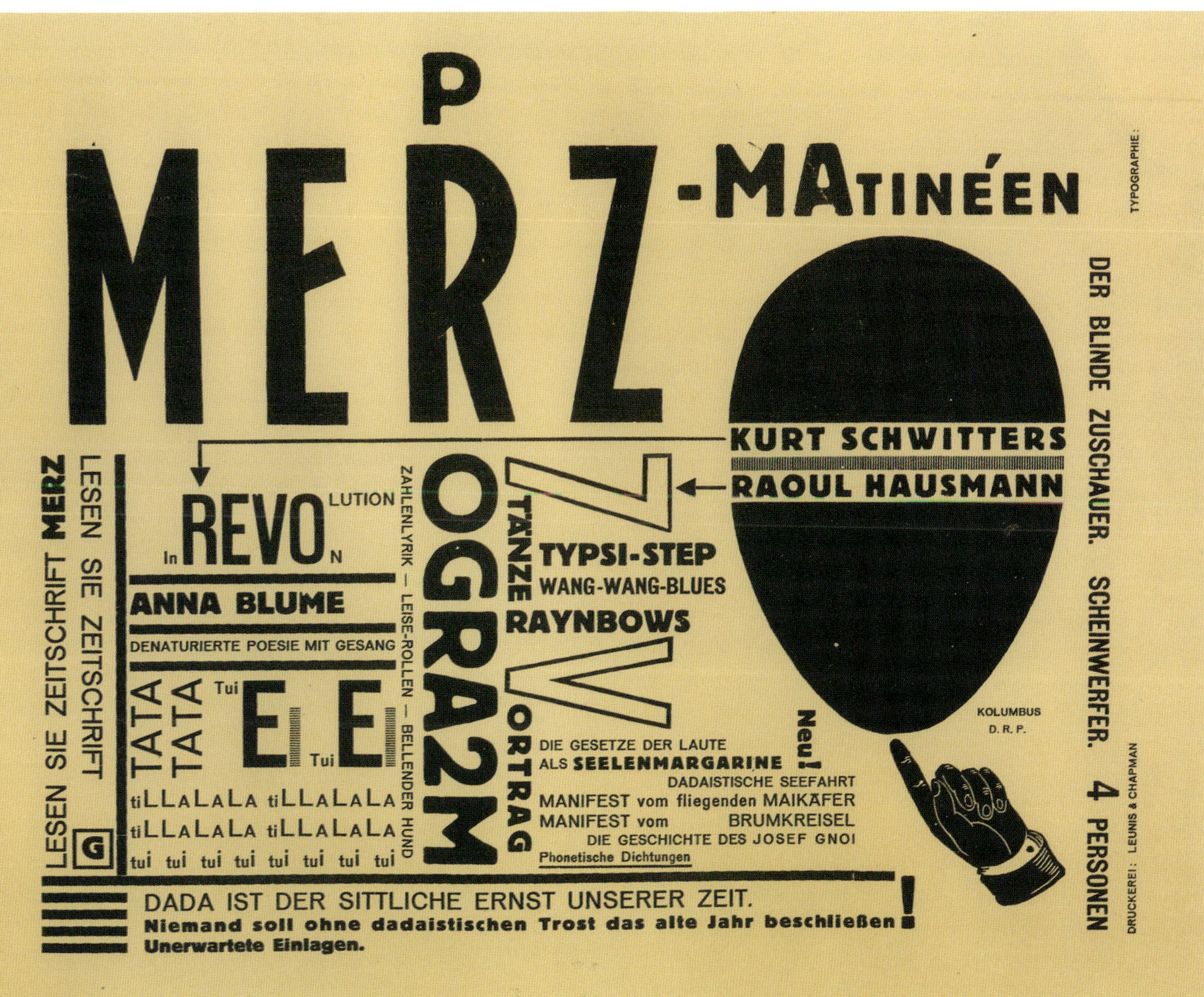

El Lissitzky
Program for 'Merz matinées' 30 Dec 1923
letterpress
Berlinische Galerie, Landesmuseum für Moderne Kunst, Fotografie und Architektur

BAUHAUS

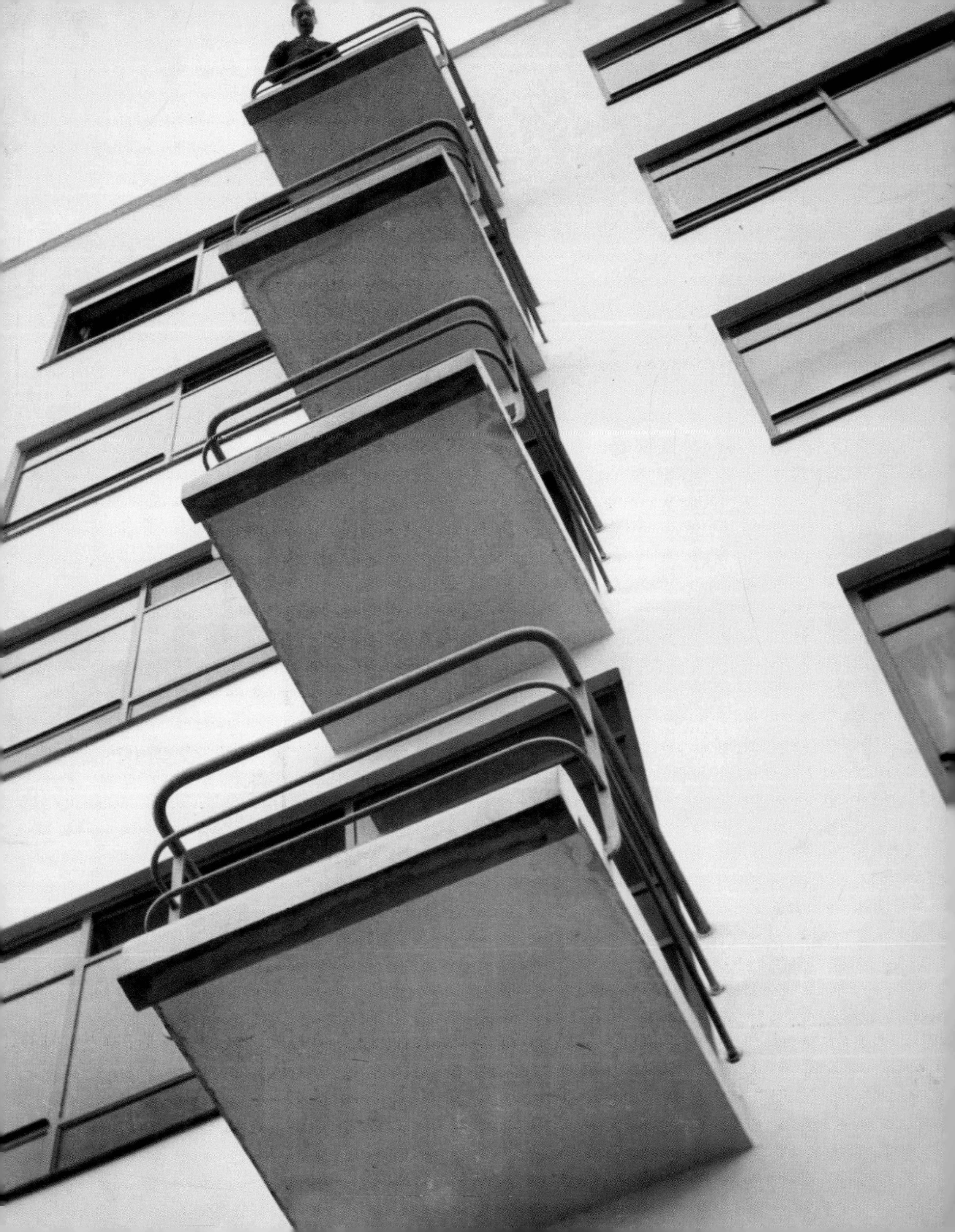

BAUHAUS OBJECTS, BAUHAUS VISIONS

Karen Koehler

In recent years, art history has witnessed a paradigmatic shift: the proverbial 'isms' have been replaced by less categorical, more complex modes of historical engagement. Even the term 'modernism' is under scrutiny when it is used to delineate specific stylistic properties. In setting out to plot a course through the complicated art world of the Weimar Republic, this exhibition demonstrates that there was not a single type of Weimar modernism, but multiple kinds of artistic practice in Germany during the 1920s and 1930s. Taken as a whole, the works in this exhibition demonstrate that modernism was not (is not) a style; rather, modernism was a way of engaging with the world – simultaneously energised, vigilant, questioning and utopian – set on distinguishing itself from the past.[1]

Germany struggled to come to terms with modernity – economically, socially and politically – and the Weimar Republic was an era of catastrophic reformation and renewal.[2] As Germany turned into an urban, industrial nation (with a concomitant mass culture), art, architecture and design came to play pivotal roles in that transformation. Many historians point to what has been called the *Sonderweg*, or 'special way', of German history – citing the late industrialisation of Germany as the cause for everything from roaring twenties fashion to the rise of National Socialism. While this is now regarded as an overstatement, there is no question that Germany's delayed democratisation and industrialisation created a different path to the 20th century. All of these issues are ubiquitous in the art of the Bauhaus, where multiple kinds of art could be found. Its troubled relationship with politics and affiliation with manufacturing underscores the inextricable and sometimes thorny exchanges between Bauhaus art and Weimar.

When most people think of the Bauhaus, the kinds of images that immediately come to mind are tubular steel chairs (pp 148–9), furnishings in primary colours, and boxy, white, flat-roofed buildings. While major exhibitions in Berlin and New York in 2009 did much to advance our understanding of the Bauhaus as a complex institution, even reviews of those exhibitions continued to imply that the word 'Bauhaus' designates a codified style.[3] Bauhaus continues to be used interchangeably with any kind of modernist design, in places as diverse as Chicago, Tel Aviv and Tokyo; South Melbourne is even home to a contemporary street-wear line named Bauhaus Clothing.[4] Arguably the most important art school in the 20th century, the Bauhaus was not a style – it was a place where some of the most important international artists taught and studied. Their work varied considerably: cubistic paintings, experimental theatre, multiple kinds of photography and decorative objects, and in only a few instances, the construction of actual buildings. Made up of classes and critiques, the energies of the school extended into festivals, parties and impromptu antics. There was even a jazz band, and students took part in everything from chanting and fasting, to soccer and fencing.

Founded in 1919 and closed in 1933, the history of the Bauhaus paralleled the Weimar Republic. These years bore witness to a revolution that brought the end to a

László Moholy-Nagy
Bauhaus balconies 1926
gelatin silver photograph
Collection of George Eastman House,
International Museum of Photography and Film

brutal European war and the overthrow of the monarchy, a civil war and the formation of a democratic Germany, economic depression, multiple kinds of social transformation, and the rise of Nazism. Based on a belief that art needed to be involved in bringing about social change, the very modernity of the Bauhaus caused the school to be deeply involved in these momentous changes. But just as there was no normative kind of Weimar modernism, there was no singular Bauhaus philosophy or practice. There were, in fact, many different 'Bauhauses': the school moved three times in Germany and each phase was complicated, contradictory and multifaceted. Founded by the German architect Walter Gropius, the Bauhaus quietly made a start in the provincial town of Weimar, Germany. Students and teachers began arriving in the spring of 1919, at the same time as representatives of the new German Government, who came to this small town to avoid the continued political tensions of Berlin. Weimar gave the republic its name, and although the site was mostly coincidence, the Bauhaus was forever linked to the new Social Democratic government in the minds of reactionaries.

While the politicians gathered to write the republic's constitution, Bauhaus students and teachers settled into the former Art Academy and the School of Arts and Crafts, two separate schools that Gropius had merged together into one integrated institution. Gropius sought to do away with what he called the 'class distinctions' between the fine arts and craftwork, and to forge an entirely new kind of creative designer, skilled in both the conceptual aesthetics of art and the technical skills of handcrafts. There were essentially two parts to the pedagogy in these early years. Rather than study colour, line, shape, materiality and composition in relationship to a story being told, these properties were studied in the *Vorkurs* (preliminary course) in and of themselves – as more essentialist and meaningful. Alongside these foundation studies, all students were assigned to a workshop – in metals, ceramics, textiles, wood, bookmaking, printing or wall painting, for example – where they matriculated from apprentice, to journeyman, to master craftsman. Each workshop was headed by a form master (artist), who taught the aesthetic properties of design, and a crafts master (technician), who enabled the students to learn the skills necessary to complete their assignments. Gropius believed that this two-part instruction was necessary because the artist who could combine the artistic with the technical did not yet exist; these were the new kind of hybrid creative workers that the Bauhaus would turn out. Bauhaus art and products included paintings, prints, photographs, drawings, furniture, metal work, sculpture, graphic design, ceramics, tapestries, stage design, theatrical performances and films, and in all cases the artists at the Bauhaus were synthetic and inventive – they were avant-garde. There were art objects made as part of a class assignment, by the teachers at the school as part of their professional practice, and as extracurricular experiments; the boundaries between academics and free creative expression were, by intention, porous.

In each phase of its existence, the school was considered to be both politically and artistically radical, and charges of cultural bolshevism hounded the school from start to finish. Following years of political strife in Weimar, in 1925 the school moved to the industrial city of Dessau, where confrontations between the artists and political events continued. When the Dessau Bauhaus was forced to shut down following the Nazi

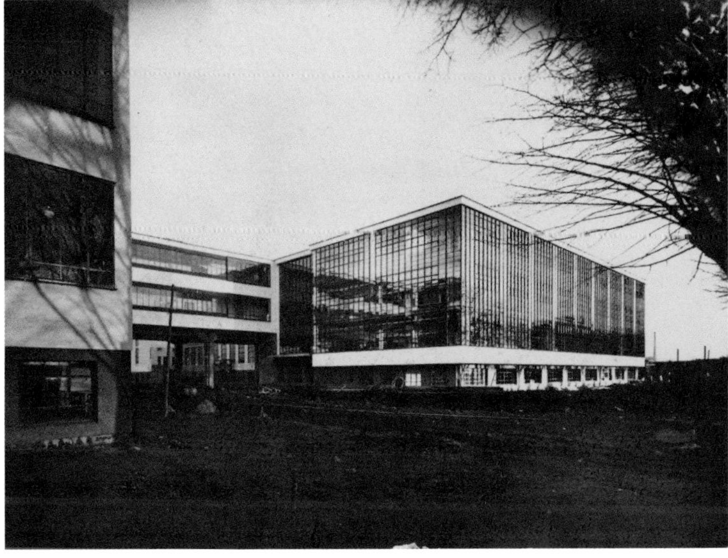

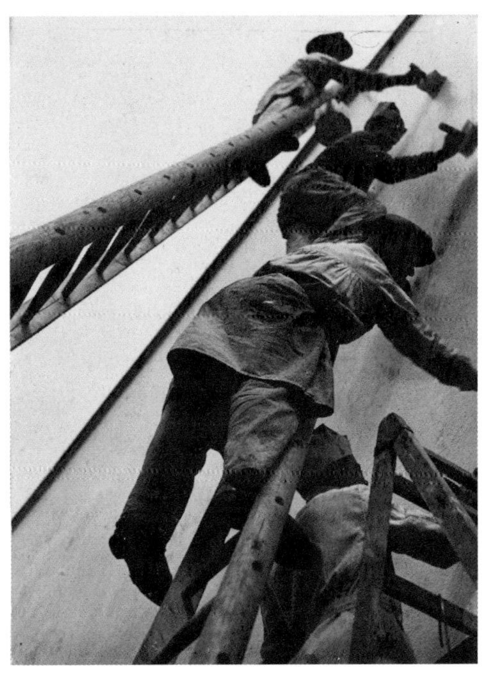

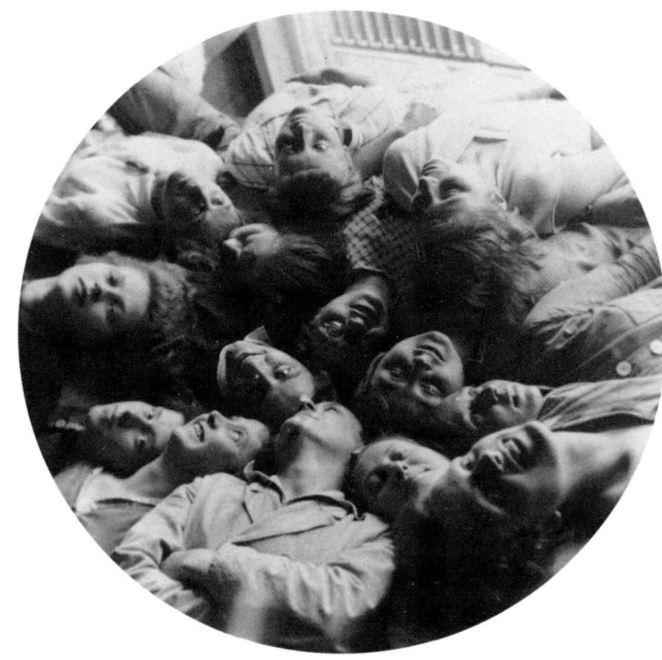

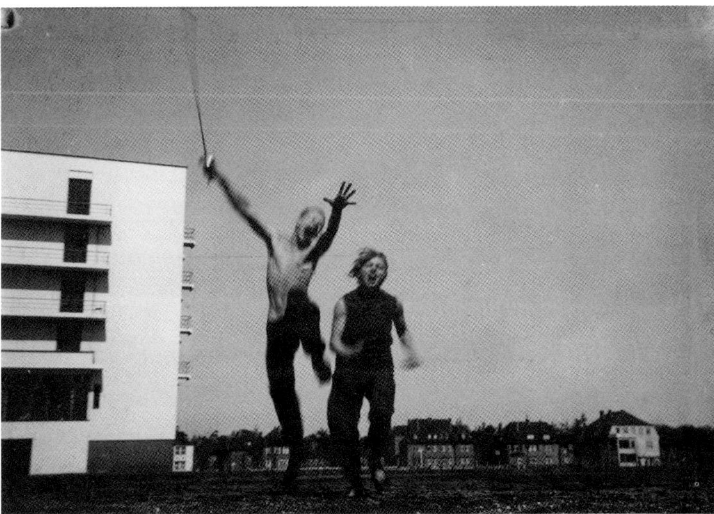

Lucia Moholy
Bauhausneubau, Dessau (New Bauhaus building, Dessau) 1926
gelatin silver photograph
J Paul Getty Museum, Los Angeles

Lotte Stam-Beese
Group-portrait, weaving workshop at the Bauhaus, Dessau 1928
gelatin silver photograph
National Gallery of Australia, Canberra

Gertrud Arndt
Wall painting workshop, Bauhaus Dessau 1930
gelatin silver photograph
National Gallery of Australia, Canberra

T Lux Feininger
[Georg Hartmann with foil and Karla Grosch running] 1929
gelatin silver photograph
J Paul Getty Museum, Los Angeles

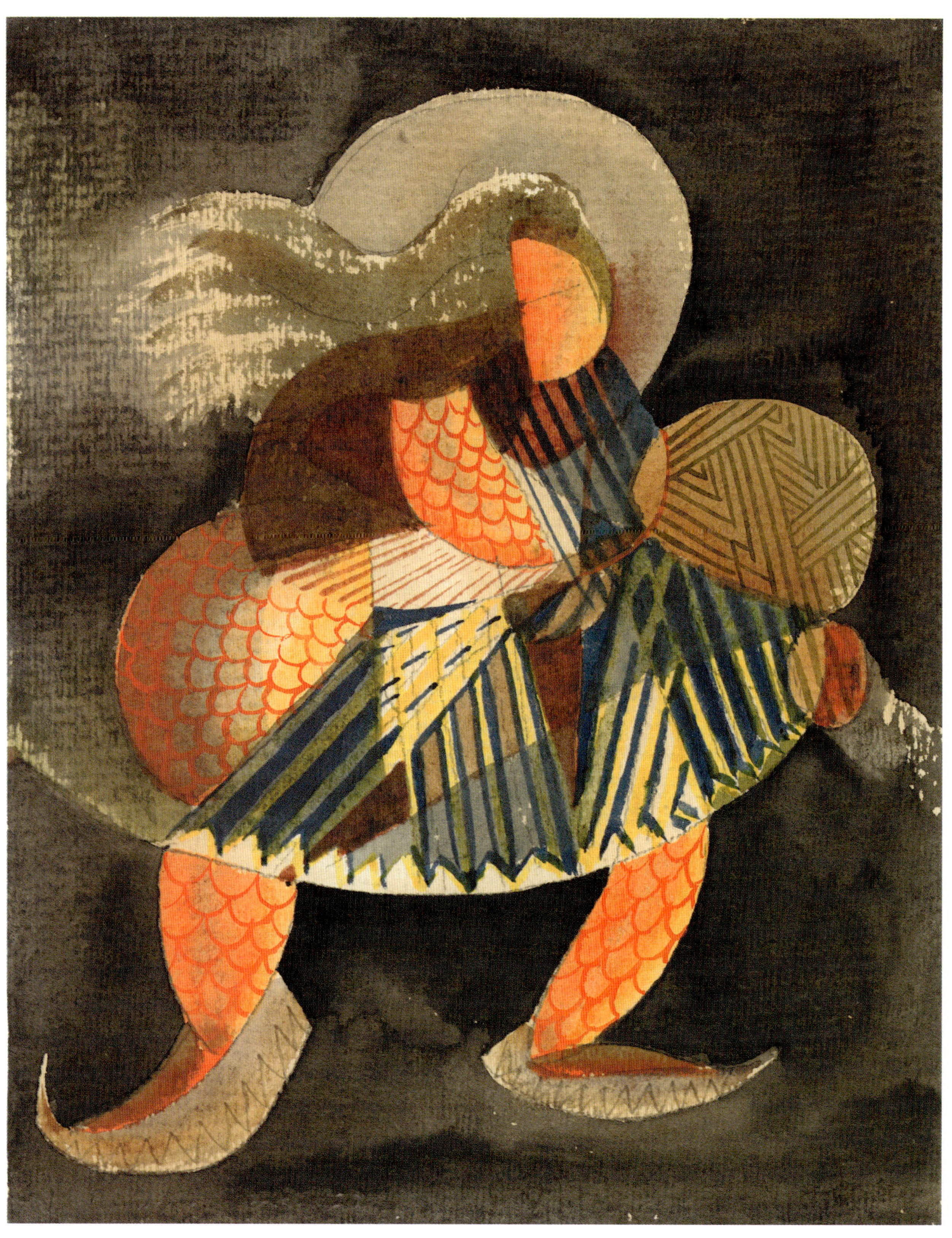

Ludwig Hirschfeld Mack
Untitled [Study for costume design] 1920
watercolour, pencil
National Gallery of Australia, Canberra

takeover of the city council in 1932, the school moved to Berlin and briefly operated out of an empty factory building. In 1933, when Nazi police raided the building in search of subversive literature, and arrested those without proper identification, it set off a series of events that caused the Bauhaus to close permanently.

The architects Walter Gropius, Hannes Meyer and Ludwig Mies van der Rohe all served as director of the Bauhaus at various times, each creating their own vision for the school and changing its direction. Following a period of utopian experimentation, based on handcrafts and expressionistic imagery, the school moved towards a greater involvement with industry. As early as 1923, Gropius steered the school towards the making of prototypes for mass production, a direction furthered under Meyer. Meyer, however, is best known for his communist leanings, and for the creation of *Kostufra* (student cells) at the school. While his own principal focus was on socially concerned planning, the school continued to work with manufacturing firms, and teachers and students continued to create individual works of art. Meyer was dismissed as director in a swirl of controversy, and was replaced by Mies, who immediately expelled the activist students. Mies transformed the school into a more conventional architecture school, with an emphasis on creating private homes and interiors.

Ludwig Hirschfeld Mack offers a provocative case study for the diversity of styles and subjects that were present at the Bauhaus, as well as the perpetual political turmoil that surrounded the *Bauhäusler*. Hirschfeld Mack started to study art in Munich in 1912, until he was called to serve as an infantry officer. After the armistice of November 1918, he was one of the 8 million returning soldiers seeking a new way of life. As Gropius wrote: 'It was as if struck by a ray of light ... After the war, I realised the old rubbish was all over.'[5]

In 1919, Hirschfeld Mack was drawn to the Weimar Bauhaus by the radical, innovative promise of the Bauhaus program. He worked principally in the print studio, helped to produce many of the official Bauhaus portfolios and was the first student to pass to the rank of journeyman. His lithograph *Reaching the stars* 1922 (p 131), for example, is technically inventive and reveals a complex patterning that is clearly drawn from the formal language of Cubistic faceting and Dadaist collage; areas of wash are interwoven with graphic patterning, simultaneously representing a map or wallpaper, while also perhaps reminiscent of camouflage. Could the object in the lower left be the infantryman's steel helmet, leaning on a stick?[6] Who, then, is striding the globe and reaching for the stars? A dead soldier? Or perhaps Hirschfeld Mack himself, now reaching for a new world from the decimation of the old world? His watercolour *The accordion player* c1922 (p 132) could be read as a studio still life, yet it also shows the influence of French artists, such as Fernand Léger, in terms of its basic geometric shapes, multiple light sources, unclear sense of spatial relationships and prismatic shading. Even though we know he played the accordion in the Bauhaus band, what the work illustrates is unclear, demonstrating that for Hirschfeld Mack it was less of an issue whether he was an abstract artist or a representational one. His concerns were of an entirely different nature – and that had to do with the relationship between colour and sound.[7] Hirschfeld Mack did not travel with the school to Dessau, but went on to teach at a number of different art schools until 1932, when his Jewish heritage forced him into exile. He travelled to England, where he joined an enclave of Bauhaus émigrés, until 1940 when he was identified as an 'enemy alien' and sent to Australian internment camps. Eventually granted citizenship there, he went on to teach art in Victoria.

The Bauhaus master Paul Klee also contests what some regard as the different narrative categories of abstraction or representation. In his lithograph *Hoffmannesque scene* (p 120), made in 1921 (the year after he joined the Bauhaus faculty as a teacher of colour theory), Klee alluded to the opera *Tales of Hoffmann* by Jacques Offenbach. Strange and curious creatures, swirling flora and architectural motifs appear against a background of brightly coloured, rectangular planes, perhaps referencing a stage set, while not quite illustrating a story. Similarly, his *Thistle picture* (p 134), a watercolour from 1924, is made of large, painterly passages that create an indistinct sense of depth and surface, against which a number of hieroglyphic forms are suspended. Ghostlike figures hover above plant-like shapes that seem as if they are part of a secret code or a palimpsest of primitive wall paintings. Whether it is a highbrow European opera, a mysterious primeval moment, or even Klee's postcard advertising one of the infamous Bauhaus festivals (p 120), the mix of abstracted, geometric and gestural forms exist alongside childlike drawings of figures and objects. These idiosyncratic works, made by one of the most influential Bauhaus teachers, make it clear that there is more to the Bauhaus than hard-edged geometry or industrial-inspired images and objects. If we look further into Bauhaus imagery and begin to consider works such as Johannes Itten's images of abstract swirling lines (opposite) or Schlemmer's *Group on banister I* 1931 (p 125), the expansiveness of Bauhaus pictorial imagery begins to reveal itself. Schlemmer's automaton figures meld into their architectural surroundings because they have been reduced to geometric shapes. Yet, this abstraction also enhances the profound alienation of Schlemmer's characters, an affect sometimes read as a portent of the rise of Nazism and the closure of the Bauhaus – surely evidence of the complicated triangulation of form, content and historical context in Bauhaus art.

An essential aspect of art made at the Bauhaus was that it was to be part of an architectural context – *everything* was to be seen as part of an architectural ensemble, as part of a *Gesamtkunstwerk*, or total work of art. Starting in the early 1920s, the school sought out commissions with manufacturing firms to mass-produce its designs, and consequently the Bauhaus had a complex connection to the professionalisation of the making of goods, from the production of handcrafts to the new vocations of the product and graphic designer. Bauhaus decorative arts also dramatise the dialectical conflicts of the object culture of Weimar Germany. Functional objects mediate human relationships, and simultaneously reflect and influence issues of production, consumption and spectatorship.[8] The move from a folk culture to a popular culture, and from the craftsman and small workshop to the factory and department store (along with other transformations in the economic class structure of Germany) were part of the increased industrialisation that was a catalyst for Bauhaus art. However, the relationship between the Bauhaus and mass production was consistently complicated. Both pragmatic and idealistic, the school sought contracts with industry in order to become more self-supporting, but also to fulfil the basic principal that beautifully designed objects would bring about a better world.

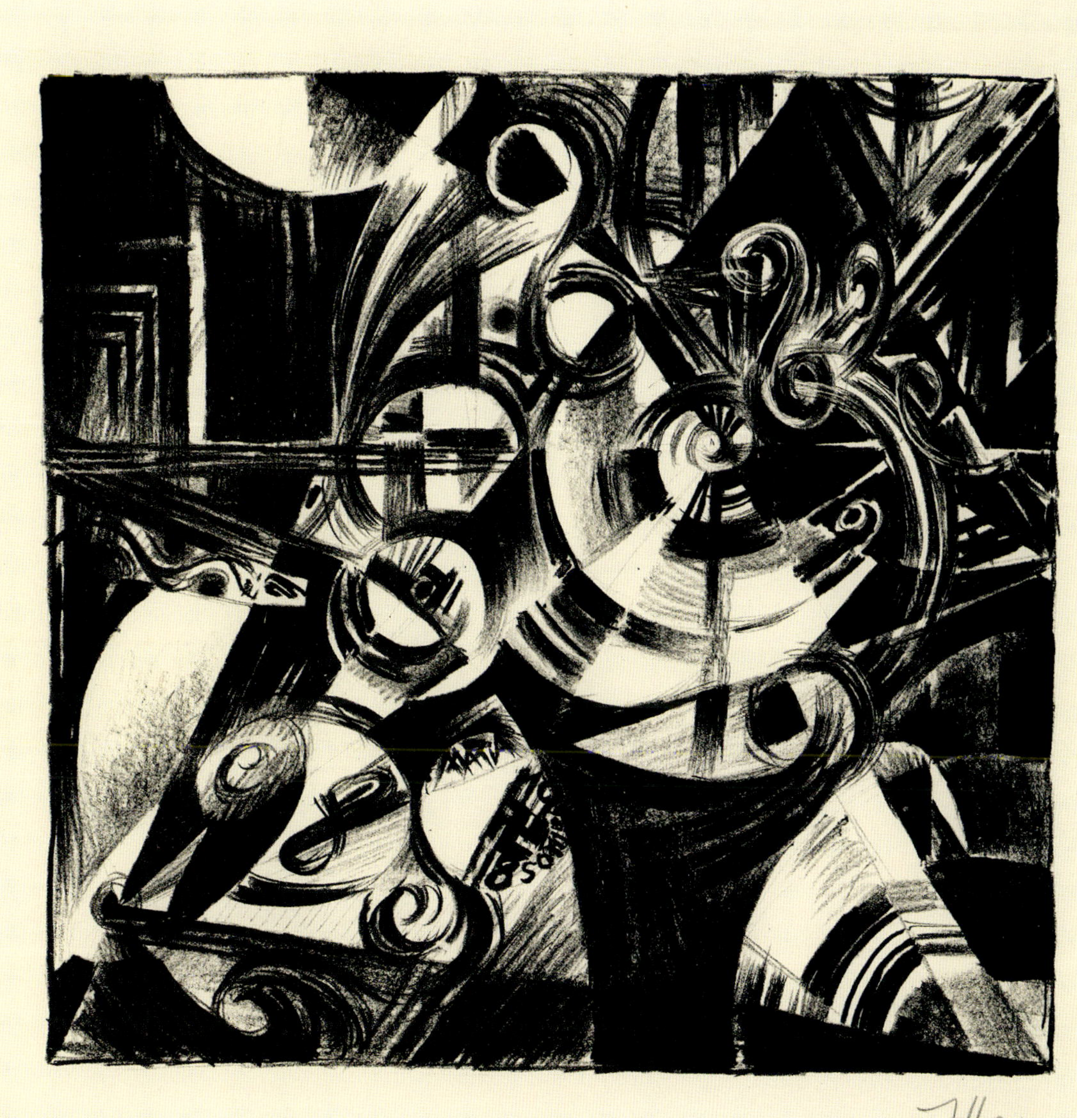

Johannes Itten
Composition 1919
lithograph
Art Gallery of New South Wales, Sydney

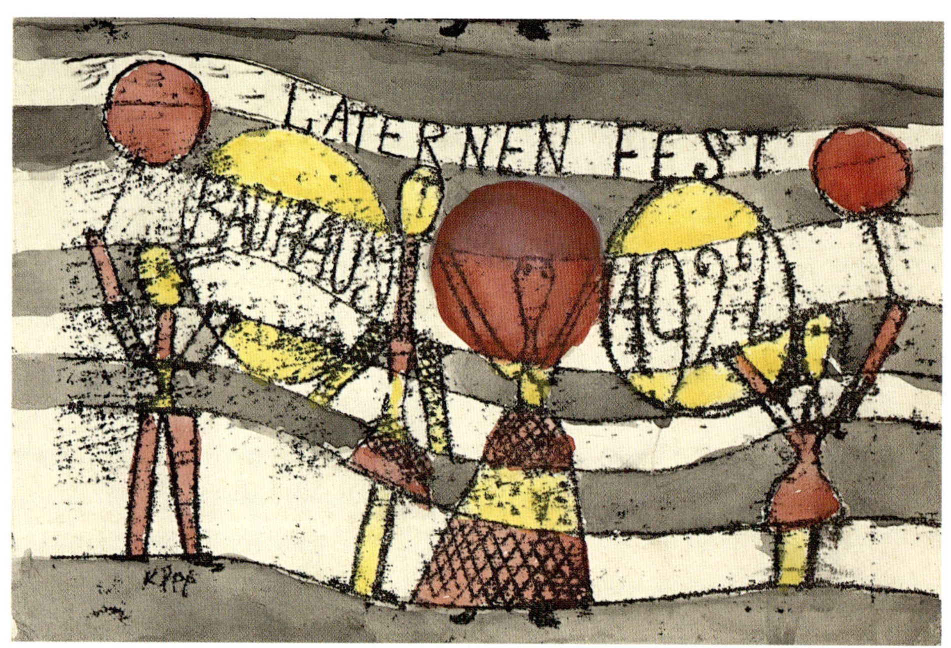

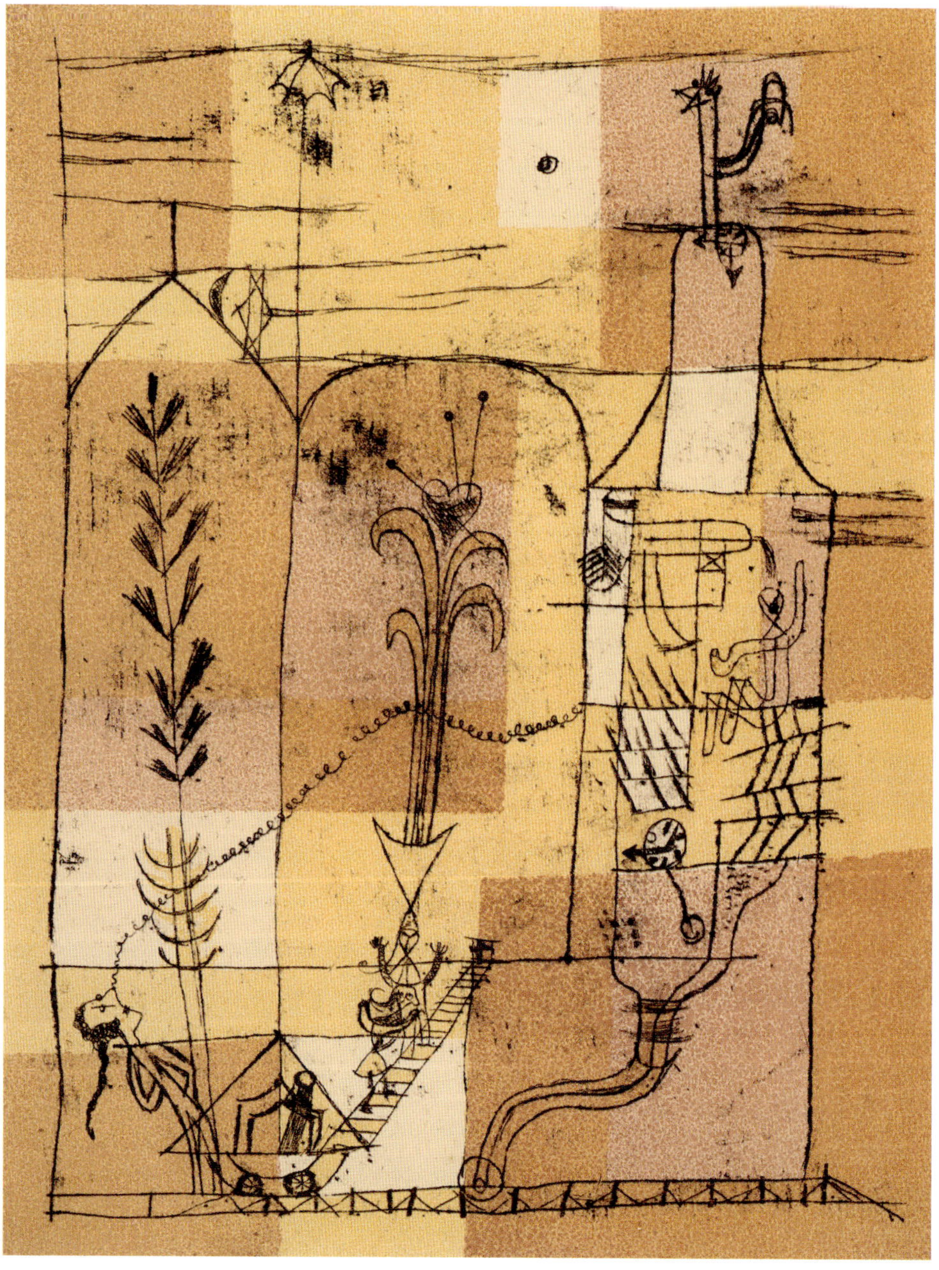

Paul Klee
Lantern festival Bauhaus 1922
colour lithograph
National Gallery of Victoria, Melbourne

Paul Klee
Hoffmannesque scene 1921
from the portfolio Bauhaus prints: new European graphic art I: masters of the State Bauhaus in Weimar 1921–22
colour lithograph
Los Angeles County Museum of Art

During the Weimar years, the ceramics studio was located in Dornburg, on the outskirts of the city, and students lived communally above the studio. Otto Lindig's earthenware represents the rustic, brown, one-of-a-kind ceramic objects that were produced there as prototypes for mass production (p 122).[9] Regardless of the number made or the materials used, all Bauhaus ceramics demonstrate the influence of the foundation courses on workshop production. There is inventiveness in the composition, and a sense of unusual shapes and patterns, often combined with a clear functionalism. These properties can also be seen in the metal work of Marianne Brandt (p 155), the containers designed by Wilhelm Wagenfeld for the German glass industry (pp 152–3), and the ceramics of Margarete Marks for the ceramics factory that she owned and operated (p 123).

The Bauhaus began with the idea that gender would not play a role in the admissions policy, in keeping with the shifting role of women in Weimar Germany. Women had gone to work in the munitions factories in large numbers, and after the war many returned to more conventional domestic roles, while others remained in the workforce, by desire or by necessity. Yet it was not an easy transition, either nationally or at the Bauhaus, where most of the women were directed to work in the weaving workshop (p 115).[10] While this was a biased designation, their successes simultaneously served to empower the women working there. Bauhaus textiles were among the most visually complex, technologically innovative and commercially successful works produced. Many of the textiles are clearly related to the work of the Bauhaus painters, while much of the ingenuity can also be seen as an extension of the theories of contrasts and colour interaction learned in the *Vorkurs*. The preliminary fabric drawings in particular demonstrate that the foundation courses and workshops were meant to be symbiotic (pp 157–8). The students produced wall hangings, carpets and blankets using weaving, knotting and appliqué methods, as well as innovative dying and surface-design techniques. Mechanical looms were introduced in 1923, which enabled the designs to become more complex, and for the studio to begin accepting outside commissions. After the school moved to Dessau, the workshop was overseen by a single master – Gunta Stölzl, a student who had trained in Weimar. By 1930, the weaving workshop had entered into an exclusive contract with Polytexil, a large manufacturing company that marketed the works under the Bauhaus-Dessau label. Bauhaus textile artists wanted to reach a mass audience with their work and support themselves as private craftswomen. This occupational quandary demonstrates the frictions of Bauhaus handcraft and industrial design – a professional hybrid that grew out of tensions between the artist as designer, the artist as a maker of fine art, and the artist as a contributor to the production of a modern, industrialised culture.[11]

The costumes, sets and choreography of the theatre workshop are considered by many to be the most experimental at the Bauhaus (pp 142–5).[12] Lothar Schreyer led the theatre workshop for two years, and was replaced by Oskar Schlemmer, whose theatrical works for the Bauhaus were in many ways closer to what we today would call performance art. The most famous piece was the *Triadic ballet*, composed by Schlemmer and performed throughout Germany. The costumes were composed of geometric forms and android masks, and the movements of the dancers were executed in a robotic adagio.

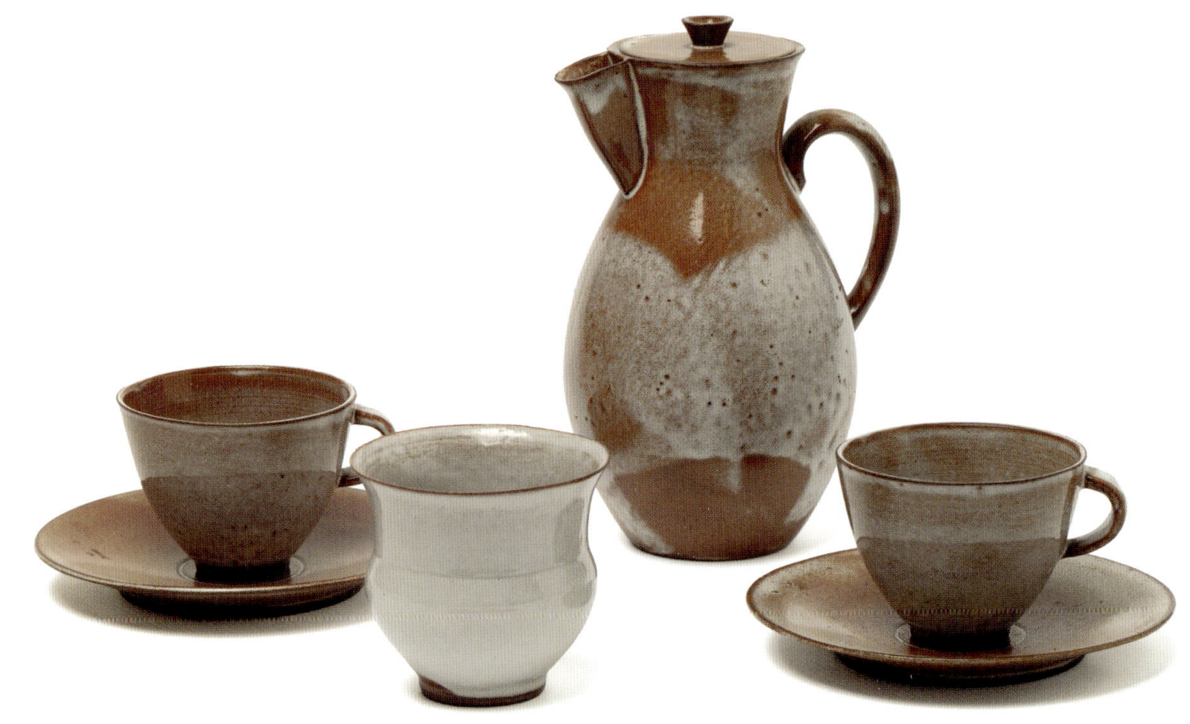

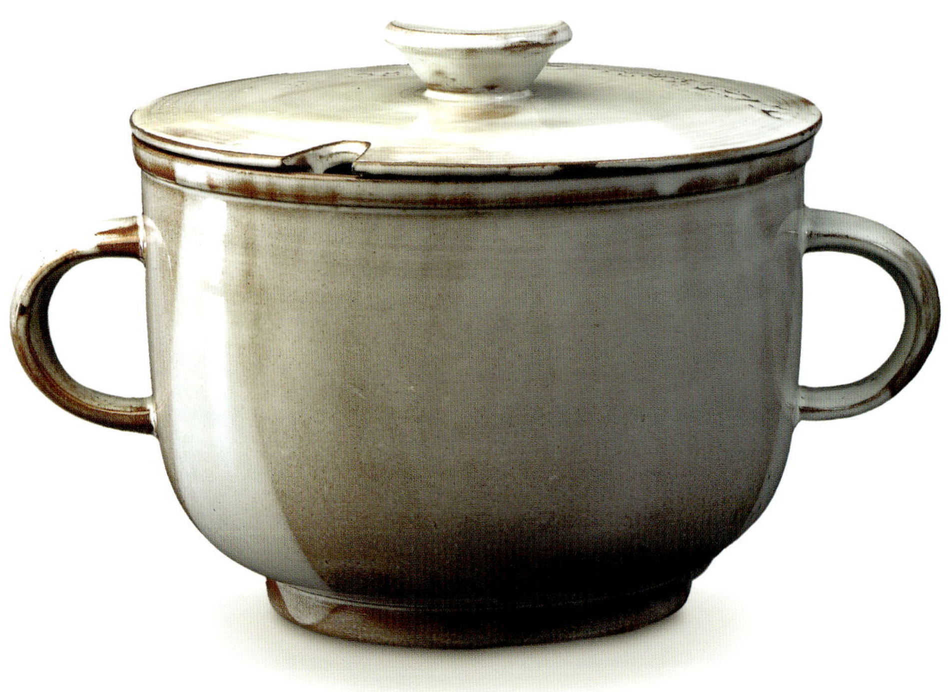

Otto Lindig
Cocoa pot, sugar bowl and two cups and saucers c1923
glazed earthenware
National Gallery of Australia, Canberra

Otto Lindig
Covered punch bowl 1926
earthenware
National Gallery of Victoria, Melbourne

The Spiral costume (p 143) raises the question of the relationship between the new and avant-garde, and the expected and conventional. Simultaneously clown-like and ghostly, the costume is manifestly unique and bizarre; the wire can surely be seen as referencing industrial materials – the stuff of mass production – yet it also clearly cites the tutu of classical ballet. In its combination of the historical and modern, this Bauhaus costume can be seen as evidence of what the German theorist Ernst Bloch referred to as the 'non-simultaneous', the dialectic of the future and the past from which Weimar modernism derived.[13] In fact, it is in the uncanny mixture of something that is both recognisably traditional and unexpectedly radical that the multi-layered disposition of Weimar modernism begins to fully reveal itself.

Photographs of Bauhaus performances also reveal the way in which light came to be seen as a material to be designed for and with (p 144). However, except for documentary shots, photography initially played no official role at the Bauhaus[14] and it was not until 1923, when László Moholy-Nagy joined the faculty, that photography began to take on a much more integral role. As an artform that is made by a machine, photography is also a medium that is inherently reproducible. This hybridity of the subjective eye of the artist and the undeniable actuality of what is being photographed was a dialogue that was manipulated by Bauhaus photographers – whether they were making photographs as individual artistic expressions, or as part of the school's advertising and book design. For Moholy-Nagy, the proliferation of photography and film had forever changed the way that we actually, physically, biologically perceive the world – we can never go back to pre-photographic perception. Moreover, photography made possible nothing less than a new way of believing, of being human.

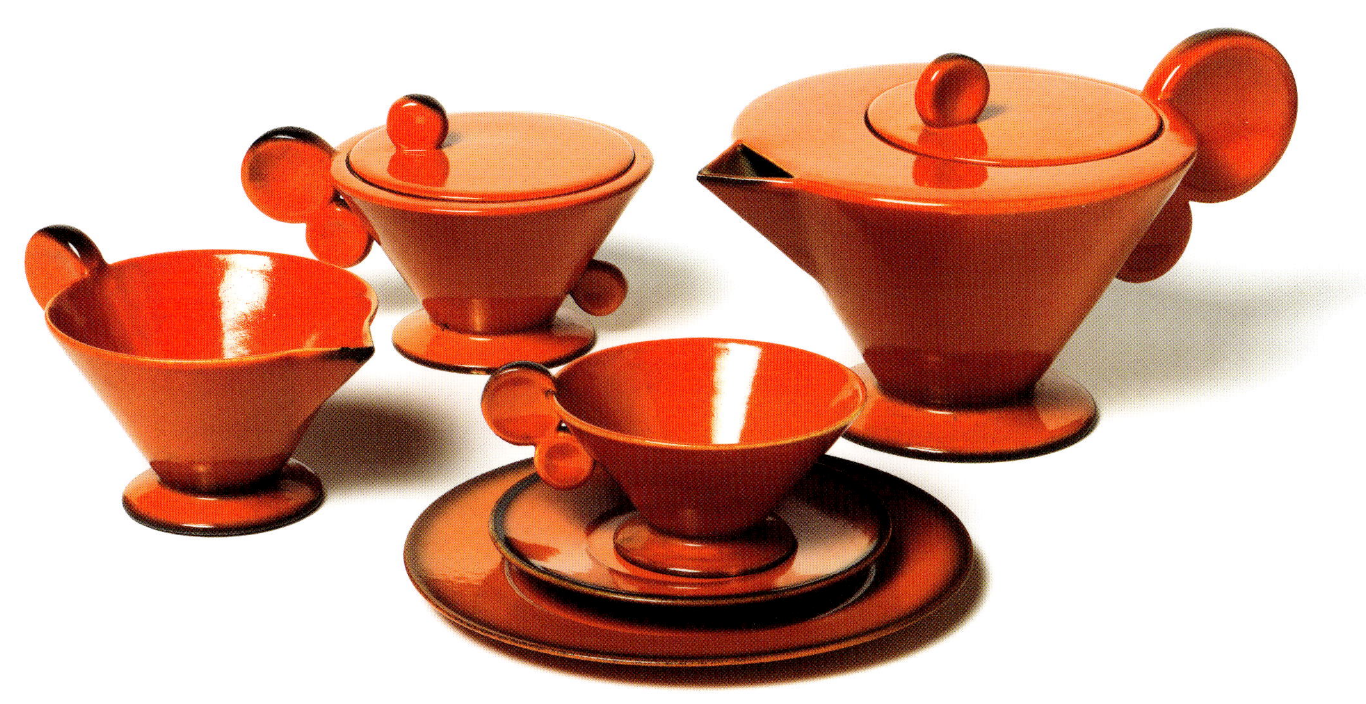

Margarete Marks
Tea set c1928
glazed earthenware slip cast
National Gallery of Australia, Canberra

Moholy-Nagy's complex philosophical approach is evidenced in many of his works. Although photograms are often regarded as a primitive form of photography, because they are camera-less, Moholy-Nagy produced photograms that were profoundly sophisticated. Created by placing objects on light-sensitive paper and briefly exposing the paper to light so that the shadow of the objects is recorded, Moholy-Nagy's photograms have an 'essential ambiguity' – while they literally record the presence the object, the things are dematerialised.[15] These ghostlike traces are more a record of light than of material (pp 126–8). The influence of Moholy-Nagy's photograms, photomontages and straight photographs can be traced in the work of many Bauhaus artists; the impact of his use of obtuse, obscuring angles in particular can be traced in the photographs of Gertrud Arndt and Walter Funkat (pp 115, 145).

According to Moholy-Nagy, '*Fotografie ist lichtgestaltung*'. This phrase is intentionally polysemantic: photography is a thing (a light form), but it is also a process, the action of designing with light. The proliferation of artificial lighting has been identified as a defining aspect of Weimar culture – the phenomenon of illuminated spaces and the mass production of related products were important components of Germany's industrial growth.[16] Film and photography are linked to the design of lamps and lighting fixtures at the Bauhaus, particularly the iconic designs of Brandt, Carl Jakob Jucker and Wilhelm Wagenfeld (whose Bauhaus lamp is still in production today, p 153).

Architectural design was not officially taught at the Bauhaus until 1927, although there were important building commissions both before and after – the most influential being the Bauhaus buildings in Dessau (p 115). Moreover, Bauhaus artists were deeply engaged in a kind of architectural thinking; in a number of works from the print studio, it is clear that students were responding to some kind of prompt that was architectural in nature (pp 130, 133). In some cases, architectural concepts extended beyond the confines of the building and into utopian realms. Wassily Kandinsky's lithographs *Small worlds III* 1922 (p 137) and *Composition* 1922 (p 139), for example, demonstrate how architecture was embedded in the veiled imagery and constructed compositions that inform his work. Both prints contain numerous utopian tropes, such as islands, satellite cities and a shifting sense of perspective, where we are simultaneously above and in front of the world depicted. We are no place and every place.[17]

Whether a pot, lamp, chair, painting, print, photograph or an entire building – and whether abstract, representational or something in between – all Bauhaus art underscored a core belief in the ability of art to bring about social change. After the Nazi seizure of power in the 1930s, it was precisely their belief in the power of art that forced many Bauhaus artists into exile. The diaspora of the artists and the objects they made have contributed to collections of Bauhaus art around the world, including many of the museums and galleries that have shared their Bauhaus art for this exhibition. Is there a message in this art for us? The enduring legacy of the Bauhaus is not a kind of modernist fashion or even a conception of spatial dynamics; it is the basic desire to create – in and of itself – a hopeful gesture towards a world beyond conflict and distrust.

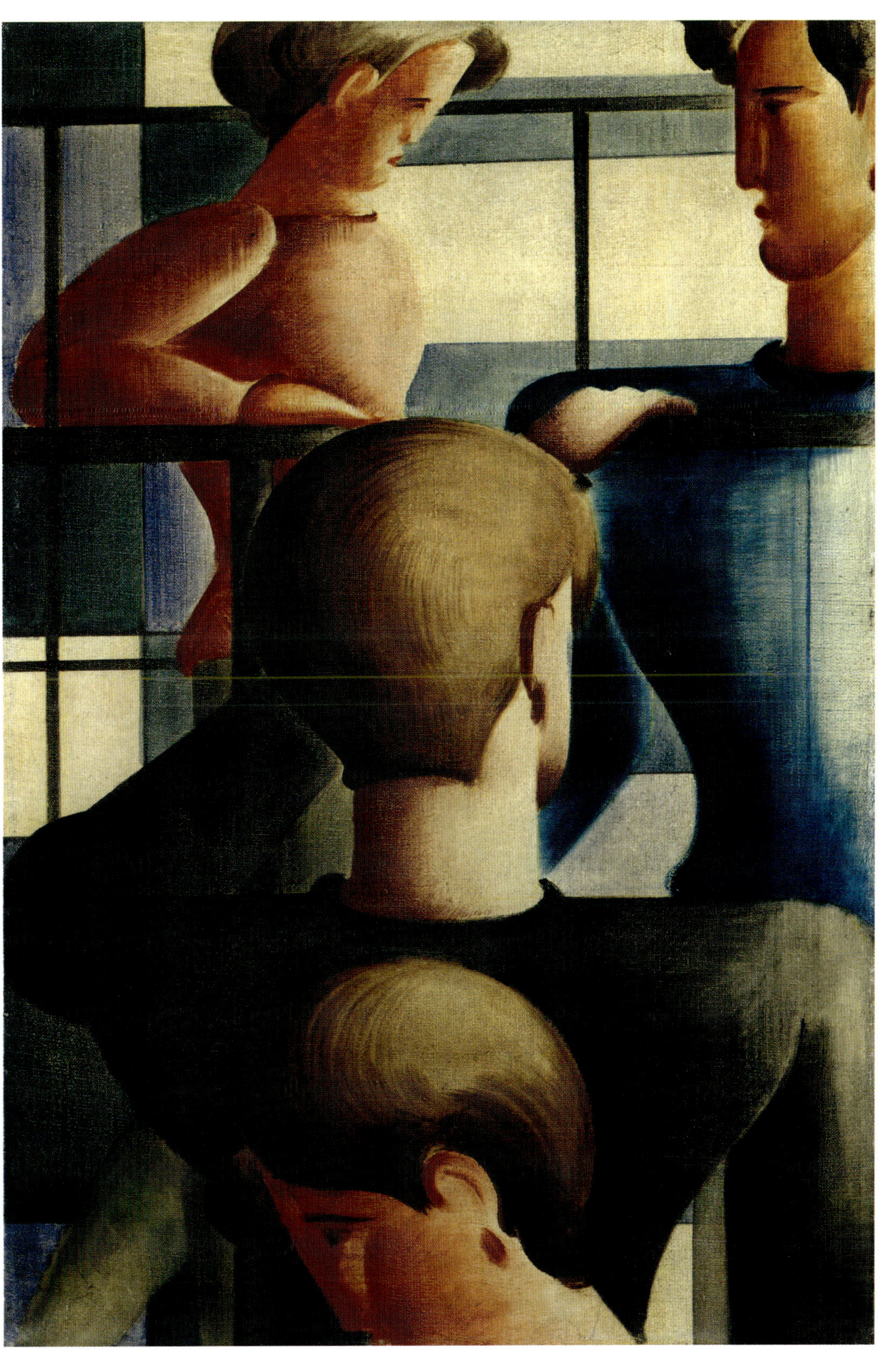

Oskar Schlemmer
Group on banister I 1931
oil on canvas
Kunstsammlung Nordrhein-Westfalen, Düsseldorf

LÁSZLÓ MOHOLY-NAGY

Photograms

Hungarian artist László Moholy-Nagy arrived in Berlin in early 1920, during a time when the German capital was emerging as a meeting place for avant-garde artists from across Europe. By the time he arrived in Germany, Moholy-Nagy had already made the crucial shift from figurative painting to works that combined lines and geometric shapes with iconic elements, letters and numbers. Technology became his primary subject and machine-like objects featured prominently in his work. Moholy-Nagy shared the utopian belief of the Constructivists that the creation of new abstract forms of art could pave the way towards a better society, and he articulated theories about the relationships between art and society in numerous essays.

Moholy-Nagy and his wife, Lucia, joined the Bauhaus in 1923, shortly after taking part in the Congress of Constructivists and Dadaists in Weimar. He served as head of the metal workshop from 1923 to 1928 and was simultaneously appointed director of the preliminary course. Through his teaching and writings, he profoundly influenced the new direction taken by students at the Bauhaus towards the creation of art objects inspired by the machine aesthetic. In one of his most famous statements, he emphasised the importance of developing artforms that represented and responded to the new machine age:

> The reality of our century is technology: the invention, construction, and maintenance of machines. To be a user of machines is to be of the spirit of this century. It has replaced the transcendental spiritualism of past eras. Everyone is equal to the machine.[1]

Photograms, or camera-less photography, created both in Berlin and Weimar from around 1922, provided the perfect medium through which Moholy-Nagy conducted his radical, formalist experimentation.[2] The photograms included in this exhibition exemplify his mastery in taking fragments from the world of technology and creating new structures and spatial relationships from the reassembled parts. In the early photograms, three-dimensional objects such as screws, bolts and pieces of machinery have been laid upon light-sensitive paper and gradually exposed to produce beautifully nuanced compositions. Moholy-Nagy's unusual

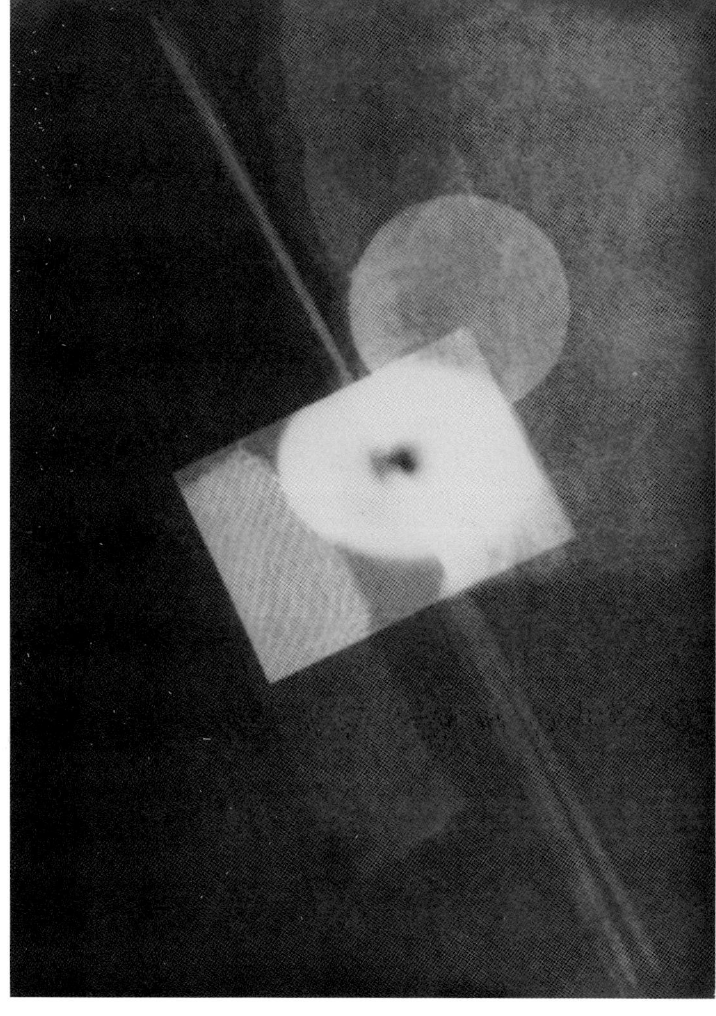

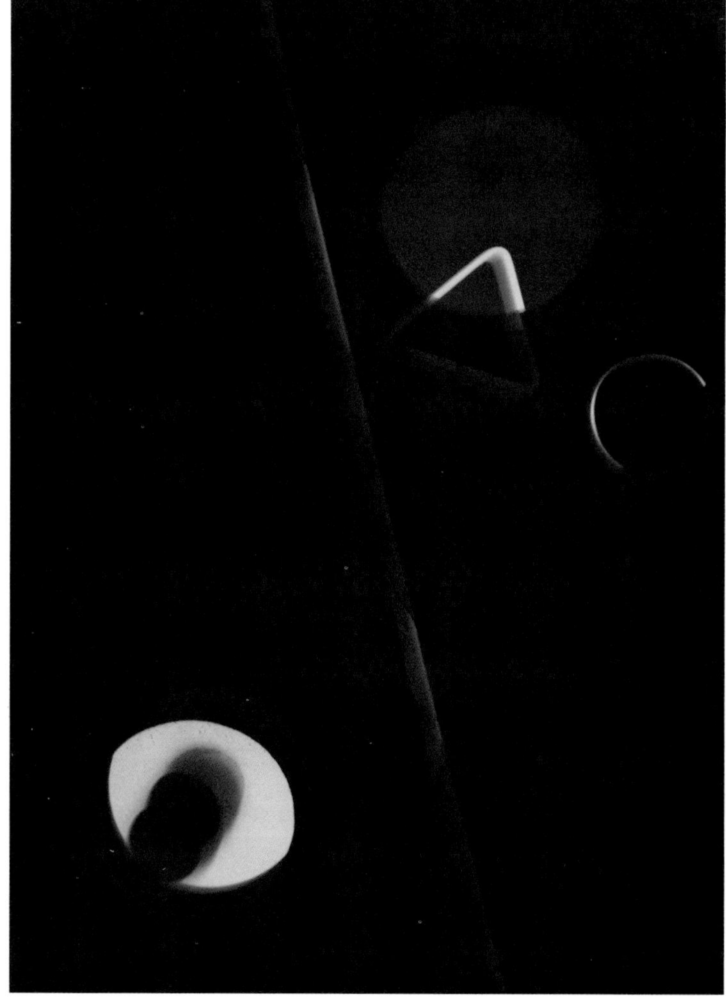

arrangement of forms through light can also be seen in *Photogram self-portrait* 1926 (p 128), where paper cut-outs and projected lights have been used to render the artist's distinctive facial features in the shape of a translucent crescent moon.

Although Moholy-Nagy and many of the Bauhaus students continued to experiment with photography extensively throughout the 1920s, photography did not form part of the Bauhaus curriculum until 1928. This is surprising, given the range of photography that was produced to not only capture daily life at the Bauhaus but also the people – or *Bauhäusler* as they were affectionately known – architecture, design products and prevailing atmosphere of the school that combined light-hearted fun with the newest artistic endeavours. This omission also marked a controversial point of departure from the belief, largely promoted by Moholy-Nagy through Bauhaus publications, that photography was the medium through which 'the new vision' could be forged. In other words, photography was propagated as a revolutionary extension of human sight, and the camera was proposed as the vehicle through which artists could best capture a glimpse of the brave new world.[3] By the time a photography workshop was finally formed in 1928, Moholy-Nagy had moved to Berlin to develop his interests in film, photography, and stage and costume design, thus ending the most radically experimental phase of photography at the Bauhaus. JS

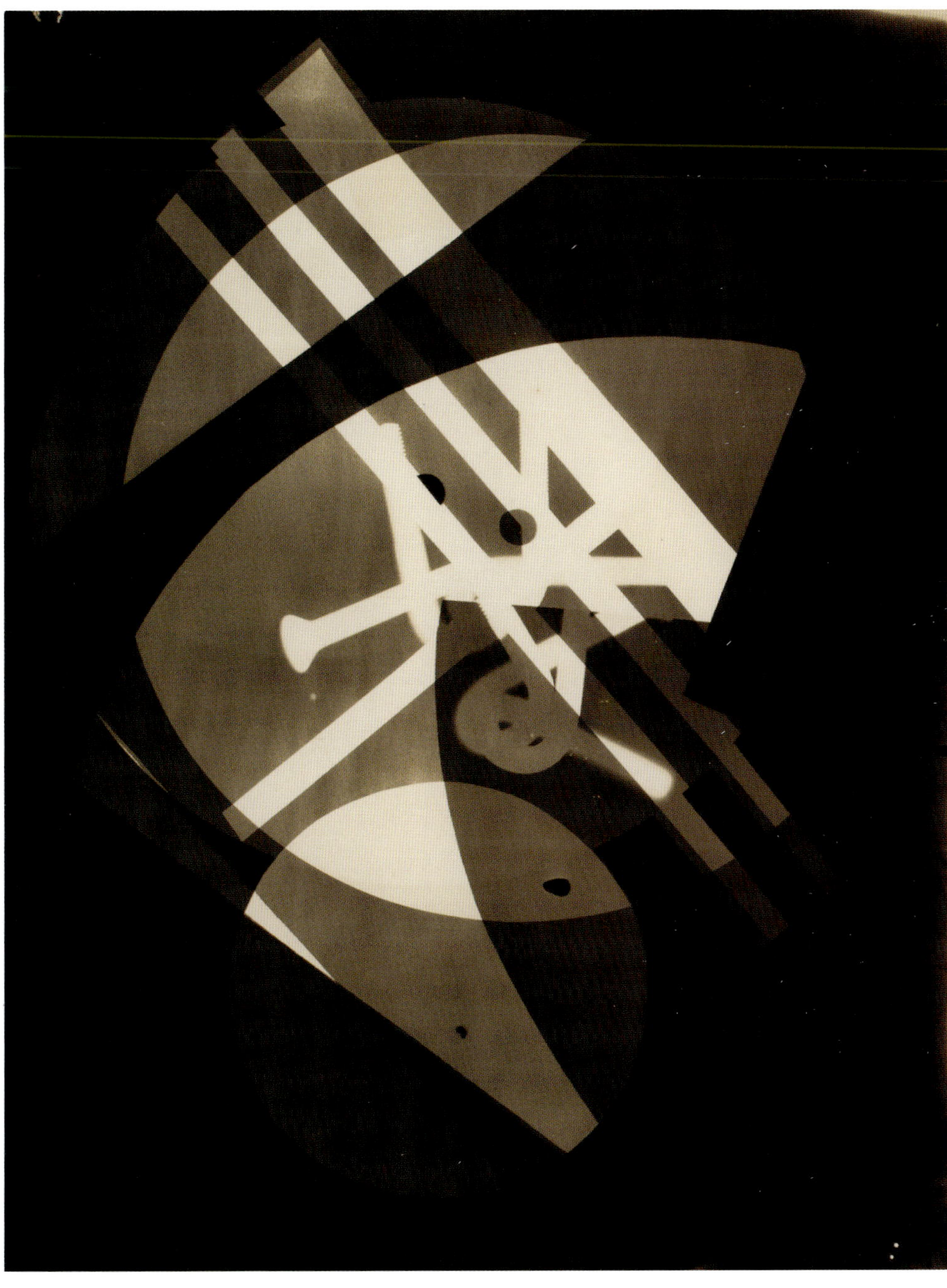

left to right:

László Moholy-Nagy
Untitled, Weimar 1923–25
photogram, bromide gelatin silver print
Museum Folkwang, Essen

László Moholy-Nagy
Untitled, Weimar 1923–25
photogram, bromide gelatin silver print
Museum Folkwang, Essen

László Moholy-Nagy
Fotogramm 1926
photogram, gelatin silver print
Collection of George Eastman House, International Museum of Photography and Film

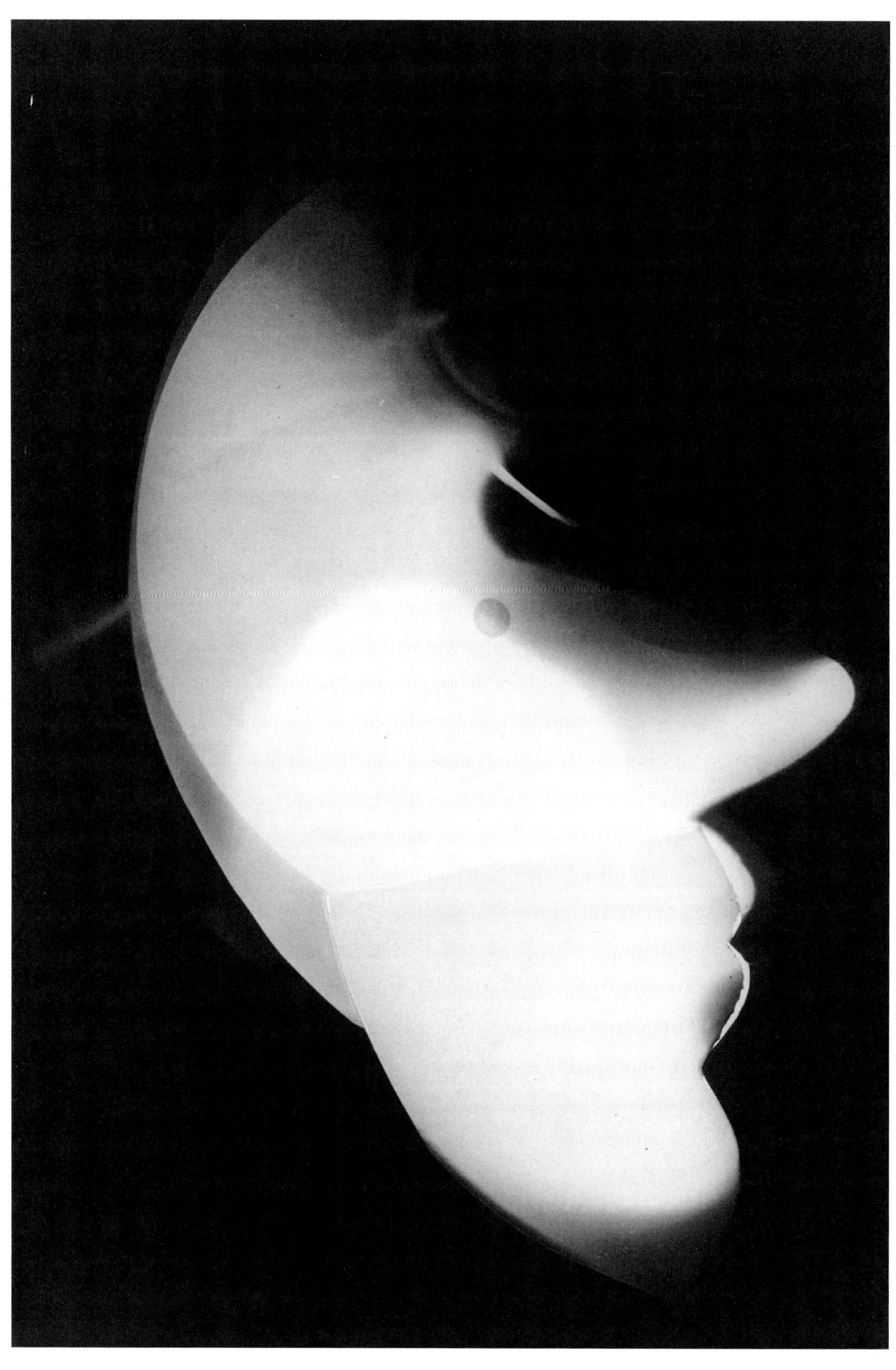

László Moholy-Nagy
Photogram self-portrait 1926
photogram
National Gallery of Australia, Canberra

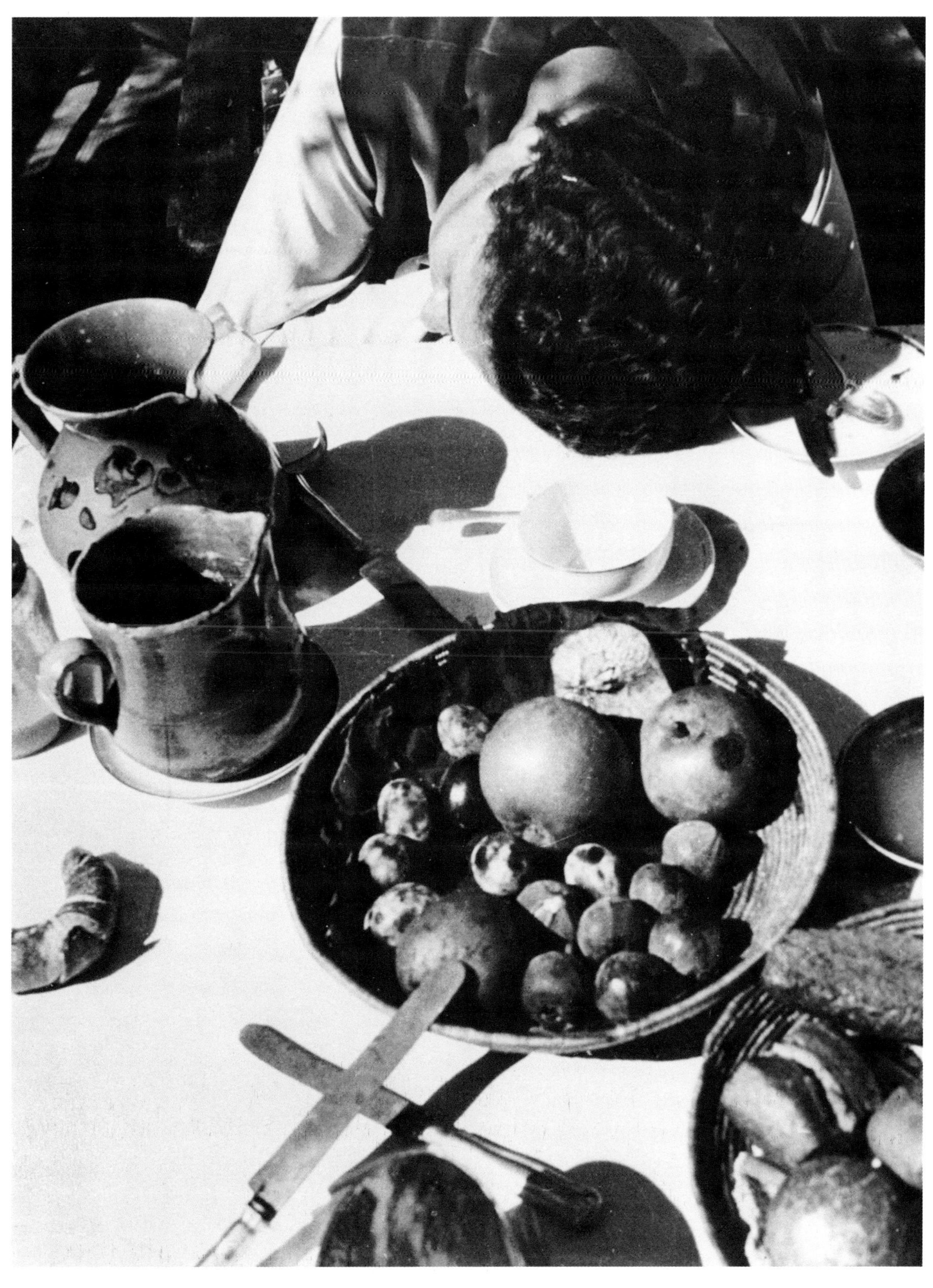

László Moholy-Nagy
Lucia at the breakfast table 1926
gelatin silver photograph
National Gallery of Australia, Canberra

LUDWIG HIRSCHFELD MACK

Reaching the stars

Ludwig Hirschfeld Mack joined the Bauhaus in the winter semester of 1919–20 as an apprentice in the printmaking workshop under Lyonel Feininger. His early work at the Bauhaus is characterised by formal inventiveness and a light-hearted playfulness as he explored a range of techniques, including drawing, watercolour painting and printmaking. Like Johannes Itten, Paul Klee and Wassily Kandinsky, Hirschfeld Mack became fascinated with the study of colour, and he developed a practical seminar on colour theory to accompany Klee's course. He also produced colour wheels and colour light plays, and conducted research into colour symbolism and the relationships between colour and musical tones. Hirschfeld Mack reiterated the fundamental belief of the Bauhaus masters that 'colours, like lines, have feeling values of their own' and this idea continued to profoundly influence his work.[1] Hirschfeld Mack left the Bauhaus when it moved to Dessau, deciding instead to establish a career in art education.

During the six years he worked at the Bauhaus, Hirschfeld Mack produced numerous watercolours and prints that capture the sense of creativity and innovation that was encouraged at the school. The printing technique of *Durchdrückzeichnung*, which he developed from 1921 onwards with Klee, was a form of monotype and was used in *City* c1922 and *Architecture* 1923 (p 133). This technique involved drawing with a pencil or other tool on the reverse of a sheet of paper that was placed over a lithographic stone and then printed. Hirschfeld Mack almost always embellished these prints with watercolour to create intimate and subtly textured works.[2] His most significant lithograph from this period, *Reaching the stars* 1922, is a complex assemblage of abstract, geometric shapes and soft, subtle colour combinations. The spirit of utopian idealism, on which the Bauhaus was founded, may provide a clue to the meaning of this work, where the stars are used to represent hope for the future in the age of modernity, or even 'a higher state of consciousness'.[3]

Hirschfeld Mack moved to London in 1936 to escape persecution by the Nazis and there continued his involvement with art education and colour theory experimentation. Declared an 'enemy alien' in 1940, he was deported to Australia aboard the *Dunera* with many other German artists, intellectuals and scientists. He was sent to intern camps in Hay, Orange and later Tatura, where he produced images of desolation and isolation.

In 1942, Hirschfeld Mack was released from Tatura and became the art master at Geelong Grammar School, where he remained until his retirement in 1957. He continued to practice as an artist, producing numerous paintings, watercolours and prints that used colour to achieve pictorial harmony and dynamism, and which are now held in public art collections around Australia. Hirschfeld Mack remained passionately involved in art education, promoting Bauhaus principles and ideas within the Australian art community and advocating his long-held belief in individual creativity as benefiting the common good. JS

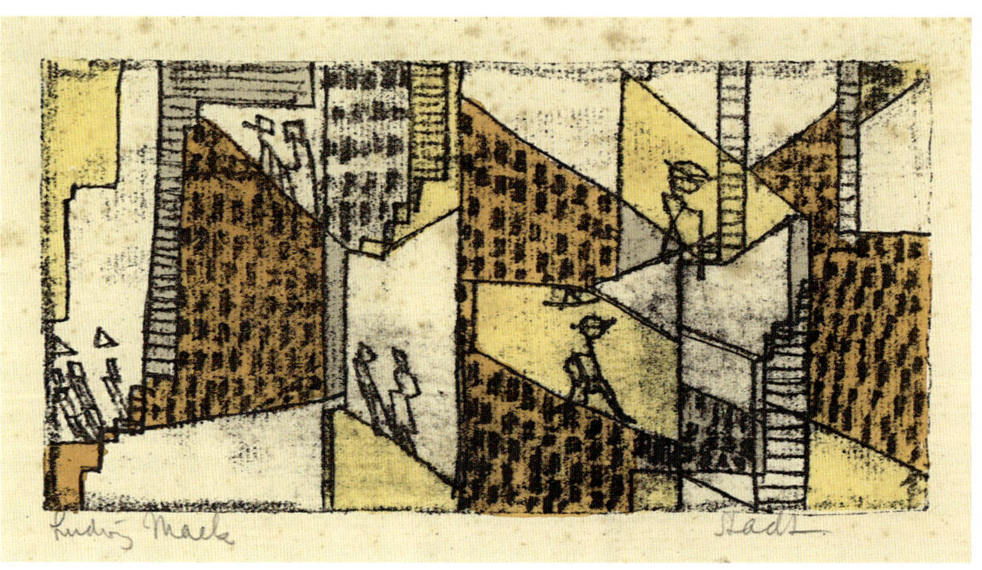

Ludwig Hirschfeld Mack
City c1922
colour lithograph
National Gallery of Victoria, Melbourne

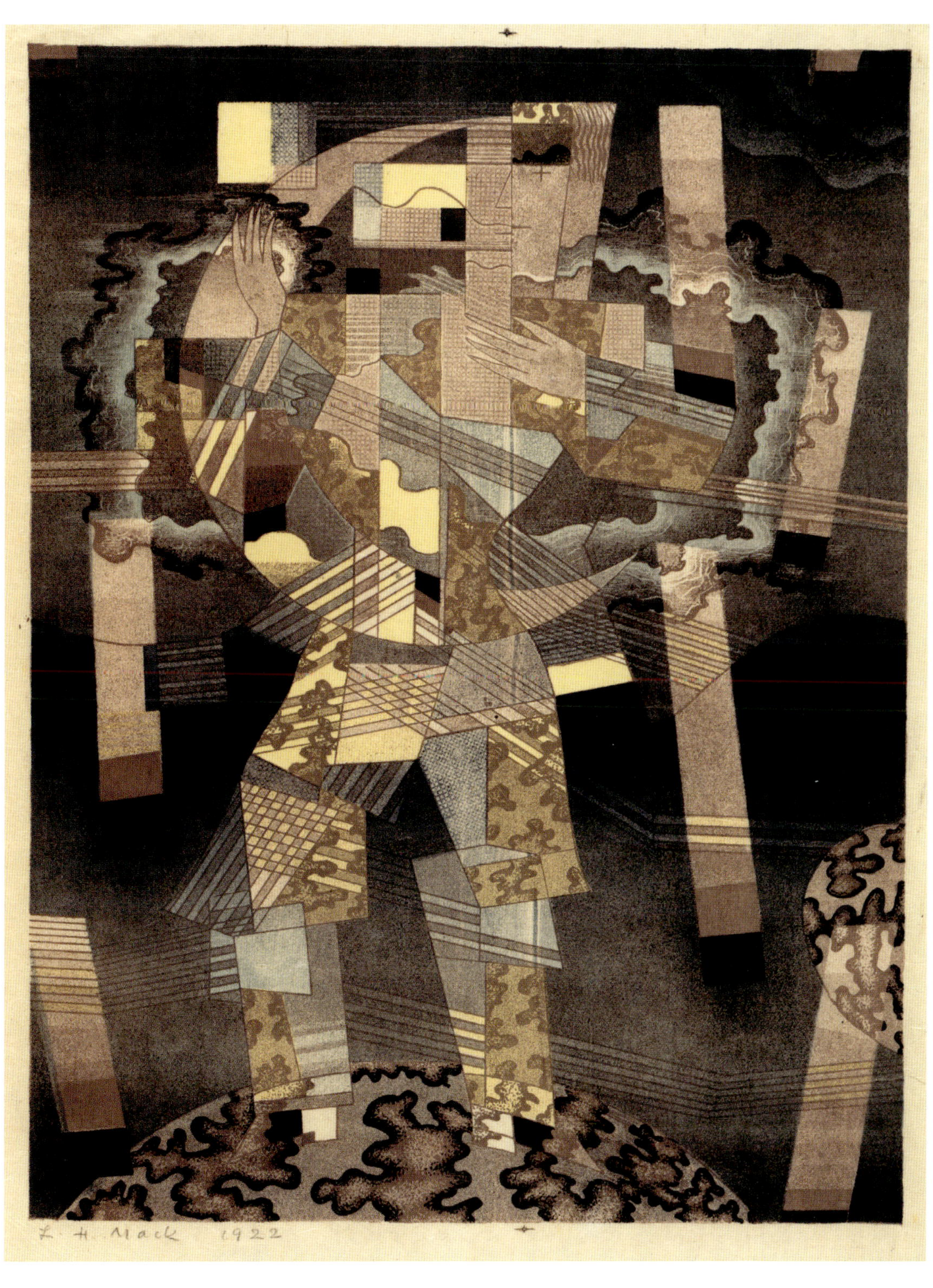

Ludwig Hirschfeld Mack
Reaching the stars 1922
colour lithograph
Art Gallery of New South Wales, Sydney

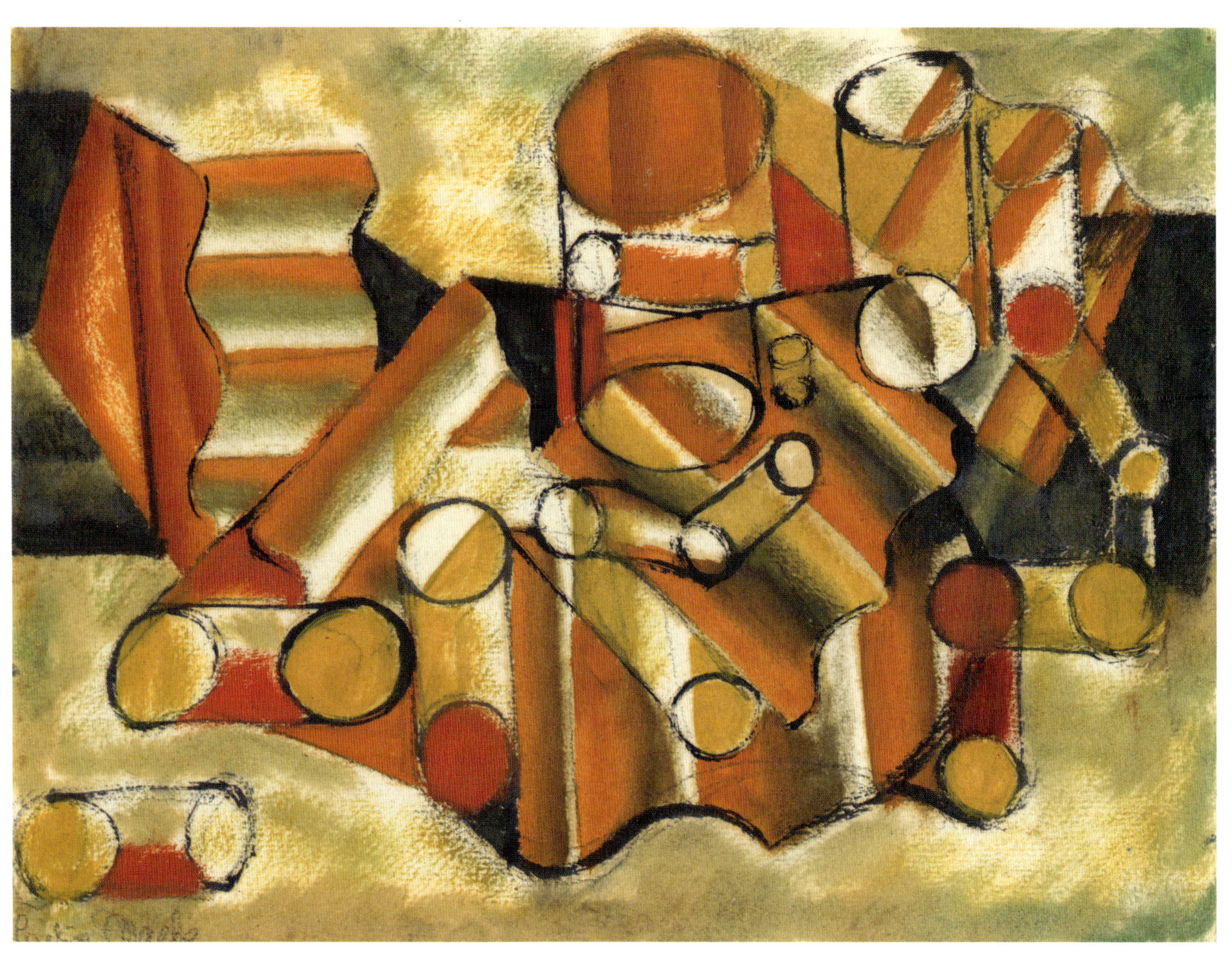

Ludwig Hirschfeld Mack
The accordion player c1922
watercolour, gouache, pencil
National Gallery of Australia, Canberra

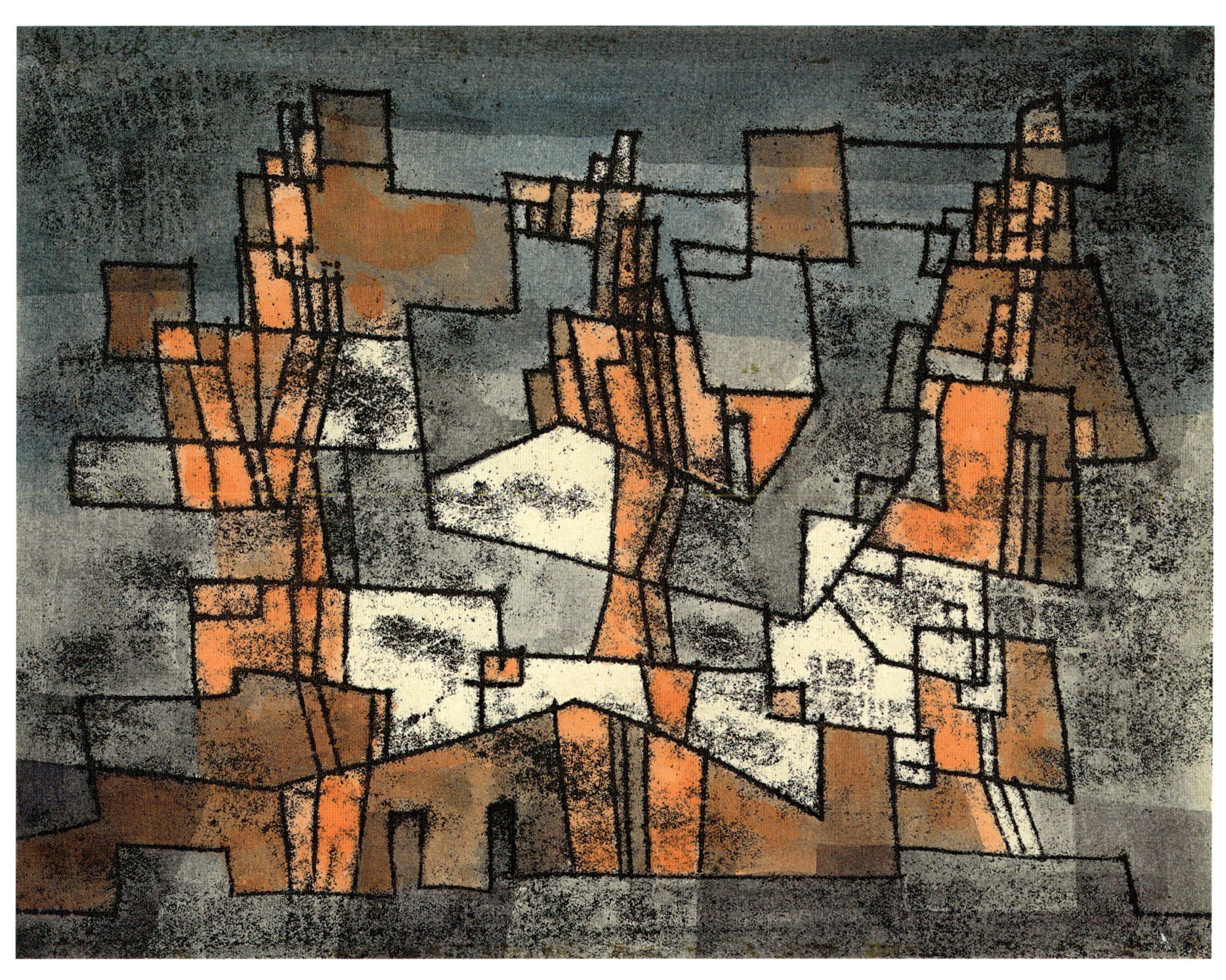

Ludwig Hirschfeld Mack
Architecture 1923
colour lithograph
National Gallery of Victoria, Melbourne

PAUL KLEE

Thistle picture

Paul Klee had been closely associated with the influential expressionist movements the Blaue Reiter and the *Sturm* before he joined the Bauhaus at the age of 40. On arriving at the Bauhaus in 1921, Klee became master of the bookbinding workshop and began teaching a course on composition as part of the preliminary instruction. Klee's influential teachings on the principles of pictorial form began by invoking 'an active line on a walk, moving freely, without goal. A walk for walk's sake.'[1] The other fundamental principle of Klee's preliminary-course teaching was colour theory. He was concerned, above all, with achieving compositional harmony by experimenting with combinations of complementary colours.[2]

Thistle picture 1924, created during Klee's early years at the Bauhaus, is an important example of his unique use of line and colour to create whimsical, dreamlike compositions. Cathy Leahy has eloquently described the watercolour as follows:

> the work presents a mysterious world of ambiguous, floating forms. Some of these, such as the central flower-like shape with jagged leaves, are suggestive of the natural world; others, such as the ladder, derive from the constructed world; while others still, such as the hovering bellows-shaped form that bears a schematic face, are purely imaginary. Although the meaning of the work is enigmatic, the sense of an 'other' world – perhaps underwater, perhaps aerial – is strongly conveyed, not only through the forms but also through the work's construction. The dominant colour is a subtly modulated blue-grey, which varies in translucency, opacity and tonality, creating an undulating spatial depth in which the forms float. The forms themselves are picked out in delicate washes of purple, brown, crimson and orange that have been brushed over paper stencils. The resulting shadowy haloes that surround the crisp outline of the forms contribute to their ethereal nature.[3]

Klee left the Bauhaus in 1931 to devote himself more fully to his art and continued to practise as an artist throughout the 1930s, even as the political climate in Europe intensified. Klee went into inner exile during this period and created mysterious and enigmatic works that evoked the loss of freedom and painful sense of alienation experienced by modernist artists whose work was being discredited by the Nazis as 'degenerate' art. JS

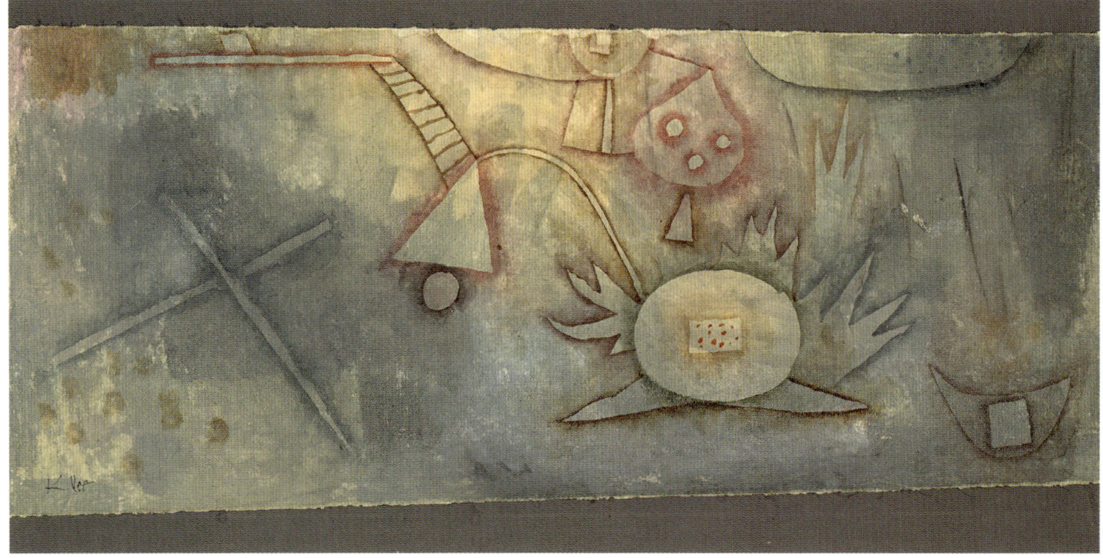

Paul Klee
Thistle picture 1924
gouache, watercolour on linen laid on card
National Gallery of Victoria, Melbourne

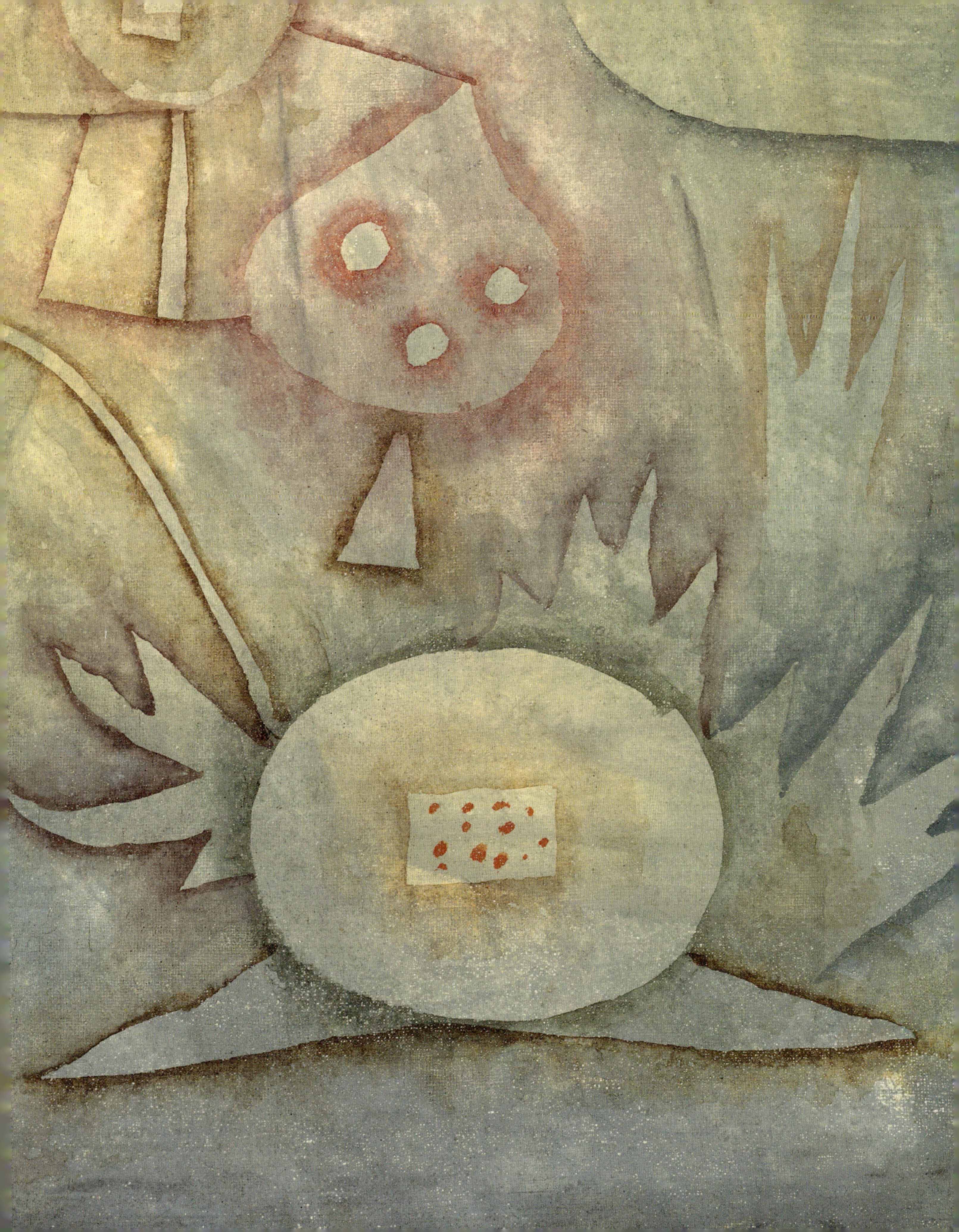

WASSILY KANDINSKY

Small worlds III

Wassily Kandinsky emerged as a major figure within the German avant-garde during the years before the First World War, when he founded the Blaue Reiter, together with Franz Marc, in Munich in 1912. Kandinsky's paintings, watercolours and prints are among the most compelling and important works of this era, as he pioneered the move away from figurative to abstract art using colour and forms derived from the imagination rather than nature. His highly symbolic and often monumental compositions were very much linked to his utopian belief in the coming of a new spiritual epoch that would be free of the selfish materialism of the modern world.

After returning to his native homeland in Russia during the war years, Kandinsky decided to move back to Germany after the war, excited by the opportunity to influence revolutionary developments in art education that were opening up in Weimar. He joined the Bauhaus in 1922, at the age of 56, and began teaching form and colour as part of the compulsory preliminary course. A new style of geometric abstraction emerged in his work in 1922 when he became master of the wall-painting workshop, and this stylistic tendency became the defining characteristic of his art over the next decade.

The *Small worlds* portfolio of six lithographs created during the time that Kandinsky joined the Bauhaus exemplifies the artist's growing interest in more rigidly defined forms and colours. In the third print from this series, he quite literally portrays a small world – a self-contained cosmos comprising dynamic arrangements of lines, patterns, geometric shapes and primary colours that emanate from the centre of the composition. Kandinsky's exploration of dynamic formal arrangements can also be seen in *Composition* 1922 (p 139), which appeared in the portfolio *Bauhaus prints: new European graphic art IV: Italian & Russian artists* 1923–24. These exquisite and intimate compositions are convincing representations of Kandinsky's passionate belief in the elemental power of colour and form.

Kandinsky produced large-scale, abstract murals that were specifically designed for architectural spaces, yet the paintings he produced at the Bauhaus largely remained in the realm of art rather than the applied arts. Together with Klee, he managed to uphold the belief in the work of art as a unique object, as opposed to designing works for mass production, even though this view contrasted strongly with the coexisting tendency towards mechanised production encouraged by fellow members of the Bauhaus, such as László Moholy-Nagy. Kandinsky was the longest-serving teacher at the Bauhaus, and he continued to teach in Dessau and then Berlin, until the school was forced to close under the National Socialists in 1933. JS

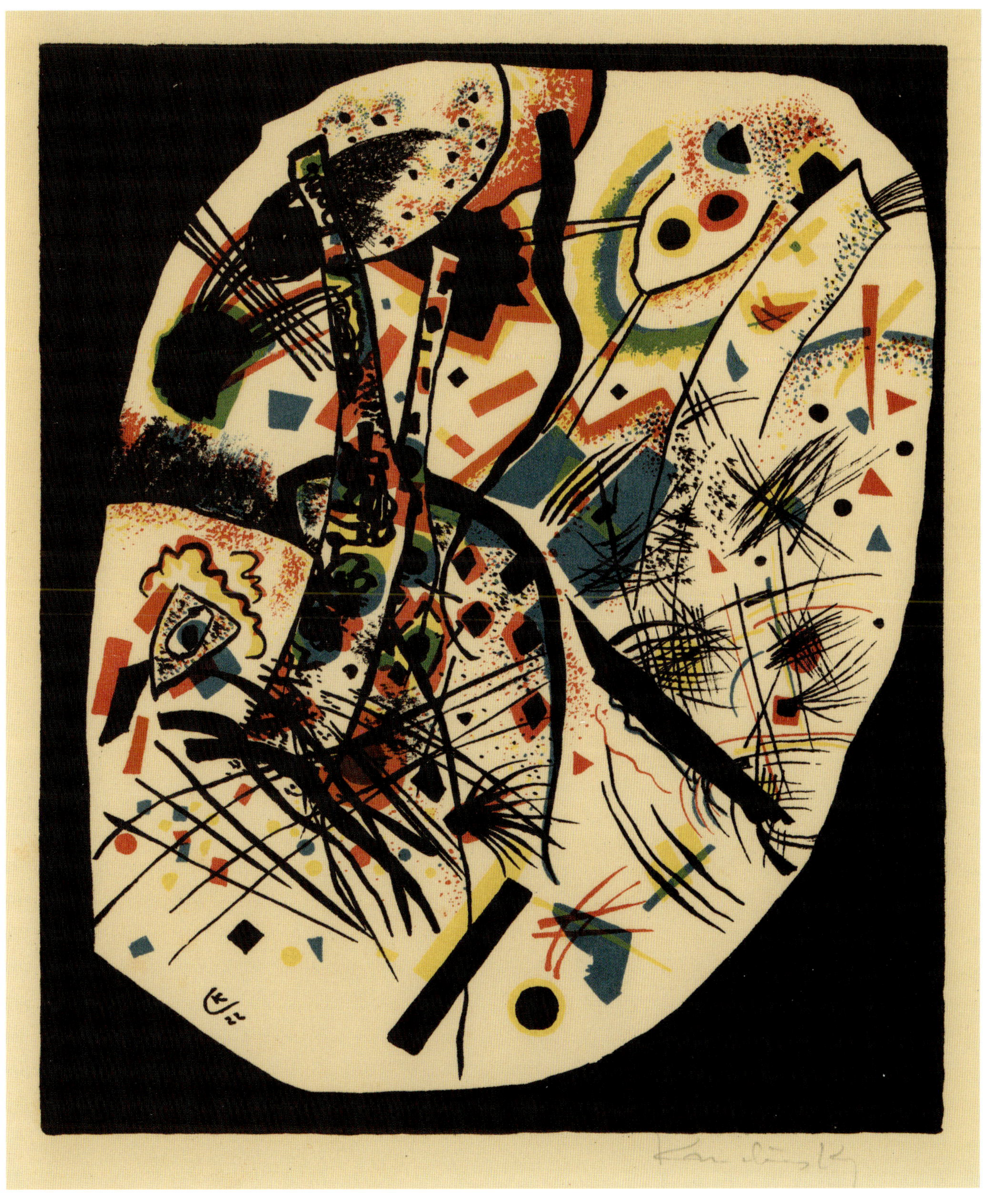

Wassily Kandinsky
Small worlds III 1922
from the portfolio Small worlds 1922
colour lithograph
National Gallery of Australia, Canberra

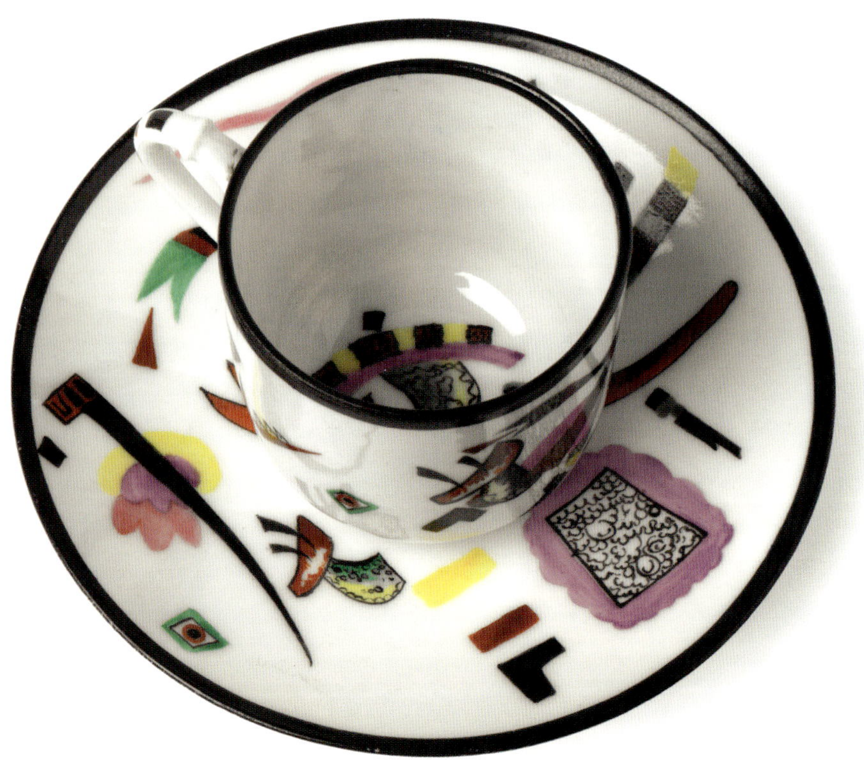

Wassily Kandinsky
Cup and saucer c1921–23
porcelain, painted overglaze decoration
National Gallery of Australia, Canberra

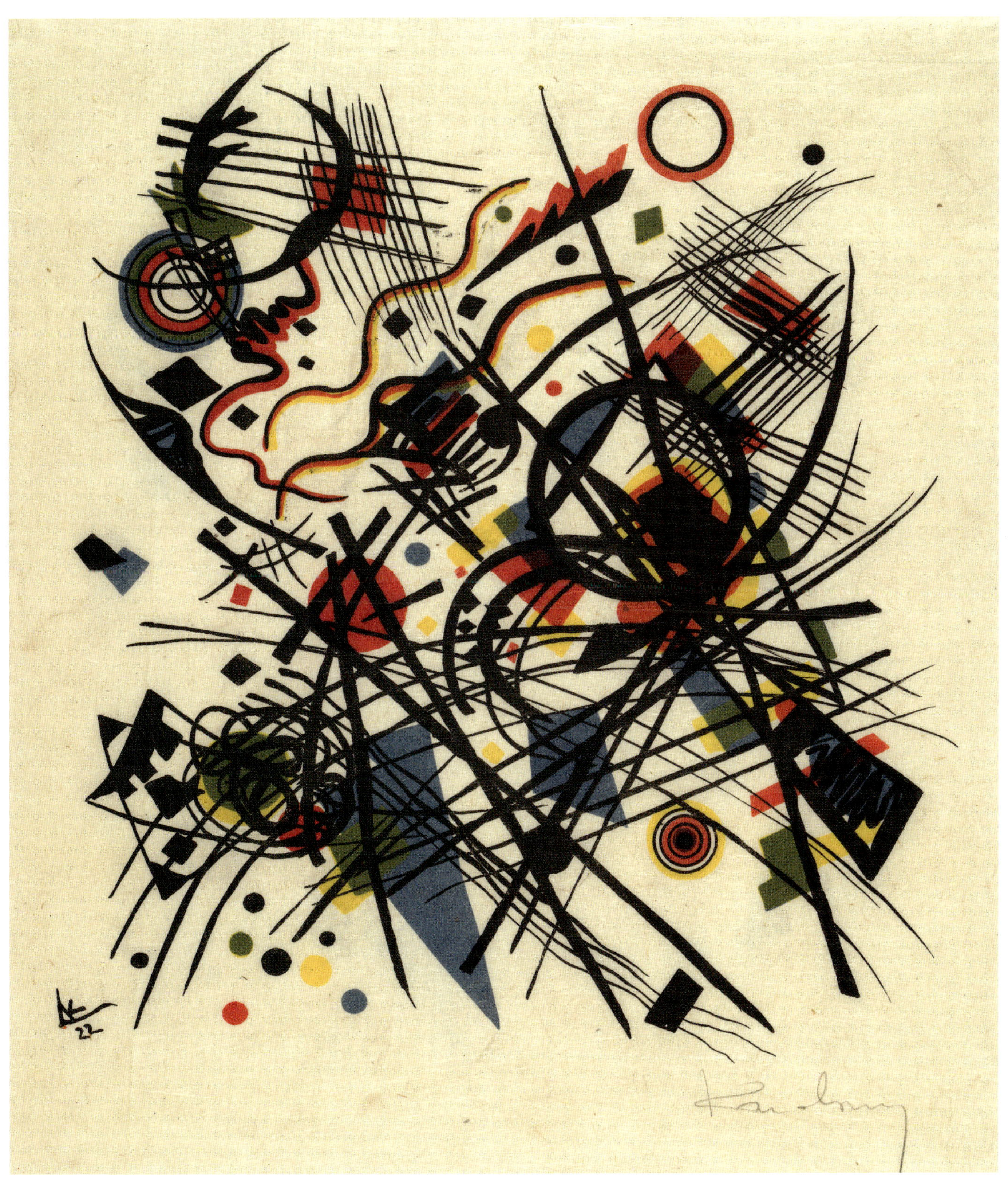

Wassily Kandinsky
Composition 1922
from the portfolio Bauhaus prints: new European graphic art IV: Italian & Russian artists 1923–24
colour lithograph
National Gallery of Australia, Canberra

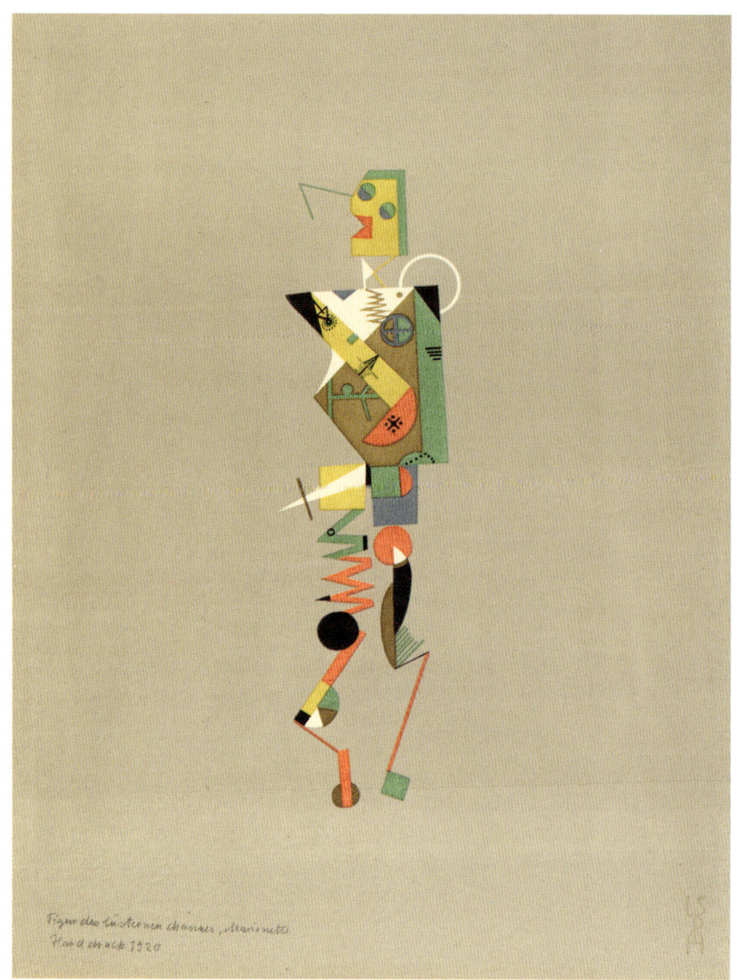

Lothar Schreyer
Figure of a lustful man for marionette theatre 1920
colour lithograph
National Gallery of Australia, Canberra

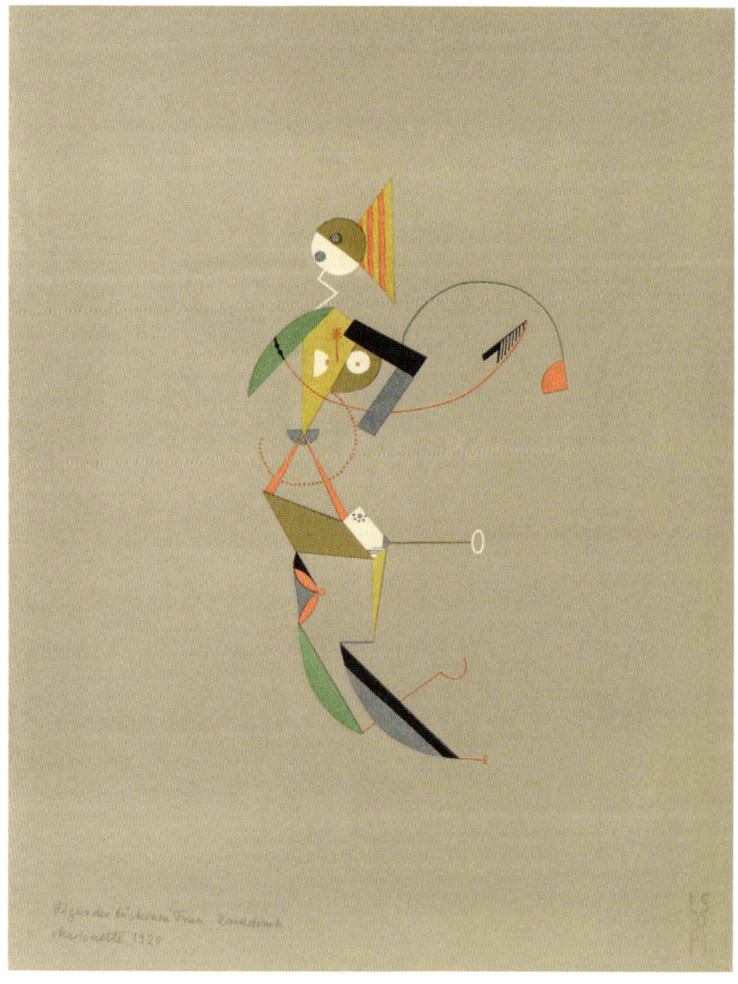

Lothar Schreyer
Figure of a lustful woman for marionette theatre 1920
colour lithograph
National Gallery of Australia, Canberra

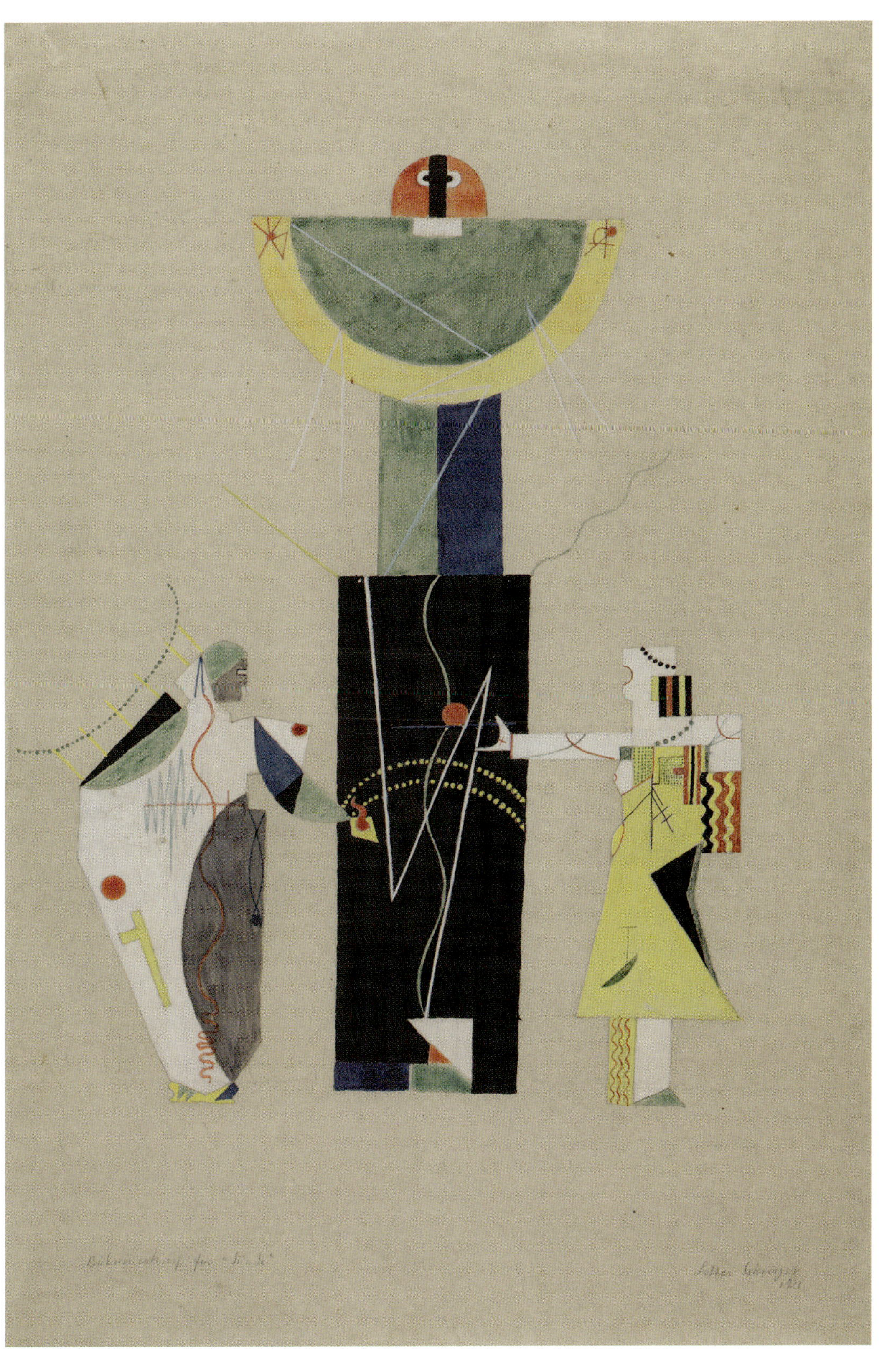

Lothar Schreyer
Stage design for 'Sin' 1921
watercolour
National Gallery of Australia, Canberra

OSKAR SCHLEMMER

Triadic ballet

Experimental dance and performance art flourished at the Bauhaus during the 1920s, inspired by Walter Gropius's call for a synthesis of all the arts, as well as the broader engagement of modernism with the performing arts. Artists worked across a range of disciplines to produce a varied and exciting program of performances that depicted, challenged and responded to the forces of modernity. There was a strong emphasis on the idea of performance as a 'total art' that combined the visual arts, dance, music, architecture and costume design, and on experimenting with light and the human body's spatial relationships to its surroundings.

The most well-known and widely performed dance production at the Bauhaus was Oskar Schlemmer's *Triadic ballet* 1922. Schlemmer had joined the Bauhaus as a painter and sculptor in the early 1920s. During these early years he introduced students to theatre and was master of the theatre workshop from 1923 to 1929. In Herbert Bayer's photograph *Theatre group on the Bauhaus roof* c1920 (below) we see Schlemmer – with his distinctive bald head and profile – clearly visible in the middle of the composition, surrounded by students and teachers. The mood is one of light-hearted playfulness, as students pose and joke around in costumes, figurines, masks and props partially based upon the *Triadic ballet*. Schlemmer asserted himself as a major figure at the school and Bauhaus performances, festivals and parties featured prominently in the calendar under his guidance.

The Bauhaus Theatre Group performed the *Triadic ballet* in Weimar in 1923, after a successful premier of the performance at the Stuttgart Landestheater in 1922. It was based upon the idea of the triad, or composites of three: three acts (yellow, pink and black); three dancers (one female, two male); the three dimensions of space (height, depth and breadth); the three basic geometric forms (ball, cube and pyramid); and the three primary colours (red, blue and yellow). The combination of dance, costume and music completed the symbolism of the triad in Schlemmer's innovative work.[1]

While there are no known photographs or film footage of the original Bauhaus performance, the ballet has been well documented through the many studies, sketches and presentation drawings that Schlemmer produced over a 15-year period. The elaborate costumes for *Triadic ballet* (now housed in the Staatsgalerie, Stuttgart) were, for Schlemmer, the most important component of the ballet.[2] These remarkable costumes exaggerate the abstract geometry generated by the human form and are themselves experimental studies in the rhythms between colour, abstract form and line. Grill's photograph – taken around the time the ballet toured to the music festival in Donaueschingen in 1926 – documents the costume worn by the female dancer in the third, and by far the most dramatic, act of the ballet (opposite).[3] The final act evoked a mystical and theatrical mood, as the dancers performed their last dance sequences against a stark black setting. The Spiral costume typically conveys Schlemmer's interest in the abstract geometry of the human form, however, it also references the feminine forms and traditional tutus of classical ballet. JS

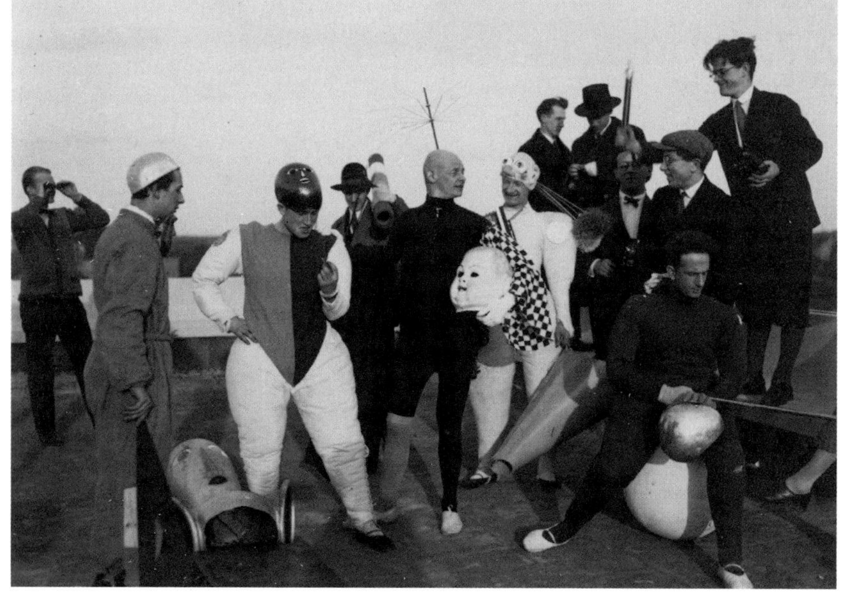

Herbert Bayer
Theatre group on the Bauhaus roof c1920
gelatin silver photograph
National Gallery of Australia, Canberra

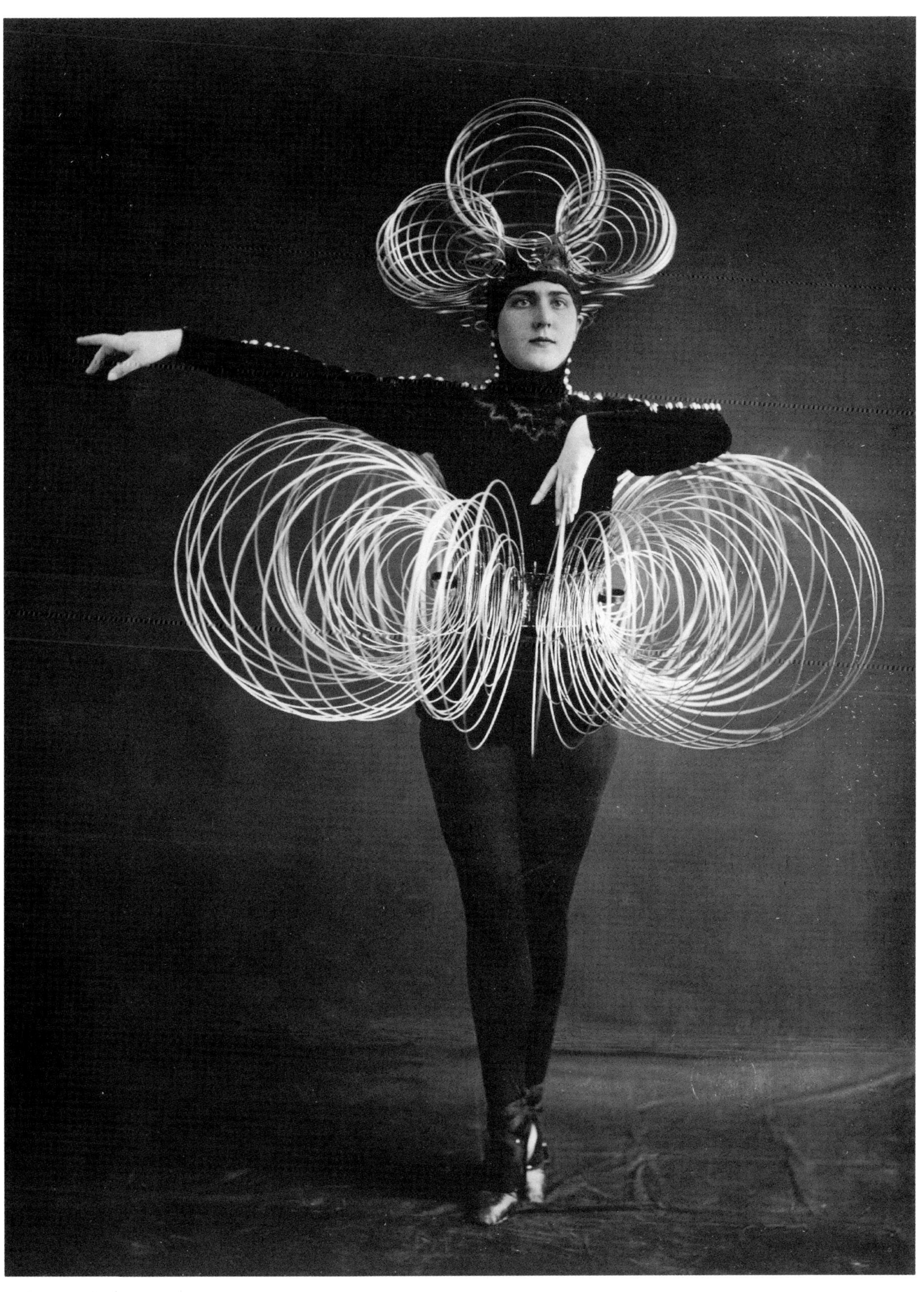

Karl Grill
[Spiral costume, from the *Triadic ballet*]
c1926–27
gelatin silver photograph
J Paul Getty Museum, Los Angeles

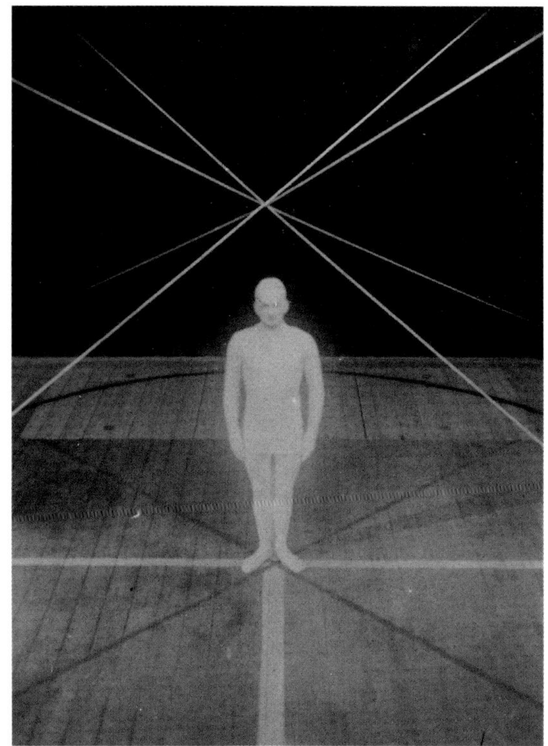

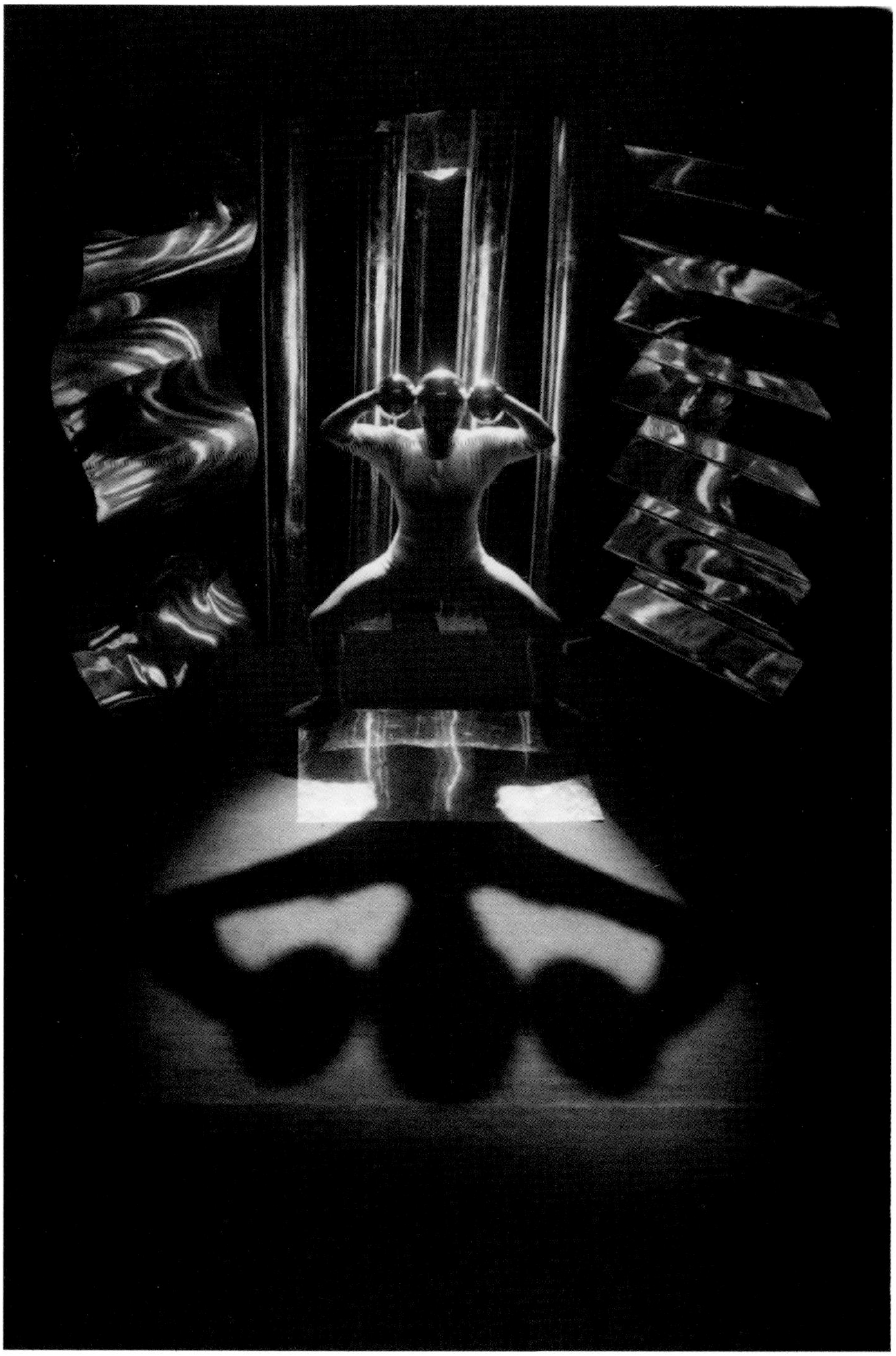

Irene Bayer
[Man on stage] c1927
gelatin silver photograph
National Gallery of Australia, Canberra

T Lux Feininger
[Metaltanz] c1928–29
gelatin silver photograph
J Paul Getty Museum, Los Angeles

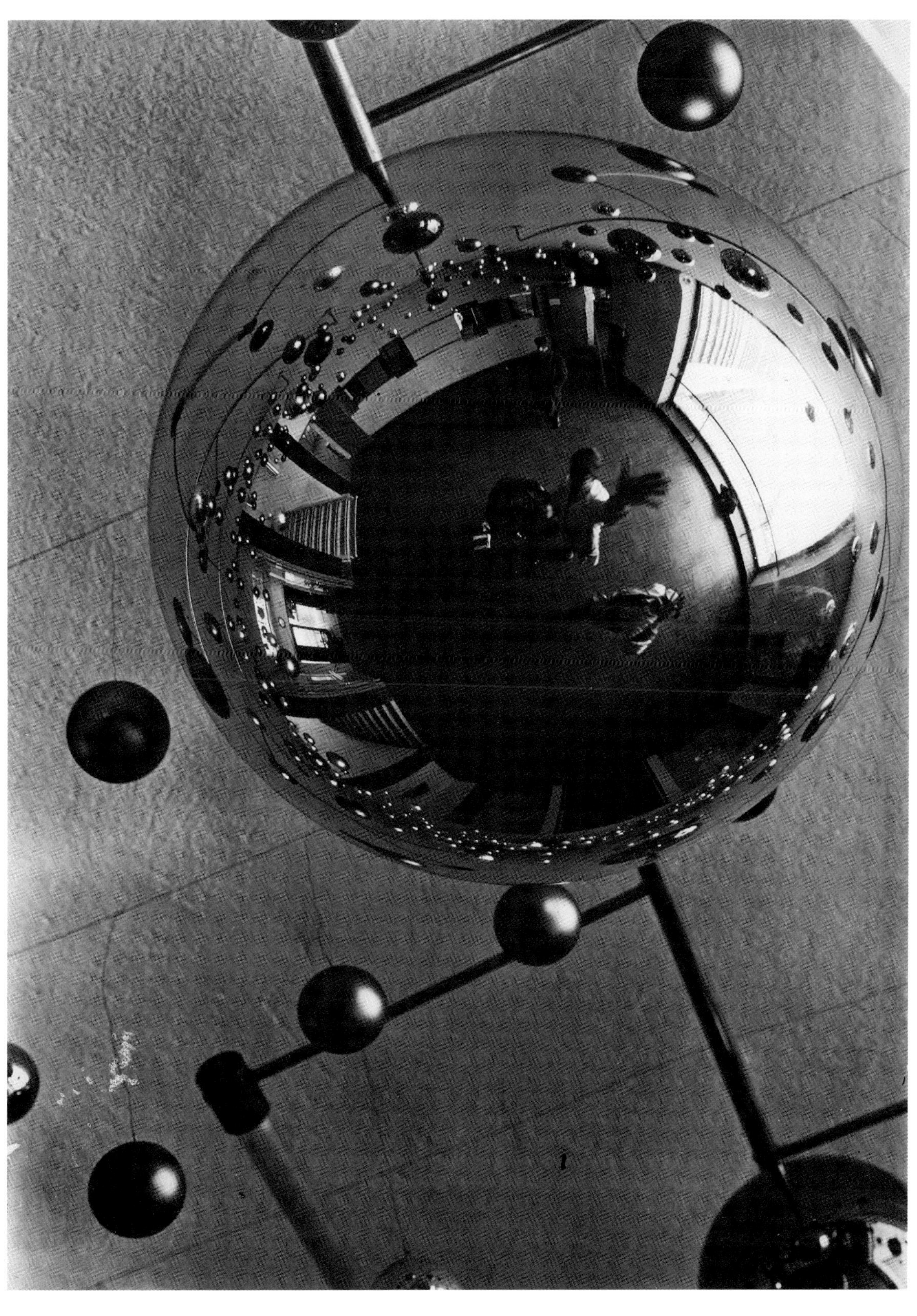

Walter Funkat
Vestibule, metallic festival 1929
gelatin silver photograph
Art Institute of Chicago, Chicago

WEISSENHOF HOUSING ESTATE EXHIBITION, STUTTGART 1927

The fact that the directors of the Bauhaus – Walter Gropius, Hannes Meyer and Ludwig Mies van der Rohe – were all architects reinforced the significant role played by architecture at the school and the profound influence that the Bauhaus has continued to exert upon international artistic developments in the areas of urban design and architecture. The terms 'modern movement' and 'international style' are still widely perceived to refer to the architecture of simple, geometric forms and plain, undecorated surfaces that are free of historical styles, as pioneered by the Bauhaus architects.

Architecture, and Gothic architecture in particular, became a crucial utopian symbol for many postwar German artists and architects. Just as the building of cathedrals provided a social and economic utopian ideal during medieval times, many believed that architecture would help restore social order in the modern era. As Gropius stated in April 1919, in his founding manifesto of the State Bauhaus in Weimar: 'Together let us desire, conceive, and create the new structure of the future, which will embrace architecture and sculpture and painting in one unity and which will one day rise toward heaven from the hands of a million workers like the crystal symbol of a new faith.'[1]

The initial tendency towards Expressionist architecture, however, soon gave way to a pre-occupation with developing a rational modern architecture constructed with new building techniques and materials. When the Bauhaus moved to Dessau, an even greater emphasis was placed on developing standardised modern housing and designing interiors in the most efficient and economic way possible.

Willi Baumeister's poster promoting *The dwelling* exhibition (right), held in Stuttgart in 1927 and organised by the *Werkbund* (German Work Association), boldly illustrates the definitive break that avant-garde architects and designers sought from all traditional living spaces, with their ornate and cluttered interiors. This internationally recognised exhibition brought together architects from around Europe, including Gropius and Mies, and involved the construction of a completely new housing estate in Weissenhof, comprising 21 separate buildings, each designed by a different architect. The aim of the housing exhibition was to radically transform all aspects of modern living in the shift towards new architectural forms and domestic interiors. The emphasis on rationalised architecture and redesigning new interiors inclusive of furniture, lamps, textiles, pictures and modern appliances, reflected the massive social changes brought about by urbanisation and modernisation.

An international exhibition promoting this utopian ideal of transforming society and developing new architectural forms for modern living was taken even further in the Frankfurt exhibition *The dwelling for minimal existence*, held in 1929. Hans Leistikow's depiction of the floor plan for the two-storey terrace houses comprising the housing estates built in Frankfurt in the 1920s starkly illustrates the contemporary ideal of 'minimal existence' (left). This term was used within the context of social policy developed during the Weimar Republic and referred to the bare essentials needed for a decent, everyday existence.[2] Since then, leading German architects of the 1920s, such as Bruno Taut, Martin Wagner and Hans Scharoun, have become renowned for their creation of urban buildings and estates that were sympathetic to the needs of the individual but also effectively solved social issues in a collective sense. JS

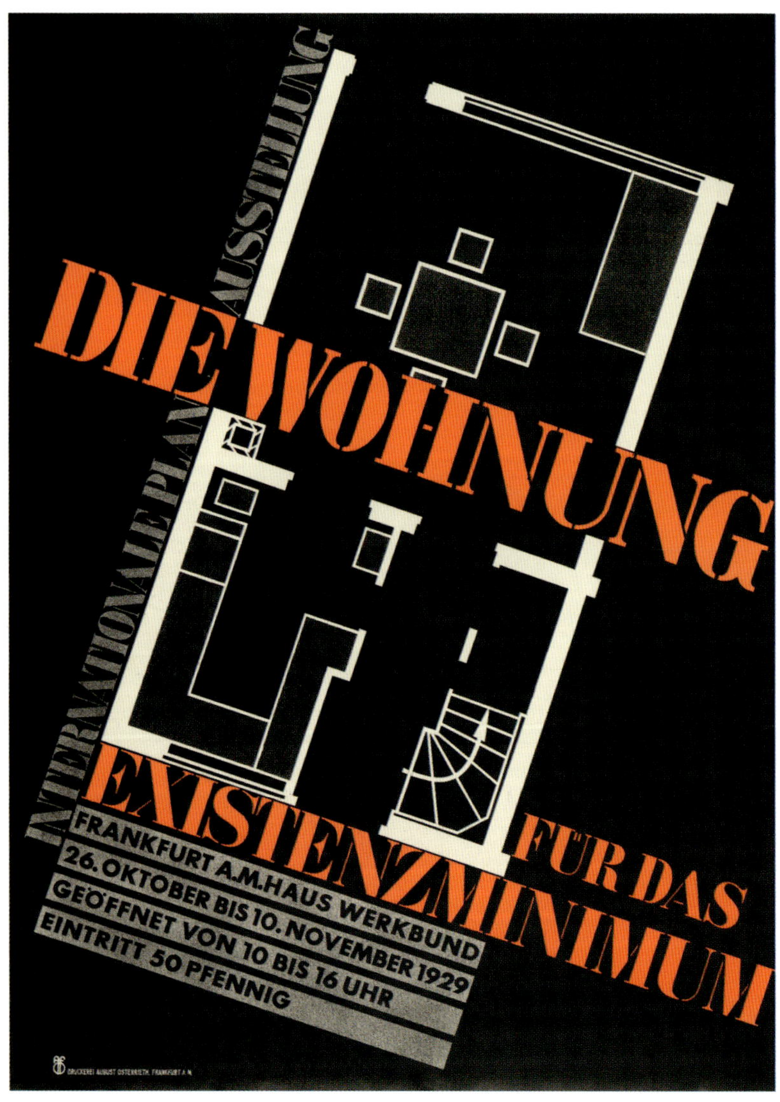

Hans Leistikow
The dwelling for minimal existence 1929
colour lithograph, poster
Kunstbibliothek Berlin, Staatliche Museen zu Berlin

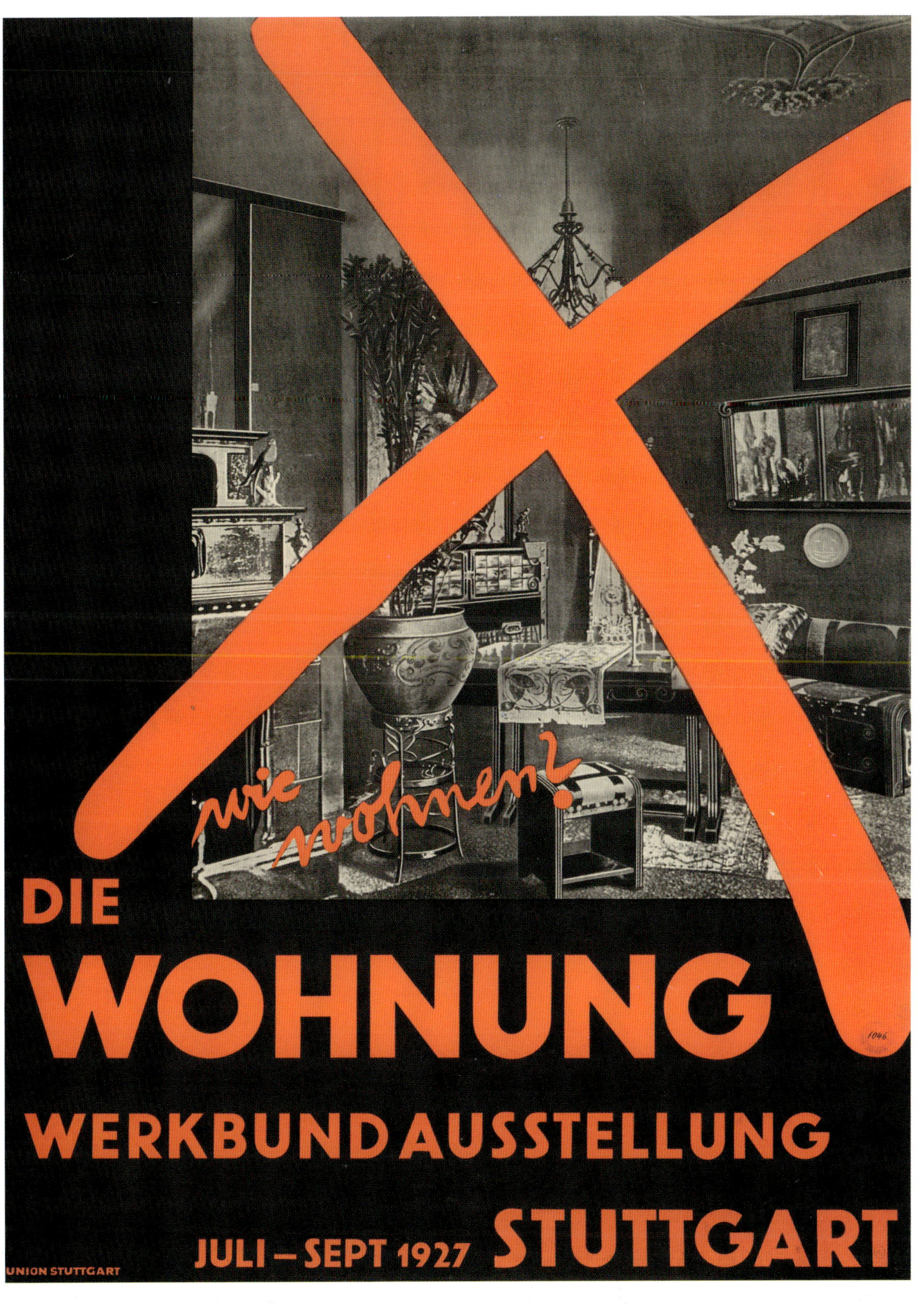

Willi Baumeister
The dwelling [*Werkbund* exhibition, Stuttgart]
1927
colour lithograph, poster
Kunstbibliothek Berlin, Staatliche Museen zu Berlin

MARCEL BREUER

Club chair (B3)

Marcel Breuer developed the first modern tubular steel furniture at the Bauhaus in 1925. He began his career as an apprentice in the furniture workshop in 1920 and was invited by Walter Gropius to join as master of the furniture workshop when the Bauhaus relocated from Weimar to Dessau in 1925. Breuer's first tubular steel chair – the *Club chair (B3)*, otherwise known as the 'Wassily' chair – was inspired by the functionalism of the machine aesthetic and the curved handlebars of his Adler bicycle. This final version, produced in c1928–29, typically featured a nickel-plated, tubular steel frame and easy-to-clean fabric body supports that created an illusion of lightness and visual transparency. However, unlike the original 1925 model, which appeared clumsy and handmade with several visible welds on the frame, this example provided an elegant, modern alternative to traditional chairs and rested upon bent tubular steel runners rather than four legs.[1]

Breuer created the B5 chair in c1926, as a simplified version of his tubular steel chair without armrests. Initially designed to furnish interiors at the Dessau Bauhaus school and the purpose-built houses of the Bauhaus masters, the B5 chair was widely reproduced in Breuer's furniture catalogues of the period. This B5 chair – together with the first cantilevered chairs by Mart Stam and Ludwig Mies van der Rohe – was exhibited at the Weissenhof Housing Estate exhibition held in Stuttgart in 1927 and promoted the idea of standardised product types that were designed for smaller and more efficient living spaces. Breuer produced model interiors for living rooms, based upon standardised workshop-assembled furniture that could be made in different colours with stained, polished or lacquered finishes, such as the wooden table included in this exhibition.[2]

Although he developed his designs at the Bauhaus, Breuer considered his tubular furniture to be his own private endeavour and not the work of the Bauhaus. Tensions erupted when Gropius sought the legal rights to produce and market Breuer's tubular steel furniture on behalf of the Bauhaus in 1926. Breuer attempted to maintain control of his designs and founded the Standard Möbel company in Berlin, arguing that his tubular steel chairs were like paintings created by other Bauhaus masters, which were sold on the open market. Gropius conceded, and the production and marketing of tubular steel furniture remained with Breuer. Despite Gropius's efforts to keep him at the Bauhaus, Breuer resigned in April 1927 and moved to Berlin to work as an architect.

Breuer's use of tubular steel provided functional, lightweight and hygienic pieces of furniture that could be mass-produced and incorporated into any room or setting. Unfortunately, due to economic troubles, Breuer lost control of his designs and few original models of his tubular steel furniture exist today. His designs continue to inspire designers to use contemporary materials and create innovative, functional objects for the modern world. JS

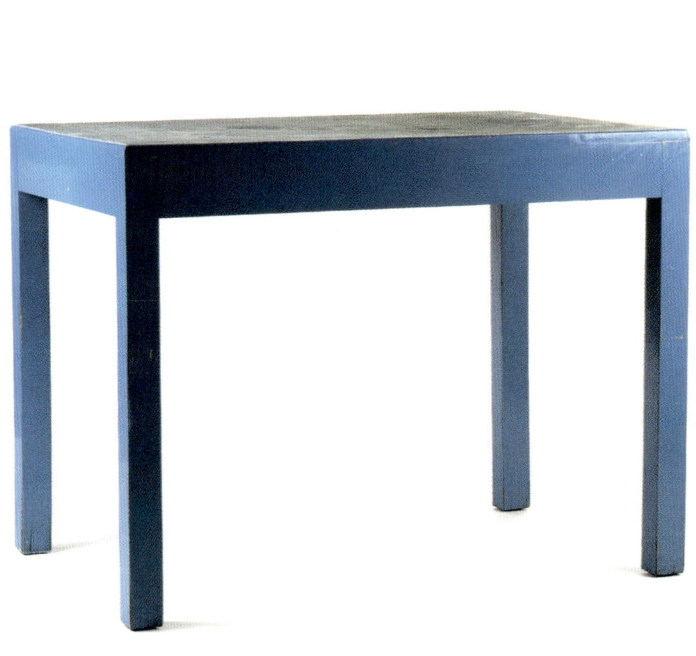

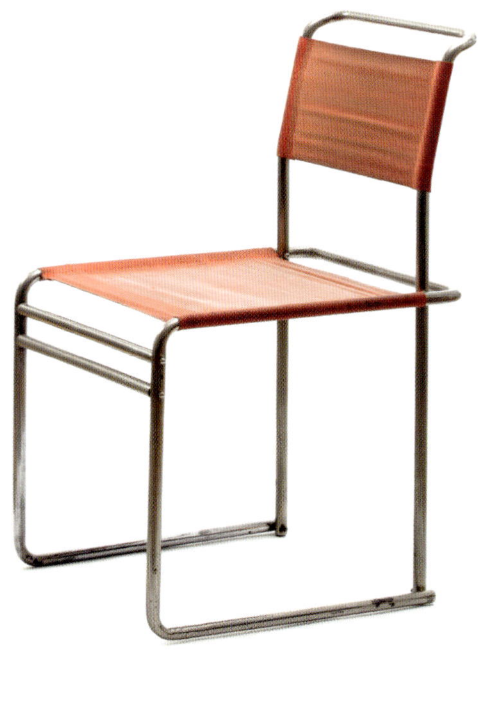

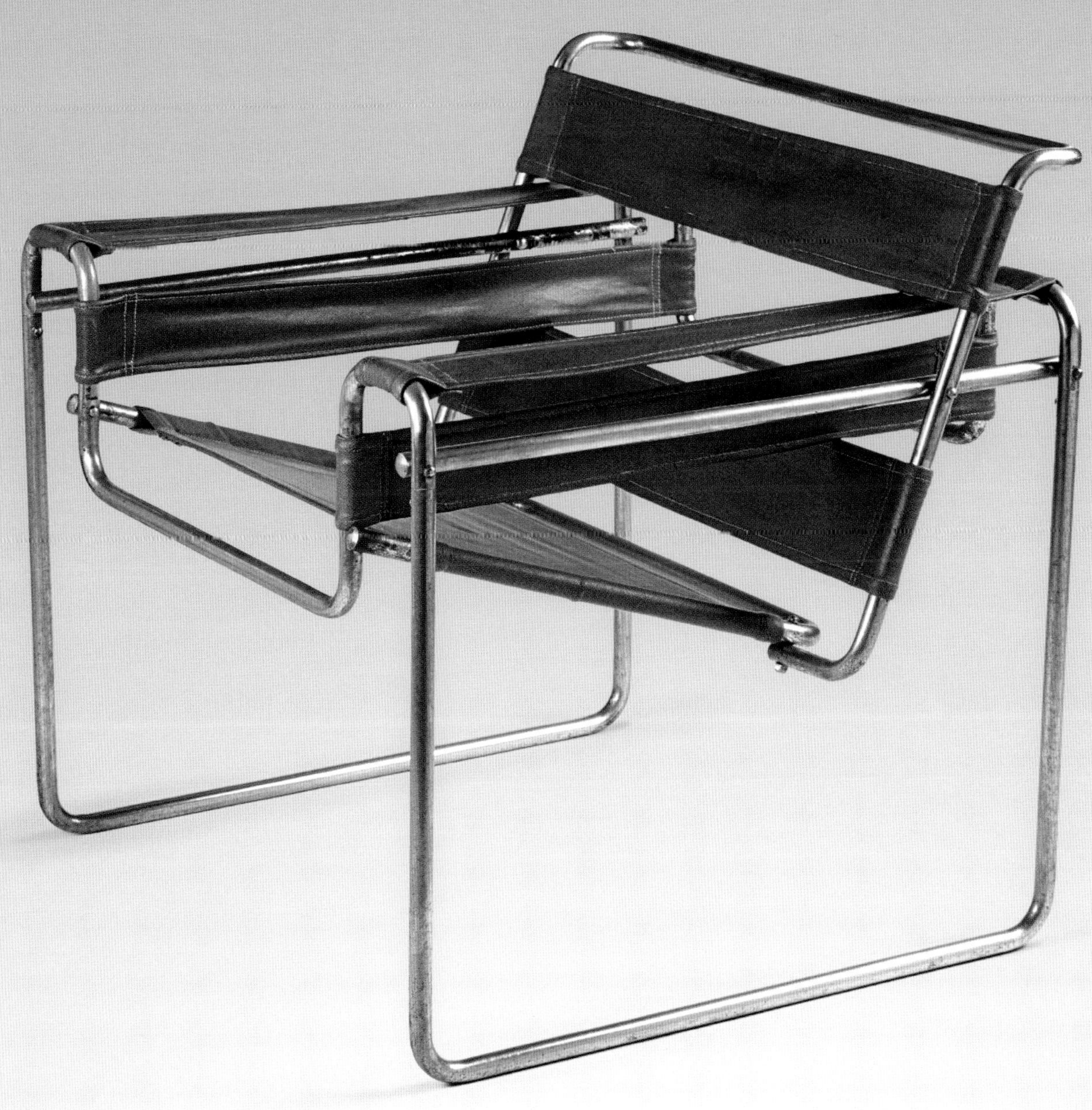

opposite:

Unknown maker
Table c1925–27
lacquered wood
Collection Vitra Design Museum

Marcel Breuer
Chair (B5) designed c1926
nickel-plated tubular steel with red fabric
Collection Vitra Design Museum

Marcel Breuer
Club chair (B3) designed 1925
nickel-plated tubular steel with dark blue oil cloth fabric
Collection Alexander von Vegesack

ERICH DIECKMANN

Dining room suite

Erich Dieckmann made a significant contribution as a designer at the Bauhaus with his pioneering ideas on modular furniture construction. He is primarily known for his standardised wood furniture and designed entire ensembles of dining and living room furniture, characterised by stringent geometric forms. His use of quality hardwoods, such as oak and cherry, and innovative use of cane matting for seat furniture create an impression of sophisticated, modern design that was appropriate for contemporary interiors. However, Dieckmann also drew upon the Bauhaus principles of standardisation and mass production to keep the prices of these pieces of furniture as low as possible.

Joining the Bauhaus in Weimar in 1921, Dieckmann served his apprenticeship in the furniture workshop from 1921 to 1925, together with Marcel Breuer. He remained in Weimar when the Bauhaus moved to Dessau in 1925 and transferred to the *Staatliche Bauhochschule Weimar* (State Building College in Weimar), serving as director of the cabinet-maker's workshop from 1925 to 1930. There his designs for modular furniture types were promoted and manufactured by the Weimar company Bau- und Wohnungskunst. In 1931 Dieckmann was forced to resign from his position, when the National Socialists seized power in Thuringia, although he did continue to work as a freelance cabinet-maker throughout the 1930s. His decision to continue to stay and work in Germany under the Nazi regime may partially account for the fact that he has been excluded from standard histories of modernist design. However, his reputation as a leading designer of early modern furniture is gradually being restored as museums acquire his pieces.

This *Dining room suite* c1927–28 is one of the few complete surviving sets recorded from Dieckmann's early application of modern design ideas. It was purchased by the Souhami family in Heidelberg in 1927 and brought to Sydney when the family immigrated to Australia from Germany in 1938. The furniture remained in the family home at 14 The Parapet, Castlecrag (designed by Walter Burley Griffin in 1924), and has been in a private collection in Melbourne since 1997.[1] The suite has recently been restored to its original colour – according to the current owner, traces of orange paint were found underneath the previous layers of pale grey-green paint – and the use of a bright orange colour scheme recalls the colour theories taught at the Bauhaus and represented in other objects included in this exhibition.[2] JS

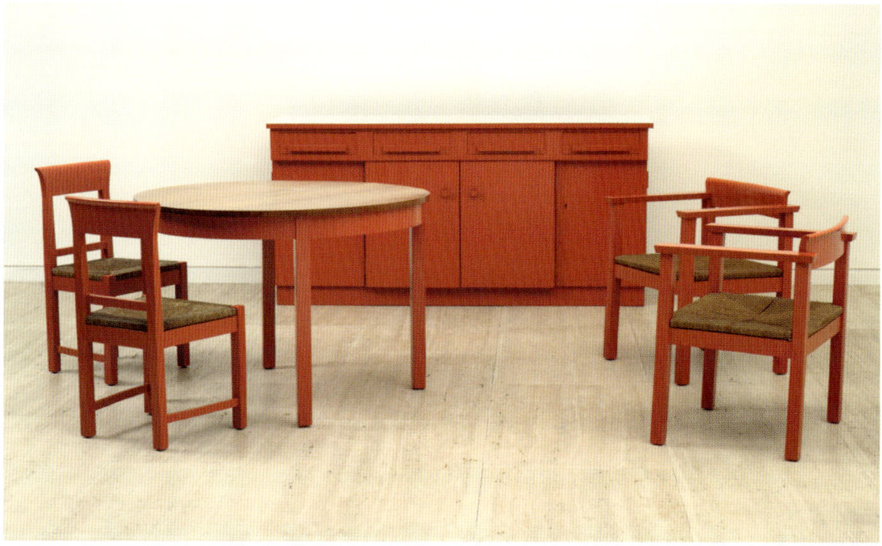

Erich Dieckmann
Dining room suite designed c1926, this example produced c1927–28
Private collection, Melbourne

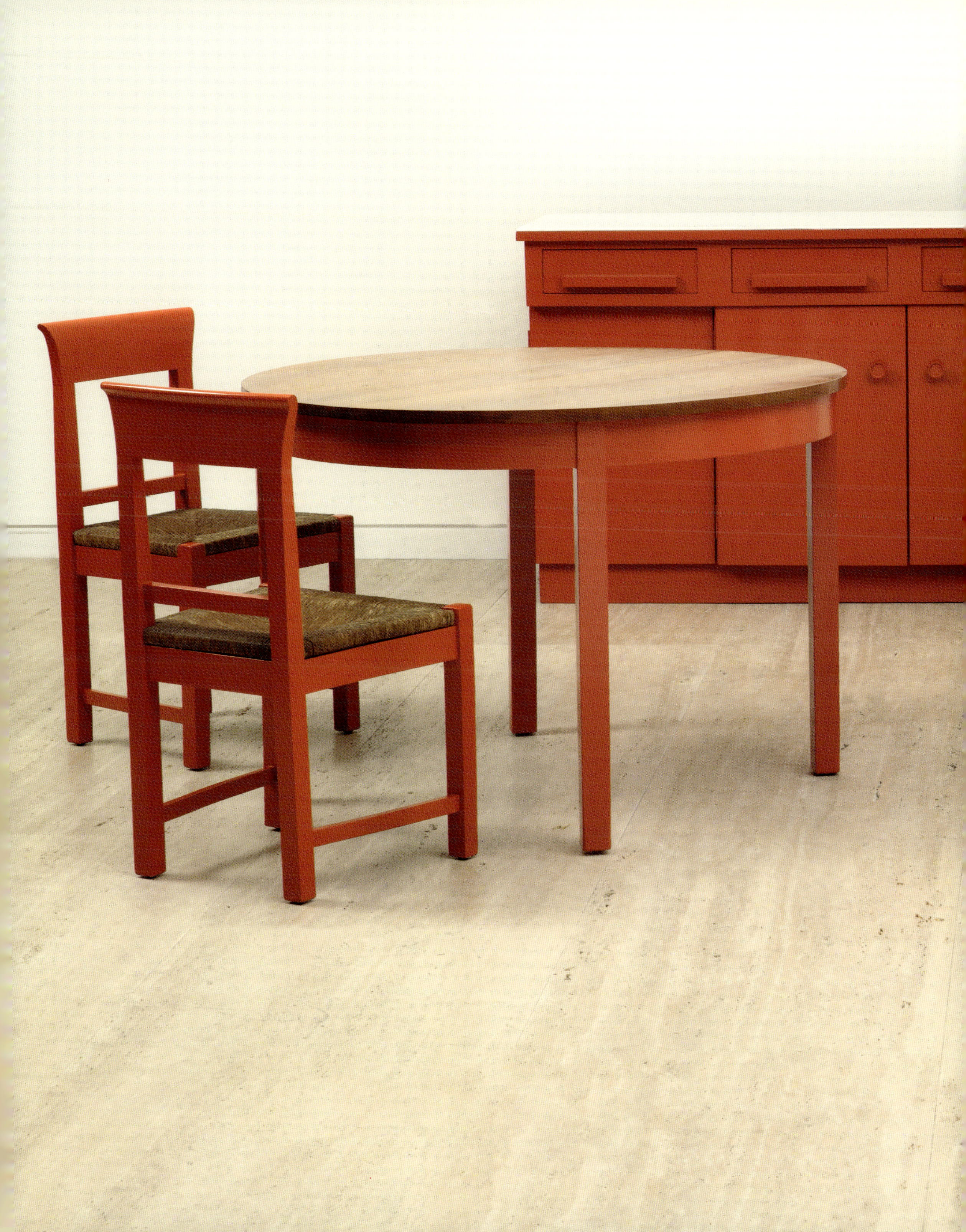

WILHELM WAGENFELD and CARL JAKOB JUCKER

Table lamp (MT 9/ME 1)

Wilhelm Wagenfeld and Carl Jakob Jucker's *Table lamp (MT 9/ME 1)*, manufactured in the metal workshop of the Weimar Bauhaus in 1924, has become an icon of modern industrial design, with its simplified form, perfect geometry and economic use of materials. The lamp embodies the essential ideal of the Bauhaus: that form follows function.

Wagenfeld and Jucker studied at the Bauhaus following the reorganisation of the metal workshop under László Moholy-Nagy in 1923. Together with embracing the machine aesthetic espoused by Moholy-Nagy, students were encouraged to use unusual metal combinations and explore new materials, such as glass and plexiglass, to create utilitarian objects. When it came to the creation of objects that could be mass-produced, Moholy-Nagy encouraged a collaborative approach, rather than an individual one. In this instance, Jucker created the preliminary designs and conducted experiments for the jointly designed table lamp, while Wagenfeld executed the final product in two variations: one designed in 1923–24 with a glass base and stem (MT 9/ME 1) and the other designed in 1924 with a metal base and stem (MT 8/ME 2). The ME 1 featured glass components that emphasised the functionality of design by allowing viewers to see the inner workings of the lamp, while the ME 2 featured nickel-plated brass components that created a sleek, industrial look. The translucent glass dome used on both versions allowed for a mixture of ambient light and direct light for reading.

Objects created in the Bauhaus metal workshop appeared finished and smooth, as if they had been machine-manufactured,

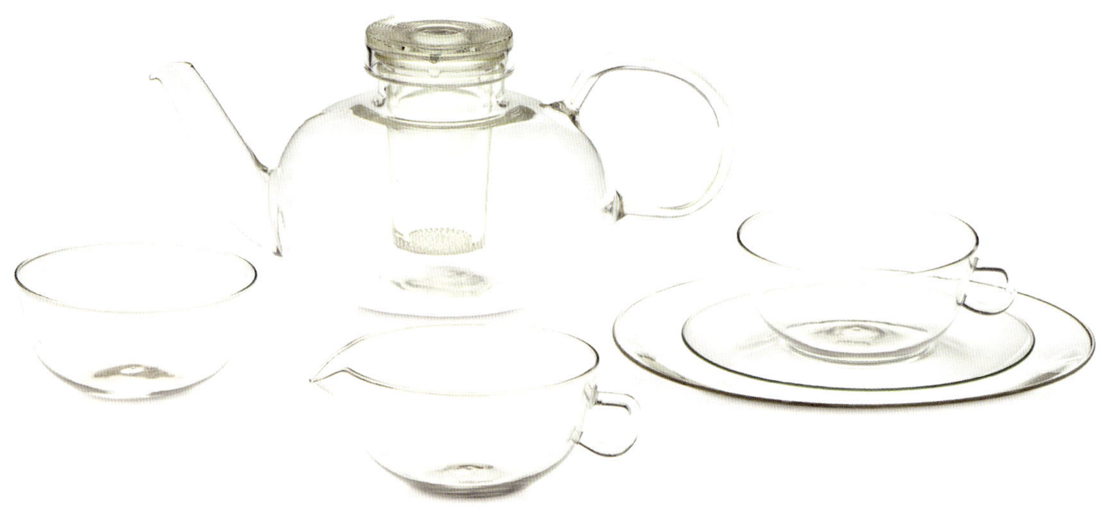

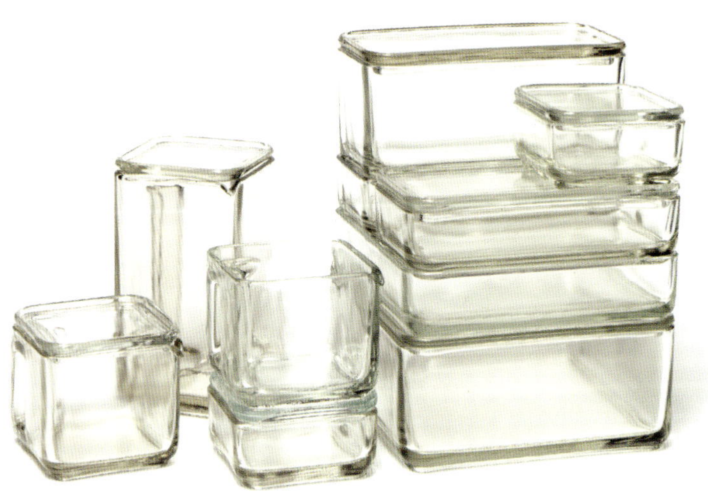

yet they were made by hand and expensive to produce. This exceptionally rare and early example of the lamp was owned by the avant-garde photographer Florence Henri, who had herself been a student at the Bauhaus before she moved to Paris to concentrate on photography. Henri acquired the lamp in 1927, following her studies at the Bauhaus, and took it with her to her studio in Paris. The lamp remained in her possession until Die Neue Sammlung – The International Design Museum Munich, purchased it from her estate in 2006.

Wagenfeld went on to become one of the most successful Bauhaus designers of metal and glassware, and his popularity allowed him to continue working throughout the years under the Nazi regime. He worked as both a teacher and product designer in the 1930s, creating modernist design classics such as his heat-resistant tea service in 1930 and his well-known *Kubus-Geschirr* stacking containers in 1938 (both opposite), which are still in production today. In these designs he continued to adhere to the functionalist principles of modernism, yet some aspects of his work in the 1930s have been controversially associated with forms of art promoted by the Nazis, thus illustrating the dilemma faced by modernist artists who continued to work in Germany during the Third Reich.[1] JS

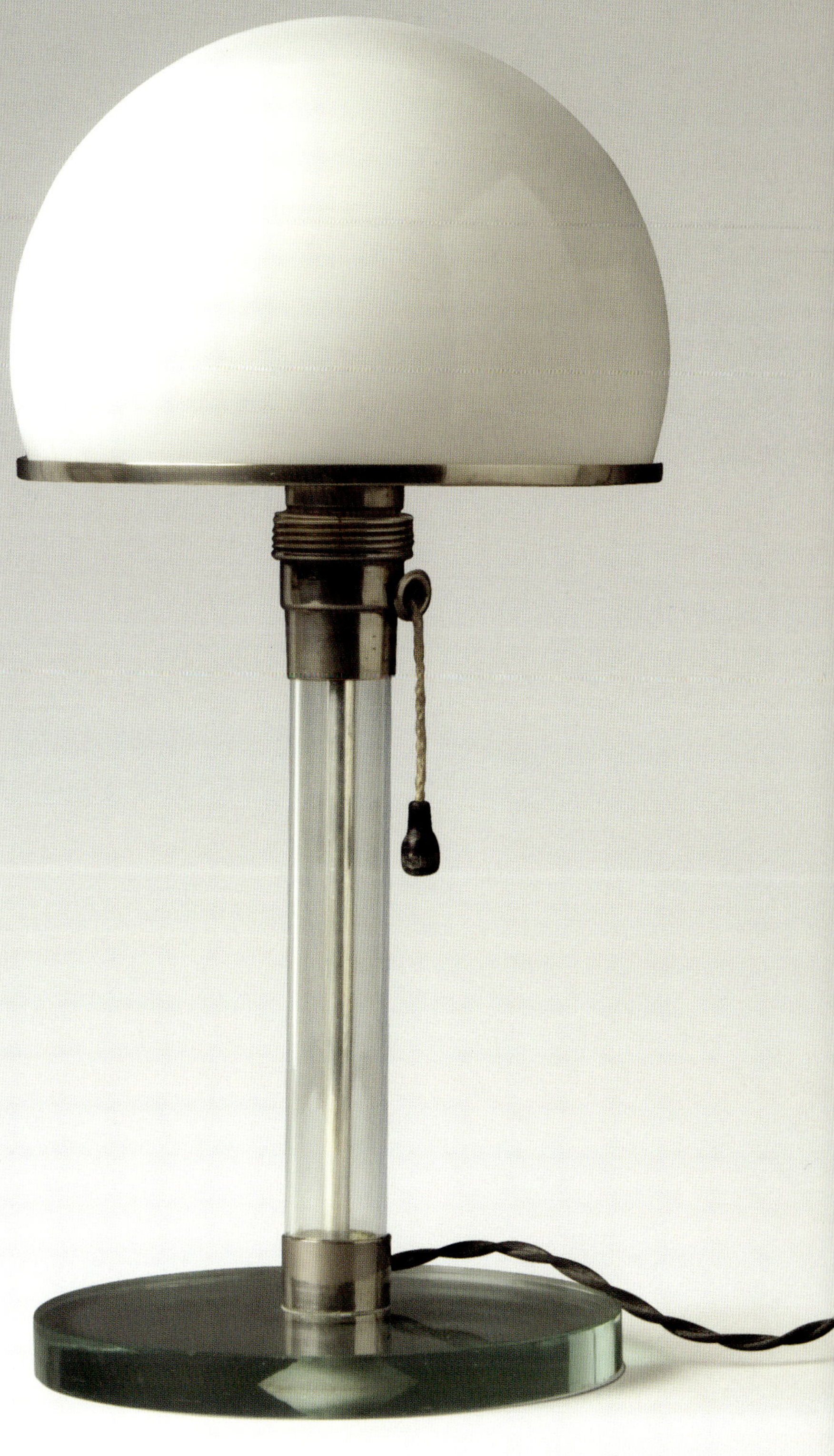

opposite:

Wilhelm Wagenfeld
Tea service 1930
heat-resistant glass
National Gallery of Victoria, Melbourne

Wilhelm Wagenfeld
'Kubus-Geschirr' stacking set of containers 1938
pressed glass
National Gallery of Australia, Canberra

Wilhelm Wagenfeld and Carl Jakob Jucker
Table lamp (MT 9/ME 1) 1923–24
nickel-plated brass, opalescent glass with plate-glass base
Die Neue Sammlung – The International Design Museum Munich

MARIANNE BRANDT

Desk set

Marianne Brandt was one of the Bauhaus's most talented students and metalwork designers. Encouraged by László Moholy-Nagy to design objects for mass production, Brandt produced a range of functional, geometric-inspired works that successfully exemplified the ways in which art and machine technology could come together. Elegant, smooth and streamlined in appearance, as well as highly original from a design perspective, many of the objects she created for use in the modern home or office have become icons of 20th-century design.

Brandt joined the metal workshop at the Bauhaus in 1923, having already earned a degree in painting. She belonged to the new generation of Bauhaus students who seized the opportunity to explore the new possibilities of creating everyday objects inspired by machine-age aesthetics and technology. After completing her studies, Brandt continued to follow Moholy-Nagy's example of combining geometric forms based on the influence of International Constructivism with mechanised manufacture.[1] In 1927, after spending nine months in Paris, she returned to Dessau and became an associate of the metal workshop, conducting negotiations with outside firms who had been assigned to manufacture Bauhaus designs.[2] Brandt continued to play a prominent role in the history of the Bauhaus Dessau, serving as acting head of the metal workshop from April 1928 until June 1929, when the metal studio merged with the furniture and murals workshops.

This desk set was produced around 1930, at the time that Brandt was asked to modernise products for Ruppelwerk, a large metalware manufacturer in Gotha, Thuringa. She was responsible for the design of small objects made of enamelled sheet metal, such as napkin holders, stamp boxes, clocks, ashtrays and the objects included in this set – pen trays, inkwells and blotters. Affordable, distinctively modern and finished in a range of bold, attractive colours, Brandt's designs of the early 1930s proved to be highly marketable, and these objects represent the successful application of the Bauhaus ideal of conceiving objects for industrial serial production. JS

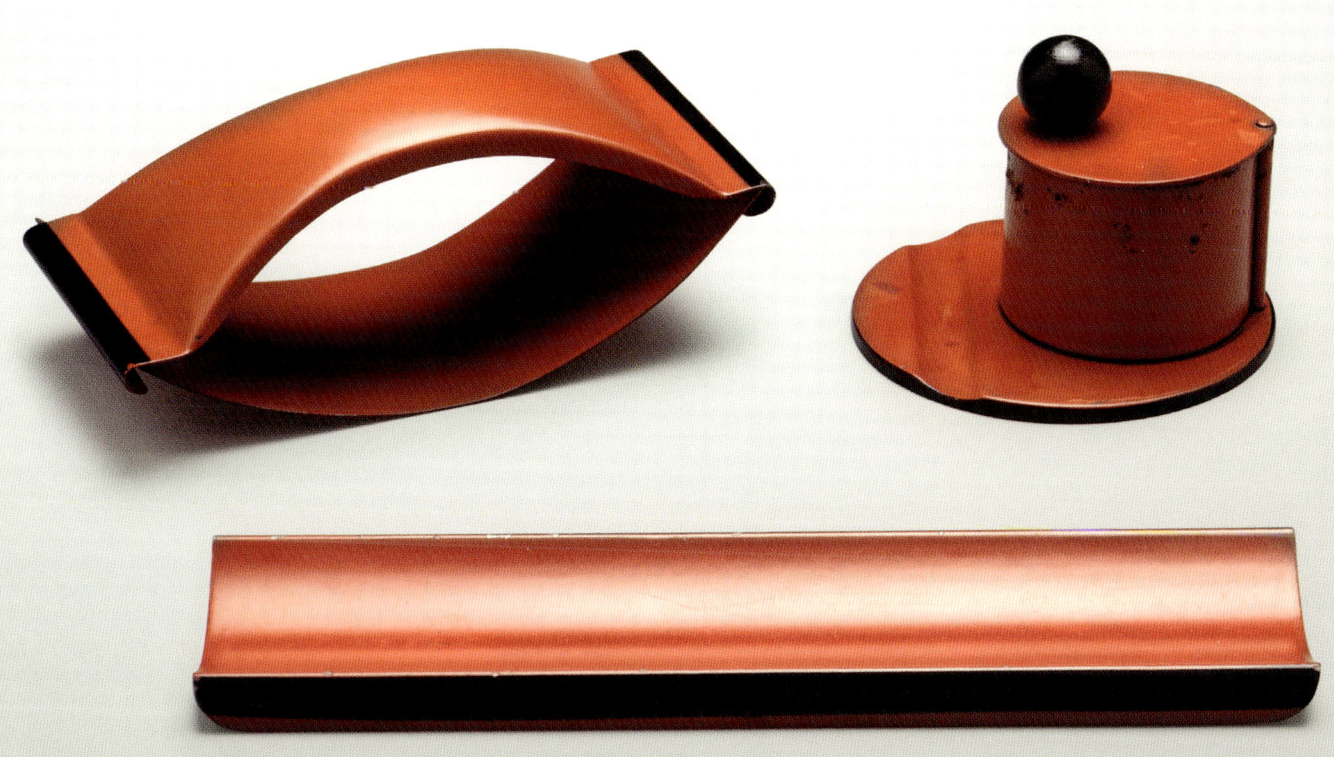

Marianne Brandt
Desk set 1930–31
enamelled metal, glass, paper
Powerhouse Museum, Sydney

GUNTA STÖLZL

Textile design

Gunta Stölzl was the first and only woman to become a Bauhaus master, and achieved the position of master of the textile workshop when the school moved to Dessau. Her textile designs, wall hangings and rugs are highly regarded in the history of modern design and explore the infinite possibilities of geometric abstraction that was inherent in so many objects created in the textile workshop. *Textile design* c1926 is the most highly resolved composition included among the striking group of textile designs in this exhibition. Stölzl's formalist emphasis on colour harmonies and grid-like arrangements of geometric shapes reveals the influence of Paul Klee, who taught preliminary courses at the Weimar Bauhaus on colour and composition, and whose teachings found particular resonance with works produced in the textile workshop.[1]

Stölzl played a prominent role as a student in the weaving workshop, which provided female art students with the opportunity to participate at the Bauhaus. In 1920, it evolved into a textile workshop and specialised in embroidery, decorative edging, crocheting, sewing and macramé, with a strong emphasis on decoration, decorative drawing and textile techniques. These traditions continued at the Dessau Bauhaus, however, the emphasis shifted from the creation of handcrafted and woven objects to the production of innovative textile designs that could stand on their own as decorative items or be utilised in the production of Bauhaus objects from other workshops.

Members of the textile workshop collaborated with students in the joinery workshop to provide furnishing fabrics, carpets and wall coverings that complemented Bauhaus furniture. An even greater emphasis was placed on developing fabric prototypes for manufacture when Hannes Meyer succeeded Walter Gropius as director of the Bauhaus in 1928. Students such as Hilde Reindl and Lena Bergner experimented with new materials and processes which resulted in the production of textile designs with unique patterns that were based on innovative arrangements of elementary forms and complementary colours. These textile samples combine fibres with diverse properties – such as wool, silk, cotton and synthetic materials – as students were encouraged to experiment with creating durable and inexpensive fabrics for mass production. The commercial application of these designs led to the establishment of the *Bauhausstoffe* (Bauhaus Fabrics) brand.[2]

During the late 1920s, female students continued to dominate the textile workshop, reinforcing conventional attitudes towards gender stereotypes that were at odds with the supposed modern values of the Bauhaus. Yet women such as Marianne Brandt, Margarete Marks and Anni Albers played a leading role at the Bauhaus, producing innovative and highly original designs in metal, ceramics and textiles. Stölzl's 12-year affiliation with the school ended in 1931, as the political atmosphere intensified, and a commemorative issue in the series of Bauhaus publications was devoted to her in honour of her distinguished career at the school.[3] JS

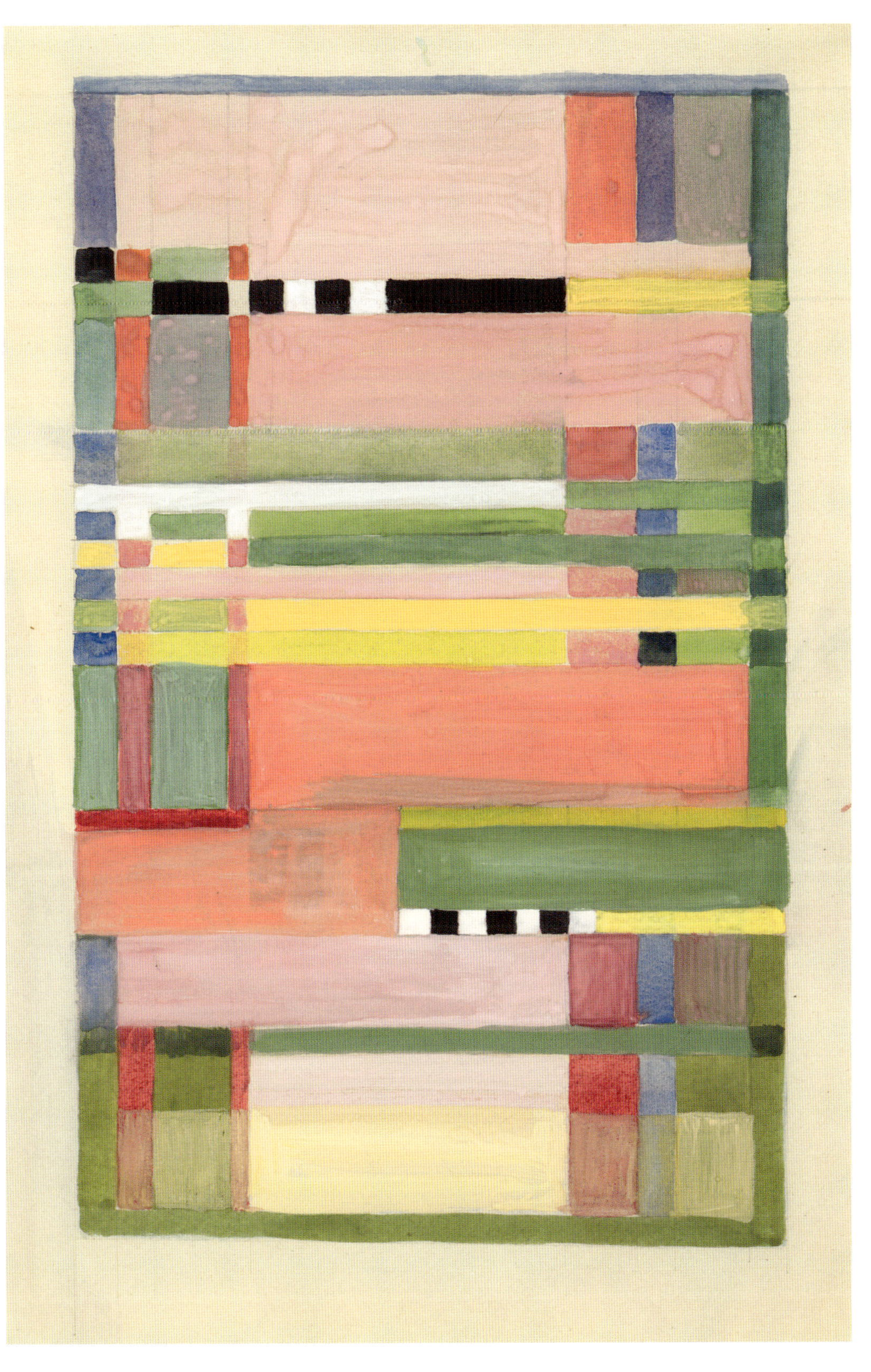

Gunta Stölzl
Textile design c1926
watercolour, gouache, pencil
National Gallery of Australia, Canberra

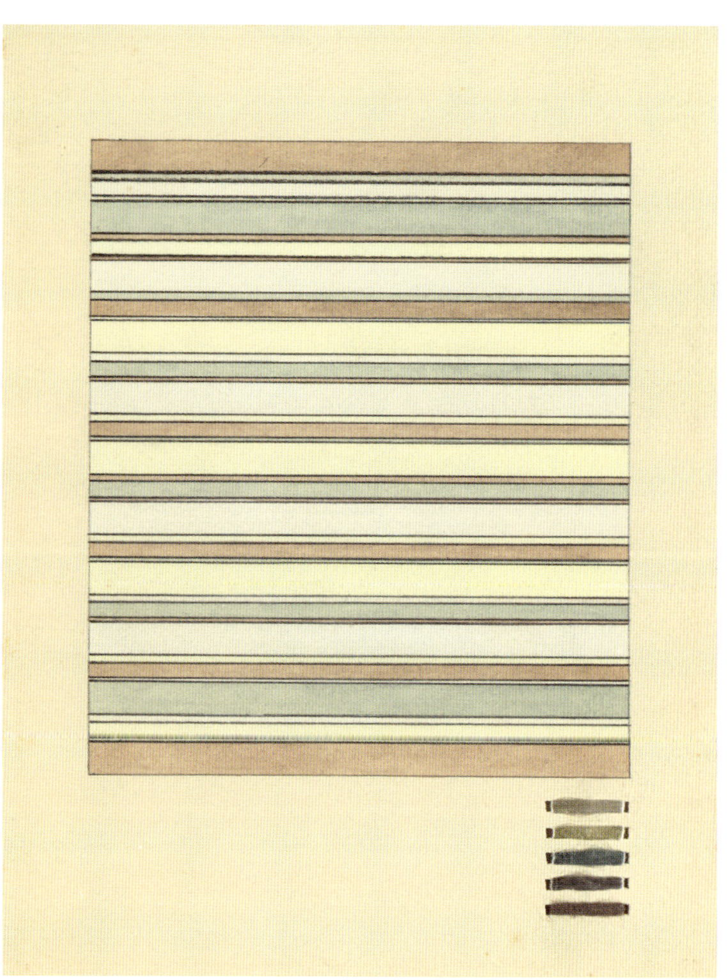

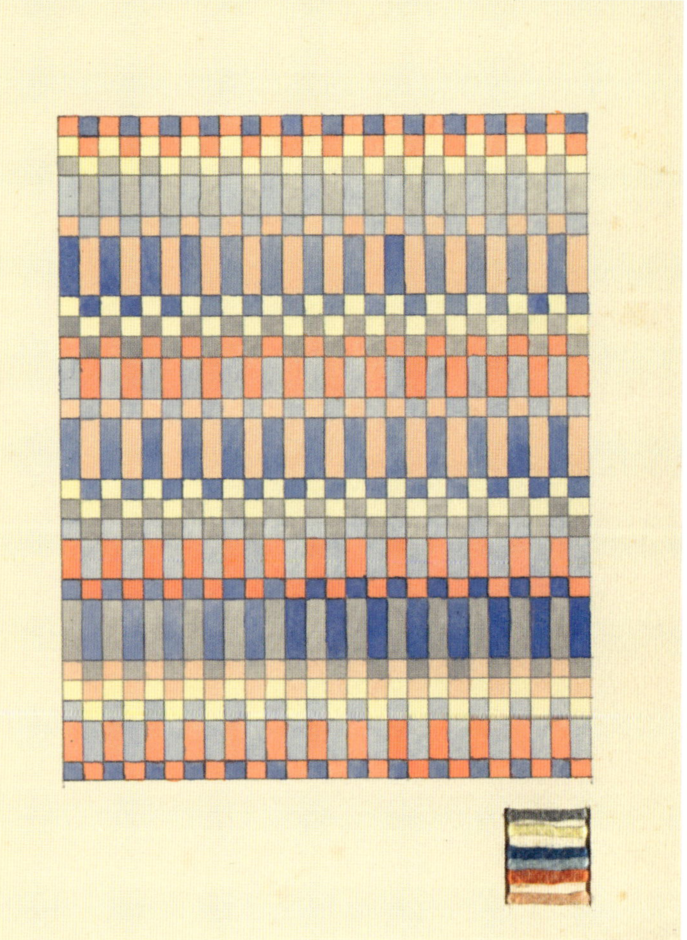

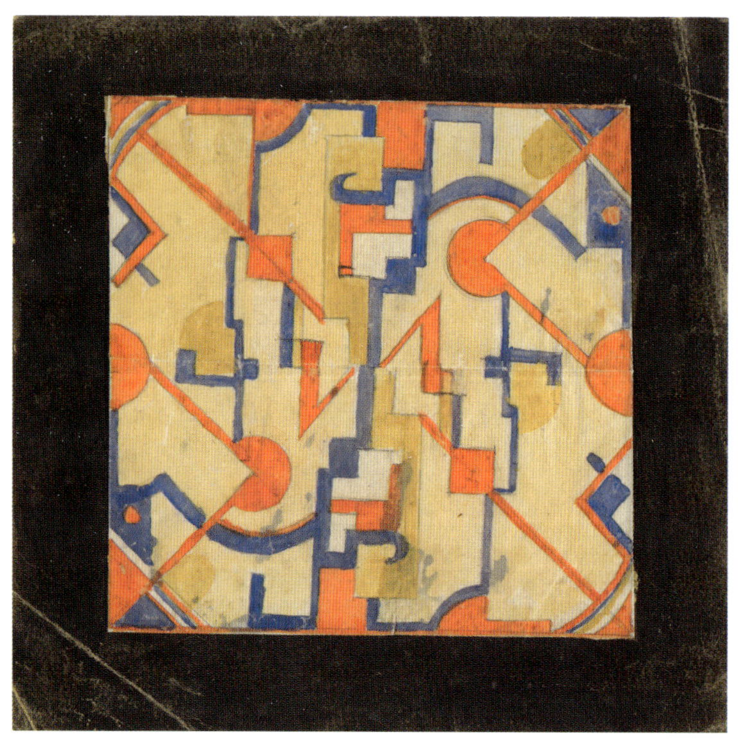

above:

Lena Bergner
Textile designs with yarn samples 1928
watercolour, pencil, wool
National Gallery of Australia, Canberra

left:

Hilde Reindl
Textile design c1928
watercolour, pencil
National Gallery of Australia, Canberra

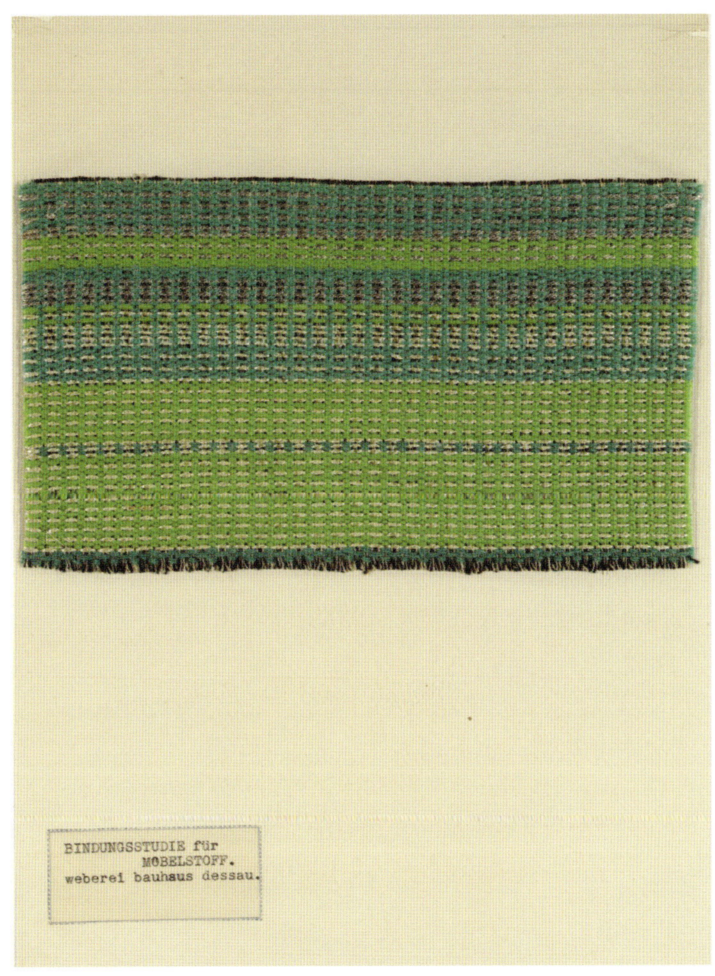

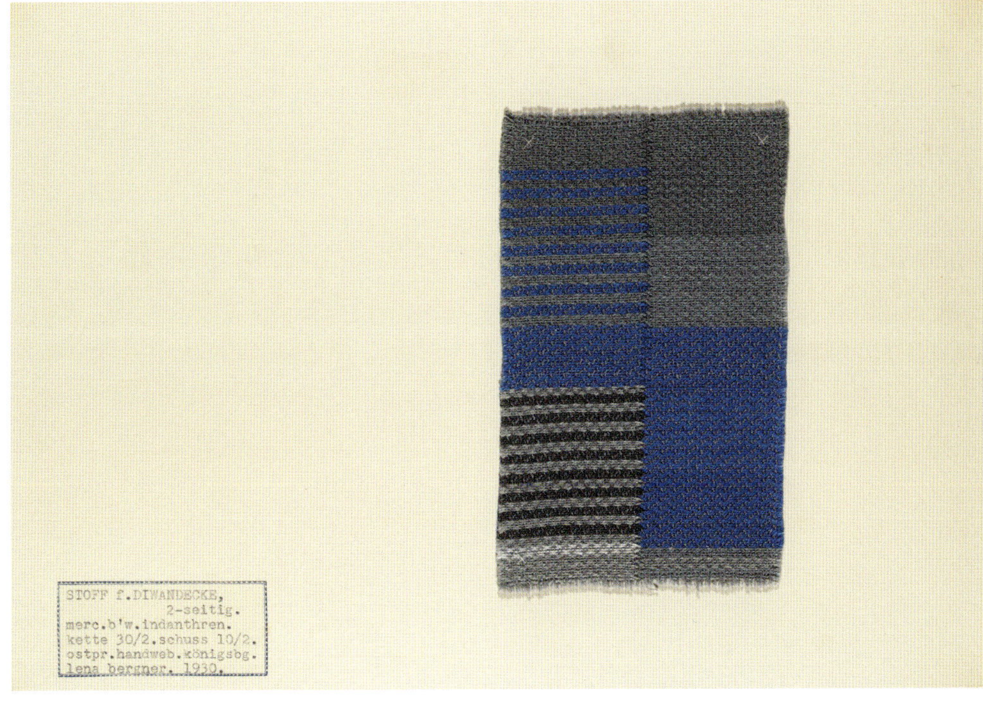

above:

Bauhaus Dessau
Weaving study, furnishing fabric swatch c1926
wool, cotton, rayon fabric
National Gallery of Australia, Canberra

left:

Lena Bergner
Fabric swatch c1926
silk, mercerised cotton
National Gallery of Australia, Canberra

CONSTRUCTIVISM

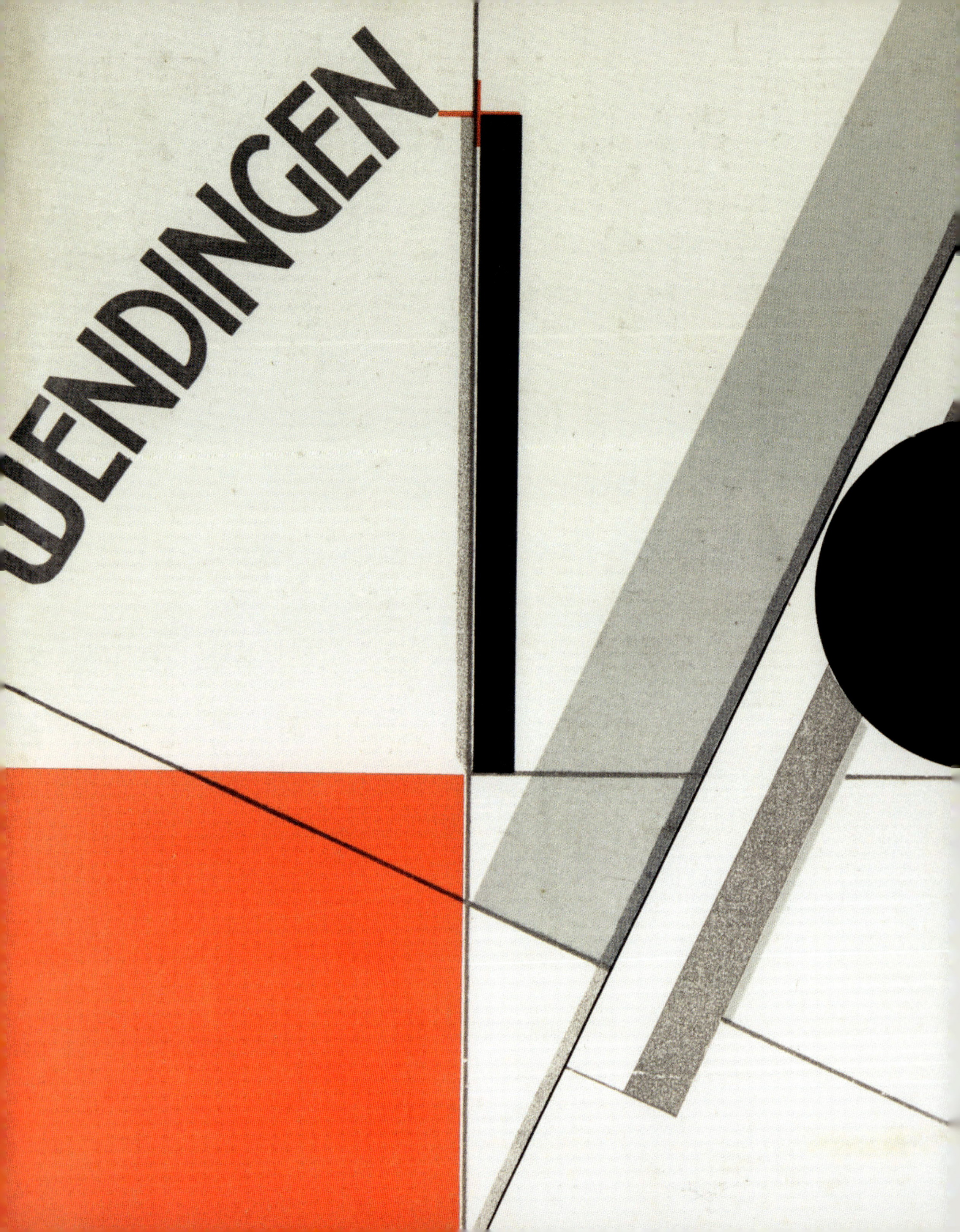
WENDINGEN

CONSTRUCTIVISM AND THE MACHINE AESTHETIC

Petra Kayser

For a brief period from 1922 to 1923, Germany was the centre of the art movement that came to be known as International Constructivism. Having emerged in Russia after the First World War through the work of Vladimir Tatlin, Alexander Rodchenko and El Lissitzky, Constructivism developed in Germany around the ideas and practices of three artists: Lissitzky, László Moholy-Nagy and Theo van Doesburg. They came from abroad to be part of the vibrant culture of artistic experimentation in the young Weimar Republic. Each had a distinct formal and theoretical approach to abstraction, and their ideas were published and debated in avant-garde circles. Constructivists were not, however, mere formalists, aloof from the political and social realities of their day. They shared a utopian belief in social reform, and saw abstract art as playing a central role in this process.

Lissitzky arrived in Berlin in late 1921, having left a teaching position at Russia's state art and technical school Vkhutemas in Moscow, the Russian equivalent of the Bauhaus. Inspired by Kazimir Malevich and Suprematism, Lissitzky developed his idea of non-objective art through *Prouns*, pictorial constructions of geometric forms, lines and planes arranged in relationships of dynamic tension (pp 176–7). Lissitzky was committed to a radical transformation of art on all fronts: painting, typography and book design, interior and stage design, and architecture. He was instrumental in making Russian modernism accessible to European audiences through publications and exhibitions, including the *First Russian art exhibition* at Berlin's Van Diemen Gallery in 1922. This was the earliest large-scale exposure of Russian Constructivism in the West, which brought the movement to the attention of the German press and public, and helped to establish it as an international movement.

Hungarian artist Moholy-Nagy came to Berlin in 1920, attracted not only by the avant-garde art produced in the city, but also by Germany's highly developed technology and print industry. Like Lissitzky, he was committed to creating a new abstract art for a dynamic, modern society. Moholy-Nagy investigated formal issues of visual representation through line, colour, light and transparency. He promoted the unity of art and technology, and explored new techniques in the production of images. Few artists have worked in such a broad range of media as Moholy-Nagy, who experimented in painting, drawing, graphic design, typography, stage design, sculpture, film and photography. Invited by Walter Gropius to join the Bauhaus in 1923, Moholy-Nagy taught there for the following five years, instructing students in the preliminary course and the metal workshop. His teaching during this vibrant period at the Bauhaus, along with his art practice and writings, made him a particularly influential figure in avant-garde art of the 1920s.

Van Doesburg established his career as an artist and critic in Leiden. In 1917 he formed de Stijl, a movement directed towards the creation of a visual language based on geometric form, line and primary colours, and also published a journal under this name

El Lissitzky
Cover for the journal *Wendingen*
no 11, 1921 (detail)

that promoted abstract art. In 1922 van Doesburg moved to Weimar, the home of the Bauhaus, and became involved in debates and events, including the first International Congress of Progressive Artists held in Düsseldorf in May 1922. Instead of forming a union of avant-garde artists, however, the congress precipitated the artists' conflicting theories and intentions. At the end of a heated debate between various participants, van Doesburg, Lissitzky and the avant-garde film-maker Hans Richter signed a statement that summarised Constructivist aims. It declared their resolve to move away from the 'tyranny of the individual' and replace the traditional and romantic idea of the artist with an artists' collective, and to work on the 'systematisation of the means of expression to produce results that are universally comprehensible'.[1] Although van Doesburg organised a second International Congress of Constructivists and Dadaists in Weimar, in September 1922, the idea of a union of artists remained unrealised.

Unlike Dada, Constructivism did not attack or subvert art, but extended it in new directions through experimentation and the exploration of new technologies. Constructivists embraced the machine as a means for creating art, and were excited by the mechanical production process that had the potential to reproduce images on a mass scale. Mechanical and technological analogies were used to describe the process of making art, and artists thought of themselves as engineers or constructors. Lissitzky wanted to produce pictures without signs of individual expression, and considered his *Prouns* as articulations of space and energy. Similarly, Moholy-Nagy experimented with geometric forms and planes in abstract space to find a purely non-representational art. His criticism of such artists as Wassily Kandinsky was that their abstract compositions triggered imaginative associations. In contrast, Moholy-Nagy wanted to create a visual language without reference to the artist's subjectivity, and aimed to remove all traces of the artist's hand. This culminated in his enamel pictures of 1923, which were made by a machine according to instructions that the artist gave to a factory supervisor over the telephone.

In his book *Painting, photography, film*, first published in 1925, Moholy-Nagy covers various techniques that can be used to produce new images, including the photogram, or 'camera-less photograph', in which objects are placed directly onto photographic paper and exposed to light to create an image. Moholy-Nagy goes on to argue that the camera should be utilised in more innovative ways. He explains that photography and film were still used in an imitative manner, reproducing what we see and hear around us: 'The new function is shrouded in traditional form' because photographic images are composed according to 'the painterly trend of the moment'.[2] Moholy-Nagy saw the camera as a means to break habits of perception that had been reinforced by a long history of pictorial representation. Just as painting could now 'free itself with increasing confidence from the representation of objective elements'[3], the possibilities of the camera could be exploited in order to produce new images and experiences.

The camera records an optical truth that we do not normally perceive. Our vision is programmed to recognise objects; we register visual data, and concepts are imposed in the act of perception in order to make sense of the world. In contrast, as Moholy-Nagy stated, 'the camera reproduces the purely optical image and therefore shows the optically true distortions, deformations, foreshortenings'.[4] Moholy-Nagy exploited the effect of

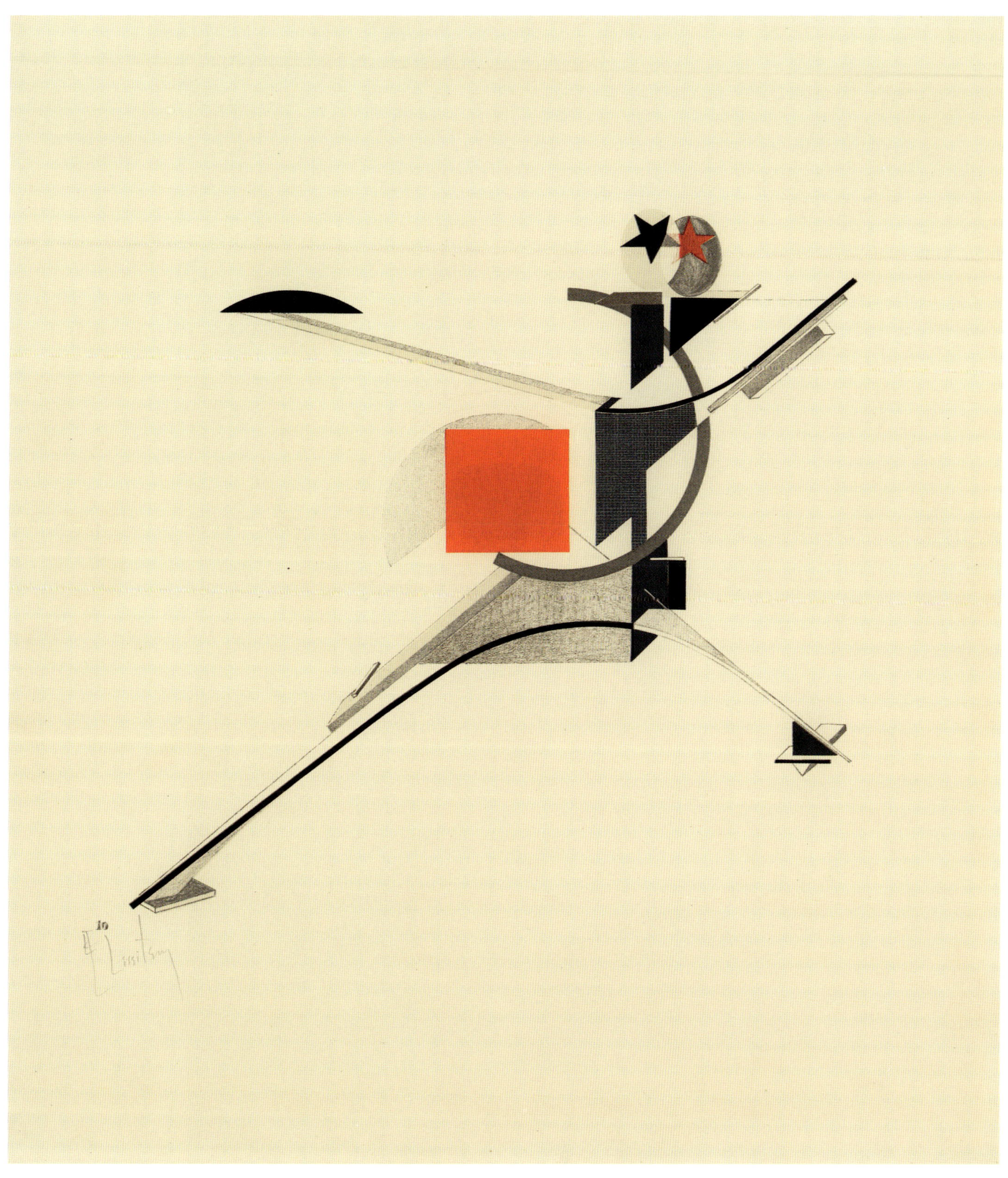

El Lissitzky
New man 1923
from the portfolio **Victory over the sun** 1923
colour lithograph
National Gallery of Australia, Canberra

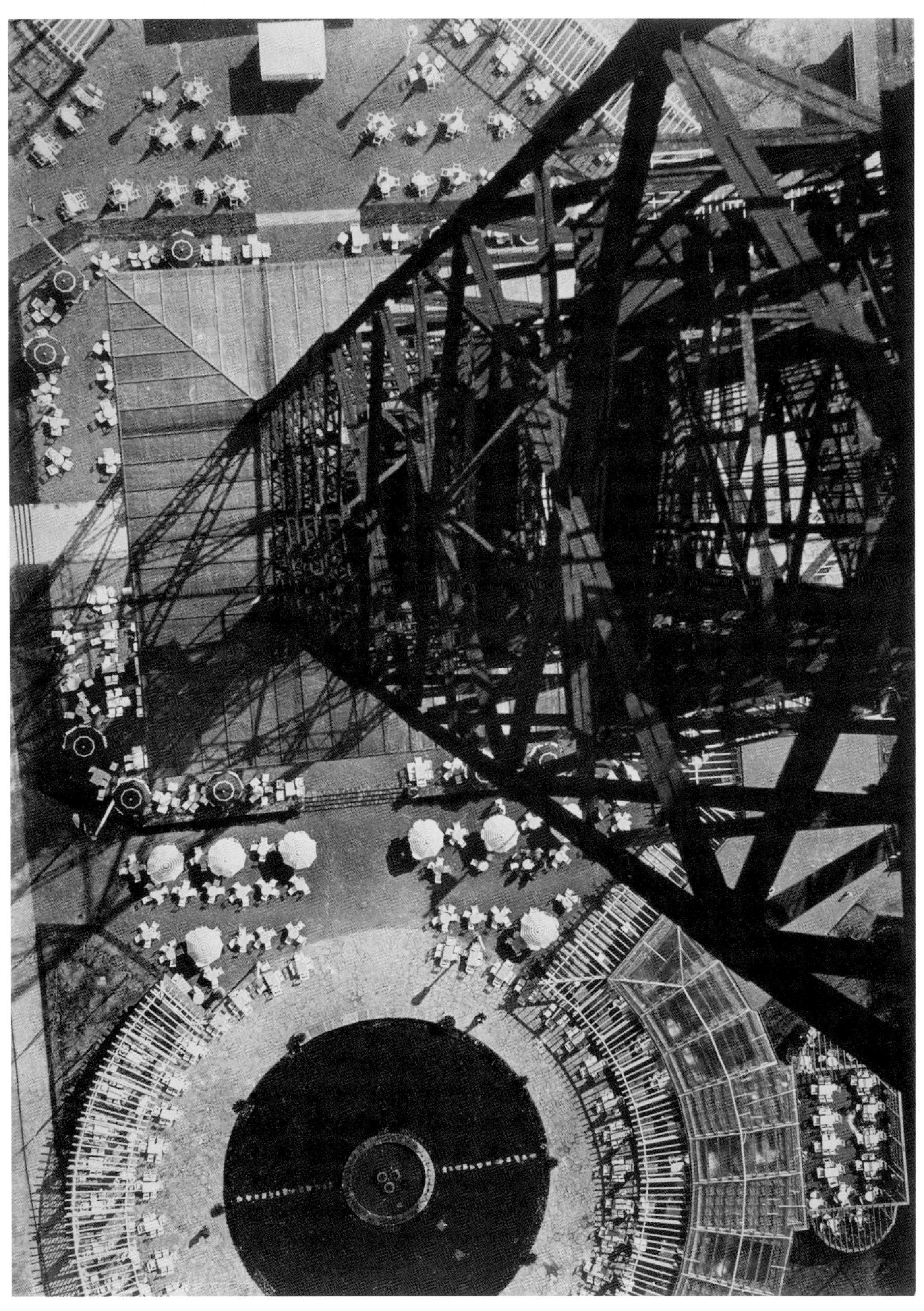

László Moholy-Nagy
Berlin radio tower c1928
gelatin silver photograph
Art Institute of Chicago, Chicago

unusual perspectives and extreme close-ups to make familiar objects look strange, deferring recognition to allow us to see the world in a new way. In *Berlin radio tower* c1928 (opposite), the perspective flattens the objects in such a way that a composition of lines, planes and contrasts is created. The structure of the tower forms an angular shape and the public space below forms a circle, creating an abstract composition with a characteristically Constructivist dynamic. Although the radio tower was a popular subject for avant garde artists in the late 1920s and 1930s, few painters managed the level of abstraction that Moholy-Nagy achieved in the medium of photography.

Moholy-Nagy was instrumental in creating a new photographic style, and was accordingly celebrated by the supporters of the New Photography movement. In the late 1920s, his work featured prominently in major exhibitions that brought modern photography to wider public attention, including *New directions in photography* held at the Jena Kunstverein in 1928, and the 1929 exhibition *Film und Foto* (FiFo) in Stuttgart, organised by the *Werkbund* (German Work Association). The first survey of international modern photography held in Germany, this exhibition included 1200 works that showed the range of recent innovations in the medium, as well as promoting the use of photography in book design, advertising and propaganda. Moholy-Nagy acted as advisor on the project, while Lissitzky designed the Russian room and later took the exhibition on an international tour. Photographs by Moholy-Nagy and Lissitzky were included, along with works by Hannah Höch, Man Ray, Marcel Duchamp and Rodchenko, and numerous images by unknown photographers, which were taken from books and newspapers. The exhibition showed the potential of these new forms of visual communication to reach a mass audience. Avant-garde photography was not only highly successful in advertising, but also in social documentation, and there was a rising market for such images in illustrated weekly magazines and the rapidly expanding mass media.

In the period between the wars, the machine was a favourite subject for avant-garde photographers, including Albert Renger-Patzsch, E O Hoppé and Wolfgang Sievers. Renger-Patzsch highlighted the structure and texture of plants, buildings and machines in his beautifully balanced compositions. Hoppé was a documentary photographer who recorded German industrial sites in the late 1920s, when heavy industry was expanding. The angle and framing of his photographs work to aestheticise technology and represent the machine as an icon of the dynamic modern age. A similar monumental aesthetic is evident in Sievers' image *Blast furnace in the Ruhr, Germany* 1933 (p 172). The machines celebrated in the photographs of the 1920s and 1930s are now ruins of the modern world. The industrial sites of the Ruhr, including the furnace depicted in Sievers' photograph, are no longer operational; however, their aesthetic and historic value is formally recognised, and some industrial sites are preserved as museums. The Ruhr region was awarded the prestigious title of European cultural capital in 2010, and the Zollverein coalmine and coking plant near the city of Essen are now UNESCO world heritage sites. In this sense, the modernist machine aesthetic has endured, as the preserved ruins of modern industry can be visited in a museum context, and the photographs of industrial monuments from the 1920s and 1930s still convey the fascination with technology.

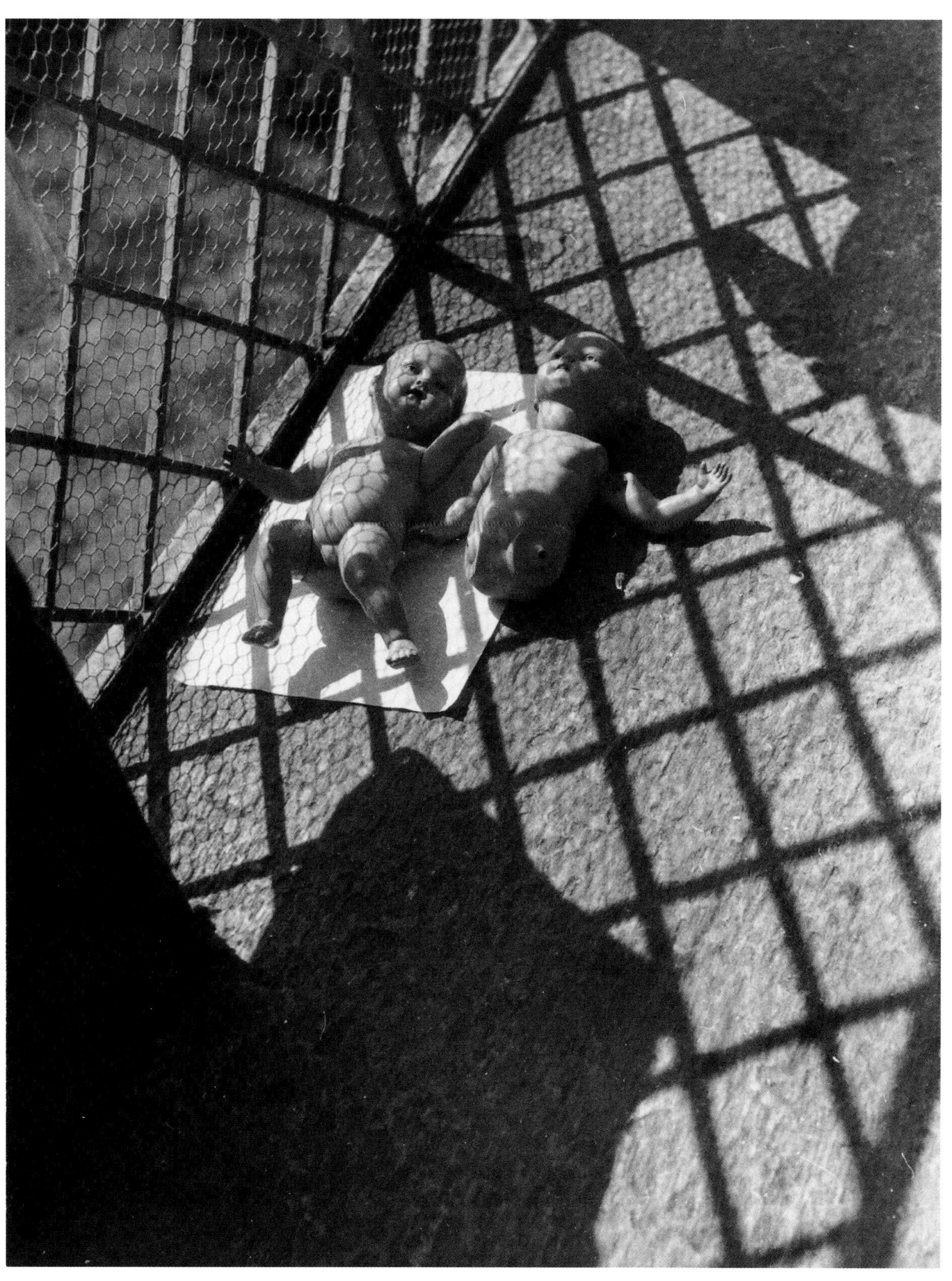

László Moholy-Nagy
[Puppen (Dolls)] 1926–27
gelatin silver photograph
J Paul Getty Museum, Los Angeles

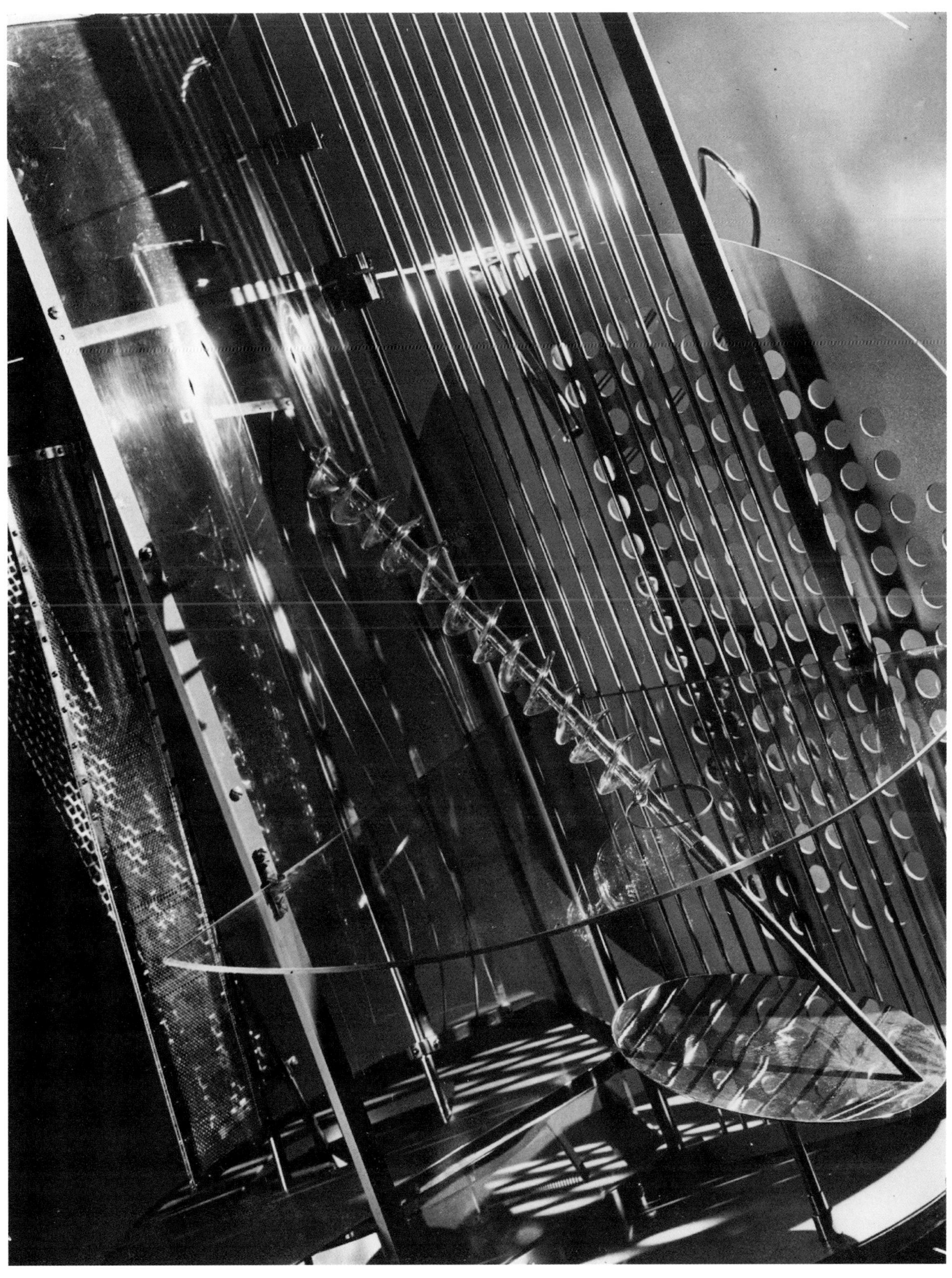

László Moholy-Nagy
Das Lichtrequisit [Light-space modulator/
Light prop/Requisite light for an electric stage]
1930

gelatin silver photograph
J Paul Getty Museum, Los Angeles

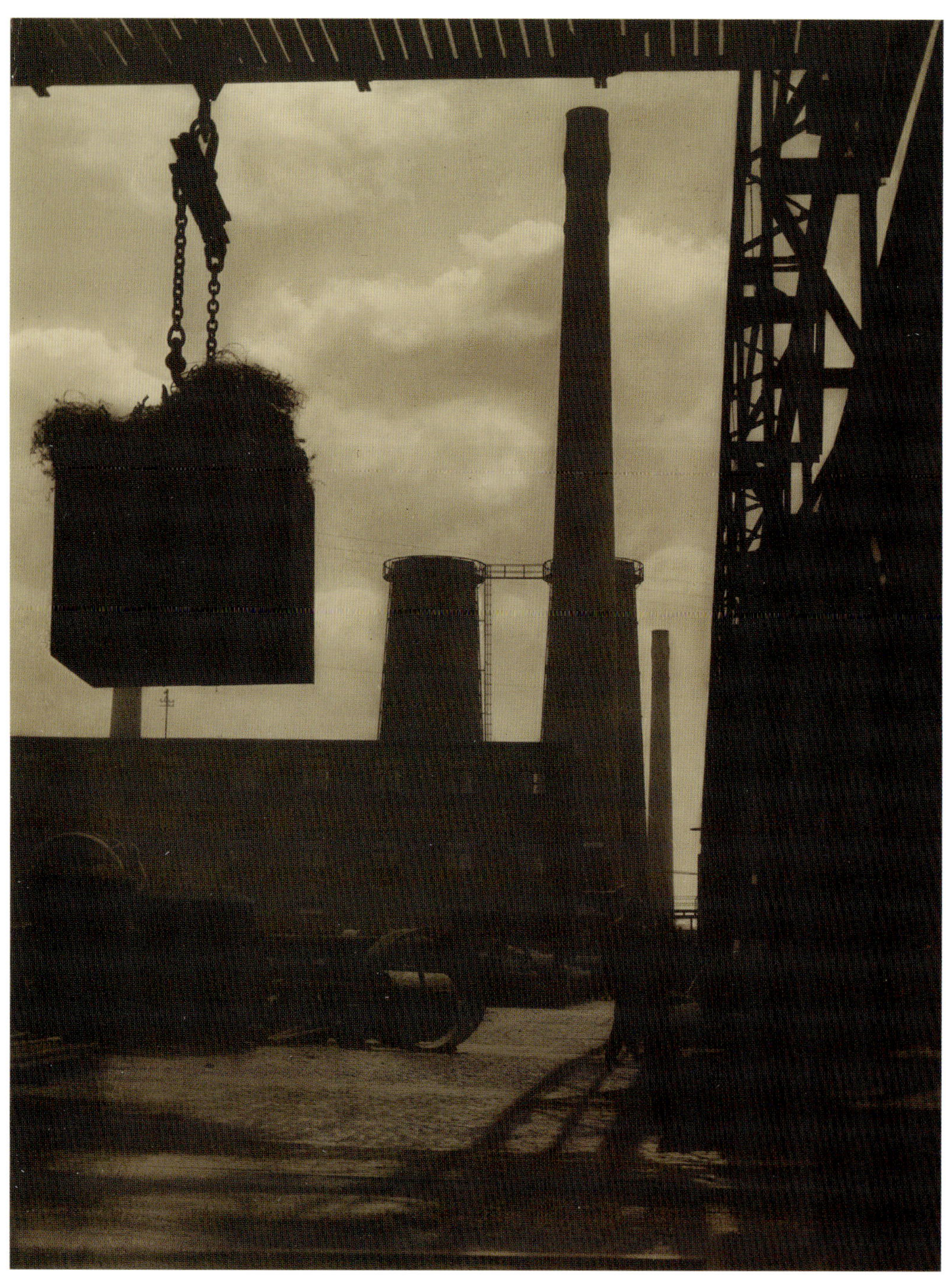

E O Hoppé
Rotating crane in a shipyard
(Turmdrehkran auf einer Werft) 1928
gelatin silver photograph
National Gallery of Australia, Canberra

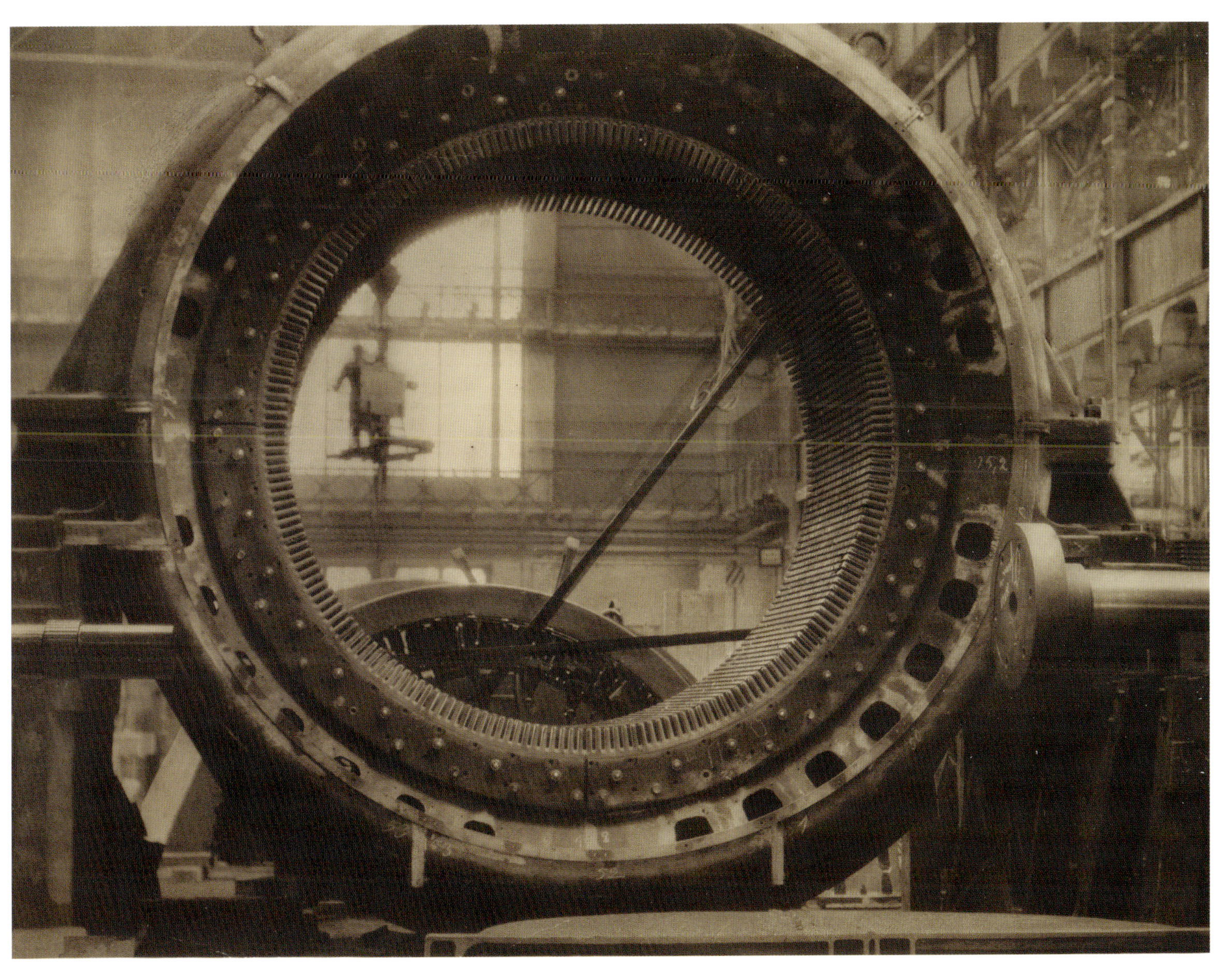

E O Hoppé
Bearing in an AC generator ('Ständer' einer Wechselstrommaschine) 1928
gelatin silver photograph
National Gallery of Australia, Canberra

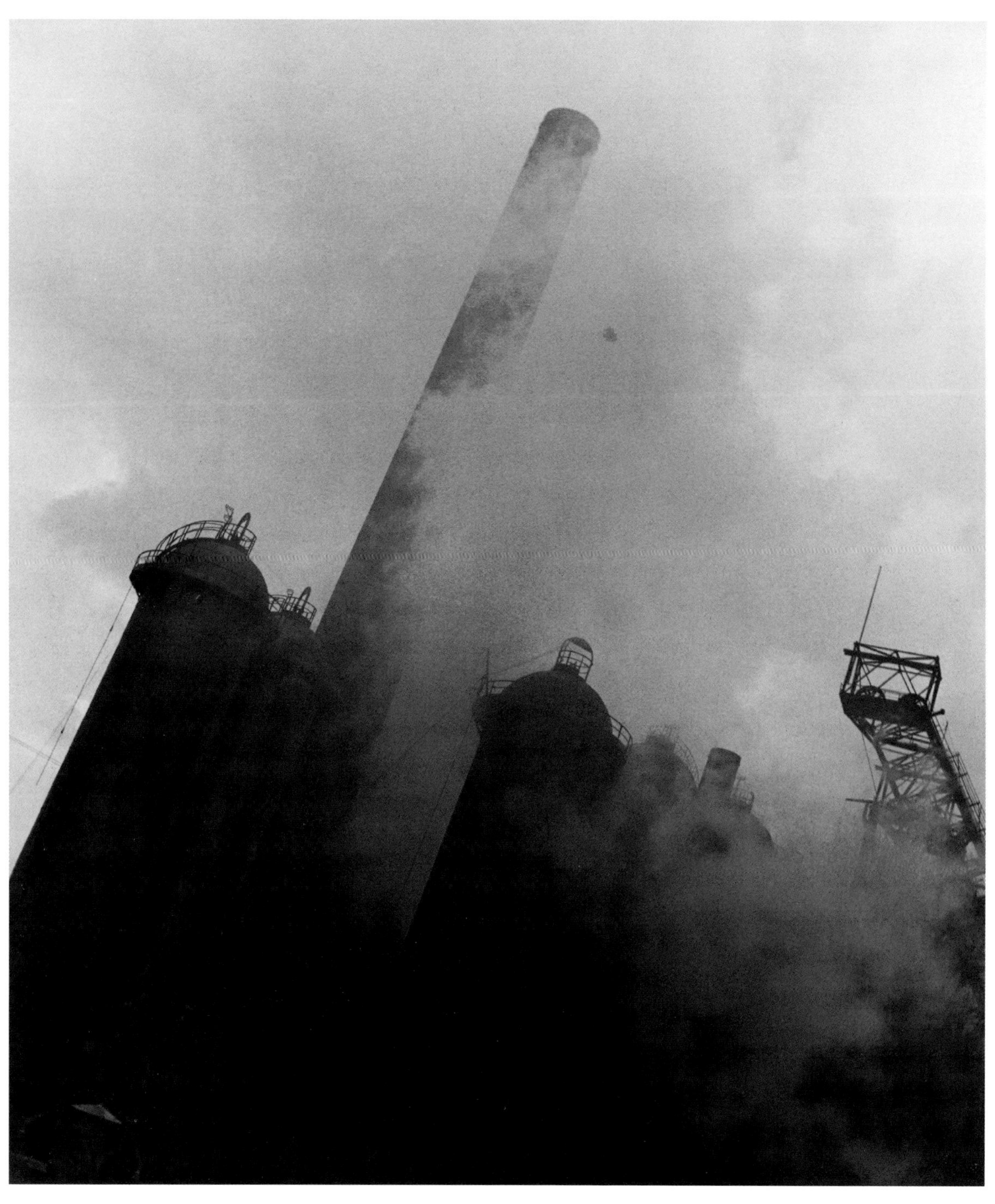

Wolfgang Sievers
Blast furnace in the Ruhr, Germany 1933
gelatin silver photograph
National Gallery of Australia, Canberra

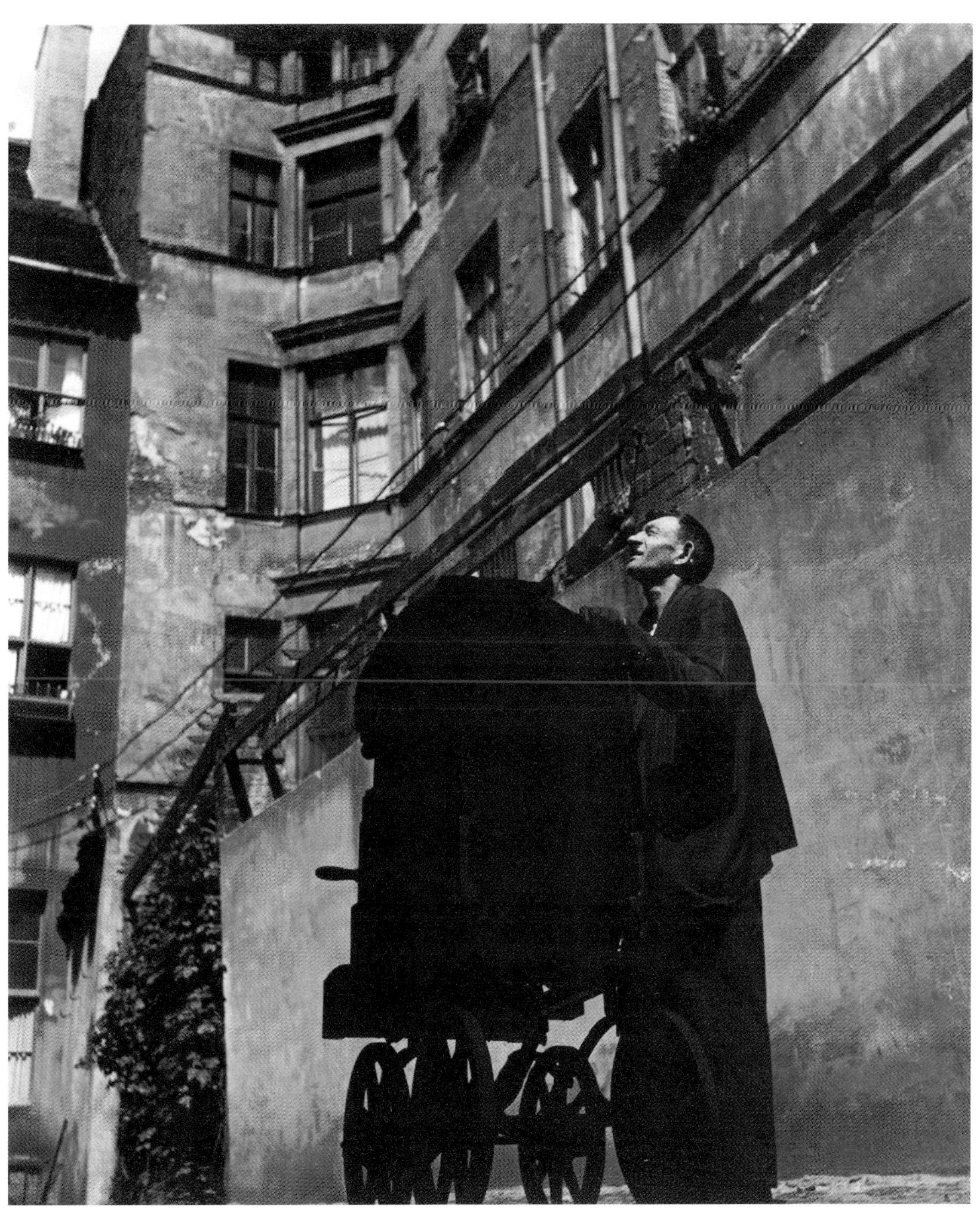

Wolfgang Sievers
Total poverty in Berlin, Germany 1933
gelatin silver photograph
National Gallery of Australia, Canberra

ERICH BUCHHOLZ

Sign P

Erich Buchholz moved to Berlin in 1915 to study art and briefly experimented with Expressionism in a manner reminiscent of Wassily Kandinsky and Franz Marc. By 1918–19, Buchholz had arrived at his own form of abstraction, well before Constructivism emerged as a major avant-garde movement in Germany. Though Buchholz's work shared some of the stylistic attributes of Constructivism, he resisted his work being categorised under this label and refused to take part in the Constructivist exhibitions. His belief in the importance of individual creativity strongly contrasted with leading Constructivist El Lissitzky's views on the utilitarian role of art.

During 1918–24, Buchholz worked in an astonishing range of media, including oil painting, drawing, watercolour, printmaking, typography, architectural design and sculpture. He also produced a series of remarkable painted wooden reliefs, which were at first conceived as blocks for woodcuts. Drawn to the materiality of carved wood, Buchholz soon realised that these objects were an independent medium in themselves. *Sign P* 1922 is one of Buchholz's major achievements and represents an important moment in the evolution of his own style, as well as the broader artistic debates that were taking place in Berlin. Created during the same year that he became acquainted with the work of Lissitzky through the *First Russian art exhibition*, Buchholz synthesised current ideas about abstract art with his own experiments on balancing the formal elements of colour – red, black and gold – with geometric forms. The enigmatic title draws upon earlier cryptic titles used in his work. However, the letter 'P' may also quite literally refer to 'plate' or 'plane', from the German *Platte*, which was inscribed on the back of other painted wood reliefs of the period and is an abbreviation of 'wood relief', from the German *Holzplatte*.[1] Through the creation of these visually compelling forms of abstract art, Buchholz fulfils the modernist view of the artist as a unique visionary who created previously unimagined and even transforming works of art.

Buchholz's reputation as one of the pioneers of geometric abstraction in Germany has been revived in recent years.[2] His work is held in collections throughout Germany and he is especially well represented in Australia through holdings in the Art Gallery of New South Wales, National Gallery of Australia, Queensland Art Gallery and Art Gallery of Western Australia.[3] JS

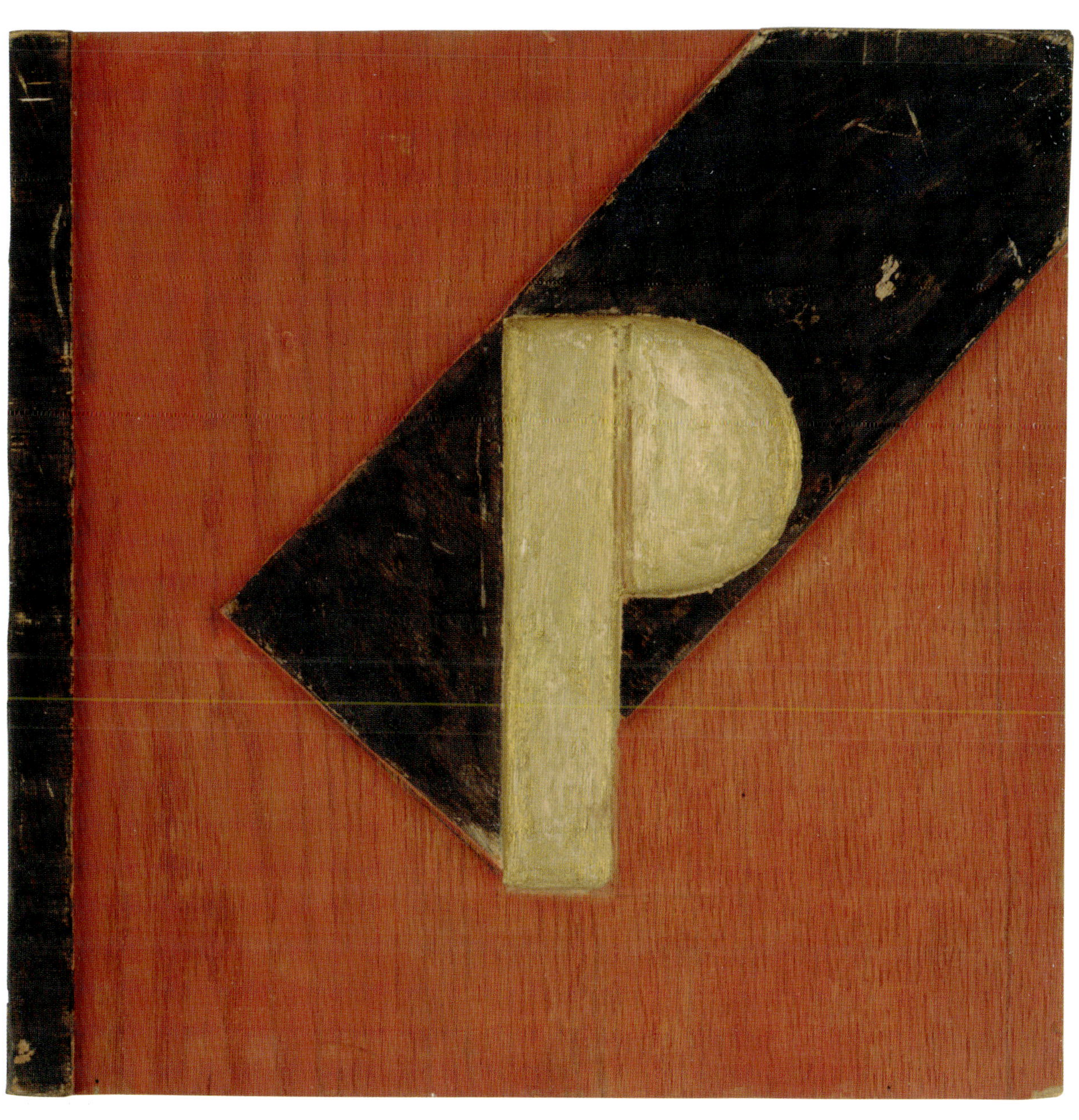

Erich Buchholz
Sign P 1922
oil on wood relief
Art Gallery of New South Wales, Sydney

EL LISSITZKY

Prouns

El Lissitzky arrived in Berlin from the new Soviet Union in 1922 to promote avant-garde art from Russia. Like many progressive artists and intellectuals, he was attracted to the thriving, cosmopolitan metropolis and found the art scene in Germany to be open and receptive to the newest ideas about revolutionary artforms paving the way towards the creation of a better society. Influenced by the purist and almost mystic Suprematist theories of Kazimir Malevich, Lissitzky initially embraced the principles of non-representational art, in which the universe was interpreted through a geometric harmony of rectangles, circles and squares, mostly using a limited range of colour that was restricted to black, red and white.[1] Lissitzky had, however, become one of the leading proponents of Constructivism by the time he arrived in Berlin and advocated the utopian view that new forms of abstract art could revolutionise social relations.

Lissitzky's most richly productive period occurred during the brief moment from 1922 to 1923 when International Constructivism flourished in Germany. His pioneering ideas about the development of radical artforms that crossed traditional boundaries between architecture, design and fine art were at the centre of debates taking place around the range of artistic practices and theories that were grouped together under the term 'Constructivism'. He was astonishingly versatile as an artist and facilitated the exchange of ideas between Russian and western European artists through the publication of avant-garde journals and the founding of the artists group The Abstracts, which continued to organise exhibitions of Constructivist art throughout

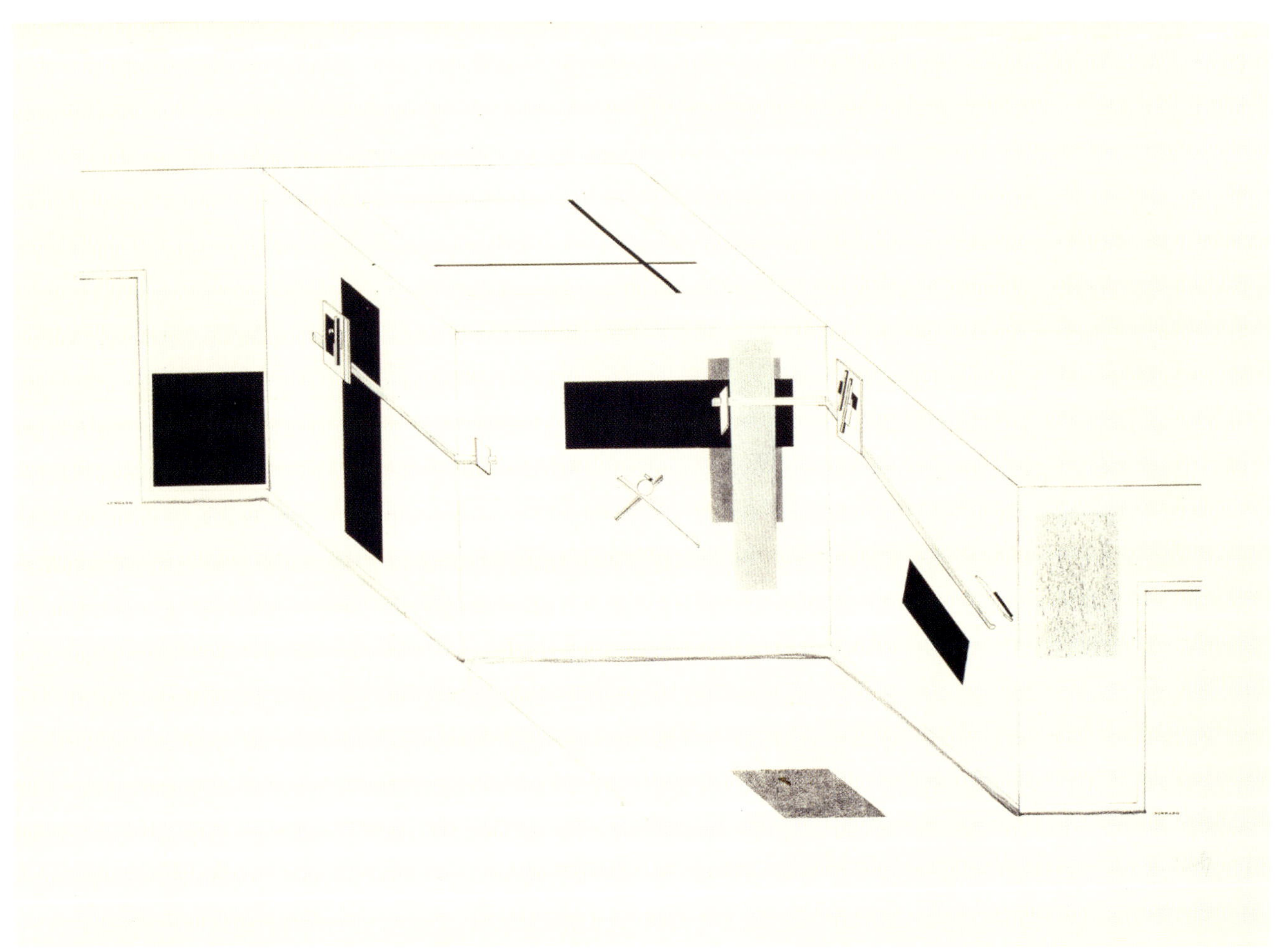

El Lissitzky
Proun 1923
from the portfolio Proun 1 Kestnermappe 1923
lithograph
State Art Collection, Art Gallery of Western Australia, Perth

the 1920s. Lissitzky's portfolio of ten large, colour lithographs designed for the Futurist opera *Victory over the sun* is one of his finest works from this period (p 178). The 'new man' of the modern age is represented as a dynamic, pseudo-mechanical figure, striding bravely forward to face the future. Lissitzky's highly inventive abstract designs of the main characters create an optimistic view of man's relationship with technology and the machine.

Lissitzky's *Proun* – an abbreviation from Russian words meaning 'projects for the affirmation of the new in art' – paintings and prints were intended as utopian statements that represented not only the new aesthetic values of geometric precision, structural emphasis and transparency, but also the corresponding socialist values of clarity, order and the possibility of collective human progress.[2] The *Proun* images were the culmination of his ideas about freeing art from representation and they opened up exciting new formal possibilities about three-dimensionality and spatial complexity in art – concepts that he took even further in the *Proun* room created for the *Grosse Berliner Kunstausstellung* (*Great Berlin art exhibition*) in 1923. The lithographic version of the *Proun room* (opposite) remains readable as the plan for the room where, Lissitzky noted, 'the six surfaces (floor, four walls, ceiling) are the given surfaces, they are to be designed.'[3] The radical, formal experimentation of the *Proun* works and their emphasis on the abstract construction of three-dimensional space continues to reinforce the importance of Lissitzky as one of the most influential modernist artists of the early 20th century. JS

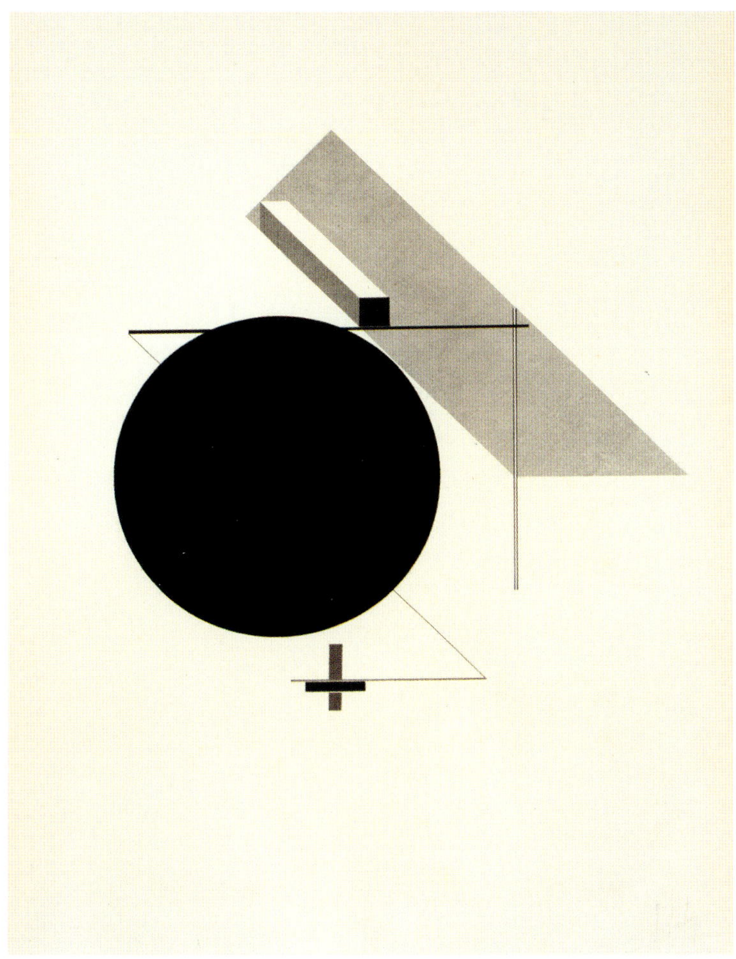

El Lissitzky
Proun 1923
from the portfolio Proun 1 Kestnermappe 1923

lithograph with black collage
State Art Collection, Art Gallery of Western Australia, Perth

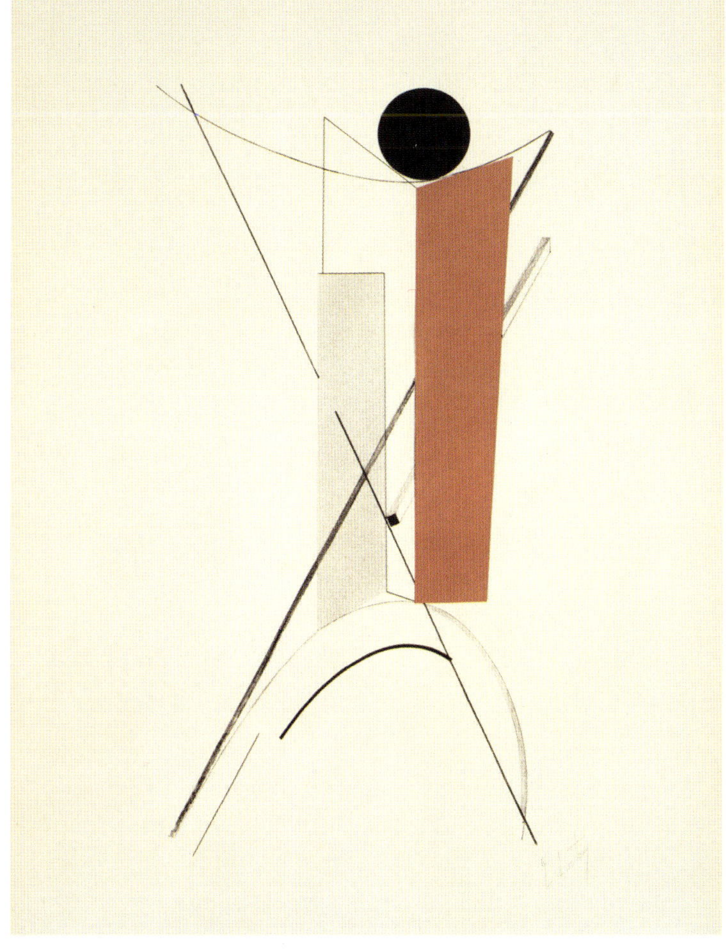

El Lissitzky
Proun 1923
from the portfolio Proun 1 Kestnermappe 1923

lithograph with red collage
State Art Collection, Art Gallery of Western Australia, Perth

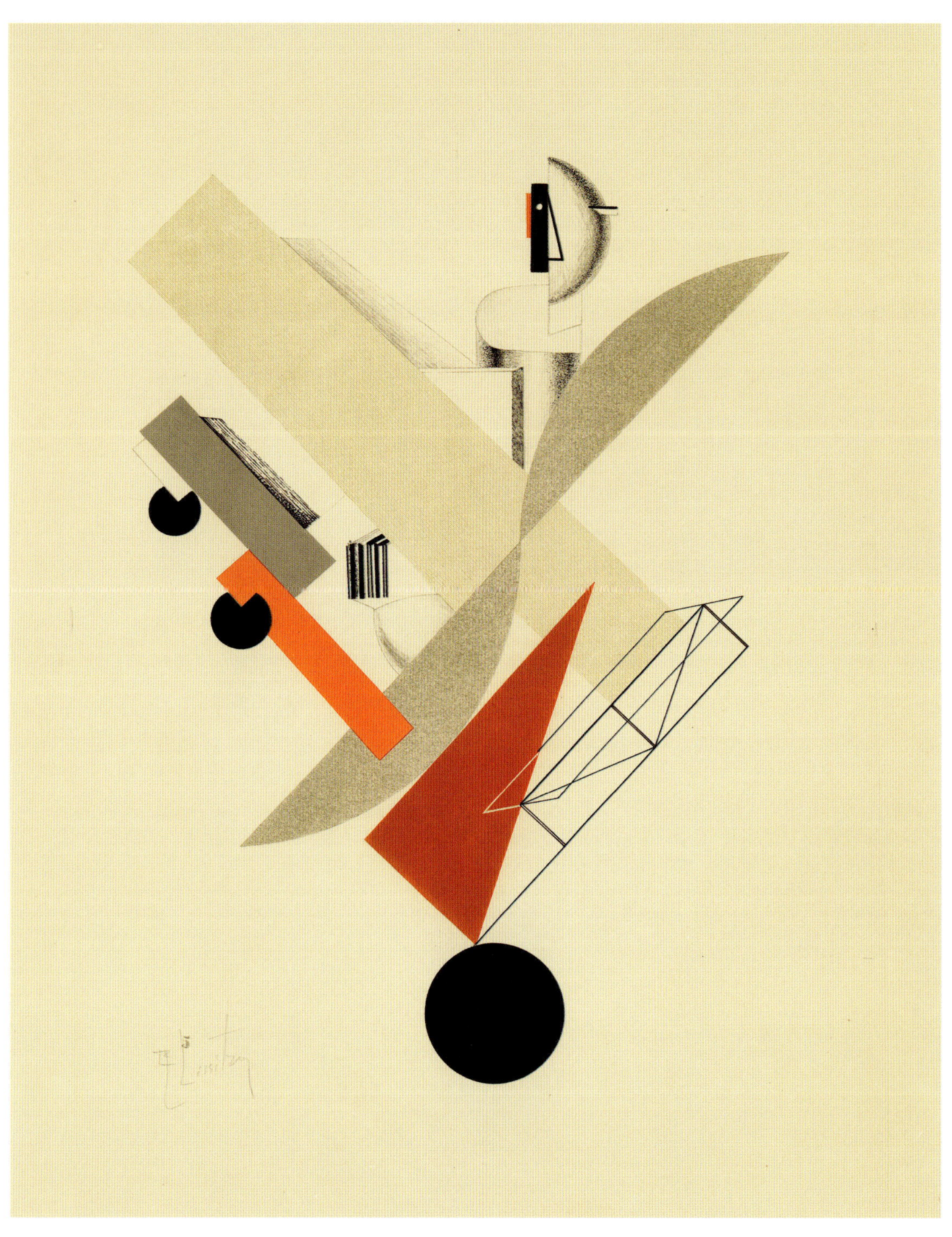

El Lissitzky
Globetrotter (in time) 1923
from the portfolio **Victory over the sun** 1923
colour lithograph
National Gallery of Australia, Canberra

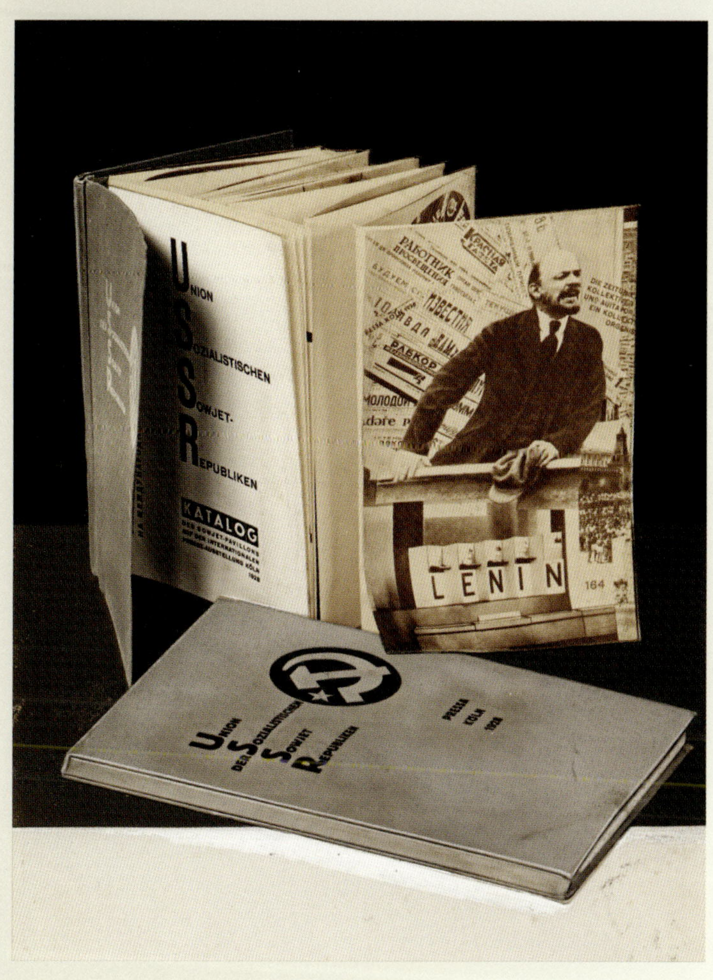

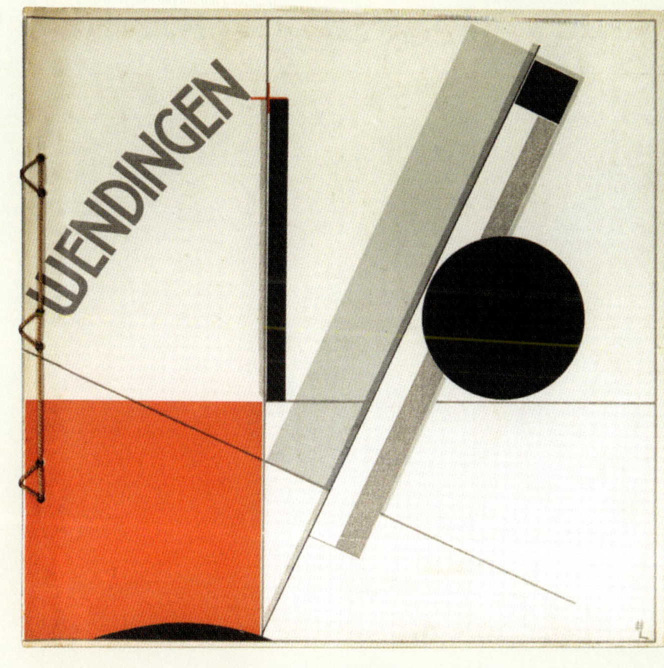

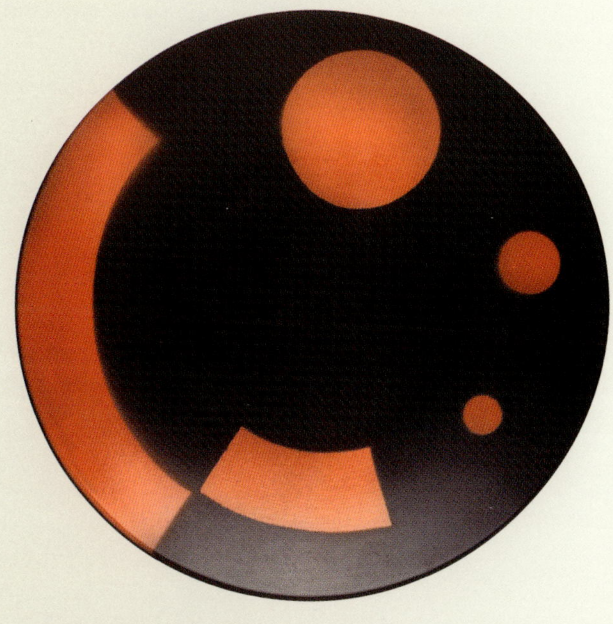

clockwise from top left:

El Lissitzky
Untitled [Pressa catalogue] 1928
photocollage, ink, paint
Art Gallery of New South Wales, Sydney

El Lissitzky
Cover for the journal *Wendingen* no 11, 1921
lithograph
Powerhouse Museum, Sydney

El Lissitzky
Plate c1923
unglazed earthenware
Powerhouse Museum, Sydney

CARL GROSSBERG

White pipes

Carl Grossberg grew up in the industrial area around Wuppertal and studied architecture before serving in the army between 1914 and 1918. After a brief time at the Bauhaus in the early 1920s, where he studied under Lyonel Feininger, Grossberg arrived at a form of heightened realism through a series of meticulous drawings and paintings that depicted industrial interiors in Germany and the Netherlands.[1] Grossberg distanced himself from avant-garde associations, and his prosaic views of heavy industry differed significantly from the utopian visions of a machine-age world that the Constructivists were simultaneously exploring through increasingly abstract forms.

From 1933 to 1939, Grossberg was engaged in painting the most important industrial plants and factories in Germany. This extensive series of paintings – produced both for himself and as commissions – offer an almost encyclopaedic view of the age of heavy industry. Grossberg's distinctive rendition of the machine aesthetic can be characterised as precise, crisp, sharply delineated and generally devoid of human presence[2], and an atmosphere of ambivalence towards the machine is successfully created in *White pipes* 1933. The inherent beauty of technology is expressed through the artist's fascination with the structure of this machine-like organism. It is represented through a labyrinthine system of bulky, white pipes contrasted against an intricately detailed assemblage of oddly shaped metallic parts. At the same time, the threatening nature of the machine is revealed through the dominating and impenetrable presence of this structure in an environment that appears cold and sterile. Grossberg manages to create an interesting tension between celebrating modernity and the threat of the modern, even though the painting appears, at first glance, to be a relatively straightforward depiction of modern technology.

In Grossberg's paintings it is possible to see close stylistic and iconographic links to 1920s German photography, as represented in this exhibition through the work of Werner Mantz, E O Hoppé, Albert Renger-Patzsch, and Wolfgang Sievers. The work of these photographers shows an extraordinary range of attitudes towards the machine, ranging from romantic idealism to documentary realism. Grossberg's shared interest in the aestheticisation of technological motifs was, however, most strongly related to the kinds of images that were published in Renger-Patzsch's large volume of photographs, *Die Welt ist schön* (*The world is beautiful*) of 1928. There is also a striking resemblance between this group of works and the commitment of late-20th-century German photographers Bernd and Hilla Becher in emphasising the order and clarity of the industrial world. JS

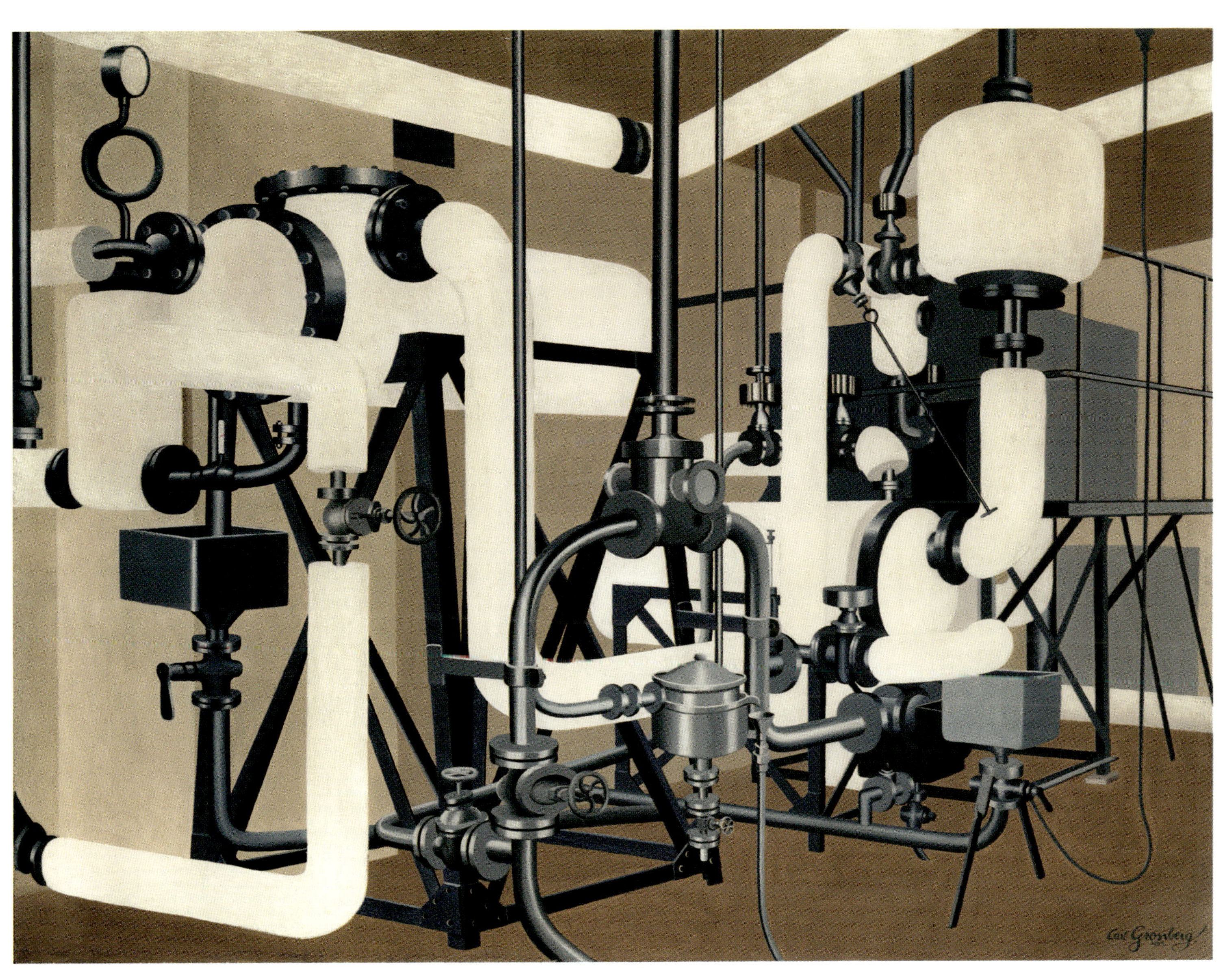

Carl Grossberg
White pipes 1933
oil on wood
Private collection

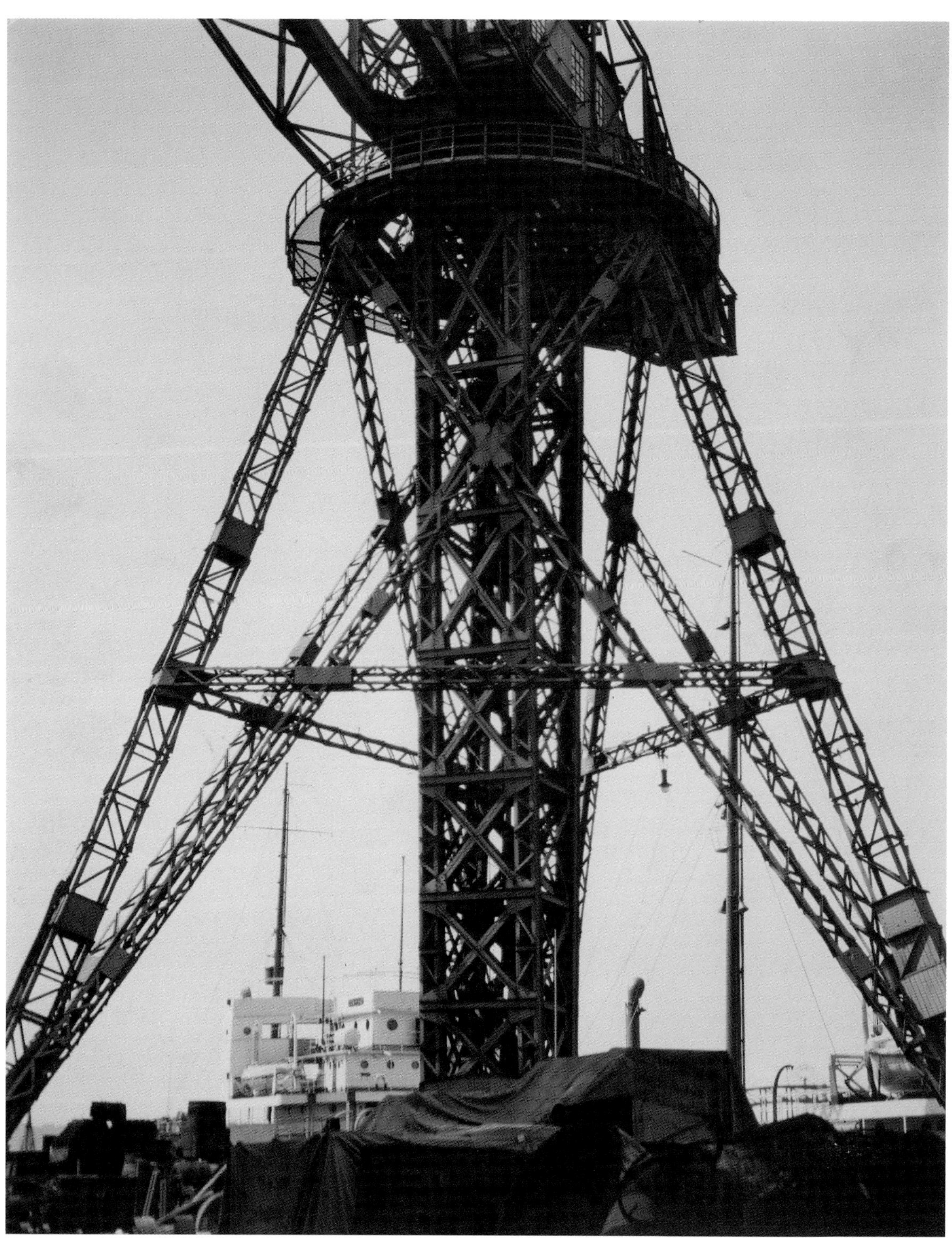

E O Hoppé
A box containing wood fibres suspended from a crane in the background, chimneys and freezer towers of the UAN power station 1928
gelatin silver photograph
National Gallery of Australia, Canberra

Werner Mantz
Two towers, transport structure, commissioned by Staatsmijnen Heerlen, Netherlands 1937–38
gelatin silver photograph
National Gallery of Australia, Canberra

Werner Mantz
Street in Cologne – Zollstock 1928
gelatin silver photograph
National Gallery of Australia, Canberra

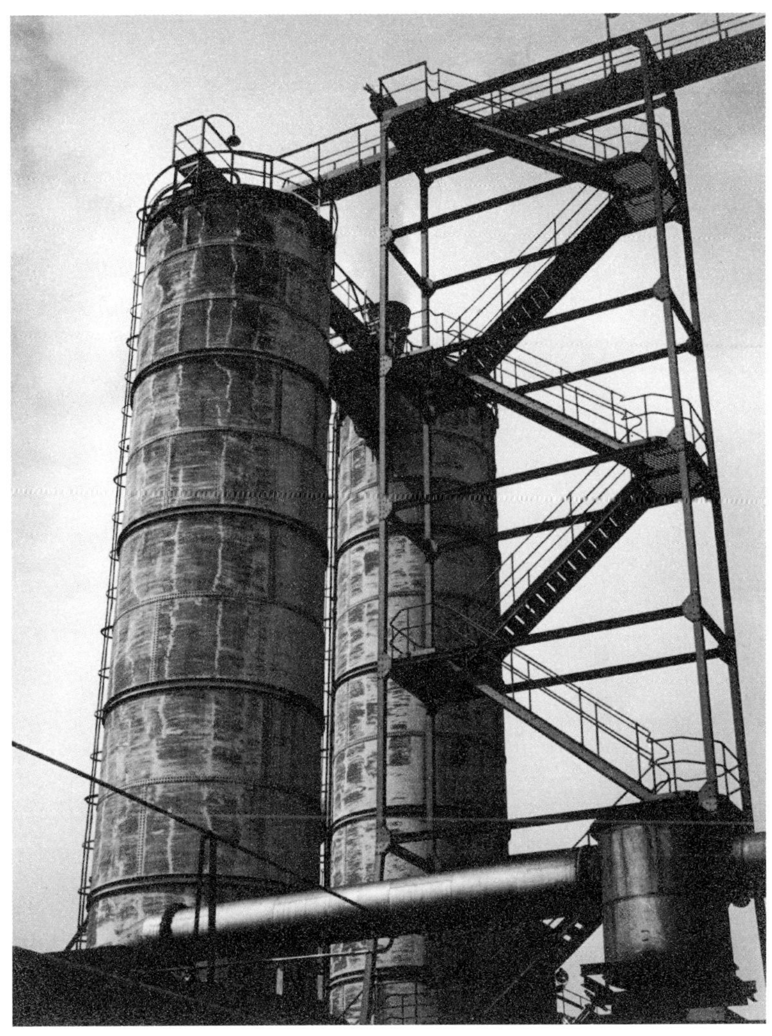

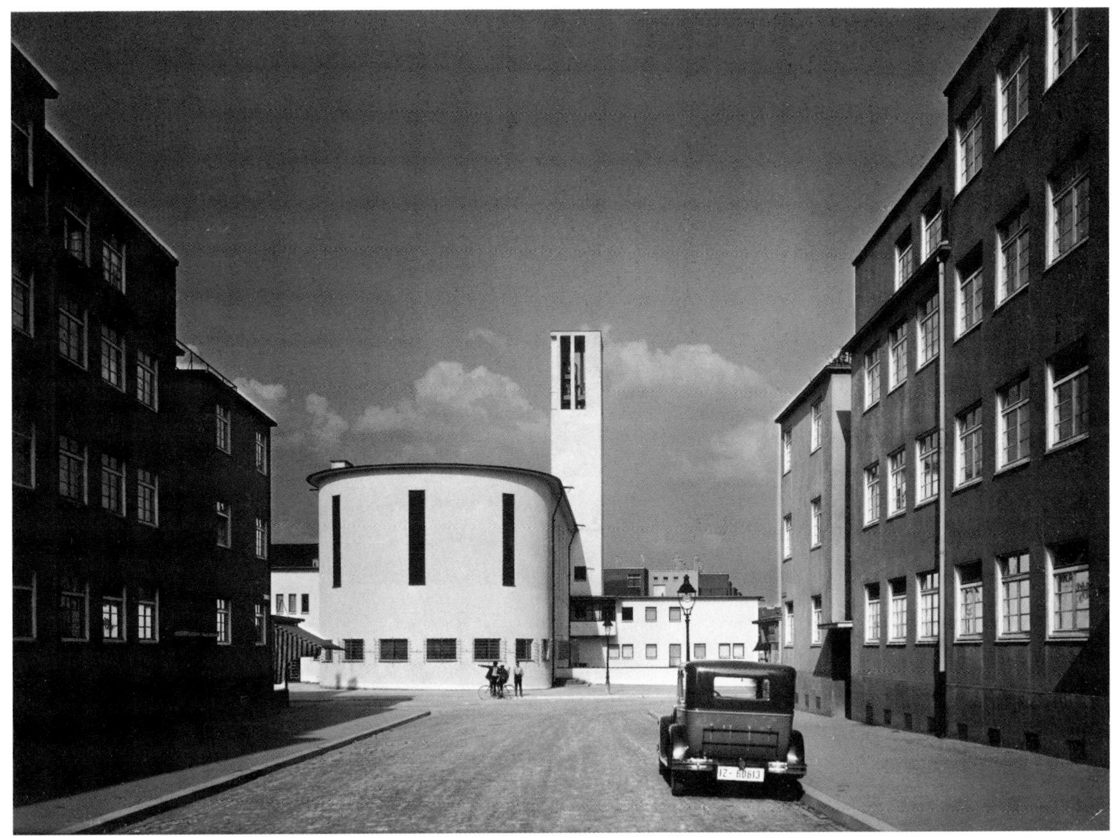

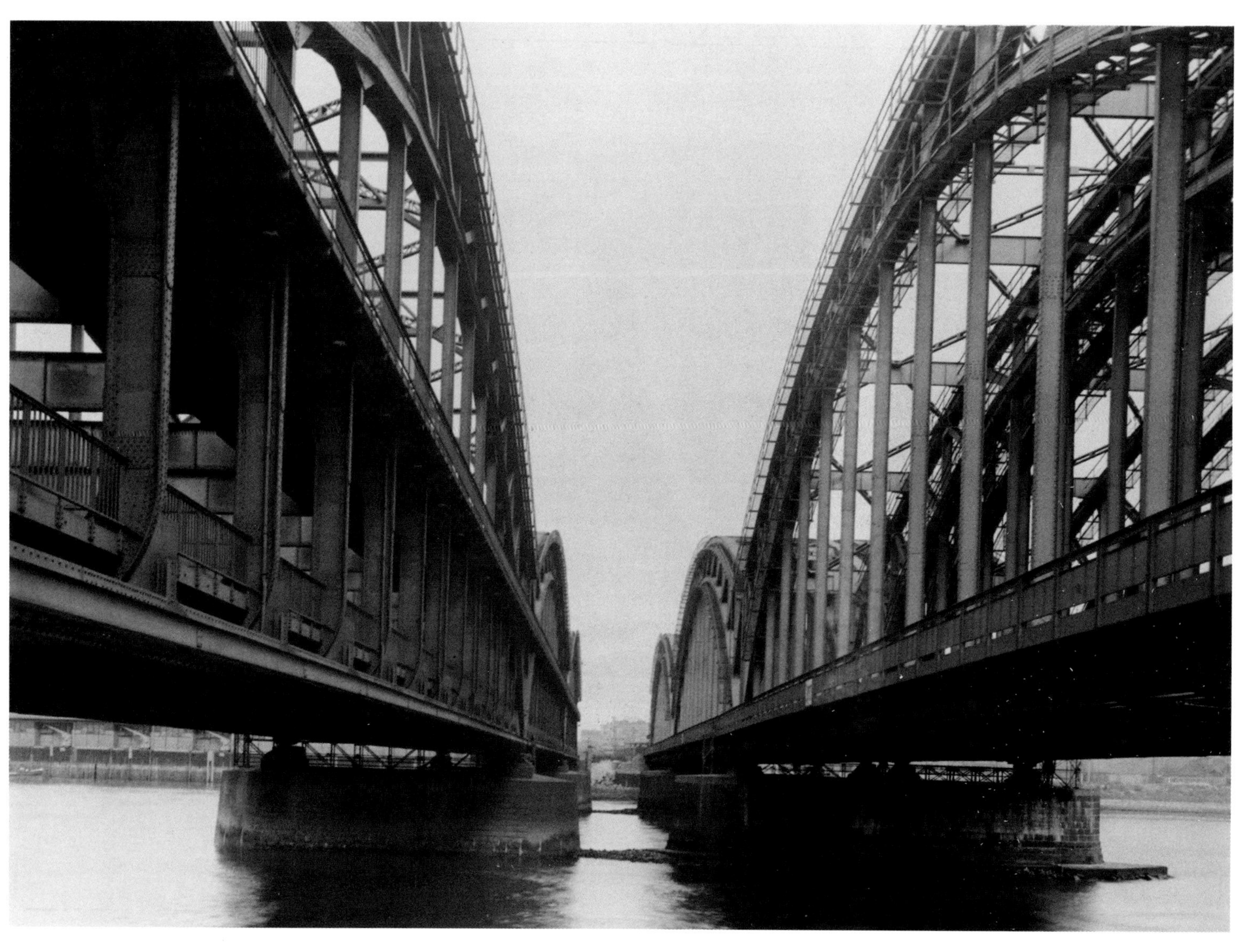

Albert Renger-Patzsch
Railroad bridge c1927
gelatin silver photograph
National Gallery of Australia, Canberra

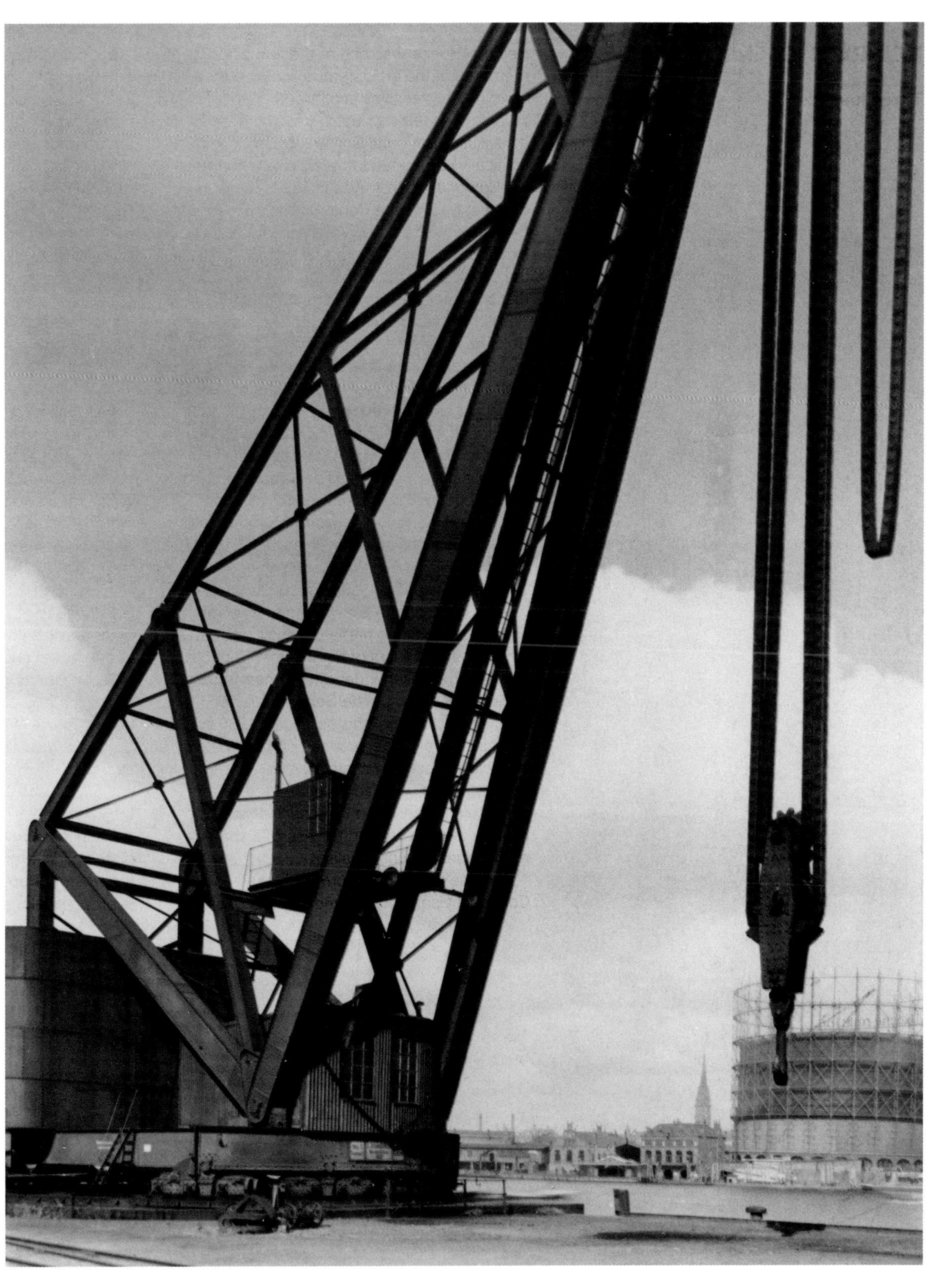

Albert Renger-Patzsch
Harbour with crane c1927
gelatin silver photograph
National Gallery of Australia, Canberra

HEINRICH HOERLE

Three invalids

Heinrich Hoerle was one of the founding members of the artists group known as the Cologne Progressives and, together with Franz Wilhelm Seiwert and Gerd Arntz, he developed a new form of figural Constructivism. These politically committed left-wing artists formed the Cologne Progressives in 1924, along very different lines to the Constructivist movements that had emerged elsewhere in Germany; they aimed to connect their radical politics with the development of revolutionary forms of art that sought to reconcile Constructivism with Realism.[1] Like many avant-garde groups, the Cologne Progressives sought to create new audiences for their art but they also hoped that their work would reveal truths about current social and political relations.

Hoerle painted *Three invalids* twelve years after the end of the First World War. During this time, war cripples had become one of the most frequently depicted motifs in modern German art, as represented in this exhibition through works by artists such as Otto Dix (p 38), George Grosz (p 53) and Max Beckmann (p 41). One-and-a-half million crippled and wounded veterans returned to Germany after the war and their ubiquitous presence on city streets throughout the years of the Weimar Republic was a powerful reminder of the enormous suffering endured by the German people.[2] Hoerle's depiction of this subject in 1930 was particularly poignant given the current state of social misery that characterised German society, which had been exacerbated by the collapse of the economy, mass unemployment, political uncertainty and the rise of a sharper, more aggressive nationalism.

Hoerle's distinctive form of figural Constructivism incorporated aspects of several avant-garde movements, including Dada and Constructivism, but also reflected the shift that took place in painting around 1925 from abstract to representational art. While the composition is dominated by the cool sharpness and sober observation of reality that characterised *Neue Sachlichkeit* (New Objectivity) there are also raw, expressive elements – such as the depiction of the foreboding night sky – that hark back to Expressionism. Hoerle has typically employed a large-format, schematic design comprising simplified, hard-edged forms and blocks of flat, bright colour. This unsentimental portrayal of war invalids as dehumanised, almost identical robots, made up of machine parts and devoid of emotion and intellect, differs from the socially critical views of postwar society portrayed by the Expressionists in earlier images. Hoerle's view of the modern world as soulless and devoid of character and individuality also contrasted strongly with the utopian views of the Constructivists in the early 1920s.

Through their art, the Cologne Progressives continued to make political statements about what they perceived to be the injustices of capitalism and the evils of fascism until 1933, when the group was forced to dissolve under the Nazi regime. Hoerle may well have intended this painting to have a distinct political purpose, as was the case with Arntz's well-known woodcuts of the late 1920s and early 1930s. It is more likely, however, that the work captured the prevailing sense of disillusionment that characterised modernist painting in Germany towards the final years of the Weimar Republic, rather than delivering an overt political message. JS

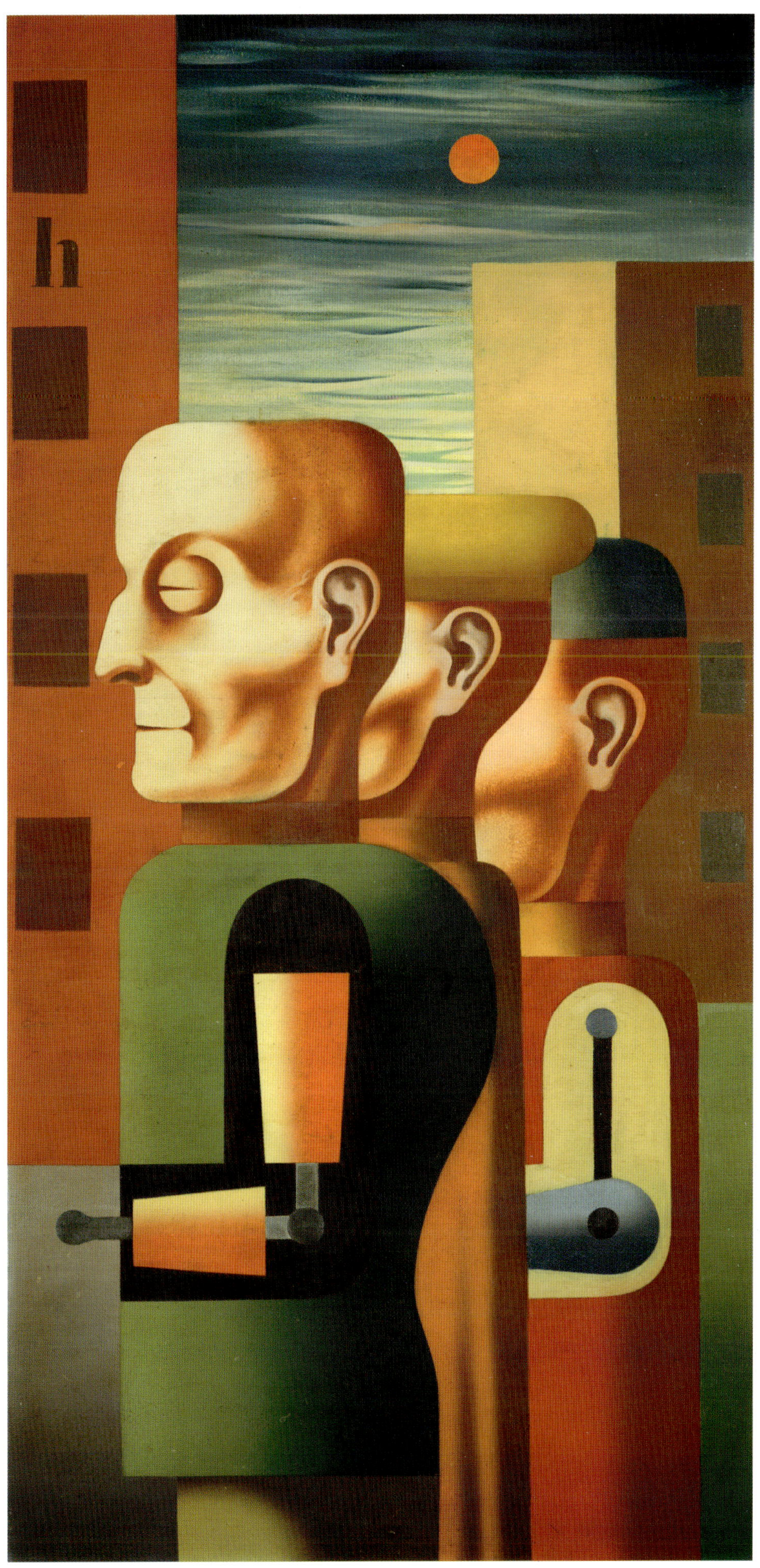

Heinrich Hoerle
Three invalids c1930
oil on plywood
Private collection

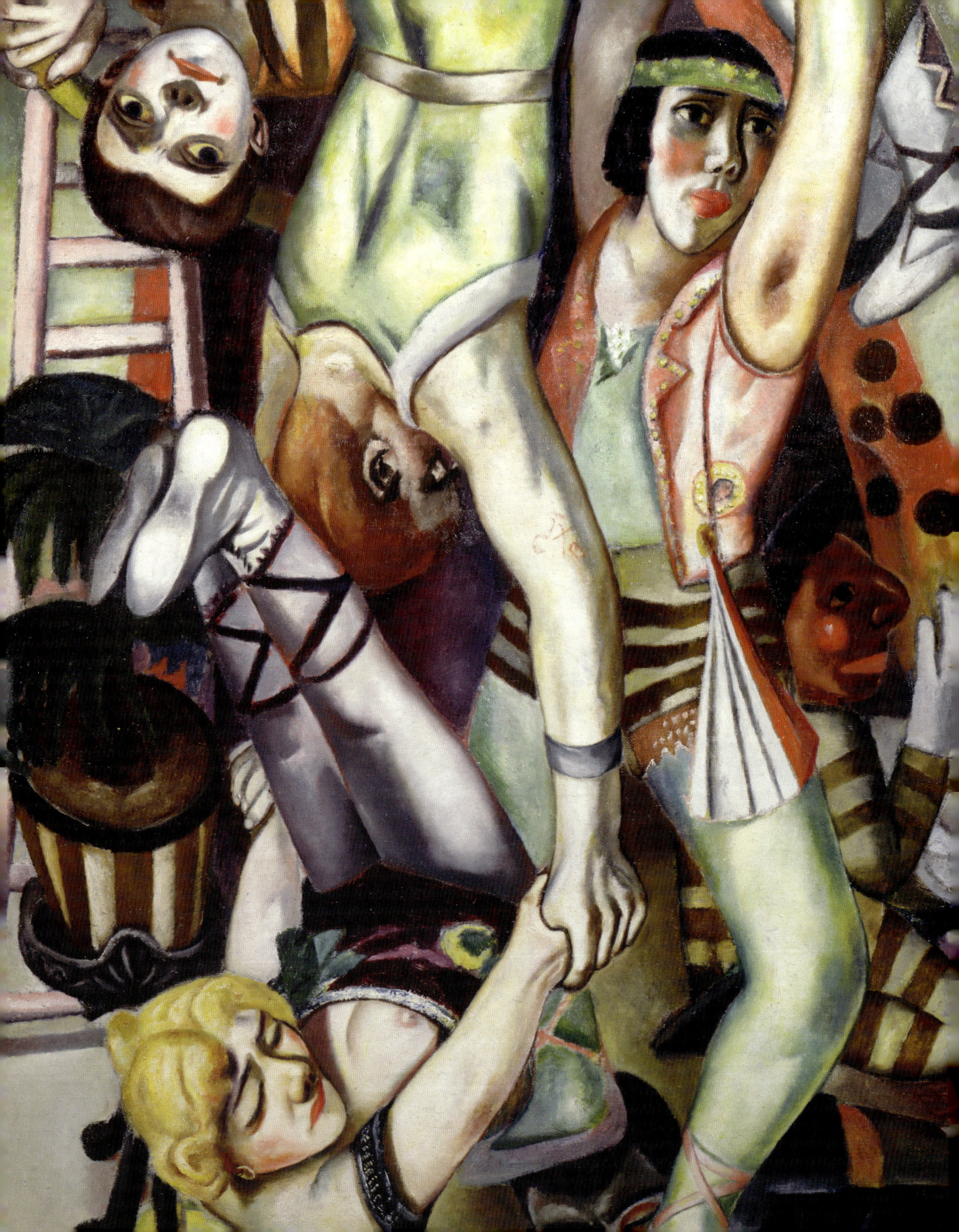

METROPOLIS: THE BRILLIANT AND SINISTER ART OF THE 1920s

Maggie Finch

Berlin in the 1920s was a unique, bustling, creative metropolis that had grown to be one of the largest cities in Europe. The implementation of the *Greater Berlin Act* of 1920 led to a rapid expansion of the boundaries, incorporating neighbouring towns and rural communities into one city, divided into 20 boroughs. This amalgamation of districts resulted in a dramatic increase in the population of Berlin – rising from under 600 000 residents in the mid 1860s, to over 4 million by the 1920s – transforming it from a large city, or *Grossstadt*, into a *Weltstadt*, a thriving, cosmopolitan metropolis.[1] The new, expanded city had become the political, business and industrial capital of Germany. It was also, unofficially, the cultural and entertainment capital, with a night-life that was notorious for being wild and uninhibited. The influx of people from rural regions and nearby countries created a unique urban demographic who lived a rapid pace of life in a city that was characterised by all who experienced it as pulsating with movement and energy.

The new Berlin inspired hope and excitement but was also a cause of anxiety, as its cultural vibrancy and technical advances were underpinned by a sense of dysfunction and danger. The city during the Weimar period was, after all, recovering from the traumas of the First World War, experiencing political unrest and hyperinflation, all overshadowed by the gradual rise of the National Socialist Party. Beneath the seductive surface of modernity and industrial progress lay a dark underbelly of social and political vices, as the increases in population were matched by high rates of overcrowding, poverty, crime and prostitution. Traditional values and social relationships within German culture were being completely rewritten by the new modes of urban life.

From the end of the 19th century, many German intellectuals considered what they saw as a crisis of culture occurring in the West as a result of aspects of modernity. This included the rapid onslaught of technological development, and political and economic upheavals – conservative ideas that were compounded by philosophers such as Oswald Spengler in his publication of 1918, *Der Untergang des Abendlandes* (*The decline of the West*). Such theories were naturally suspicious of the effects of progress and the expansion of the metropolis. Urbanisation was viewed by many as a force of corruption that was dividing country and city, and as a cause of degeneration of the mind and soul, resulting in the weakening of national values and culture.[2] For others, however, the opportunities for social change and personal liberation brought about by modernity in the city were embraced, and Berlin quickly became a hub for artists, writers and people of ambition.[3]

Artists were sensitive to the cultural anxieties brought about by the changes in lifestyle within the metropolis. Acting as diarists and observers, they documented and translated the new urban spaces and the dynamism of life. The metropolis inspired insightful and empathetic responses but also derogatory ones, as the promise of a modern utopia was both revered and scorned. As such, there was not one unified,

Max Beckmann
The trapeze 1923 (detail)

aesthetic response; rather, artists adopted diverse, pluralist approaches to create dynamic views of mass society that explored the human condition within the urban environment.

The changing role of women in the city was a subject of particular interest for artists. With the signing of the Weimar Constitution in 1919, men and women were afforded equal rights and those over the age of 20 were awarded the right to vote. Germany remained a patriarchal state, however, with equality between the sexes being a legal obligation but not necessarily a social reality. Women were undoubtedly becoming more visible in everyday life, with many entering the workforce for the first time and with (limited) incomes, they were able to become consumers and partake in urban forms of entertainment, such as attending the cinema.[4] This new role and status of women in the Weimar Republic was encapsulated in the concept of the *neue Frau*, or new woman. However, as will become evident upon discussion of works in this section of the exhibition, the presence of women in the public realm – during the day and in the shadows of the night – was often represented by male artists with ambivalence and anxiety.

While Berlin was considered to be the quintessential metropolis of Germany during the Weimar period, it was not isolated as an urban site of avant-garde activity. Rather, artists were responding to the new pace of life in cities such as Dresden, Frankfurt, Weimar, Dessau, Munich, Hanover and Cologne to name a few. It should also be acknowledged that despite the rapid industrialisation and urbanisation occurring in Germany early in the 20th century, the majority of the population continued to live

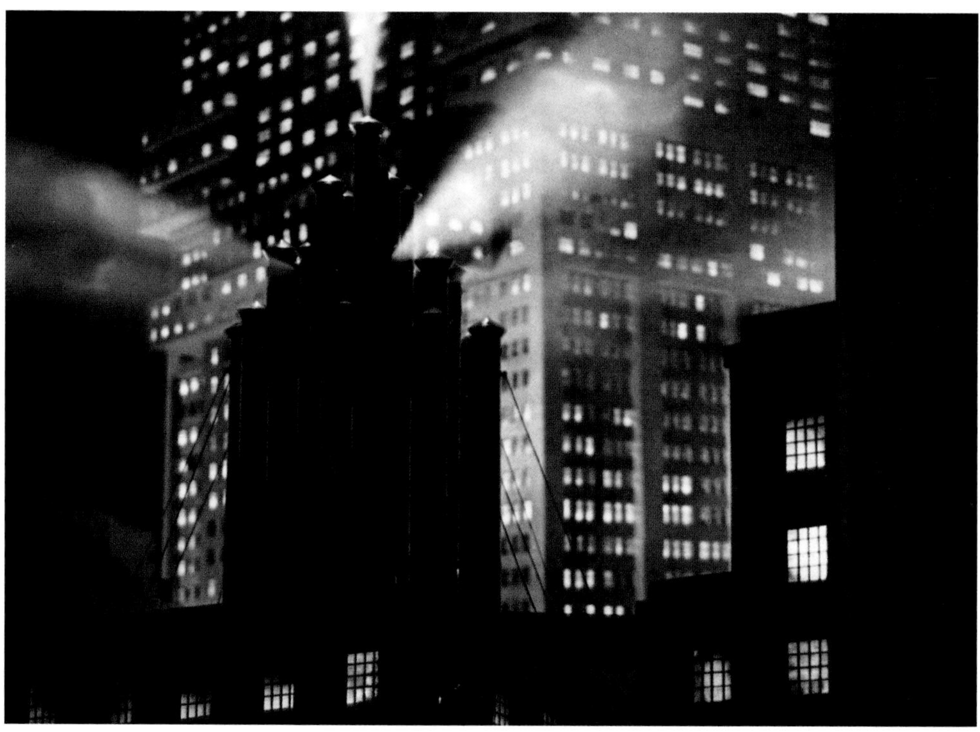

Fritz Lang
Metropolis 1927
film still

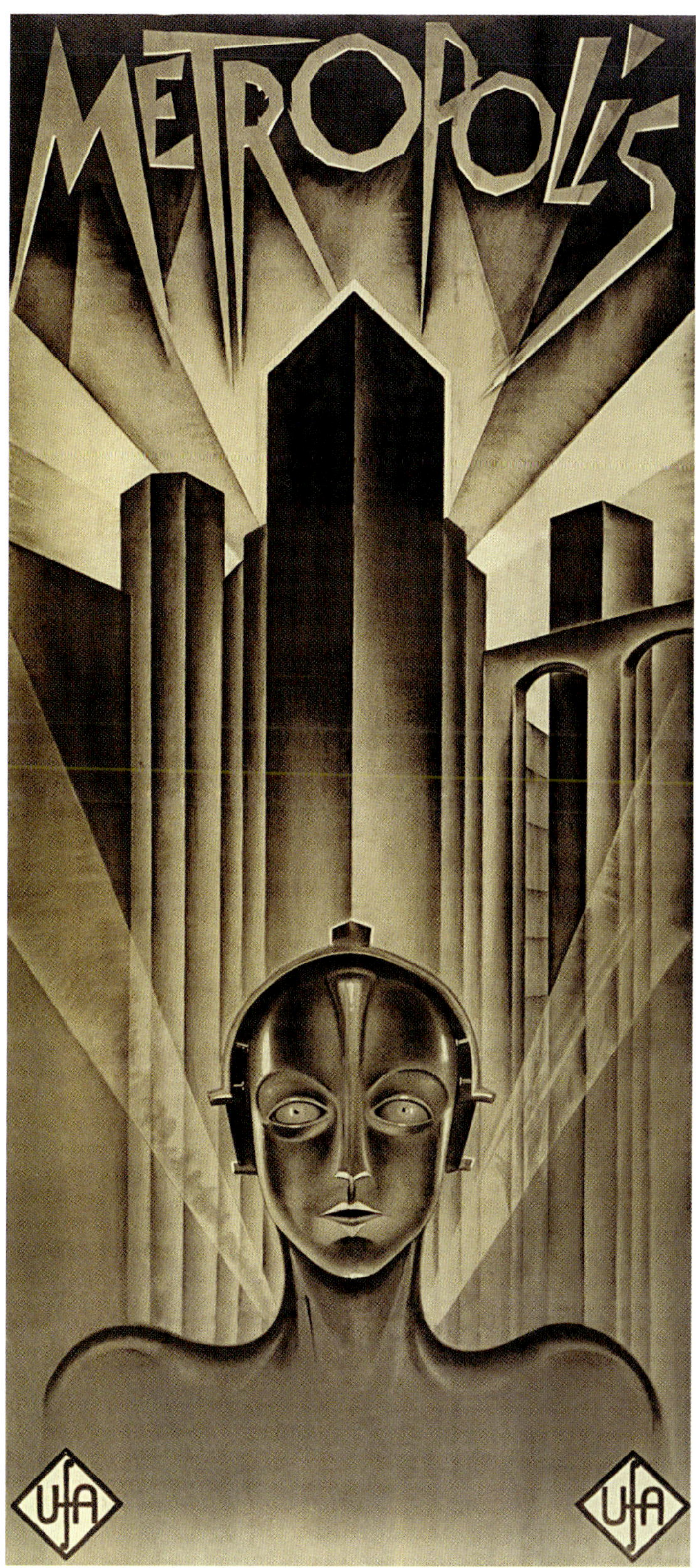

Heinz Schulz-Neudamm
Metropolis 1926
colour lithograph, poster
Austrian National Library, Vienna

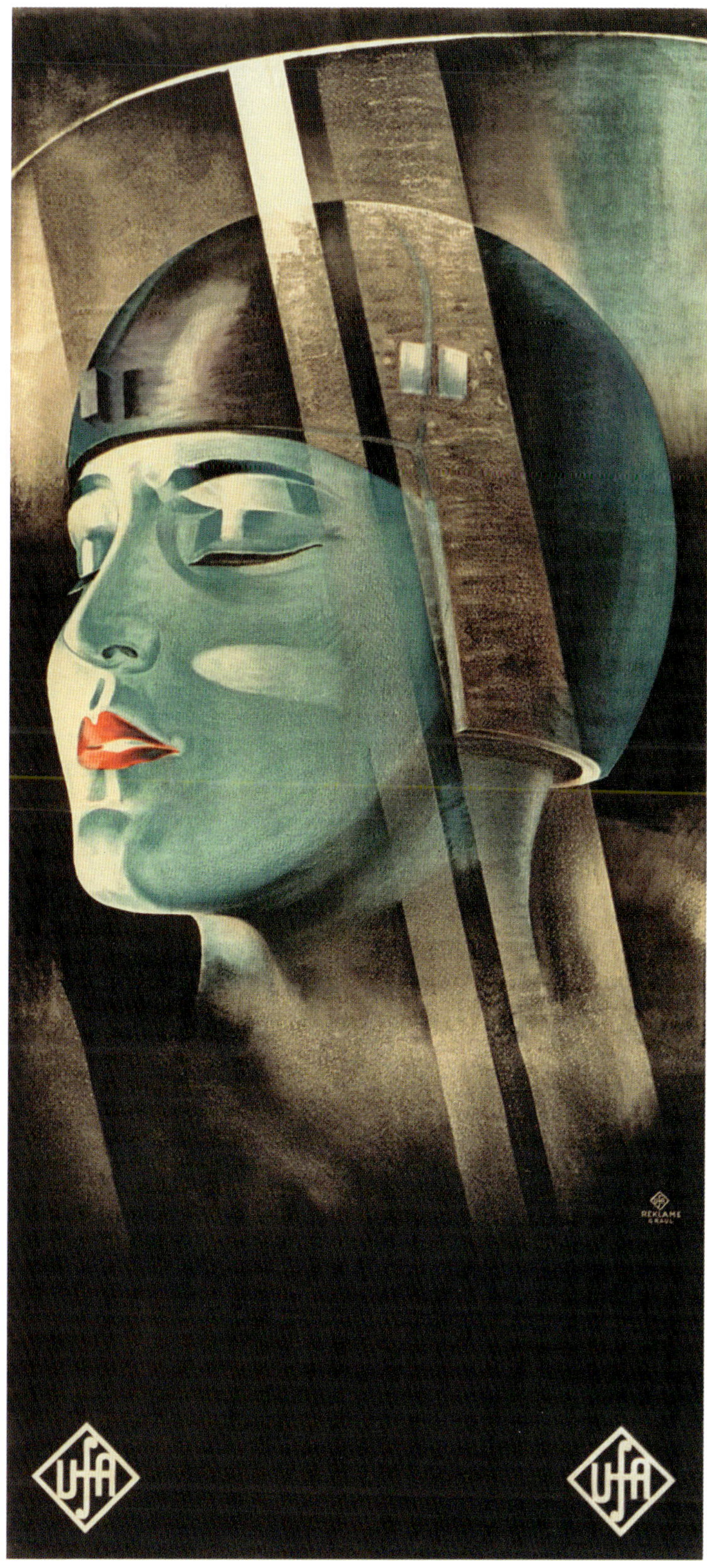

Werner Graul
Metropolis 1926
colour lithograph, poster
Austrian National Library, Vienna

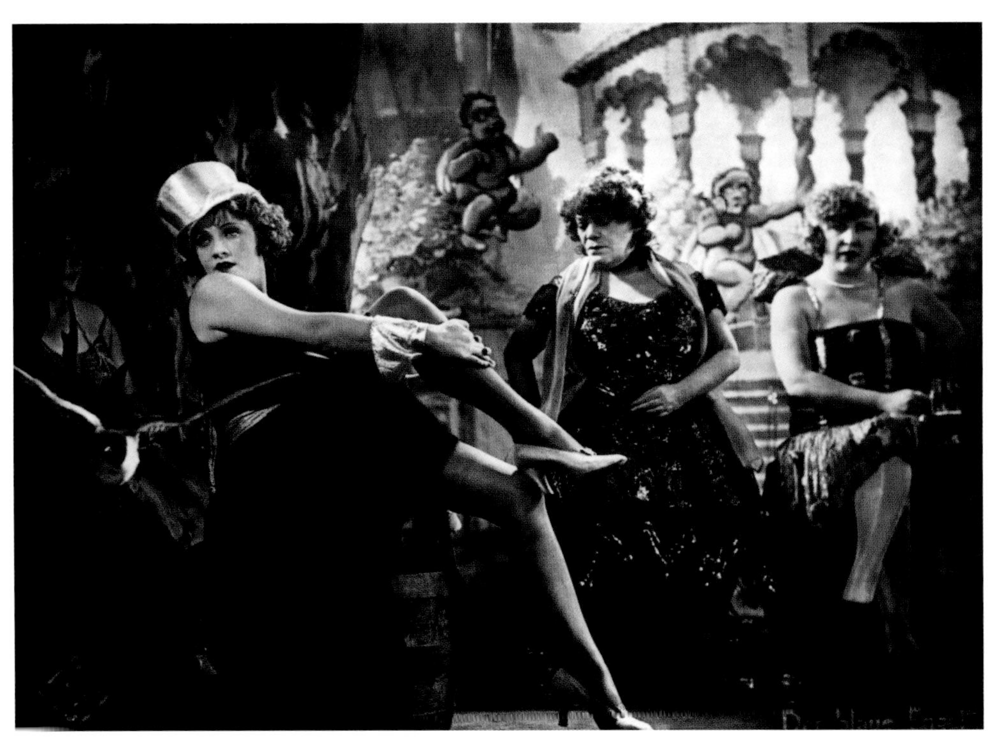

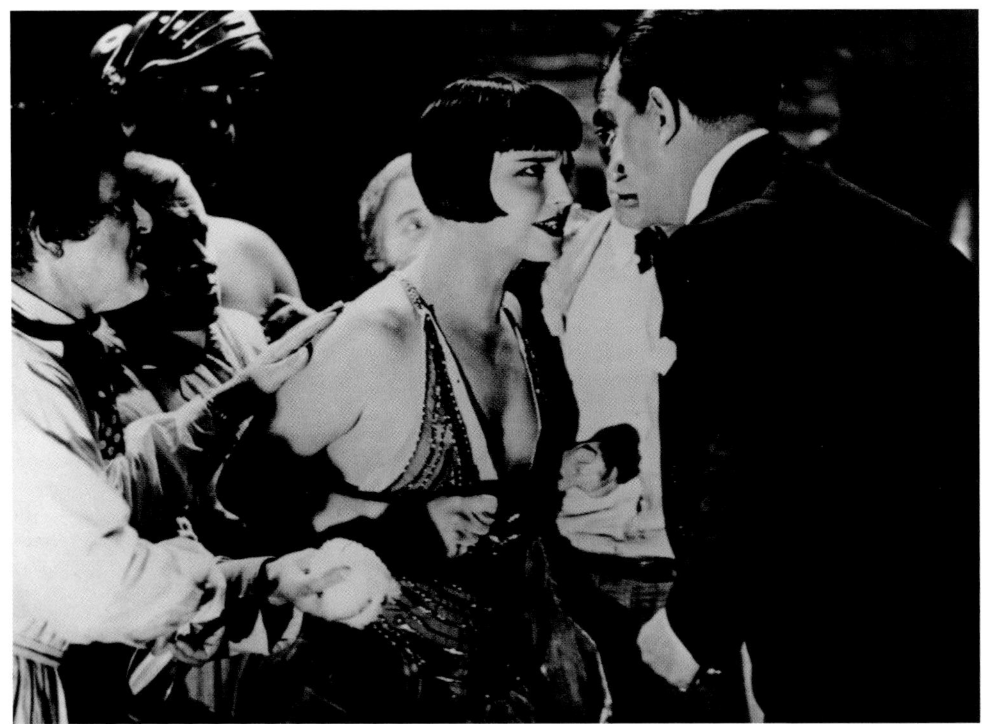

Josef von Sternberg
Blue angel 1930
film still

Georg Wilhelm Pabst
Pandora's box 1929
film still

in largely rural settings.[5] Nevertheless, every aspect of the old ways of life were being challenged by the development of the thriving cities, throwing traditional values and culture into flux.

The perceived excitement and simultaneously destructive possibilities of the machine-age were powerful themes of the fantastical film *Metropolis* of 1927, directed by Fritz Lang (p 192). Lang used the Expressionistic backdrop of a futuristic and technologically advanced city, which is 'powered' by helpless mechanical underground workers, to tell the love story of Freder (the son of an industrialist) and Maria (a spiritual leader of the workers). Fredersen (the ruler of the city) orders for Maria to be transformed into a robot to prevent a planned revolt and control the workers through deception. While remaining morally ambiguous, the dramatic juxtaposition of the workers toiling underground while the industrialists and managers enjoy the splendours above was seen as a comment on modern capitalism, and the rift between high and low classes that was emerging in the large German cities in the interwar period. Both utopian and dystopian, the city in *Metropolis* is ultimately depicted as a terrifying machine founded on greed and as the cause of the repression of human individuality.

This fear of a loss of humanity and social decline caused by modernisation was also evident in Josef von Sternberg's *Blue angel* 1930 (opposite). This melancholic and seductive film depicts the collapse of the once-respected Professor Dr Immanuel Rath after he falls madly in love with the beautiful cabaret performer Lola Lola, played by Marlene Dietrich. The professor's love for Lola Lola slips gradually out of control, resulting in an infatuation that reduces him to the humiliation of playing the role of a clown in the cabaret. He is stripped of his wealth, his profession, his social standing and eventually his life. Dietrich's Lola Lola is a formidable character, at once an emblem of the liberated *neue Frau* and a parable of the dangers of uninhibited female sexuality. The male desire towards her is undercut by a sense of anxiety – a tension that was played out as a common subject of Weimar cinema.[6] Lola Lola is the ultimate femme fatale, who 'traps' her male prey while relishing her vampish status in the spotlight of the cabaret. The voyeurism towards Dietrich's Lola Lola is reminiscent of the Englishman Harold Nicholson's romantic characterisation of Weimar Berlin as an intoxicating female. As Nicholson wrote, 'Berlin is a girl in a pullover, not too much makeup on her face ... One walks with her among the lights and in the shadows. And after an hour or so, one is hand-in-hand.'[7]

For contemporary German audiences watching this film, the liberated setting of the Blue Angel club would have been reminiscent of many such venues operating in Berlin and the major German cities during the 1920s. Indeed, one of the radical effects of industrialisation and denser city living was the development of a mass culture and entertainment industry that broke from traditional forms of art and recreation in Germany. City dwellers flocked to newly built cinemas, theatres and outdoor cafés. Mass culture was associated with modernity and, for the younger urban population, promised a fresh perspective and opportunity for escapism. Felix H Man, a pioneer of photojournalism, walked the city streets with his camera, using the modern photographic media to record all aspects of life in the dynamic new Germany: musical rehearsals for performances of the operas of Richard Wagner (p 199); night revellers out at one of the many cafés that lined the Kurfürstendamm (p 199); and playful scenes of Berliners frolicking at their beloved Lunapark amusement park, which when it opened in 1909 was the largest of its kind in Europe (opposite, p 198).

While Berlin in the 1920s afforded a prosperous lifestyle for some, the large influx of inhabitants within the metropolis, which coincided with increasing economic and political instability in the latter years of the Weimar Republic, resulted in widespread poverty and social alienation. Margaret Michaelis, who had moved from Vienna to Berlin in the late 1920s, observed these darker aspects of city life and the effects of homelessness and unemployment that had become a grim reality for many.[8] Michaelis's photograph *Untitled* [*Column with posters*] c1932 is a vivid representation of the time (p 19). Using the visual language of New Photography, she created a graphic image of an otherwise typical city street scene: an advertising pillar adorned with posters for the numerous shows that were on offer on a daily basis. Michaelis has used the sharp angle of the composition to draw our attention to a small, handwritten note adhered to the pillar. The note reads *Notruf!* (Emergency!) and is a plea for help and food – a stark reminder of the darker aspects of city life and the tragic state of poverty in the metropolis.

In Frankfurt am Main, Max Beckmann was drawn to marginalised aspects of the entertainment industry – the life and characters of the theatres, carnivals and circuses that he frequented regularly. His paintings and drypoint prints depicting scenes from the carnivals of the 1920s reveal his personal response to these colourful characters, who played an important role in entertaining a society in need of distraction after the traumas of the First World War. Carnival season saw the beginning of boisterous parties, dancing, music and performances, and Beckmann depicted these events with dynamic lines in compressed compositions, crammed scenes that were frenzied and at times grotesque (pp 203, 205). For Beckmann, a new means of representation was essential to articulate the chaos felt in Germany after the devastation of the war. His carnival scenes are expressions of his view of the modern condition: claustrophobic, chaotic and often masked.[9]

Any apparent sentiment in the representations of Beckmann is stripped away in the watercolours and drawings of Rudolf Schlichter, Otto Dix and George Grosz, as they portrayed the night-life and sex trade of the big cities with brutal realism. In their visual representations, the 'metropolis of pleasure' was seen as entirely dark, decadent and sinister; any pleasure gained was rendered pathetic or dangerous. Schlichter depicted scenes of vicious sex crimes, which were prevalent in the city at the time, with a curious mix of empathy and voyeurism. In 1919–20 he painted *Tingel tangel* (p 209), an interior scene of a cabaret, similar to that operated by Friedrich Hollaender, the prolific songwriter whose music was made famous in Marlene Dietrich's renditions in *Blue angel*. Schlichter's depiction of the cast of characters at the cabaret in a naive style was not intended as a caricature. Rather, he was at pains to render it a study of their thoughts and behaviours. The resulting image creates a tableau of desperate and disengaged characters where no gaze is met; they are each psychologically isolated.

Grosz also roamed the streets of Berlin seeking subjects for his often savage, satirical drawings and watercolours that form a scathing picture of society in the Weimar Republic. His contempt is evident in works such as *The powder-puff* c1930 (p 211), where the

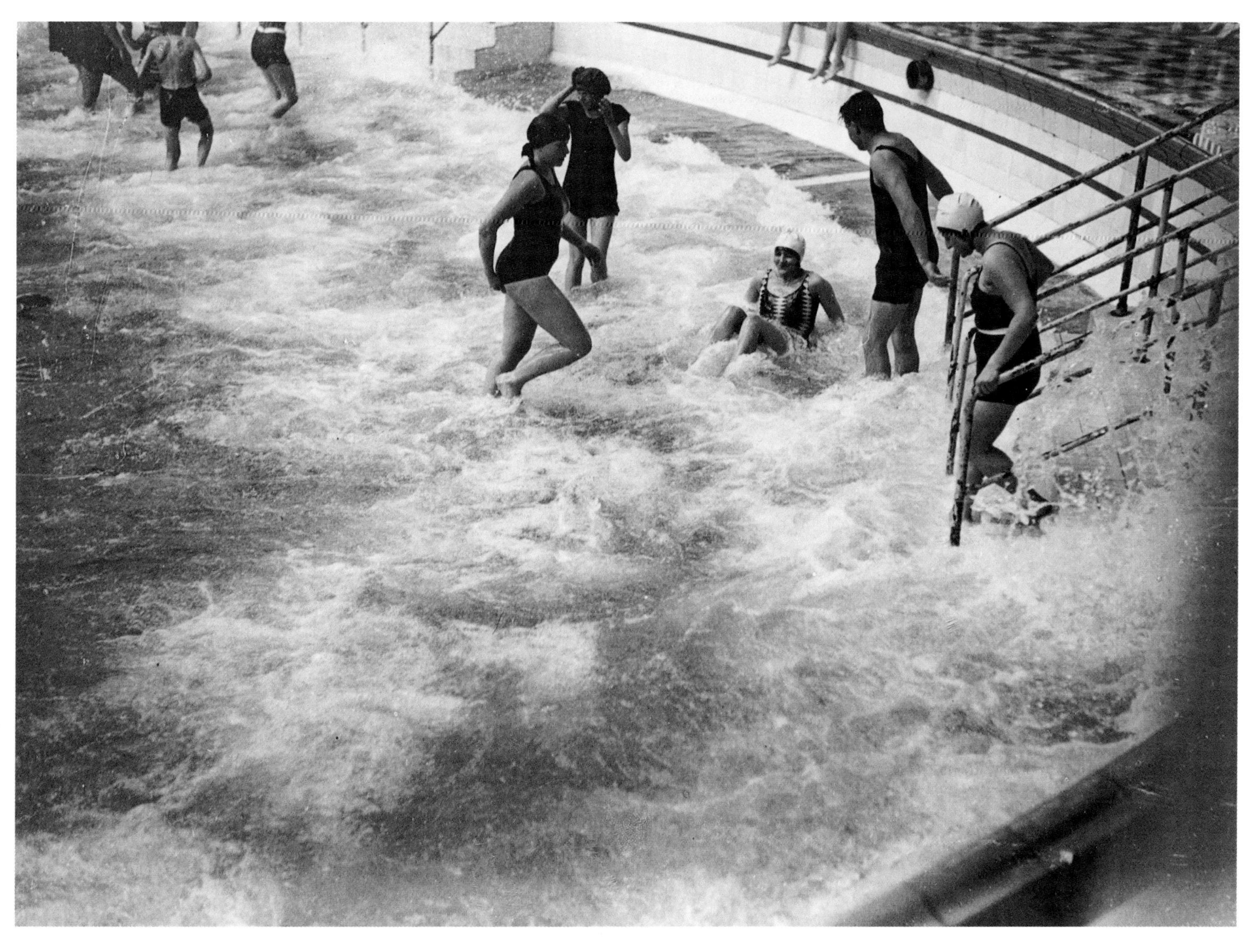

Felix H Man
Lunapark 1929
gelatin silver photograph
National Gallery of Victoria, Melbourne

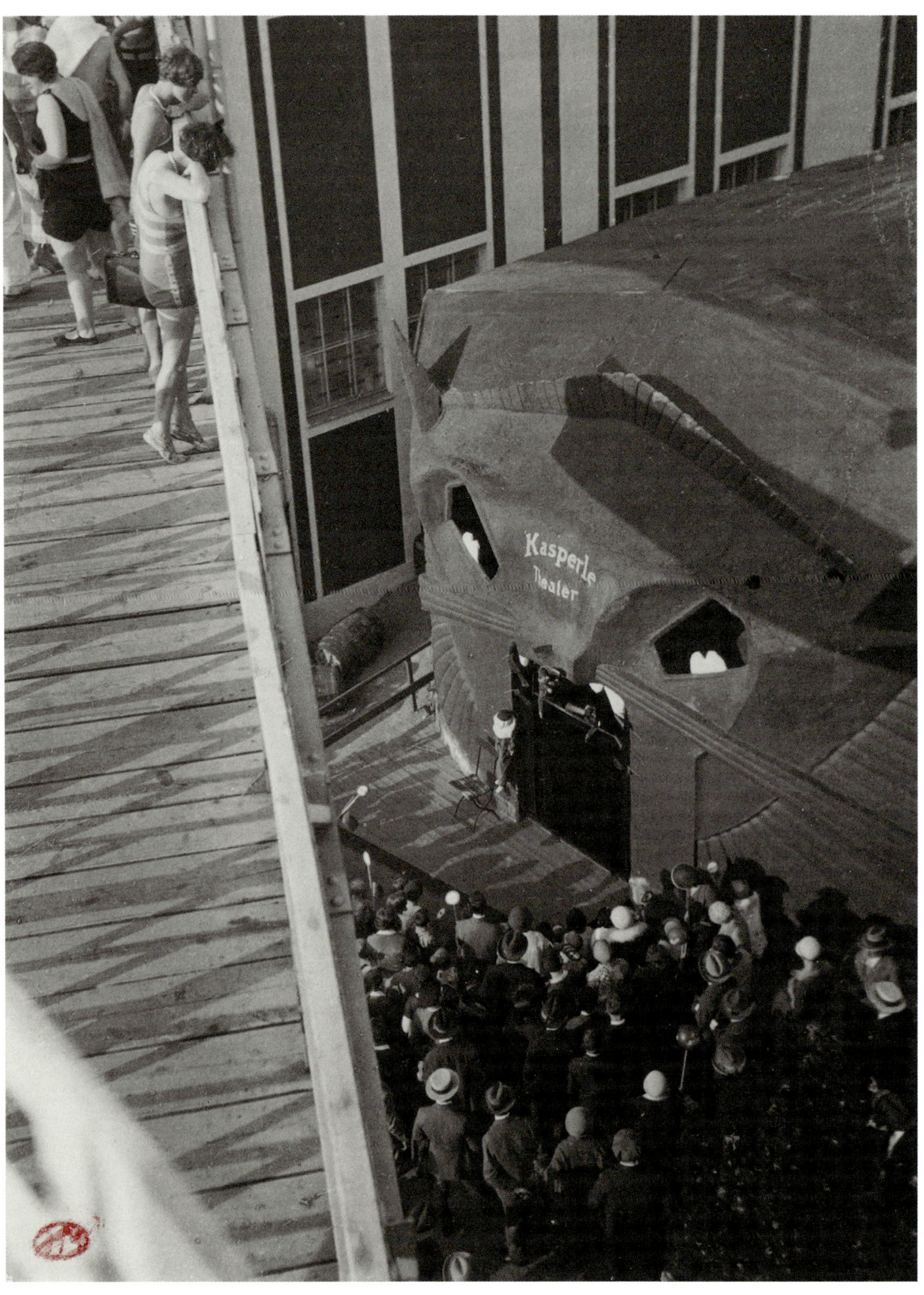

Felix H Man
Entrance to Lunapark, Berlin 1929
gelatin silver photograph
National Gallery of Australia, Canberra

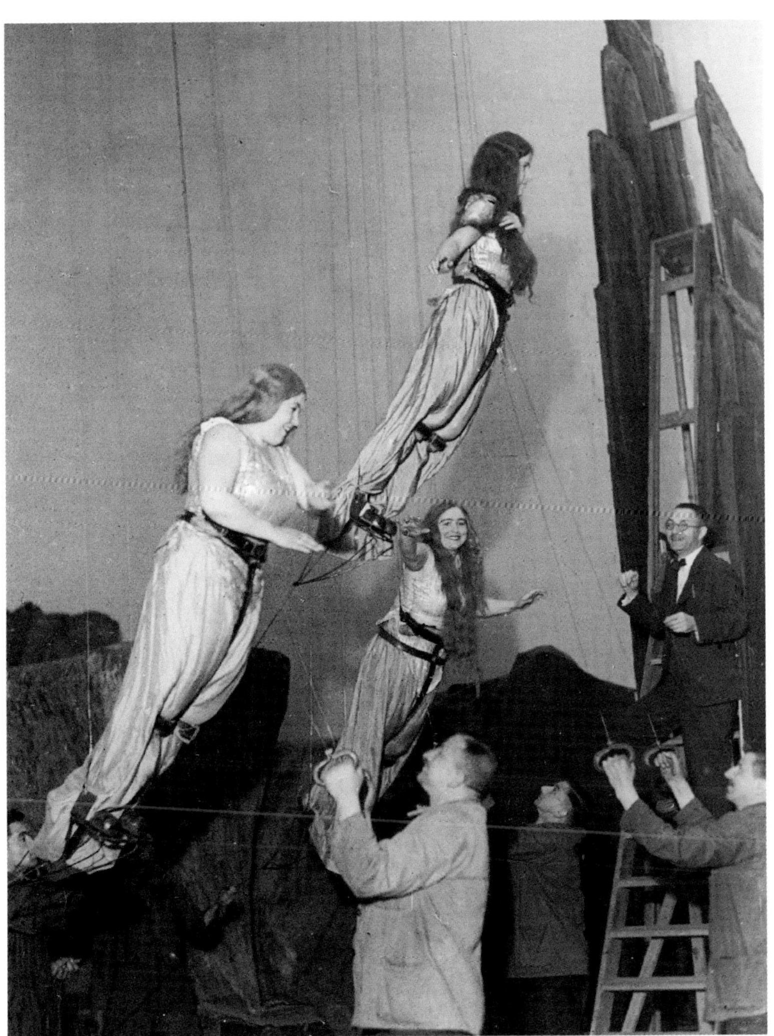

Felix H Man
Swimming rehearsal for Rhinemaidens, Bayreuth 1930
gelatin silver photograph
National Gallery of Victoria, Melbourne

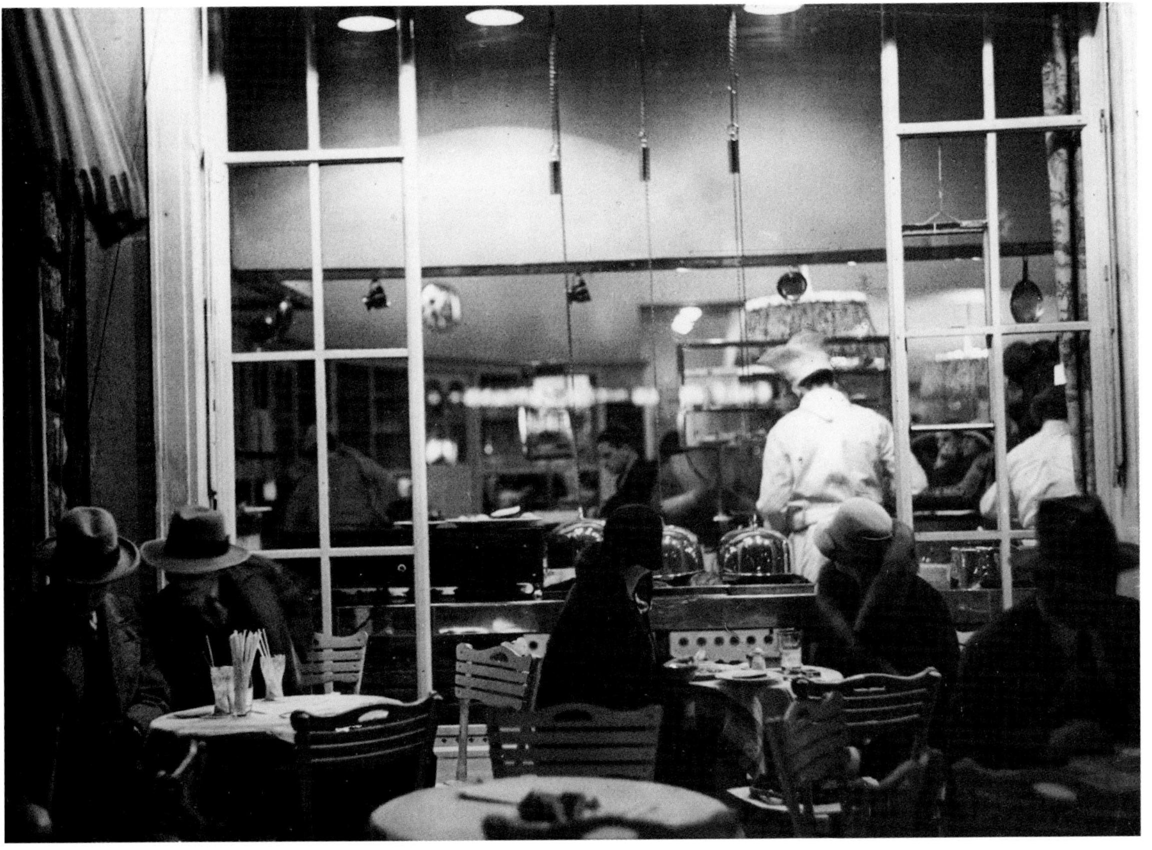

Felix H Man
Kurfürstendamm after midnight, Berlin 1929
gelatin silver photograph
National Gallery of Australia, Canberra

women are depicted with both eroticism and disgust. Grosz was a leading figure of the *Neue Sachlichkeit* (New Objectivity) movement, and was uncompromising in his depiction of the degradation of life and culture occurring in the metropolis. His images show a city of artifice that is without soul or humanity following the atrocities and hypocrisies of war, a city crowded with vacant characters united only by their desire to profit.

Human subjects, the many and varied participants of the extraordinary Weimar era cities, were also the focus of scrutiny through the camera lenses of August Sander and Hugo Erfurth. Sander had a highly specific vision for photography; he used it as a means to quietly and soberly document the entire spectrum of German life, creating typologies of human subjects. Begun prior to the First World War, Sander worked throughout the Weimar period on his quest to create his ambitious project *People of the 20th century*. Sander's portraits were consistent in their aesthetic composition, with clean lines and uncontrived poses, and an emphasis on realism that aligned his practice to the *Neue Sachlichkeit* artists. Although Sander ranked his subjects according to social status, his photographs remained sincere, with a humanitarian intent. Sander's consistent approach created an extraordinary document of the mutability of society in the modern cities of Germany, ranging from vagabond performers, as in *Circus artistes* 1926–32 (p 217), to the jaunty society figures and artists in *The painter Otto Dix and his wife, Martha* 1925–26 (p 215).

While Sander was encyclopaedic in approach, Erfurth was highly selective in his representation of the figures he felt contributed significantly to the cultural life of the time. Working in Dresden, Erfurth created beautifully composed images of architects, painters and art dealers, with a focus on representing the psyche of the sitters. Using natural light sources within the studio, his graphic photographs were then skilfully enhanced using the bromoil process to create iconic portraits that mirror the dominant personalities of the subjects. Erfurth's photographs, while using somewhat traditional techniques, form a dynamic record of some of the most forward-thinking citizens that shaped the cities of the Weimar era (pp 219–23).

The evolution of dense, urban cities in the turbulent period of the Weimar Republic was the subject of endless fascination for artists of the time, who depicted the metropolis with intrigue, attraction, lust and loathing. The city was seen as both the site and cause of the excesses of human behaviour. Berlin was the ultimate metropolis of the time and it was an emblem of modernity in the Weimar period – restless, stimulating and ultimately fragile.

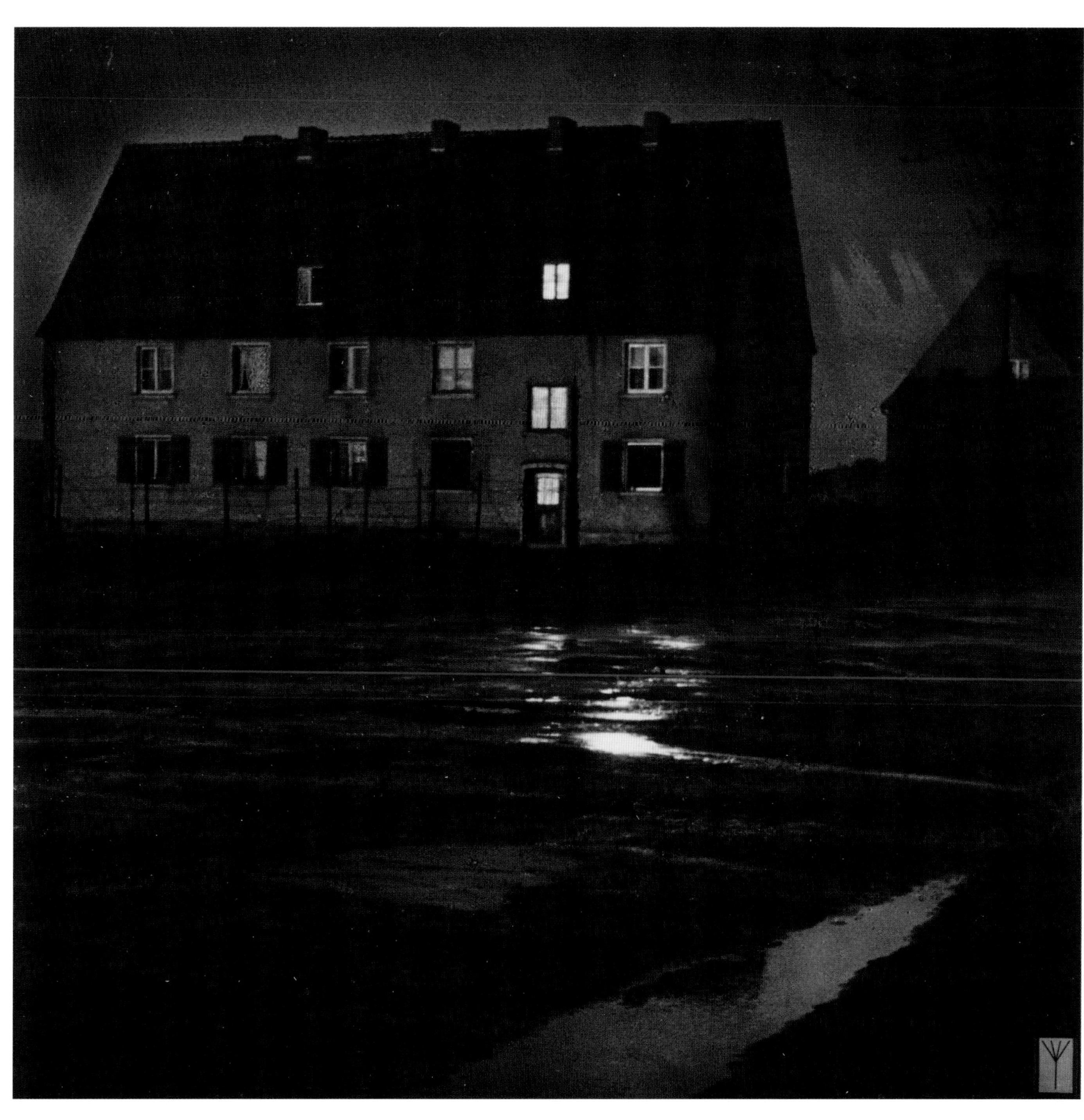

Willy Zielke
Light in the night 1930
gelatin silver photograph
Art Gallery of New South Wales, Sydney

MAX BECKMANN

The trapeze

Max Beckmann's extraordinary and unique series of paintings and prints depicting circus performers offers fascinating insights into the ways in which one of Weimar Germany's leading artists responded to modernity. In these works, which were created in Frankfurt am Main in the early 1920s, Beckmann turned away from the 'big city' subjects favoured by George Grosz and Otto Dix, and concentrated on circus and carnival scenes, depicting acrobats, trapeze artists, tightrope walkers and dancers who existed on the margins of urban society. Beckmann's enigmatic portrayals of this exotic milieu focused on creating an atmosphere of psychic unease through the construction of claustrophobic spaces and constrained relationships. These works have long been interpreted as representing universal truths about human behaviour and Beckmann certainly does emphasise the physicality of the costumes, and the attributes and activities of the performers to show the superficiality of the external reality they represent.[1] In the context of this exhibition, *The trapeze* 1923 and related works on paper allude more specifically to the prevailing sense of anxiety, uncertainty and change experienced in the modern era.

Beckmann has drawn upon many of the pictorial elements employed in earlier scenes of contemporary life, most notably *The dream*, which had been painted two years earlier, in 1921 (p 61). In both works he uses the same tight crowding of intertwined figures in a narrow, vertical space that appears compressed and highly constructed, like a stage set. The theatricality and complexity of the composition is taken even further in *The trapeze*, where seven acrobats are assembled upon a trapeze-like contraption, poised and elaborately dressed for their performance. However, the figures are unable to move and appear psychologically distant from each other; Beckmann's use of acidic colour, dominated by a palette of bright green, purple and orange contrasts, heightens this feeling of oppression.[2] The intense gaze of the upside-down acrobat dressed in orange-and-brown stripes – which is widely regarded as a self-portrait – draws the viewer not only

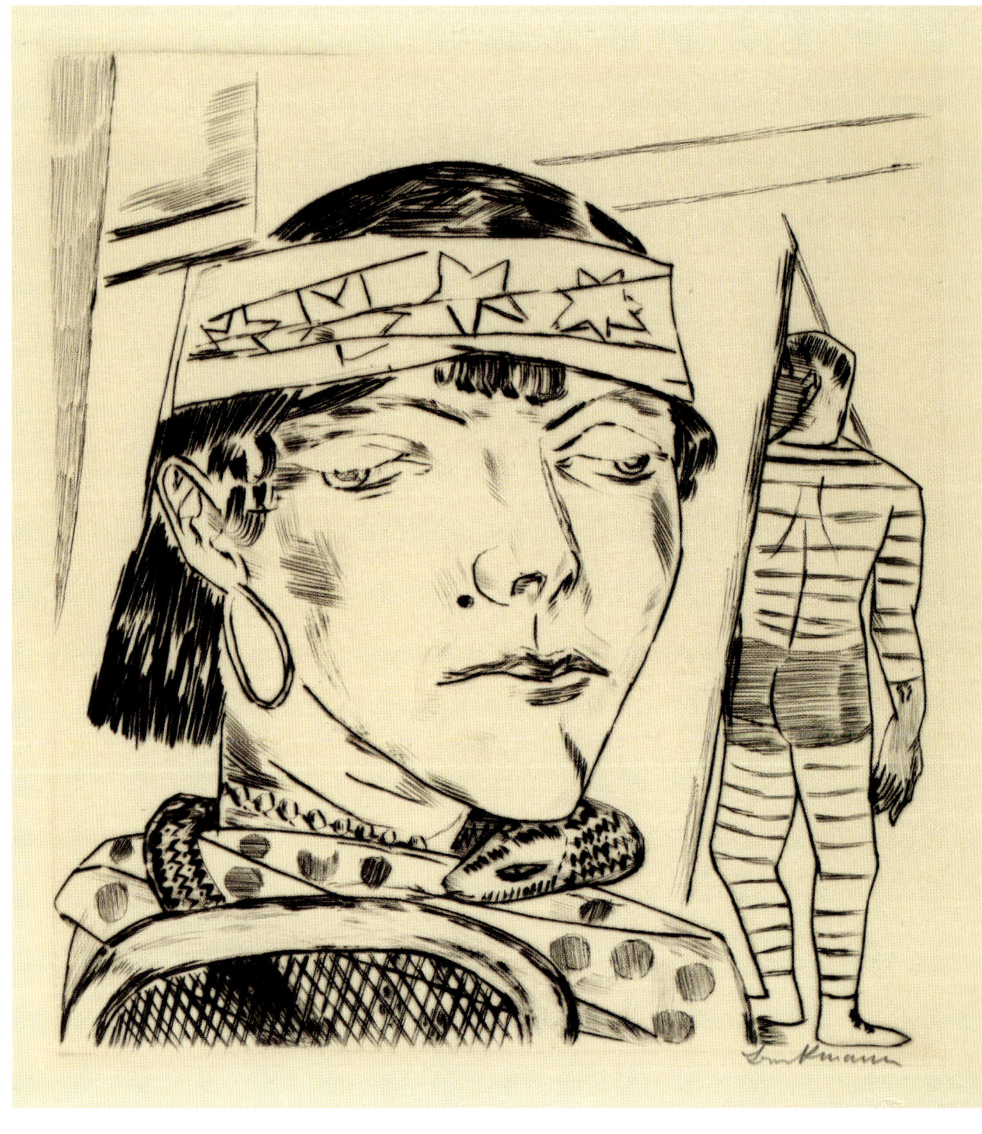

into the world of the circus performers, but also to what Beckmann saw as the role of the artist: taking risks, thrilling the viewers and astonishing the mind and senses.[3]

Though Beckmann is considered one of the towering figures of 20th-century art, his work remains relatively isolated in the context of German modernism and resists categorisation in terms of any single avant-garde movement. His work from this period is often compared with *Neue Sachlichkeit* (New Objectivity), in that it reinforced the representational aspects of painting and emphasised traditional artistic elements. Yet his continuing interest in the distorted angles, intense colour and tilted perspectives of the Expressionists was anathema to the supposed 'objectivity' of realist painting. Beckmann's major contribution to modernism was the development of a highly personal and complex symbolism that embodied the profound sense of creative individualism that helped to shape Weimar culture. JS

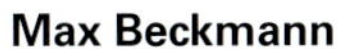

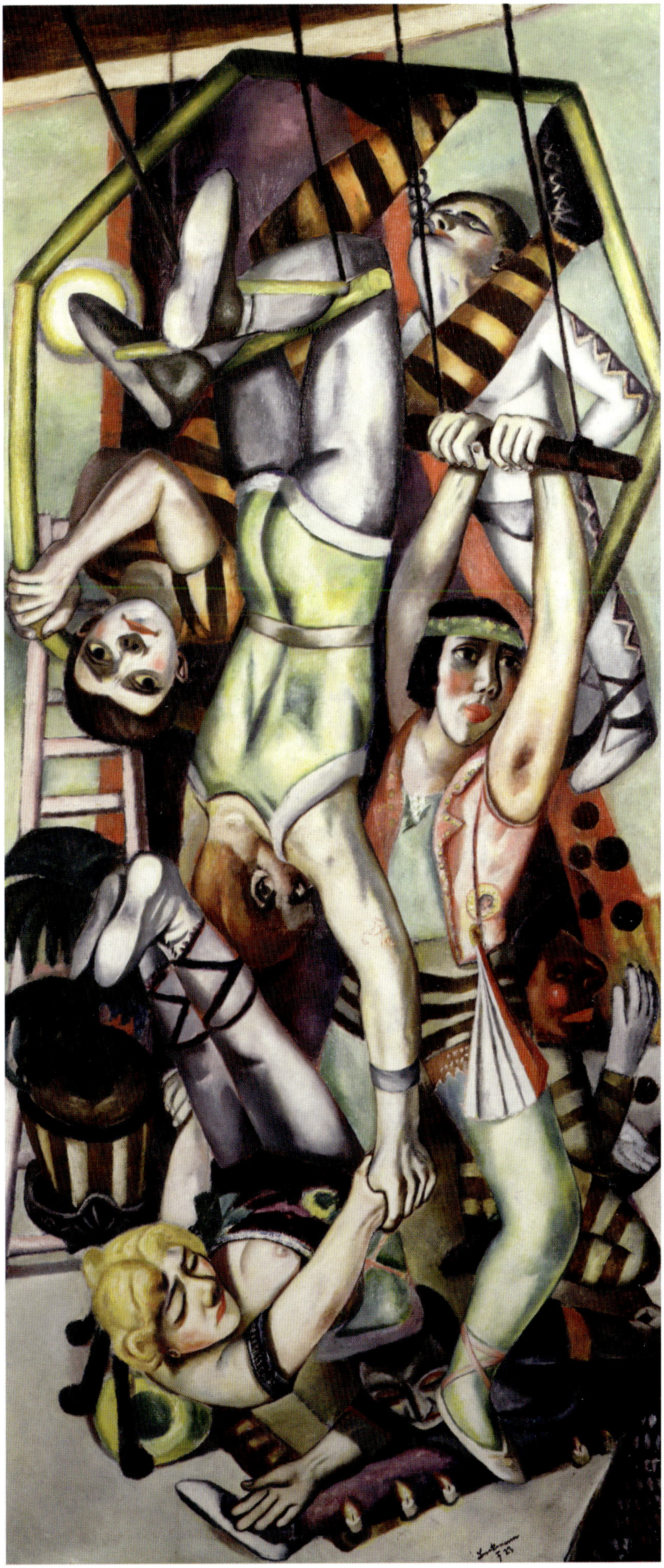

Max Beckmann
The trapeze 1923
oil on canvas
Toledo Museum of Art

opposite:

Max Beckmann
The snake woman 1921
from the portfolio Carnival 1922
drypoint
Art Gallery of New South Wales, Sydney

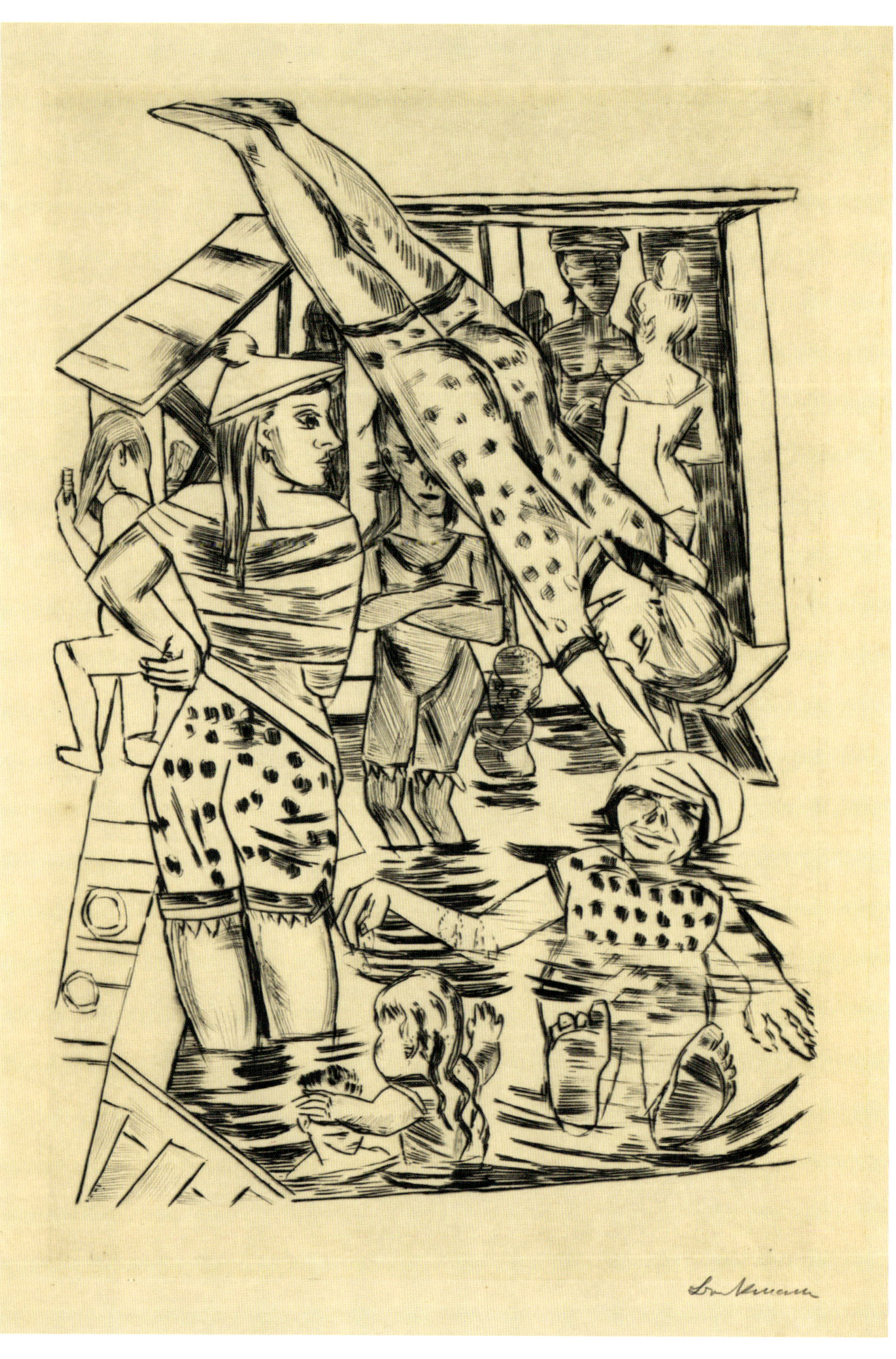

Max Beckmann
Women's bath 1922

drypoint
Art Gallery of New South Wales, Sydney

Max Beckmann
Negro dance 1921
from the portfolio **Carnival** 1922
drypoint
Private collection, Melbourne

Max Beckmann
Behind the scenes 1921
from the portfolio **Carnival** 1922
drypoint
Private collection, Melbourne

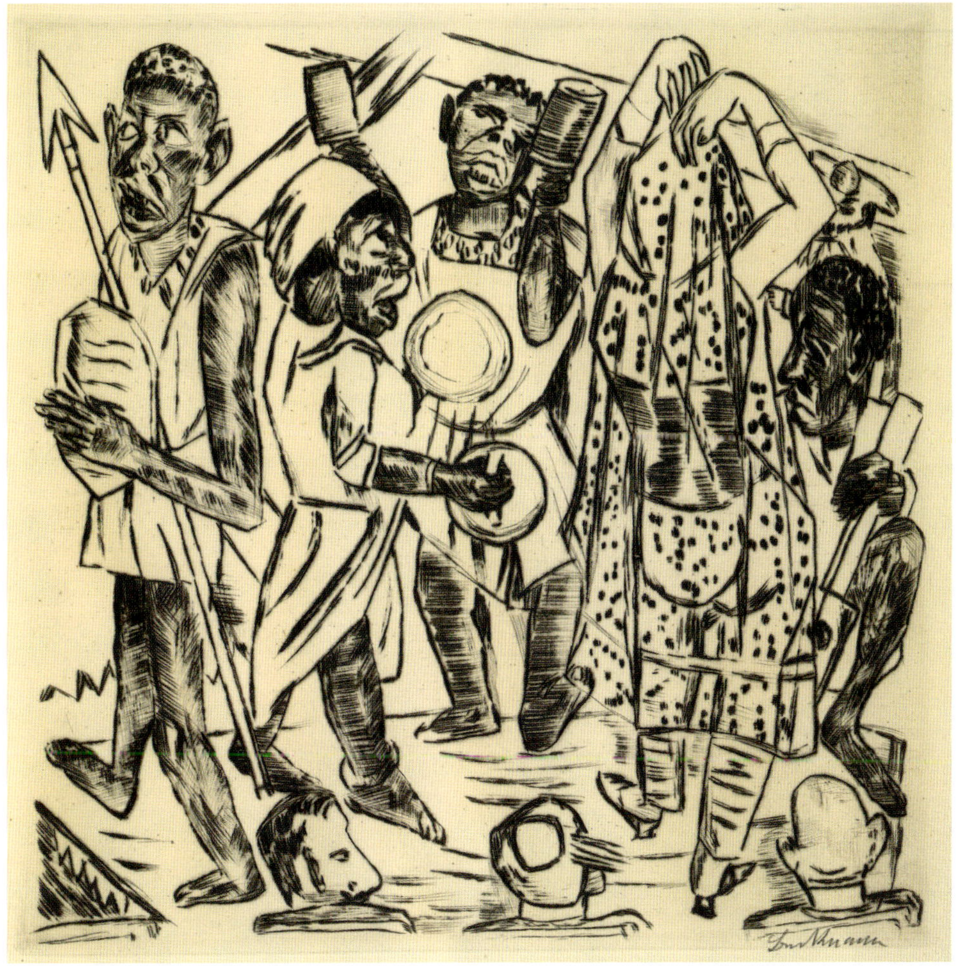

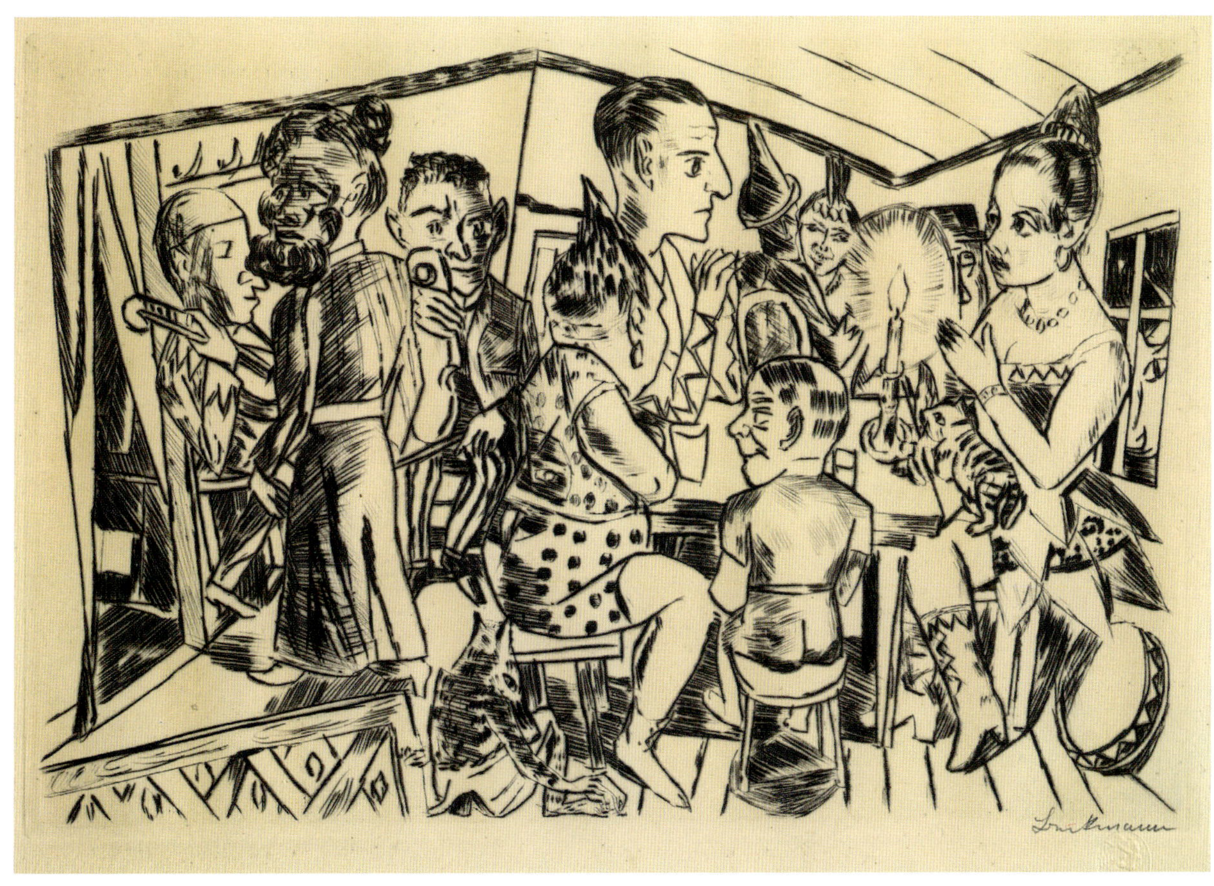

RUDOLF SCHLICHTER

Sex murder

While artists such as Otto Dix and George Grosz produced images that satirised Berlin's infamous and sinister night-life during the Weimar era, others – such as Rudolf Schlichter – focused on the grim realism of the city's seedy underbelly. Schlichter's gruesome and often disturbing paintings and drawings of the 1920s reveal the artist's fascination with depicting the vices, narcissism and excesses of the metropolis. His emphasis on representing the stark reality of his subjects often served to heighten rather than detract from the shocking nature of his work.

Schlichter moved to Berlin from the southern provinces in 1919, having studied art in Stuttgart and then at the Karlsruhe Academy from 1911 to 1916. His training in traditional academic draughtsmanship, combined with his desire to escape bourgeois conventions, proved enormously influential factors in the development of his art. He became one of the founding members of Berlin Dada and produced superb Dada collages, as well as extremely provocative objects, including *Prussian archangel* 1920 that he made with John Heartfield. This scandalous work consisted of a stuffed figure of a solider with a pig's head, and hung from the ceiling at the First International Dada Fair in 1920 (see p 81).

Schlichter joined the Communist Party and a number of left-wing artists groups through which he came into contact with Otto Dix, George Grosz, Bertolt Brecht and Alfred Döblin. Schlichter's political activism manifested itself through his empathetic representation of the working classes. His sensitive, matter-of-fact depictions of waiters, prostitutes, the unemployed and other socially disadvantaged people – as well as contemporary writers who sympathised with the plight of the workers, such as Bertolt Brecht and Egon Erwin Kisch – were intended to expose the harsh realities of contemporary society. Of equal importance were the range of erotically graphic water-colours and drawings he produced during the years he spent in Berlin in the 1920s (pp 208–9). Schlichter was particularly drawn to the subject of sex murder, which had emerged in the work of the Expressionists (pp 37, 49) and developed throughout the 1920s in German realist painting, literature and avant-garde cinema. Sexual violence occurred with greater frequency in Weimar Germany, and the fact that artists chose to prominently feature themes of sexual violence suggests that this motif expressed underlying anxieties about living in the metropolis.

Schlichter's *Sex murder* of 1924 is uncompromising in its objective and unsentimental portrayal of this brutal act. The essential details of the composition have been drawn with fine, black outlines to which transparent colour washes have been sparingly, yet confidently applied, exposing the dingy interior and the prostitute's bloodstained body and exhausted facial features. The stark simplicity of Schlichter's technique makes the subject of the murdered woman seem all the more horrific. This technique was refined further in *The embrace* c1927–28 (p 210) – believed to be a study for a now-lost painting of two women scuffling – confirming Schlichter's ability to brilliantly portray even the most daring and disturbing subjects.[1] JS

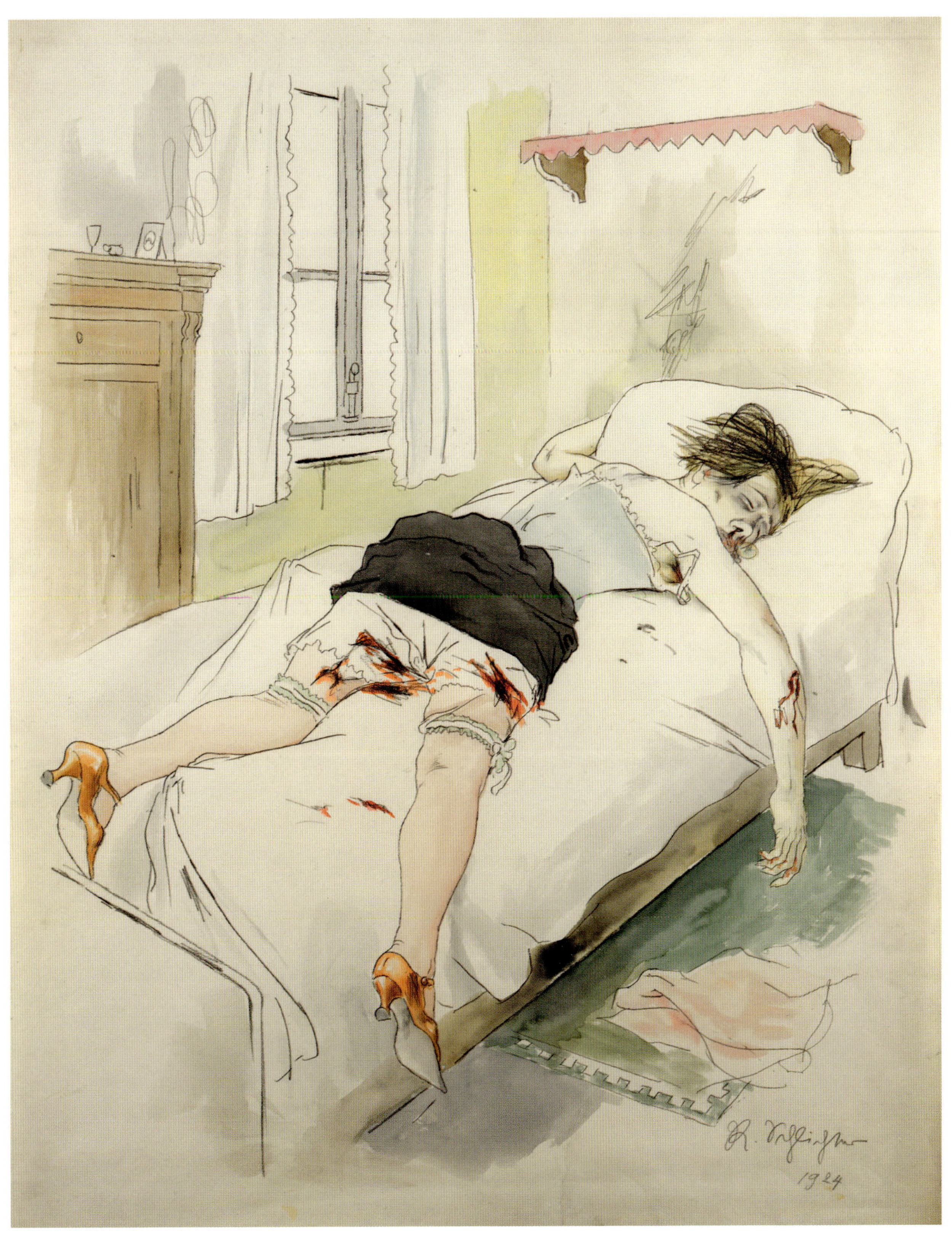

Rudolf Schlichter
Sex murder 1924
watercolour, black chalk
Private collection

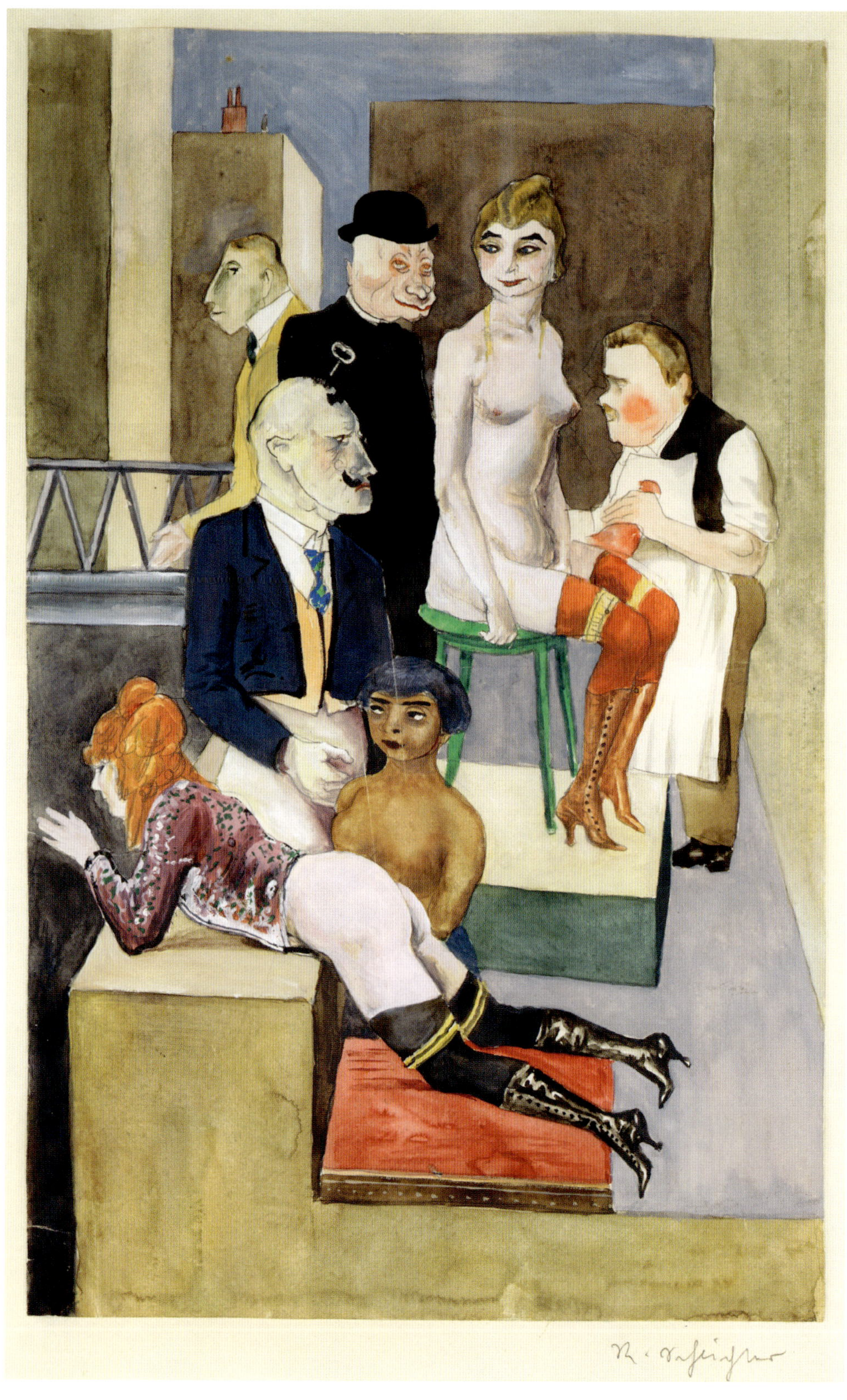

Rudolf Schlichter
Meeting of fetishists and maniacal flagellants
c1923
watercolour
Private collection

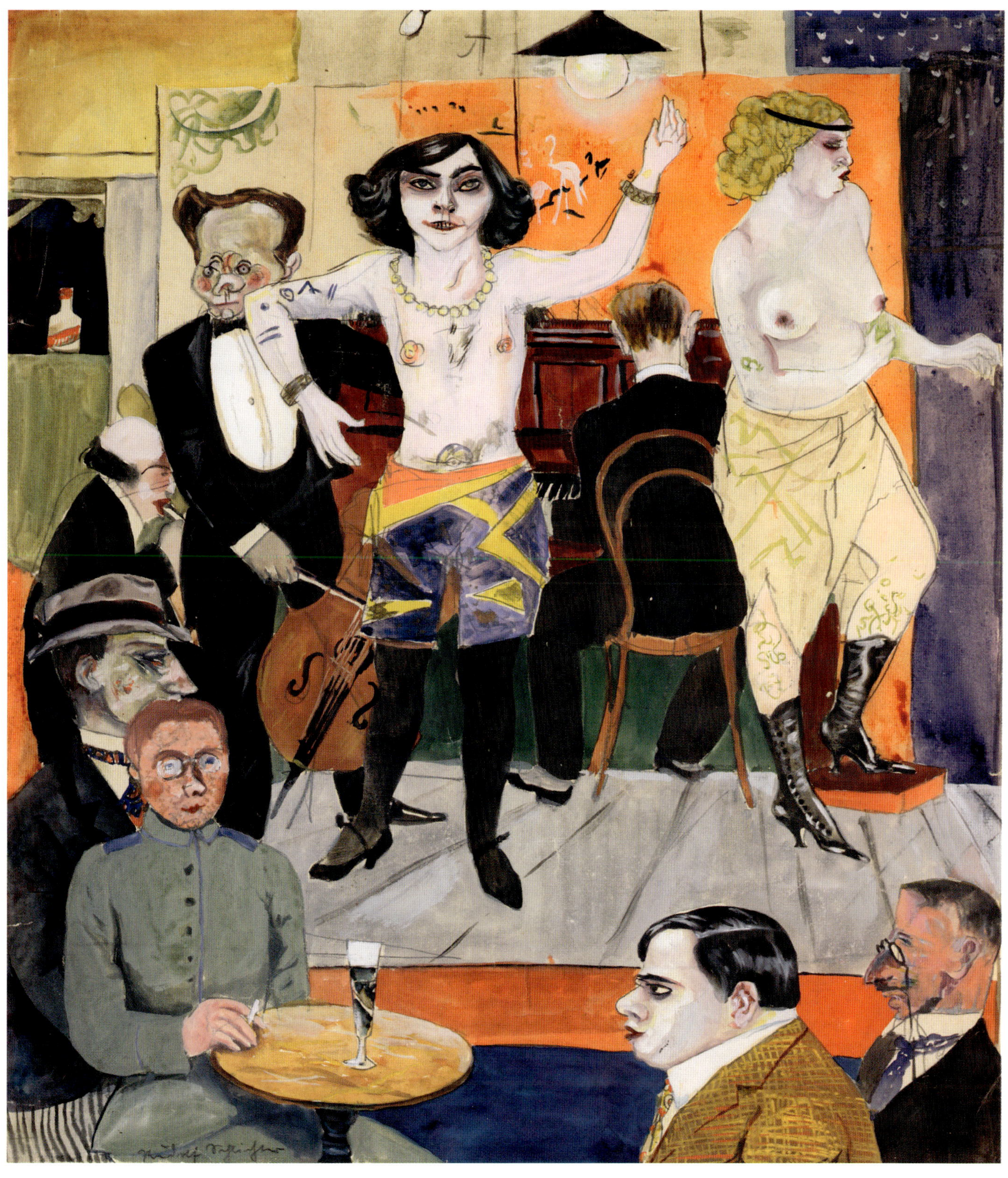

Rudolf Schlichter
Tingel tangel 1919–20
watercolour
Private collection

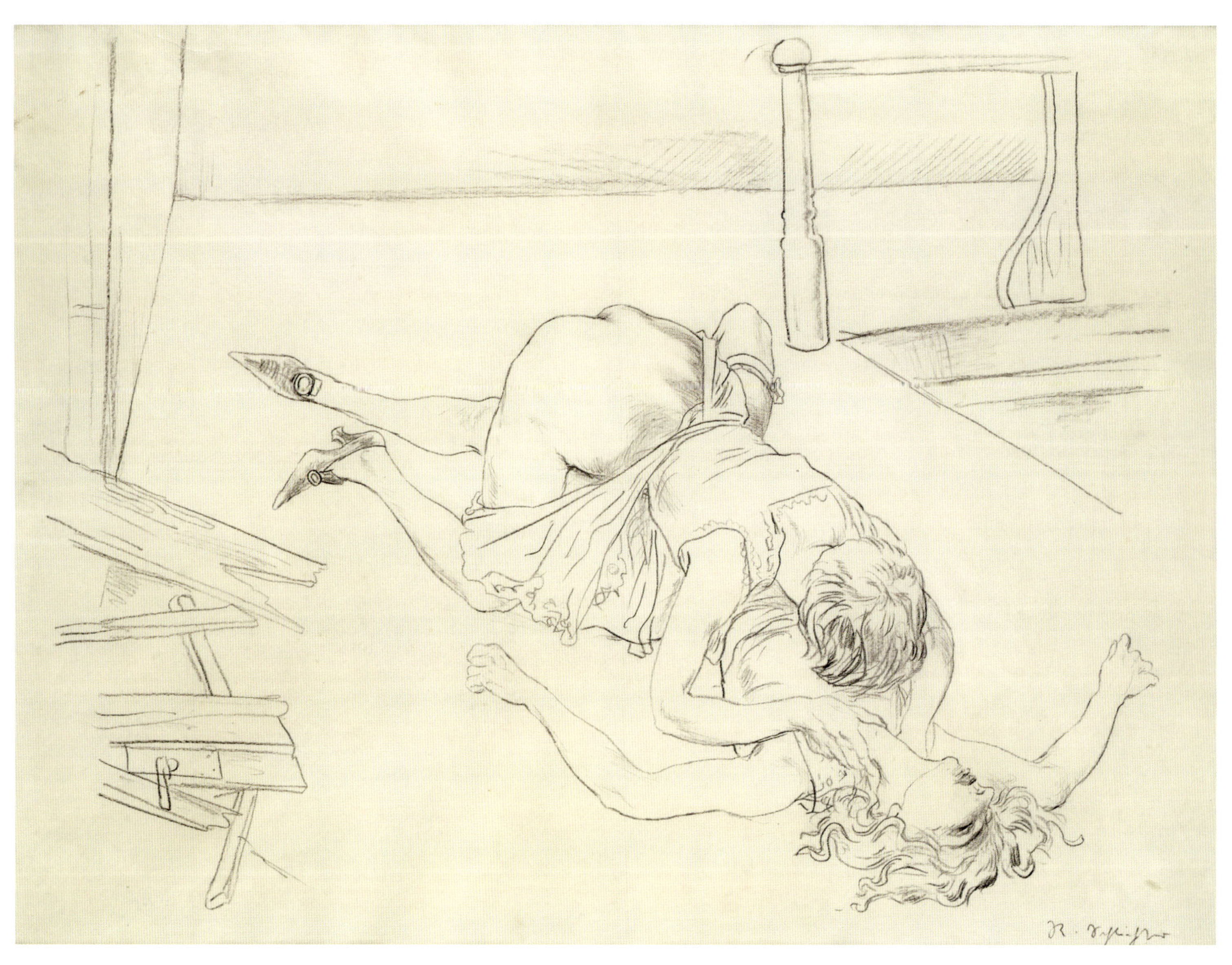

Rudolf Schlichter
The embrace c1927–28

pencil
Private collection, London

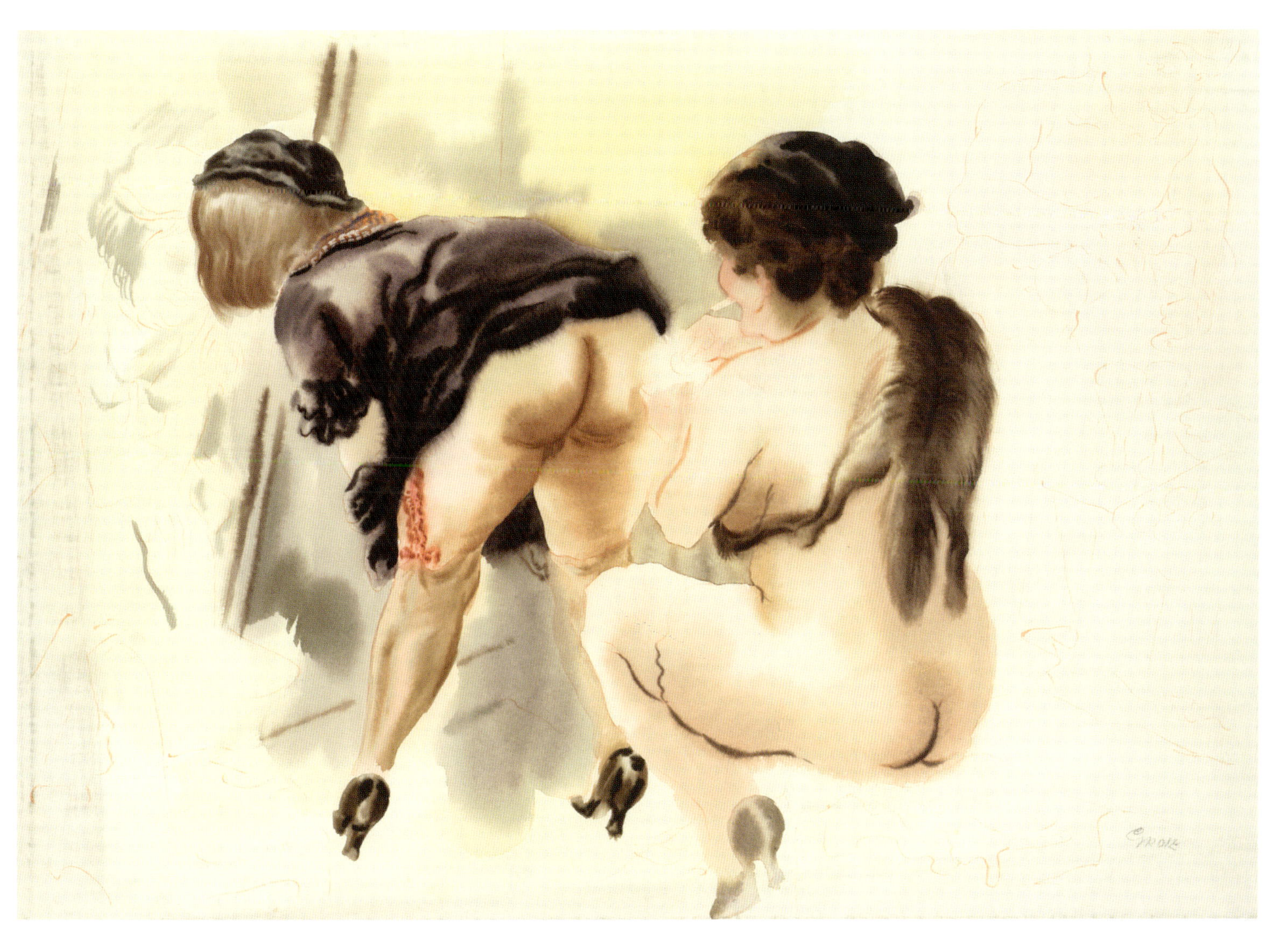

George Grosz
The powder-puff c1930
watercolour
Private collection, London

AUGUST SANDER

Secretary at West German Radio in Cologne

The small selection of photographs by August Sander in this exhibition formed part of an extraordinary, lifelong project to produce a collective portrait of the German people. Sander's ambitious photographic project evolved around the idea of representing 'types' of people, either professional or social, rather than portraits of individuals. First exhibited in Cologne in 1927, and followed by the publication of a selection of 60 images in 1929, Sander worked towards producing what would eventually appear posthumously as a seven-volume publication entitled *People of the 20th century: a cultural history in photographs*. This project included more than 600 photographs that Sander selected from about 2000 negatives.

Sander's unemotional and sharply focused images are among the most compelling photographs of the 20th century, and offer unique and enduring impressions of life in Germany during a period of rapid urbanisation and modernisation. The images appear straightforward and objective, capturing Sander's aim 'to be honest and tell the truth about our age and its people'.[1] Sander typically followed the conventions of the full-length standing figure or the three-quarter seated pose. He presented his subjects within familiar environments, or against a neutral backdrop in his studio, and dressed in their everyday professional or social attire.

Sander combined photographs of farmers, craftsmen and workers in the countryside near Cologne with tradespeople and professionals in the city, and classified the images of these 'types' into seven sections: Farmer, Skilled Tradesman, Woman, Classes and Professions, Artists, City, and Last People. His engagement with modernity is fully explored in this massive project, which he undertook from 1892 until 1954. Sander's ambiguity towards modernity is evocatively portrayed in *Secretary at West German Radio in Cologne* 1931, which he categorised as 'The woman in intellectual and practical occupation'. Centrally placed in the composition against a neutral, softly lit background, the sitter fully commands the viewer's attention. The mesmerising beauty and elegant dress of the woman adhere to traditional feminine attributes, yet her short, bobbed haircut, half-smoked cigarette and professional status indicate that she belonged to the new generation of independent, emancipated women who were breaking away from traditional female roles. The so-called *neue Frau* (new woman) was a motif frequently depicted in 1920s German art and came to represent a progressive view of the modern woman in Weimar Germany. Women could now vote, were able to work in a professional capacity outside the domestic sphere, could wear short hair and the newest fashions, and be seen alone in public. However, the emergence of the *neue Frau* was also perceived as a potential threat to the whole of society. Sander presents a positive picture of the *neue Frau* but also reveals her vulnerability through her uncertain gaze and stooped posture, as well as general fears about living in the modern age and breaking with the certainty of the past. JS

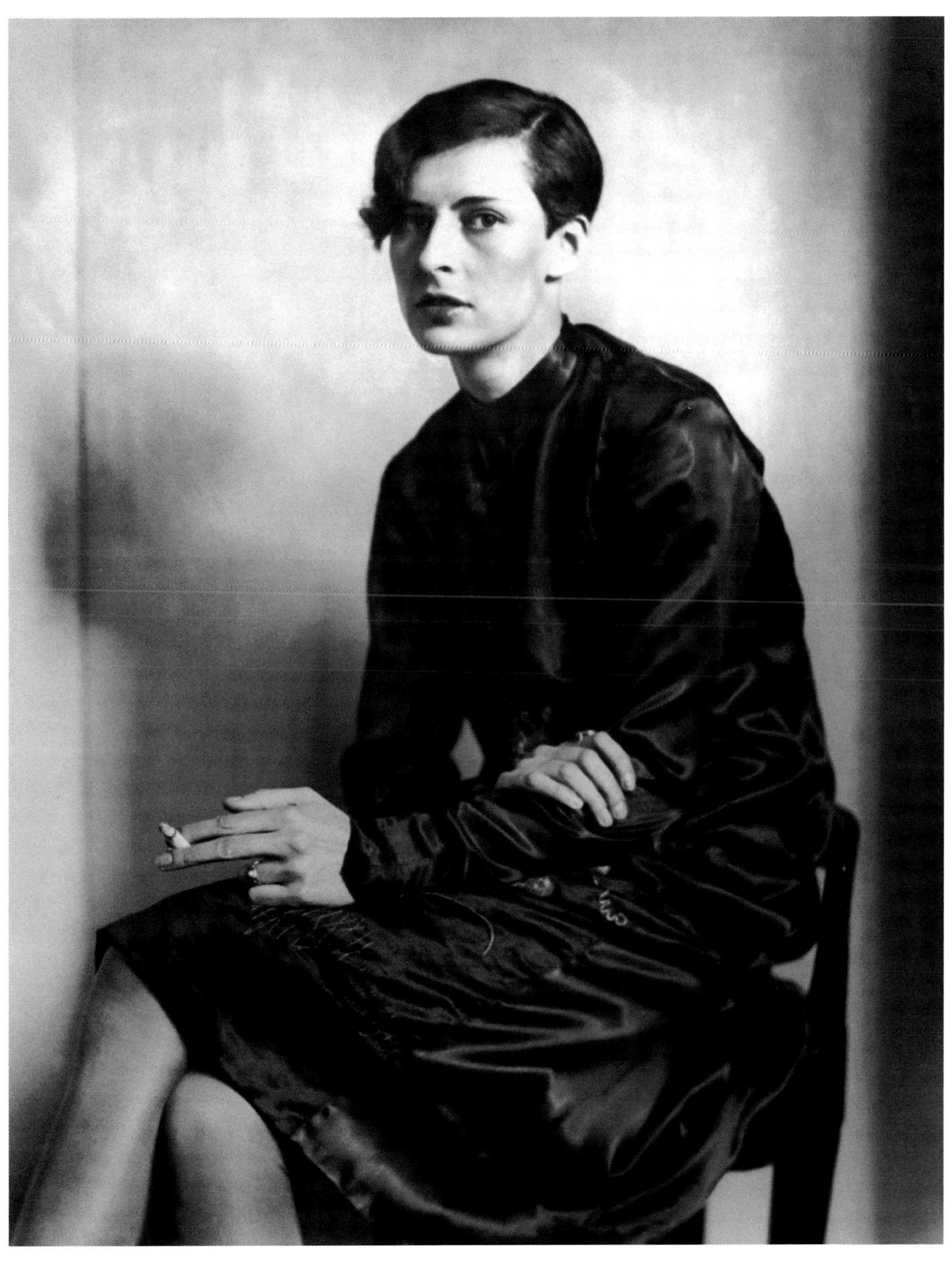

August Sander
Secretary at West German Radio in Cologne
1931
from the project People of the 20th century
gelatin silver photograph
Die Photographische Sammlung/SK Stiftung Kultur,
August Sander Archiv, Cologne

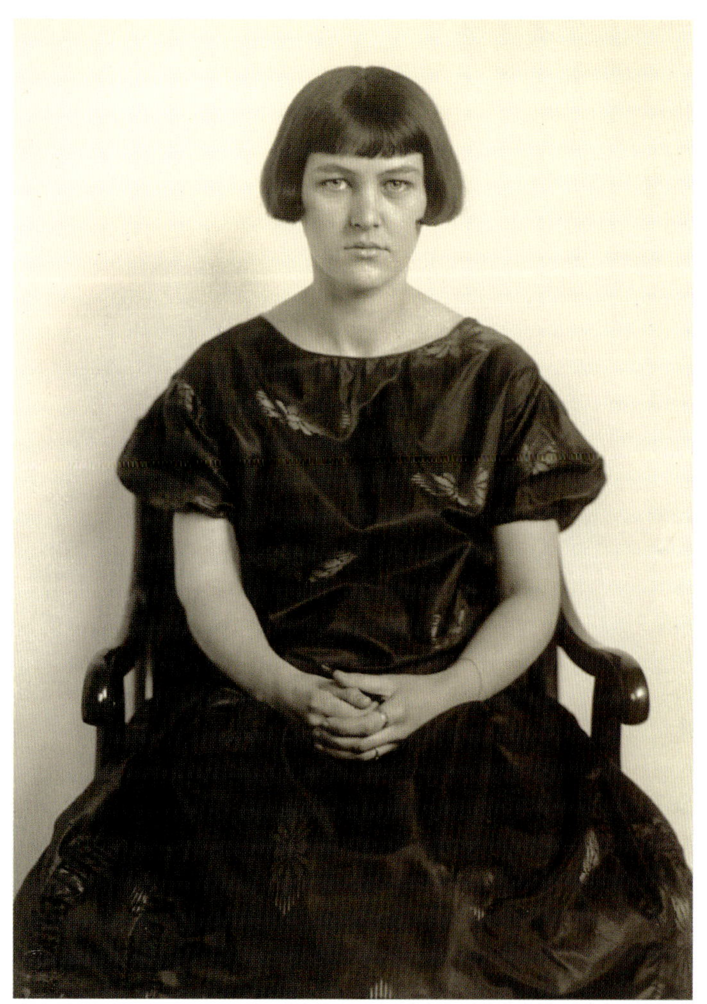

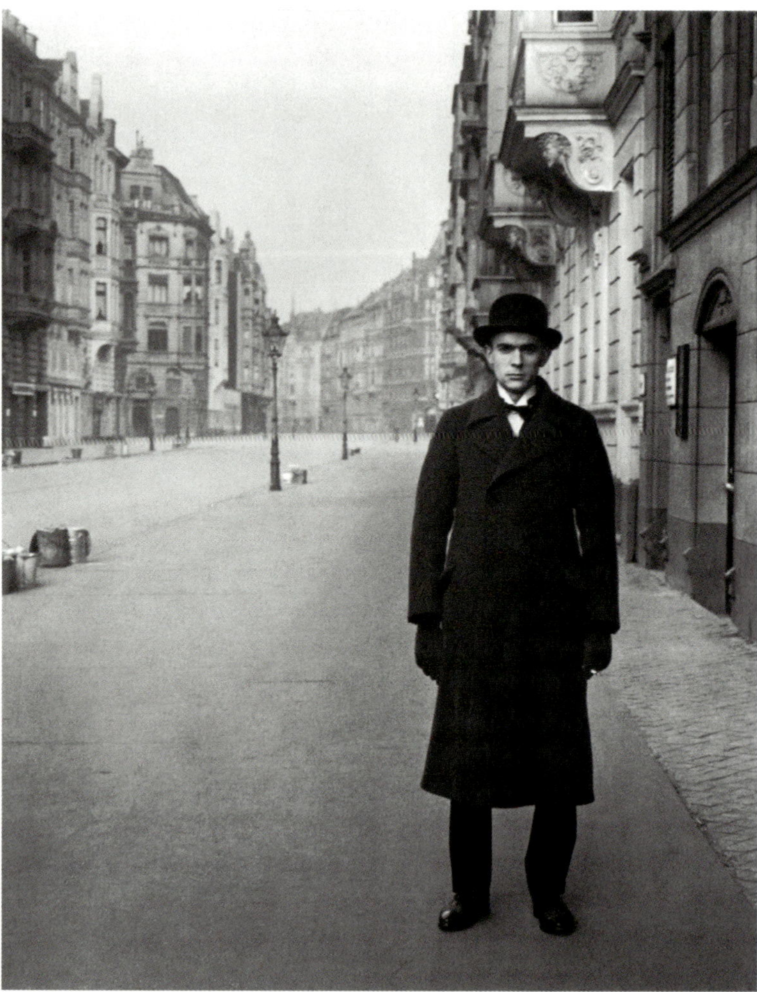

August Sander
Painter's daughter 1925
from the project **People of the 20th century**
gelatin silver photograph
National Gallery of Victoria, Melbourne

August Sander
Painter (Anton Räderscheidt) 1926
from the project **People of the 20th century**
gelatin silver photograph
Die Photographische Sammlung/SK Stiftung Kultur, August Sander Archiv, Cologne

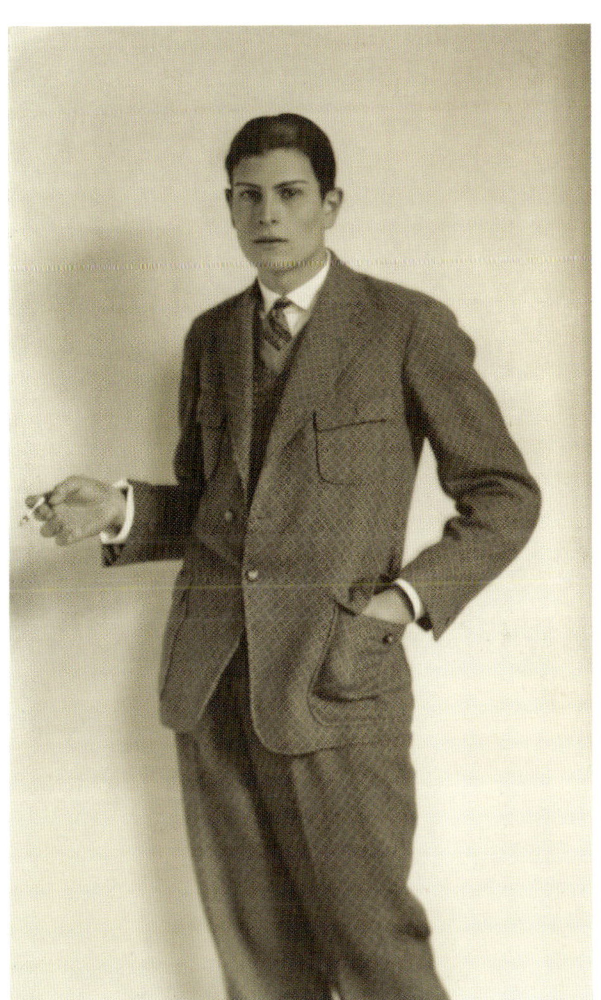

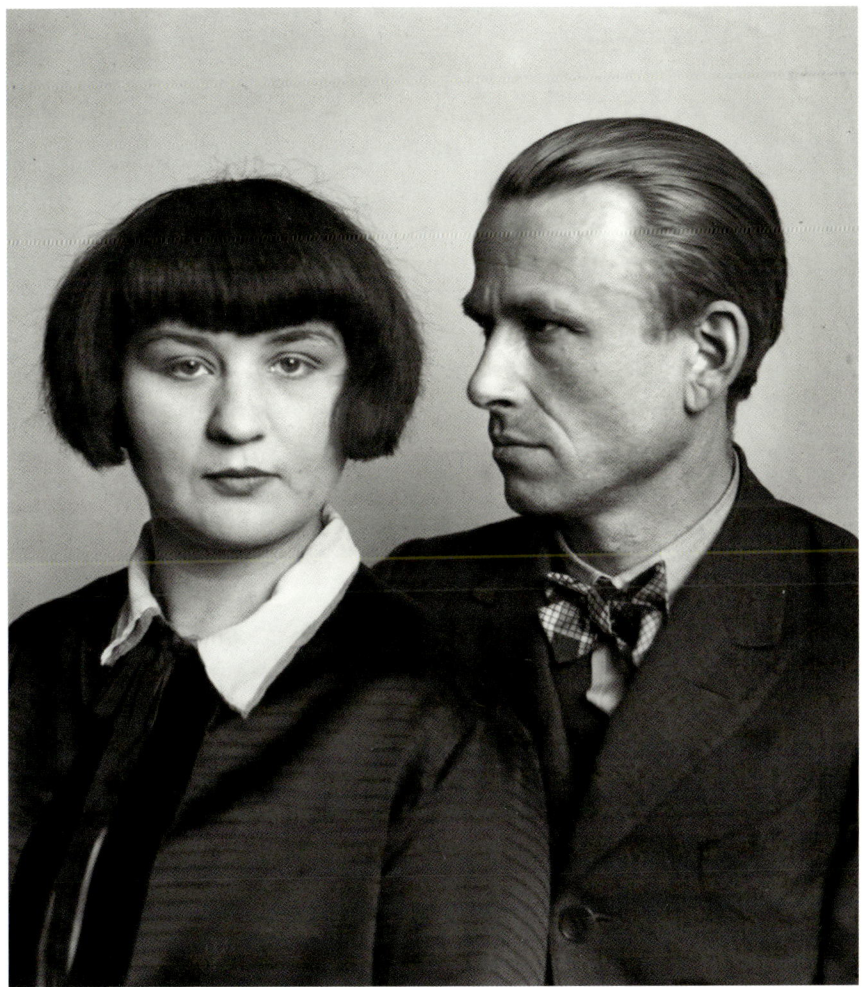

August Sander
High school student, Cologne 1927
from the project **People of the 20th century**
gelatin silver photograph
J Paul Getty Museum, Los Angeles

August Sander
The painter Otto Dix and his wife, Martha
1925–26
from the project **People of the 20th century**
gelatin silver photograph
Art Institute of Chicago, Chicago

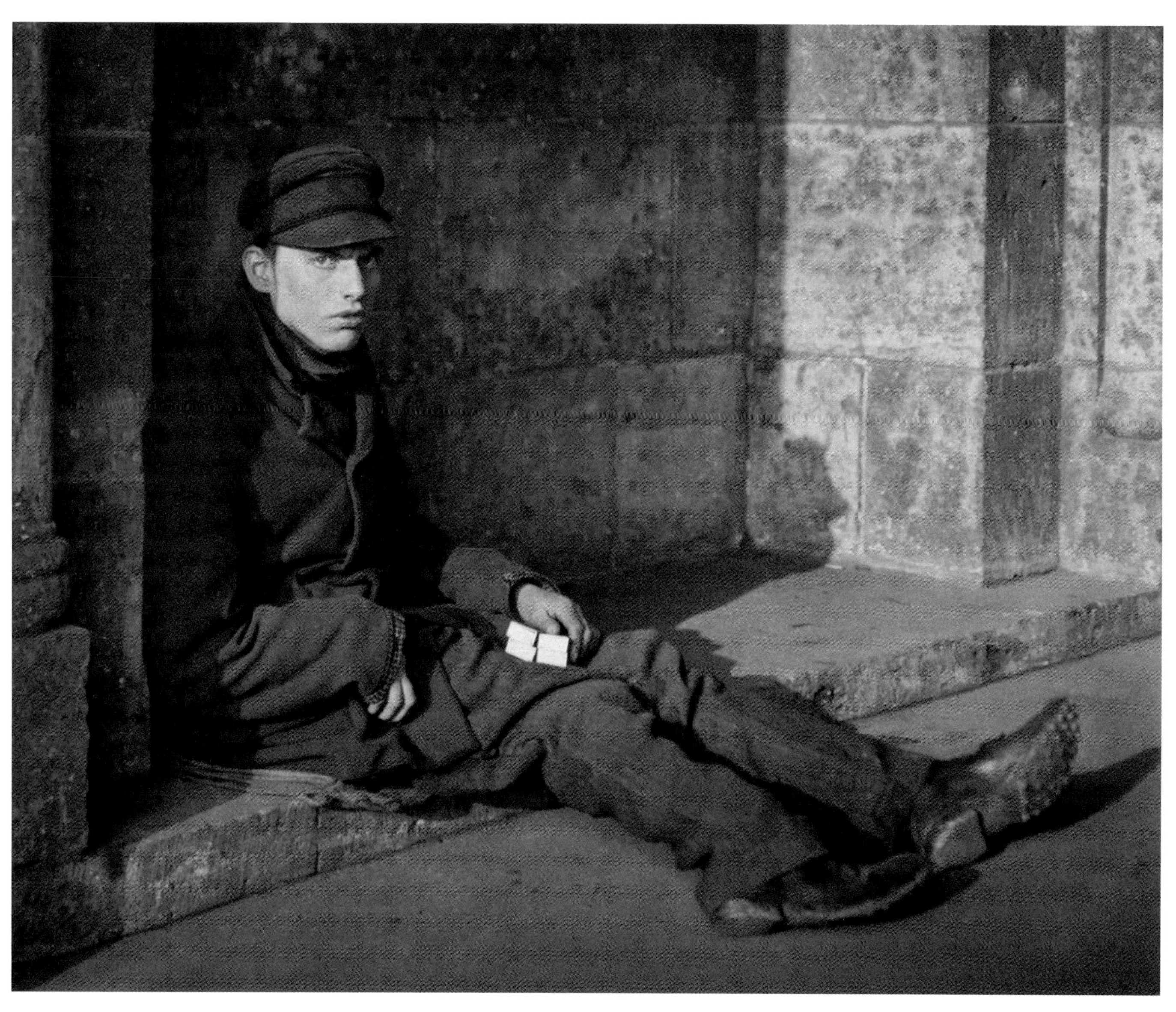

August Sander
Match-seller 1927
from the project People of the 20th century
gelatin silver photograph
Die Photographische Sammlung/SK Stiftung Kultur,
August Sander Archiv, Cologne

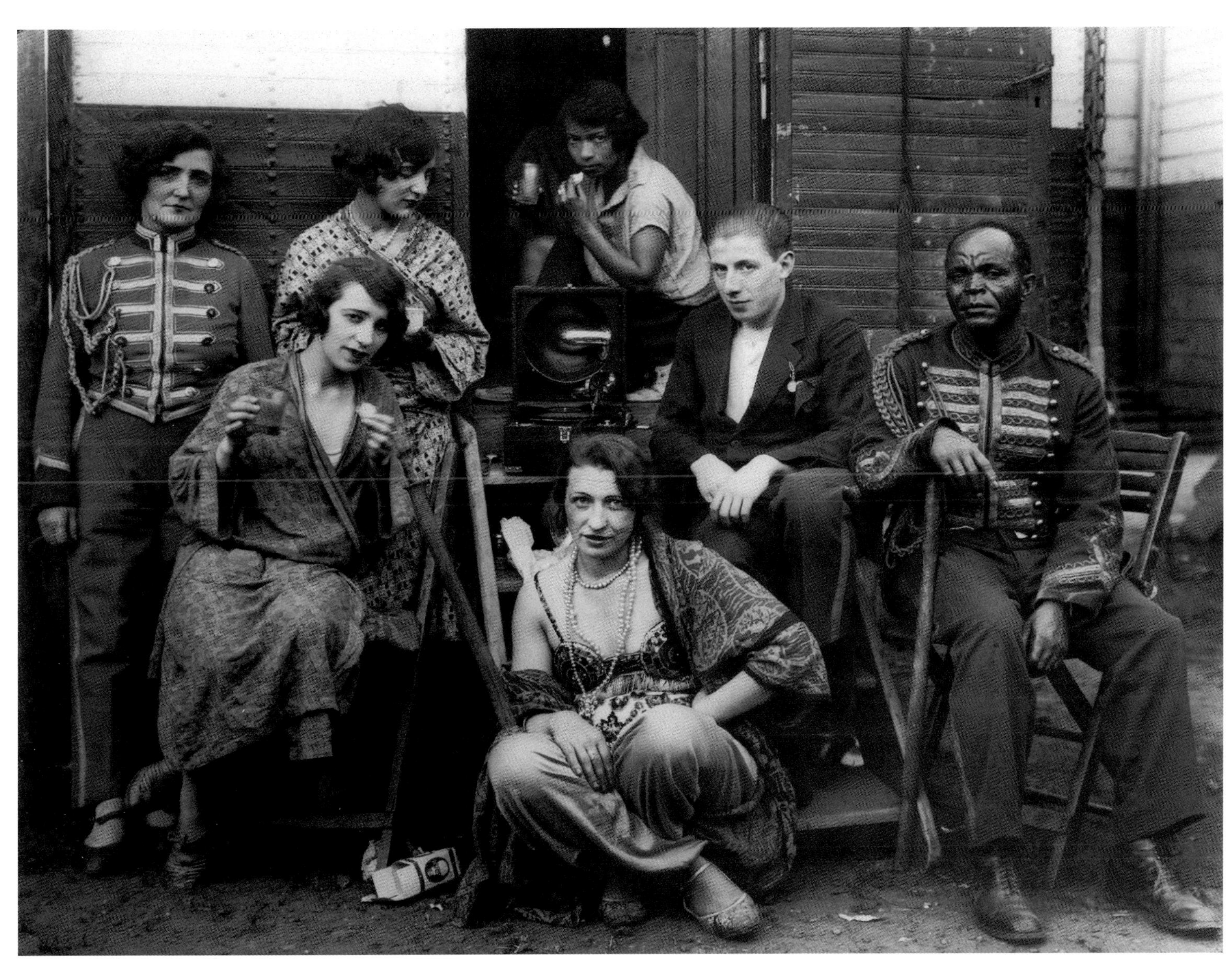

August Sander
Circus artistes 1926–32
from the project **People of the 20th century**
gelatin silver photograph
Die Photographische Sammlung/SK Stiftung Kultur, August Sander Archiv, Cologne

HUGO ERFURTH

Alfred Flechtheim

Hugo Erfurth worked from his Dresden studio during the early years of the 20th century, photographing the most prominent members of German society from the areas of art, culture, science and politics. Though he produced more than 500 photographic portraits of the most influential and important people who helped to shape modern German culture, his work is not usually discussed in the context of modernist photography. In contrast to many artists and photographers who embraced the newest avant-garde trends in the 1920s, Erfurth's work was strongly influenced by late 19th-century photography. He remained faithfully committed to traditional elements of Impressionist photography, which aimed to achieve a painterly aesthetic through the use of soft-focus lenses and the bromoil process. However, Erfurth also embraced the realist principles of 1920s German photography and sought to represent the modernity of his subjects.

Erfurth's portraits are important in the context of this exhibition, as they offer interesting comparisons with August Sander's monumental project *People of the 20th century*. In contrast to Sander's preoccupation with documenting general 'types', Erfurth focused on prominent citizens and attempted to capture the uniqueness and individuality of these people. He developed his own distinctive style of portrait photography, which concentrated on the faces of his sitters, often set against plain white backgrounds.[1] His mastery in manipulating images was achieved by touching up many of his photographs with oil pigments or producing bromoil prints, which are made by bleaching and fixing a gelatin silver photograph, and then applying a greasy ink to the wet print until the required density is achieved.[2] These techniques could increase the quality and effect of the portrait, and enhance certain characteristics of the sitter through the manipulation of light, graininess, tonality and contrasts.[3]

Contemporary debates around the question of whether a photograph could capture the psychological depth of a person were played out in these photographs. Otto Dix – who lived and worked in Dresden from 1919 to 1922 and was a friend of Erfurth's – fiercely maintained that it was only possible to capture the essence of a person in a painted portrait.[4] Erfurth managed, however, to capture a likeness as well as portray a sense of the sitter's personality in portraits such as *Alfred Flechtheim* 1928. Flechtheim was a renowned Berlin-based Jewish art dealer, who specialised in avant-garde French painting and was described by a contemporary colleague as having 'a fascinating head that inspired many artists to portray him. Once you saw this man, you never forgot him.'[5] Erfurth chose to highlight Flechtheim's distinctive profile in a traditional three-quarter length, seated studio portrait. The sitter is posed in an informal manner, just as he might appear during a moment of pause midway through a conversation. Erfurth's intriguing portrait invites the viewer to study Flechtheim's fascinating physical appearance, but to also consider his worldly and sophisticated personality. Erfurth was one of the few artists to objectively portray Flechtheim's character in a way that was neither flattering nor condescending, and that did not resort to racial stereotypes. In stark contrast, the Nazis later used caricatures of Flechtheim to symbolise all that was wrong with contemporary German art on posters for their infamous *Degenerate art* exhibition (p 277). JS

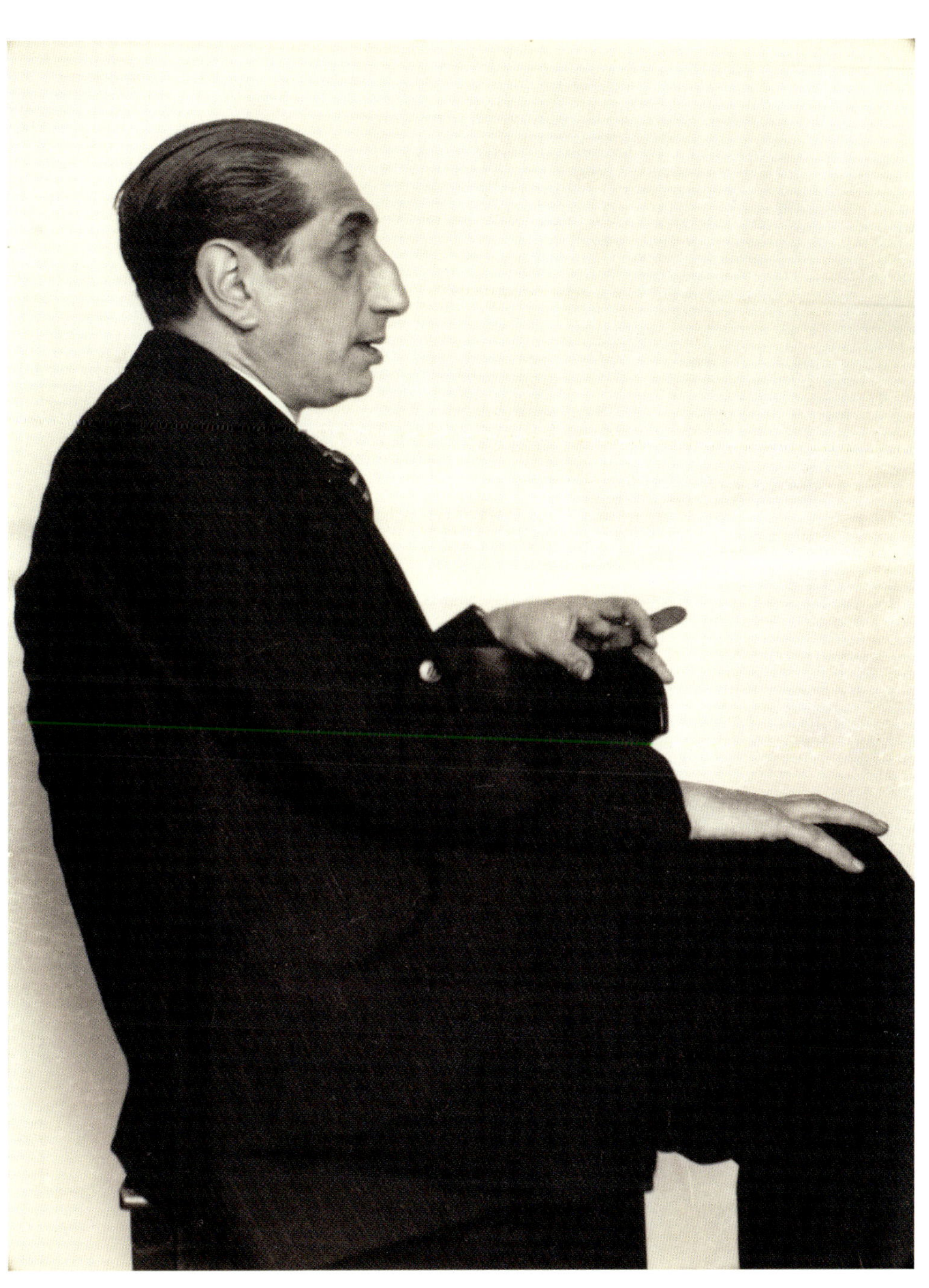

Hugo Erfurth
Alfred Flechtheim 1928
gelatin silver photograph
Museum Ludwig, Cologne

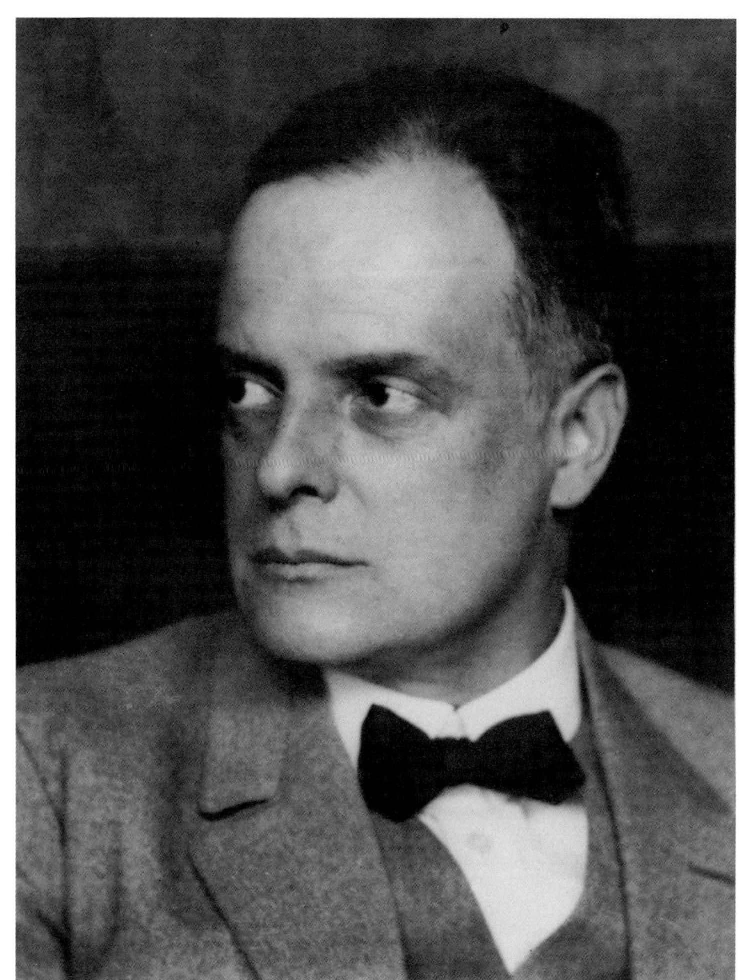

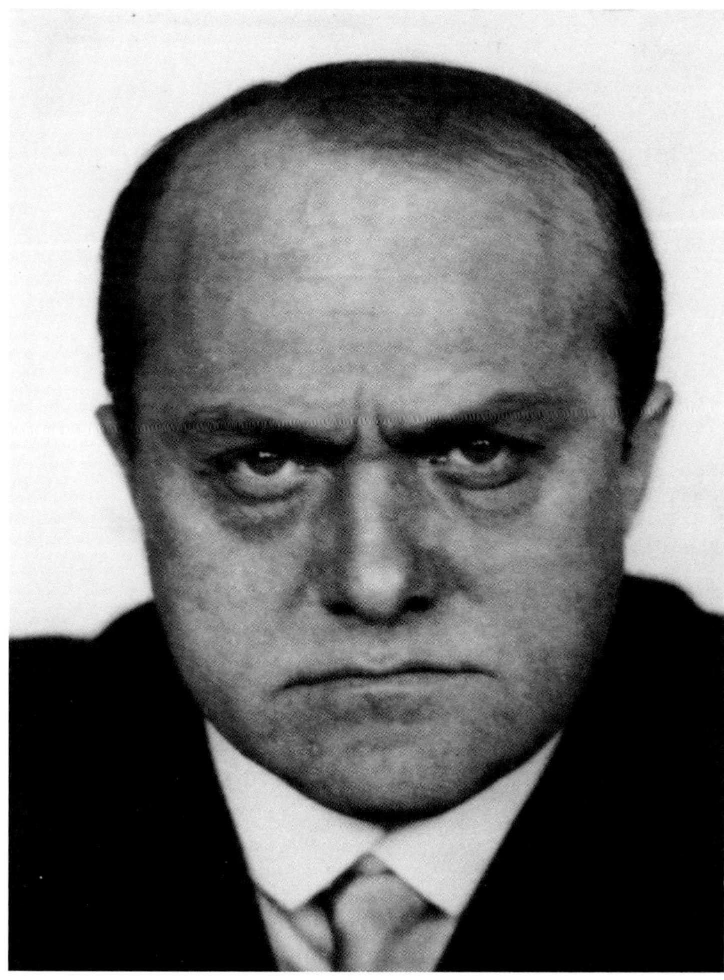

Hugo Erfurth
Paul Klee 1922–27
bromoil photograph, bromide gelatin silver print
Museum Folkwang, Essen

Hugo Erfurth
Max Beckmann 1928
bromoil photograph
Museum Ludwig, Cologne

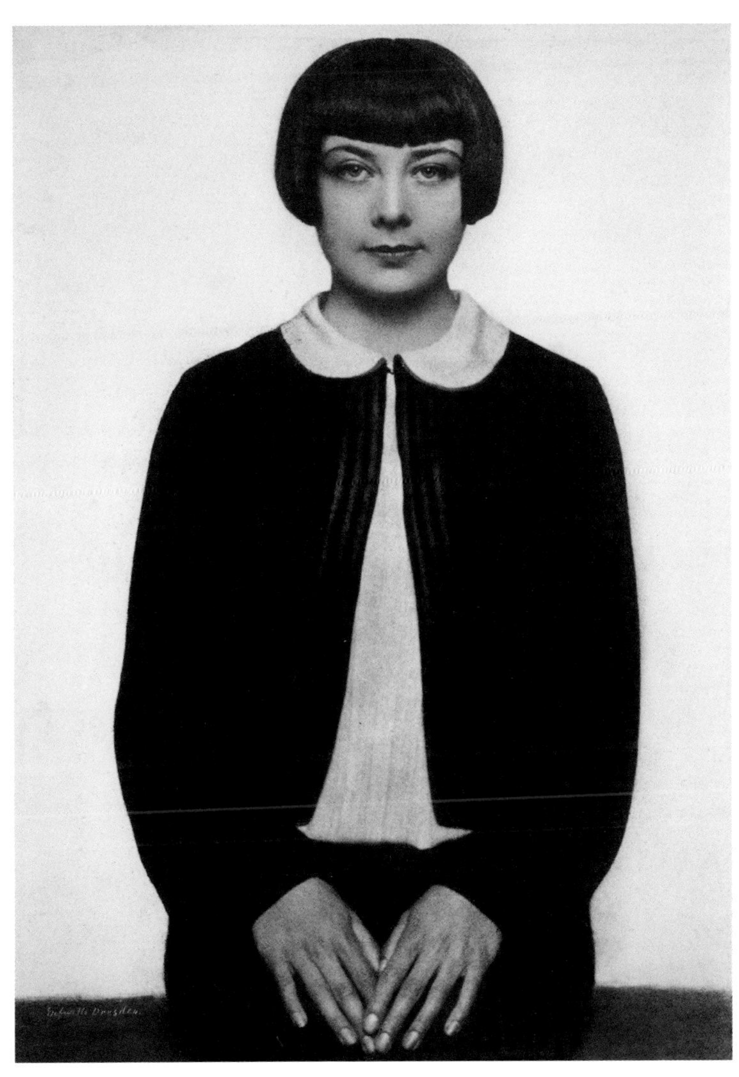

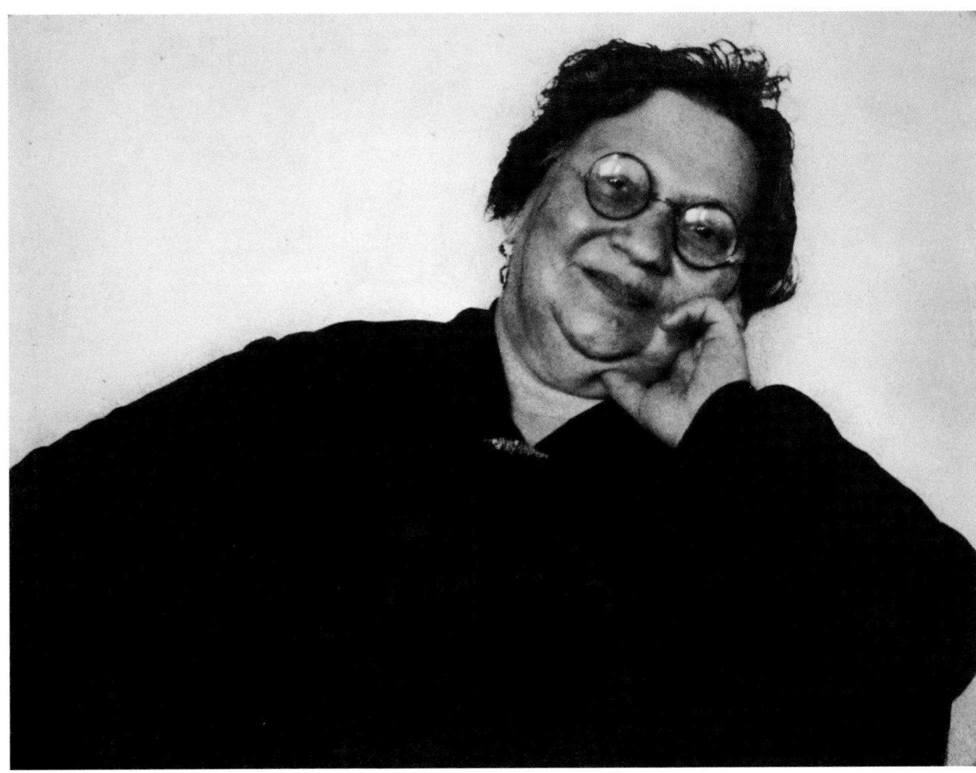

Hugo Erfurth
Hilde Wächler 1929
bromoil photograph
Museum Ludwig, Cologne

Hugo Erfurth
Johanna Ey c1930
bromoil photograph
Museum Ludwig, Cologne

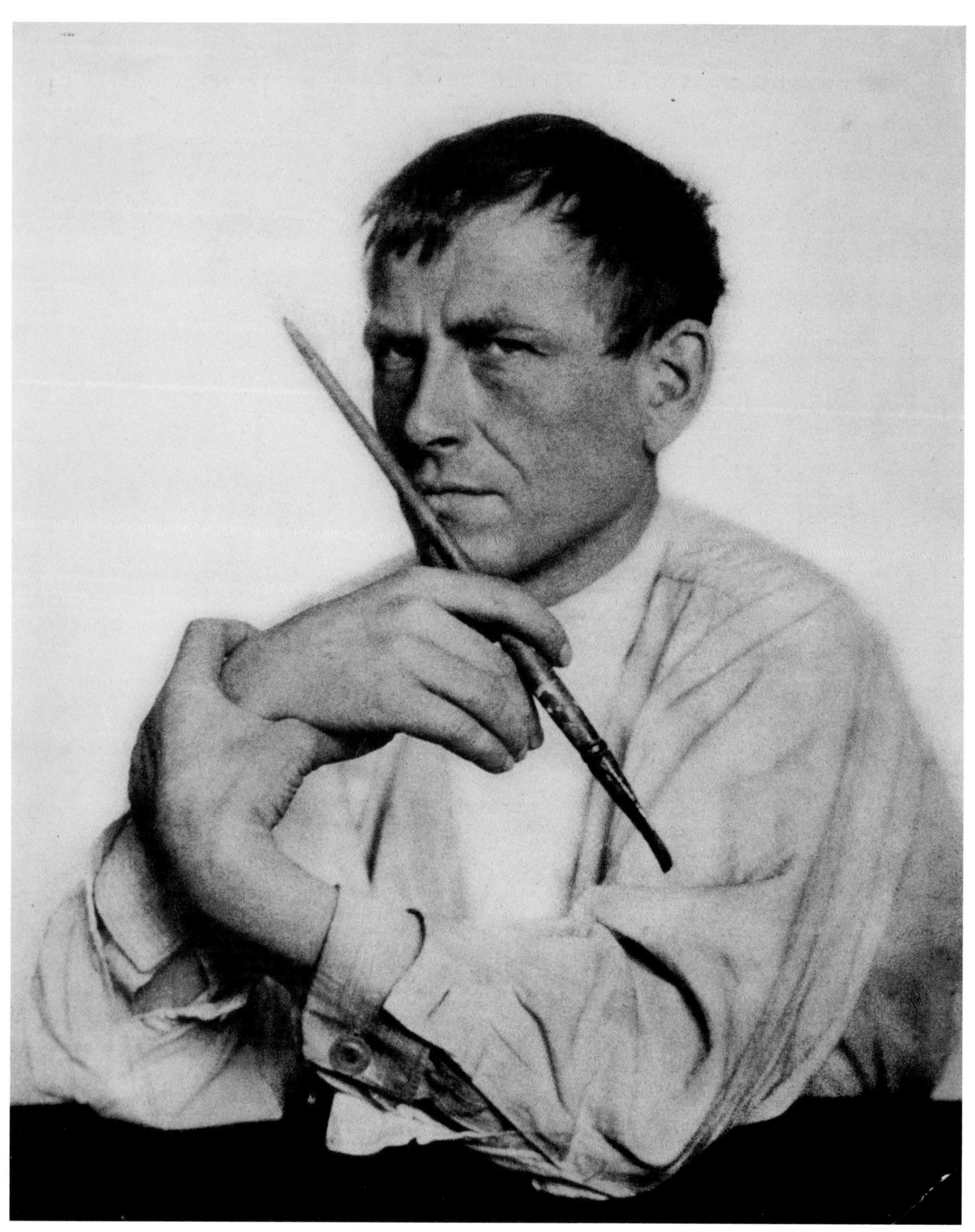

Hugo Erfurth
Otto Dix with brush 1929
bromoil photograph
Museum Ludwig, Cologne

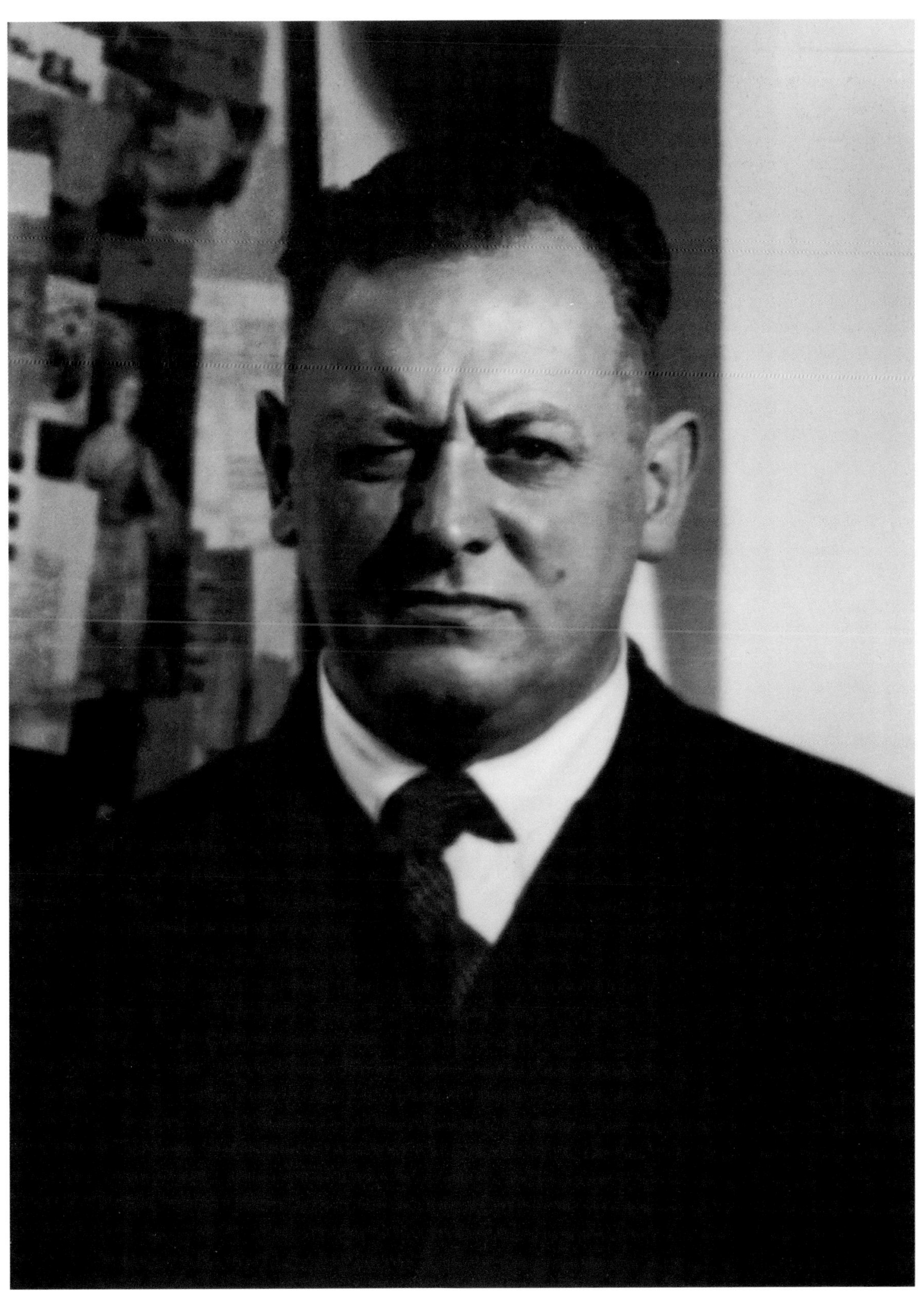

Hugo Erfurth
Kurt Schwitters c1930
gelatin silver photograph
Museum Ludwig, Cologne

NEW OBJECTIVITY

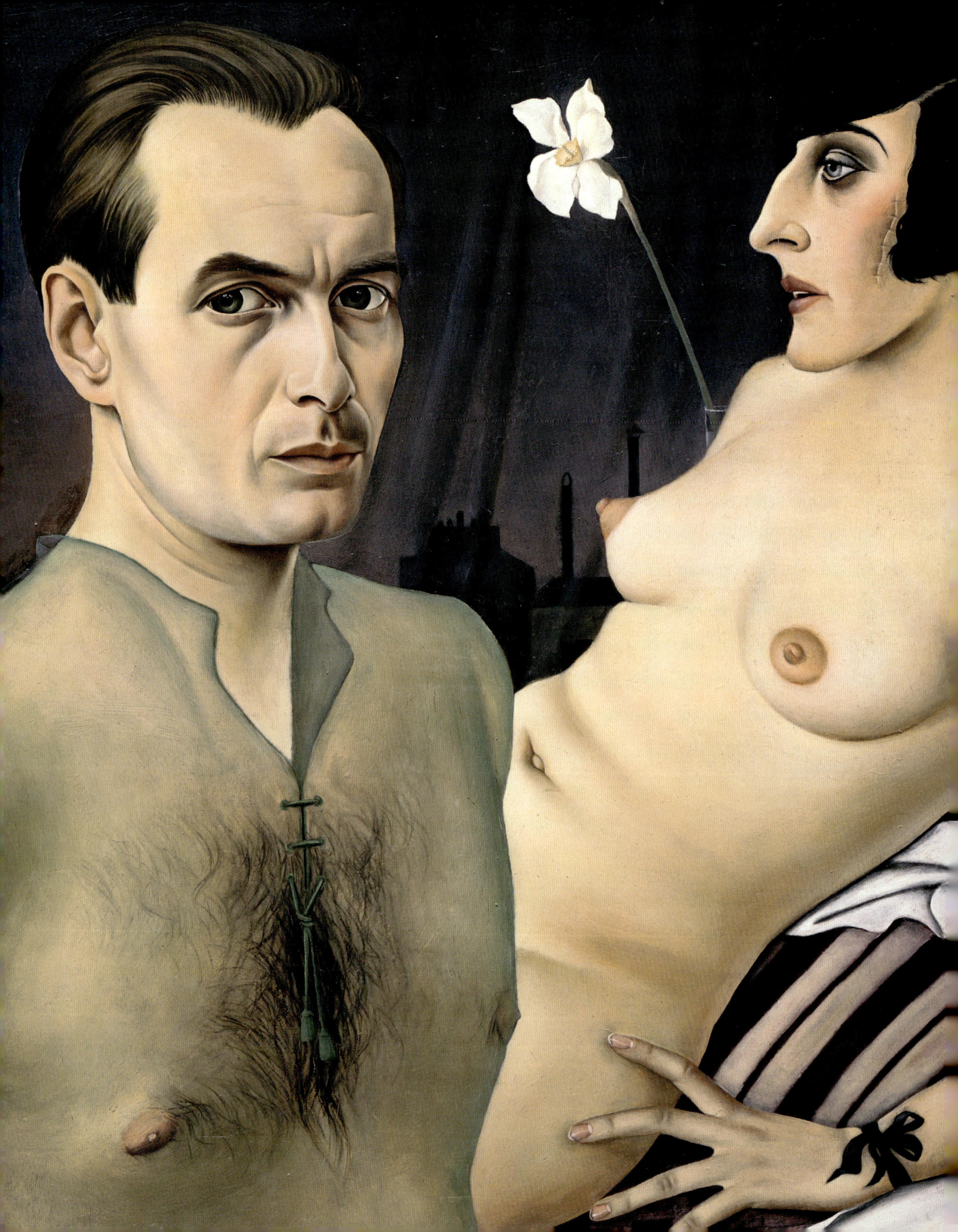

GERMAN REALIST PORTRAITS OF THE 1920s

Matthias Eberle

If the main characteristics of the movement *Neue Sachlichkeit* (New Objectivity) can be described as clear, sharp contours and smooth, highly finished surfaces, then this points to two fundamental positions taken by the painters who fostered this style: an astute awareness and an emphasis on traditional craftsmanship.[1] This awareness contrasted sharply with the chaos and aftermath of the war, and craftsmanship stood in competition with industry and the machine, not least in opposition to the camera. The painter could now use a picture that was manually generated rather than machine-made – as a contrast to the uncontrolled, frighteningly fast-moving times – which would allow the viewer to take a step back and gain insight into the self and to recognise one's emotions more clearly.

Neue Sachlichkeit was a phenomenon of the city. It was the so-called sober painting style that was committed to objectively portraying reality and practised by different artists throughout Germany in the 1920s. Major painters of the 19th century, including Jean-François Millet, Gustave Courbet, Wilhelm Leibl and Max Liebermann, portrayed the farmer in opposition to the city dweller as a representative of a large and important section of society; after the First World War, the factory worker took over this role. This subject featured in the works of politically engaged artists, while others represented city dwellers. The urban resident, male or female, remained the most prominent figure, the most important model, and it was not until Hitler and Stalin came to power that the farmer became a notable subject in painting again. In the metropolis of the 1920s, artists painted portraits of colleagues, secretaries, doctors, photographers and fashionable women, who all stood or sat as models as well as businessmen, actors, dancers and writers. The milieu in which these artists mingled were the middle-class circles – they were not interested in suburban or rural idylls, or in the lives of the upper classes. Notable individuals, such as the chancellor, president, major industrialists, financiers and Nobel Prize winners, all had their portraits painted by artists of the older generation, such as Liebermann, Lovis Corinth, Max Slevogt and others. Their style was rejected by the younger artists, who therefore lost this important clientele. Most of these younger painters did not earn much money and were not able to travel long distances, but they had little else in common. They viewed themselves as independent individuals with very different views of people and the world. They were only loosely connected to each other and shared no common theory. Although some were attracted to extreme leftist politics for a short period immediately after the war, these artists did not share common political interests. They did not publish any manifestoes, nor did they establish any artists association or have a clear geographic centre. Some of them, such as Alexander Kanoldt, lived and worked in Breslau, while others, including Carlo Mense and Georg Schrimpf, were based in Munich. However, most of these young artists – George Grosz, Otto Dix, Jeanne Mammen and Christian Schad, for example – resided in Berlin or Dresden.

Christian Schad
Self-portrait 1927 (detail)

It was the museum directors and art critics who invented the name *Neue Sachlichkeit* for the movement, and who also wrote about the works of this mostly 30-year-old generation of artists in various art magazines. Otto Dix – who did not flatter anyone except himself in his portraits – is represented by several works in this exhibition, in which he portrays writers and representatives of the museum profession. *Dr Paul Ferdinand Schmidt* (p 241) is an early portrait from 1921, which dates from the time when Dix studied painting. The work depicts the art writer and museum director, and son of a senior bureaucrat, Paul Ferdinand Schmidt. Schmidt had studied law and art history in Munich, Paris and Strasbourg, and later worked at various museums and published studies on 19th- and early 20th-century German art. As director of the Stadtmuseum in Dresden, he especially nurtured young Expressionist painters, in particular Dix. In this work the artist depicts the man who supported his art on a ridiculously narrow, superficially altered, old-fashioned chair in an empty corner of the room. The pinstriped suit, crossed arms and stiff, upright collar signify distance and a kind of artificial elegance. The sitter lifts his right eyebrow and the right corner of his mouth in a mocking way. Two enormous eyes stare out at us like intense, glaring headlights from a head that is much too large in relation to the lanky body. This man examines the person in front of him very closely before shaking his hand.

Six years later, Dix painted *Portrait of the poet Theodor Däubler* (opposite). The sitter directs his gaze at us, but is oblivious to us; he is completely absorbed in himself and in another, ideal world. Däubler was a wandering scholar, had no fixed address and lived off the kindness and support of others, occasionally writing for magazines about art and travel. The portrait was painted in September 1927 in Dresden, where Dix had been teaching at the academy since spring. Däubler had just returned from a trip to Greece and stayed with the family of the painter. He amazed everyone with his immense appetite and when he summoned the power of the ancient gods with his booming voice.

Born in Trieste – the most important port of the Austro-Hungarian Empire – Däubler was raised bi-lingual in German and Italian, and spent his youth there and in Venice. These formative years shaped him for the rest of his life. The culture, art and literature of the south captivated him and he kept returning to it. Of all the great arts of antiquity, Däubler was particularly impressed by high poetry and the epic. His own epic poem, entitled *Das Nordlicht* (*The northern light*) – a monumental work with 30 000 verses – was published in 1910. Däubler was friends with the heroes of the avant-garde in Italy and France. He spent the war years with friends in Dresden and, when peace was restored, he re-established his contacts abroad and educated the German public about the development of the arts in neighbouring Roman countries through the art magazine *Cicerone* in 1920. Not least of all, it was he who made famous in Germany the names of Carlo Carrà, Giorgio de Chirico and others. Däubler stood above borders and the petty questions of everyday existence – therefore, Dix painted him as a kind of Jupiter who looks down from Olympus onto the world and right through us. The view across the river to the other bank is the view from the painter's Dresden studio; the Corinthian columns on the left of the picture honour him as a poet of the epic and a friend of antiquity. The somewhat bizarre cloud formation above the poet's head is typical of the deep irony

Otto Dix
Portrait of the poet Theodor Däubler 1927
tempera on plywood
Museum Ludwig, Cologne

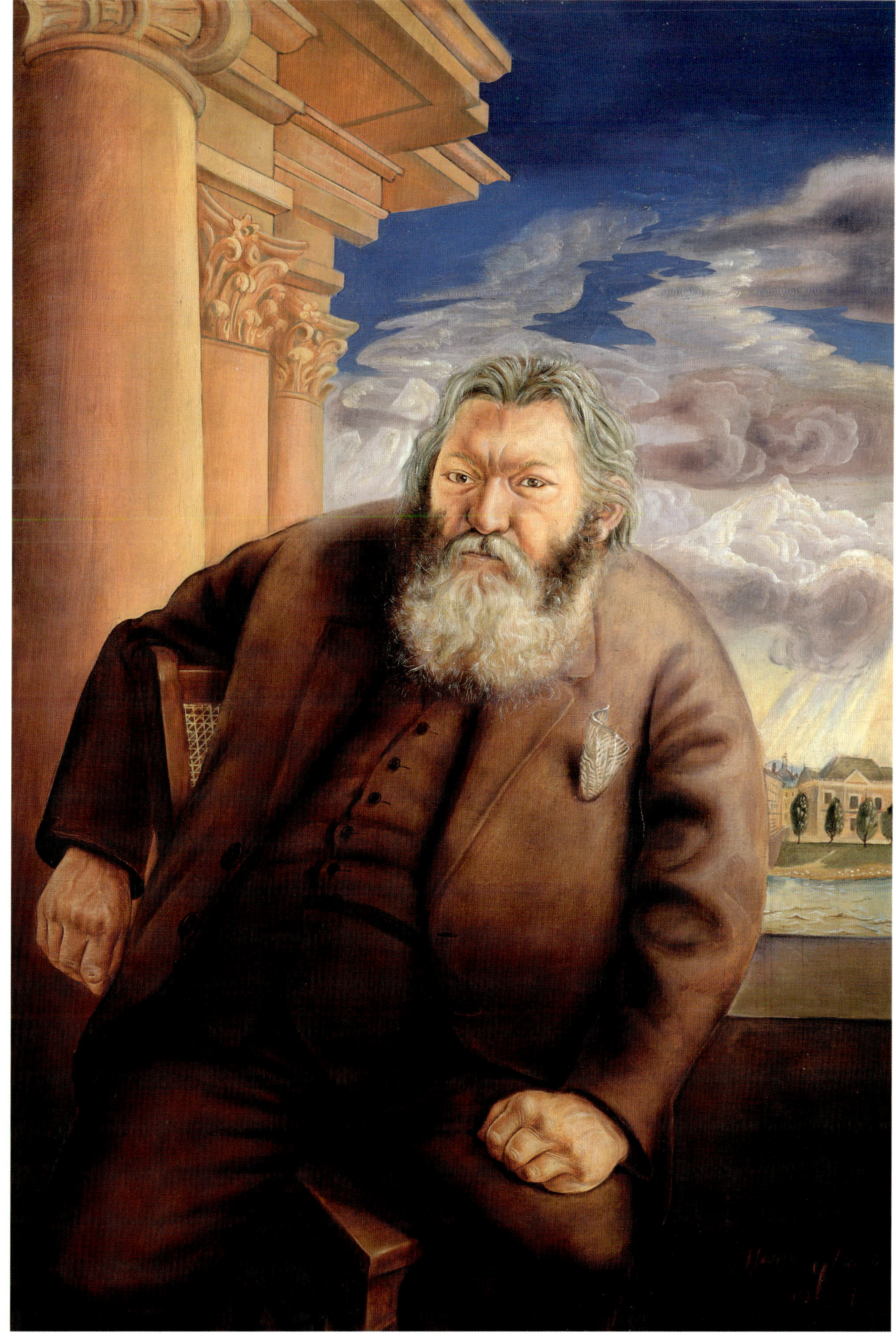

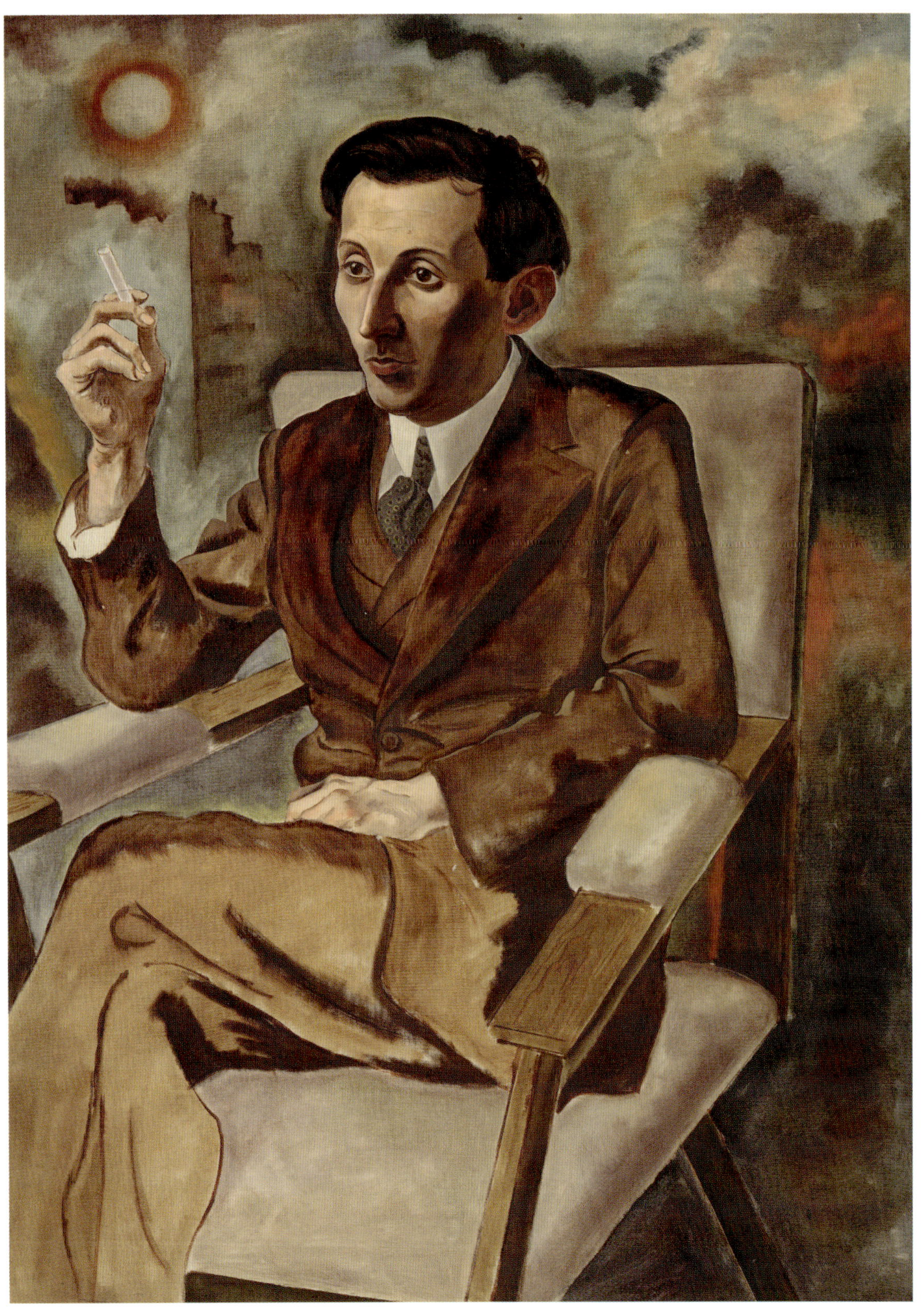

George Grosz
Portrait of Walter Mehring 1926
oil on canvas
Koninklijk Museum voor Schone Kunsten, Antwerp

of Dix, who emphasised what to him seemed exaggerated with a sharpened realism. He also treated the posture of the subject ironically: we can tell that this man does not completely belong here, as he sits at an angle and appears rather uncomfortable – furthermore, his weight would have been too much for the delicate chair.

In Berlin around the same time, Grosz also painted a writer, his somewhat younger friend Walter Mehring (opposite). Mehring had been suspended from his high school in 1914 due to unpatriotic behaviour; he had studied art history and written for the magazine *Der Sturm* (*The Storm*), which advocated Expressionist painting. After the war, he wrote critical texts for small revues and cabaret. Taking stylistic elements from Expressionism and Dada, he developed these into biting satires in which he ridiculed philistinism, politics and the church. He enjoyed experimenting with language, for example, by letting texts flow in rhythms like those familiar from jazz music. His intention was to capture the complexity of life in the modern metropolis. Although he avoided any political involvement, Mehring was forced to emigrate as a Jew in 1933 and ended up in the United States in 1941. He and Grosz remained close friends in exile, and Grosz painted a second portrait of him in 1944. In the later portrait the subject is again shown on a chair and leaning to the left but he places his head in his propped-up, right hand and looks anxiously at the viewer. In this picture he sits in front of us, neatly dressed, wearing a cravat, waistcoat and cufflinks; his gaze evades us but his mind seems to be active. He has placed his right elbow on the armrest of the chair and is holding up a cigarette. The room in which he finds himself is not clearly defined and transforms into the unknown, into a kind of sky. Storm clouds threaten in the top left of the picture where the cigarette points to a planet, circled in red. Does Mehring suspect an impending disaster?

These three portraits of writers and poets show very different characters in diverse roles. How did the painters view themselves? Christian Schad, who spent a couple of years during the war in Switzerland, travelled through Italy after the war, arrived in Vienna in 1925 and relocated to Berlin in 1927. His *Self-portrait* 1927 (p 243) – one of the most well-known images of *Neue Sachlichkeit* – was painted in Vienna while he was travelling, during a period of personal crisis after the breakdown of his marriage. It shows the painter sitting on an unmade bed that he shares with a woman. Sharply, almost bitterly, he looks out of the picture. Each person is alone; there is nothing to say to each other. The different directions of the figures' gazes and facial orientation lead us to suspect that Schad might have caught a glimpse of himself in the mirror and was therefore forced to consider his reflection, that is, himself. He surprises himself in a situation that we would normally try to hide and which, precisely because of its intimacy, reveals more about the person than bare skin. Schad's partner is a woman who is well aware of her physical attractiveness, and because of the black ribbon on her left wrist and the red stocking on her right leg, appears consciously undressed but not naked; Schad has kept on his transparent shirt. It seems that this was not a passionate act, but a fleeting encounter, and it cannot be said who used who as an object. It is certainly not the kind of passionate encounter from which scars such as the one on this woman's face would result. In Naples, where Schad had lived for a while, many girls and women were proud of the scars on their faces made by jealous husbands or lovers; these scars were seen as evidence of passionate affection.

The woman in this painting, branded as an object by the scar on her left cheek, has come out of this encounter as unaffected as Schad is. For both of them, the attempt to escape the prison of their own selves was in vain. In the background Schad painted the silhouette of rooftops in Paris, a place of longing for bohemians. Can the dream for an independent and easy life still be realised now that he recognises his marriage has failed?

Grosz also painted himself in the late 1920s. Immediately after the war, he joined the German Communist Party (KPD) in order to use his art effectively in the class struggle. For many years he drew and painted caricatures of philistines, extortionists, vain militarists and the clergy. After travelling for several months through the Soviet Union in 1922, where he also saw Lenin, Grosz gradually withdrew from strict party line politics. Orthodox comrades no longer seemed to him to be better people than those he had satirised. Around the middle of the decade he became tame and enjoyed a good income – *Self-portrait with hat* 1928 (opposite) stems from this period. He stands before us in three-quarter-length format, in a dark blue suit, wearing a tie and scarf, with his left hand placed casually in the side pocket of his jacket while holding a pipe in his right hand. His gaze evades us. He is a normal citizen now, no longer a revolutionary, and has distanced himself from all political camps. He confesses that he wants to be nothing other than a painter.

The only artist of the *Neue Sachlichkeit* who could be considered a painter of idyllic subjects was Schrimpf. He lived in Munich and was friends with the painters Carlo Mense and Heinrich Maria Davringhausen, who are also represented in this exhibition. Schrimpf drew his inspiration from Romanticism and contemporary Italian painting. Profound human relationships, particularly women's relationship to nature, were his general theme, resulting in motifs of young girls in simple, often rural surroundings, and images of mother and child, playing children and landscapes. In an early picture dating from the beginning of the 1920s, he painted a portrait of his second wife, simply titled *Hedwig Schrimpf* (p 234). Our gaze wanders past her straight, self-contained and seemingly devoted posture, to the wide, populated land. The space is almost empty, the woman is quiet and nothing distracts her; she shows no reaction to the viewer and appears to look inwards. In the advanced stages of her pregnancy, she seems like a calm pillar between home and nature. Schrimpf often painted young women in front of a window, looking at the outside world, who functioned as intermediaries between inside and outside, maintaining a connection with nature without giving up culture. Maintaining this balance is not always an easy task, as represented in this painting, which shows the enormous distance between the person and the external landscape beyond the window.

The solitude and loneliness of people in the modern world is a recurring theme in portraits of this time. Max Beckmann was particularly drawn to characters and people who epitomised the distant relationship between the individual and the world. Towards the end of the 1920s, he was quite successful and earned a good income; in addition, his wife came from a wealthy family. The couple travelled to Saint Moritz in Switzerland for their winter holidays in 1929, where they lodged at the Grand Hotel. There the painter noticed a young man from a family of Argentineans who were among the hotel guests. Beckmann painted the young man, in a work entitled *Young Argentine* 1929 (p 245). The artist's wife later wrote that 'he was interested in the nature and the appearance of this young

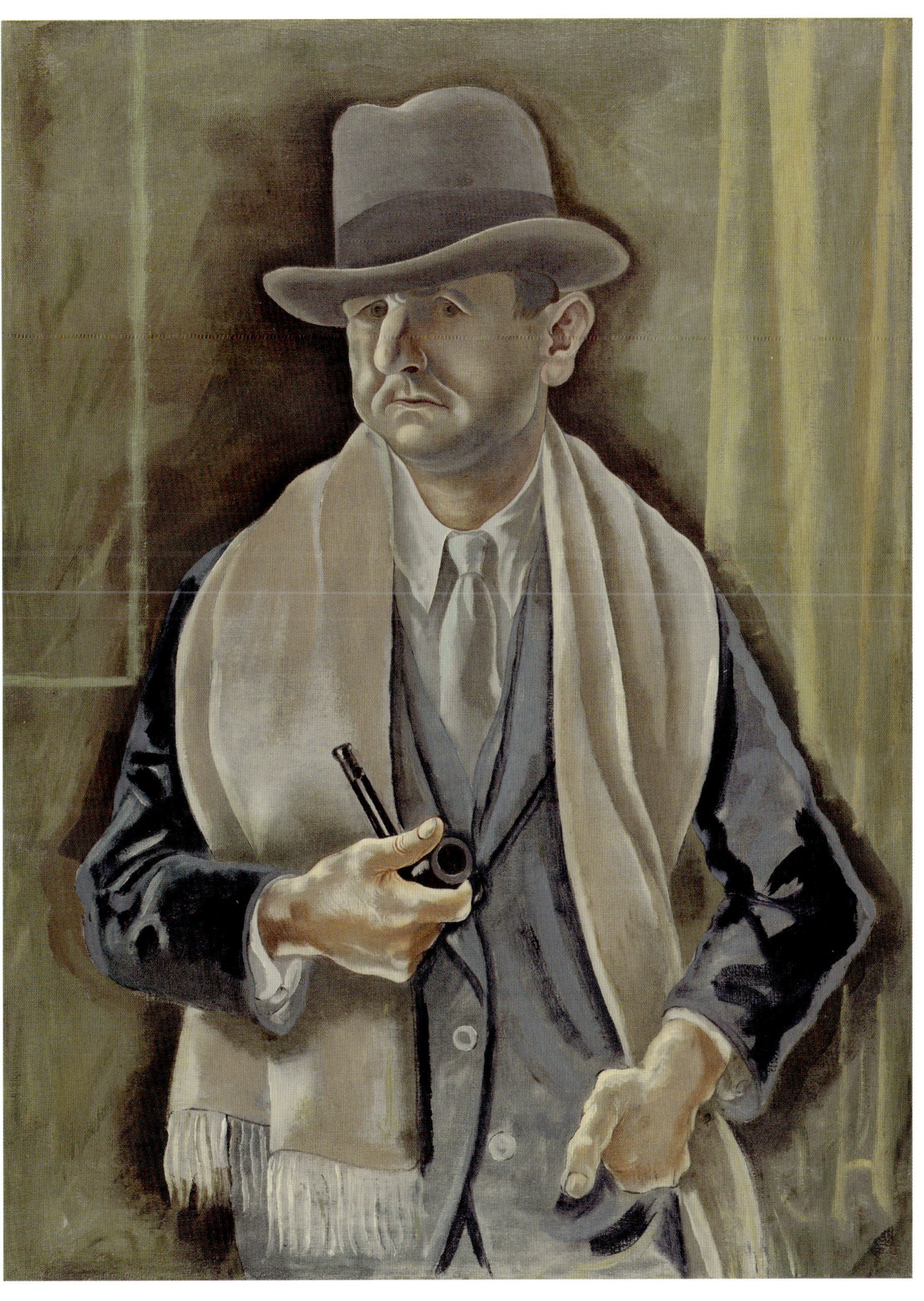

George Grosz
Self-portrait with hat 1928
oil on canvas
Berlinische Galerie, Landesmuseum für Moderne Kunst, Fotografie und Architektur

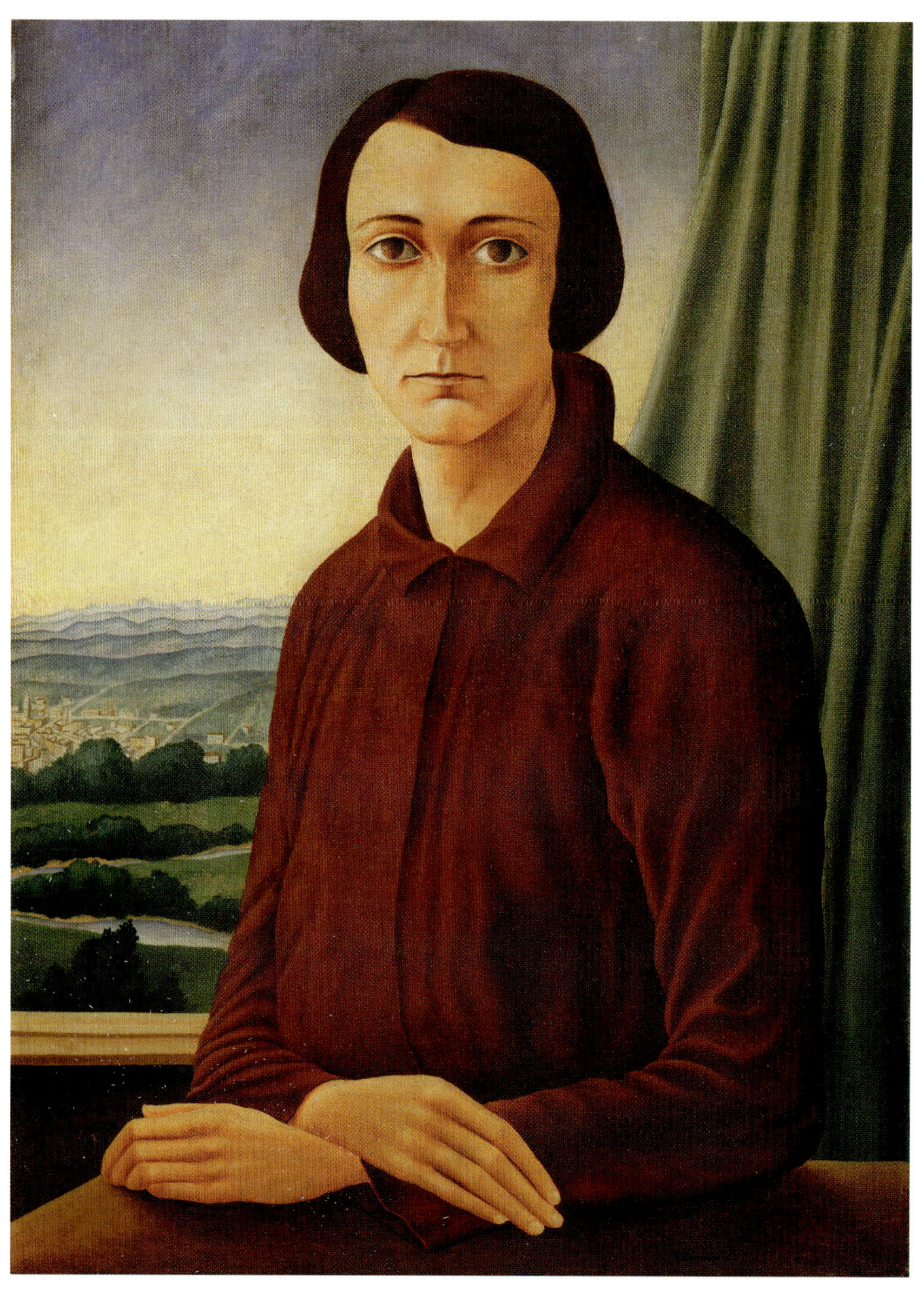

Georg Schrimpf
Hedwig Schrimpf 1922
oil on hardboard
Städtische Galerie im Lenbachhaus, Munich

man who, in contrast to his loud and temperamental family, seemed quiet, introverted and mysterious. He painted the picture immediately after our return to Frankfurt'.[2]

The isolation of this privileged, civilised man from his lively family and his environment fascinated the painter. The unbridgeable gap between the sitter and his surroundings is made apparent in the composition of the painting. Clad in a black tuxedo, the young man is seated on a chair and shown in three-quarter profile, crammed into the slim portrait-format of the picture. His body shape is angular and hostile. His left hand is half-hidden in his trouser pocket; the right hand in which he holds his cigarette is equally awkward. He has placed his hand in front of his body to the far right of his thigh, as if he was trying to build a barricade against others. His gaze evades us as he looks into nothingness. No picture hangs on the ochre-coloured wall in the background, which might have been used to point to an interest or distinguishing feature of the sitter. There seems to be no other furniture apart from the chair. The broad, black stripe on the left-hand side of the picture, which does not represent anything tangible, opens up the room towards the back, leading into uncertainty. The lower edge of the composition cuts off the legs of the chair as well as the legs of the man so that he is not easily situated. Where does he belong? Where is he? He does not appear to have spoken with the artist, who drew him from memory and later painted him; furthermore, the young man never sat as his model. The art dealer who represented Beckmann later found out that the young Argentine had committed suicide shortly after his stay in Switzerland.[3]

Very few of the artists represented in this exhibition were able to escape the verdict that was imposed after 1933: *entartet* (degenerate). The mass movement of left- and right-wing groups, who were concerned with cultivating or breeding a certain type of person, did not find their ideal in these paintings. Almost all of the artists discussed here were forced to flee to the provinces and therefore into inner emigration within Germany (Dix, Schrimpf and Schad) or to escape into exile abroad (Grosz and Beckmann). Although they had a clearer view of the individual in the modern world and arguably produced better paintings than the artists who complied with the regime, that did not protect them. This makes it easier for us to appreciate their work today.

ALEXANDER KANOLDT

Half nude II

Alexander Kanoldt was, to a large extent, the most typical of the *Neue Sachlichkeit* (New Objectivity) painters who embraced the 'call to order' declared by Picasso in 1920. His hard-edged and almost airless paintings are characterised by a sharpened focus and a very cold, sober depiction of things as they really were. More than any other painter of his generation, Kanoldt remained obsessed with the traditional academic principles of line and detail, clarity and precision. He carefully constructed pictorial compositions that were inspired more by Cubist forms and the work of André Derain and Paul Cézanne than by modern German painting.

Kanoldt studied at the Karlsruhe Academy from 1901 to 1904, and shortly afterwards moved to Munich where he came into contact with the newest and most innovative developments taking place within the avant-garde. He made a decisive break away from the pure abstraction of Wassily Kandinsky and Franz Marc, continuing his association with the modern, yet stylistic conservative Munich New Secession from 1913 to 1920. During these years he fought in the First World War and travelled throughout Italy. Kanoldt was deeply impressed by the Italian landscape, and many of his works from the early 1920s were influenced by classical Italian painting. His work had been described by Gustav Friedrich Hartlaub, the director of the Städtische Kunsthalle in Mannheim and one of the most influential figures in the German museum world, as representing the so-called right wing of *Neue Sachlichkeit* and was featured in Hartlaub's well-known exhibition in 1925 titled *Neue Sachlichkeit: Deutsche Malerei seit dem Expressionismus* (*The New Objectivity: German painting since Expressionism*). More than 50 of the 124 works in the exhibition were by the Munich painters Kanoldt, Carlo Mense, Georg Schrimpf and Heinrich Maria Davringhausen, and the term 'right wing' was used to refer to the general stylistic tendency of these artists towards pre-modern, figurative Classicism rather than the socially critical realism of the Verists.[1] Unlike their 'left wing' contemporaries George Grosz and Otto Dix, the Munich artists generally had no interest in politics and were not aligned with right-wing politics, as suggested by Hartlaub's rather misleading label.

Painted in 1926, shortly after Kanoldt was appointed a professor at the Breslau Academy, *Half-nude II* was a complete antithesis to Expressionist painting, which many believed had outlasted its importance and was perceived to be an indulgence of the emotions. This half-length nude was one of the few paintings of the human figure by Kanoldt and depicts a prostitute devoid of eroticism, emotion and sensuality. Kanoldt distanced himself from the toughness and modernity of the subject matter by concentrating on the external appearance of the woman as she presents herself to the viewer. He refrains from making judgments about his subject, yet the woman's sense of despondency and sadness is revealed through her downcast gaze, unflattering boudoir attire and sagging, frumpy physique. The sense of detachment is further emphasised through Kanoldt's sharpened realism and use of Classical portraiture conventions, such as the half-length, seated portrait format and austere studio setting. The mirror held in the woman's hand is the only symbolic attribute in the painting and makes reference to the *vanitas* symbol – frequently depicted in late Renaissance painting – as a metaphor for the transience of life and the vanity of earthly achievements and pleasures.[2] JS

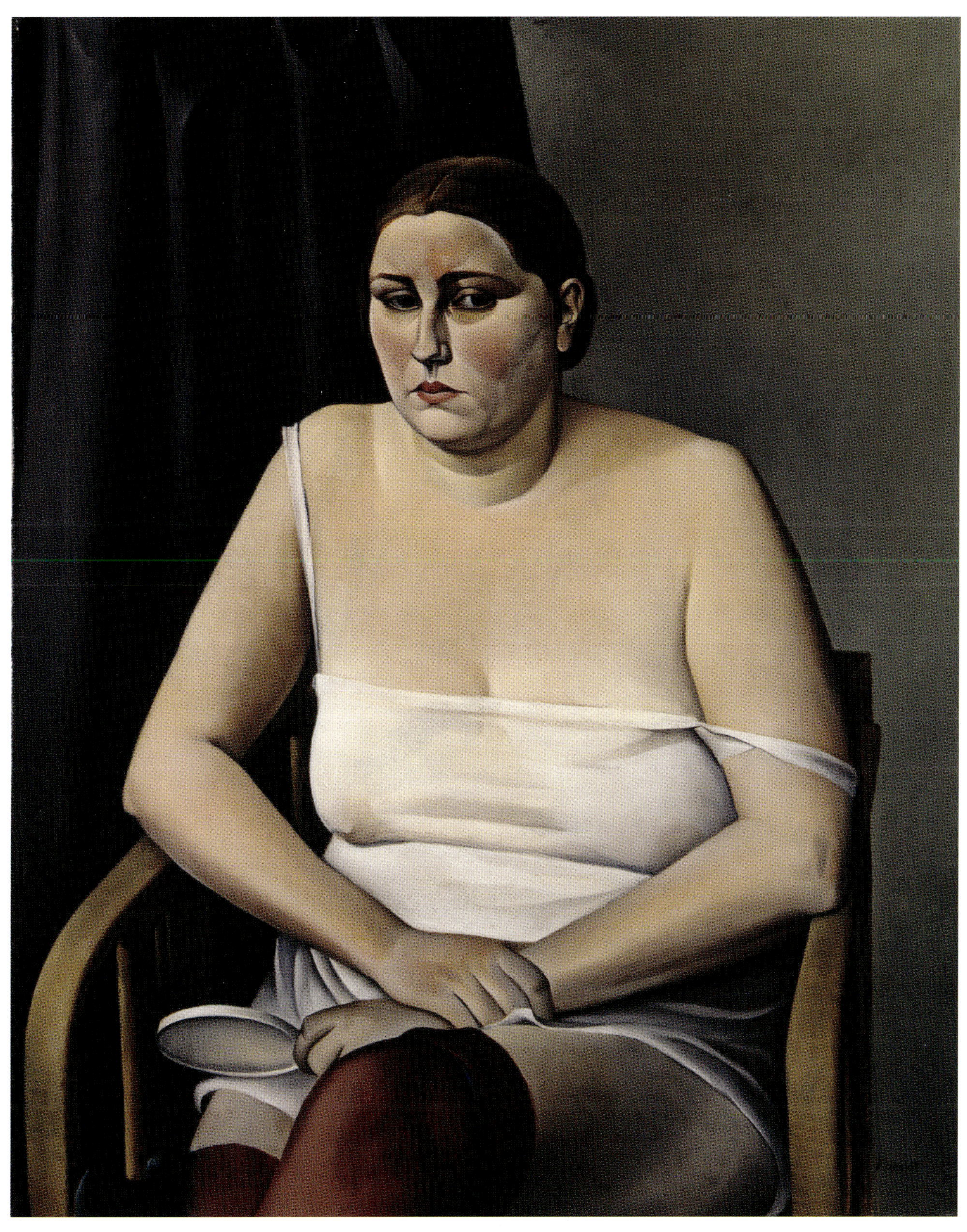

Alexander Kanoldt
Half nude II 1926
oil on canvas
Bayerische Staatsgemäldesammlungen, Munich
Pinakothek der Moderne

CARLO MENSE

The painter Heinrich Maria Davringhausen

The close stylistic and iconographic links between the work of the Munich artist Carlo Mense and the *Pittura metafisica* artists Giorgio de Chirico and Carlo Carrà have been widely understood as underpinning the 'magic realism' of the early 1920s. Mense, Georg Schrimpf and Heinrich Maria Davringhausen were particularly influenced by the synthesis of Realism and Surrealism that was explored in the paintings of their Italian contemporaries, which had been publicised in Munich from 1919 onwards through the magazine *Valori Plastici*. They also drew their inspiration from

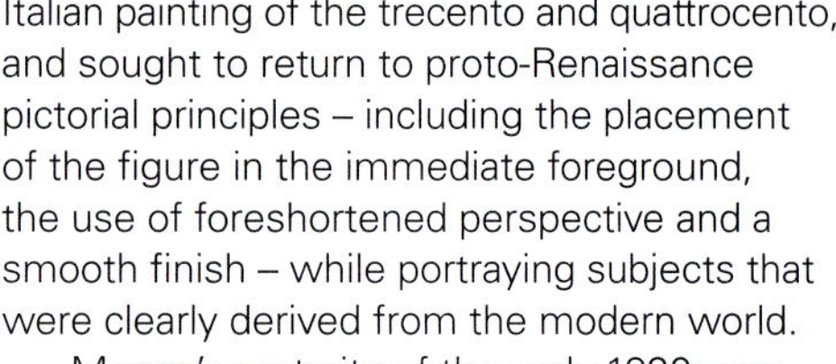

Italian painting of the trecento and quattrocento, and sought to return to proto-Renaissance pictorial principles – including the placement of the figure in the immediate foreground, the use of foreshortened perspective and a smooth finish – while portraying subjects that were clearly derived from the modern world.

Mense's portraits of the early 1920s are striking examples of this encounter between traditional and modern artforms. *Portrait of Underberg* c1925 (left) was most probably a commissioned portrait of the businessman Gottfried Underberg, who was an owner of a family company that produced spirits and liqueurs, most notably the well-known Underberg herbal digestive.[1] Underberg's confident and commanding presence is conveyed not only through the formality of his expression, attire and pose, but through references to his aristocratic background, suggested by the inclusion of the large hunting dog, the family coat of arms in the upper right-hand corner and a miniaturised version of the family's grand, Renaissance-style residence. However, rather than presenting these status symbols in a familiar and intimate context, Mense has created an atmosphere that makes them appear strange and isolated by employing de Chirico's use of dramatic lighting and stage-like construction of a classicised architectural space, comprising an arcaded interior and a chequered floor.

The painter Heinrich Maria Davinghausen 1922 (opposite) is a more typical portrait in that the subject was drawn from Mense's immediate circle of friends and acquaintances. Both a friend and fellow artist, Davringhausen worked in an Expressionist style before moving to Munich in 1919, when his style shifted towards the new form of emerging realism. Davringhausen behaved in a dandyish manner in his private life and is presented in this portrait as an elegantly dressed, upper-class gentleman.[2] His sideways glance, however, gives the work an enigmatic meaning clearly derived from the work of de Chirico. Many artists associated with *Neue Sachlichkeit* (New Objectivity) explored the theme of urban alienation, and in this work the deserted streets behind the artist create a prevailing sense of the loss of one's identity, particularly male identity, in modern life. JS

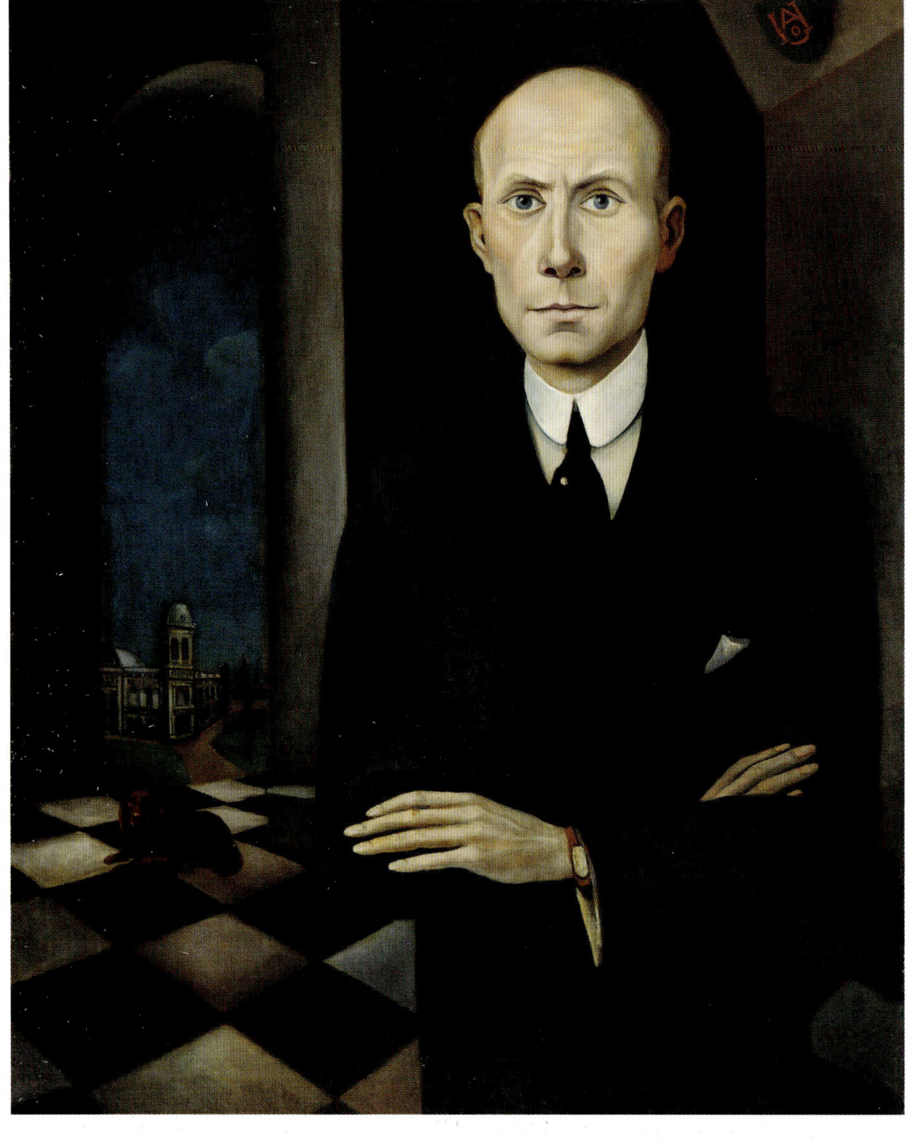

Carlo Mense
Portrait of Underberg c1925
oil on canvas
Private collection

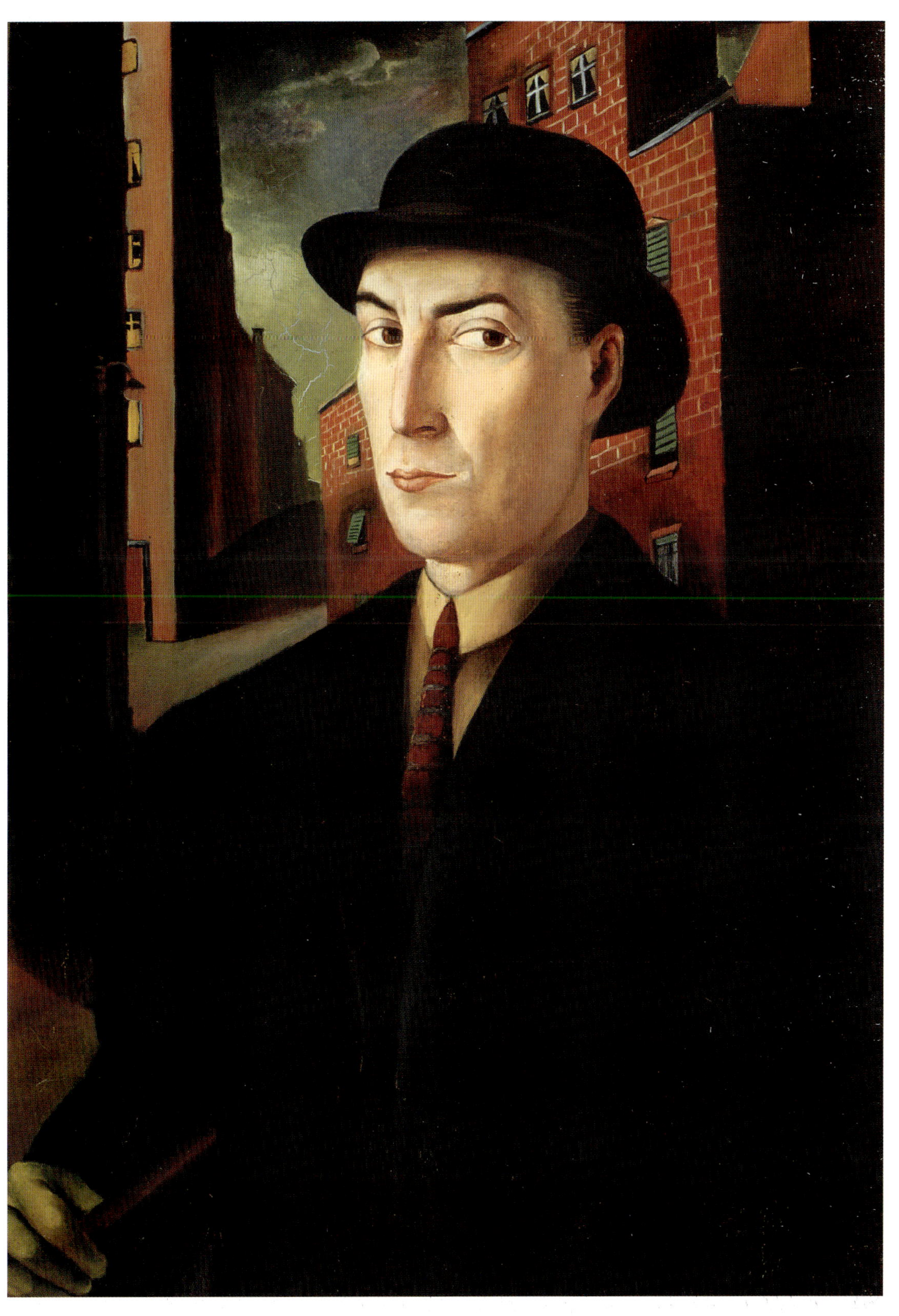

Carlo Mense
The painter Heinrich Maria Davringhausen
1922
oil on canvas
Museum Ludwig, Cologne

OTTO DIX

Dr Paul Ferdinand Schmidt

Otto Dix returned to Dresden in 1919, having served as a machine-gunner during the war. He turned to portraiture at the same time he began working on his major painting *Trench* 1920–23 (location unknown, probably destroyed) and cycle of prints titled *War* 1924, depicting the horrors of modern warfare. While his portraits of the early 1920s share the same immediacy and intensity of his war images, they generally represent the more restrained tendency that emerged in Dix's art, and European painting in general, towards a more objective and straightforward representation of the external world. These portraits combined Realist detail with a subdued sense of Expressionist emotion and typically exemplified Dix's exceptional ability to distil the physical attributes of his sitters into striking portraits that collectively represent the intellectual sophistication and cultural freedom of the Weimar Republic.

Portraiture became a major vehicle of expression for the postwar generation of German artists, with its emphasis on the representation of the human figure and the traditional artistic qualities of drawing and technical precision.[1] Dix, in particular, felt the need to return to traditional modes of representation after experiencing the atrocities of the First World War, and portraiture was well suited to his sound academic training in the principles of drawing as a student at the Dresden Academy from 1919 to 1922. He was fascinated, above all, with themes drawn from modern life, and portraiture allowed him the opportunity to depict his contemporaries – mostly acquaintances and patrons from his immediate circle in Dresden, Düsseldorf and later Berlin. Throughout the 1920s, he almost always chose his own models rather than seeking out commissions.

Dr Paul Ferdinand Schmidt 1921 was one of Dix's earliest painted portraits and remains an astonishingly fresh and compelling work. In this portrait, the distinguished art historian and critic is portrayed in an incredibly sparse and monochromatic interior. Painted during Schmidt's term as director of the Stadtmuseum in Dresden, Dix's portrait conveys a sense of the sitter's quick intelligence and sharp wit by focusing the viewer's attention on his lively facial expression and features.[2] Dix was particularly influenced by the techniques of the Old Masters, and the slight distortion of the figure that is evident in Schmidt's twisted smile, elongated hands and tightly intertwined posture creates an impression of hyper-realism that harks back to 16th-century German painting. There is an atmosphere of familiarity and intimacy in Dix's portrait, and it was no coincidence that he was one of Dix's earliest supporters. He was one of a handful of museum directors in the 1920s to acquire major avant-garde works by the Brücke artists and more recent modernist works by artists such as Kurt Schwitters, Max Beckmann, George Grosz and Dix. Schmidt's progressive collecting policies, however, proved ultimately too radical for Dresden's conservative establishment and he was dismissed from his post in 1923. By focusing on the objective representation of external detail, Dix alluded to the stark contrast between Schmidt's engaging and intellectually vibrant personality, and the uninspiring, institutional space that surrounded him. JS

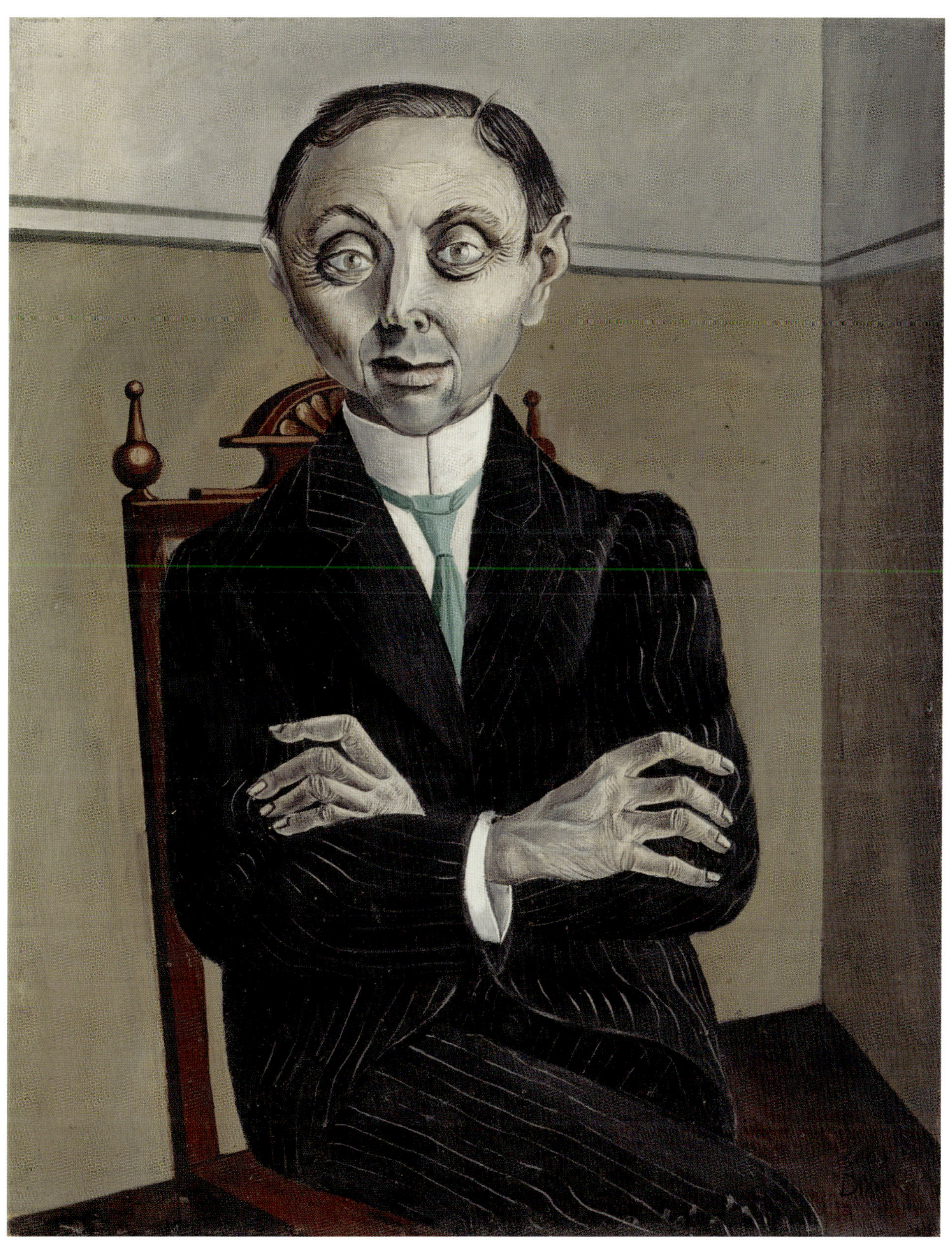

Otto Dix
Dr Paul Ferdinand Schmidt 1921
oil on canvas
Staatsgalerie Stuttgart

CHRISTIAN SCHAD

Self-portrait

Christian Schad's iconic *Self-portrait* of 1927 singularly exemplifies the cool objectivity and cynicism towards cosmopolitan culture that had emerged in many works by modernist German artists during the late 1920s. This extraordinary and paradoxical self-portrait was painted shortly before Schad moved from Vienna to Berlin in 1928, and during a time of a personal crisis when he decided to leave his wife and son. Schad lived for the most part in Naples and Rome between 1921 and 1925, and this resulted in the crucial shift in his work from earlier experimentations with abstract, Dadaist forms of art – including the wood relief (p 95) and photogram (p 94) included in this exhibition – towards representational oil painting strongly influenced by the clarity and light of Renaissance panel painting.[1] In Schad's hard-edged portraits of the mid to late 1920s, for which he is best known, there was a very conscious attempt to sharpen the artist's gaze through an emphasis on the absolute clarity of form and a fastidious attention to small details. His works relate very closely to *Neue Sachlichkeit* (New Objectivity) in a formal sense, but they also stand apart as independent and highly original paintings that chronicle the glamour and decadence of upper-middle-class society in the 1920s.

It was not unusual for artists during the Weimar Republic to depict intimate interior scenes representing casual sexual encounters, but what is most striking about Schad's depiction of this subject is the complete absence of emotion during this most private and intimate of moments. In *Self-portrait*, Schad presents himself as a cold lover next to a reclining female nude who may be a model, mistress or prostitute. In this provocative and somewhat ambiguous representation, the lovers remain physically connected but psychologically isolated from each other, with the woman gazing out beyond the realm of the painting and the artist staring with a strained expression at the viewer. The transparent green shirt worn by the artist, strongly reminiscent of fabrics and colours found in Renaissance painting, draws attention to the superficial nature of the liaison and exposes the loss of the artist's identity in the fleeting, modern world of the metropolis.

The single narcissus portrayed next to the woman would traditionally refer to vanity and self-love, but here this symbol makes ironic reference to the woman's acute sense of her own sexuality, conveyed through Schad's highly stylised image of her sexually available body. The intense focus on the details of her external appearance – her heavy make up, modern bob, underarm hair, manicured nails, black ribbon, red stocking and smooth, creamy skin – draw attention to her sexually explicit role in this painting. Schad makes further reference to his sexual ownership of the woman by marking her cheek with a *fregio* – a type of disfiguring scar inflicted by jealous Neapolitan lovers on their mistresses' cheeks, which were worn proudly as proof of the passion the women inspired.[2] The night view of rooftops and chimneystacks behind the couple is most probably Montmartre, representing the artist's 'vague longing for Paris'.[3] As Schad said in a later statement about this work: 'All these different elements to do with the mind or the body may be banal and nothing on their own, but together they make a good painting, in my view'.[4] JS

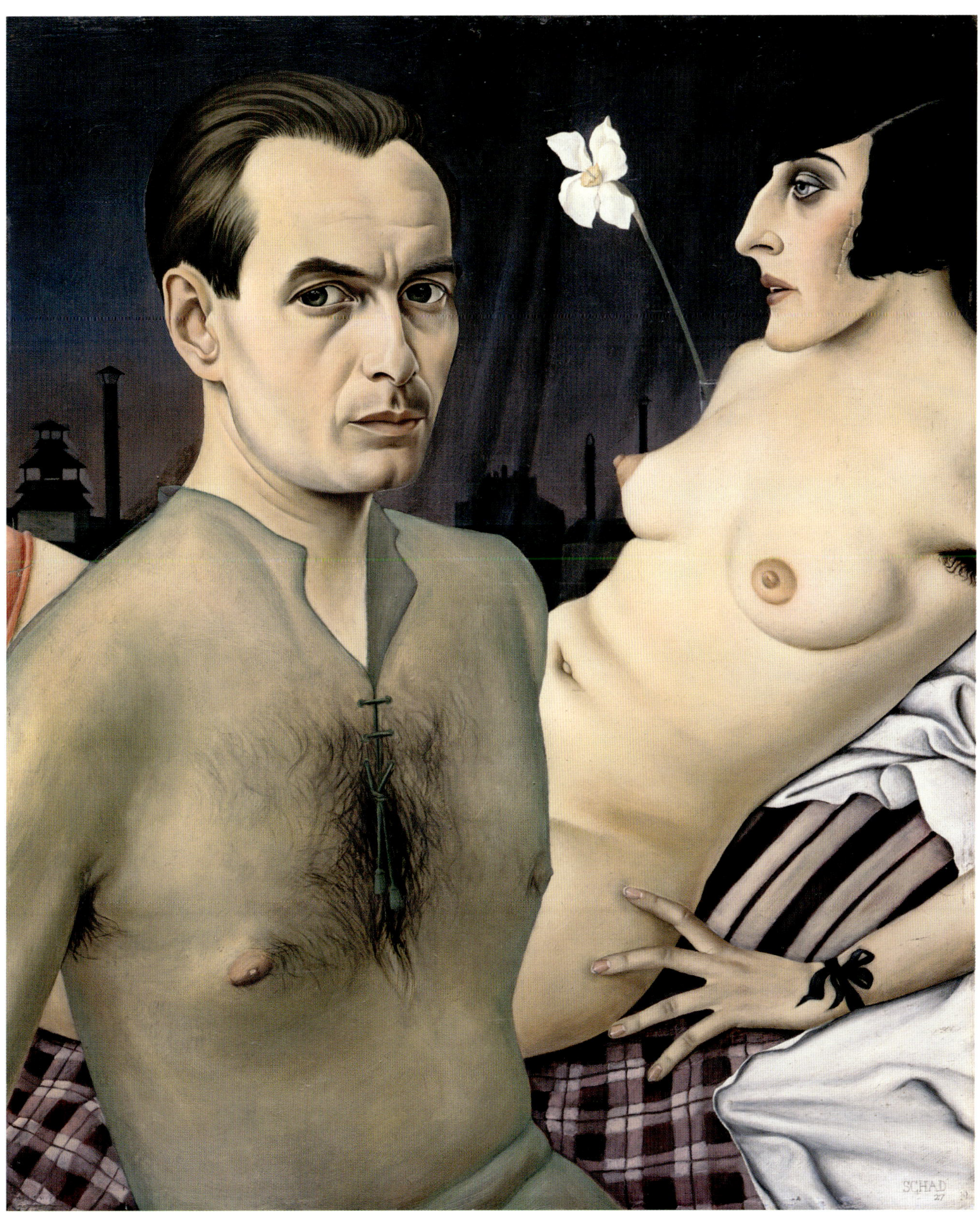

Christian Schad
Self-portrait 1927
oil on wood
Private collection, courtesy Tate London

MAX BECKMANN

Young Argentine

While Max Beckmann's work had been closely associated with *Neue Sachlichkeit* (New Objectivity) in the mid 1920s, he had begun to distance himself from 'the style of the era' as early as 1926.[1] Unlike many of his contemporaries, Beckmann sought an active engagement with French avant-garde art of the 1920s, and after 1926 his work began to display interesting connections with artists such as Pablo Picasso, through a heightened emphasis on the physicality of the sitter. There had also been significant changes in Beckmann's personal life around this time. In 1925 he married his second wife, 'Quappi' (Mathilde von Kaulbach), and his entrée into new aristocratic circles coincided with a period of great artistic success for him.[2]

Young Argentine 1929 was painted from memory after Beckmann returned to Frankfurt following a three-week stay with Quappi at the Grand Hotel in Saint Moritz, Switzerland.[3] Beckmann had seen the blond Argentine with his family at the chic and fashionable resort, and was intrigued by his withdrawn and mysterious demeanour. As in his finest self-portrait of the mid 1920s, Beckmann presents a three-quarter length image of a gentleman dressed elegantly in a black tuxedo and white shirt. The figure holds a cigarette and is posed in front of a fairly neutral interior, leading to a doorway that slices abruptly through the left-hand side of the composition. Despite the striking formal similarities between the way in which Beckmann portrayed the young man and himself, the sense of confidence and success that is asserted so powerfully in *Self-portrait in tuxedo* of 1927 (Harvard University Art Museums) is replaced here by a mood of melancholy and sadness.

Beckmann often sought to show the surface nature of things in a self-conscious manner, and in this work he typically accentuates the sitter's painted white face to draw attention to the superficiality of the 'mask' worn in social situations by members of the upper class. Yet the man's pensive, faraway gaze conveys a sense of anxiety and even despair, traits that were buried within Beckmann's own psyche and which later emerged in his self-portraits of the 1930s.[4] The profound sense of disillusionment conveyed in this intriguing portrait can also be seen in other portraits of the 1920s by Dix and George Grosz (pp 230, 233). JS

Max Beckmann
Young Argentine 1929
oil on canvas
Bayerische Staatsgemäldesammlungen, Munich
Pinakothek der Moderne

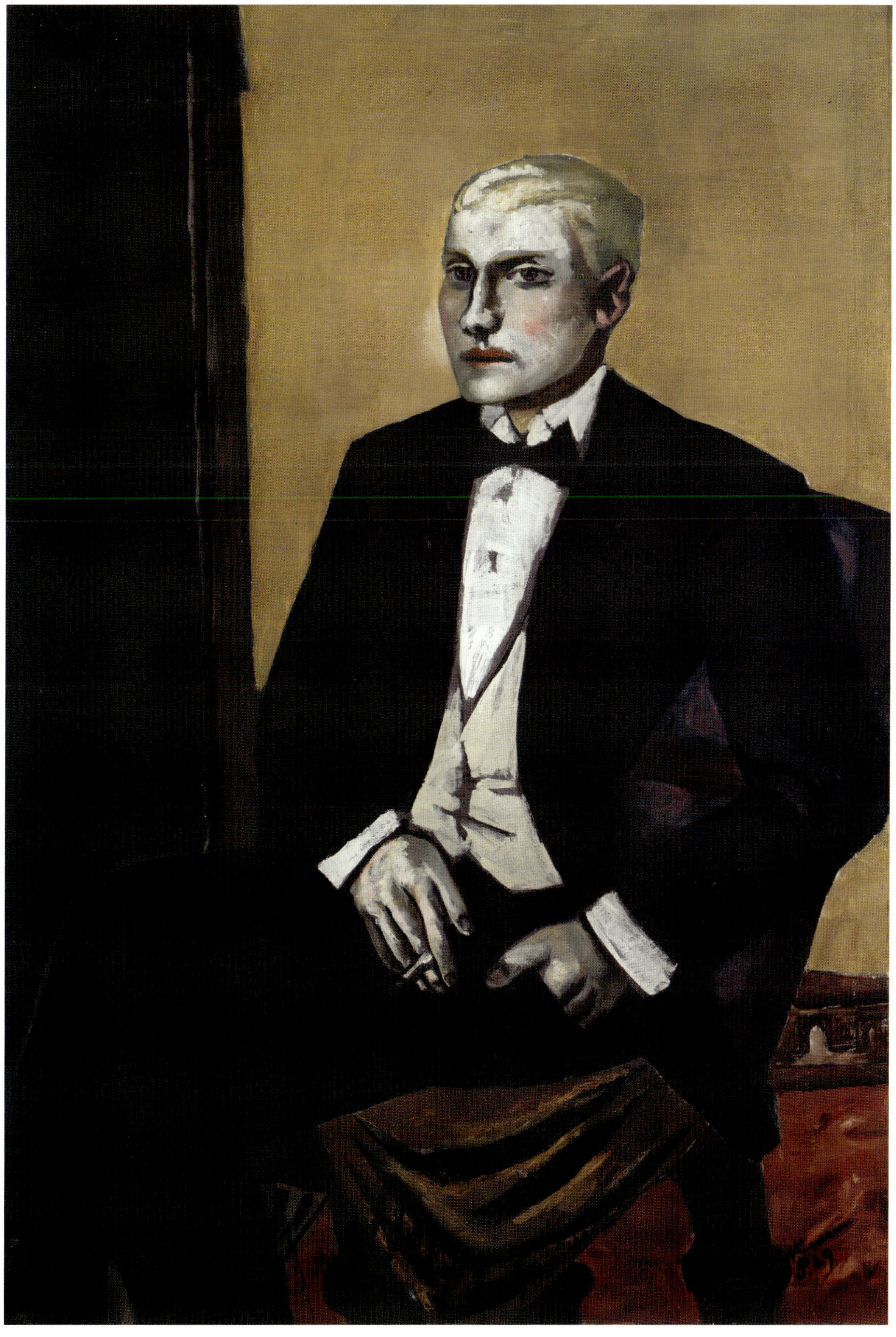

KARL HUBBUCH

Twice Hilde II

Karl Hubbuch emerged as one of the leading artists of the 1920s to develop a form of socially critical realism that combined cool social analysis with the traditional artistic qualities of drawing and technical precision. Hubbuch had studied at the Karlsruhe Academy alongside Rudolf Schlichter and Georg Scholz from 1908 to 1912, and then moved to Berlin where he continued his studies under the master graphic artist Emil Orlik. During this time he met George Grosz, and both artists were encouraged to use their considerable graphic skills to depict life in prewar Berlin. Hubbuch served as a driver and telephone operator in the First World War, and suffered from an attack of malaria that left him seriously ill for several years. In 1920, he resumed his studies at the Karlsruhe Academy and produced a large number of intricately detailed drawings, etchings and engravings that focused on the female form in often melodramatic and bizarre settings (pp 58–9).[1] Hubbuch moved between Berlin and Karlsruhe in the early 1920s, and his work resisted classification in terms of any single avant-garde movement. He settled in Karlsruhe in 1924, where he began teaching drawing classes at the academy.

Hubbuch's influence as a teacher and major artist of *Neue Sachlichkeit* (New Objectivity) was profoundly felt at this time. *Twice Hilde II* c1929 is a rare and fascinating example of Hubbuch's ability to produce large-scale figure paintings. This painting forms the left-hand section of a double-panelled work that presents four different views of the artist's student, model and wife Hilde Isai. While two versions of Hilde posing as a flamboyant bohemian can be seen in the pendant to this painting, *Twice Hilde I* 1929 (Pinakothek der Moderne, Munich), she is portrayed in this painting in two completely different guises.[2]

Hilde appears both as a prim and proper bourgeois citizen, conservatively dressed in a fur-trimmed coat and tight-fitting cap, and as a self-consciously modern woman of the 1920s. Her modernity, and hence her rebelliousness, are conveyed through her unruly hairstyle, thick spectacles, short skirt, boldly patterned top and, not least of all, the Marcel Breuer Bauhaus chair which is included as the only prop in an otherwise sparse interior. Hilde was, by all accounts, a self-assured and fiercely independent woman, and Hubbuch's sharply accentuated depiction of her gazing thoughtfully downwards offers an illuminating insight into her character, as well as presenting a generalised image of the *neue Frau* (new woman) who emerged during the late years of the Weimar Republic.[3] Shortly after Hubbuch painted this work, Hilde left Karlsruhe to study photography at the Dessau Bauhaus. She divorced Hubbuch in 1933 and – sensing the increasingly hostile anti-Semitic climate in Germany – migrated to New York, where she worked as a photographer until the 1960s. Karl Hubbuch remained in Germany and continued to produce socially critical, Realist works during the early 1930s. JS

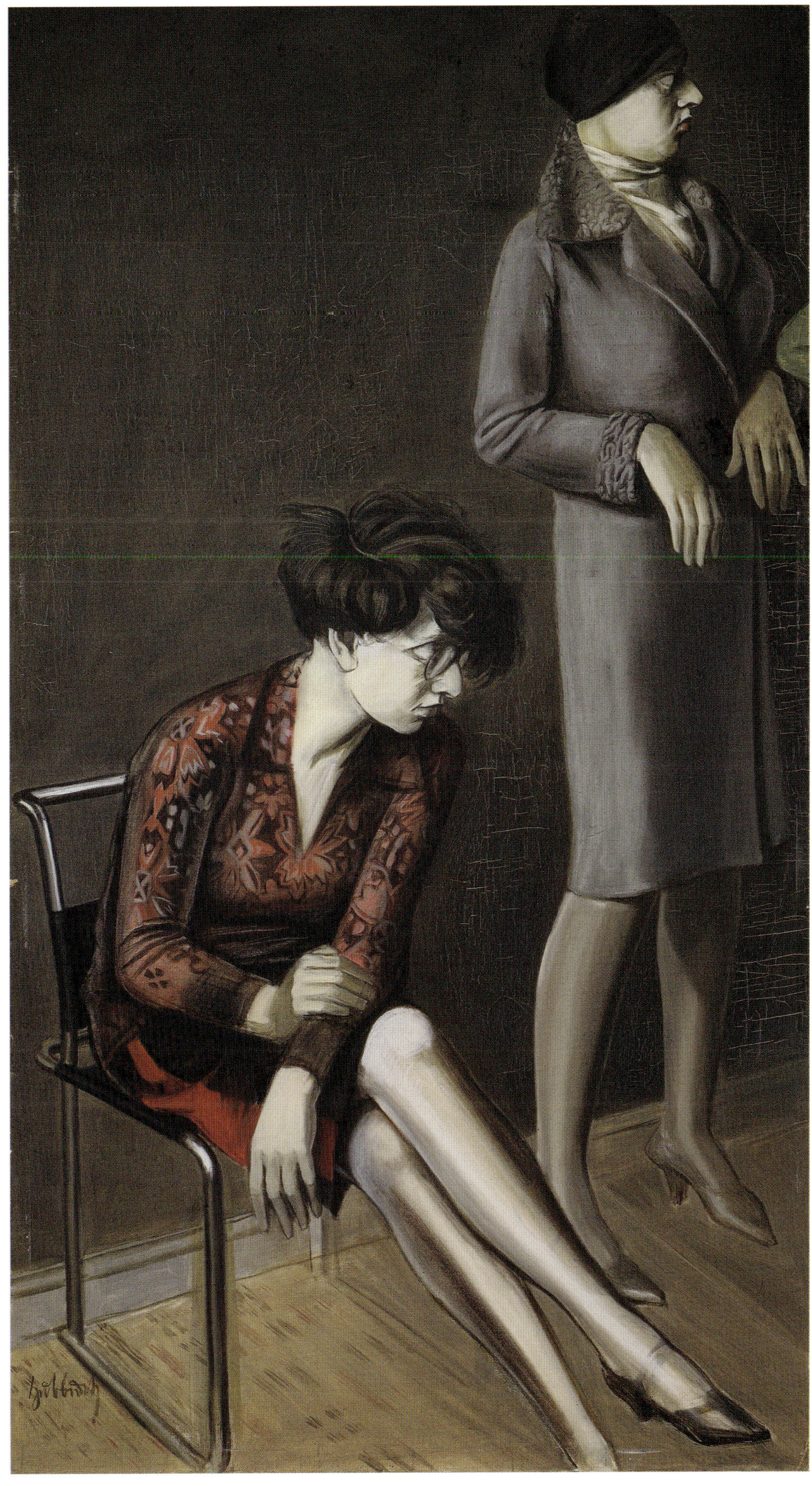

Karl Hubbuch
Twice Hilde II c1929
oil on canvas
Museo Thyssen-Bornemisza, Madrid

JEANNE MAMMEN

Valeska Gert

Jeanne Mammen's portrait *Valeska Gert* c1928–29 was one of the few painted portraits of a woman by a woman to appear in German art of the 1920s. Having studied art in Paris, Brussels and Rome, Mammen moved to Berlin in 1919 and supported herself by producing numerous illustrations and drawings for magazines, depicting the fast-paced life of Berlin between the wars. Her studio was located near Berlin's notorious Kurfürstendamm and it was here, in the bars, cafés, cabarets and night-clubs, that Mammen found her subject matter.

Women figure predominantly in Mammen's most highly regarded works from 1920 to 1933, and while she is mildly critical of the plight of her female protagonists, she also infuses her subjects with a sense of gracefulness and compassion seldom seen in the work of the Berlin Verists. Her extremely rare painted portrait of the dancer, cabaret artist and actress Valeska Gert is an unusual and very alluring work. Gert invented a form of grotesque, Expressionist dance and is presented here as if mid-way through a performance with her head thrown back, eyes tightly closed and a strained expression that suggests intense concentration.[1] Her heavily rouged lips and daring red dress were the trademark symbols of the contemporary femme fatale who featured prominently in film, posters, paintings and books. Mammen also makes specific reference to Gert's wayward character and unconventional form of self-expression through her wildly individual hairstyle and bizarre, transparent neckpiece.

This painting celebrates the possibility of women living out their independence and fantasies in the metropolis, yet it also hints at the superficiality and illusionary nature of this existence by emphasising the details of the dancer's appearance. JS

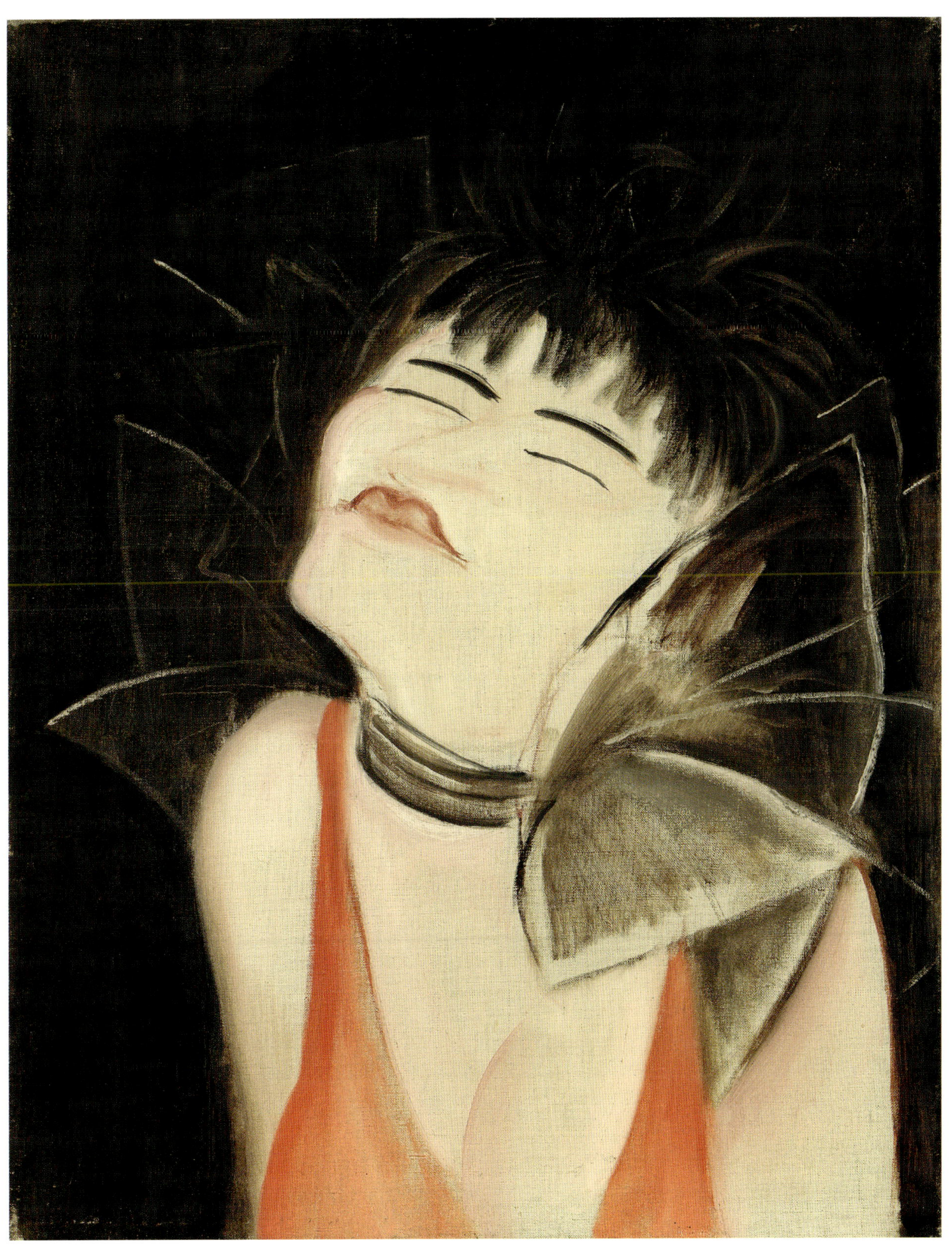

Jeanne Mammen
Valeska Gert c1928–29
oil on canvas
Berlinische Galerie, Landesmuseum für Moderne Kunst, Fotografie und Architektur

OTTO DIX

Portrait of the dancer Tamara Danischewski

By the time Otto Dix painted *Portrait of the dancer Tamara Danischewski* in 1933, it had become increasingly dangerous for him to continue working as an artist in Dresden. Earlier that year he had been dismissed without notice from his teaching position at the Dresden Academy, and in September 1933 his works were exhibited in the first *Degenerate art* exhibition held in Dresden Town Hall's inner courtyard. Dix moved to Lake Constance with his family later that year, and for him the 1930s and 1940s were characterised by a state of inner exile.

In this increasingly hostile if not impossible environment, Dix produced what has been described as one of his 'happiest portraits'.[1] The slim dancer is shown carrying a white iris and wearing a single pearl earring to suggest her burgeoning sexuality. In contrast to many of Dix's views of women throughout the 1920s, which revealed an explicit and threatening sexuality, this image presents a surprisingly natural and spontaneous impression of a young woman in the prime of her youth.[2] The urban context of many of Dix's earlier representations of women is substituted here by a natural setting, where an intricate arrangement of leaves on a grapevine can be seen as further suggesting sexual innocence. Yet Dix hints at the woman's awareness of her own attractiveness by accentuating her blonde curls, graceful figure, delicate facial features and cheerful smile. Dix's portrait brilliantly captures the dancer's individuality and carefree nature – qualities that contrasted strongly with idealised depictions of women that conformed to the racial and gender stereotypes that would soon be propagated by the National Socialists. Contemporary political events are further highlighted, somewhat ironically, in the inscription in the left-hand corner of the composition, which incorporates the artist's initial 'd' into the form of a swastika. JC

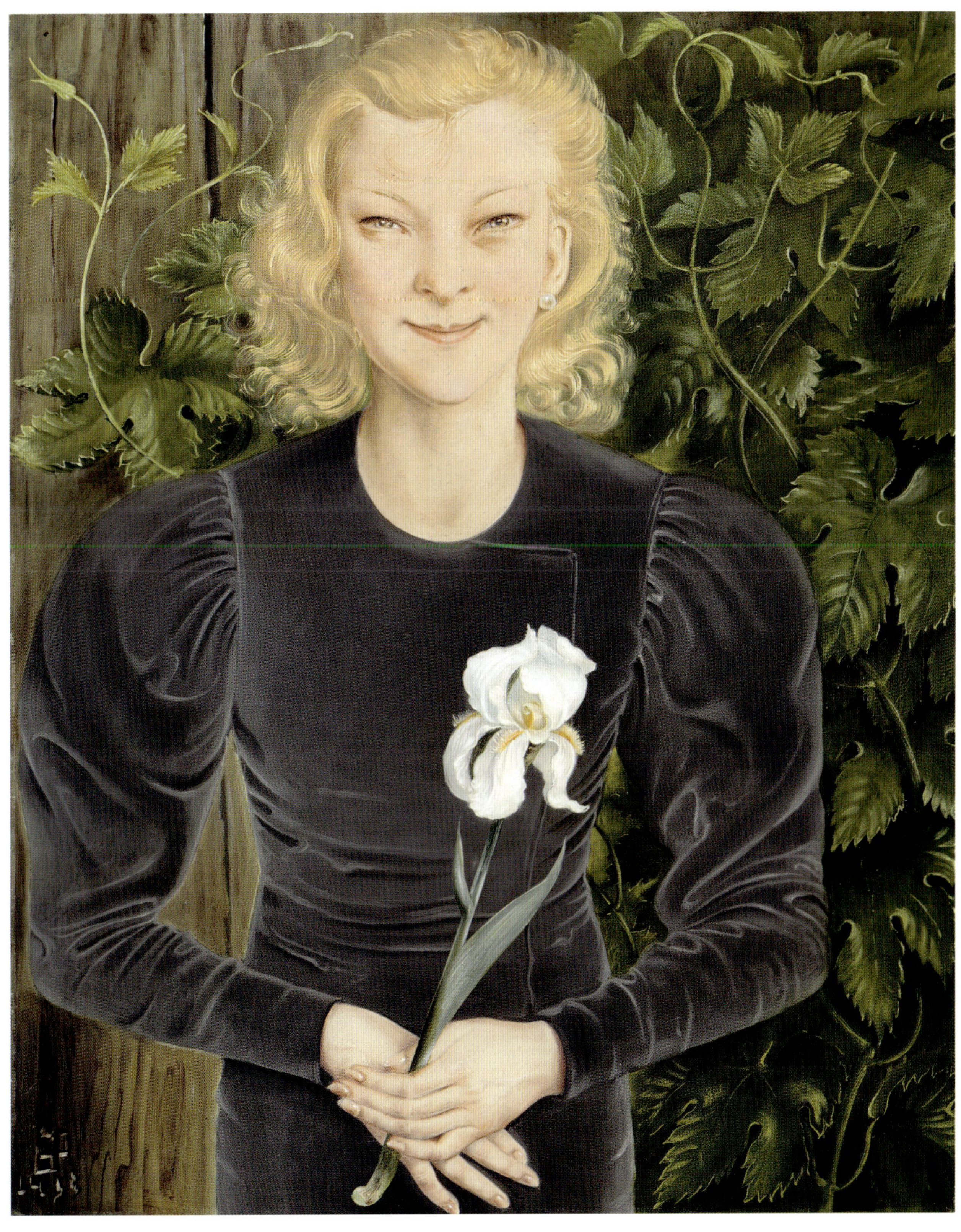

Otto Dix
Portrait of the dancer Tamara Danischewski
1933
oil, tempera on wood
Kunstmuseum, Stuttgart

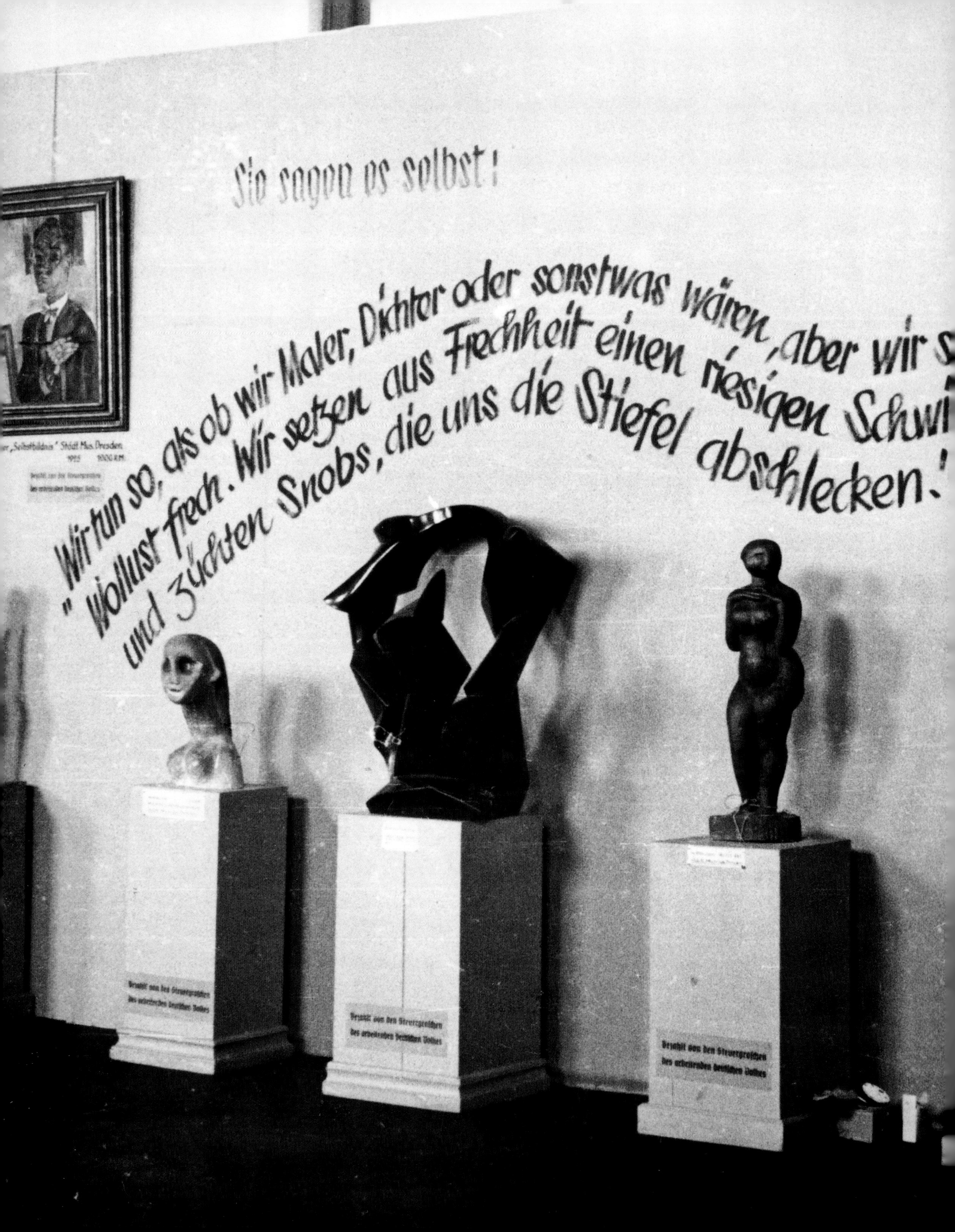

Sie sagen es selbst!
Wir tun so, als ob wir Maler, Dichter oder sonstwas wären, aber wir s
„Wollust frech. Wir setzen aus Frechheit einen riesigen Schwi
und züchten Snobs, die uns die Stiefel abschlecken."
„Selbstbildnis" Städt. Mus. Dresden
Bezahlt von den Steuergroschen des arbeitenden deutschen Volkes
Bezahlt von den Steuergroschen des arbeitenden deutschen Volkes
Bezahlt von den Steuergroschen des arbeitenden deutschen Volkes

IN THE TWILIGHT OF POWER: THE CONTRADICTIONS OF ART POLITICS IN NATIONAL SOCIALIST GERMANY

Uwe Fleckner

When visitors entered the *Degenerate art* exhibition – which opened on 19 July 1937 in the exhibition rooms of the Archäologisches Institut (Archaeological Institute) of Munich's Hofgarten and rapidly received record attendances – they would have been confronted with a demagogic arrangement that must have reminded them of certain manifestations of the European avant-garde, such as the First International Dada Fair in Berlin in 1920. Under the direction of the academic painter and committed National Socialist Adolf Ziegler, who was also president of the Reich Chamber of Visual Arts, the organisers took the opportunity of juxtaposing various genres and media, including originals and reproductions, words and images, in order to create an antithesis between modern artforms – such as montage or collage – and their original progressive intentions. Perverted in this way, these stylistic techniques were utilised to attack modern art; hundreds of works by important painters and sculptors, from Jankel Adler to Otto Dix, from Wilhelm Lehmbruck to Gert Wollheim, were confiscated from leading German museums and publically condemned. Presented under perfidious slogans, such as 'Revelation of the Jewish racial soul', and accompanied by demeaning comments, including 'Paid for by the taxes of the German working people', the artists were defamed on the basis of racial and political grounds, and their aesthetic and philosophical beliefs rendered absurd.[1]

Subsequently shown in varying configurations until 1941 in at least a dozen cities throughout Germany and Austria, this exhibition attained a somewhat propagandistic highpoint in a room on the upper level of the building. Exhibited there were paintings and sculptures by important Expressionists, such as Ernst Barlach, Ernst Ludwig Kirchner, Emil Nolde and Karl Schmidt-Rottluff, together with works of equally provocative artistic forms that left the National Socialist demagogues bewildered. George Grosz, Kurt Schwitters, Paul Klee, Richard Haizmann, Wassily Kandinsky, Conrad Felixmüller, Walter Dexel, Heinrich Campendonk and other artists were represented on three walls, one of them being the famous-infamous 'Dada wall' (p 257). The exhibition organisers tried to further denigrate the work of these artists through the addition of selected quotes, such as 'massive sham'.[2]

A closer examination of the treatment of one of the defamed artists, sculptor Rudolf Belling, perfectly exemplifies the contradictions of the art-critical and political foundations of the propaganda machine unleashed by the National Socialists. Belling's wooden version of his sculpture *Triad* of 1918–19 (opposite), executed in 1924, had been acquired that same year by the National Gallery in Berlin, and was confiscated in July 1937 for inclusion in the *Degenerate art* exhibition; it occupied a central position on one of the walls with its abstract Expressionist forms and was accompanied by sculptures by Otto Baum and Eugen Hoffmann, as well as Belling's *Head (Portrait of Toni Freeden)* of 1925 (Neue Nationalgalerie, Berlin).[3] Although these five sculptures hardly shared any stylistic similarities, they were presented in one row at an even height and, together with

Georg Schödl
A view of room 3 in the *Degenerate art* exhibition (with Rudolf Belling's *Triad*) held at the Archäologisches Institut, Munich, 19 July – 30 Nov 1937 (detail)

below left:

Georg Schödl
A view of room 3 in the *Degenerate art* exhibition (with Rudolf Belling's *Triad*) held at the Archäologisches Institut, Munich, 19 July – 30 Nov 1937
Research Library, Getty Research Institute, Los Angeles, California

fig 4

Unknown photographer
Hitler visiting the *Degenerate art* exhibition stops at the *Dada wall*, Munich 1937, *Völkischer Beobachter*, 17 July 1937
Heidelberg, Universitätsbibliothek

paintings by Nolde, Felixmüller and Dexel on the left-hand side, and Campendonk on the right-hand side, were headed by a band of text that constituted an exhibition panel which entailed an 'unmasking' motto expressed in a polemic quote of 1915, taken from the magazine *Die Aktion*: 'We act as if we were painters, poets, or whatever, but what we are is simply and ecstatically impudent. In our impudence we take the world for a ride and train snobs to lick our boots!'[4] This was obviously meant to highlight the moral inferiority of the creators of these works, the deceptive nature of their images, as well as the social irresponsibility from which these artists supposedly drew their motivation.

The exhibition organisers had, however, overlooked – or conveniently ignored – the fact that Belling was simultaneously represented with one of his bronze sculptures at the first *Great German art exhibition*, which opened one day earlier than *Degenerate art* in the specially built Haus der Deutschen Kunst (House of German Art) in Munich, and was organised as a counter event to the exhibition of 'degenerate' art. Opened by Adolf Hitler himself, with great pomp and ceremony, the exhibition aimed to give an overview of the official art of the Third Reich, and this clear and generously spaced display was designed in complete contrast to the exhibition of defamed works in the Hofgarten (fig 5 p 258).[5] On display were paintings and sculptures depicting rural and military subjects, homeland landscapes, and portraits of worthy personalities from political, cultural and social circles of Germany, as well as representative works that epitomised the world view propagated by the National Socialists. Belling's sculpture *The boxer (Portrait of Max Schmeling)*, created in 1929 towards the end of the Weimar Republic (fig 6 p 259), was included in a selection of human figures in the House of German Art, which were obviously intended to demonstrate the athleticism and military eagerness of the *neue Mensch* (new man) of National Socialist origin. This momentary impression portrays the boxer while fighting and, despite its figurative composition, can hardly be contextualised within the academic, classicised monumentalism of National Socialist art because of its cautious abstract treatment of form, as well as its small size. This example alone demonstrates that appreciation or rejection of a work of art by Hitler and his followers was not solely based on aesthetic characteristics.

Belling was not the only artist whose defamation remained by no means beyond doubt. Nolde and Barlach – both castigated in the *Degenerate art* exhibition – had, for example, been advocated by Joseph Goebbels, Minister of Propaganda, for years after the seizure of power by the National Socialist German Workers Party (NSDAP), as he acknowledged German Expressionism as a source of prospective German art. The National Socialist League of German Students also supported the more moderate

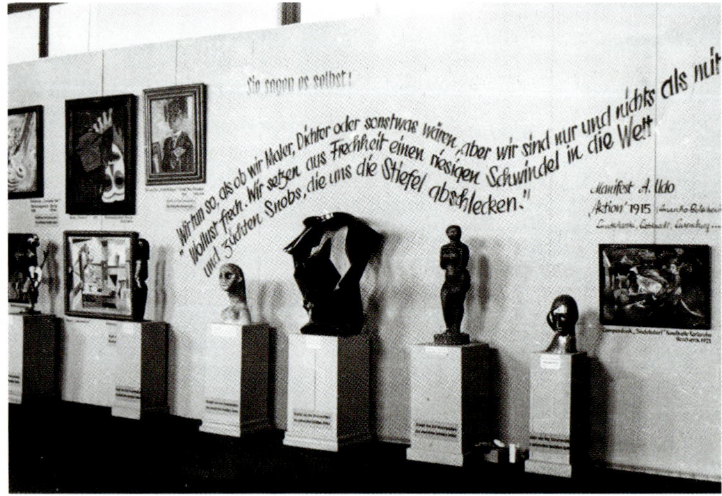

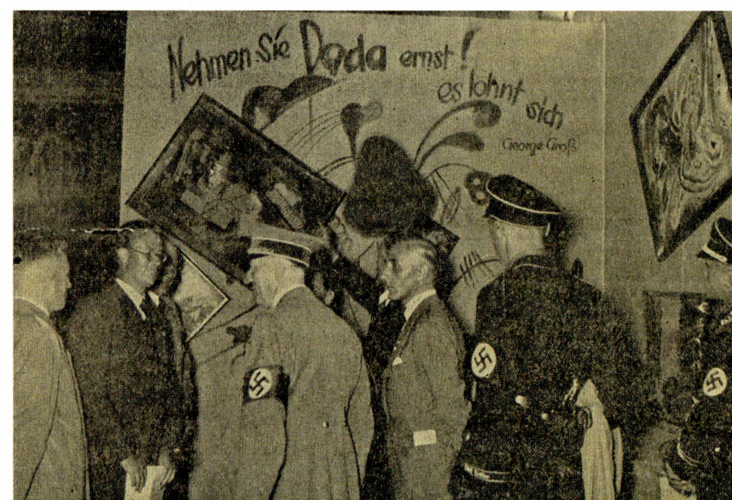

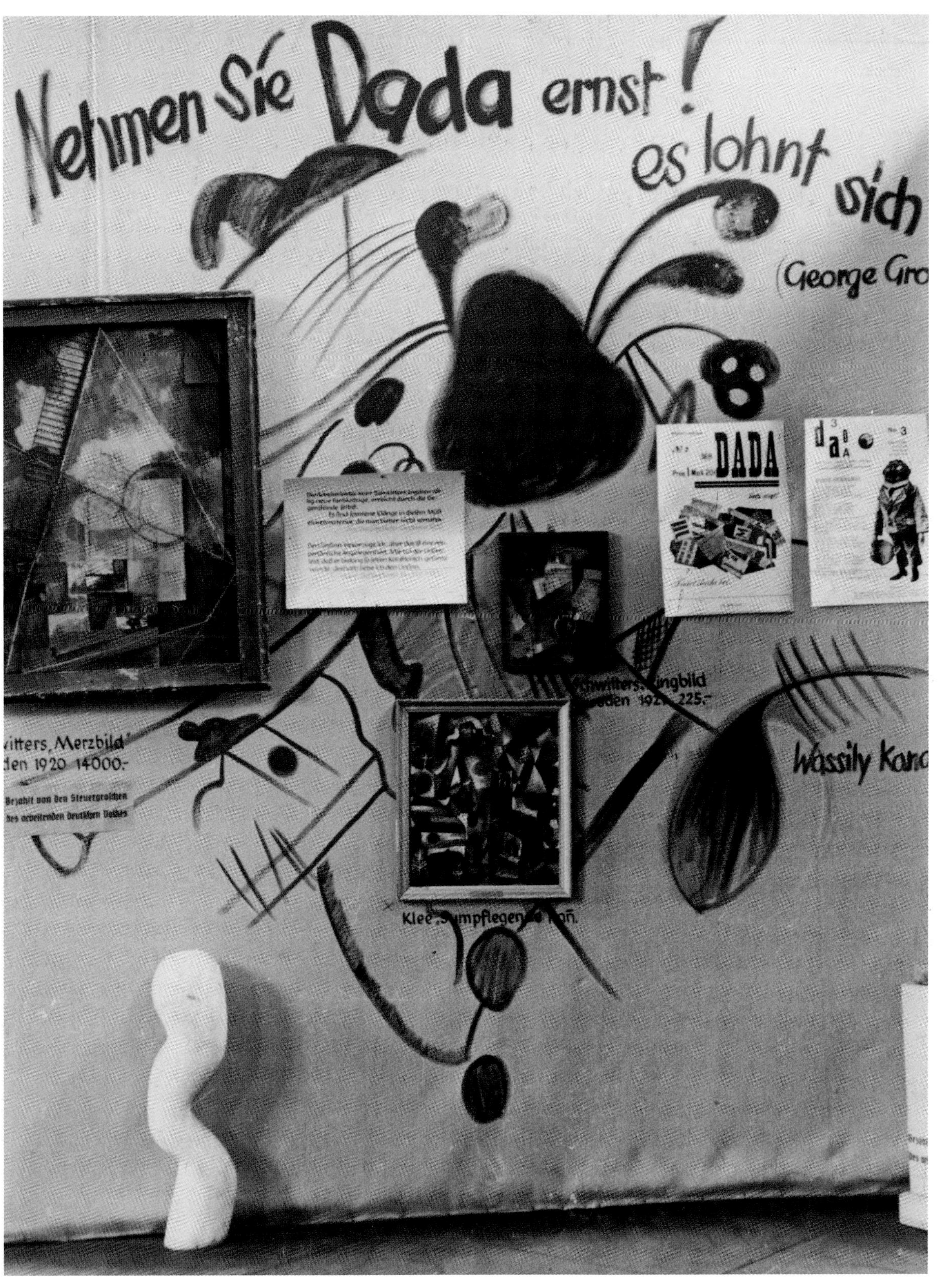

Georg Schödl
A view of the 'Dada wall' in room 3 in the *Degenerate art* exhibition held at the Archäologisches Institut, Munich, 19 July – 30 Nov 1937
Research Library, Getty Research Institute, Los Angeles, California

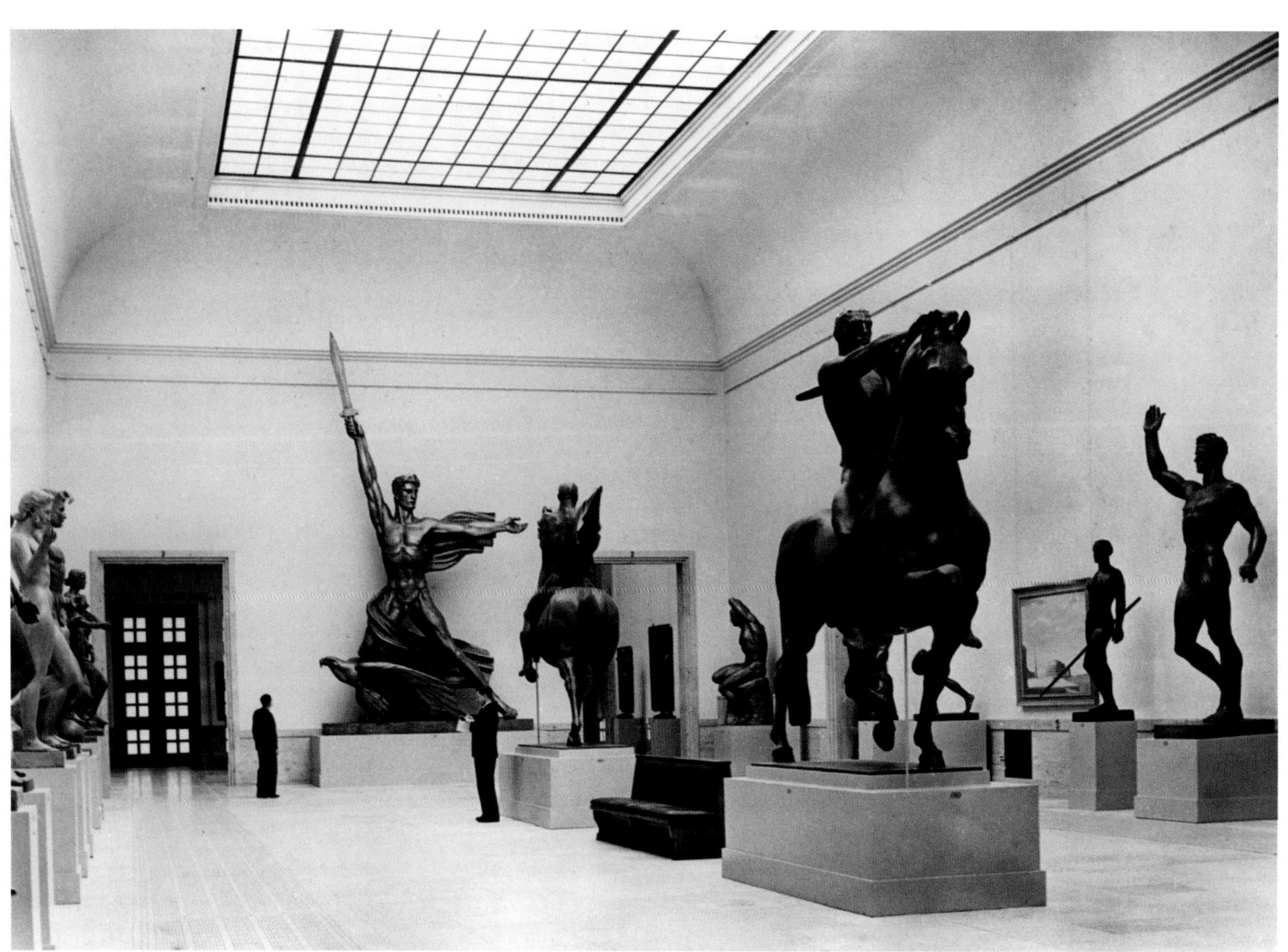

fig 5

Unknown photographer
View of the first *Great German art exhibition* at the Haus der Deutschen Kunst with works by Josef Thorak, Arno Breker and Fritz Klimsch, Munich 1937

Staatliche Museen Preussischer Kulturbesitz, Zentralarchiv, Berlin

Expressionist artists during the mid 1930s and Georg Schrimpf – a representative of *Neue Sachlichkeit* (New Objectivity), who had been discredited as a 'degenerate' artist in Munich – was able to place some of his works within the collections of high-ranking National Socialists like Rudolf Hess, Hitler's deputy, and Walter Darré, the Minister for Welfare and Agriculture.[6] The sculptor Gerhard Marcks was also represented by two works in the *Degenerate art* exhibition, while another work, his bronze *Swimmer II* of 1938 (Neue Nationalgalerie, Berlin), won a prize in the official touring exhibition *Contemporary German sculpture* in 1940.[7] Even Franz Marc, whose *Tower of blue horses* from 1913 (location unknown) was one of the major works in the defamatory exhibition, was defended – in spite of his use of daring colours and compositions – in a protest by influential military officials; they pleaded for the immediate removal of works by the German officer, who had died during the First World War.[8] This contradictory position towards individual artists resulted in consequences for the *Degenerate art* exhibition that are hardly conceivable today: some works were hung elsewhere in the exhibition or removed altogether (one of them being *Tower of blue horses*), and in some instances entire rooms had to be temporarily closed. The confiscation commission for the 'degenerate' art campaign – which at first targeted 30 German museums for the 1937 exhibition but, during the course of the year, visited around 100 collections and confiscated approximately 20 000 works by more than 1400 artists – did not proceed in a consequential manner at all. The standards of the 'cleansing' changed from one museum to the next: works by some artists were not confiscated with the same rigour at each location, works were randomly overlooked, and others were hidden from the commission by brave museum officials. Finally, in May 1938, a 'law effecting the confiscation of products of degenerate art' retrospectively legalised the confiscation of works of art so that they were not only available from then on for exhibition purposes but so they could also be sold for foreign currency abroad. This responsibility was given to four German art dealers, who conducted this task with varying degrees of success, not always based on economic interests, but at least to some extent, based on an interest in preserving the works.[9]

The astonishing heterogeneity of National Socialist art politics originated in deep-seated power struggles between the supporters of a *Blut-und-Boden* (blood-and-soil) ideology and those who supported modernism within the NSDAP, which had tried to gain unlimited control over all aspects of cultural life immediately after the seizure of power by the National Socialists in January 1933. During the first years of the Third Reich these conflicts were mostly played out in arguments about differing interpretations of art and culture.[10] In March, for example, the Ministry for Public Enlightenment and Propaganda was founded, headed by Goebbels, and the *Professional Civil Service Restoration Act* was passed in April, which enabled the new officials to dismiss undesirable museum directors and university professors. In September the Reich Chamber of Culture was created, which would regulate all work-related practices of artists, writers and musicians. The fight against the 'destructive influence on our daily lives' of works of modern art and literature – a fight that originated during the German empire – was already outlined in the so-called '25-point program' by Hitler's party in 1920. From 1933 onwards, however, the folkish wing of the NSDAP associated with Alfred Rosenberg's Combat League

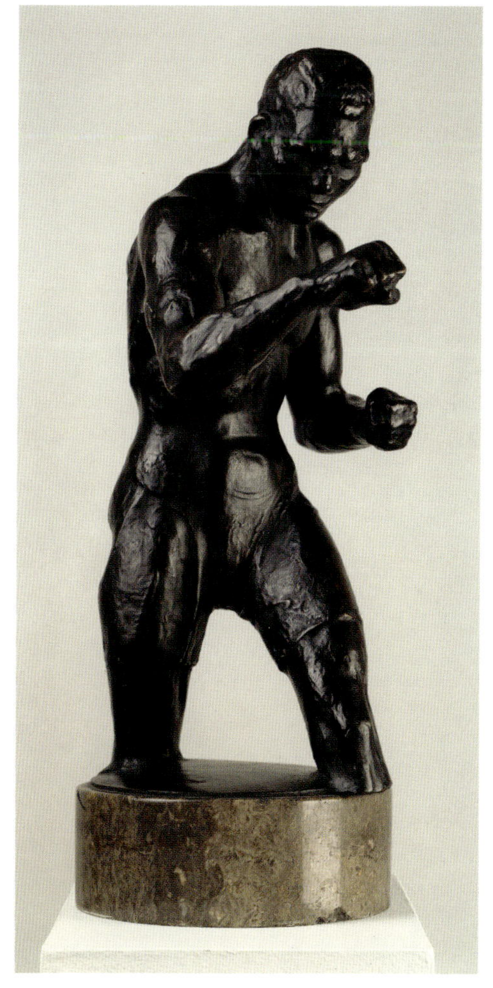

fig 6
Rudolf Belling
The boxer (Portrait of Max Schmeling) 1929
bronze
Museum of Modern Art, New York

for German Culture fought bitterly with the so-called 'Berlin Opposition', which saw National Socialism as a socio-cultural revolutionary movement, over the right way to replace the despised artistic achievements of the Weimar Republic with their own goals. While the folkish movement supported a 'Nordic-Germanic' art of pre-industrial times, the art-political front of the opposition within the NSDAP supported Expressionist and Futurist tendencies.[11] The Führer and new chancellor disregarded both artistic antagonists in his speech at a party rally in September 1934, in which he spoke of the dangers of artistic sabotage by the Cubists, Futurists, Dadaists and others, but also cautioned against excessively retrograde German art.[12]

Henceforth, the power struggles officially ended and, although the NSDAP curtailed its extremist factions during a phase of political consolidation, modernist art and culture was still perceived as a danger because of its potential to remind people of the free and democratic past of the Weimar Republic, which led to the intensification of the systematic 'cleansing' of German museums, libraries, universities and art schools. In his speech at the opening of the first *Great German art exhibition* on 18 July 1937, Hitler finally sharpened his assault against the defamed moderns. The chancellor had visited the *Degenerate art* show during its installation two days earlier (fig 4 p 256), and in his speech kept coming back to *Kunstzwerge* (art gnomes), *Kunstmißhandler* (art abusers), *Kunstfabrikanten* (art manufacturers), *Kunstbetrüger* (art phonies) and *Kunststotterer*

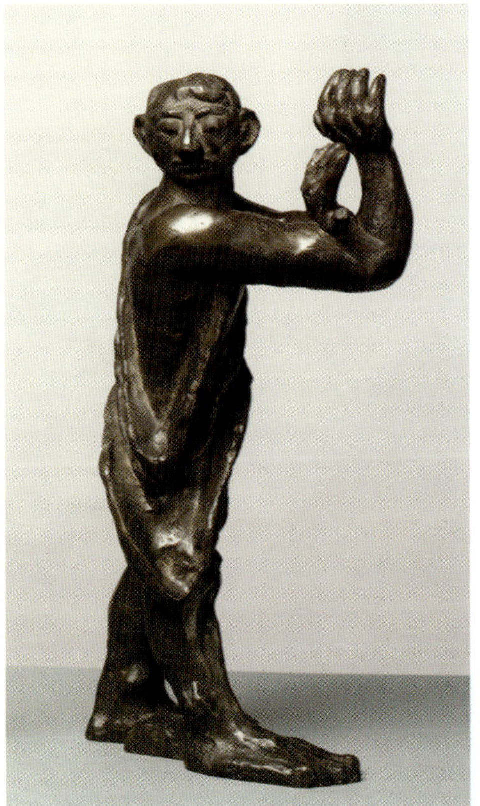

fig 7

Max Beckmann
Man in the dark 1934
bronze, patinated
Bayerische Staatsgemäldesammlungen, Munich
Pinakothek der Moderne

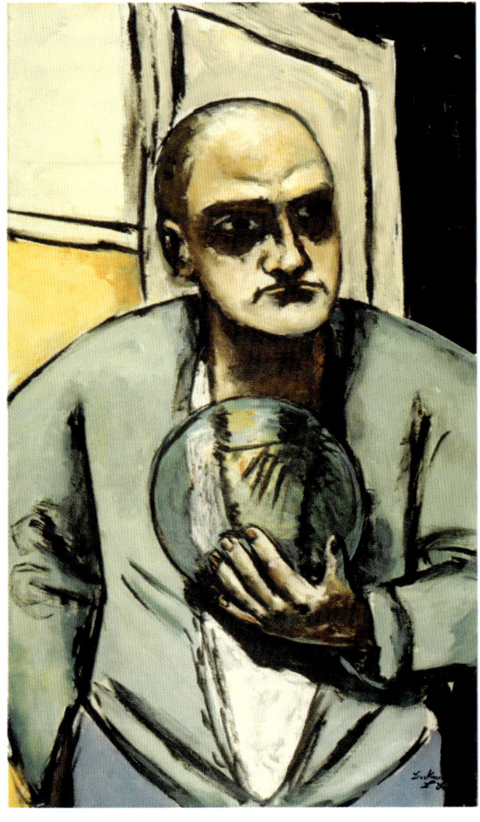

fig 8

Max Beckmann
Self-portrait with glass ball 1936
oil on canvas
Private collection

(art stutterers), whose works he had found so effectively arranged.[13] In contrast to modernism's 'Jewish discovery of art's life expectancy', he pointed to the 'emergence of eternity' of an art whose foundations were rooted not in historical change, but rather its opposite – the unchangeable characteristics of a people.[14] In his speech, Hitler explicitly mentioned the *Degenerate art* exhibition, which was to open the next day, to highlight the general worthlessness of the defamed artworks, but he also pointed to the opportunity to use the display of these works didactically as 'documents of the deepest demise'.[15] He repeated his attack on modern and avant-garde art in this context and left no doubt about his intentions to act decisively:

> Cubism, Dadaism, Futurism, Impressionism and so on have nothing to do with our German people. For all of these terms are neither old nor modern, they are simply the artificial babble of people whom God did not grace with true artistic talent and who instead were given the gift of chatter and deception. Therefore I want to confess in this hour that it is my unwavering decision to clean up the phrases in German artistic life just like the ones in areas of political confusion ... From now on we will fight an unrelenting cleansing war against the last elements of our cultural demise.[16]

Hitler, who as a failed painter had an obsessive love-hate relationship with avant-garde art, shamelessly announced a radicalisation of the already existing art-political measures of the National Socialist government in addition to his defamation of condemned artists and their supporters in museums, galleries and art criticism. The dramatic consequences for painters and sculptors of the attacked art movements were persecution, imprisonment, exile and murder, and their works were ridiculed, sold or destroyed.

One of these 'art abusers', Max Beckmann, fled with his wife from Germany and went into exile in Amsterdam in the days before the opening of the *Degenerate art* exhibition.[17] This visionary artist, whose professorship at the Frankfurt Art School had already been revoked in the spring of 1933, was well aware that it was no longer just the appreciation of his work that was at stake in a more and more tightened art political situation, but also his survival. At the beginning of the 1930s, Beckmann had been waiting, almost strategising, and also had sympathisers within the National Socialist elite.[18] However, as early as 1934 he reacted in artistic terms to the beginning of the Third Reich with his first bronze sculpture, *Man in the dark* (fig 7).[19] Interestingly, it is the metaphor of the dark – a metaphor of no longer being able to see – which the clear-sighted Beckmann represents through this figure. With his arms carefully lifted in a defensive gesture and his eyes closed, the man feels his way through an imaginary space, which alludes to the general problem of depicting space in the work of the artist but also unavoidably contextualises the work within the new political reality of National Socialism. Later paintings, such as *Self-portrait with glass ball* of 1936 (fig 8) – which shows the painter as a fortune teller with a grim expression – illustrate the uncertainty of the times. Similarly, *The liberated man* 1937 (Pinakothek der Moderne, Munich) – which was painted in exile and expresses a feeling of sceptical relief brought about by his successful escape, represented in the motif of the broken chains – and numerous enigmatic triptychs of the 1930s and 1940s show that Beckmann constantly referred to his own situation, broken in the prism of contemporary

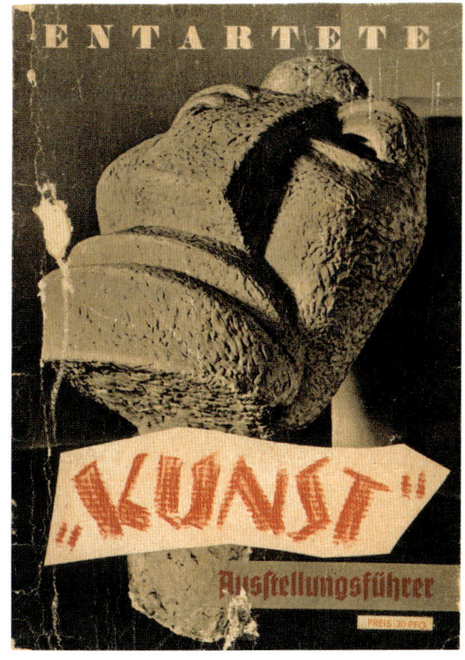

fig 9

Cover of the brochure for the *Degenerate art* exhibition, Berlin 1938 (with Otto Freundlich's The new man 1912)

political circumstances. Although the totalitarian state was able to confiscate his works – almost 600 of his paintings and works on paper were removed from German museums – Beckmann was able to live and stoically affirm his artistic strength while in exile, despite the ever-present danger of deportation. However, even in Germany a few collectors, art dealers and art historians dared to remain in secret contact with the artist, so that at least some of his works entered private collections during the Third Reich and were even shown, from time to time, in semi-public exhibitions.

Many other artists also fled into exile: George Grosz, for example, went to the United States in 1933; Paul Klee left for Switzerland; John Heartfield went to Czechoslovakia, and later to England, continuing the publication of his political photomontages from abroad; Heinrich Campendonk emigrated to Belgium in 1934; Rudolf Belling went to Turkey in 1937; Kurt Schwitters left for Norway in that same year and went later to England; and Ludwig Meidner was able to flee to England at the last minute, in 1939. But not everyone who left Germany was able to save their life. The painter and sculptor Otto Freundlich, whose sculpture *The new man* of 1912 (location unknown) was mistreated by the National Socialists as a negative icon during their hate campaign (fig 9 p 261), was temporarily interned at the outbreak of war in France, arrested during his escape through the south west of the country in 1943 and murdered in the concentration camp Majdanek, in Poland.[20] Felix Nussbaum, who first went into exile in Italy and then in Belgium after 1935, was deported in 1944 and died in Auschwitz. The fate of Nussbaum, who was particularly endangered due to his Jewish heritage, demonstrates the extraordinary manner in which condemned artists – whose existence the National Socialists saw as having no ethical foundation and who allegedly only strived for economic advantage – continued to embrace their work, even under life-threatening conditions and the worst circumstances. Indeed, it shows that painting was a means of resistance and a survival strategy.[21] After the invasion of German troops into Belgium, Nussbaum – who had critically highlighted the conflict between academic and progressive artists in his satirical painting *The mad square* 1931 (p 264–5) – lived in hiding with his wife in temporary lodgings but continued to paint until the bitter end, and represented his increasingly untenable situation without illusion in works such as *Fear (Self-portrait with Marianne)* of 1941, *Self-portrait with Jewish passport* of 1943 (both Felix-Nussbaum-Haus, Osnabruck) and *The triumph of death (The skeletons play for the dance)* of 1944 (fig 10).

The despairing, oppositional paintings of Beckmann and Nussbaum, together with the many paintings, sculptures, works on paper and photographs created by the condemned artists abroad or during their inner emigration in Germany, stood in clear contrast to the official creations of the Third Reich. The anaemic nude figures by Ziegler or the vastly monumental, artistically inferior, sculptures by Arno Breker, Fritz Klimsch or Josef Thorak, were a type of art that was irreconcilably different and finally victorious from a historical perspective in this unequal battle. Many works by the persecuted painters and sculptors have gone down in the history of art as evidence of artistic as well as moral integrity, of resistance and often-uncompromising modernity. The works of the National Socialist Party followers, on the other hand, can only be seen today as documents of an authoritarian understanding of art that was exhausted in the service of the ideology.

But why was it that the attack on modernism by Hitler and his followers had been conducted so rigorously in some instances, and with so many contradictions in others? Why were art and culture given such a high status in public life during the Third Reich? We first have to come to terms with the specific psychological disposition of Adolf Hitler when answering these questions. In his continual tirades of hatred about any form of modern or avant-garde art, particularly those that represented the democratic pluralism of the Weimar Republic, it becomes apparent that the art-critical interferences of the Führer – who saw himself as an artist, but who was doomed to be unsuccessful due to his lack of talent even in the field of academic landscape painting – were the obsession of a failed artist directed against the envied representatives of an art scene of which he was never allowed to be a part. More important, though – and in contradiction to this personal attitude – is the National Socialists' insight into the effect of modern art and culture on the masses. In the first decades of the 20th century, modes of communication such as exhibitions, museums, film and theatre, as well as architectural and urban design with its public monumental sculpture, were of particular importance. And finally it was the intention of the new rulers, at least until the beginning of the Second World War, to impress national and international elites by showing them that National Socialist Germany still saw itself in the tradition of the great cultural achievements of the 19th century. The conflict between hateful barbarity on the one hand and the self-image as a cultural nation on the other finally exposes the fact that the cultural politics of the National Socialists had to remain a construct of extreme contradictions.

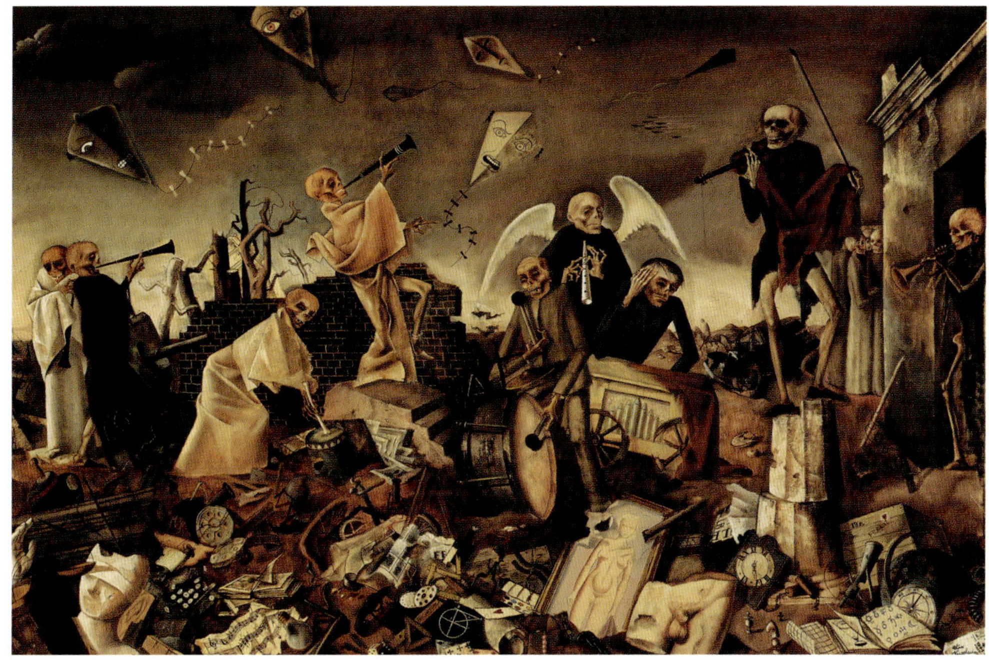

fig 10
Felix Nussbaum
The triumph of death (The skeletons play for the dance) 1944
oil on canvas
Felix-Nussbaum-Haus, Osnabruck

FELIX NUSSBAUM

The mad square

In *The mad square* 1931, Felix Nussbaum portrays Pariser Platz, the site of Berlin's official art establishment, as a crazy place. Indignant young artists gather outside the entrance of the Prussian Academy of Arts, surrounded by a haphazard display of freshly painted canvasses by Nussbaum, who appears in the left-hand corner of the group holding a note of protest. The young artists' demonstration against the exclusion of their work from the prestigious academy exhibition is directed towards the established artists – including Käthe Kollwitz, who can be seen in the middle of the second row – whose arrival at the academy is heralded by pomp and ceremony. Ignoring the protest, the academicians turn their attention towards the institution while, equally oblivious to the demands of the young artists, the academy's president, Max Liebermann, works on a large self-portrait from his rooftop studio.

In this work Nussbaum not only satirised the overriding conservatism of the academy, he was also a critic of the times. *The mad square* was painted during a period of intense political polarisation in the years immediately before the cataclysm, and in retrospect it is difficult to avoid seeing it as a forewarning. History has shown all too well that the structures representing the old world, which Nussbaum presents as crumbling and disintegrating, were soon to be revived with a vengeance. Yet it would have been impossible for the artist to foretell such realities, and recent suggestions that this work contains symbols of death and destruction – for example, in the machine-like row of drumming figures entering the scene from

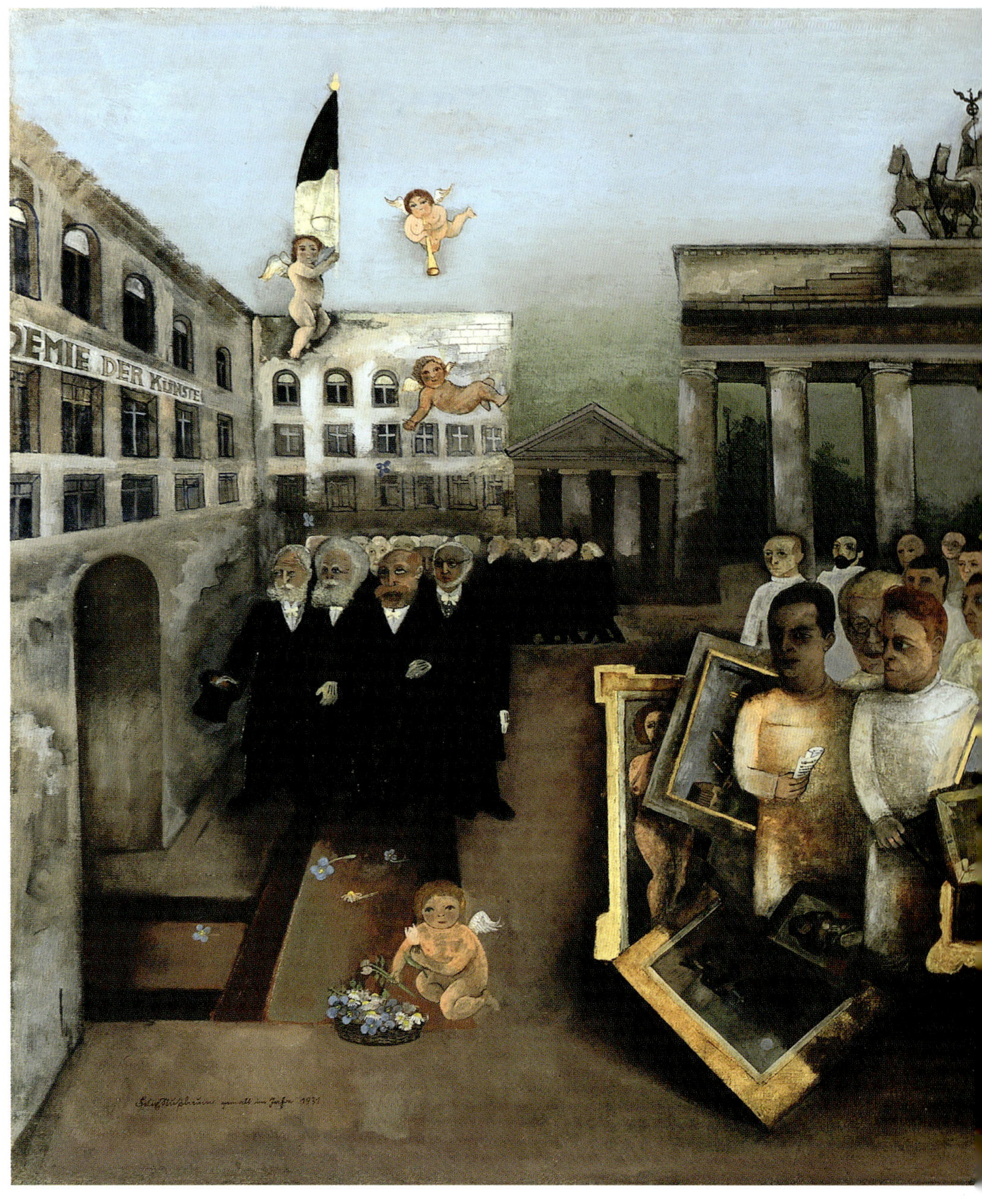

the back right-hand corner or in the crosses in the windows – are simply inadequate.[1] Nonetheless, Nussbaum does allude to Germany's recent past, the years of the Weimar Republic through which he lived and experienced the collapse of society. He hinted at the loss of traditional structures of authority by portraying them in ruins – as with the statue of Victory, who has become detached from her column and flies through the air losing her wreath – as well as the death of art, by showing Liebermann's house as a crumbling structure and placing crosses in the windows of other outmoded institutions, such as the academy.

An artist of Jewish descent, and from the northern German provinces, Nussbaum arrived in Berlin during the 1920s to pursue a career in art. He studied at the United State School for Free and Applied Art in 1925 and held solo shows as early as 1926, as well as exhibiting frequently in group exhibitions, such as the Berlin Secession. His status as a promising young artist was confirmed in 1932, when he was invited to study at the Villa Massimo in Rome; however, in 1933 his residency was terminated by Joseph Goebbels, who banned Jewish artists from studying there. Nussbaum spent the ensuing years in exile and lived in terror for the last four years of his life in German-occupied Brussels. While in hiding, he painted a number of powerful images that portray the fear, despair, isolation and constant threat of death he experienced throughout the early 1940s. Nussbaum was captured by the Nazis in July 1944 and deported to Auschwitz, where he died on 2 August. JS

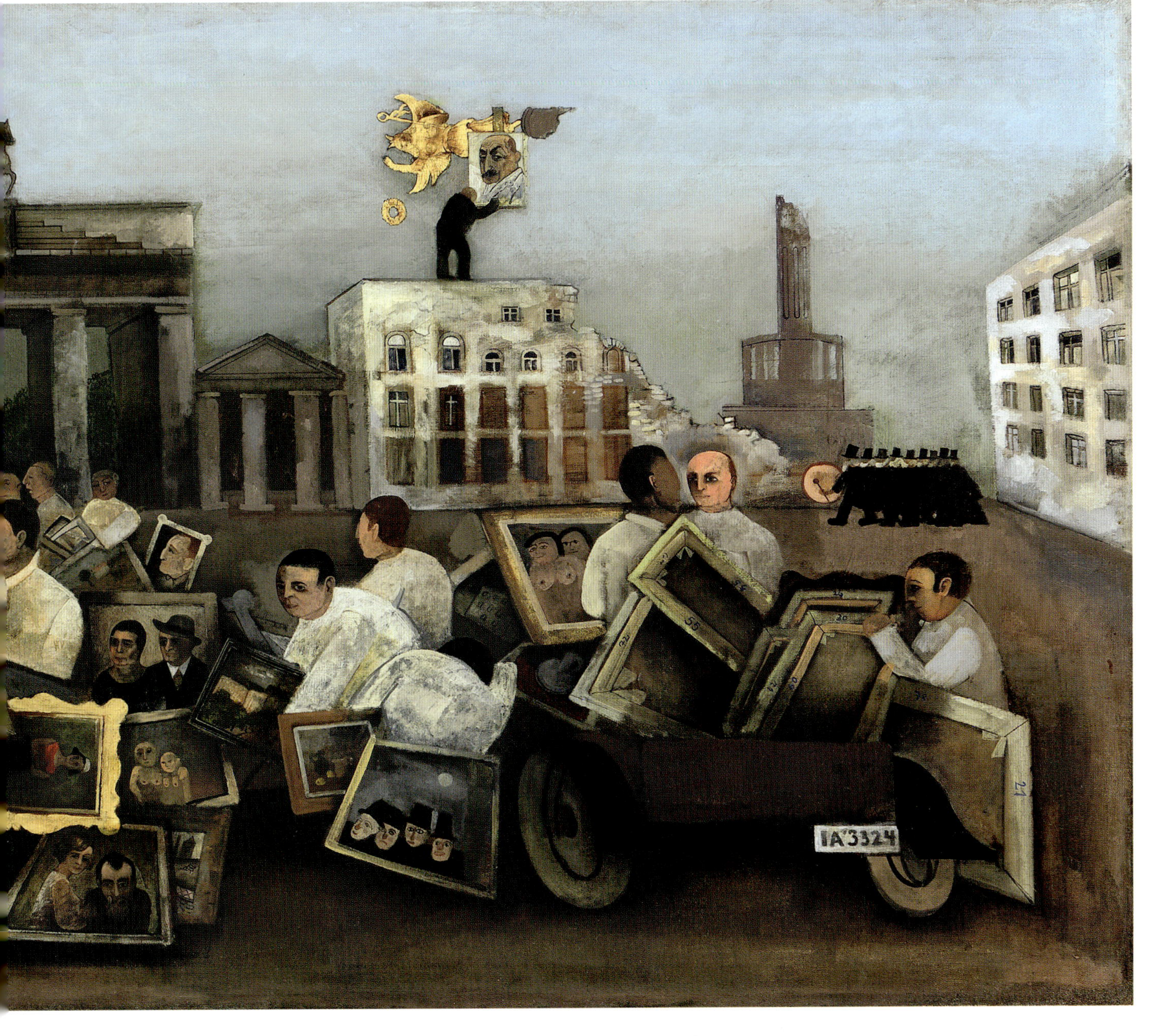

Felix Nussbaum
The mad square 1931
oil on canvas
Berlinische Galerie, Landesmuseum für Moderne Kunst, Fotografie und Architektur

JOHN HEARTFIELD

Photomontage

John Heartfield stated that the idea of creating critical photomontages exposing hidden agendas in politics, commerce and international events originated during his time as a solider in the war:

> I started making photomontages during the First World War. There are a lot of things that got me into working with photos. The main thing is that I saw both what was being said and not being said with photos in the newspapers. The most important thing for me was that I intrinsically became involved in the opposition and worked with a medium I didn't consider to be an artistic medium, photography ... I found out how you can fool people with photos, really fool them ... You can lie and tell the truth by putting the wrong title or captions under them, and that's roughly what was being done.[1]

Following on from his involvement with the Berlin Dadaists, Heartfield emphasised the dialectical tendency of photomontage, as well as its anarchic potential to affirm and negate contemporary political arguments. Since becoming a communist in 1918, Heartfield worked exclusively in photomontage and his work appeared regularly during the 1920s in the German Communist Press, which included the Malik Verlag's publications and the *Arbeiter Illustrierte Zeitung* (AIZ, or *Workers' Illustrated Paper*), which had a circulation of 450 000 by the end of the 1920s.[2]

Between 1930 and 1938, Heartfield produced more than 200 photomontages that appeared on either the front or back covers of the *AIZ*, or as occasional double-page spreads. His engaging and highly provocative cover images ensured the paper's viability, as

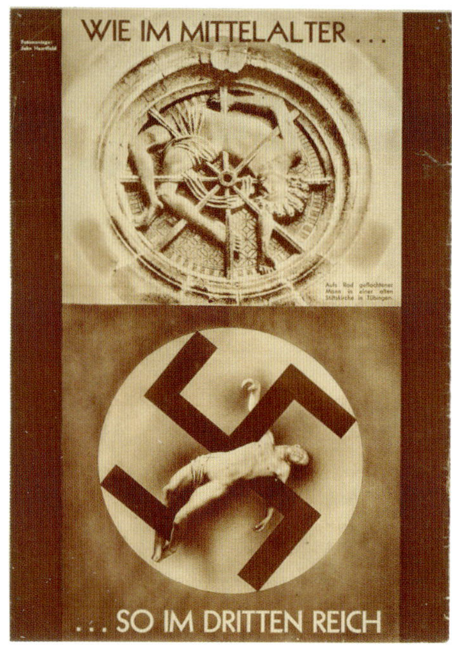

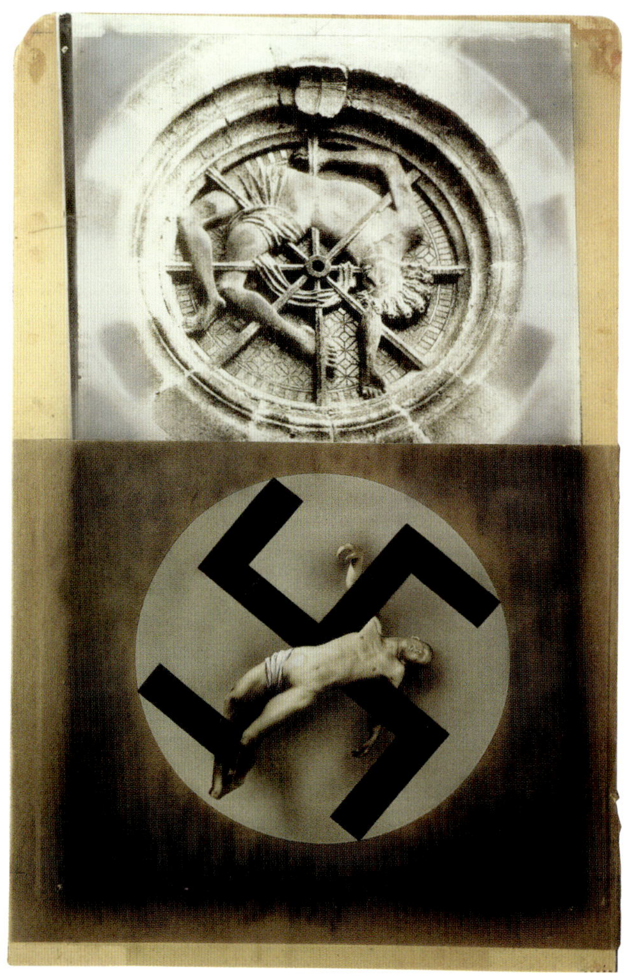

above:

John Heartfield
As in the Middle Ages ... so in the Third Reich
from the Workers' Illustrated Paper May 1934
photolithograph
Akademie der Künste, Berlin, Kunstsammlung

fig 11

John Heartfield
Design for 'As in the Middle Ages ... so in the Third Reich' c1934
photomontage, retouched
Akademie der Künste, Berlin, Kunstsammlung

many readers bought the newspapers from newsstands. Heartfield relentlessly opposed the Nazi propaganda machine, and his anti-fascist photomontages of the early 1930s are among the most compelling and powerful images he created. In 1933 he was forced into exile and fled to Prague, where he continued to create a multitude of scathing critiques of contemporary political and social issues for the *AIZ*.

Heartfield's designs for the photomontages *Adolf, the superman: swallows gold and spouts rubbish* c1932 (below) and *As in the Middle Ages … so in the Third Reich* c1934 (fig 11) are important examples of the way in which he constructed his photomontages from images taken from the mass media. The rapid growth of the mass print media during the Weimar Republic had provided Heartfield with endless possibilities to create montages that comprised seemingly unrelated, juxtaposed fragments. In his now-famous satirical representation of Hitler giving a speech to Rhineland industrialists, Heartfield conceals the fact that this is a picture constructed from a number of different elements. He does this with such clever craftsmanship and technical brilliance that the overall effect is both deceptive and completely convincing. By drawing attention to the fact that meaning is created through the addition of the text 'Adolf, the superman: swallows gold and spouts rubbish', as well as the inscription in the upper-right corner 'X ray by John Heartfield', the artist exposes the highly constructed and ideologically manipulative nature of contemporary political discourse. JS

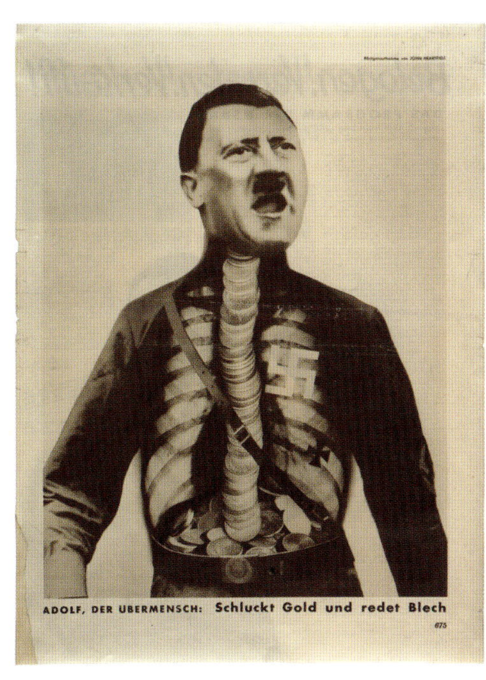

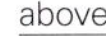

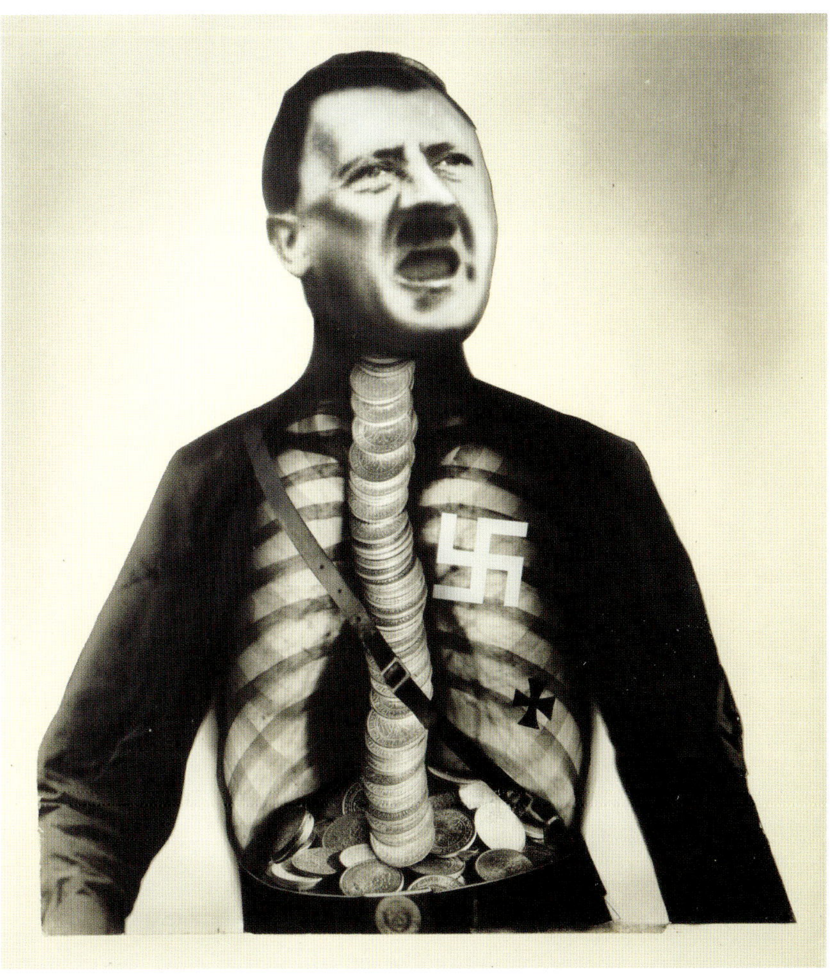

above:

John Heartfield
Adolf, the superman: swallows gold and spouts rubbish
from the Workers' Illustrated Paper July 1932
photolithograph
Akademie der Künste, Berlin, Kunstsammlung

John Heartfield
Design for 'Adolf, the superman: swallows gold and spouts rubbish' c1932
photomontage, retouched
Akademie der Künste, Berlin, Kunstsammlung

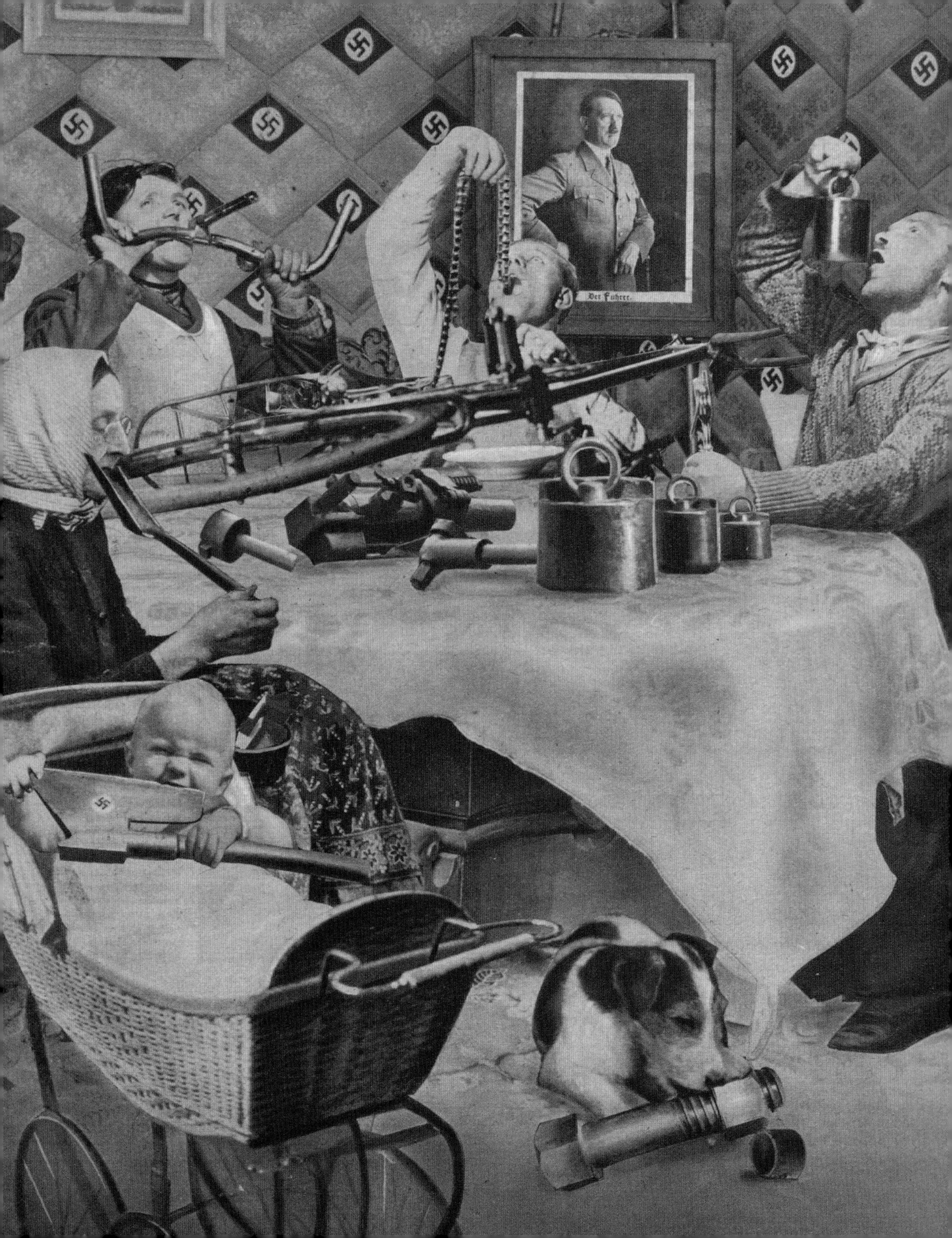
Der Führer.

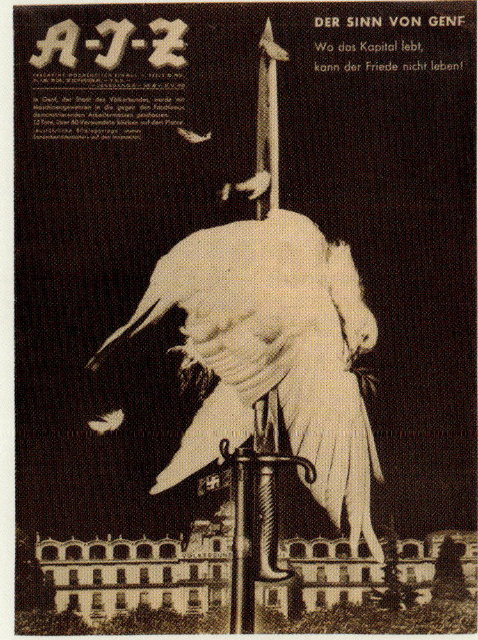

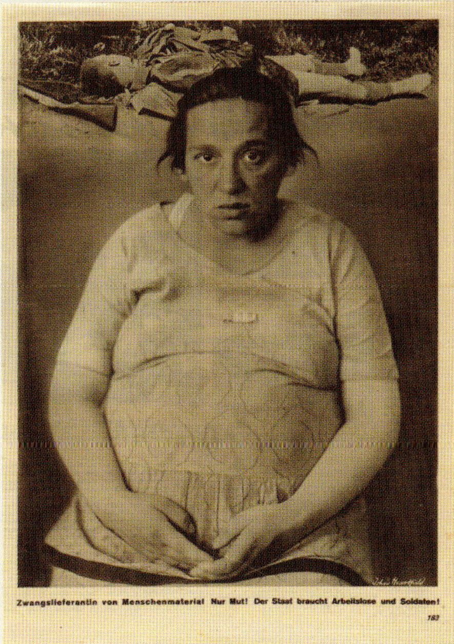

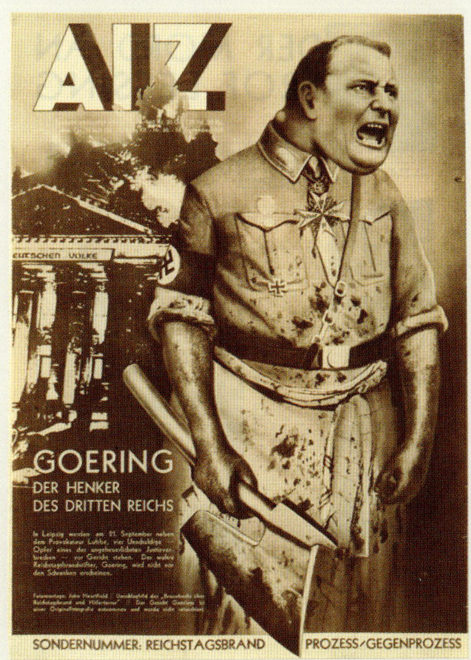

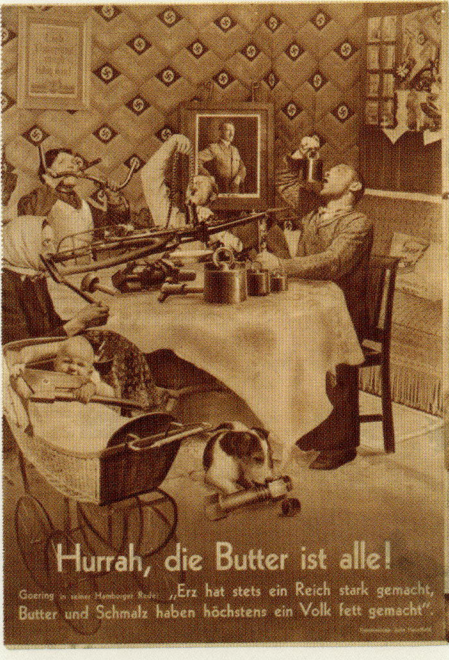

John Heartfield
The meaning of Geneva: where capital lives, peace cannot live!
from the Workers' Illustrated Paper, Nov 1932
photolithograph
Akademie der Künste, Berlin, Kunstsammlung

John Heartfield
Forced supplier of human material, take courage!
from the Workers' Illustrated Paper, 1930
photolithograph
Akademie der Künste, Berlin, Kunstsammlung

John Heartfield
Goering: the executioner of the Third Reich
from the Workers' Illustrated Paper, Sept 1933
photolithograph
Akademie der Künste, Berlin, Kunstsammlung

John Heartfield
Hurray, the butter is finished!
from the Workers' Illustrated Paper Dec 1935
(detail opposite)
photolithograph
Akademie der Künste, Berlin, Kunstsammlung

ERNST LUDWIG KIRCHNER

Brown figures in café

In 1938, Ernst Ludwig Kirchner took his own life in the Swiss Alpine village of Davos, which had been his principal residence since 1918. His suicide was brought about by the physical decline he experienced after suffering a nervous breakdown during the First World War, but also through the personal and professional rejection he suffered as one of the principal targets of the Nazi's assault against modern art and artists. His continuing addiction to alcohol, morphine and the commonly prescribed sedative Veronal, combined with the extreme hostility towards his work in Germany in the 1930s, created an impossible situation for Kirchner. Though he had been elected a member of Prussian Academy of Arts in Berlin in 1931, to honour his achievement as a leading exponent of Expressionism, he renounced his membership in 1937 to protest against the politicisation of modern art and its institutions. Between 1937 and 1938, an astounding total of 639 works by Kirchner were confiscated from German museums and 32 were included in the *Degenerate art* exhibition.[1] Kirchner continued to work in a state of inner exile in Davos, yet the onset of illness and the stress of artistic circumstances led him to destroy many of his works before his death on 15 June.

Brown figures in café 1928–29, departs quite significantly from many of Kirchner's late paintings of mountain landscapes, portraits and nudes that characteristically employ bright, high-keyed colours and simplified, expressionistic forms. The setting is unusual in that it is neither urban nor alpine, but a non-specific scene of a café, where the silhouetted forms of two people engaged in a conversation can be seen surrounded by an almost frieze-like arrangement of simplified forms and figures. By the mid 1920s, Kirchner had evolved his earlier experimentation with 'primitivism' into an identifiable artistic style that combined a severe flattening of form with the use of broad, heavily defined contours.[2] Yet the drastically reduced palette of orange-brown, black, green and whitish tones gives this painting a unique quality that is both edgy and striking.

On the one hand, the painting is suggestive of the renewed sense of artistic creativity that Kirchner experienced when he moved to the Swiss Alps to recuperate after the war. The scene hints at the feeling of tranquillity and contentment that could be found in the natural environment and at the sense of unity that could be forged through male–female relationships. On the other hand, there is an underlying tension between the foreground figures, with their featureless, unidentified faces, and the way in which they are crammed into the tightly defined space, which appears both stage-like and cinematic. Many modernist artists sensed a prevailing loss of direction in avant-garde art by 1929 and this enigmatic painting can also be seen as representing a turning point in Kirchner's own work during the crisis of modernism. JS

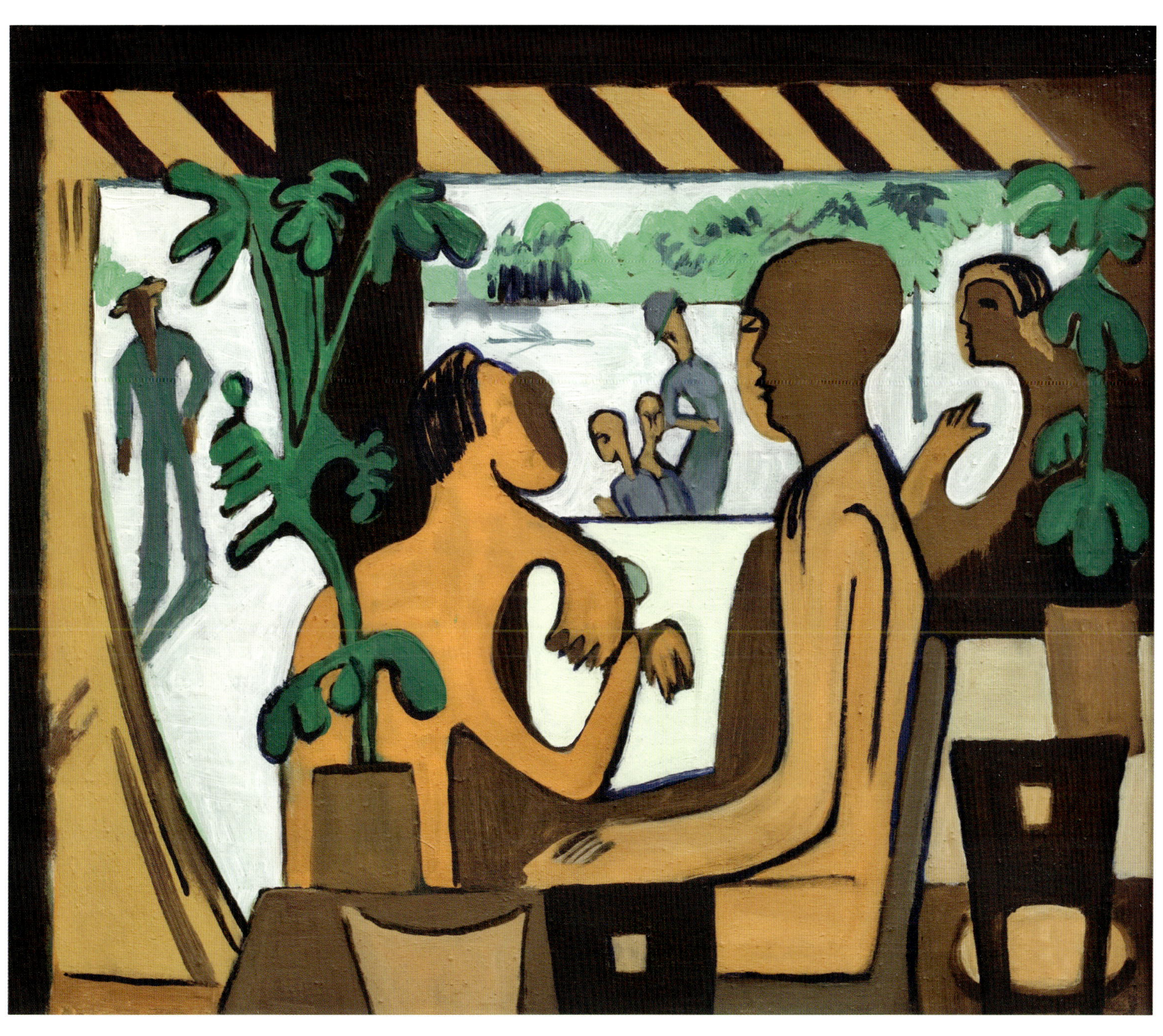

Ernst Ludwig Kirchner
Brown figures in café 1928–29
oil on canvas
Museum Ludwig, Cologne

MAX BECKMANN

Crouching woman

The relatively small number of sculptures created by Max Beckmann in comparison to the large number of paintings, prints and drawings he produced over his lifetime has led some commentators to describe his sculpture as merely an extension of his work as a painter.[1] It was, however, through his sculptures of the human form that Beckmann pushed the physicality of the figure beyond the constrained construction of the body represented in his paintings, and achieved a clarity and openness not found in his tightly constructed two-dimensional works. In a letter to his wife, dated 16 March 1915, Beckmann expressed his aim:

> to produce ever more simple work, to develop a more concentrated mode of expression, but I will never … abandon the ideas of fullness, of roundness, of the vibrantly pulsating … no arabesques … but fullness and plasticity.[2]

Beckmann had moved to Berlin in 1934 after being dismissed from his professorship at the Städelschule in Frankfurt am Main, with his work labelled 'degenerate' art by the National Socialists. Though he refrained from exhibiting in Germany in the mid 1930s, it was during this very difficult period of enforced inner exile that he turned to sculpture. Beckmann produced a total of eight small plaster sculptures in the mid 1930s and in 1950, and only after his death was the decision taken by his wife and a New York gallery owner to produce a series of five bronze castings for each of these sculptures, and to have the plaster works destroyed subsequently.[3] *Crouching woman* 1935 was among the first five sculptures Beckmann created in Berlin between 1934 and 1936. There is an awkward sense of unease about the striking and unusual pose of Beckmann's fleshy model as she crawls on all fours – a pose not found in traditional sculpture and not entirely unlike the crawling movement of his second wife, Quappi, depicted in a painting of 1930 that has recently come to light.

The heightened sense of eroticism that found its way into Beckmann's work in the 1930s is also conveyed in this posthumous cast of *Crouching woman*. While Beckmann's coarse modelling of the female form related to many traditions of modern sculpture, from Rodin to Degas, the kind of open sexuality expressed in this sculpture was more influenced by sculptural representations of the female nude created during the Weimar era, by artists such as Georg Kolbe and Gerhard Marcks.

Crouching woman exemplifies Beckmann's extraordinary ability to develop a new and unsettling form of art during a period when his artistic creativity and personal freedom were coming increasingly under threat. By 1937, the situation in Germany had become so hostile to modern artists that on the day following the opening of the *Degenerate art* exhibition, Beckmann and his wife fled to Amsterdam. They migrated to the United States in 1947 and Beckmann never returned to Germany. In his poignant and now-famous speech delivered at the *Exhibition of 20th century German art*, held in London's New Burlington Galleries in 1938, Beckmann aptly stressed the need for artistic transcendence: 'I have never been politically active in any way. I have tried only to realize my conception of the world as intensely as possible.'[4] JS

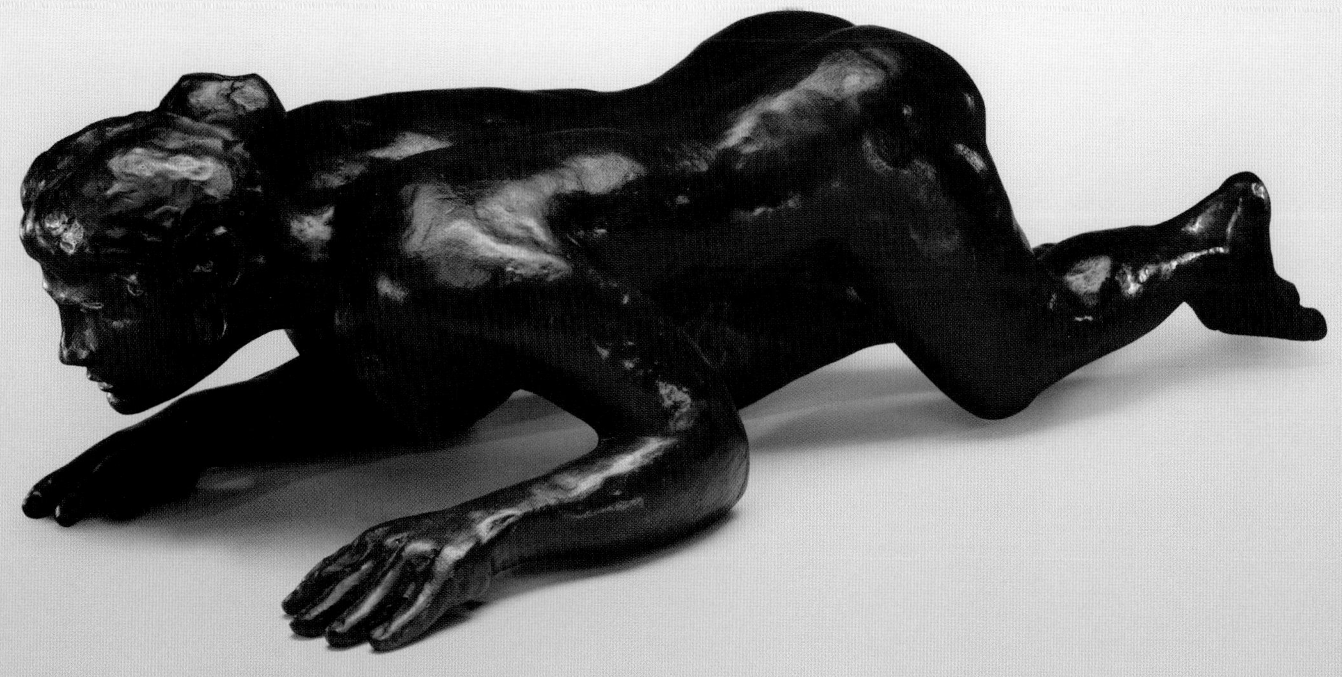

Max Beckmann
Crouching woman 1935
bronze
Private collection, courtesy Richard Feigen, New York

'DEGENERATE' ART

Jacqueline Strecker

The *Degenerate art* exhibition, held in Munich in 1937, is widely acknowledged as representing the culmination of the National Socialists' brutal campaign against modernism. It is also interesting to consider the immediate model and forerunner of this exhibition, which was held in the inner courtyard of the Dresden Town Hall from 23 September to 18 October 1933. This *Degenerate art* exhibition was organised by Richard Müller, the newly appointed director of the Dresden Art Academy. Dresden had been one of Germany's most politically conservative cities and Saxony, together with Thuringia, were among the first states to embrace National Socialism. Given that Hitler was appointed as chancellor on 30 January 1933, it is extraordinary to note the speed with which the local government set about to discredit modern art by confiscating works from Dresden's state museum and blacklisting modern artists in order to prevent them from teaching and exhibiting their work publically.

A short archival film in our exhibition takes viewers on a tour around the Dresden exhibition of 1933, and a range of paintings by Otto Dix, George Grosz, Erich Heckel, Ernst Ludwig Kirchner, Paul Klee, Wassily Kandinsky, Emil Nolde, Kurt Schwitters and others can be seen on display on temporary walls. The Lord Mayor of Dresden, dressed in full National Socialist uniform, is seen walking through the exhibition, while some of the onlookers shake their heads in disapproval as they view the art on display. The listing of purchase prices against each work was intended as a further indictment against what the Nazis considered to be misguided collecting policies of museum directors during the Weimar era. By contrast, the second part of the exhibition comprised sugary landscapes, naturalistic still-lifes and portraits, heroic generalised views of soldiers, and a bronze bust of Hitler. These were presented as positive examples of contemporary German art that had been recently acquired 'under the direction of the National Socialists'. This exhibition toured to at least eight German cities between 1934 and 1936 before it was finally incorporated into the much larger *Degenerate art* exhibition held in Munich.[1]

The negative press generated by the series of *Degenerate art* exhibitions held throughout Germany in the late 1930s created an insatiable appetite in the public to see modern art for themselves. In Munich, more than 2 million people visited the exhibition, while far fewer saw the *Great German art exhibition* held in the nearby Nazi-designed Haus der Deutschen Kunst (House of German Art). It was bizarre but quite astute that the Nazis chose to promote *Degenerate art* through the same forms of art that they sought to denigrate, as in the poster for the display of the exhibition in Hamburg in 1938 (p 277). The sculpture depicted here was based on Otto Freundlich's *The new man* 1912, which was also reproduced on the cover of the *Degenerate art* exhibition guide (fig 9 p 261). The exaggeration of features such as the narrow eyes and enlarged nose, features which are echoed in the head in the background (supposedly modelled on the profile of the Jewish art dealer Alfred Flechtheim), reveal the insidious racism of the National Socialists.[2]

Following the conclusion of the exhibition in Munich, and during its subsequent tour, most of the confiscated paintings, sculptures and works on paper were destroyed. Works of 'international value' were sold at auction and many of these are now fortunately held in collections around the world. The final section of this exhibition and publication bring together a small group of these works to celebrate the achievements of artists such as Nolde, Kirchner, Franz Marc, Dix, Grosz and Max Beckmann and their great contribution to modernism. Additional works from the *Degenerate art* exhibition, or that were condemned by the Nazis as 'degenerate', are included in other sections of this publication and in the exhibition. See the 'List of works' (pp 301–7).

It is important not to judge what happened to modern German art in the light of *Degenerate art* as an isolated event but to acknowledge that art and politics had been closely intertwined since the emergence of modernism in Germany. This conflict was intensified during the Weimar years and came to an ugly head after 1933, representing a continuation of past, unresolved tensions played out in the cultural sphere rather than an abrupt and unexpected departure from the history of modern art and its institutions in Germany.

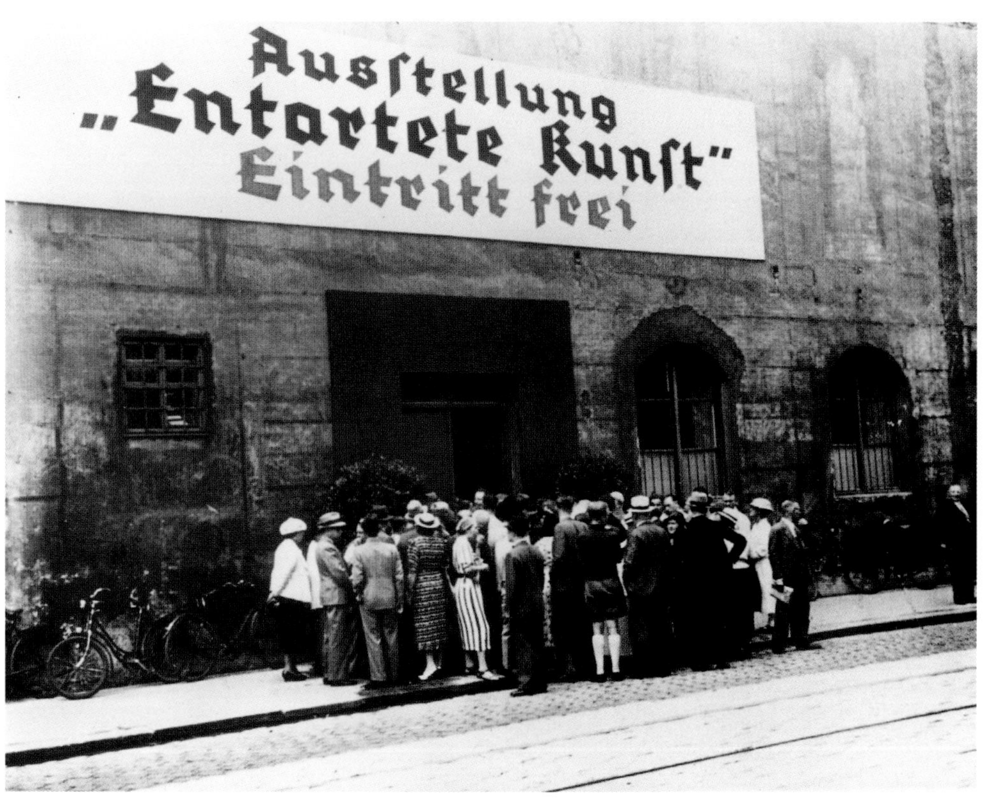

fig 12

Photographer unknown
The Nazi curated *Degenerate art* (Entartete Kunst) travelling exhibition at its first stop at the Hofgarten, Munich, Germany, 19 July 1937

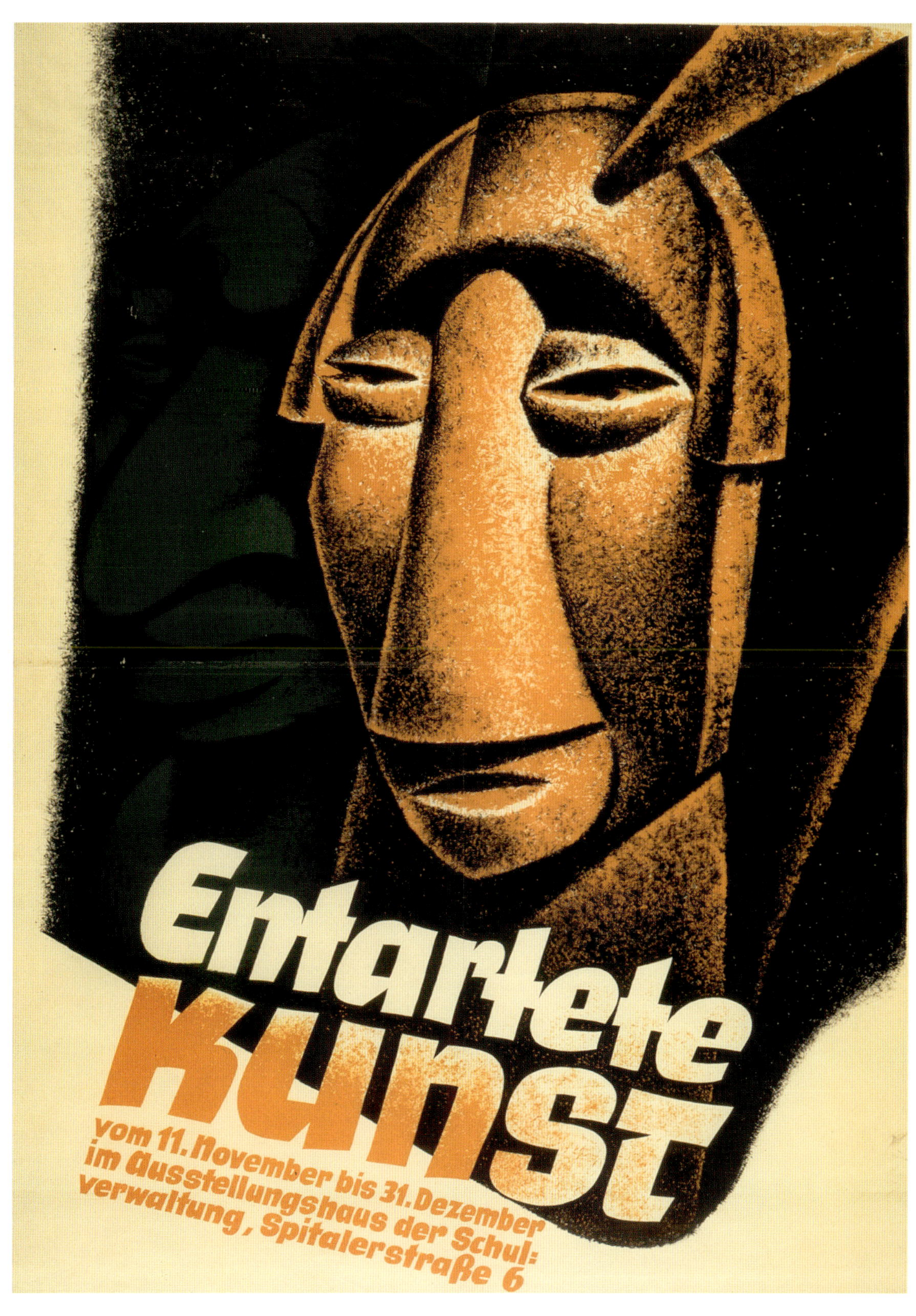

Rudolf Herrmann
Degenerate art 1938
colour lithograph, poster
Los Angeles County Museum of Art

RUDOLF BELLING

Triad

Rudolf Belling trained as a sculptor and modeller in Berlin before the war. After completing his service, he became one of the founding members of the revolutionary Workers Council for Art and the *Novembergruppe* (November Group). These groups of politically committed artists and architects believed in the capacity of art to forge social and political change, and they embraced a number of avant-garde directions, including Expressionism, Cubism, Futurism, Constructivism and Realism. Belling created *Triad* in 1918–19 during a time of extreme political upheaval and during a period that was strongly influenced, certainly in avant-garde artistic circles, by an atmosphere of utopian idealism.

Triad is often attributed as being the first abstract sculpture created in Germany. The work is based on the idea of a sculptural form composed of three interrelated, geometric figures that twist and turn in a dynamic, rhythmic arrangement. Belling produced the original plaster cast of *Triad* – upon which the present bronze was based – as a model for a much larger and ultimately unrealised sculpture that was to stand six-metres high.[1] Not only does the work engage with ideas emerging at the time about artistic forms finding their parallel in musical sounds or notes, but it represents a highly resolved and compelling response to the emergence of abstraction in Berlin. *Triad* combines geometric abstraction with modernist figuration, while incorporating Futurist, Cubist and Expressionist elements. It is characterised by a harmonious synthesis of formal elements and an emphasis on the three-dimensionality of the object, which can be viewed from all angles in fascinating and completely different configurations.

Belling's *Triad* has attained a somewhat iconic status in the canon of modernist art history. Purchased in 1924 by Ludwig Justi, the progressive director of Berlin's National Gallery, the sculpture featured prominently in displays of contemporary German art in the 1920s as an icon of modernism. Belling's reputation as one of Germany's foremost sculptors during the Weimar years was confirmed in 1931, when he was elected a member of the Prussian Academy of Arts; an honour he later renounced following the politicisation of the academy. *Triad* was confiscated in 1937 and then displayed in the *Degenerate art* exhibition, at the centre of a row of sculptures that were grouped together under the thematic heading 'The cultural Bolsheviks' order of battle'. It often appears in documentary photographs of this notorious exhibition (p 254, 256). The bizarre and often contradictory nature of the confrontation between modern and official art in the 1930s was clearly demonstrated when *Triad*, together with Belling's *Head (Portrait of Toni Freeden)* 1928 (Neue Nationalgalerie, Berlin), were removed from *Degenerate art* after it became apparent that Belling's bronze of the boxer Max Schmeling was on display simultaneously at the *Great German art exhibition* as a positive example of the 'new' German art (fig 6, p 259).[2] The removal of these works was not only ironic but pointed to the ill-conceived logic of the organisers in promoting officially sanctioned works of art in one context, while vehemently condemning works by the same artist in another. JS

Rudolf Belling
Triad 1918–19
bronze
Bayerische Staatsgemäldesammlungen, Munich
Pinakothek der Moderne

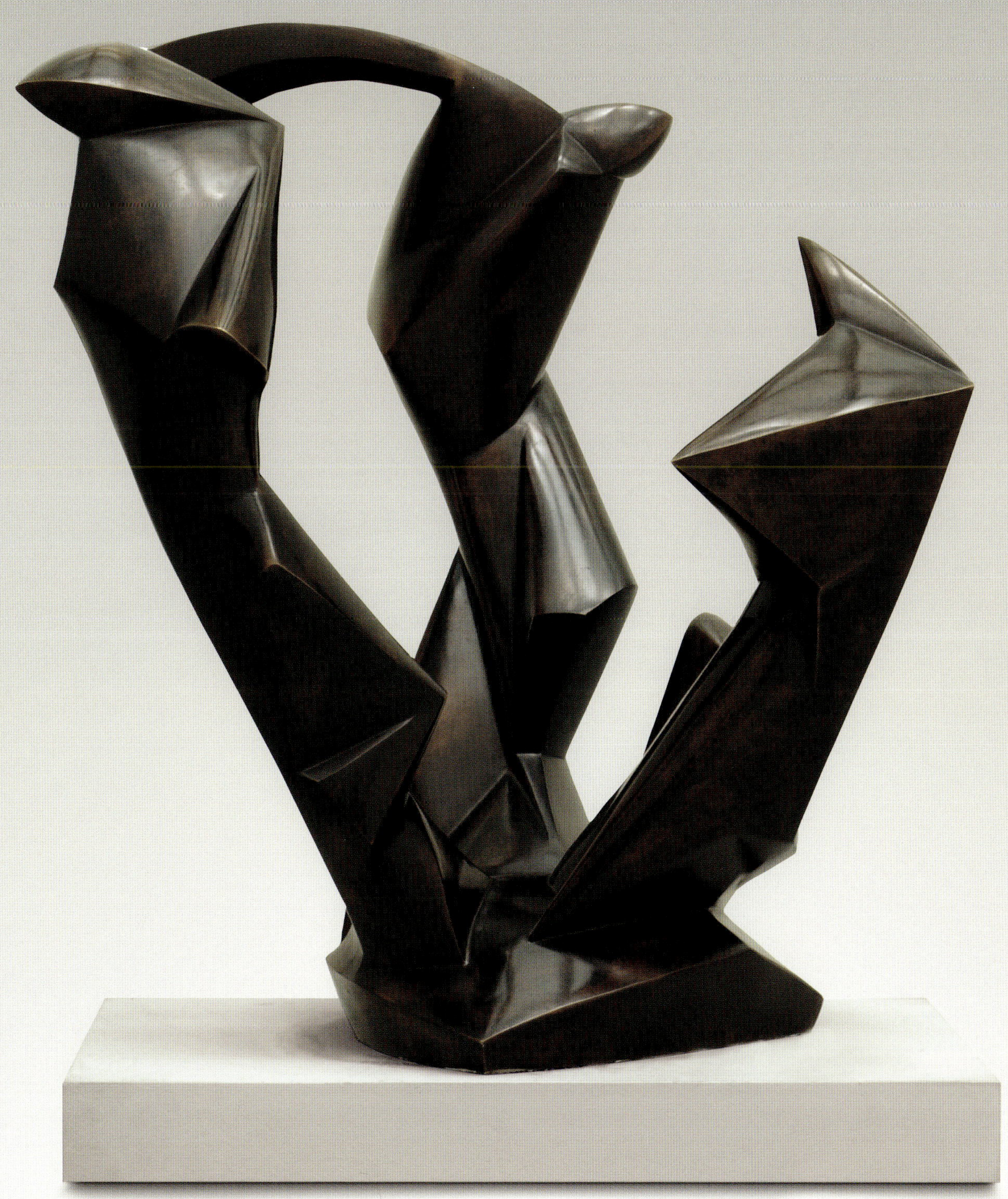

EMIL NOLDE

Conversation

The Expressionists, and the work of Emil Nolde in particular, were targeted by the Nazis in the *Degenerate art* exhibition, held in Munich in 1937, as representing the deterioration of the purportedly pure values of German art and culture. Thirty-six paintings and prints by Nolde, with their emphasis on the distortion of form and colour that departed from naturalistic modes of representation, were featured as evidence of the mental deficiency and moral decay that had supposedly infiltrated modern German art.[1]

Nolde's *Conversation* 1917 (opposite) was one of a number of woodcuts on display that had been confiscated from the *Kupferstichkabinett* (Museum of Prints and Drawings) in Berlin (below). This work, depicting a 'conversation' between a naked man and woman who are shown seated in a tightly constructed landscape while a dog howls nearby, would have been perceived as an affront to bourgeois morality. It is not difficult to see how the gawkish facial expressions of the figures could have been misconstrued as evidence of their racial and intellectual inferiority. *Conversation* is a striking example of the way in which Nolde, and the Brücke artists in general, 'primitivised' form through crude contours and accentuating the rough and raw quality of the woodcut medium, as well as emphasising the mask-like quality of the faces, inspired by Oceanic and African sculpture. Created during a cathartic moment when European civilisation was undergoing a massive transformation, this work testifies to the great contribution made by Expressionism to modernism in its complete rejection of western traditions of representation and the development of radically new and more direct forms of expression that were based on intuitive and emotional responses.

The strong presence of works by Nolde in the context of *Degenerate art* ultimately highlighted one of the enormous paradoxes of the Nazis' campaign against modern art. Despite Nolde's formal radicalism, he had always been politically conservative and held a lifelong belief in nationalism and racial purity.[2] The fact that by 1920 he had become a member of the National Socialist Party had no bearing on Hitler's condemnation of his work as 'degenerate'. The case of Nolde points to the highly political nature of *Degenerate art* as a propaganda exercise that singularly aimed to convince the population of the alleged 'degeneracy' of German culture brought about by 'Jewish-bolshevist' influences. Like many of his contemporaries, Nolde was forbidden to engage in any 'activity, professional or amateur, [in] the realm of art' because of what was considered to be his 'cultural irresponsibility'.[3] He did, however, continue to work on a series of watercolours after 1938, but these sensual and contemplative landscapes lacked the bold innovation that characterised his earlier work. JS

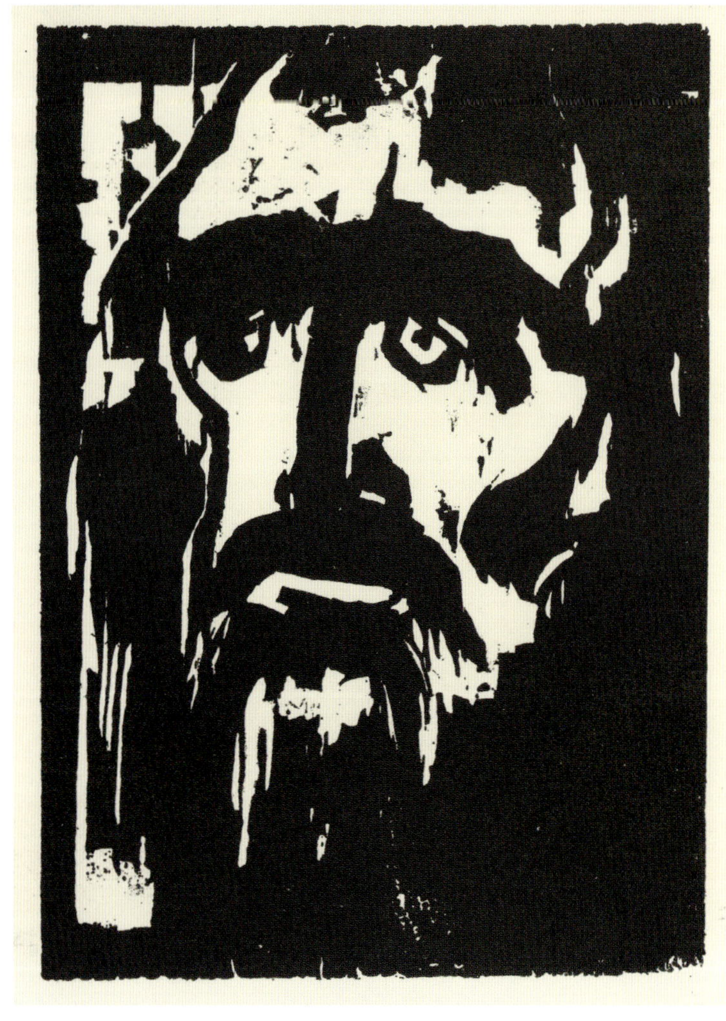

Emil Nolde
Head of a prophet 1912
from the portfolio **Genius I** 1919
woodcut
National Gallery of Australia, Canberra

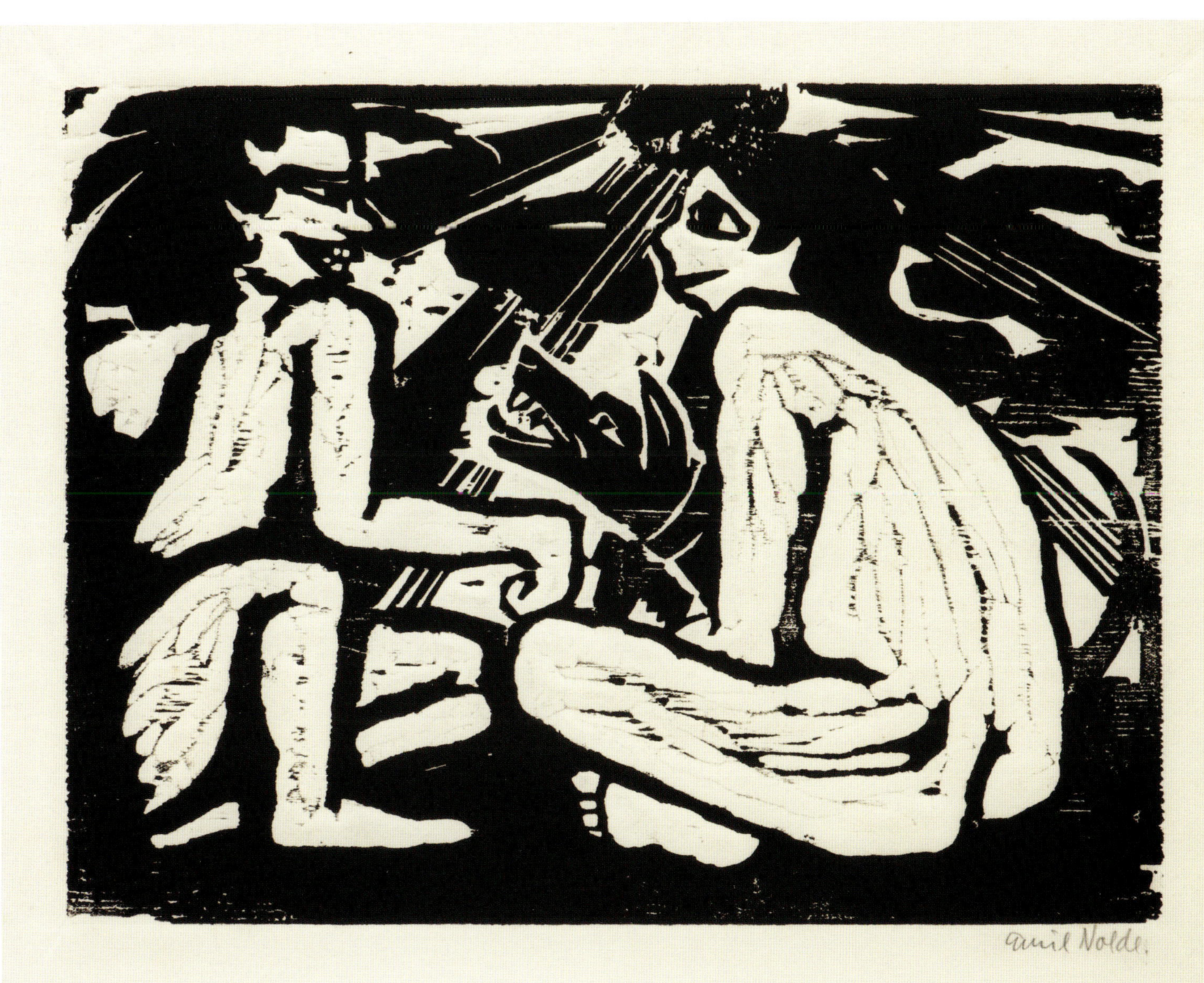

Emil Nolde
Conversation 1917
woodcut
Sprengel Museum, Hanover

ERNST LUDWIG KIRCHNER

Nude looking over her shoulder

At least 32 works by Ernst Ludwig Kirchner were displayed in the *Degenerate art* exhibition, including three wooden sculptures that were featured prominently. The earliest sculpture, *Bather* 1905–10, was included in the third room of the exhibition under the heading 'An insult to German womanhood'. *The couple* 1923–24 was displayed with George Grosz's *Adventure* 1920 and Christoph Voll's undated sculpture *Pregnant woman*. These works came under particular attack, as they were placed next to the following quote from Adolf Hitler's speech at the opening of the Haus der Deutschen Kunst (House of German Art) on 18 July 1937:

> It is not Bolshevist art collectors or their literary henchmen who have laid the foundations for the existence of a new art or safeguarded the very survival of art in Germany, but we, we to whom this state owes its life ... We shall now wage inexorable war to eliminate the last elements of our cultural decay.[1]

To further highlight what the Nazis perceived to be Kirchner's status as a 'degenerate' artist, his *Blacksmith of Hagen* 1915–16 was displayed in a central position in the ground-floor lobby with Otto Freundlich's *The new man* 1912, which was later reproduced on the cover of the *Entartete Kunst* exhibition guide.

Comparable to these confiscated and now lost wooden sculptures is Kirchner's *Nude looking over her shoulder* c1912. Typical of the sculptures he created during the prewar years in Berlin, Kirchner depicted the naked female form in a primitivised and simplified style that was clearly derived from the African and Oceanic art that he had seen in the ethnographic museums in Dresden and Berlin. The figure's sharply contorted body, mask-like face, smoothly contoured breasts, and enlarged buttocks, thighs and feet imbue this work with a totemic quality that conveys an image of a modern fertility goddess. Kirchner, Erich Heckel and other members of the Brücke had been experimenting with wood sculpture from as early as 1906. These sculptures were carved directly from a single tree trunk and, while the rough physical texture of the wood was intentionally accentuated, this sculpture has an unusually smooth and more finished surface that was typical of the sculptures Kirchner carved from the oak he collected from the beach during a summer visit to the island of Fehmarn in the Baltic Sea.[2] Kirchner often painted his sculptures with bright colours and it has been suggested that this work was originally conceived to be painted completely blue.[3] By bringing together sculpture and painting, Kirchner challenged the prevailing Classical ideal of sculpture that emphasised form rather than colour. This sculpture was also unique in drawing attention to the representation of the subject from several angles so that it could be seen from multiple perspectives rather than a single viewpoint, as had been the established tradition of western art since the Renaissance.

Kirchner's sculptures are not generally as well known as his paintings and prints; however, they provide a fascinating insight into a previously neglected aspect of his work during the high point of Expressionism. During the mid 1920s, when his work was being acquired by major museums in Germany and his reputation as the leading Expressionist was being established, Kirchner's Swiss students created figurative wooden sculptures that directly emulated his woodcarvings. These sculptures also profoundly influenced the work of neo-Expressionist artists, such as Georg Baselitz, in the 1980s. JS

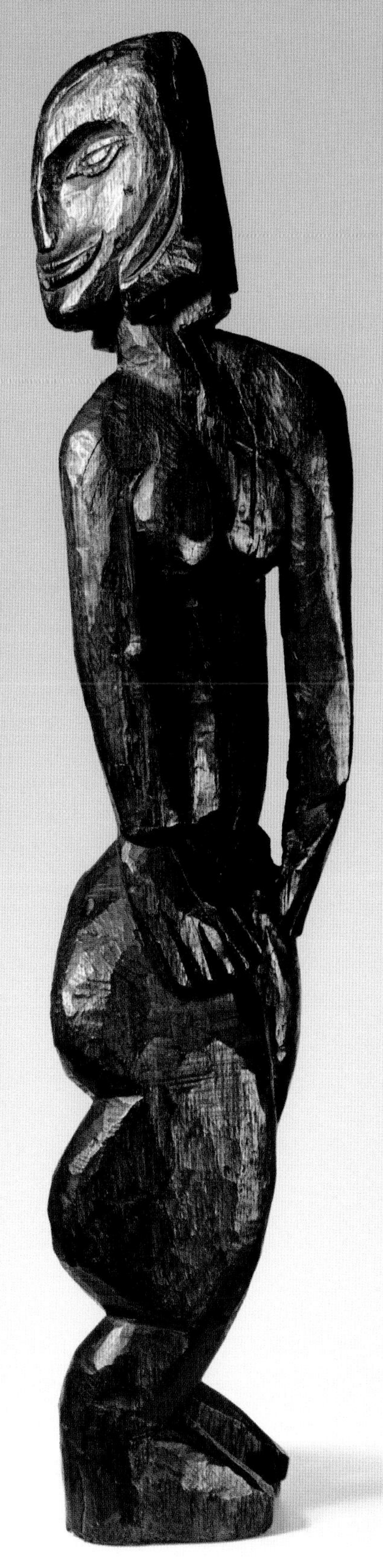

Ernst Ludwig Kirchner
Nude looking over her shoulder c1912
black-dyed oakwood
Stiftung Museum Kunst Palast, Düsseldorf

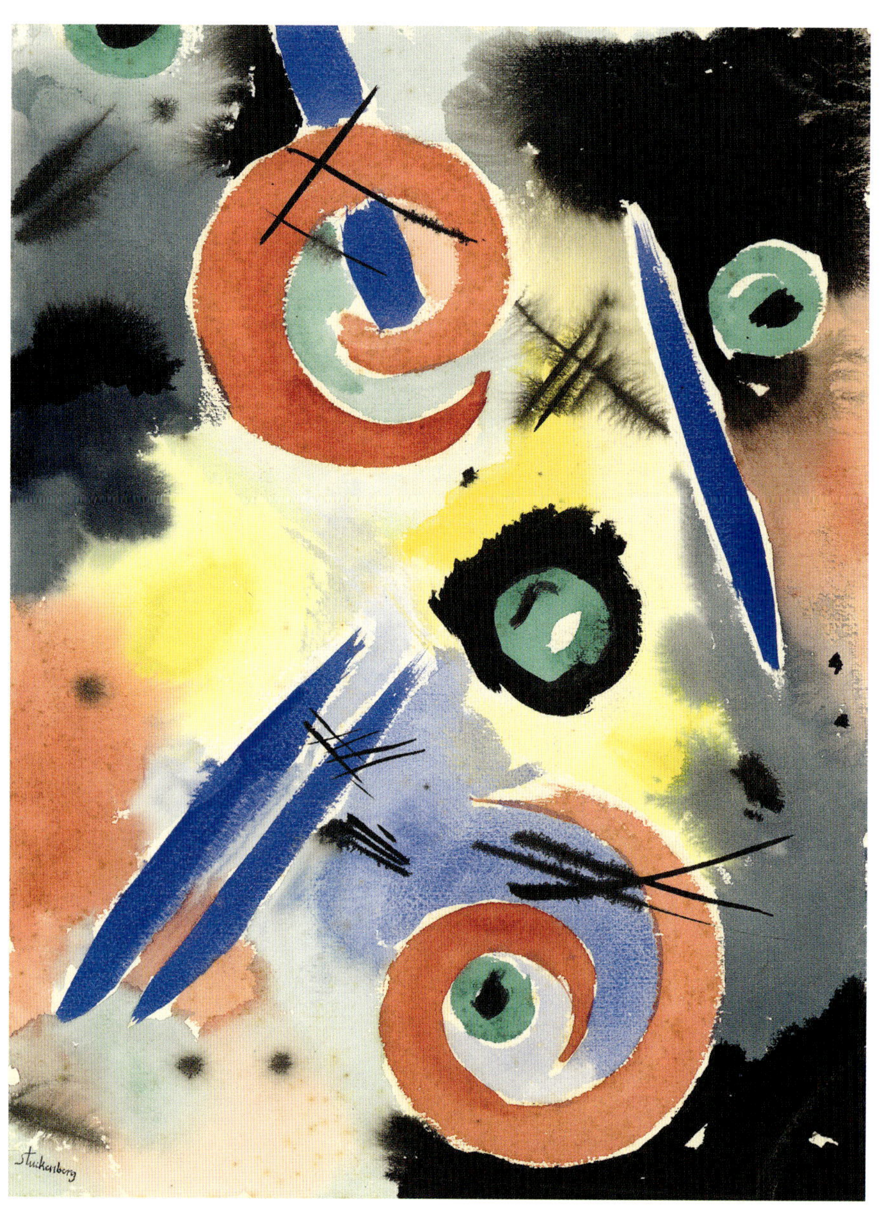

Friedrich Stuckenberg
Swimming and painting c1920–21
watercolour
Private collection, Melbourne

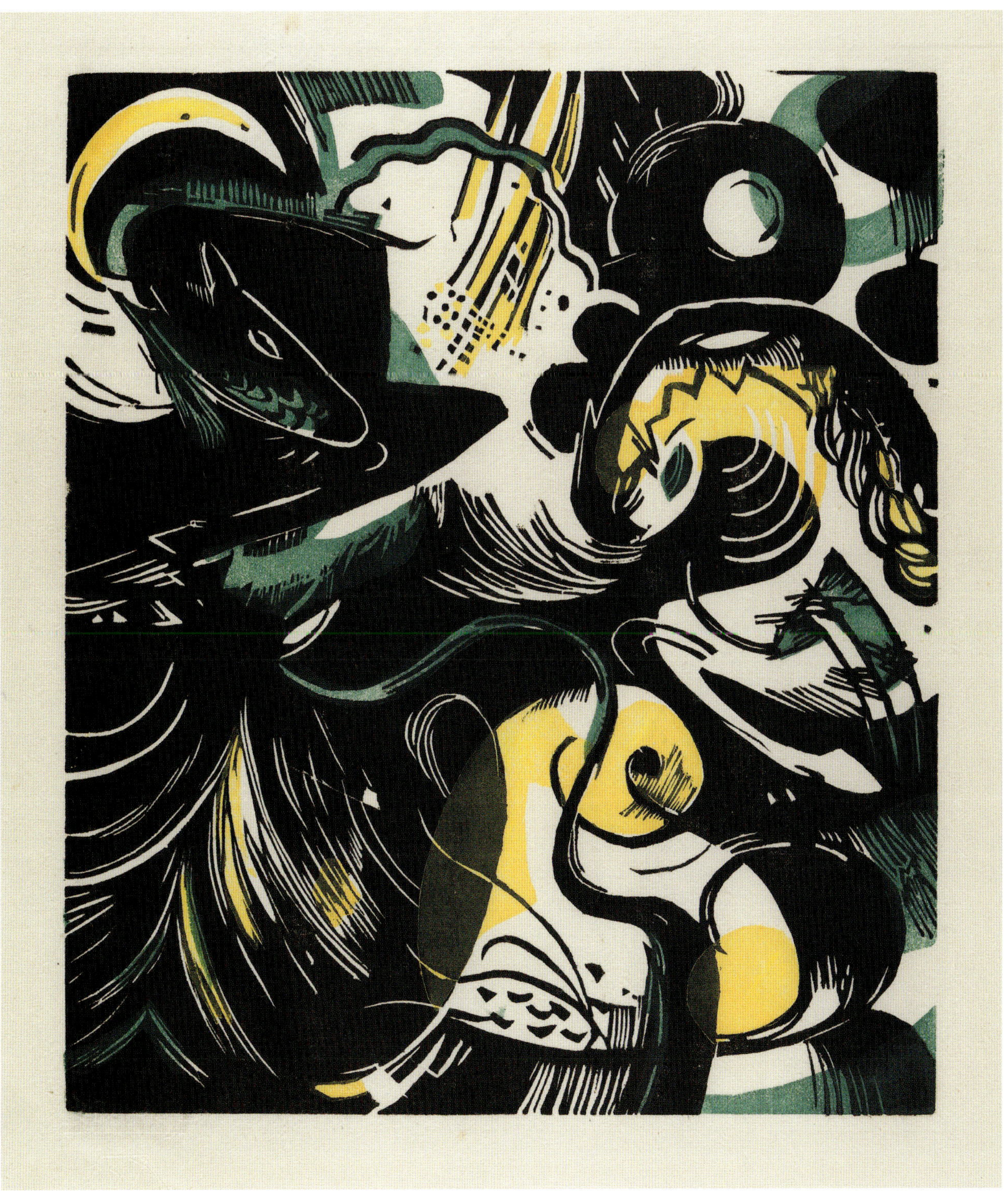

Franz Marc
Story of creation II 1914
colour woodcut
Queensland Art Gallery, Brisbane

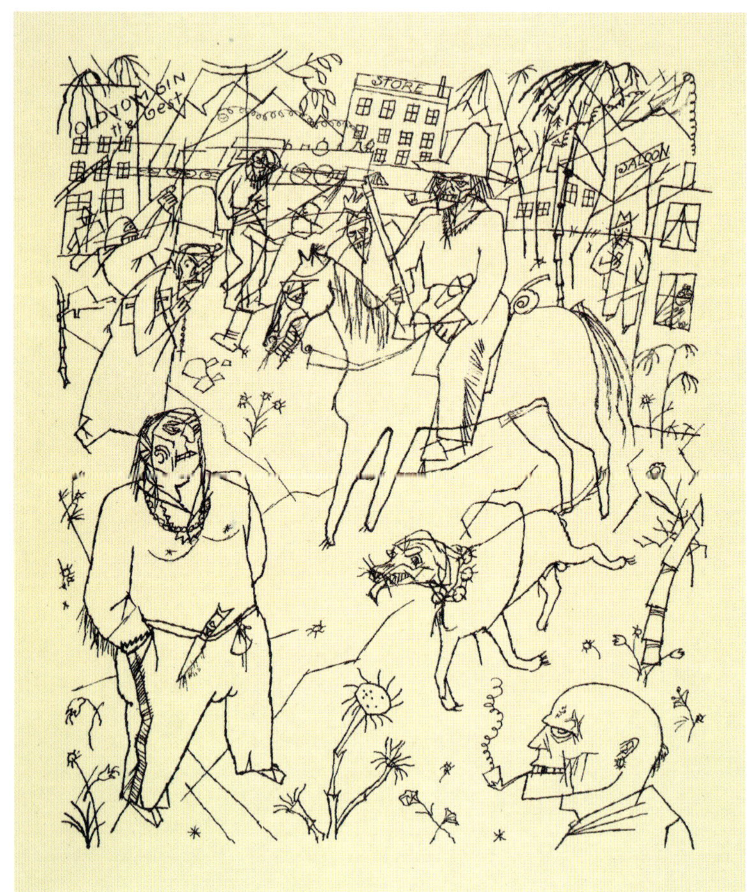

George Grosz
Texas picture for my friend Chingachgook 1915–16
from the First George Grosz portfolio 1917
lithograph
Private collection, Melbourne

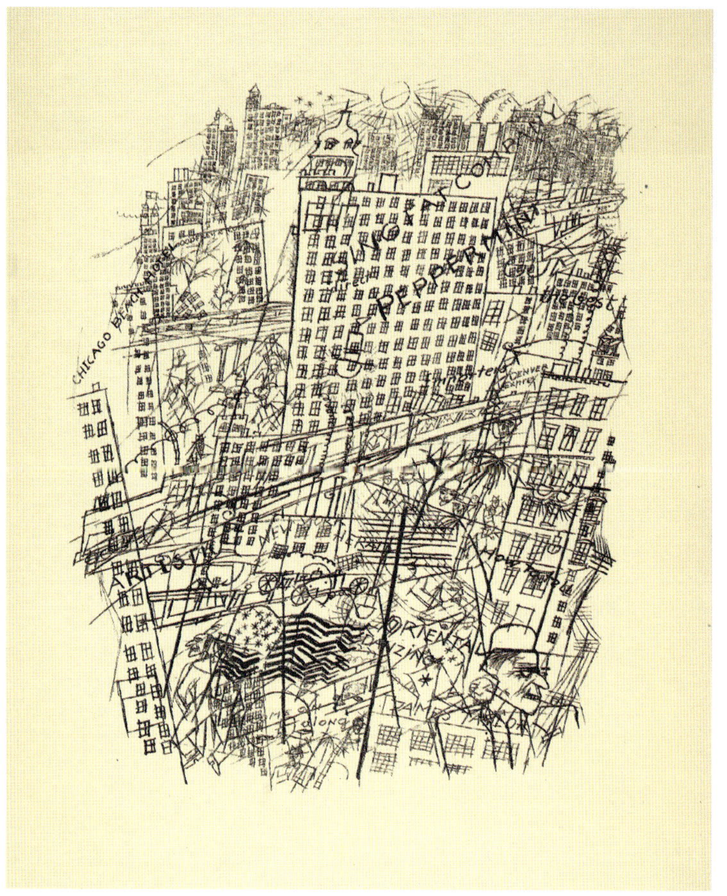

George Grosz
Memory of New York 1915–16
from the First George Grosz portfolio 1917
lithograph
Private collection, Melbourne

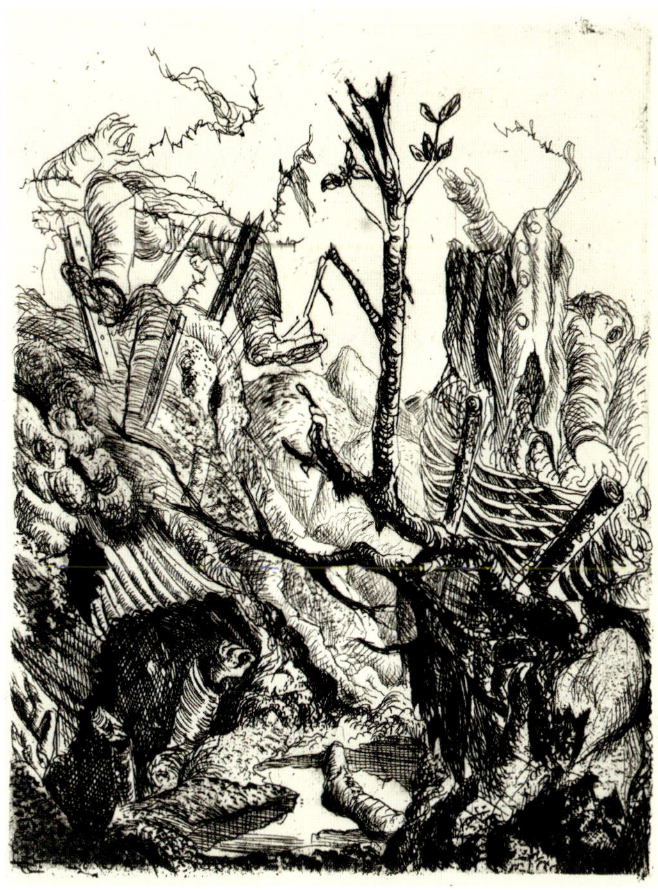

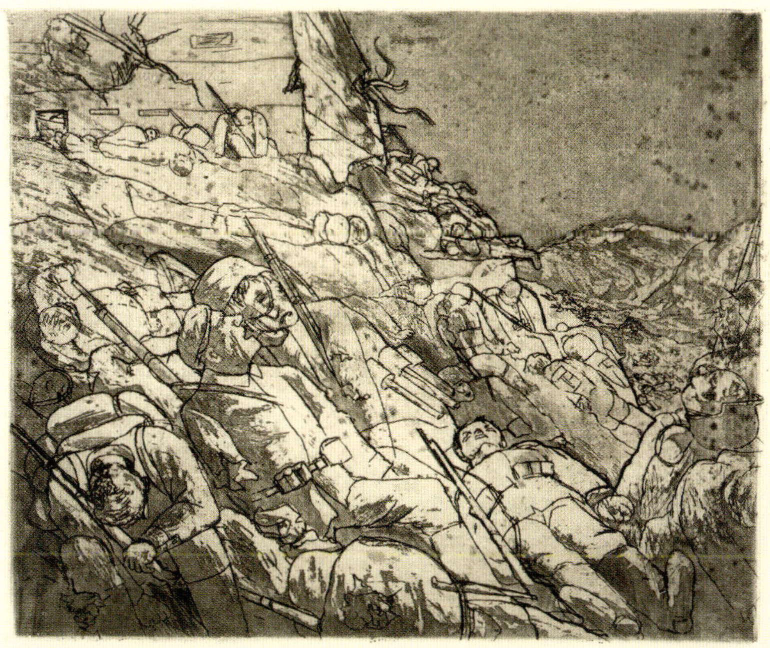

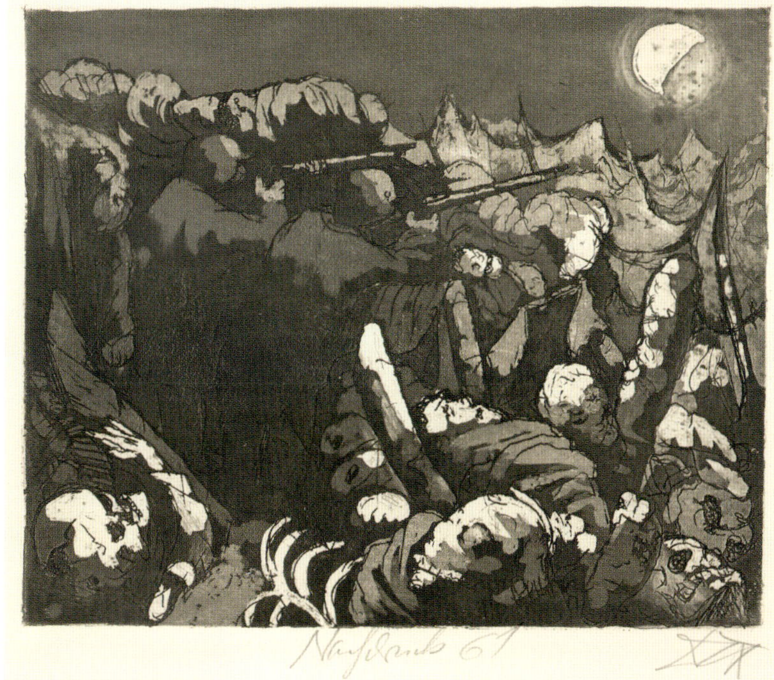

above:

Otto Dix
Abandoned position near Neuville
from the portfolio War 1924
etching, drypoint, aquatint
Australian War Memorial, Canberra

above right:

Otto Dix
The sleepers of Fort Vaux – gas deaths
from the portfolio War 1924
etching, aquatint, drypoint
Australian War Memorial, Canberra

Otto Dix
At night the men in the trenches have to keep firing
from the portfolio War 1924
etching, aquatint, drypoint
Australian War Memorial, Canberra

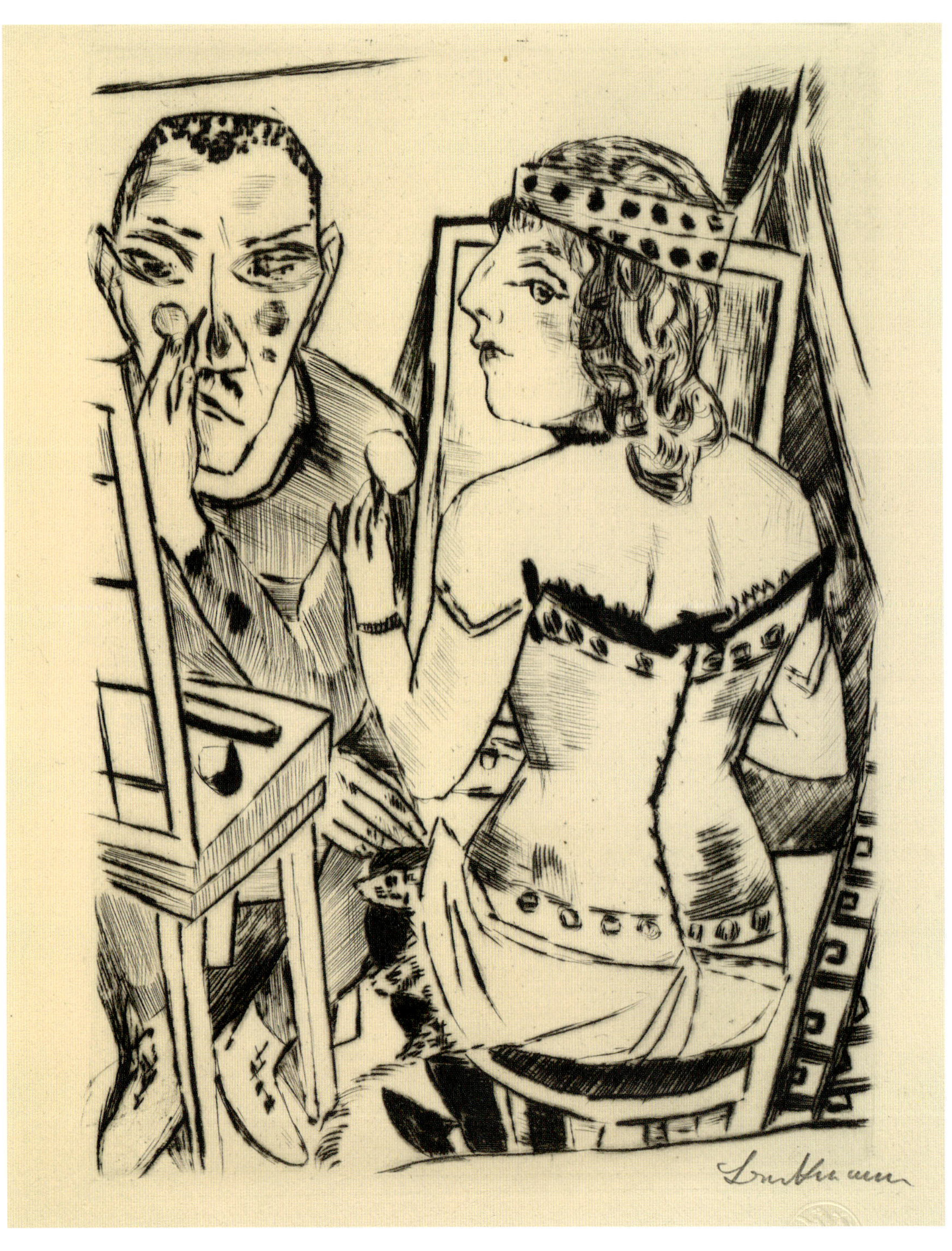

Max Beckmann
Dressing room 1921
from the portfolio Carnival 1922
drypoint
Private collection, Melbourne

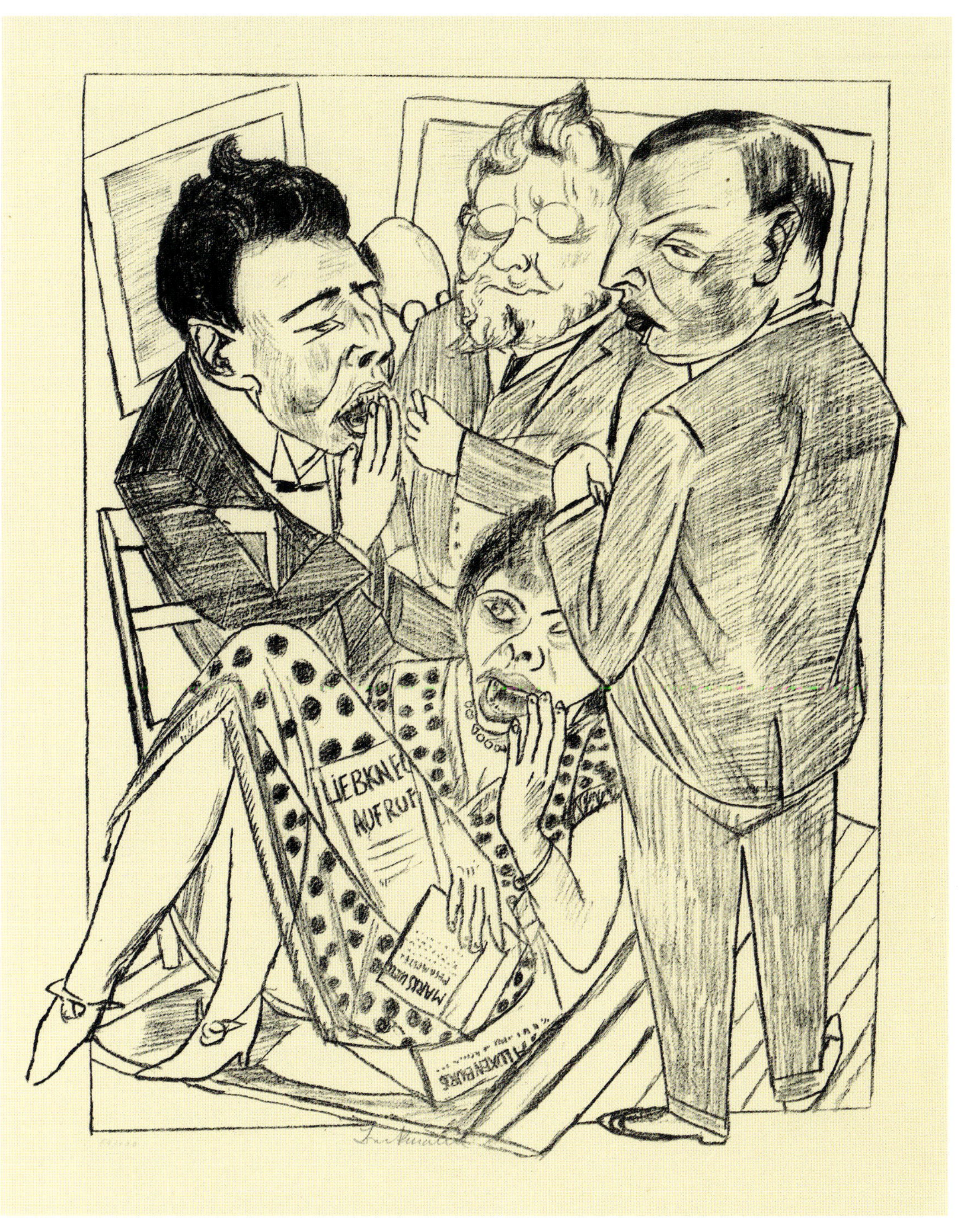

Max Beckmann
The disillusioned II 1922
lithograph
National Gallery of Australia, Canberra

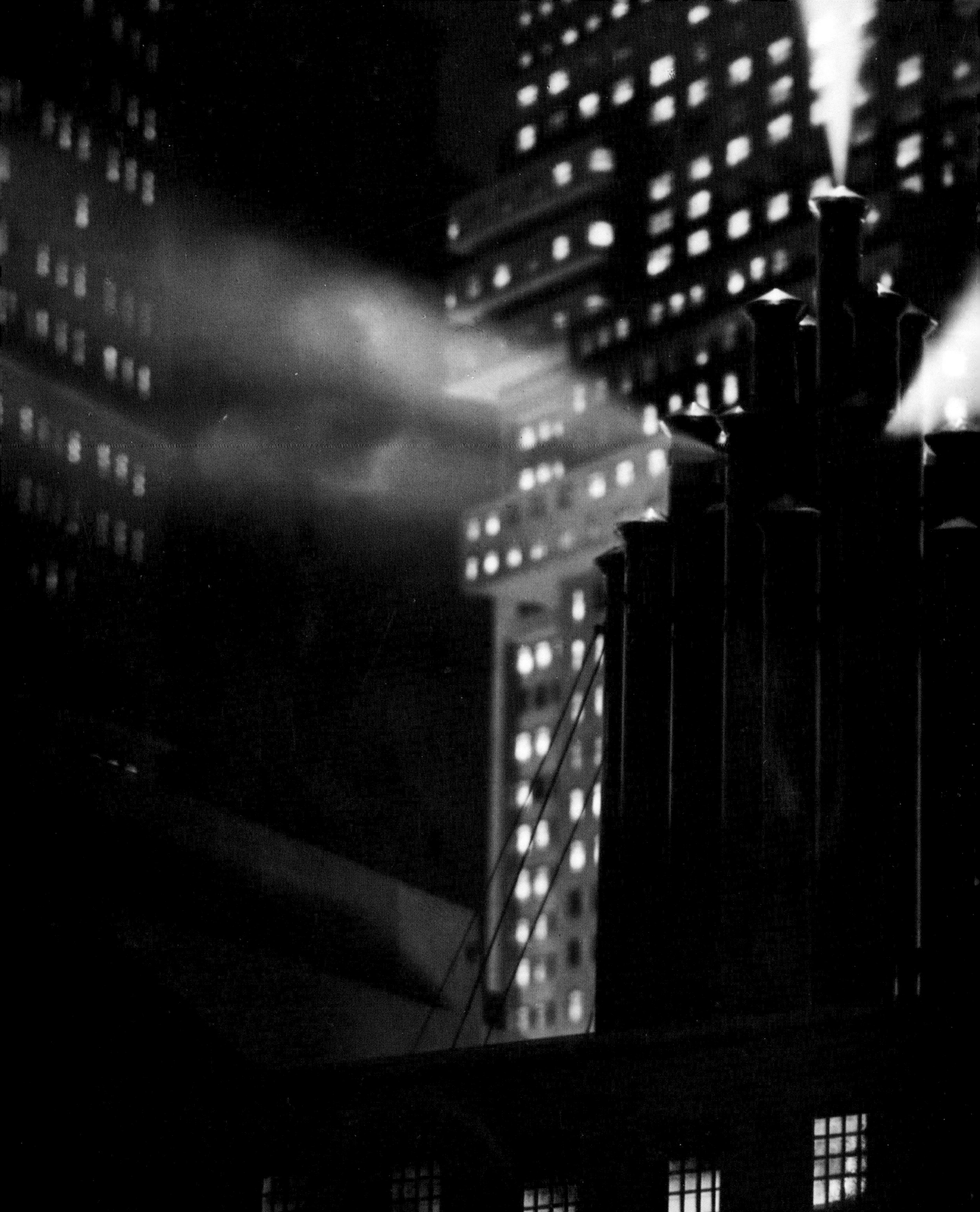

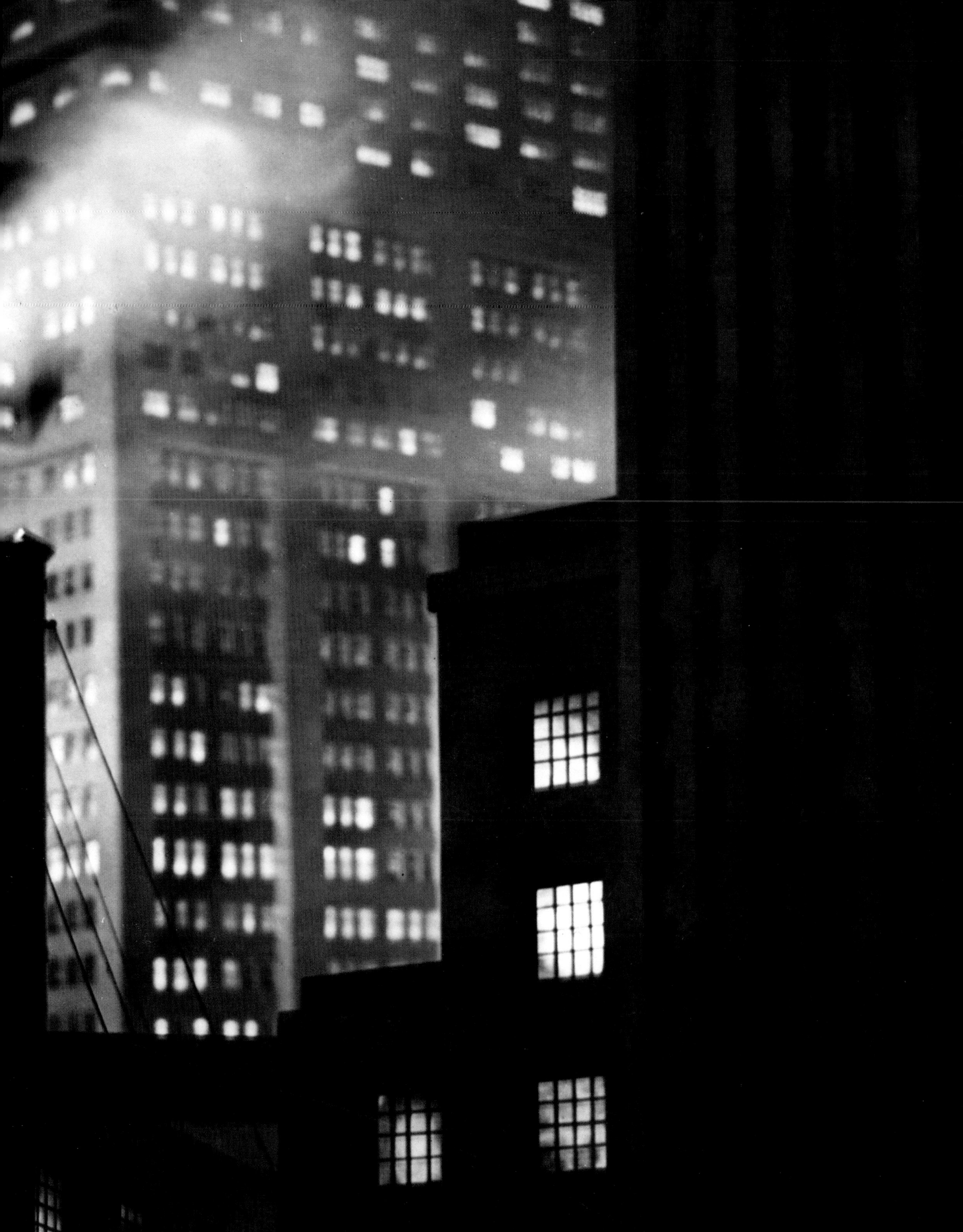

INTRODUCTION

The mad square: modernity in German art 1910–37

1 See Eric D Weitz, *Weimar Germany: promise and tragedy*, Princeton University Press, Princeton 2007; Rainer Metzger, *Berlin in the 20s: art and culture 1918–1933*, Thames and Hudson, London 2007; and John Willett, *The Weimar years: a culture cut short*, Thames and Hudson, London 1984. For general histories of modern Germany, see Volker R Berghahn, *Modern Germany: society, economy and politics in the twentieth century*, Cambridge University Press, Cambridge 1987; and Gordon A Craig, *Germany 1866–1945*, Oxford University Press, Oxford 1981

2 Terry Smith has summarised modernism as a 'term applied to the invention and the effective pursuit of artistic strategies that seek not just close but essential connections to the powerful forces of social modernity'. He has defined modernity as a 'term applied to the cultural condition in which the seemingly absolute necessity of innovation becomes a primary fact of life, work, and thought'. Terry Smith, in Jane Turner (ed), *Dictionary of art*, Macmillan, London 1996, vol 21, pp 775–9. See also Christopher Wilk, 'Introduction: What was Modernism?', in Christopher Wilk (ed), *Modernism: designing a new world* 1914–1939, exh cat, Victoria and Albert Museum, London, 6 Apr – 23 July 2006, pp 12–21

3 Wassily Kandinsky & Franz Marc (eds), *The 'Blaue Reiter' Almanac*, Klaus Lankheit (ed), Thames and Hudson, London 1974 (1965), p 154

4 'Chronology' in Stephanie Barron, *'Degenerate art': the fate of the avant-garde in Nazi Germany*, exh cat, Los Angeles County Museum of Art, Los Angeles, 17 Feb – 12 May 1991, p 392

5 Weitz 2007, p 41

6 See, for example, the following exhibition catalogues: Barry Bergdoll & Leah Dickerman, *Bauhaus 1919–1933: workshops for modernity*, Museum of Modern Art, New York, 8 Nov 2009 – 25 Jan 2010; Deborah Wye, *Kirchner and the Berlin street*, Museum of Modern Art, New York, 3 Aug – 10 Nov 2008; Sabine Rewald, *Glitter and doom: German portraits from the 1920s*, Metropolitan Museum of Art, New York, 14 Nov 2006 – 19 Feb 2007; Leah Dickerman (ed), *Dada: Zurich, Berlin, Hannover, Cologne, New York, Paris*, exh cat, National Gallery of Art, Washington, 19 Feb – 14 May 2006 and Museum of Modern Art, New York, 18 June – 11 Sept 2006; Jill Lloyd & Michael Peppiatt (eds), *Christian Schad and the Neue Sachlichkeit*, Neue Galerie, New York, 14 Mar – 9 June 2003; and Sean Rainbird, *Max Beckmann*, Tate Modern, London, 12 Feb – 5 May 2003

EXPRESSIONISM

German expressionism: apocalypse, war and revolution

1 Hans Wilderotter gives an account of how avant-garde idealism overlapped with official propaganda in his essay 'L'Invention de la première guerre mondiale: expectatives et expériences, visions et constructions,' in *Allemagne, les années noires*, exh cat, Musée Maillol, Paris, Oct 2007 – Feb 2008, pp 36–8

2 Max Beckmann, 'Wartime Letters: Roeselare, Wervicq, Brussels', translated in Barbara Copeland Buenger (ed), *Max Beckmann: self-portrait in words, collected writings and statements* 1903–1950, University of Chicago Press, Chicago 1997, p 169

3 See Wilderotter 2007–08, p 41

4 I am grateful to Starr Figura from the department of prints and illustrated books at MoMA, New York, for sharing this information with me.

5 Cited by Reinhold Heller, 'Otto Dix', Grove Art Online, Oxford University Press 2009, www.oxfordartonline.com (accessed Dec 2010)

6 'Novembergruppe: Rundschreiben vom 13. Dezember 1918', in Helga Kliemann (ed), *Die Novembergruppe*, Gebr. Mann, Berlin 1969, p 55

7 Max Pechstein, 'What We Want', translated in Victor H Miesel (ed), *Voices of German Expressionism*, Prentice-Hall, New Jersey 1970, pp 179–80

Ernst Ludwig Kirchner
Woman in a hat

1 Deborah Wye, *Kirchner and the Berlin street*, exh cat, Museum of Modern Art, New York, 3 Aug – 10 Nov 2008, p 19

2 Janda Gooding, 'Ernst Ludwig Kirchner *Woman in a Hat* and *The Pledge – Hutten Greets Sickingen*', in Gary Dufour (ed), *State art collection: Art Gallery of Western Australia*, Art Gallery of Western Australia, Perth 1997, p 38

Ludwig Meidner
Apocalyptic landscape

1 Ludwig Meidner, 'Vision des apokalyptischen Sommers', quoted in Carol S Eliel & Eberhard Roters, *The apocalyptic landscapes of Ludwig Meidner*, exh cat, Los Angeles County Museum of Art, Los Angeles, 12 Oct – 17 Dec 1989, p 65

2 Dagmar Grimm, 'Ludwig Meidner', in Stephanie Barron, *'Degenerate art': the fate of the avant-garde in Nazi Germany*, exh cat, Los Angeles County Museum of Art, Los Angeles, 17 Feb – 12 May 1991, p 298

Ernst Barlach
The avenger

1 Marc Scheps (ed), *20th century art: Ludwig Museum*, Benedikt Taschen, Cologne 1996, pp 61, 62

2 Dagmar Grimm, 'Ernst Barlach', in Barron 1991, p 196

3 Dagmar Grimm, 'Ernst Barlach', in Barron 1991, p 197

Heinrich Maria Davringhausen
The sex murderer

1 For further reading on this subject, see Maria Tatar, *Lustmord: sexual murder in Weimar Germany*, Princeton University Press, Princeton 1995; and Beth Irwin Lewis, 'Lustmord: Inside the Windows of the Metropolis', in Katharina von Ankum (ed), *Women in the metropolis: gender and modernity in Weimar culture*, University of California Press, Berkeley, Los Angeles and London 1997, pp 202–32

2 See, for example, Sergiusz Michalski, *New Objectivity: painting, graphic art and photography in Weimar Germany 1919–1933*, Benedikt Taschen, Cologne 1994, pp 82–3

3 Joachim Kaak, 'Heinrich Maria Davringhausen: Der Lustmörder', in Carla Schulz-Hoffmann (ed), *Pinakothek der Moderne: Malerei, Skulptur, Fotographie, Neue Medien*, Pinakothek-Dumont, Munich 2006, p 92

George Grosz
Suicide

1 Robin Reisenfeld, *The German print portfolio 1890–1930: serials for a private sphere*, exh cat, David and Alfred Smart Museum of Art, Chicago, 5 Oct – 12 Dec 1993, p 105

Otto Dix
The Felixmüller family

1 Carol O Selle & Peter Nisbet, *German realist drawings of the 1920s*, exh cat, Busch-Reisinger Museum, Cambridge, 26 July – 28 Sept 1986, p 218

2 Joan Weinstein, *The end of expressionism: art and the November Revolution in Germany 1918–19*, University of Chicago Press, Chicago and London 1990, pp 129–31

3 Charles Werner Haxthausen, 'Modern German Masterpieces: Otto Dix', *Winter Bulletin*, Saint Louis Art Museum, 1985, pp 38–9

Max Beckmann
The dream

1 Peter Selz, *Max Beckmann*, Museum of Modern Art, New York 1964, p 35, quoted in Charles Werner Haxthausen, 'Modern German Masterpieces: Max Beckmann The Dream', *Winter Bulletin*, Saint Louis Art Museum, Saint Louis 1985, p 11

Käthe Kollwitz
Memorial for Karl Liebknecht

1 Quoted in René Block & Erna Haist, *Prints and drawings of the Weimar Republic*, Institute for Foreign Cultural Relations, Stuttgart 1985, p 65

2 See 'Käthe Kollwitz *Memorial Sheet for Karl Liebknecht*, 1919–1920', Los Angeles County Museum of Art, http://collectionsonline.lacma.org/mwebcgi/mweb.exe?request=record;id=81151;type=101 (accessed Jan 2011)

Expressionist posters

1 Jean McAuslan & Simon Forrester, *Poster art 1914–20: in Britain, France and Germany*, exh cat, Australian War Memorial, Canberra, 11 Nov 1992 – 11 Nov 1993, np

previous pages:

Fritz Lang
Metropolis 1927 (film still, detail)

DADA

Dada in Germany: 'the disfiguration of the contemporary world'

1 Hugo Ball, *Flight out of time: a Dada diary*, edited and with an introduction by John Elderfield (Ann Raimes trans), University of California Press, Berkeley, Los Angeles and London 1996, p 67

2 Ball 1996, p 65

3 Ball 1996, p 63

4 Ball 1996, p 77

5 Wieland Herzfelde, 'Introduction to the First International Dada Fair', translated and introduced by Brigid Doherty, *October*, 105, summer 2003, p 102

6 See Barbara McCloskey, *George Grosz and the Communist Party: art and radicalism in crisis*, Princeton University Press, Princeton 1997, p 55

7 On the Dada Fair, see Helen Adkins, 'Erste Internationale Dada-Messe', in *Stationen der Moderne*, exh cat, Berlinische Galerie, Berlin 1988, pp 157–83; and Hanne Bergius, *Montage und Metamechanik: Dada Berlin, Artistik von Polaritäten*, Mann, Berlinvv 2000, pp 233–304, 349–414

8 Ticket number 310 was sold on 16 July, and number 389 on 4 August. See Bergius 2000, p 289

9 Herzfelde 2003, pp 101–2

10 Herzfelde 2003, p 102

11 On the significance of Grosz's notion of 'materialisation' in relation to other uses of the term in German culture of the period, see Brigid Doherty, '"See: *We Are All Neurasthenics*!" or, the Trauma of Dada Montage', *Critical Inquiry*, 24, autumn 1997, pp 84–5

12 Herzfelde 2003, p 102

13 See Raoul Hausmann, Rudolf Schlichter, George Grosz & John Heartfield, 'Die Gesetze der Malerei', a manifesto published posthumously in Thater-Schulz (ed), *Hannah Höch: Eine Lebenscollage*, vol 1, part 2 (1919–1920), Argon, Berlin 1989, pp 696–8

14 Walter Benjamin, 'The Work of Art in the Age of its Technological Reproducibility (Second Version)', in Michael W Jennings, Brigid Doherty & Thomas Y Levin (eds), *The work of art in the age of its technological reproducibility and other writings on media*, Harvard University Press, Cambridge 2008, p 38

Christian Schad
Portrait of a woman

1 Olaf Peters, '"A Voluntary International Madman": Christian Schad and the Avant-Garde 1915–20', in Jill Lloyd & Michael Peppiatt (eds), *Christian Schad and the Neue Sachlichkeit*, exh cat, Neue Galerie, New York, 14 Mar – 9 June 2003, pp 33–4

2 Bettina Schad, quoted in Leah Dickerman, (ed), *Dada: Zurich, Berlin, Hannover, Cologne, New York, Paris*, exh cat, Museum of Modern Art and National Gallery of Art, Washington, 19 Feb – 14 May 2006, p 41

3 Leah Dickerman, 'Zurich', in Dickerman 2006, p 41

Hannah Höch
Collage

1 Maria Makela, 'The Misogynist Machine: Images of Technology in the Work of Hannah Höch', in Katharina von Ankum (ed), *Women in the metropolis: gender and modernity in Weimar culture*, University of California Press, Berkeley, Los Angeles and London 1997, p 121

2 Amanda L Hockensmith & Sabine T Kriebel, 'Hannah Höch', in Dickerman 2006, p 475

3 Maud Lavin, 'Strategies of Pleasure and Deconstruction: Hannah Höch's Photomontages in the Weimar Years', in Irit Rogoff (ed), *The divided heritage: themes and problems in German modernism*, Cambridge University Press, Cambridge 1990, pp 93–115

Kurt Schwitters
Merz

1 Dorothea Dietrich, 'Hannover', in Leah Dickerman (ed) 2006, p 157

BAUHAUS

Bauhaus objects, Bauhaus visions

1 See Stephen J Lee, *The Weimar Republic*, Routledge, London and New York 2010; Stuart Taberner & Frank Finlay (eds), *Recasting German identity: culture, politics and literature in the Berlin Republic*, Camden House, Rochester 2002; Kathleen Canning, Kerstin Barndt & Kristin McGuire (eds), *Weimar publics/Weimar subjects*, Berghahn Books, New York 2010; Janet Ward, *Weimar surfaces: urban visual culture in 1920s Germany*, University of California Press, Berkeley 2001; Eric D Weitz, *Weimar Germany: promise and tragedy*, Princeton University Press, Princeton 2007

2 Alan E Steinwis, 'Conservatism, National Socialism and the Cultural Crisis of the Weimar Republic', in Larry Eugene Jones & James Retallack (eds), *Between reform, reaction and resistance: studies in the history of German conservatism from 1789 to 1945*, Berg, Providence 1993, p 329

3 Bauhaus-Archiv Berlin/Museum für Gestaltung, Stiftung Bauhaus Dessau and Klassik Stiftung Weimar, in cooperation with the Museum of Modern Art, New York (eds), *Bauhaus: a conceptual model*, Hatje Cantz, Ostfildern 2009; Barry Bergdoll & Leah Dickerman, *Bauhaus 1919–1933: workshops for modernity*, exh cat, Museum of Modern Art, New York, 8 Nov 2009 – 25 Jan 2010

4 See Bauhaus Clothing, www.bauhausclothing.com (accessed Dec 2010)

5 Quoted in Reginald Isaacs, *Walter Gropius: Der Mensch und sein Werk*, Gebr. Mann Verlag, Berlin 1983, p 188

6 One of the earliest uses of this kind of camouflage, these Stahlhelm helmets were often painted in brown and green patterns by the soldiers themselves in the trenches.

7 In 1922 Hirschfeld Mack built what he called a *Farbenlichtspiele* (coloured light instrument). This complicated apparatus, also called a 'light organ', projected coloured forms on a transparent screen that would overlap in different tonal gradations. Coloured light was projected through liquids, reflected from mirrors and shot through moving lenses in performances in which the organ was sometimes played by as many as four people. Hirschfeld Mack performed with his instrument in Weimar, Vienna and Leipzig, and was included in the early Absolute Film show in Berlin in 1925, alongside some of the most experimental examples of early cinema. Gregory Zinman, 'Painting with Light: the Bauhaus Influence on the Cinematic Avant-Garde', Museum of the Moving Image, www.movingimagesource.us/articles/painting-with-light-20091119 (accessed Sept 2010). The artist described his process and intentions in Ludwig Hirschfeld Mack, *Farben Licht-Spiele: Wesen, Ziele, Kriterien*, Adler and Heyer, Weimar 1925

8 For a theoretical introduction to the complexities of 'object culture', see Bill Brown, 'The Refabrication of Things', *Critical Inquiry*, vol 36, no 2, winter 2010, pp 188–92

9 Cornelia von Buol, 'The Ceramics Workshop', in Jeannine Fiedler & Peter Feierabend (eds), *Bauhaus*, Könemann, Cologne 1999, pp 439–49; see also Magdalene Droste, *Bauhaus: 1919–1933*, Bauhaus-Archiv Museum für Gestaltung, Berlin 1990, pp 68–72

10 See T'ai Smith, 'Unknown Weaver, Possibly Else Mögelin "Wall Hanging" 1923', in Bergdoll & Dickerman 2009–10, pp 116–19; Droste 1993, pp 73–4; Monika Stadler & Yael Aloni, *Gunta Stölzl: Bauhaus master*, Museum of Modern Art, New York 2009; and Ulrike Müller, *Bauhaus women: art, handicraft, design*, Flammarion, Paris 2009

11 Sigrid Wortman Weltge, *Women's work: textile art from the Bauhaus*, Chronicle Books, San Francisco 1993

12 See Paul Paret, 'Oskar Schlemmer "Study for the Triadic Ballet" 1924', in Bergdoll & Dickerman 2009–10, pp 168–71; Arnd Wesemann, 'The Bauhaus Theater Group', in Fiedler & Feierabend 2000, pp 532–51

13 See Frederic J Schwartz, *Blind spots: critical theory and the history of art in twentieth century Germany*, Yale University Press, New Haven 2005; Ernst Bloch, *Heritage of our times*, University of California Press, Berkeley 1991

14 Katherine Ware, 'Photography at the Bauhaus', in Fiedler & Feierabend 2000, pp 506–29; Jeannine Fiedler, *Photography at the Bauhaus*, MIT, Cambridge 1990

15 Michael W Jennings, 'Lázló Moholy-Nagy: Photograms', in Bergdoll & Dickerman 2009–10, pp 216–19. See also Louis Kaplan, *Lázló Moholy-Nagy: biographical writings*, Duke University Press, Durham and London 1995; and Michel Frizot, 'The Metamorphoses of the Image: Photo-Graphics and the Alienation of Meaning', in Michel Frizot (ed), *A new history of photography*, Könemann, Cologne 1998, pp 431–55

16 Frances Guerin, *A culture of light: cinema and technology in 1920s Germany*, University of Minnesota Press, Minneapolis 2005

17 See Karen Koehler, 'Kandinsky's Kleine Welten and Utopian City Plans', *Journal of Society of Architectural Historians*, vol 57, no 4, Dec 1998, pp 432–47

László Moholy-Nagy
Photograms

1 László Moholy-Nagy, 'Constructivism and the Proletariat', *MA*, May 1922, reprinted in Sibyl Moholy-Nagy, *Moholy-Nagy: experiment in totality*, Harper, New York 1950, p 19

2 Michael W Jennings, 'László Moholy-Nagy: Photograms', in Bergdoll & Dickerman 2009–10, pp 216–19

3 Adrian Sudhalter, 'Walter Gropius and László Moholy-Nagy: Bauhaus Book Series 1925–30', in Bergdoll & Dickerman 2009–10, pp 196–9; Achim Borchardt-Hume, 'Two Bauhaus Histories', in *Albers and Moholy-Nagy: from the Bauhaus to the new world*, exh cat, Tate Modern, London, 9 Mar – 4 June 2006, p 73

Ludwig Hirschfeld Mack
Reaching the stars

1 Hirschfeld Mack 1925, quoted in Joanna Boose, *Ludwig Hirschfeld Mack: Bauhaus artist and innovator*, text panel, Ian Potter Museum of Art, University of Melbourne, Melbourne, 15 May – 31 Aug 2008

2 Nicholas Draffin, *Two masters of the Weimar Bauhaus: Lyonel Feininger and Ludwig Hirschfeld Mack*, exh cat, Art Gallery of New South Wales, Sydney, 4 July – 6 Oct 1974, p 42; Jeanne Klovdahl, 'Ludwig Hirschfeld Mack: Australia's Bauhaus Master', *Imprint*, vol 23, no 4, Dec 1988, p 2

3 Magdalene Keaney, 'Images of Displacement: Art from the Internment Camps', in Roger Butler (ed), *The Europeans: émigré artists in Australia* 1930–1960, National Gallery of Australia, Canberra 1997, p 89

Paul Klee
Thistle picture

1 Paul Klee, *Pedagogical sketchbook*, 1925, quoted in Alex Potts, 'Paul Klee: Fire in the Evening', in Bergdoll & Dickerman 2009–10, p 302

2 Hal Foster, 'Exercises for Color Theory Courses', in Bergdoll & Dickerman 2009–10, pp 266–9

3 Cathy Leahy, *Prints and drawings in the international collections of the NGV*, National Gallery of Victoria, Melbourne 2003, p 110

Oskar Schlemmer
Triadic ballet

1 Oskar Schlemmer, 'Diary Entry', 5 July 1926, in Tut Schlemmer, *The letters and diaries of Oskar Schlemmer*, Wesleyan University Press, Middletown 1972, p 196

2 Jana Scholze, 'Triadic Ballet', in Christopher Wilk (ed), *Modernism: designing a new world 1914–1939*, exh cat, Victoria and Albert Museum, London, 6 Apr – 23 July 2006, p 134

3 Tag Gronberg, 'Performing Modernism', in Wilk 2006, p 126

Weissenhof Housing Estate exhibition, Stuttgart 1927

1 Walter Gropius, 'Program of the Staatliches Bauhaus in Weimar', in Anton Kaes, et al, *The Weimar Republic sourcebook*, University of California Press, Berkeley and Los Angeles 1994, p 435

2 Tim Benton, in Wilk 2006, p 186

Marcel Breuer
Club chair (B3)

1 Christopher Wilk, 'Club Chair', in Wilk 2006, p 103

2 Frederic J Schwartz, 'Marcel Breuer: Club Chair', in Bergdoll & Dickerman 2009–10, pp 228–35

Erich Dieckmann
Dining room suite

1 *20th century art and design*, Phillips, Sydney, auction catalogue, 27 Oct 1997, lots 223–31

2 Hal Foster, 'Exercises for Color Theory Courses', in Bergdoll & Dickerman 2009–10, pp 266–73

Wilhelm Wagenfeld and Carl Jakob Jucker
Table lamp (MT 9/ME 1)

1 David Crowley, 'Kubus Stacking Storage Containers', in Wilk 2006, p 362

Marianne Brandt
Desk set

1 Christopher Wilk, 'Ashtray' and 'Tea Infuser', in Wilk 2006, p 101

2 Adrian Sudhalter, '14 Years Bauhaus: a Chronicle', in Bergdoll & Dickerman 2009–10, pp 331–2

Gunta Stölzl
Textile design

1 Leah Dickerman, 'Bauhaus Fundaments', in Bergdoll & Dickerman 2009–10, p 21

2 Ulrich Lehmann, 'Gunta Stölzl: Prototype Samples for Furnishing Fabric and Wall Coverings', in Wilk 2006, p 218

3 For further information, see Adrian Sudhalter, '14 Years Bauhaus: a Chronicle', in Bergdoll & Dickerman 2009–10, p 335

CONSTRUCTIVISM

Constructivism and the machine aesthetic

1 'Statement by the International Faction of Constructivists', reprinted in Stephen Bann (ed), *The tradition of Constructivism: documents of 20th-century art*, Thames and Hudson, London 1974, p 68

2 László Moholy-Nagy, *Painting, photography, film*, Lund Humphries, London 1969, p 27 (originally published as *Malerei Fotografie Film*, vol 8, Bauhausbücher, Munich 1925)

3 Moholy-Nagy 1969, p 35

4 Moholy-Nagy 1969, p 28

Erich Buchholz
Sign P

1 Michael Lloyd & Michael Desmond, *European and American paintings and sculptures 1870–1970 in the Australian National Gallery*, Australian National Gallery, Canberra 1992, pp 136–9

2 Anne Kirker (ed), *Erich Buchholz: the restless avant-gardist*, exh cat, Queensland Art Gallery, Brisbane, 25 June – 17 Sept 2000; and Andrew McNamara, 'Erich Buchholz: the Inconvenient Footnote within Art History', *Art and Australia*, vol 39, no 2, summer 2001, pp 256–63

3 The author would like to acknowledge the generosity of the artist's daughter, Mo Wedd-Buchholz, in donating many of these works to public collections in Australia.

El Lissitzky
Prouns

1 Christine Dixon, *Victory over the sun: Russian books and prints 1912–1935*, exh cat, National Gallery of Australia, Canberra, 13 Aug – 30 Oct 1994, np

2 Christina Lodder, 'Searching for Utopia', in Christopher Wilk (ed), *Modernism: designing a new world 1914–1939*, exh cat, Victoria and Albert Museum, London, 6 Apr – 23 July 2006, pp 38–9

3 El Lissitzky, 'Exhibition Rooms: Proun Room, Great Berlin Art Exhibition, 1923', in Sophie Lissitzky-Küppers, *El Lissitzky: life, letters, texts*, Thames and Hudson, London 1968, p 365

Carl Grossberg
White pipes

1 Carol O Selle & Peter Nisbet, *German realist drawings of the 1920s*, exh cat, Busch-Reisinger Museum, Cambridge, 26 July – 28 Sept 1986, pp 220–1

2 Selle & Nisbet 1986, p 221

Heinrich Hoerle
Three invalids

1 Lynette Roth, *Köln Progressiv 1920–33: Seiwert, Hoerle, Arntz*, exh cat, Museum Ludwig, Cologne, 15 Mar – 15 June 2008, p 17; and Wieland Schmied, 'Neue Sachlichkeit: German Realism of the Twenties', in René Block & Erna Haist, *Prints and drawings of the Weimar Republic*, Institute for Foreign Cultural Relations, Stuttgart 1985, p 28

2 Sabine Rewald, *Glitter and doom: German portraits from the 1920s*, exh cat, Metropolitan Museum of Art, New York, 14 Nov 2006 – 19 Feb 2007, p 238

METROPOLIS

Metropolis: the brilliant and sinister art of the 1920s

1 Dorothy Rowe, 'Desiring Berlin: Gender and Modernity in Weimar Germany', in Marsha Meskimmon & Shearer West (eds), *Visions of the 'neue Frau': women and the visual arts in Weimar Germany*, Scolar Press, Aldershot 1995, p 145

2 The notion of *Blut-und-Boden* (blood-and-soil) was an ideology later promoted by the Nazis as a means of justifying the racial purity of the German people. It promoted ethnicity through genetic descent (blood) and through the inheritance of land (soil), and celebrated rural traditions and customs.

3 Eric D Weitz, *Weimar Germany: promise and tragedy*, Princeton University Press, Princeton 2007, p 41

4 Shearer West, 'Introduction', in Meskimmon & West 1995, p 2

5 Anton Kaes, Martin Jay & Edward Dimendberg (eds), *The Weimar Republic sourcebook*, University of California Press, California 1994, p 412

6 For analysis of the representation of anxieties of gender roles and responsibilities in Weimar cinema, see: Patrice Petro, 'Modernity and Mass Culture in Weimar: Contours of a Discourse on Sexuality in Early Theories of Perception and Representation', *New German Critique*, no 40 (special issue on Weimar film theory), winter 1987, pp 115–46

7 Harold Nicholson, 'The Charm of Berlin', *Der Querschnitt*, vol 9, no 5, 1932, pp 345–6; reproduced in Kaes, Jay & Dimendberg 1994, p 426

8 See Helen Ennis, *Margaret Michaelis: love, loss and photography*, National Gallery of Australia, Canberra 2005

9 It was this honesty of representation of human life that was later condemned by the Nazi Party, and Beckmann was one of many contemporary German artists whose works were displayed in the *Degenerate art* exhibition of 1937.

Max Beckmann
The trapeze

1 Cornelia Stabenow, 'The Trapeze', in Carla Schulz-Hoffmann & Judith C Weiss (eds), *Max Beckmann: retrospective*, exh cat, Saint Louis Art Museum, Saint Louis, 7 Sept – 4 Nov 1984, pp 220–1

2 Robert F Phillips, 'Max Beckmann: The Trapeze', in Don Bacigalupi et al, *Toledo Museum of Art: masterworks*, Toledo Museum of Art, Toledo 2009, p 303

3 This concept was explored in the text panel for Max Beckmann's *Acrobats* 1939 in Saint Louis Art Museum (on display in June 2008).

Rudolf Schlichter
Sex murder

1 Götz Adriani (ed), *Rudolf Schlichter: Gemälde, Aquarelle, Zeichnungen*, exh cat, Kunsthale Tübingen, 13 Sept – 23 Nov 1997, p 197

August Sander
Secretary at West German Radio in Cologne

1 August Sander, *August Sander: 'In photography there are no unexplained shadows!'* (organised by the August Sander Archive, Kulturstiftung Stadtsparkasse, Cologne), exh cat, National Portrait Gallery, London, 28 Feb – 9 June 1997, p 21

Hugo Erfurth
Alfred Flechtheim

1 Bodo von Dewitz, 'Hugo Erfurth: Ein Photograph und die vielen "Köpfe seiner Zeit"', in Bodo von Dewitz & Karin Schuller-Procopovici (eds), *Hugo Erfurth 1874–1948: Photograph zwischen Tradition und Moderne*, Wienand, Cologne 1992, p 9

2 Judy Annear (ed), *Photography: Art Gallery of New South Wales collection*, Art Gallery of New South Wales, Sydney 2007, p 337

3 Klaus Pollmeier, 'Zur photograpischen Technik Hugo Erfurths', in Dewitz & Schuller-Procopovici 1992, p 482

4 Sabine Rewald, *Glitter and doom: German portraits from the 1920s*, exh cat, Metropolitan Museum of Art, New York, 14 Nov 2006 – 19 Feb 2007, pp 7, 120

5 Gustav Kahnweiler, quoted in Rewald 2006–07, p 118

NEW OBJECTIVITY

German realist portraits of the 1920s

1 For a closer examination of *Neue Saclichkeit*, see Matthias Eberle, 'Neue Sachlichkeit in Germany: a Brief History', in Sabine Rewald, *Glitter and doom: German portraits from the 1920s*, exh cat, Metropolitan Museum of Art, New York, 14 Nov 2006 – 19 Feb 2007, pp 21–38; and Sergiusz Michalski, *New Objectivity: painting, graphic art and photography in Weimar Germany 1919–1933*, Benedikt Taschen, Cologne 1994

2 Erhard Göpel & Barbara Göpel, *Max Beckmann: Katalog der Gemälde*, Schriften der Max Beckmann Gesellschaft, Bern 1976, vol 1, no 305, pp 219–20

3 Göpel & Göpel 1976, p 220

Alexander Kanoldt
Half nude II

1 Sergiusz Michalski, *New Objectivity: painting, graphic art and photography in Weimar Germany 1919–1933*, Benedikt Taschen, Cologne 1994, pp 18–19

2 Cornelia Stabenow, 'Alexander Kanoldt: Halbakt II', in Carla Schulz-Hoffmann (ed), *Pinakothek der Moderne: Malerei, Skulptur, Fotografie, Neue Medien*, Pinakothek-Dumont, Munich 2006, p 176

Carlo Mense
The painter Heinrich Maria Davringhausen

1 Brigitte Lohkamp, 'Zu einer Kunstgeografie der zwanziger Jahre in Deutschland', in Joachim Heusinger von Waldegg (ed), *Die zwanziger Jahre im Porträt: Porträts in Deutschland 1918–1933 Malerei, Graphik, Fotographie, Plastik*, exh cat, Rheinisches Landesmuseum, Bonn, 10 Sept – 24 Oct 1976, p 204 (cat 75)

2 Michalski 1994, p 82

Otto Dix
Dr Paul Ferdinand Schmidt
1 Sabine Rewald, 'I must paint you!', in Rewald 2006–07, p 5

2 Rewald 2006–07, pp 76–9 (cat 14)

Christian Schad
Self-portrait
1 Rewald 2006–07, pp 74–6 (cat 13)

2 Rewald 2006–07, p 76

3 Jill Lloyd & Michael Peppiatt (eds), *Christian Schad and the Neue Sachlichkeit*, exh cat, Neue Galerie, New York, 14 Mar – 9 June 2003, p 230

4 Lloyd & Peppiatt 2003, p 230

Max Beckmann
Young Argentine
1 Olaf Peters, 'Max Beckmann', in Renée Price (ed), *New worlds: German and Austrian art 1890–1940*, exh cat, Neue Galerie, New York, 16 Nov 2001 – 18 Feb 2002, p 298
2 Sean Rainbird, 'A gathering storm: Beckmann and cultural politics 1925–38', in *Max Beckmann*, exh cat, Tate Modern, London, 12 Feb – 5 May 2003, p 158
3 Carla Schulz-Hoffmann, 'Max Beckmann: Junger Argentinier', in Schulz-Hoffmann 2006, p 44
4 Rewald 2006–07, pp 148–50 (cat 40)

Karl Hubbuch
Twice Hilde II
1 Carol O Selle & Peter Nisbet, *German realist drawings of the 1920s*, exh cat, Busch-Reisinger Museum, Cambridge, 26 July – 28 Sept 1986, p 225

2 Joachim Kaak, 'Karl Hubbuch: Zweimal Hilde (I)', in Schulz-Hoffmann 2006, p 158

3 Rewald 2006–07, p 251

Jeanne Mammen
Valeska Gert
1 Klara Drenker-Nagels, 'Die zwanziger und frühen dreissiger Jahre', in Jörn Merkert & Freya Mülhaupt (eds), *Jeanne Mammen 1890–1976: Gemälde, Aquarelle, Zeichnungen*, exh cat, Berlinische Galerie, Berlin, 8 Nov 1997 – 4 Jan 1998, p 48

Otto Dix
Portrait of the dancer Tamara Danischewski
1 Fritz Löffler, *Otto Dix: life and work*, Holmes & Meier, New York 1982, p 84

2 Keith Hartley, *Otto Dix 1891–1969*, exh cat, Tate Gallery, London, 11 Mar – 17 May 1992, p 188 (cat 105)

POWER

In the twilight of power: the contradictions of art politics in National Socialist Germany
1 Mario-Andreas von Lüttichau, 'Entartete Kunst', in Eberhard Roters & Bernhard Schulz (eds), *Stationen der Moderne: Die bedeutendsten Kunstausstellungen des 20. Jahrhunderts in Deutschland*, exh cat, Berlinische Galerie, Berlin, 25 Sept 1988 – 8 Jan 1989, pp 288–313; Stephanie Barron, *'Degenerate art': the fate of the avant-garde in Nazi Germany*, exh cat, Los Angeles County Museum of Art, 17 Feb – 12 May 1991; Christoph Zuschlag, *'Entartete Kunst': Ausstellungsstrategien im Nazi-Deutschland*, Heidelberger Kunstgeschichtliche Abhandlungen, vol 21, Wernersche Verlagsgesellschaft, Worms 1995

2 For information on the 'Dada wall', see Uwe Fleckner, 'Sie nahmen Dada ernst. Das "Merzbild" von Kurt Schwitters und seine Inszenierungen als Werk "entarteter" Kunst', in Uwe Fleckner (ed), *Das verfemte Meisterwerk: Schicksalswege moderner Kunst im 'Dritten Reich'*, Schriften der Forschungsstelle 'Entartete Kunst', vol 4, Akademie Verlag, Berlin 2009, pp 75–101

3 For information on works shown on this wall, see Mario-Andreas von Lüttichau, 'Rekonstruktion der Ausstellung "Entartete Kunst", Munich, 19 Juli – 30 November 1937', in Peter-Klaus Schuster (ed), *Nationalsozialismus und 'Entartete Kunst': Die 'Kunststadt' München 1937*, Prestel, Munich 1987, pp 120–81, 138f

4 A Undo [pseudonym, possibly Franz Jung, Hugo Kersten or Franz Pfemfert], 'Der Impertinentismus: Ein Manifest', in *Die Aktion: Wochenschrift für Politik, Literatur, Kunst*, no 5, 1915, pp 448–50. See also Thomas Anz & Michael Stark (eds), *Expressionismus: Manifeste und Dokumente zur deutschen Literatur 1910–1920*, Metzler, Stuttgart 1982, p 63f

5 Ines Schlenker, *Hitler's salon: the 'Grosse Deutsche Kunstausstellung' at the Haus der Deutschen Kunst in Munich 1937–1944*, German Linguistic and Cultural Studies, vol 20, Oxford 2007

6 Ulrich Gerster, 'Der Schützling des Stellvertreters: Georg Schrimpf und sein Gemälde "Mädchen vor dem Spiegel"', in Fleckner 2009, pp 335–63; for further information on Expressionism and National Socialism, see Christian Saehrendt, *Die Brücke zwischen Staatskunst und Verfemung: Expressionisische Kunst als Politikum in der Weimarer Republik, im Dritten Reich und im Kalten Krieg*, Pallas Athene, vol 13, Franz Steiner, Stuttgart 2005

7 Zuschlag 1995, p 34

8 For information on the ambivalent response to the artists, see Isgard Kracht, 'Verehrt und verfemt: Franz Marc im Nationalsozialismus', in Uwe Fleckner (ed), *Angriff auf die Avantgarde: Kunst und Kunstpolitik im Nationalsozialismus*, Schriften der Forschungsstelle 'Entartete Kunst', vol 1, Akademie Verlag, Berlin 2007, pp 307–77; Roland März, 'Spuren und Legenden: "Der Turm der blauen Pferde" von Franz Marc', in Fleckner 2009, pp 565–96, 576ff

9 Andreas Hüneke, 'Bilanzen der "Verwertung" der "Entarteten Kunst"', in Eugen Blume & Dieter Scholz (eds), *Überbrückt. Ästhetische Moderne und Nationalsozialismus: Kunsthistoriker und Künstler 1925–1937*, Walther König, Cologne 1999, pp 265–74; Meike Hoffmann (ed), *Ein Händler 'entarteter' Kunst: Bernhard A Böhmer und sein Nachlass*, Schriften der Forschungsstelle 'Entartete Kunst', vol 3, Akademie Verlag, Berlin 2010

10 For information on National Socialist art politics, see Hildegard Brenner, *Die Kunstpolitik des Nationalsozialismus*, Rowohlt, Reinbek bei Hamburg 1963; and Joseph Wulf, *Die Bildenden Künste im Dritten Reich: Eine Dokumentation*, Mohn, Gütersloh 1963

11 Brenner 1963, p 63ff

12 Adolf Hitler, '"Kunst verpflichtet zur Wahrhaftigkeit": Rede auf der Kulturtagung des Parteitags der NSDAP in Nürnberg' (1934), in Adolf Hitler, *Reden zur Kunst- und Kulturpolitik. 1933–1939* (Robert Eikmeyer, ed), Revolver, Frankfurt am Main 2004, pp 63–79, 74f

13 Adolf Hitler, '"Programmatische Kulturrede des Führers": Rede zur Eröffnung der Grossen Deutschen Kunstausstellung in München' (1937), in Hitler 2004, pp 123–43; Anonymous, 'Adolf Hitler weiht den Tempel für wahre und ewige deutsche Kunst', in *Völkischer Beobachter*, 19 July 1937, pp 1–4. For information on Hitler's visit to the *Degenerate art* exhibition, see Fleckner 2009, p 75ff

14 Hitler 2004, p 128

15 Hitler 2004, p 132

16 Hitler 2004, pp 136f, 141

17 It has been generally accepted that Beckmann was forced into exile one day after Hitler's speech in the House of German Art; see Stephan Lackner, 'Exil in Amsterdam und Paris', in Carla Schulz-Hoffmann & Judith C Weiss (eds), *Max Beckmann: Retrospektive*, exh cat, Haus der Kunst, Munich, 25 Feb – 23 Apr 1984, pp 147–58; Uwe M Schneede, *Max Beckmann: der Maler seiner Zeit*, C H Beck, Munich 2009, p 177ff. New information has come to light that suggests that the artist had already left Germany one day earlier; see Christian Lenz: *Max Beckmann-Archiv. Erwerbungen 2008–2010*, Hefte des Max Beckmann Archivs, vols 11–12, Munich 2010, p 19

18 In a letter from Günther Franke, dated 23 October 1930, Beckmann wrote: 'Don't forget to teach the Nazis that I am a *German* painter if you have the chance'. Quoted in Max Beckmann, *Briefe* (Klaus Gallwitz, Uwe M Schneede & Stephan von Wiese, eds), Piper, Munich and Zurich 1993–96, vol 2, p 178; see also Barbara Copeland Buenger, 'Max Beckmann: "Der Künstler im Staat"', in Blume & Scholz 1999, pp 191–200

19 Thomas Noll, 'Max Beckmann "Mann im Dunkeln"', in *Max Beckmann: Aufsätze*, Hefte des Max-Beckmann-Archivs, vol 6, Munich 2002, pp 26–59

20 Isgard Kracht, 'Vom Symbol der Freiheit zum Sinnbild "entarteter" Kunst: Otto Freundlichs Plastik "Der neue Mensch"', in Fleckner 2009, pp 3–27

21 Karl Georg Kaster (ed), *Felix Nussbaum: art defamed – art in exile – art in resistance. A biography*, Overlook Press, Woodstock 1997; Sabine Eckmann, 'Felix Nussbaums ästhetische Strategien im Exil: Hybride Erinnerungen und radikaler Illusionismus', in Rosamunde Neugebauer (ed), *Zeit im Blick: Felix Nussbaum und die Moderne*, exh cat, Felix-Nussbaum-Haus, Osnabruck, 5 Dec 2004 – 28 Mar 2005, pp 123–31

Felix Nussbaum
The mad square
1 For separate accounts of *The mad square*, see Max Osborn, 'Akademie und Secession in Berlin', *Deutsche Kunst und Dekoration*, vol 34, Apr–Sept 1931, p 200; Paul Westheim, 'Felix Nussbaum: Der tolle Pariser Platz', *Kunstblatt*, vol 15, 1931, p 159; Klaus Märtens, 'Felix Nussbaum: Der tolle Platz Berlin 1931 – oder die Situation der Zeit im Bild', *Berliner Kunstblatt*, vol 5, no 13, 1976; Reinhart Strecke, et al, '*… zusammenkommen, um von den Künsten zu räsonieren'. Materialien zur Geschichte der Preussischen Akademie der Künste*, Archiv-Dependance der Akademie der Künste, Berlin, 12 Apr – 31 Aug 1991, pp 233–5; Peter Junk & Wendelin Zimmer, *Felix Nussbaum: Leben und Werk*, DuMont, Cologne 1982, pp 80–5; Ursula Prinz & Eberhard Roters, 'Felix Nussbaum', in *Berlinische Galerie 1913–1933: Bestände – Malerei, Skulptur, Graphik*, exh cat, Berlinische Galerie, Berlin nd, pp 171–3 (cat 305); Maiken Schmidt, 'Felix Nussbaum', in Eva-Maria Amberger et al, *100 Jahre Kunst im Aufbruch: Die Berlinische Galerie zu Gast in Bonn*, Wienand, Cologne 1998, pp 144–5

John Heartfield
Photomontage
1 John Heartfield (1967), quoted in Peter Pachnicke & Klaus Honnef (eds), *John Heartfield*, Harry N Abrams, New York 1992, p 14

2 Anton Kaes et al, *The Weimar Republic sourcebook*, University of California Press, Berkeley and Los Angeles 1994, p 643

Ernst Ludwig Kirchner
Brown figures in café
1 Peter Guenther, 'Ernst Ludwig Kirchner', in Barron 1991, p 269

2 Beat Stutzer, 'Expressionism from the mountains?', in Beat Stutzer et al, *Ernst Ludwig Kirchner and friends: Expressionism from the Swiss mountains*, Scheidegger & Spiess, Zurich 2007, p 15

Max Beckmann
Crouching woman
1 See, for example, Cornelia Stabenow, 'Metaphors of helplessness: the sculpture of Max Beckmann', in Schulz-Hoffmann & Weiss 1984, p 137

2 Max Beckmann, *Briefe im Kriege* 1914–15, 1955 (1916), R Piper, Munich 1984, p 23, quoted in *European Masters: Städel Museum: 19th–20th century*, exh cat, National Gallery of Victoria, Melbourne, 19 June – 10 Oct 2010, p 240

3 Ursula Grzechca-Mohr, 'Max Beckmann', *European Masters: Städel Museum: 19th–20th century*, exh cat, National Gallery of Victoria, Melbourne, 19 June – 10 Oct 2010, p 240

4 Max Beckmann, 'On My Painting', first read in London, 21 July 1938, reproduced in Barbara Copeland Buenger (ed), *Max Beckmann: self-portrait in words: collected writings and statements 1903–50*, University of Chicago Press, Chicago 1997, p 302

'Degenerate' art
1 Christoph Zuschlag, 'An "Educational Exhibition": the Precursors of "Entartete Kunst" and its Individual Venues', in Barron 1991, pp 85, 100

2 Wall text for Rudolf Herrmann's poster advertising the 1938 *Degenerate art* exhibition in Hamburg, Los Angeles County Museum of Art (on display June 2008)

Rudolf Belling
Triad
1 Joachim Kaak, 'Rudolf Belling: Dreiklang', in Carla Schulz-Hoffmann (ed), *Pinakothek der Moderne: Malerei, Skulptur, Fotografie, Neue Medien*, Pinakothek-Dumont, Munich 2006, p 55

2 Mario-Andreas von Lüttichau, '"Entartete Kunst" Munich 1937: a reconstruction', in Barron 1991, p 55

Emil Nolde
Conversation
1 This concept was explored in the wall text for Rudolf Herrmann's poster advertising the 1938 *Degenerate art* exhibition in Hamburg, Los Angeles County Museum of Art (on display June 2008).

2 Dagmar Grimm, 'Emil Nolde', in Barron 1991, p 315

3 Dagmar Grimm, 'Emil Nolde', in Barron 1991, p 319

Ernst Ludwig Kirchner
Nude looking over her shoulder
1 Mario-Andreas von Lüttichau, '"Entartete Kunst" Munich 1937: a reconstruction', in Barron 1991, p 57

2 Wolfgang Henze, *Die Plastik Ernst Ludwig Kirchners*, Galerie Henze and Ketterer, Wichtrach and Bern 2002, pp 154–8

3 Wolfgang Henze, 'The Sculptures of Ernst Ludwig Kirchner', in Jill Lloyd & Magdalene M Moeller (eds), *Ernst Ludwig Kirchner: the Dresden and Berlin years*, exh cat, Royal Academy of Arts, 28 June – 21 Sept 2003, p 35

Ades, Dawn. *Art and power: Europe under the dictators 1930–1945*, exh cat, Hayward Gallery, London, 26 Oct 1995 – 21 Jan 1996

Adriani, Götz (ed). *Rudolf Schlichter: Gemälde, Aquarelle, Zeichnungen*, exh cat, Kunsthalle Tübingen, 13 Sept – 23 Nov 1997

Amberger, Eva-Maria, Ulrich Domröse, Janos Frecot, Ursula Prinz, Jörn Merkert, Freya Mülhaupt, Ursula Müller & Eva Züchner. *100 Jahre Kunst im Aufbruch: Die Berlinische Galerie zu Gast in Bonn*, exh cat, Kunst- und Ausstellungshalle der Bundesrepublik Deutschland, Bonn, 25 Sept 1998 – 10 Jan 1999

Ankum, Katharina von (ed). *Women in the metropolis: gender and modernity in Weimar culture*, University of California Press, Berkeley, Los Angeles and London 1997

Annear, Judy (ed). *Photography: Art Gallery of New South Wales collection*, Art Gallery of New South Wales, Sydney 2007

Barron, Stephanie (ed). *German expressionism 1915–1925: the second generation*, exh cat, Los Angeles County Museum of Art, Los Angeles, 9 Oct – 31 Dec 1988

Barron, Stephanie. *'Degenerate art': the fate of the avant-garde in Nazi Germany*, exh cat, Los Angeles County Museum of Art, Los Angeles, 17 Feb – 12 May 1991

Bergdoll, Barry & Leah Dickerman. *Bauhaus 1919–1933: workshops for modernity*, exh cat, Museum of Modern Art, New York, 8 Nov 2009 – 25 Jan 2010

Block, René & Erna Haist. *Prints and drawings of the Weimar Republic*, Institute for Foreign Cultural Relations, Stuttgart 1985

Boose, Joanna. *Ludwig Hirschfeld Mack: Bauhaus artist and innovator*, Ian Potter Museum of Art, University of Melbourne, Melbourne, 15 May – 31 Aug 2008, www.art-museum.unimelb.edu.au/art_exhibitions_browse.aspx?year=2008 (viewed June 2008)

Buenger, Barbara Copeland (ed). *Max Beckmann: self-portrait in words: collected writings and statements 1903–50*, University of Chicago Press, Chicago 1997

Dewitz, Bodo von & Karin Schuller-Procopovici (eds). *Hugo Erfurth 1874–1948: Photograph zwischen Tradition und Moderne*, Wienand, Cologne 1992

Dickerman, Leah (ed). *Dada: Zurich, Berlin, Hannover, Cologne, New York, Paris*, exh cat, National Gallery of Art, Washington, 19 Feb – 14 May 2006 and Museum of Modern Art, New York, 18 June – 11 Sept 2006

Dixon, Christine. *Victory over the sun: Russian books and prints 1912–1935*, exh cat, National Gallery of Australia, Canberra, 13 Aug – 30 Oct 1994

Draffin, Nicholas. *Two masters of the Weimar Bauhaus: Lyonel Feininger and Ludwig Hirschfeld Mack*, exh cat, Art Gallery of New South Wales, Sydney, 4 July – 6 Oct 1974

Droste, Magdalene. *Bauhaus 1919–1933*, Bauhaus-Archiv Museum für Gestaltung, Berlin 1990

Eberle, Matthias. *World War I and the Weimar artists: Dix, Grosz, Beckmann, Schlemmer*, Yale University Press, New Haven 1985

Eliel, Carol S & Eberhard Roters. *The apocalyptic landscapes of Ludwig Meidner*, exh cat, Los Angeles County Museum of Art, Los Angeles, 12 Oct – 17 Dec 1989

Evans, David. *John Heartfield: Arbeiter-Illustrierte Zeitung/Volks Illustrierte 1930–38*, Kent Gallery, New York 1992

Fabre, Gladys & Doris Wintgens Hötte (eds). *Van Doesburg and the international avant-garde: constructing a new world*, exh cat, Tate Modern, London, 4 Feb – 16 May 2010

Fiedler, Jeannine & Peter Feierabend (eds). *Bauhaus*, Könemann, Cologne 1999

Frascina, Francis & Charles Harrison (eds). *Modern art and modernism: a critical anthology*, Open University, London 1982

Friedrich, Otto. *Before the deluge: a portrait of Berlin in the 1920s*, Harper Perennial, New York 1995

Gay, Peter. *Weimar culture: the outsider as insider*, Secker & Warburg, London 1969

Gay, Peter. *Modernism: the lure of heresy from Baudelaire to Beckett and beyond*, William Heinemann, New York and London 2007

German expressionism: the colours of desire, exh cat, Art Gallery of New South Wales, Sydney, 11 Oct – 10 Dec 1989; National Gallery of Victoria, Melbourne, 20 Dec 1989 – 18 Feb 1990

Goettl, Helmut, Wolfgang Hartmann & Michael Schwarz (eds). *Karl Hubbuch 1891–1979*, exh cat, Badischer Kunstverein Karlsruhe, 4 Oct – 29 Nov 1981

Grosz, George. *The autobiography of George Grosz: a small yes and a big no*, Allison & Busby, London and New York 1982

Hartley, Keith. *Otto Dix 1891–1969*, exh cat, Tate Gallery, London, 11 Mar – 17 May 1992

Hartley, Keith (ed). *The romantic spirit in German art 1790–1990*, exh cat, Scottish National Gallery of Modern Art, Edinburgh, 28 July – 7 Sept 1994

Heckert, Virginia & Judy Annear. *Extraordinary images of ordinary people: the photographs of August Sander from the J Paul Getty Museum, Los Angeles*, exh cat, Art Gallery of New South Wales, Sydney, 17 Nov – 3 Feb 2008

Kaes, Anton, Martin Jay & Edward Dimendberg (eds). *The Weimar Republic sourcebook*, University of California Press, Berkeley and Los Angeles 1994

Karcher, Eva. *Otto Dix: 1891–1969*, Taschen, Cologne 2002

Keaney, Magdalene. 'Images of Displacement: Art from the Internment Camps', in Roger Butler(ed), *The Europeans: émigré artists in Australia 1930–1960*, National Gallery of Australia, Canberra 1997, pp 85–101

Kirker, Anne (ed). *Erich Buchholz: the restless avant-gardist*, exh cat, Queensland Art Gallery, Brisbane, 25 June – 17 Sept 2000

Lange, Susanne, Gabriele Conrath-Scholl & Gerd Sander (eds). *August Sander: Menschen des 20. Jahrhunderts: Ein Kulturwerk in Lichtbildern eingeteilt in sieben Gruppen [People of the 20th century: a cultural history in photographs]*, Die Photographische Sammlung/SK Stiftung Kultur, Cologne 2002

Leahy, Cathy. *Prints and drawings in the international collections of the NGV*, National Gallery of Victoria, Melbourne 2003

Lewis, Beth Irwin. *George Grosz: art and politics in the Weimar Republic*, University of Wisconsin Press, Madison 1971

Lissitzky-Küppers, Sophie. *El Lissitzky: life, letters, texts*, Thames and Hudson, London 1968

Lloyd, Jill & Magdalena M Moeller (eds). *Ernst Ludwig Kirchner: the Dresden and Berlin years*, exh cat, Royal Academy of Arts, London, 28 June – 21 Sept 2003

Lloyd, Jill & Michael Peppiatt (eds). *Christian Schad and the Neue Sachlichkeit*, exh cat, Neue Galerie, New York, 14 Mar – 9 June 2003

Löffler, Fritz. *Otto Dix: life and work*, Holmes & Meier, New York 1982

Lohkamp, Brigitte. 'Zu einer Kunstgeografie der zwanziger Jahre in Deutschland', in Joachim Heusinger von Waldegg (ed), *Die zwanziger Jahre im Porträt: Porträts in Deutschland 1918–1933 Malerei, Graphik, Fotographie, Plastik*, exh cat, Rheinisches Landesmuseum, Bonn, 10 Sept – 24 Oct 1976

McNamara, Andrew. 'The Bauhaus in Australia: interdisciplinary confluences in modernist practices', in Ann Stephen, Philip Goad and Andrew McNamara (eds), *Modern times: the untold story of modernism in Australia*, exh cat, Powerhouse Museum, Sydney, 8 Aug – 15 Feb 2008, pp 2–15

Merkert, Jörn & Freya Mülhaupt. *Jeanne Mammen 1890–1976: Gemälde, Aquarelle, Zeichnungen*, exh cat, Berlinsiche Galerie, Berlin, 8 Nov 1997 – 4 Jan 1998

Meskimmon, Marsha & Shearer West (eds). *Visions of the 'neue frau': women and the visual arts in Weimar Germany*, Scolar Press, Aldershot 1995

Metzger, Rainer. *Berlin in the 20s: art and culture 1918–1933*, Thames and Hudson, London 2007

Michalski, Sergiusz. *New Objectivity: painting, graphic art and photography in Weimar Germany 1919–1933*, Benedikt Taschen, Cologne 1994

Milner, John. *El Lissitzky design*, Antique Collectors' Club, Suffolk 2009

Moholy-Nagy, László. *Painting, photography, film*, Lund Humphries, London 1969 (originally published as *Malerei Fotografie Film*, vol 8, Bauhausbücher, Munich 1925)

Nicholas, Lynn H. *The rape of Europa: the fate of Europe's treasures in the Third Reich and the Second World War*, Macmillan, London 1994

Pachnicke, Peter & Klaus Honnef (eds). *John Heartfield*, Harry N Abrams, New York 1992

Price, Renée (ed). *New worlds: German and Austrian art 1890–1940*, exh cat, Neue Galerie, New York, 16 Nov 2001 – 18 Feb 2002

Rainbird, Sean. *Max Beckmann*, exh cat, Tate Modern, London, 12 Feb – 5 May 2003

Reisenfeld, Robin. *The German print portfolio 1890–1930: serials for a private sphere*, exh cat, David and Alfred Smart Museum of Art, Chicago, 5 Oct – 12 Dec 1993

Remmele, Mathias & Alexander von Vegesack. *Marcel Breuer: design and architecture*, Vitra Design Museum, Weil am Rhein 2003

Rewald, Sabine. *Glitter and doom: German portraits from the 1920s*, exh cat, Metropolitan Museum of Art, New York, 14 Nov 2006 – 19 Feb 2007

Rogoff, Irit (ed). *The divided heritage: themes and problems in German modernism*, Cambridge University Press, Cambridge 1990

Roth, Lynette. *Köln Progressiv 1920–33: Seiwert, Hoerle, Arntz*, exh cat, Museum Ludwig, Cologne, 15 Mar – 15 June 2008

Scheps, Marc (ed). *20th century art: Ludwig Museum*, Benedikt Taschen, Cologne 1996

Schmidt, Johann-Karl (ed). *Otto Dix: Bestandskatalog*, Galerie der Stadt, Stuttgart 1989

Schulz-Hoffmann, Carla & Judith C Weiss. *Max Beckmann: retrospective*, exh cat, Haus der Kunst, Munich, 25 Feb – 23 Apr 1984

Schulz-Hoffmann, Carla (ed). *Pinakothek der Moderne: Malerei, Skultpur, Fotografie, Neue Medien*, Pinakothek-Dumont, Munich 2006

Schuster, Peter-Klaus. *George Grosz: Berlin-New York*, exh cat, Neue Nationalgalerie, Berlin, 21 Dec 1994 – 17 Apr 1995

Schwartz, Frederic J. *Blind spots: critical theory and the history of art in twentieth-century Germany*, Yale University Press, New Haven 2005

Selle, Carol O & Peter Nisbet. *German realist drawings of the 1920s*, exh cat, Busch-Reisinger Museum, Cambridge, 26 July – 28 Sept 1986

Selz, Peter. *Beyond the mainstream: essays on modern and contemporary art*, Cambridge University Press, New York 1997

Spanke, Daniel & Marion Ackermann. *Getroffen: Otto Dix und die Kunst des Porträts*, exh cat, Kunstmuseum Stuttgart, 1 Dec 2007 – 6 Apr 2008

Stadler, Monika & Yael Aloni. *Gunta Stölzl: Bauhaus master*, Museum of Modern Art, New York 2009

Stephen, Ann, Philip Goad & Andrew McNamara. *Modern times: the untold story of modernism in Australia*, exh cat, Powerhouse Museum, Sydney, 8 Aug – 15 Feb 2008

Strecker, Jacqueline. '"The trench" (1920–23) by Otto Dix: "A masterpiece of unspeakable horror"', *Apollo: the international magazine of arts*, no 428, 1997, pp 22–6

Strecker, Jacqueline. '"Two Pair": Otto Dix to Andy Warhol', *Portrait 27*, National Portrait Gallery, Canberra, autumn 2008, pp 11–13

Weinstein, Joan. *The end of Expressionism: art and the November Revolution in Germany 1918–19*, University of Chicago Press, Chicago and London 1990

Weitz, Eric D. *Weimar Germany: promise and tragedy*, Princeton University Press, Princeton 2007

Whitford, Frank. *Bauhaus*, Thames and Hudson, London 1984

Wilk, Christopher (ed). *Modernism: designing a new world 1914–1939*, exh cat, Victoria and Albert Museum, London, 6 Apr – 23 July 2006

Willett, John. *The new sobriety 1917–1933: art and politics in the Weimar period*, Thames and Hudson, London 1978

Willett John. *The Weimar years: a culture cut short*, Thames and Hudson, London 1984

Wye, Deborah. *Kirchner and the Berlin street*, exh cat, Museum of Modern Art, New York, 3 Aug – 10 Nov 2008

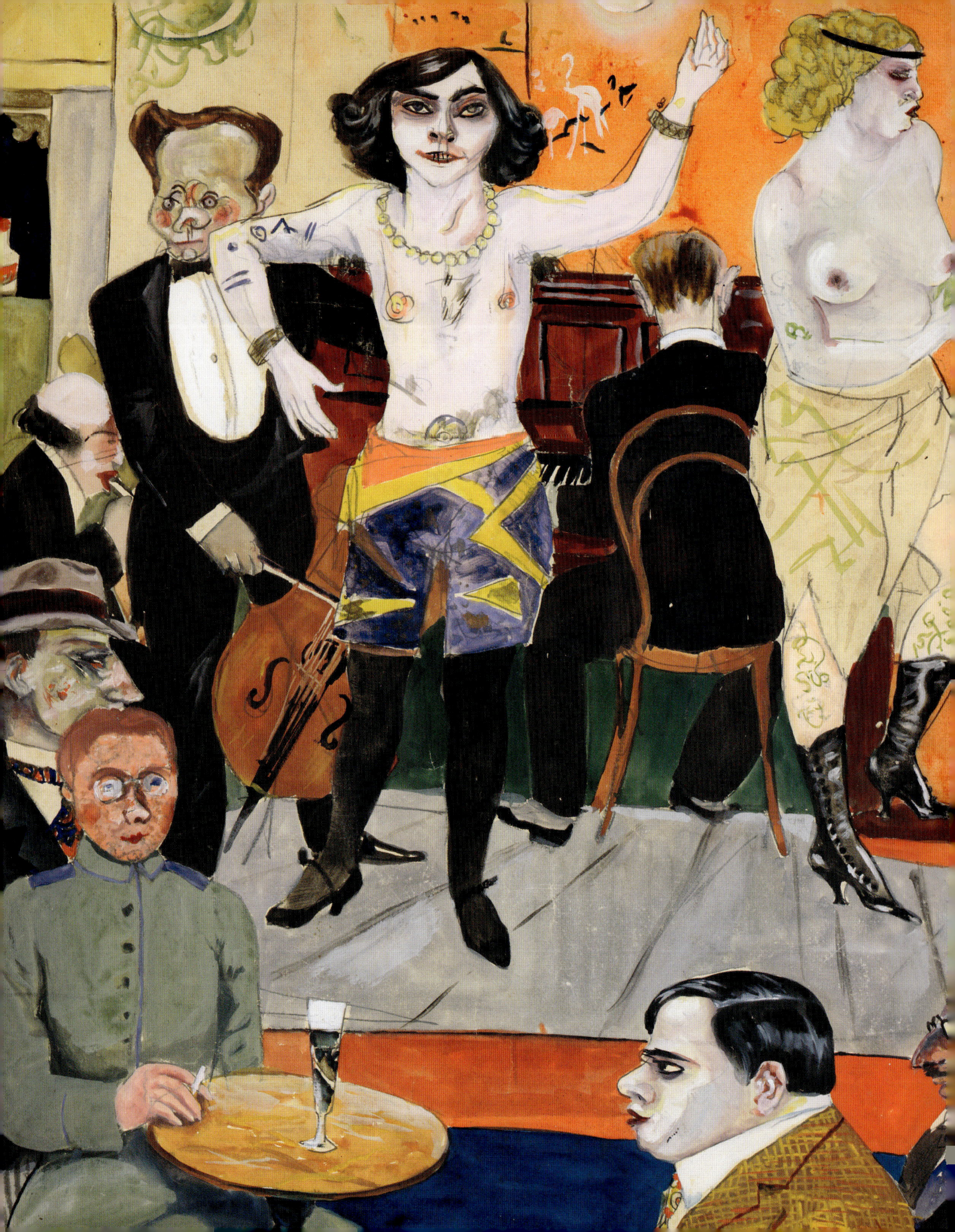

LIST OF WORKS

- • Only on display at the Art Gallery of New South Wales
- •• Only on display at the National Gallery of Victoria
- ^ Included in the *Degenerate art* exhibition, Munich, 1937

Titles of works are in English and have been given by the lenders. In some cases, where no English translation exists or where a descriptive title has been attributed to a work, the title is given in brackets [ ]. Parentheses ( ) are used in titles given by the artists.

Dimensions are given in centimetres in the following order: height, width, depth. For drawings and collages, sheet size is used; for intaglio prints, plate size is given; and for woodcuts and lithographs, image size is used. Image size is given for photographs (unless otherwise specified) and all photographs are assumed to have been printed within five years of their given date unless otherwise stated. Similarly, sculptures are assumed to have been cast within five years of their given dates unless otherwise stated.

GERTRUD ARNDT (1903–2000)

Wall painting workshop, Bauhaus Dessau 1930
gelatin silver photograph, 8.2 x 6 cm
National Gallery of Australia, Canberra
Purchased 1984 84.2942

ATELIER LEDL & BERNHARD

Rudolf Ledl and Fritz Bernhard
(active in Berlin 1901–25)

The cabinet of Dr Caligari 1920
colour lithograph, poster, 125.7 x 94.9 cm
Austrian National Library, Picture Archives and Graphics Department, Vienna

ERNST BARLACH (1870–1938)

The avenger 1914, cast 1930
bronze, 44 x 58 x 22 cm
Museum Ludwig, Cologne ML 76/SK 0046

BAUHAUS DESSAU (1925–32)

Weaving study, furnishing fabric swatch c1926
wool, cotton, rayon fabric, 20.2 x 11.8 cm
National Gallery of Australia, Canberra
Purchased with the assistance of Dame Elizabeth Murdoch 1988 88.1680

WILLI BAUMEISTER (1889–1955)

The dwelling ['Werkbund' exhibition, Stuttgart] 1927
colour lithograph, poster, 115 x 81 cm
Kunstbibliothek Berlin, Staatliche Museen zu Berlin

HERBERT BAYER (1900–1985)

Theatre group on the Bauhaus roof c1920
gelatin silver photograph, 7.5 x 10.5 cm
National Gallery of Australia, Canberra
Purchased 1985 85.257

IRENE BAYER (1898–1991)

[Man on stage] c1927
gelatin silver photograph, 10.6 x 7.6 cm
National Gallery of Australia, Canberra
Purchased 1983 83.3175

MAX BECKMANN (1884–1950)

The night 1919 •
from the portfolio **Hell** 1919
lithograph, 55.5 x 70.3 cm
Kupferstichkabinett, Staatliche Museen zu Berlin

The way home 1919 ••
from the portfolio **Hell** 1919
lithograph, 73 x 48.5 cm
Kupferstichkabinett, Staatliche Museen zu Berlin

Behind the scenes 1921
from the portfolio **Carnival** 1922
drypoint, 21 x 30.6 cm
Private collection, Melbourne

The dream 1921
oil on canvas, 182 x 91 cm
Saint Louis Art Museum
Bequest of Morton D May 841:1983

Dressing room 1921 ^
from the portfolio **Carnival** 1922
drypoint, 20.8 x 14.4 cm
Private collection, Melbourne

Here is intellect 1921
drypoint, 33.8 x 25.7 cm
Collection of James Fairfax, Sydney

Negro dance 1921
from the portfolio **Carnival** 1922
drypoint, 25.9 x 25 cm
Private collection, Melbourne

The snake woman 1921
from the portfolio **Carnival** 1922
drypoint, 28.7 x 25.3 cm
Art Gallery of New South Wales, Sydney
Purchased 1989 306.1989

Children at the window 1922
drypoint, 32.2 x 22.7 cm
Art Gallery of New South Wales, Sydney
Purchased 2004 262.2004

The disillusioned II 1922 •^
lithograph, 48 x 38 cm
National Gallery of Australia, Canberra
Purchased 1986 86.1309

Women's bath 1922
drypoint, 43.7 x 28.5 cm
Art Gallery of New South Wales, Sydney
Purchased 1989 307.1989

The trapeze 1923
oil on canvas, 196.5 x 84 cm
Toledo Museum of Art
Purchased with funds from the Libbey Endowment, Gift of Edward Drummond Libbey 1983.20

Rudolf Schlichter
Tingel tangel 1919–20 (detail)

Young Argentine 1929
oil on canvas, 125.5 x 83.5 cm
Bayerische Staatsgemäldesammlungen, Munich
Pinakothek der Moderne, 1974
Stiftung Günther Franke 14375

Crouching woman 1935, cast after 1962
bronze, 17.8 x 22.9 x 50.8 cm
Private collection
Courtesy Richard L Feigen and Co, New York

RUDOLF BELLING (1886–1972)

Triad 1918–19, cast after 1950 ^
bronze, 90 x 85 cm
Bayerische Staatsgemäldesammlungen, Munich
Pinakothek der Moderne, acquired 1963 B388

LENA BERGNER (1906–1981)

Fabric swatch c1926
silk, mercerised cotton, 8.6 x 14.6 cm
National Gallery of Australia, Canberra
Purchased with the assistance of Dame Elizabeth Murdoch 1988 88.1684

Textile design with yarn sample 1928
watercolour, pencil, wool, 24 x 18 cm
National Gallery of Australia, Canberra
Purchased with the assistance of Dame Elizabeth Murdoch 1988 88.1674

Textile design with yarn sample 1928
watercolour, pencil, wool, 24 x 18 cm
National Gallery of Australia, Canberra
Purchased with the assistance of Dame Elizabeth Murdoch 1988 88.1675

MARIANNE BRANDT (1893–1983)

Desk set 1930–31
manufactured by Ruppelwerk, Gotha
enamelled metal, glass, paper
ink blotter 7 x 15 x 7 cm
inkwell 7.5 x 9 cm diam
pen tray 1.2 x 21 x 6.3 cm
Lent by the Powerhouse Museum, Sydney
Purchased 2002 2003/137/2

MARCEL BREUER (1902–1981)

Club chair (B3) designed 1925,
this example produced c1928–29
manufactured by Standard Möbel, Berlin
nickel-plated tubular steel with dark blue oil cloth fabric, 73.5 x 77.8 x 70.4 cm
Collection Alexander von Vegesack VST-1001-1

Chair (B5) designed c1926
manufactured by Standard Möbel, Berlin
nickel-plated tubular steel with red fabric
86.5 x 59 x 45.5 cm
Collection Vitra Design Museum MST-1004-3

ERICH BUCHHOLZ (1891–1972)

Sign P 1922
oil on wood relief, 26 x 26 cm
Art Gallery of New South Wales, Sydney
Purchased 1991 340.1991

HEINRICH MARIA DAVRINGHAUSEN

(1894–1970)

The sex murderer 1917
oil on canvas, 119.5 x 148.5 cm
Bayerische Staatsgemäldesammlungen, Munich
Pinakothek der Moderne, acquired 1972 14292

ERICH DIECKMANN (1896–1944)

Dining room suite designed c1926, this example produced c1927–28
manufactured by Bau- und Wohnungskunst, Weimar
circular dining table, natural oak top with lacquered wood base, 76 x 108.5 x 110 cm
two arm chairs, lacquered wood with rush seats, each 73 x 62 x 52.5 cm
two side chairs, lacquered wood with rush seats, each 82.3 x 44.5 x 40.5 cm
sideboard, lacquered wood with white glass top (later addition), 90 x 184.5 x 50 cm
Private collection, Melbourne

OTTO DIX (1891–1969)

The Felixmüller family 1919
oil on canvas, 75.9 x 91.4 cm
Saint Louis Art Museum
Bequest of Morton D May 882:1983

Dr Paul Ferdinand Schmidt 1921
oil on canvas, 83 x 63 cm
Staatsgalerie Stuttgart 2764

The suicide 1922
from the portfolio **Death and resurrection** 1922
drypoint, 35 x 28.2 cm
Art Gallery of New South Wales, Sydney
Purchased 2004 259.2004

Prostitute and war wounded 1923
pen, ink, 46.9 x 37.3 cm
LWL-Landesmuseum für Kunst und Kulturgeschichte
Westfälisches Landesmuseum, Münster KdZ 1006 LM

Abandoned position near Neuville ^
from the portfolio **War** 1924
etching, drypoint, aquatint, 19.5 x 14.5 cm
Australian War Memorial, Canberra ART50211

At night the men in the trenches have to keep firing ^
from the portfolio **War** 1924
etching, aquatint, drypoint, 24.5 x 29.5 cm
Australian War Memorial, Canberra ART50159

The sleepers of Fort Vaux – gas deaths ^
from the portfolio **War** 1924
etching, aquatint, drypoint, 24.6 x 29.4 cm
Australian War Memorial, Canberra ART50158

Storm troopers advancing under a gas attack ^
from the portfolio **War** 1924
etching, aquatint, drypoint, 19.4 x 29 cm
Australian War Memorial, Canberra ART50157

Transplantation [Skin graft] ^
from the portfolio **War** 1924
etching, aquatint, drypoint, 19.9 x 14.9 cm
Australian War Memorial, Canberra ART50209

Portrait of the poet Theodor Däubler 1927 ^
tempera on plywood, 152 x 102 cm
Museum Ludwig, Cologne ML 76/2738

Portrait of the dancer Tamara Danischewski 1933
oil, tempera on wood, 80.3 x 64.1 cm
Kunstmuseum, Stuttgart O-2174

HUGO ERFURTH (1874–1948)

Paul Klee 1922–27
bromoil photograph, bromide gelatin silver print
26 x 19.5 cm
Museum Folkwang, Essen 100/45

Alfred Flechtheim 1928
gelatin silver photograph, 23.9 x 17.8 cm
Museum Ludwig, Cologne FH 1164, RBA 216 885

Max Beckmann 1928
bromoil photograph, 26 x 20 cm
Museum Ludwig, Cologne FH 1162, RBA 216 843

Hilde Wächler 1929
bromoil photograph, 38.3 x 26.6 cm
Museum Ludwig, Cologne FH 1161, RBA 216 602

Otto Dix with brush 1929
bromoil photograph, 47 x 37.5 cm
Museum Ludwig, Cologne FH 1371, RBA 216 782

Johanna Ey c1930
bromoil photograph, 31 x 39.2 cm
Museum Ludwig, Cologne FH 246, RBA 216 467

Kurt Schwitters c1930
gelatin silver photograph, 38.3 x 27.5 cm
Museum Ludwig, Cologne FH 1184, RBA 216 398

T LUX FEININGER (1910–)

[Metaltanz] c1928–29
gelatin silver photograph, 16.7 x 10.9 cm
J Paul Getty Museum, Los Angeles 84.XM.127.20

[Georg Hartmann with foil and Karla Grosch running] 1929
gelatin silver photograph, 8.3 x 11.4 cm
J Paul Getty Museum, Los Angeles 86.XM.689.2

RUDI FELD (1896–1994)

The danger of bolshevism c1920
colour lithograph, poster, 97.1 x 72 cm
Australian War Memorial, Canberra
Presented through the Cultural Gifts Program 2006
ARTV09320

WALTER FUNKAT (1906–2006)

Vestibule, metallic festival 1929
gelatin silver photograph, 17.2 x 12.1 cm
Art Institute of Chicago, Chicago
Restricted Gift of the Rice Foundation and Photography Purchase Account 1982.1410

WERNER GRAUL (1905–1984)

Metropolis 1926
colour lithograph, poster, 210 x 95 cm
Austrian National Library, Picture Archives and Graphics Department, Vienna

KARL GRILL (active at the Bauhaus 1920–29)
[Spiral costume, from the 'Triadic ballet'] c1926–27
gelatin silver photograph, 22.5 x 16.2 cm
J Paul Getty Museum, Los Angeles 84.XM.127.8

ARTHUR GRIMM (1883–1948),
GEORG SCHÖDL (nd) **AND UNKNOWN ARTISTS**
Archival photographs of the *Degenerate art* exhibition held at the Archäologisches Institut, Munich, 19 July – 30 Nov 1937
obtained through the courtesy of the Research Library, Getty Research Institute, Los Angeles, California (840001); Bildarchiv Preussischer Kulturbesitz, Berlin; and Ullstein Bild

---

CARL GROSSBERG (1894–1940)
White pipes 1933
oil on wood, 70 x 90 cm
Private collection

GEORGE GROSZ (1893–1959)
Taverne du Midi 1915
lithograph, 24.5 x 18.2 cm
National Gallery of Victoria, Melbourne
Purchased 1984 P85-1984

City street 1915–16
from the **First George Grosz portfolio** 1917
lithograph, 26 x 37.4 cm
Private collection, Melbourne

Memory of New York 1915–16 ^
from the **First George Grosz portfolio** 1917
lithograph, 37.8 x 29.7 cm
Private collection, Melbourne

Moonlit night 1915–16
from the **First George Grosz portfolio** 1917
lithograph, 37.4 x 30 cm
Private collection, Melbourne

People in the street 1915–16
from the **First George Grosz portfolio** 1917
lithograph, 27.5 x 21.7 cm
Private collection, Melbourne

Texas picture for my friend Chingachgook 1915–16 ^
from the **First George Grosz portfolio** 1917
lithograph, 26.8 x 21.5 cm
Private collection, Melbourne

Suicide 1916
oil on canvas, 100 x 77.5 cm
Tate London
Purchased with assistance from The Art Fund 1976
T02053

Murder in Ackerstrasse 1916–17
lithograph, 42.5 x 33.8 cm (sheet)
Art Gallery of New South Wales, Sydney
Purchased under the terms of the Florence Turner Blake Bequest 1984 164.1984

The convict 1919
photolithograph, 46.3 x 34.4 cm
National Gallery of Victoria, Melbourne
Purchased 1984 P86-1984

Tatlinesque diagram 1920
watercolour, collage, ink on paper, 41 x 29.2 cm
Museo Thyssen-Bornemisza, Madrid 1978.6(570)

'Under my rule, it shall come to pass, that potatoes and small beer shall be considered a holiday treat; and woe to him who meets my eye with the audacious front of health. Haggard want, and crouching fear, are my insignia; and in this livery will I clothe ye.' 1920–21 ••
from the portfolio **The robbers** 1922
photolithograph, 49 x 37.6 cm
National Gallery of Australia, Canberra
Purchased 1986 86.1069.3

'I've done my bit ... the plunder is your affair!' 1922 ••
from the portfolio **The robbers** 1922
photolithograph, 49 x 37.2 cm
National Gallery of Australia, Canberra
Purchased 1986 86.1069.5

Portrait of Walter Mehring 1926 ^
oil on canvas, 110 x 78 cm
Koninklijk Museum voor Schone Kunsten, Antwerp 2454

Self-portrait with hat 1928
oil on canvas, 109.5 x 79 cm
Berlinische Galerie, Landesmuseum für Moderne Kunst, Fotografie und Architektur BG-M 3545/84

The powder-puff c1930
watercolour, 45.5 x 65 cm
Private collection, London

GEORGE GROSZ AND WIELAND HERZFELDE (1896–1988)
Cover of the journal 'Bankruptcy' no 3, 1919
letterpress, gillotage, 40 x 29 cm
National Gallery of Australia, Canberra
Purchased 1992 92.1346

RAOUL HAUSMANN (1886–1971)
Cover of the journal 'Der Dada' no 2, Dec 1919 ^
edited by Raoul Hausmann, John Heartfield and George Grosz, Malik-Verlag, Berlin
photolithograph, 29.2 x 22.8 cm
Berlinische Galerie, Landesmuseum für Moderne Kunst, Fotografie und Architektur BG-HHE I 12.55

Untitled [Portrait of Hannah Höch] 1931
gelatin silver photograph, 12.9 x 16.7 cm
Berlinische Galerie, Landesmuseum für Moderne Kunst, Fotografie und Architektur BG-FS 022/97

JOHN HEARTFIELD (1891–1968)
Cover of the newspaper 'Everyone His Own Football' vol 1, 15 Feb 1919
edited by Wieland Herzfelde, Malik-Verlag, Berlin and Leipzig
photomontages on front cover by John Heartfield and George Grosz, 42.8 x 29.3 cm
Akademie der Künste, Berlin, Kunstsammlung
JH 5279 •
DR 5600.2 ••

Cover of the journal 'Der Dada' no 3, Apr 1920
edited by Raoul Hausmann, John Heartfield and George Grosz, Malik-Verlag, Berlin
photolithograph, 23.2 x 15.7 cm
Akademie der Künste, Berlin, Kunstsammlung
JH 3800 •
JH lfd no 346 ••

Forced supplier of human material, take courage!
from the **Workers' Illustrated Paper**, vol 9, no 10, 1930, p 183
photolithograph, 36.2 x 25 cm
Akademie der Künste, Berlin, Kunstsammlung
JH 1244 •
JH 4 ••

Design for 'Adolf, the superman: swallows gold and spouts rubbish' c1932 •
photomontage, retouched, 70.5 x 59 cm
Akademie der Künste, Berlin, Kunstsammlung
JH 524

Adolf, the superman: swallows gold and spouts rubbish ••
from the **Workers' Illustrated Paper**, vol 11, no 29, 17 July 1932, p 675
photolithograph, 38 x 27 cm
Akademie der Künste, Berlin, Kunstsammlung
JH 2261

The meaning of Geneva: where capital lives, peace cannot live!
from the **Workers' Illustrated Paper**, vol 11, no 48, 27 Nov 1932, p 1137
photolithograph, 38 x 27 cm
Akademie der Künste, Berlin, Kunstsammlung
JH 29 •
JH 1258 ••

Goering: the executioner of the Third Reich
from the **Workers' Illustrated Paper**, vol 12, no 36, 14 Sept 1933, p 609
photolithograph, 38 x 27 cm
Akademie der Künste, Berlin, Kunstsammlung
JH 1261 (lfd no 426) •
JH 769 ••

As in the Middle Ages ... so in the Third Reich
from the **Workers' Illustrated Paper**, vol 13, no 22, 31 May 1934, p 352
photolithograph, 38 x 27 cm
Akademie der Künste, Berlin, Kunstsammlung
JH 71 •
JH 780 ••

Hurray, the butter is finished!
from the **Workers' Illustrated Paper**, vol 14, no 51, 19 Dec 1935, p 816
photolithograph, 38 x 27 cm
Akademie der Künste, Berlin, Kunstsammlung
JH 124 •
JH 1383 ••

RUDOLF HERRMANN (1879–1964)
Degenerate art 1938
colour lithograph, poster, 117.3 x 82.3 cm
Los Angeles County Museum of Art
Gift of the Robert Gore Rifkind Collection, Beverly Hills, CA M.2003.115.28

WIELAND HERZFELDE
SEE GEORGE GROSZ

LUDWIG HIRSCHFELD MACK
(1893–1965)

Untitled [Study for costume design] 1920 •
watercolour, pencil, 25.2 x 19.3 cm
National Gallery of Australia, Canberra
Gift of Olive Hirschfeld 1979 79.856

The accordion player c1922 ••
watercolour, gouache, pencil, 20.2 x 26 cm
National Gallery of Australia, Canberra
Gift of Olive Hirschfeld 1979 79.865 AB

City c1922
colour lithograph, 8.8 x 17.2 cm
National Gallery of Victoria, Melbourne
Gift of Mrs Olive Hirschfeld 1971 P70-1971

Reaching the stars 1922
colour lithograph, 42.3 x 31.6 cm
Art Gallery of New South Wales, Sydney
Purchased 1961 DA13.1961

Architecture 1923
colour lithograph, 18.7 x 23.6 cm
National Gallery of Victoria, Melbourne
Gift of Mrs Olive Hirschfeld 1971 P71-1971

HANNAH HÖCH (1889–1978)

Heads of state 1918–20
collage on iron-on embroidery pattern
16.2 x 23.3 cm
Institute for Foreign Cultural Relations, Stuttgart

On gold paper c1920 •
collage, 23.6 x 20.2 cm
National Gallery of Australia, Canberra
Purchased 1981 81.736

The coquette I 1923–25
collage, 18.5 x 20.5 cm
Institute for Foreign Cultural Relations, Stuttgart

Half-caste 1924
collage, 11 x 8.2 cm
Institute for Foreign Cultural Relations, Stuttgart

Balance 1925
collage, 30.5 x 20.3 cm
Institute for Foreign Cultural Relations, Stuttgart

Imaginary bridge 1926
oil on canvas, 65.5 x 72.5 cm
National Gallery of Australia, Canberra
Purchased 1983 83.3005

Love 1931 ••
from the series **Love**
photomontage, 21.8 x 21 cm
National Gallery of Australia, Canberra
Purchased 1983 83.15

Made for a party 1936
collage, 36 x 19.8 cm
Institute for Foreign Cultural Relations, Stuttgart

HEINRICH HOERLE (1895–1936)

Three invalids c1930
oil on plywood, 100 x 50 cm
Private collection

E O HOPPÉ (1878–1972)

A box containing wood fibres suspended from a crane in the background, chimneys and freezer towers of the UAN power station 1928
gelatin silver photograph, 29.1 x 21.6 cm
National Gallery of Australia, Canberra
Purchased 1980 80.3198

Bearing in an AC generator ('Ständer' einer Wechselstrommaschine) 1928
gelatin silver photograph, 20.5 x 26 cm
National Gallery of Australia, Canberra
Purchased 1980 80.3200

Rotating crane in a shipyard (Turmdrehkran auf einer Werft) 1928
gelatin silver photograph, 29.6 x 22.9 cm
National Gallery of Australia, Canberra
Purchased 1980 80.3185

KARL HUBBUCH (1891–1979)

The clairvoyant of Pristina 1921
etching, drypoint, 23.0 x 15.6 cm
Art Gallery of New South Wales, Sydney
Purchased 1989 50.1989

The longing for anyone 1922
etching, drypoint, 14.9 x 12.4 cm
Art Gallery of New South Wales, Sydney
Purchased 1989 52.1989

Twice Hilde II c1929
oil on canvas, 150 x 77 cm
Museo Thyssen-Bornemisza, Madrid 1978.88 (596)

JOHANNES ITTEN (1888–1967)

Composition 1919
lithograph, 29.2 x 29.5 cm
Art Gallery of New South Wales, Sydney
Purchased 1984 266.1984

CARL JAKOB JUCKER
SEE WILHELM WAGENFELD

WASSILY KANDINSKY (1866–1944)

Cup and saucer c1921–23
manufactured by the State Porcelain Factory, St Petersburg
porcelain, painted overglaze decoration
cup 6 x 8.1 x 6.1 cm diam
saucer 2.4 x 13 x 13 cm diam
National Gallery of Australia, Canberra
Purchased 1978 78.1291.a–b

Composition 1922 •^
from the portfolio **Bauhaus prints: new European graphic art IV: Italian & Russian artists** 1923–24
colour lithograph, 28 x 24 cm
National Gallery of Australia, Canberra
Felix Man Collection, Special Government Grant 1972
72.509.201

Small worlds III 1922 ••^
from the portfolio **Small worlds** 1922
colour lithograph, 27.8 x 23 cm
National Gallery of Australia, Canberra
The Poynton Bequest 2007 2007.1309

ALEXANDER KANOLDT (1881–1939)

Half nude II 1926
oil on canvas, 90.5 x 71 cm
Bayerische Staatsgemäldesammlungen, Munich
Pinakothek der Moderne, acquired 1971 14157

RICHARD KAUFFMANN (1887–1958)

Durchdringe Dich selbst oder: Ich umarme mich [I embrace myself] 1922
gelatin silver photograph, 10 x 7.8 cm
Berlinische Galerie, Landesmuseum für Moderne Kunst, Fotografie und Architektur BG-HHC-F 262/79

ERNST LUDWIG KIRCHNER (1880–1938)

Woman in a hat 1911
oil on canvas, 95 x 85 cm
State Art Collection, Art Gallery of Western Australia, Perth
Gift of Baron H H Thyssen-Bornemisza 1979

Nude looking over her shoulder c1912
black-dyed oakwood, 81 cm high
Stiftung museum kunst palast, Düsseldorf O.1957.9

Brown figures in café 1928–29
oil on canvas, 60.5 x 70 cm
Museum Ludwig, Cologne ML 10263

PAUL KLEE (1879–1940)

Hoffmannesque scene 1921 ^
from the portfolio **Bauhaus prints: new European graphic art I: masters of the State Bauhaus in Weimar** 1921–22
colour lithograph, 31.7 x 23 cm
Los Angeles County Museum of Art
Los Angeles County Fund 63.18

Lantern festival Bauhaus 1922
colour lithograph, 9.3 x 14.5 cm
National Gallery of Victoria, Melbourne
Gift of Mrs Olive Hirschfeld 1971 P55-1971

Thistle picture 1924
gouache, watercolour on linen laid on card
38.1 x 54.3 cm
National Gallery of Victoria, Melbourne
Purchased 1953 2999-4

CÉSAR KLEIN (1876–1954)

Workers citizens farmers soldiers ... 1919
colour lithograph, poster, 68.2 x 100 cm
Australian War Memorial, Canberra ARTV06638

Whoever does not work is the gravedigger for his own children nd
colour lithograph, poster, 114.9 x 78.4 cm
Los Angeles County Museum of Art
Gift of the Robert Gore Rifkind Foundation, Beverly Hills, CA M.2003.114.74

KÄTHE KOLLWITZ (1867–1945)

Memorial for Karl Liebknecht 1919–20
woodcut, 40.3 x 53.6 cm
Los Angeles County Museum of Art
Gift of Clifford Odets 60.65.4

Help Russia 1921 ••
lithograph, poster, 67 x 46.6 cm
National Gallery of Australia, Canberra
Purchased 1986 86.1068

The parents 1923
from the portfolio War 1924
woodcut, 47.8 x 59.4 cm
Australian War Memorial, Canberra ART50253

FRITZ LANG (1890–1976)

Metropolis 1927
10min excerpt, 16mm transferred to DVD
black and white, silent, German/English intertitles
original musical score by Gottfried Huppertz
Courtesy Potential Films, Melbourne
Production still courtesy of the British Film Institute and Transit Film GmbH

HANS LEISTIKOW (1892–1962)

The dwelling for minimal existence 1929
colour lithograph, poster, 117 x 84 cm
Kunstbibliothek Berlin, Staatliche Museen zu Berlin

OTTO LINDIG (1895–1966)

Cocoa pot, sugar bowl and two cups and saucers c1923
glazed earthenware
pot 19.6 x 14 x 12 cm
sugar bowl 8.4 x 9 cm diam
cup and saucer 7.6 x 15 cm diam
cup and saucer 7.8 x 15 cm diam
National Gallery of Australia, Canberra
Purchased 1988 88.1954.1–4

Covered punch bowl 1926
earthenware, 21.1 x 33.7 x 25 cm
National Gallery of Victoria, Melbourne
The LW Thompson Collection Bequest, 2004 2004.781.a–b

EL LISSITZKY (1890–1941)

Cover for the journal 'Wendingen' no 11, 1921
issue devoted to Frank Lloyd Wright, written by Dr H P Berlage, typography by H T Wijdeveld, Amsterdam, Holland, 1921
lithograph, 32.7 x 33.2 x 5 cm
Lent by the Powerhouse Museum, Sydney
Purchased 1997 97/242/1

Globetrotter (in time) 1923 •
from the portfolio **Victory over the sun** 1923
colour lithograph, 35.8 x 25.6 cm
National Gallery of Australia, Canberra
Purchased 1980 80.2319.6

New man 1923 ••
from the portfolio **Victory over the sun** 1923
colour lithograph, 31.1 x 32.1 cm
National Gallery of Australia, Canberra
Purchased 1980 80.2319.11

Plate c1923
manufactured by an unknown maker
unglazed earthenware, 2.6 x 11.9 cm diam
Lent by the Powerhouse Museum, Sydney
Purchased 2002 2003/137/1

Program for 'Merz matinées' 30 Dec 1923
letterpress, 22.5 x 27.9 cm
Berlinische Galerie, Landesmuseum für Moderne Kunst, Fotografie und Architektur
BG-HHE II 23.54 •
BG-HHE II 23.54a ••

Proun 1923
from the portfolio **Proun 1 Kestnermappe** 1923
lithograph with black collage, 60.6 x 44.4 cm
State Art Collection, Art Gallery of Western Australia, Perth
Purchased 1985 1985/00Q2.3

Proun 1923
from the portfolio **Proun 1 Kestnermappe** 1923
lithograph with red collage, 60.5 x 44.2 cm
State Art Collection, Art Gallery of Western Australia, Perth
Purchased 1985 1985/00Q2.6

Proun 1923
from the portfolio **Proun 1 Kestnermappe** 1923
lithograph, 44.2 x 60.5 cm
State Art Collection, Art Gallery of Western Australia, Perth
Purchased 1985 1985/00Q2.7

Kurt Schwitters 1924–25
gelatin silver photograph, 18.1 x 13 cm
J Paul Getty Museum, Los Angeles 96.XM.5

Untitled [Pressa catalogue] 1928
photocollage, ink, paint, 14.9 x 10.9 cm
Art Gallery of New South Wales, Sydney
Purchased 1997 61.1997

JEANNE MAMMEN (1890–1976)

Valeska Gert c1928–29
oil on canvas, 60 x 44 cm
Berlinische Galerie, Landesmuseum für Moderne Kunst, Fotografie und Architektur BG-M 0651/78

FELIX H MAN (1893–1985)

Entrance to Lunapark, Berlin 1929
gelatin silver photograph, 24.2 x 17.8 cm
National Gallery of Australia, Canberra
Purchased 1987 87.116

Kurfürstendamm after midnight, Berlin 1929
gelatin silver photograph, 18 x 24.3 cm
National Gallery of Australia, Canberra
Purchased 1987 87.1469

Lunapark 1929
gelatin silver photograph, 18.1 x 24.1 cm
National Gallery of Victoria, Melbourne
Purchased through The Art Foundation of Victoria with the assistance of The Herald & Weekly Times Limited, Fellow 1990 PH73.1990

Swimming rehearsal for Rhinemaidens, Bayreuth 1930
gelatin silver photograph, 20.5 x 15.2 cm
National Gallery of Victoria, Melbourne
Purchased through The Art Foundation of Victoria with the assistance of The Herald & Weekly Times Limited, Fellow 1990 PH75-1990

WERNER MANTZ (1901–1983)

Street in Cologne – Zollstock 1928
gelatin silver photograph, 17 x 22.8 cm
National Gallery of Australia, Canberra
Purchased 1984 84.554

Two towers, transport structure, commissioned by Staatsmijnen Heerlen, Netherlands 1937–38
gelatin silver photograph, 23 x 17.2 cm
National Gallery of Australia, Canberra
Purchased 1984 84.559

FRANZ MARC (1880–1916)

Story of creation II 1914
colour woodcut, 23.7 x 19.8 cm
Queensland Art Gallery, Brisbane
Purchased 1988, Queensland Art Gallery Foundation
1988.099

MARGARETE MARKS (1899–1990)

Tea set c1928
manufactured by Haël-Werkstätten
glazed earthenware slip cast
teapot 14 x 25.8 x 17.2 cm
sugar bowl 10 x 16 x 12.8 cm
milk jug 8.8 x 17 x 11.4 cm
cup 6.6 x 13.2 x 10.6 cm
saucer 13.8 cm diam
plate 19.4 cm diam
National Gallery of Australia, Canberra
Purchased with the assistance of Diana Woodlard 1988 88.1676.1–4

LUDWIG MEIDNER (1884–1966)

Apocalyptic landscape 1913
oil on canvas, 67.3 x 80 cm
Private collection, courtesy Richard Nagy, London

CARLO MENSE (1886–1965)

The painter Heinrich Maria Davringhausen 1922
oil on canvas, 86.5 x 59.5 cm
Museum Ludwig, Cologne ML 76/2777

Portrait of Underberg c1925
oil on canvas, 97 x 77.5 cm
Private collection

MARGARET MICHAELIS (1902–1985)

Untitled [Column with posters] c1932
gelatin silver photograph, 23.2 x 17.7 cm
National Gallery of Australia, Canberra
Gift of the estate of Margaret Michaelis-Sachs 1986
86.1384.130

LUCIA MOHOLY (1894–1989)

Bauhausneubau, Dessau (New Bauhaus building, Dessau) 1926
gelatin silver photograph, 8.3 x 10.7 cm
J Paul Getty Museum, Los Angeles 85.XP.384.44

LÁSZLÓ MOHOLY-NAGY (1895–1946)

Untitled, Weimar 1923–25
photogram, bromide gelatin silver print, 17.9 x 12.8 cm
Museum Folkwang, Essen 8/95

Untitled, Weimar 1923–25
photogram, bromide gelatin silver print, 17.8 x 12.8 cm
Museum Folkwang, Essen 10/95

[The law of the series] 1925
gelatin silver photograph, 21.6 x 16.2 cm
J Paul Getty Museum, Los Angeles 84.XM.997.3

Bauhaus balconies 1926
gelatin silver photograph, 49.5 x 39.3 cm
Collection of George Eastman House
Purchased from Mrs Sibyl Moholy-Nagy with funds provided by Eastman Kodak Company 1981:2163:0007

Fotogramm 1926
photogram, gelatin silver print, 23.8 x 17.7 cm
Collection of George Eastman House
Purchased from Mrs Sibyl Moholy-Nagy with funds provided by Eastman Kodak Company 1981:2163:0027

Lucia at the breakfast table 1926
gelatin silver photograph, 24.3 x 17.8 cm
National Gallery of Australia, Canberra
Purchased 1994 94.1097

Photogram self-portrait 1926
photogram, 36.1 x 24 cm
National Gallery of Australia, Canberra
Purchased 1984 84.2922

[Puppen (Dolls)] 1926–27
gelatin silver photograph, 23.5 x 17.6 cm
J Paul Getty Museum, Los Angeles 85.XP.260.194

Berlin radio tower c1928
gelatin silver photograph, 36 x 25.5 cm
Art Institute of Chicago, Chicago
Julien Levy Collection, Special Photography Acquisition Fund 1979 1979.84

Spring, Berlin 1928
gelatin silver photograph, 48 x 38 cm
Collection of George Eastman House
Gift of Katharine Kuh 1981:2164:0001

Das Lichtrequisit [Light-space modulator/Light prop/Requisite light for an electric stage] 1930
gelatin silver photograph, 24 x 18.1 cm
J Paul Getty Museum, Los Angeles 84.XP.912.3

EMIL NOLDE (1867–1956)

Head of a prophet 1912 ••^
from the portfolio **Genius I** 1919
woodcut, 22 x 15.4 cm (image), 34.8 x 25.4 cm (page)
National Gallery of Australia, Canberra
Gift of Orde Poynton Esq CMG 1990 90.1047.1

Conversation 1917 ^
woodcut, 24 x 31.5 cm
Sprengel Museum, Hanover Gr 1964/334

FELIX NUSSBAUM (1904–1944)

The mad square 1931
oil on canvas, 97 x 195.5 cm
Berlinische Galerie, Landesmuseum für Moderne Kunst, Fotografie und Architektur BG-M 0008/75

GEORG WILHELM PABST (1885–1967)

Pandora's box 1929
4min excerpt, 35mm transferred to DVD, black and white, silent, German intertitles
Courtesy Praesens-Film AG, Zurich
Production still courtesy of the British Film Institute

MAX PECHSTEIN (1881–1955)

To the lantern! c1919
colour lithograph, poster, 70.4 x 93 cm
Los Angeles County Museum of Art
Gift of the Robert Gore Rifkind Collection, Beverly Hills, CA M.2003.115.44

The National Assembly is the cornerstone of the German Socialist Republic 1919
colour lithograph, poster, 67.8 x 44.8 cm
Australian War Memorial, Canberra ARTV06661

HILDE REINDL (1909–)

Textile design c1928
watercolour, pencil, 13.8 x 13.8 cm
National Gallery of Australia, Canberra
Purchased 1988 88.1667

ALBERT RENGER-PATZSCH (1897–1966)

Harbour with crane c1927
gelatin silver photograph, 22.7 x 16.8 cm
National Gallery of Australia, Canberra
Purchased 1983 83.134

Railroad bridge c1927
gelatin silver photograph, 16.8 x 22.8 cm
National Gallery of Australia, Canberra
Purchased 1983 83.178

JOHANNES SAFIS (nd)

Bolshevism means to drown the world in blood 1919
colour lithograph, poster, 115.3 x 92.2 cm
Australian War Memorial, Canberra
Presented through the Cultural Gifts Program 2006 ARTV09316

AUGUST SANDER (1876–1964)

Painter's daughter 1925
from the project **People of the 20th century, III The woman, 16 The elegant woman**
gelatin silver photograph, 22.4 x 15.4 cm
National Gallery of Victoria, Melbourne
Purchased from admission funds 1988 PH84-1988

The painter Otto Dix and his wife, Martha 1925–26
printed by August Sander at the end of his career
from the project **People of the 20th century, III The woman, 13 Woman and man**
gelatin silver photograph, 24.7 x 21.7cm
Art Institute of Chicago, Chicago
Acquired through a grant from the Lloyd A Fry Foundation 1996 1996.91

Painter (Anton Räderscheidt) 1926
from the project **People of the 20th century, V The artists, 33 The painter**
gelatin silver photograph, 21.9 x 16.8 cm
Die Photographische Sammlung/SK Stiftung Kultur, August Sander Archiv, Cologne DGPH915

Circus artistes 1926–32
printed by August Sander in the 1950s
from the project **People of the 20th century, VI The city, 37 Travelling people – fair and circus**
gelatin silver photograph, 23.4 x 29.2 cm
Die Photographische Sammlung/SK Stiftung Kultur, August Sander Archiv, Cologne DGPH939

High school student, Cologne 1927
from the project **People of the 20th century, VI The city, 40 City youth**
gelatin silver photograph, 21.3 x 12.5 cm
J Paul Getty Museum, Los Angeles 84.XM.126.126

Match-seller 1927
from the project **People of the 20th century, IV Classes and professions, 27 The businessman**
gelatin silver photograph, 20.4 x 24.3 cm
Die Photographische Sammlung/SK Stiftung Kultur, August Sander Archiv, Cologne DGPH964

Secretary at West German Radio in Cologne 1931
printed by August Sander in the 1950s
from the project **People of the 20th century, III The woman, 17 The woman in intellectual and practical occupation**
gelatin silver photograph, 29 x 22 cm
Die Photographische Sammlung/SK Stiftung Kultur, August Sander Archiv, Cologne DGPH1016

CHRISTIAN SCHAD (1894–1982)

Schadograph no 10 1919
photogram, gelatin silver print, 7.9 x 5.6 cm
Museum of Fine Arts, Houston
Gift of Max and Isabell Smith Herzstein 88.15

Portrait of a woman 1920
painted wood, metal, 60 x 30 x 10.1 cm
Kerry Stokes Collection, Perth

Self-portrait 1927
oil on wood, 76 x 62 cm
Private collection, courtesy Tate London

OSKAR SCHLEMMER (1888–1943)

Group on banister I 1931
oil on canvas, 92.5 x 60.5 cm
Kunstsammlung Nordrhein-Westfalen, Düsseldorf 1038

RUDOLF SCHLICHTER (1890–1955)

Tingel tangel 1919–20
watercolour, 53 x 45.5 cm
Private collection

Meeting of fetishists and maniacal flagellants c1923
watercolour, 43.9 x 27.3 cm
Private collection

Sex murder 1924
watercolour, black chalk, 69 x 53 cm
Private collection

The embrace c1927–28
pencil, 45.5 x 58.5 cm
Private collection, London

GEORG SCHÖDL
SEE ARTHUR GRIMM

GEORG SCHOLZ (1890–1945)

Profiteering farming family 1920
colour lithograph, 26.5 x 35.5 cm
Private collection

Paper boy 1921
lithograph, 20.1 x 22 cm
Private collection

LOTHAR SCHREYER (1886–1966)

Figure of a lustful man for marionette theatre 1920•
colour lithograph, 39.8 x 29.8 cm
National Gallery of Australia, Canberra
Purchased 1990 90.1052

Figure of a lustful woman for marionette theatre 1920•
colour lithograph, 39.6 x 29.8 cm
National Gallery of Australia, Canberra
Purchased 1990 90.1053

Stage design for 'Sin' 1921 ••
watercolour, 48 x 31.6 cm
National Gallery of Australia, Canberra
Purchased 1981 81.2852

GEORG SCHRIMPF (1889–1938)

Hedwig Schrimpf 1922
oil on hardboard, 69 x 50 cm
Städtische Galerie im Lenbachhaus, Munich G12165

HEINZ SCHULZ-NEUDAMM (1899–1969)

Metropolis 1926
colour lithograph, poster, 211 x 96 cm
Austrian National Library, Picture Archives and Graphics Department, Vienna

KURT SCHWITTERS (1887–1948)

Untitled (Hanover and Hildesheim) 1928
collage, pasteboard, ribbon, threads, paper on paper, 11.7 x 9.1 cm (image), 29.7 x 22 cm (original mat)
Kurt und Ernst Schwitters Stiftung, Hanover
The foundation of the Kurt und Ernst Schwitters Stiftung is mainly due to the Schwitters family with the support of the NORD/LB Norddeutsche Landesbank, the Savings Bank Foundation of Lower Saxony, the Niedersächsische Lottostiftung, the Cultural Foundation of the Federal States, the State Minister at the Federal Chancellery for Media and Cultural Affairs, the Ministry for Science and Culture of the Land of Lower Saxony and the City of Hanover DISKUS obj/06830699

Merz drawing [FOX] 1930
collage, 15.6 x 14.9 cm (image), 30.8 x 22.7 cm (sheet)
National Gallery of Australia, Canberra
Purchased 1973 73.574

ROBERT SENNECKE (1885–1938)

Archival photographs of the *First International Dada Fair* held at the Otto Burchard Gallery, Berlin, 30 June – 25 Aug 1920
Obtained through the courtesy of the Berlinische Galerie, Landesmuseum für Moderne Kunst, Fotografie und Architektur, and Bildarchiv Preussischer Kulturbesitz, Berlin

WOLFGANG SIEVERS (1913–2007)

Blast furnace in the Ruhr, Germany 1933
gelatin silver photograph, 27.5 x 23 cm
National Gallery of Australia, Canberra
Purchased 1988 88.1913

Total poverty in Berlin, Germany 1933
gelatin silver photograph, 29 x 23.6 cm
National Gallery of Australia, Canberra
Purchased 1982 82.2191

LOTTE STAM-BEESE (1903–1988)

Group-portrait, weaving workshop at the Bauhaus, Dessau 1928
gelatin silver photograph, 8.4 cm diam
National Gallery of Australia, Canberra
Purchased 1984 84.2945

JOSEF VON STERNBERG (1894–1969)

Blue angel 1930
4min excerpt, 35mm transferred to DVD, black and white, English, original musical score by Friedrich Hollaender
Courtesy Transit Film GmbH
Production still courtesy Bildarchiv Preussischer Kulturbesitz, Berlin and Transit Film GmbH

GUNTA STÖLZL (1897–1983)

Textile design c1926
watercolour, gouache, pencil, 35.8 x 25 cm
National Gallery of Australia, Canberra
Purchased 1988 88.1678

LOUISE STRAUS-ERNST (1893–1944) with MAX ERNST (1891–1976)

Augustine, Thomas et Otto Flake 1920
collage, 23 x 13.5 cm
Sprengel Museum, Hanover F-B-S 16.C

FRIEDRICH STUCKENBERG (1881–1944)

Swimming and painting c1920–21 •
watercolour, 40 x 29 cm
Private collection, Melbourne

WILHELM WAGENFELD (1900–1990)

Tea service 1930
manufactured by Jenaer Glaswerk, Schott and Genossen
Jena heat-resistant glass
teapot 11.6 x 25.8 x 15.2 cm
sugar bowl 4.6 x 9.8 cm diam
milk jug 4.9 x 12 x 9.6 cm
cup 4.9 x 12 x 9.9 cm
saucer 1.3 x 14.9 cm diam
side plate 1.3 x 20 cm diam
National Gallery of Victoria, Melbourne
Helene Guilfoyle (née Steiert) Bequest, 2004 2004.700.a-g.3

'Kubus-Geschirr' stacking set of containers 1938
manufactured by Vereinigte Lausitzer Glaswerke
pressed glass, 16.5 x 18 x 18 cm
National Gallery of Australia, Canberra
Purchased from Gallery Restaurant Funds 1987 87.354.1-10

WILHELM WAGENFELD (1900–1990) AND CARL JAKOB JUCKER (1902–1997)

Table lamp (MT 9/ME 1) 1923–24
manufactured by the Bauhaus Metal Workshop, Weimar
nickel-plated brass, opalescent glass with plate-glass base, 37 x 18 x 18 cm
Die Neue Sammlung – The International Design Museum Munich
Purchased through the generosity of Osram GmbH, Munich 285/2005

ROBERT WIENE (1873–1938)

The cabinet of Dr Caligari 1919 ••
5min excerpt, 35mm transferred to DVD, black and white, silent, German intertitles (English subtitles)
Courtesy Transit Film GmbH
Production still courtesy of the British Film Institute and Transit Film GmbH

WILLY ZIELKE (1902–1988)

Light in the night 1930
gelatin silver photograph, 17.5 x 17.4 cm
Art Gallery of New South Wales, Sydney
Purchased with funds provided by the Photography Collection Benefactors' Program 2003 15.2003

UNKNOWN ARTIST

***Degenerate art* exhibition in the inner courtyard of the Dresden Town Hall** 1933
4.30min excerpt, 35mm transferred to dvcam tape, black and white, silent, German intertitles
Bundesfilmarchiv/Transit Film GmbH

UNKNOWN MAKER

Table c1925–27
lacquered wood, 80.6 x 104.8 x 70 cm
Collection Vitra Design Museum MGE-1018-C

ACKNOWLEDGMENTS

An exhibition of this scope and complexity would not have been possible without the help of many individuals and institutions. I wish to warmly thank the following colleagues, curators, scholars and lenders for their generosity and support in helping me to develop this exhibition over the many years it has taken to realise this project.

Firstly, I wish to thank Edmund Capon, director and chief curator, Art Gallery of New South Wales, and Gerard Vaughan, director, National Gallery of Victoria, for embracing and supporting this project so enthusiastically through each stage of its development. At the Art Gallery of New South Wales, I also acknowledge the generous support of Anne Flanagan, deputy director, and Erica Drew, senior exhibitions manager, for their excellent management of the exhibition. Charlotte Cox, exhibitions registrar, and Charlotte Davy, senior exhibitions registrar, have overseen the complex task of managing the loan logistics and deserve great thanks for their efforts. Donna Brett, manager, copyright, has assisted the project substantially and I thank her for dealing with all matters pertaining to copyright and image usage and for coordinating numerous enquiries regarding curatorial research. Special thanks also goes to Michelle Andringa, rights and images coordinator, for coordinating film rights and usage. I acknowledge Karen Hancock for her inspired brilliance in designing this publication, and Paige Amor for her efforts in editing such a large and multi-faceted publication. Other individuals I would like to thank at the Gallery are Tony Bond, Terence Maloon, Judy Annear, Josephine Touma, Claire Martin, Robert Herbert, Craig Brush, Molly Waugh, Lisa Franey, Cara Hickman, Tanguy Le Moing, Jenni Carter and Vivian Huang.

Special gratitude is extended to our colleagues at the National Gallery of Victoria, who have supported the exhibition since its inception: Frances Lindsay, deputy director; Nicole Monteiro, exhibitions manager; Cherie McNair, senior exhibitions coordinator; Daryl West-Moore, senior exhibitions designer; Denise McCann, senior registrar, exhibitions; Janine Bofill, registrar; Ted Gott, senior curator, international art; Gina Panebianco, head of education and programs; and Jennie Moloney, senior publications coordinator. In particular, I would like to thank Petra Kayser, curator, Department of Prints and Drawings, and Maggie Finch, assistant curator, Department of Photography, for coordinating the display of the exhibition at the National Gallery of Victoria and for contributing insightful thematic essays to the catalogue.

We have collaborated with many art galleries, museums, private collectors and other organisations around the world to bring these important works of art to Sydney and Melbourne. Museum colleagues in Germany who have been generous with loans include: Freya Mülhaupt, Heinz Stahlhut and Ulrich Domröse, Berlinische Galerie; Anita Beloubek-Hammer, Kupferstichkabinett, Berlin; Moritz Wullen, Kunstbibliothek, Berlin; Rosa von der Schulenburg and Peter Zimmermann, Kunstsammlung, Akademie der Künste, Berlin; Kasper König, Stephan Diederich and Emily Evans, Museum Ludwig Cologne; Gabriele Conrath-Scholl and Rajka Knipper, Die Photographische Sammlung/SK Stiftung Kultur, Cologne; Beat Wismer and Kay Heymer, Museum Kunst Palast, Düsseldorf; Marion Ackermann and Annette Krusinsky, Kunstsammlung Nordrhein-Westfalen, Düsseldorf; Ute Eskildsen, Museum Folkwang Essen; Ulrich Krempel and Isabel Schulz, Sprengel Museum Hanover/Kurt und Ernst Schwitters Stiftung, Hanover; Carla Schulz-Hoffmann, Bayersiche Staatsgemäldesammlungen, Pinakothek der Moderne, Munich; Florian Hufnagel and Josef Strasser, Die Neue Sammlung – The International Design Museum Munich; Karin Althaus, Lenbachhaus, Munich; Hermann Arnhold and Erich Franz, Landesmuseum für Kunst und Kulturgeschichte, Münster; Daniel Spanke, Kunstmuseum Stuttgart; Sean Rainbird, Staatsgalerie Stuttgart; Nina Bingel, Institute for Foreign Cultural Relations, Stuttgart; and Alexander von Vegesack and Serge Mauduit, Vitra Design Museum, Weil am Rhein. I would like to extend special thanks to Elisabeth Giese in Munich for coordinating the loan of an important group of works from private collections in Germany. I also acknowledge the generous assistance of the German Consul General, Hans Gnodtke, who enthusiastically supported the project and endorsed our loan requests to museums in Germany.

I would also like to acknowledge the assistance of the following colleagues in the United States: James Cuno and James Rondeau, Art Institute of Chicago; Peter Marzio and Anne Tucker, Museum of Fine Arts, Houston; Anne Lyden and Virginia Heckert, J Paul Getty Museum, Los Angeles; Thomas Gaehtgens, Getty Research Institute, Los Angeles; Stephanie Barron and Timothy Benson, Los Angeles County Museum of Art, Los Angeles; Brent R Benjamin and Andrew Walker, Saint Louis Art Museum, Saint Louis; Anthony Bannon, Alison Nordström and Joe Struble, George Eastman House, Rochester; and Don Bacigalupi and Amy Gilman, Toledo Museum of Art, Toledo. In Europe and the United Kingdom I wish to thank Paul Huvenne and Yolande Duckers, Koninklijk Museum voor Schone Kunsten, Antwerp; Vicente Todoli and Matthew Gale, Tate, London; Guillermo Solana, Museo Thyssen-Bornemisza, Madrid; and Christian Maryška, Austrian National Library, Vienna.

In Australia I wish to thank: Tony Ellwood, Queensland Art Gallery/Gallery of Modern Art, Brisbane; Steve Gower, Lola Wilkins and Warwick Heywood, Australian War Memorial, Canberra; Ron Radford, Christine Dixon, Jane Kinsman, Gael Newton, Anne O'Hehir, Robert Bell and Nick Nicholson, National Gallery of Australia, Canberra; Gerard Vaughan and Frances Lindsay, National Gallery of Victoria, Melbourne; Stefano Carboni, Gary Dufour and Melissa Harpley, Art Gallery of Western Australia, Perth; Dawn Casey and Eva Czernis-Ryl, Powerhouse Museum, Sydney; and all the staff at the Art Gallery of New South Wales, Sydney.

I am greatly indebted to Richard Nagy in London, Richard Feigen in New York and Michael Hasenclever in Munich for their help in securing critical loans from private collections. I would also like to thank Barry Humphries, James Fairfax, David Sampietro and Kerry Stokes for their generous loans. I am especially grateful to have had the opportunity to discuss the project with the late Nick Waterlow, who generously championed the exhibition. Sincere thanks goes to Frank McDonald for the many stimulating conversations we have had on German art. I also thank Andrew Schapiro for helping to locate the superb suite of Bauhaus furniture in Australia and Hannah Fink for her comments and advice regarding authors.

I have carried out scholarly and curatorial research over a number of years both in Australia and Germany, and would like to thank the University of Sydney, German Academic Exchange Service (DAAD), University of Melbourne, and Goethe-Institut for supporting my research at various critical stages. The exhibition research has been assisted by the help of many scholars and curators who have answered questions and generously offered information. In particular, I would like to thank the members of the international curatorium: Jill Lloyd, Matthias Eberle, Carla Schulz-Hoffmann and Sean Rainbird for their guidance and wide-ranging scholarly contributions to the project. In addition, the catalogue has been greatly enhanced by the contributions of Eric Hobsbawm, Brigid Doherty, Karen Koehler and Uwe Fleckner. I am indebted to Volker Weidhaas and Dirk Schaefer at the Berlinische Galerie, Landesmuseum für Moderne Kunst, Fotografie und Architektur for helping us to obtain the archival film of the 1933 *Degenerate art* exhibition in Dresden. I also acknowledge the valuable assistance of Kelly McDonald for her work on the Bauhaus artists and Victoria Tokarowski for researching works by Marcel Breuer, Wilhelm Wagenfeld, Ludwig Hirschfeld Mack, Gunta Stölzl and Oskar Schlemmer. I also warmly acknowledge the assistance of Sabine Scholz who helped to translate two of the essays. My final thanks is extended to the many people in and outside of the art world who have discussed this project with me over the years: their interest, passion and shared excitement in this highly relevant chapter in modern European art and culture have encouraged me to realise this ambitious and long-overdue exhibition and publication.

Jacqueline Strecker

LENDERS TO THE EXHIBITION

Museums and galleries

Australia	Art Gallery of New South Wales, Sydney Art Gallery of Western Australia, Perth Australian War Memorial, Canberra Gallery of Modern Art/Queensland Art Gallery, Brisbane National Gallery of Australia, Canberra National Gallery of Victoria, Melbourne Powerhouse Museum, Sydney
Austria	Austrian National Library, Vienna
Belgium	Koninklijk Museum voor Schone Kunsten, Antwerp
Germany	Akademie der Künste, Berlin, Kunstsammlung Bayerische Staatsgemäldesammlungen, Pinakothek der Moderne, Munich Berlinische Galerie, Landesmuseum für Moderne Kunst, Fotographie und Architektur, Berlin Folkwang Museum, Essen Institute for Foreign Cultural Relations, Stuttgart Kunstbibliothek, Staatliche Museen zu Berlin, Berlin Kunstmuseum Stuttgart, Stuttgart Kunstsammlung Nordrhein-Westfalen, Düsseldorf Kupferstichkabinett, Staatliche Museen zu Berlin, Berlin Kurt und Ernst Schwitters Stiftung, Hanover Landesmuseum für Kunst und Kulturgeschichte, Münster Museum Ludwig, Cologne Die Neue Sammlung – The International Design Museum Munich Die Photographische Sammlung/SK Stiftung Kultur, August Sander Archiv, Cologne Sprengel Museum, Hanover Staatsgalerie Stuttgart, Stuttgart Städtische Galerie im Lenbachhaus, Munich Stiftung Museum Kunst Palast, Düsseldorf Vitra Design Museum, Weil am Rhein
Spain	Museo Thyssen-Bornemisza, Madrid
United Kingdom	Tate, London
United States	Art Institute of Chicago, Chicago George Eastman House, International Museum of Photography and Film, Rochester J Paul Getty Museum, Los Angeles Los Angeles County Museum of Art, Los Angeles Museum of Fine Arts, Houston Saint Louis Art Museum, Saint Louis Toledo Museum of Art, Toledo
Private collections	James Fairfax, Sydney Barry Humphries, London David Sampietro, Melbourne Kerry Stokes, Perth Anonymous lenders

INTERNATIONAL CURATORIUM

Edmund Capon is director and chief curator at the Art Gallery of New South Wales, where he has curated an extensive range of exhibitions encompassing Asian, European and Australian art. Recent exhibitions include *The first emperor: China's entombed warriors*, *Giacometti: sculpture, prints and drawings from the Fondation Maeght*, *Darkness and light: Caravaggio and his world*, *Buddha: radiant awakening* and *Jeffrey Smart*. He has written numerous books and articles covering a broad range of artistic, archaeological and arts-related matters.

Matthias Eberle is professor of cultural history at the Kunsthochschule in Berlin (see opposite).

Jill Lloyd is an independent curator, lecturer and writer based in London, specialising in German modernism (see opposite).

Sean Rainbird is director of the Staatsgalerie Stuttgart. He was previously senior curator at Tate Modern, where he curated numerous exhibitions on German modernism, including *Kandinsky: the path to abstraction* and *Max Beckmann*. He has recently curated *Edward Burne-Jones: the earthly paradise* for the Staatsgalerie Stuttgart and the Kunstmuseum Bern.

Carla Schulz-Hoffmann is deputy director of the General Bavarian State Collections and chief curator at the Pinakothek der Moderne in Munich. Professor Schulz-Hoffmann has curated numerous exhibitions on 20th-century German art, including *Max Beckmann: exile in Amsterdam*, *Cy Twombly*, *The painter Max Beckmann* and *Georg Baselitz*.

Jacqueline Strecker is guest curator at the Art Gallery of New South Wales (see opposite).

Gerard Vaughan is director of the National Gallery of Victoria, Melbourne. He was previously director of the British Museum Development Trust. He has broad interests in art and architectural history, and has specialised in the history of taste and collecting in the 18th and 19th centuries.

CONTRIBUTORS

Brigid Doherty teaches the history of modern art and aesthetic theory at Princeton University. She has contributed catalogue essays for the *Dada* exhibition at the National Gallery of Art, Washington, DC, and the Museum of Modern Art, New York (2006), the *Bauhaus* exhibition at the Museum of Modern Art (2009), and for numerous exhibitions of the work of artists Hanne Darboven and Rosemarie Trockel. She is an editor of a volume of the work of Walter Benjamin, *The work of art in the age of its technological reproducibility and other writings on media* (2008).

Matthias Eberle is professor of cultural history at the Kunsthochschule in Berlin. He has organised numerous exhibitions of modern German art and has written extensively on the subject. Professor Eberle has contributed to the Metropolitan Museum of Art's exhibition catalogue *Glitter and doom: German portraits from the 1920s*.

Maggie Finch is assistant curator of photography at the National Gallery of Victoria. She has written articles and curated exhibitions on a broad range of topics including travel photography of the 19th century, photography and archives, space photography and contemporary photography.

Uwe Fleckner is professor in art history at the University of Hamburg and director of the Warburg-House in Hamburg. He recently held an appointment as the Gerda Henkel visiting professor of German Studies at Stanford University. Professor Fleckner has written on many aspects of modern German art and culture, and is widely recognised as one of the leading scholars on 'Degenerate' art.

Eric Hobsbawm is emeritus professor at the School of History, Classics and Archaeology, Birkbeck College, University of London. Professor Hobsbawm is the author of numerous publications, including *The age of revolution*, *The age of capital*, *The age of empire*, *The age of extremes* and, most recently, *How to change the world*.

Petra Kayser is curator of prints and drawings at the National Gallery of Victoria. Her research interests include the art of the Weimar Republic and 16th-century Wunderkammer collections. Dr Kayser has published numerous articles and curated exhibitions on themes including satirical art in the 18th and 19th centuries.

Karen Koehler is professor of art and architectural history at Hampshire College. She teaches courses in modern and contemporary architecture, painting, sculpture, photography and design. Professor Koehler has published widely on Bauhaus art and architecture and is currently writing a book on the Bauhaus for Phaidon Press.

Jill Lloyd is an independent curator, lecturer and writer based in London, specialising in German modernism. She has curated exhibitions on Max Beckmann, Ernst Ludwig Kirchner, Christian Schad and Van Gogh for the Neue Galerie in New York. Dr Lloyd is the author of *German Expressionism: primitivism and modernity*.

Jacqueline Strecker is guest curator at the Art Gallery of New South Wales. She has lectured and published widely on German modernism since completing her PhD on the art of the Weimar Republic. Dr Strecker has curated numerous exhibitions including *Rembrandt*, *Giacometti* and *The art of the First World War*. All entries on works in *The mad square* are by Jacqueline Strecker (JS).

IMAGE CREDITS

The Art Gallery of New South Wales thanks the copyright holders for granting permission to reproduce works illustrated in this publication. Every effort has been made to contact the copyright holders and any omissions will be corrected in future editions providing the publisher has been notified in writing.

Abbreviation: Lic Viscopy *for* Licensed by Viscopy, Sydney/Australia

Cover Photo: © Tate, London 2011. © George Grosz / VG Bild-Kunst, Bonn. Lic Viscopy

pp 4–5 © Felix Nussbaum / VG Bild-Kunst, Bonn. Lic Viscopy

pp 10, 11 Photo: Sotheby's Picture Library. © Ludwig Meidner-Archiv. Jüdisches Museum der Stadt Frankfurt am Main

p 14 Photo: Courtesy of George Eastman House, International Museum of Photography and Film. © László Moholy-Nagy / VG Bild-Kunst, Bonn. Lic Viscopy

p 19 © Estate of Margaret Michaelis-Sachs

p 22 Photo: © Karl Hubbuch, Sydney 2011. Provenance: Museo Thyssen-Bornemisza. © The artist's estate

p 25 Photo: © George Grosz, Sydney, 2011. Provenance: Museo Thyssen-Bornemisza. © George Grosz / VG Bild-Kunst, Bonn. Lic Viscopy

p 26 Photo: © bpk Berlin / Kupferstichkabinett, Staatliche Museen zu Berlin / Jörg P Anders. © Max Beckmann / VG Bild-Kunst, Bonn. Lic Viscopy

p 29 Photo: The J Paul Getty Museum, Los Angeles. © László Moholy-Nagy / VG Bild-Kunst, Bonn. Lic Viscopy

p 32 © Otto Dix / VG Bild-Kunst, Bonn. Lic Viscopy

p 35 (left) Photo: courtesy Museum Ludwig, Cologne

p 35 (right) © George Grosz/VG Bild-Kunst, Bonn. Lic Viscopy

p 37 Photo: Christopher Snee AGNSW. © George Grosz / VG Bild-Kunst, Bonn. Lic Viscopy

p 38 Photo © LWL-Landesmuseum für Kunst und Kulturgeschichte Münster / Sabine Ahlbrand-Dornseif. © Otto Dix / VG Bild-Kunst, Bonn. Lic Viscopy

p 41 Photo: © bpk Berlin / Kupferstichkabinett, Staatliche Museen zu Berlin / Jörg P Anders. © Max Beckmann / VG Bild-Kunst, Bonn. Lic Viscopy

p 43 Photo: State Art Collection, Art Gallery of Western Australia

p 45 Photo: Sotheby's Picture Library. © Ludwig Meidner-Archiv. Jüdisches Museum der Stadt Frankfurt am Main

p 46 Photo: Rheinisches Bildarchiv Köln

p 47 Photo: Rheinisches Bildarchiv Köln

p 49 Photo: © bpk Berlin / Bayerische Staatsgemäldesammlungen. © Renata Davringhausen c/o Leopold-Hoesch-Museum Düren

p 51 Photo: © Tate, London 2011. © George Grosz / VG Bild-Kunst, Bonn. Lic Viscopy

p 52, 53 (left) and (right) © George Grosz / VG Bild-Kunst, Bonn. Lic Viscopy

pp 55, 56, 57 & 58 © Otto Dix / VG Bild-Kunst, Bonn. Lic Viscopy (p 58 Photo: Diana Panuccio AGNSW)

p 59 (left) & (right) Photo: Diana Panuccio AGNSW. © The artist's estate

pp 61, 62 & 63 © Max Beckmann / VG Bild-Kunst, Bonn. Lic Viscopy (p 62 Photo: Chilin Gieng AGNSW; p 63 Photo: Jenni Carter AGNSW)

p 64 & 66 © Käthe Kollwitz / VG Bild-Kunst, Bonn. Lic Viscopy

pp 65, 67 & 69 Digital image © 2009 Museum Associates / LACMA / Art Resource, NY / VG Bild-Kunst, Bonn. Lic Viscopy (p 65 © Käthe Kollwitz; p 67 © Max Pechstein; p 69 © César Klein)

p 66 (left) © Max Pechstein / Bild-Kunst. Lic Viscopy

p 68 © César Klein / VG Bild-Kunst, Bonn. Lic Viscopy

pp 70 & 71 © The artist's estate

p 72 Production still courtesy of the British Film Institute and Transit Film GmbH © Friedrich-Wilhelm-Murnau-Foundation, Wiesbaden

p 73 Österreichische Nationalbibliothek, Vienna, Sammlung Donau

p 76 Photo: © Institut für Auslandsbeziehungen e.V., Stuttgart © Hannah Höch / VG Bild-Kunst, Bonn. Lic Viscopy

p 79 (left) Photo: Akademie der Künste, Berlin, Kunstsammlung, Heartfield 5279 / Roman März / AdK © The Heartfield Community of Heirs / VG Bild-Kunst, Bonn. Lic Viscopy

p 79 (right) © George Grosz / VG Bild-Kunst, Bonn. Lic Viscopy

p 81 (top) Courtesy Berlinische Bildarchiv Preussischer Kulturbesitz, Berlin

p 81 (bottom) © The Heartfield Community of Heirs / VG Bild-Kunst, Bonn. Lic Viscopy

p 82 Photo: courtesy Berlinische Bildarchiv Preussischer Kulturbesitz, Berlin

p 85 (top) © Friedel Scholz, Waldkirch

p 85 (bottom) © Friedel Scholz, Waldkirch

pp 86, 87, 88 & 89 © George Grosz / VG Bild-Kunst, Bonn. Lic Viscopy

p 91 Photo: © Institut für Auslandsbeziehungen e.V., Stuttgart © Hannah Höch / VG Bild-Kunst, Bonn. Lic Viscopy

p 93 (left) Photo: Akademie der Künste, Berlin, Kunstsammlung, Heartfield 1459 / Roman März / AdK © The Heartfield Community of Heirs / VG Brild-Kunst, Bonn. Lic Viscopy

p 93 (right) © Raoul Hausmann / VG Bild-Kunst, Bonn. Lic Viscopy

p 94 & 95 © Christian Schad Stiftung Aschaffenburg. VG Bild-Kunst, Bonn. Lic Viscopy

p 97 Photo: Michael Herling / Aline Gwose © Max Ernst and Louise Straus-Ernst / ADAGP. Lic Viscopy

pp 99, 100 (right) © Hannah Höch / VG Bild-Kunst, Bonn. Lic Viscopy

p 100 (left) Photo: © Institut für Auslandsbeziehungen e.V., Stuttgart © Hannah Höch / VG Bild-Kunst, Bonn. Lic Viscopy

pp 101, 102 & 103 Photo: © Institut für Auslandsbeziehungen e.V., Stuttgart© Hannah Höch / VG Bild-Kunst, Bonn. Lic Viscopy

p 104 © Hannah Höch / VG Bild-Kunst, Bonn. Lic Viscopy

p 105 (top) © Raoul Hausmann / VG Bild-Kunst, Bonn. Lic Viscopy

p 105 (bottom) © The artist's estate

p 106 Photo: The J Paul Getty Museum, Los Angeles © El Lissitzky / VG Bild-Kunst. Licensed by Viscopy, Sydney

p 107 Photo: Kurt Schwitters-Archiv. Michael Herling / Aline Gwose © Kurt Schwitters / VG Bild-Kunst, Bonn. Lic Viscopy

p 108 © Kurt Schwitters / VG Bild-Kunst, Bonn. Lic Viscopy

p 109 © El Lissitzky / VG Bild-Kunst. Lic Viscopy

p 112 Photo: Courtesy of George Eastman House, International Museum of Photography and Film. © László Moholy-Nagy / VG Bild-Kunst, Bonn. Lic Viscopy

p 115 (top left) Photo: The J Paul Getty Museum, Los Angeles © Lucia Moholy / VG Bild-Kunst, Bonn. Lic Viscopy

p 115 (top right) © Gertrud Arndt / VG Bild-Kunst, Bonn. Lic Viscopy

p 115 (bottom right) Photo: The J Paul Getty Museum, Los Angeles © T Lux Feininger

p 115 (bottom left) © The artist's estate

p 116 © Estate of Ludwig Hirschfeld Mack

p 119 Photo: Chilin Gieng AGNSW © Johannes Itten / OOAS. Lic Viscopy

p 120 (top) Photo: Courtesy National Gallery of Victoria, Melbourne

p 120 (bottom) Digital image © 2009 Museum Associates / LACMA / Art Resource, NY

p 122 (top & bottom) © Otto Lindig Estate

p 123 © Margarete Marks Estate

p 125 Photo: Walter Klein © 2011 The Oskar Schlemmer Estate and Archives, Secretariat: IT-28824 Oggebbio (VB), Italy, www.schlemmer.org

p 126 (left & right) © László Moholy-Nagy / VG Bild-Kunst, Bonn. Lic Viscopy

p 127 Photo: Courtesy of George Eastman House, International Museum of Photography and Film © László Moholy-Nagy / VG Bild-Kunst, Bonn. Lic Viscopy

pp 128 & 129 © László Moholy-Nagy / VG Bild-Kunst, Bonn. Lic Viscopy

pp 130, 131, 132, 133 © Estate of Ludwig Hirschfeld Mack (p 131 Photo: Chilin Gieng AGNSW)

pp 134 & 135 Photo: Courtesy National Gallery of Victoria, Melbourne

pp 137, 138 & 139 © Wassily Kandinsky / ADAGP. Lic Viscopy

pp 140 (left & right) **& 141** © Lothar Schreyer Estate

p 142 © Herbert Bayer / VG Bild-Kunst, Bonn. Lic Viscopy

p 143 Photo: The J Paul Getty Museum, Los Angeles © The artist's estate

p 144 (left) © Irene Bayer Estate

p 144 (right) Photo: The J Paul Getty Museum, Los Angeles © T Lux Feininger

p 145 & 322 Photograph by Greg Harris. Reproduction, The Art Institute of Chicago © The artist's estate

pp 146 & 147 Photo: © bpk / Kunstbibliothek, Staatliche Museen zu Berlin / Dietmar Katz (p 146 © Hans Leistikow Estate; p 147 © Willi Baumeister) / VG Bild Kunst, Bonn. Lic Viscopy

pp 148 (left & right) **& 149** Photo: Vitra Design Museum, Weil am Rhein

p 149 Photo: Thomas Dix / Courtesy Vitra Design Museum, Weil am Rhein

pp 150 & 151 © Erich Dieckmann Estate

p 152 (top & bottom) © Wilhelm Wagenfeld / VG Bild-Kunst, Bonn. Lic Viscopy

p 153 Photo: Die Neue Sammlung - The International Design Museum Munich © Wilhelm Wagenfeld / VG Bild-Kunst, Bonn. Lic Viscopy

p 155 Photo: Marinco Kojdanovski, Powerhouse Museum © Marianne Brandt / VG Bild-Kunst, Bonn. Lic Viscopy

p 157 © Gunta Stölzl, Lic Viscopy

pp 158 & 159 (top & bottom) © Lena Bergner Estate

p 158 (bottom) © The artist

p 159 (top) © The artist's estate

pp 162 & 165 © El Lissitzky / VG Bild-Kunst. Lic Viscopy (p 162 Photo: Sotha Bourn, Powerhouse Museum)

p 166 Photo: The Art Institute of Chicago © László Moholy-Nagy / VG Bild-Kunst, Bonn. Lic Viscopy

pp 168 & 169 Photo: The J Paul Getty Museum, Los Angeles © László Moholy-Nagy / VG Bild-Kunst, Bonn. Lic Viscopy

pp 170 & 171 © Curatorial Assistance, Inc / E O Hoppé Estate Collection

pp 172 & 173 © Estate of Wolfgang Sievers

p 175 Photo: Ray Woodbury AGNSW © Erich Buchholz Estate

pp 176, 177 (left & right) Photo: State Art Collection, Art Gallery of Western Australia © El Lissitzky / VG Bild-Kunst. Lic Viscopy

p 178 © El Lissitzky / VG Bild-Kunst. Lic Viscopy

p 179 (top left) Photo: Diana Panuccio, AGNSW © El Lissitzky / VG Bild-Kunst. Lic Viscopy

p 179 (top right & bottom) © El Lissitzky / VG Bild-Kunst. Lic Viscopy (Photo: Sotha Bourn top right & Marinco Kojdanovski bottom, Powerhouse Museum)

p 181 Photo: Courtesy private collection

p 182 © Curatorial Assistance, Inc / E O Hoppé Estate Collection

p 183 (top & bottom) © Werner Mantz / VG Bild-Kunst, Bonn. Lic Viscopy

pp 184 & 185 © Albert Renger-Patzch-Archiv / Ann und Jurgen Wilde. VG Bild-Kunst, Bonn / Lic Viscopy

p 187 Photograph: Ernst Reinhold, München © VG Bild-Kunst, Bonn

p 190 Photo: Photography Incorporated, Toledo © Max Beckmann / VG Bild-Kunst, Bonn. Lic Viscopy

p 192 Production still courtesy of the British Film Institute and Transit Film GmbH

p 193 (left & right) Photo: courtesy Austrian National Library, Vienna

p 194 (top) Production still courtesy of BPK, Berlin and Transit Film GmbH © Friedrich-Wilhelm-Murnau-Foundation, Wiesbaden

p 194 (bottom) Production still courtesy of the British Film Institute © Praesens-Film AG, Zürich

pp 197, 198 & 199 (top & bottom) © Felix H Man Estate

p 201 Photo: Diana Panuccio AGNSW © The artist's estate

p 202 Photo: Diana Panuccio AGNSW © Max Beckmann / VG Bild-Kunst, Bonn. Lic Viscopy

p 203 Photo: Photography Incorporated, Toledo © Max Beckmann / VG Bild-Kunst, Bonn. Lic Viscopy

p 204 Photo: Mim Stirling AGNSW © Max Beckmann / VG Bild-Kunst, Bonn. Lic Viscopy

p 205 (top) © Max Beckmann / VG Bild-Kunst, Bonn. Lic Viscopy

p 205 (bottom) © Max Beckmann / VG Bild-Kunst, Bonn. Lic Viscopy

pp 207, 208, 209 & 210 © Rudolf Schlichter Estate, courtesy Galerie Alvensleben, Munich

p 211 © George Grosz / VG Bild-Kunst, Bonn. Lic Viscopy

pp 213 & 214 (left & right) © Die Photographische Sammlung / SK Stiftung Kultur – August Sander Archiv, Cologne. Lic Viscopy

p 215 (left) Photo: The J Paul Getty Museum, Los Angeles © J Paul Getty Trust

pp 215, 216 & 217 © Die Photographische Sammlung / SK Stiftung Kultur – August Sander Archiv, Cologne. Lic Viscopy (p 215 right Photo: Greg Williams, The Art Institute of Chicago)

pp 219, 220 (left & right), **221** (top & bottom), **222 & 223** Photo: Rheinisches Bildarchiv Köln © Hugo Erfurth / VG Bild-Kunst, Bonn. Lic Viscopy

p 226 © Christian Schad Stiftung Aschaffenburg. VG Bild-Kunst, Bonn. Lic Viscopy

p 229 Photo: Rheinisches Bildarchiv Köln © Otto Dix / VG Bild-Kunst, Bonn. Lic Viscopy

p 230 Photo: © Royal Museum of Fine Arts Antwerp © Lukas-Art in Flanders vzw © George Grosz / VG Bild-Kunst, Bonn. Lic Viscopy

p 233 © George Grosz/VG Bild-Kunst, Bonn. Lic Viscopy

p 234 Photo: Städtische Galerie im Lenbachhaus, München

p 237 Photo: © bpk, Berlin / Bayerische Staatsgemäldesammlungen

p 238 © The artist's estate

p 239 Photo: Rheinisches Bildarchiv Köln © The artist's estate

p 241 Photo: © Staatsgalerie Stuttgart © Otto Dix / VG Bild-Kunst, Bonn. Lic Viscopy

p 243 © Christian Schad Stiftung Aschaffenburg. VG Bild-Kunst, Bonn. Lic Viscopy

p 245 Photo: © bpk Berlin / Bayerische Staatsgemäldesammlungen © Max Beckmann / VG Bild-Kunst, Bonn. Lic Viscopy

p 247 Photo: © Karl Hubbuch, Sydney 2011. Provenance: Museo Thyssen-Bornemisza © The artist's estate

p 249 © Jeanne Mammen / VG Bild-Kunst, Bonn. Lic Viscopy

p 251 Photo: Kunstmuseum Stuttgart © Otto Dix / VG Bild-Kunst, Bonn. Lic Viscopy

pp 254, 256 (left & right) & **257** Courtesy of the Research Library, Getty Research Institute, Los Angeles, California (840001)

p 258 Photo: Courtesy Staatliche Museen Preussischer Kulturbesitz, Zentralarchiv, Berlin

p 259 Photo: Bayerische Staatsgemäldesammlungen - Pinakothek der Moderne, Munich © Rudolf Belling / VG Bild-Kunst, Bonn. Lic Viscopy

p 260 (left & right) © Max Beckmann / VG Bild-Kunst, Bonn. Lic Viscopy

pp 263, 264 & 265 © Felix Nussbaum / VG Bild-Kunst, Bonn. Lic Viscopy

pp 266, 267, 268 & 269 Photo: Akademie der Künste, Berlin, Kunstsammlung © The Heartfield Community of Heirs / VG Bild-Kunst, Bonn. Lic Viscopy (p 266: left Heartfield 71 / Roman März & right Heartfield 435; p 267: left Heartfield 2261 & right Heartfield 524 / Egon Beyer; p 268: Heartfield 124 / Roman März; p 269: top left Heartfield 1258 / Roman März, bottom left Heartfield 1261 / Roman März, top right Heartfield 1244 / Foto AdK & bottom right Heartfield 124 / Roman März)

p 271 Photo: Rheinisches Bildarchiv Köln

p 273 Photo: Courtesy of Richard L Feigen and Co © Max Beckmann / VG Bild-Kunst, Bonn. Lic Viscopy

p 277 Digital image © 2009 Museum Associates / LACMA / Art Resource, NY © The artist's estate

p 279 Photo: Bayerische Staatsgemäldesammlungen - Pinakothek der Moderne, Munich © Rudolf Belling / VG Bild Kunst, Bonn. Lic Viscopy

p 280 © Nolde - Stiftung Seebüll

p 281 Photo: Michael Herling / Aline Gwose © Nolde - Stiftung Seebüll

p 283 Photo: Stiftung Museum Kunst Palast, Düsseldorf

p 284 © The artist's estate

p 285 Photo: Collection of the Queensland Art Gallery, Brisbane

p 286 (left & right) © George Grosz / VG Bild-Kunst, Bonn. Lic Viscopy

p 287 © Otto Dix / VG Bild-Kunst, Bonn. Lic Viscopy

pp 288 & 289 © Max Beckmann / VG Bild-Kunst, Bonn. Lic Viscopy

pp 290, 291 Courtesy Potential Films, Melbourne; Production still courtesy of the British Film Institute and Transit Film GmbH

p 300 © Rudolf Schlichter Estate, courtesy Galerie Alvensleben, Munich

p 316 Photo © bpk / Kunstbibliothek, Staatliche Museen zu Berlin / Dietmar Katz; © Willi Baumeister / VG Bild-Kunst, Bonn. Lic Viscopy

Endpapers © El Lissitzky / VG Bild-Kunst. Lic Viscopy.

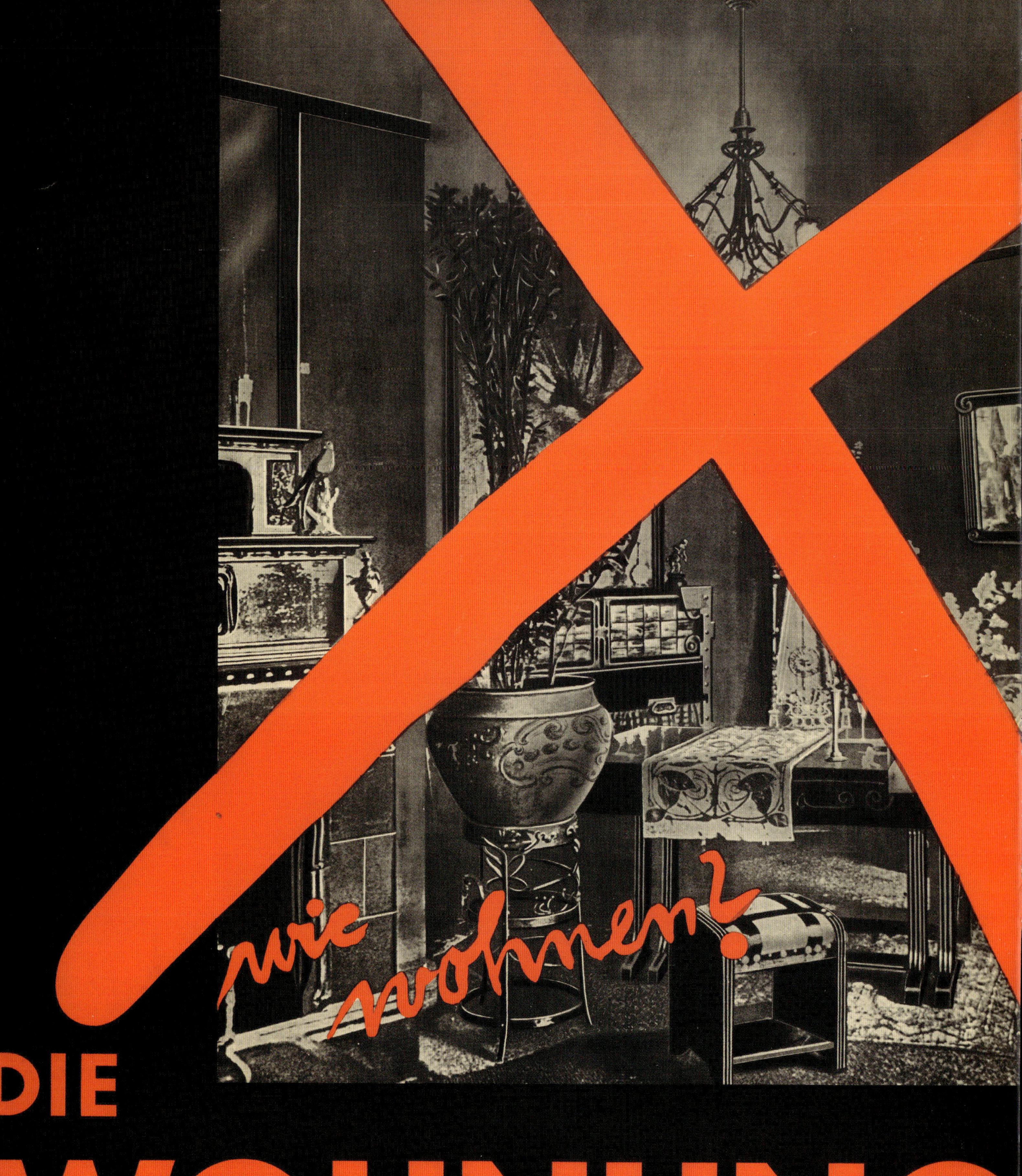

DIE
WOHNUNG

INDEX

Illustrations are indicated by italic page numbers; principal articles on catalogue works are indicated by ***bold italic*** page numbers.

Willi Baumeister
The dwelling [*Werkbund* exhibition, Stuttgart]
1927 (detail)

T

U

V

W

Z

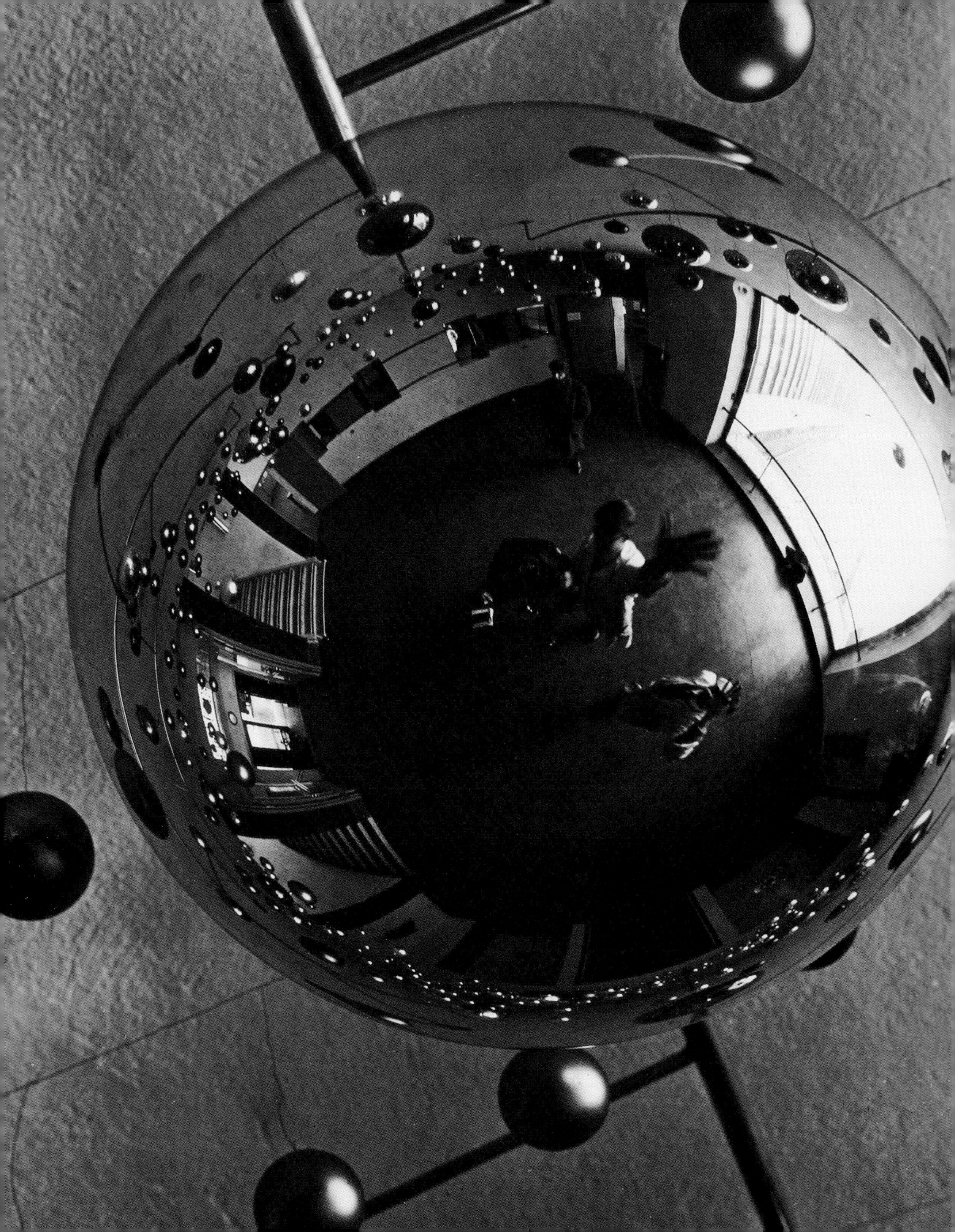

Published by
Art Gallery of New South Wales
Art Gallery Road, The Domain
Sydney 2000, Australia
www.artgallery.nsw.gov.au

in association with the exhibition
The mad square: modernity in German art 1910–37

Art Gallery of New South Wales
6 August – 6 November 2011

National Gallery of Victoria
25 November 2011 – 4 March 2012

The Art Gallery of New South Wales is a statutory body of the NSW State Government

Curator and editor: Jacqueline Strecker
Entries on works: Jacqueline Strecker
Translations: Jacqueline Strecker, Sabine Scholz, Petra Kayser
Managing editor: Julie Donaldson
Text editor: Paige Amor
Rights and permissions: Donna Brett, Michelle Andringa (film)
Index: Sherrey Quinn

Design: Karen Hancock
Production: Cara Hickman
Prepress: Spitting Image, Sydney
Printing: 1010 Printing International. Printed in China

Cataloguing-in-publication data:
ISBN 9781741740684 (pbk/flexibind)
ISBN 9783791346762 (hc)
The mad square: modernity in German art 1910-37 /
edited by Jacqueline Strecker.
Includes bibliographical references and index.
1. Art, German–20th century–Exhibitions.
2. Art–Political aspects–Germany–Exhibitions.
3. Modernism (Art)—Germany–Exhibitions.
I. Strecker, Jacqueline. II. Art Gallery of New South Wales. III. National Gallery of Victoria.

Distribution:
Paperback distributed in Australia, UK, Europe and Asia by
Thames & Hudson
181A High Holborn, London WC1V 7QX
Tel: 44 20 7845 5000
Email: sales@thameshudson.co.uk
www.thameshudson.co.uk

Hardcover distributed in North America by
Prestel Publishing
900 Broadway, Suite 603, New York, NY 10003
Tel: 212 995 2720
Email: sales@prestel-usa.com
www.prestel.com

cover: **George Grosz** Suicide 1916 (detail)
endpapers: **El Lissitzky** Program for 'Merz matinées' 30 Dec 1923 (detail)
opposite: **Walter Funkat** Vestibule, metallic festival 1929 (detail)

MAD SQUARE

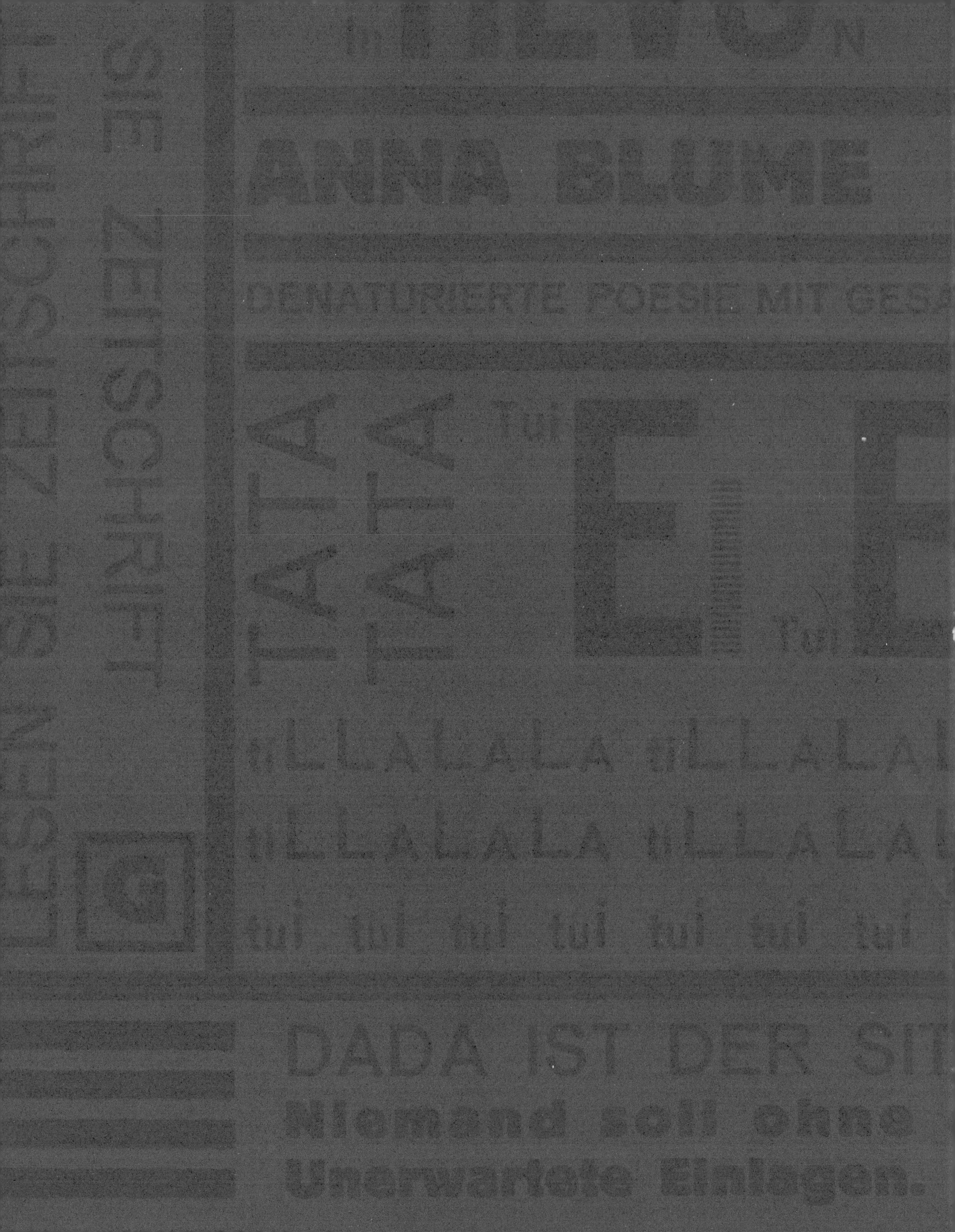

ANNA BLUME
DENATURIERTE POESIE MIT
LESEN SIE ZEITSCHRIFT
TATA
TATA
Tui
Tui
tuLLALALA
tuLLALALA
tui tui tui tui tui tui tui
DADA IST DER
Niemand soll ohne
Unerwartete Einlagen.